INSIDE RACING

A Season
With the PacWest CART Indy Car Team

By

PAUL HANEY

Published by *TV MOTORSPORTS*, 1829 Brewster Avenue, Redwood City, CA 94062.

First Printing January 1998

The information in this book is true to the best of our knowledge. All recomendations are made without any guarantee on the part of the authors or Publisher, who disclaim any liability incurred in connection with the use of any information presented here.

We recognize that some words, model names, and designations mentioned in this book are the property of the trademark holder. We use them for indentification only.

Photos included here were taken by the author unless otherwise credited.

COVER CREDITS:

Cover design by William Nagel of Redwood City, Calif., who also consulted on the layout and design of the body of the book.

The photos for the cover art were taken by the author. The pit stop photo on the front cover was taken at the Vancouver race as was the photo of Mauricio Gugelmin with the winner's trophy.

> Mark Moore, chief mechanic on Mauricio Gugelmin's 17-car always changes the right front tire. He saw an early version of the cover and said, "Look, I'm just loosening the nut and everybody else has the wheel off. That was when Mauricio stoped with his tire on top of my wheel gun. I had to wait for the car to go up on the jacks before I could grab the gun."

TABLE OF CONTENTS

LIST OF ILLUSTRATIONS

PREFACE

1997 was the best year of my life, so far. I had an idea, sold it to some people, and then got to live it and write about it. It's all here in these pages.

As usual I had a lot of help. Bruce McCaw liked the idea when I first told him about it and he sold it to the people at PacWest. Everyone at PacWest made me feel welcome. They let me stare at them and take photos and ask dumb questions.

All that travel is expensive. Thanks go to Adrian Reynard and Rick Gorne of Reynard Racing Cars, Al Speyer and Trevor Hoskins at Bridgstone/Firestone Inc., Steve Fusek at PacWest, and Tom Crawford at Motorola for contributing to my travel fund. Special thanks to Steve Potter at Mercedes-Benz of North America. These people listened to me say what I wanted to do and believed it made sense. It means a lot to me that they thought I could pull it off.

Linda Mansfield edited the text. We emailed ascii files back and forth and she made sure we were consistant and correct. I wouldn't have had time to generate the index if she hadn't kept a list of names. We put the whole thing together in four months. Her comments on style and substance were invaluable.

I created the track maps in CorelDraw with data from PacWest and help from Jim Swintal and Hank Thorpe. Except where noted I took the photos. I used PageMaker to layout the pages.

This book is a tribute to the people who work in racing. I hope I've revealed some of the hard work and dedication and no-excuses performance racing people exhude every minute of every day. If a small fraction of the people on this planet cared about their work and each other like racers do, it would be a much better world.

Paul Haney, Redwood City, Calif. January 1998.

Hat to Cover Bald Spot	Sun Block
Sunglasses	Stopwatch
Pocket Notebooks	Pen-on-a-String
Scanner and Headphones	Hardcard
Tape Recorder	Camera in Fanny Pack with Extra Film and Batteries
Tapes and Spare Batteries in Pockets	Water Bottle Hung on Belt
Comfortable Shoes	Orthotic Inserts in Shoes

The Author in
Working Uniform

CHAPTER 1
WHO IS PACWEST?

HOW DID THIS GET STARTED?

I took the idea to PacWest owner Bruce McCaw in June of '96, not because of PacWest but because Bruce had been a subscriber to my newsletter, *TV MOTORSPORTS,* since 1992 and I felt comfortable talking to him. He said he liked the idea and made the comment, "It would be interesting to see what an outsider thinks about us." At that time I was surprised by the state-ment. Now I know that kind of thinking is what makes Bruce a different kind of race team owner and PacWest a different kind of race team.

I talked to other teams about the book project and got some favorable responses. I was very comfortable with the people at Comptech and had the idea that an American driver, like Parker Johnstone, would result in better sales numbers. A month or so after our first talk, I told Bruce I would probably travel with Comptech in 1997, and to my surprise he sounded disap-pointed. I hadn't realized just how much Bruce liked the idea. When Parker left Comptech for Team Green I called Bruce to say I'd like to work with PacWest. He sent me a confirming fax right away and said he would forward my proposal to his drivers and managers. That was the first week in December 1996.

I was concerned that Bruce's support could overwhelm any negative feelings the team might have so I called VP Race Operations John Anderson and VP Business Operations Steve Fusek to give them a chance to shoot me down. I wanted to hear any bad news early on. But they both said they thought it was a great idea and we got started.

From the first day I popped into the PacWest shop in February to the end of the "Driving Experience" in October, no one at PacWest ever said anything negative to me. Sometimes they were busy when I had a question or they couldn't talk about a specific topic, but nobody got mad or even irritated. To the contrary, I had a great time hanging out with the crew, and I made some good friends. Racing is full of amazing people.

A fairy-tale story, really, my getting to hang out with a winning CART team during the 1997 season, a chance of a lifetime for sure. I've never worked so hard in my life. The travel alone is a huge hassle and drain on life's energies. In the end, all my notes and tapes and photos generated some unique stories about what goes on behind the scenes at the top of motor racing.

PACWEST HISTORY

PacWest jumped in with both feet in 1994, and was the first team ever to run two cars in every event during its first season. Most people prefer to get used to walking before they try to fly. Dominic Dobson and Scott Sharp were the drivers that first year, and Dobson earned a podium finish at the 500-mile race at Michigan Speedway. Dobson and Sharp finished the season 18th and 21st in points. Bruce McCaw, Wes Lematta, and Tom Armstrong, all successful businessmen from the Pacific Northwest, formed the team. PacWest bought Rick Galles' half of Galmer Engineering in Bicester, England, acquiring the services of Alan Mertens, the other owner, as PacWest technical director.

The drivers in 1995 were Danny Sullivan and Mauricio Gugelmin. Sullivan was injured in an accident during the race at Michigan Speedway. He missed the last four races of the season and later retired as a driver in favor of a TV announcing career. Juan Fangio II finished the season in Sullivan's place. Gugelmin ended the season 10th in points.

In 1996 Mark Blundell found himself without a ride in Formula 1, so he came to PacWest to join Mauricio Gugelmin. Blundell had a horrendous accident during the race at Rio de Janeiro, and was lucky to emerge with a broken foot. The cause of the accident was a fatigue failure of a rear brake hat, the part that attaches the brake rotor to the hub. Gugelmin's car suffered a similar failure, but did not crash. PacWest cars used Cosworth/Ford XB engines, a generation older than the XDs run by most other Cosworth/Ford teams. Gugelmin finished 14th in season points with Blundell 16th.

Prior to the 1997 season PacWest made some changes in their "package," the term used for the combination of chassis, engine, and tire manufacturer that make up the major components of the racecar. The team switched from Cosworth/Ford engines to Ilmor/Mercedes-Benz power, stayed with Reynard chassis, and switched from Goodyear to Firestone tires.

Bruce McCaw is a businessman and a racer living in Bellevue, Wash. He serves as chief executive officer of PacWest Racing Group and is president of RaceSport Management, the managing partner of PacWest. He is responsible for all the strategic decisions of the team. As an owner of a CART franchise, he serves on the board of directors of CART. He also serves on the board of directors of Alaska Airlines and Claircom Communications. He is the former chairman of Forbes Westar, Inc., and former director of McCaw Cellular Communications. Bruce is a commercial pilot and regulerly exercises racecars from his vintage car collection in vintage races all over the world. In 1996 Bruce married the former Jolene Rister.

When Bruce's brother Craig sold McCaw Cellular to AT&T for $12.5 billion, Bruce was assured of having enough money to do whatever he wants to do. Using some of that money to create PacWest has benefited a lot of racing people, including myself. Rich people are easy to resent, but frankly I'm glad Bruce has all that money. His wealth is more than money. His personal warmth and friendly support are worth a lot more than money to the people around him.

Russ Cameron and Bruce McCaw

THE ORGANIZATION

Blundell's crash at Rio precipitated changes at PacWest. Bruce McCaw took a more hands-on role in daily operations and Tom Armstrong grew less involved. Bruce chose Steve Fusek as his vice president of business operations and put him in charge of marketing, sponsor relations, public relations, and hospitality. John Anderson became vice president of race operations. Both of these guys were relatively inexperienced, neither having held jobs at that level previously. That is a hallmark of PacWest. Bruce McCaw picks people who are ready for more responsibility and gives them a chance to see what they can do. He backs them up but doesn't seem to micromanage his people as badly as other team owners.

The following charts show how PacWest is organized. Accounting services for the team are based at Bruce McCaw's office in Seattle.

PacWest Racing Group

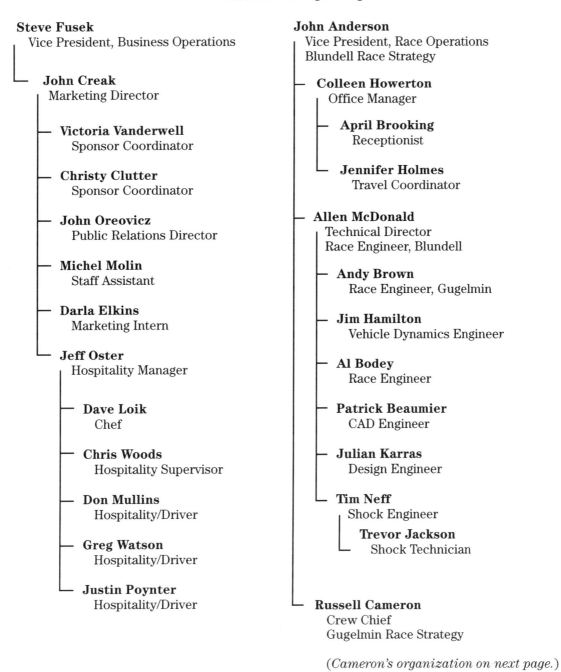

Steve Fusek
Vice President, Business Operations

— **John Creak**
Marketing Director

— **Victoria Vanderwell**
Sponsor Coordinator

— **Christy Clutter**
Sponsor Coordinator

— **John Oreovicz**
Public Relations Director

— **Michel Molin**
Staff Assistant

— **Darla Elkins**
Marketing Intern

— **Jeff Oster**
Hospitality Manager

— **Dave Loik**
Chef

— **Chris Woods**
Hospitality Supervisor

— **Don Mullins**
Hospitality/Driver

— **Greg Watson**
Hospitality/Driver

— **Justin Poynter**
Hospitality/Driver

John Anderson
Vice President, Race Operations
Blundell Race Strategy

— **Colleen Howerton**
Office Manager

— **April Brooking**
Receptionist

— **Jennifer Holmes**
Travel Coordinator

— **Allen McDonald**
Technical Director
Race Engineer, Blundell

— **Andy Brown**
Race Engineer, Gugelmin

— **Jim Hamilton**
Vehicle Dynamics Engineer

— **Al Bodey**
Race Engineer

— **Patrick Beaumier**
CAD Engineer

— **Julian Karras**
Design Engineer

— **Tim Neff**
Shock Engineer

— **Trevor Jackson**
Shock Technician

— **Russell Cameron**
Crew Chief
Gugelmin Race Strategy

(*Cameron's organization on next page.*)

Russell Cameron
Crew Chief
Gugelmin Race Strategy

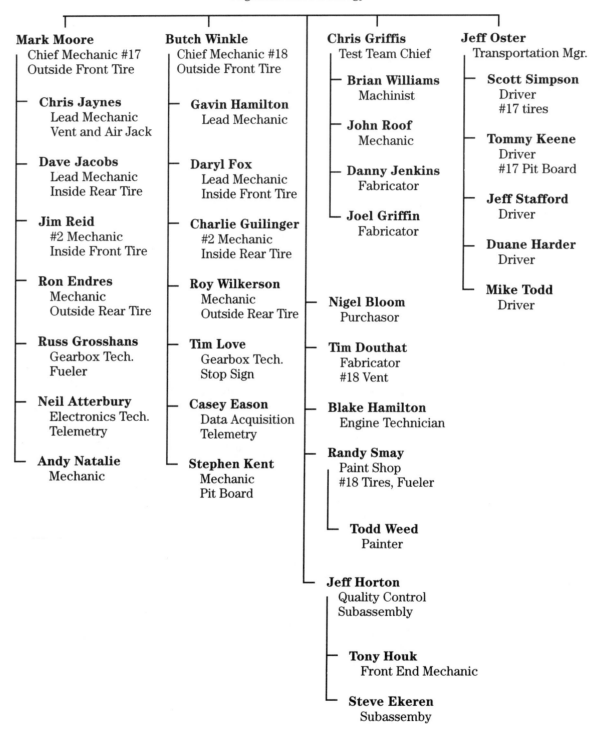

Mark Moore
Chief Mechanic #17
Outside Front Tire

- **Chris Jaynes**
  Lead Mechanic
  Vent and Air Jack

- **Dave Jacobs**
  Lead Mechanic
  Inside Rear Tire

- **Jim Reid**
  #2 Mechanic
  Inside Front Tire

- **Ron Endres**
  Mechanic
  Outside Rear Tire

- **Russ Grosshans**
  Gearbox Tech.
  Fueler

- **Neil Atterbury**
  Electronics Tech.
  Telemetry

- **Andy Natalie**
  Mechanic

Butch Winkle
Chief Mechanic #18
Outside Front Tire

- **Gavin Hamilton**
  Lead Mechanic

- **Daryl Fox**
  Lead Mechanic
  Inside Front Tire

- **Charlie Guilinger**
  #2 Mechanic
  Inside Rear Tire

- **Roy Wilkerson**
  Mechanic
  Outside Rear Tire

- **Tim Love**
  Gearbox Tech.
  Stop Sign

- **Casey Eason**
  Data Acquisition
  Telemetry

- **Stephen Kent**
  Mechanic
  Pit Board

Chris Griffis
Test Team Chief

- **Brian Williams**
  Machinist

- **John Roof**
  Mechanic

- **Danny Jenkins**
  Fabricator

- **Joel Griffin**
  Fabricator

- **Nigel Bloom**
  Purchasor

- **Tim Douthat**
  Fabricator
  #18 Vent

- **Blake Hamilton**
  Engine Technician

- **Randy Smay**
  Paint Shop
  #18 Tires, Fueler

  - **Todd Weed**
    Painter

- **Jeff Horton**
  Quality Control
  Subassembly

- **Tony Houk**
  Front End Mechanic

- **Steve Ekeren**
  Subassemby

Jeff Oster
Transportation Mgr.

- **Scott Simpson**
  Driver
  #17 tires

- **Tommy Keene**
  Driver
  #17 Pit Board

- **Jeff Stafford**
  Driver

- **Duane Harder**
  Driver

- **Mike Todd**
  Driver

CONVERSATION WITH BRUCE McCAW, PACWEST OWNER

Mark Blundell had a horrible crash at the first CART race in Rio de Janeiro in 1996. I knew that some big changes happened at PacWest after that so I started with that question.

Paul: "You made a lot of changes and decisions late last season and over the winter about people and tires and engines that have led to the team being where it is now at the start of the '97 season. Did that all start at Rio last year?"

Bruce: "I think what Rio precipitated was really two things. One was a change in our decision-making structure, also our organization. That began the day after Rio. I sat down with the key people on the team and, first off, I had to understand exactly what had happened. It became increasingly clear that we'd made a mistake. And we'd made a mistake that we shouldn't have made. Mistakes are never tolerable in this sport, but it became clear to me that we had made a mistake that we clearly could have avoided and we made a mistake for all the wrong reasons. We did something that had gotten by us and we didn't have the checks and balances in the organization that I feel are important in any business. We didn't have as clear a decision-making process as we needed. So we really needed to look at how we were organized and what it took to go forward.

"There were some reasons for our problems. We had three centers of influence between Seattle, the U.K., and Indianapolis. We really had to boil that down to one. Everything had to be managed and decided out of Indianapolis, whether it was racing related or non-racing related. We really had to shift that focus. What had evolved was a structure that was too dependent on where people lived instead of where the business needed to operate. That was the core of all the changes we made. First, I had to center our management and decision-making in Indianapolis. And second, I needed to separate the racing and the business side. That all didn't happen right after Rio. Some of it took awhile. It took a few months, actually.

"On the racing side, we left Rio with John Anderson firmly in charge so that he had the final say on the race program. Probably the next test we had outside of race weekends was the process that we started to go through to look forward to the '97 season and decide what equipment we wanted to run with. We had been reluctant to make changes over the last couple of years because we hadn't had the time to think it all out as well as we'd like to have. But by May '96 I'd started a process to start from the ground up and look at our chassis options, look at our engine options, and look at our tire options. We needed to look at it with a clean sheet of paper and decide what package we should run next year and see if we could get the package we wanted.

"That process got started. John Anderson went to the U.K.. to visit Ilmor, Cosworth, Reynard, Lola, and Galmer. I needed to break John in to getting the information and make sure he was looking at the right things while he was making those decisions. We were putting John in a more senior position and I thought that was a good way to start that process, to get him over there talking to people representing the team and thinking about the future.

"And Steve Fusek was given responsibility for organizing things better from a business standpoint. We clearly had some on-going opportunities from the marketing and hospitality side. He started working at bringing some new people in to do that. Both those guys set out to look at the future and where they thought we needed to take things."

Paul: "In there somewhere you became the sole owner of the team. Is that right?"

Bruce: "Not exactly. What really happened was the on-going support of the team was just coming from me. I didn't consciously go out and buy everybody else out. That has not happened. But from a practical standpoint my contribution effectively reduces their level of ownership. There are two key issues here. Wes Lamata's involvement was because of Dominic [Dobson]. Wes and I have known each other through aviation circles; we have a lot of mutual friends. Wes had been a sponsor of Dominic's racing efforts over time and was willing to continue to do so. Wes had put a fair chunk of money into the team, although it was less relative to my investment. Tom's [Tom Armstrong's] investment was less but he had agreed to run the team for one year in '94. I was way too busy in my business life to take on a full-time responsibility for the team. In '94 I pretty much left it to those guys.

"In '95 Dominic was no longer driving and he acted as general manager of the team. He really wanted to go back into retirement and he found out that this was really not a great way to retire [laughs]. Wes didn't have any great incentive to put money into the team if he wasn't supporting Dominic's driving career. The '94 season was a huge disappointment to us in terms of revenue. The team performed pretty well for a start-up team. We came very close to having some very good results. But for the business to continue we had to focus a lot more heavily on revenue, and that was the reason we made the driver changes we did. We were trying to find some drivers we thought would be easier to find sponsors for because of their name and experience."

Paul: "How did you get involved with Mauricio?"

Bruce: "In 1994 Mauricio came to the Mid-Ohio CART test and we sat down together and chatted. He wanted to make a move from Chip Ganassi's team. The more I talked to him I could see that he was very frustrated with Chip, for a couple of reasons. Michael Andretti wanted a one-car program and Michael told me some of this himself so I know it's true. Michael just didn't want another car around. He wanted everything focused on him and that was it. So Mauricio's car was running out of the back of the building at RNA [Reynard North America in Indianapolis] it wasn't even in the team shop. He didn't have a spare wing or much in the way of any spare parts. Chip ran the thing on a next-to-nothing budget. He told Mauricio, 'You break it, you park the car.' Mauricio brought some money into that program.

"An interesting thing happened later. At a test after we'd hired Mauricio in the winter of '95, we were at Sebring. Michael and I have been friends for a long time and he and Mauricio had always gotten along OK, but it was a difficult situation. There at Sebring Mauricio and I were together and we went over to talk to Michael. The three of us started talking and Michael and Mauricio started to compare notes in a way they had never felt comfortable doing when they were teammates. And it was funny for me to hear all this. Chip was telling them each the same story that the other guy was bringing money to the program and so it was good to have him on board. There was a lot of bullshit flying around and he was bullshitting them both. With that talk the two of them got that chapter behind them and they both understood things better and they both seemed happy they were driving for somebody other than Chip that year."

Paul: "When Mauricio came he brought the Hollywood sponsorship with him. Was that the first big sponsor PacWest got?"

Bruce: "At that Mid-Ohio test when we first talked, Mauricio told me that Hollywood had supported him for a long time and they weren't happy. They didn't feel they were getting a fair shake. There were a bunch of issues involved. Mauricio said that he thought they would support a change to PacWest. I started talking to them. One of their people came up and we met in Indianapolis. We finally shook hands on a deal in late November '94. I'd already decided that, of all the drivers we'd looked at, we liked Mauricio.

"I'd made a decision that we had to replace Scott [Sharp] with a driver that had more experience and one that we could build some revenue around. Scott had told us a lot of sponsors would follow him from Trans-Am but nobody did. We didn't get a nickel out of that deal. It was a pretty dry hole.

"Mauricio and I had spent a lot of time together and I had grown to respect him and like him. I felt that he was the guy that would really bring a lot to the team. And this is a team that had set out to run American drivers and not have tobacco sponsors. [Hollywood, Mauricio's sponsor, is the largest Brazilian cigarette company.] That was part of our goals in '94. But things change sometimes. Either you can change or you can go broke. But Mauricio really brought something to the party. I saw an inner strength in him that I felt good about.

"So we were sailing along and then, the day after Christmas, Mauricio called me and he sounded like his best friend had just died. He said Hollywood just canceled the program. They'd had a huge budget overrun from a rock concert or something. They had spent a lot of money they didn't think they were going to spend, and they had pulled the plug on our sponsorship. So Mauricio thought he was out on the street. But we'd gone so far, I thought to myself, 'I really believe in this guy.' There were some other guys we could have brought in to drive who would have brought some money, but Mauricio was who I wanted.

"I told him we would continue, but we'd have to adjust his salary some. I told him I'd run him for the season. So he ended up leading the first race at Miami, taking second, damn near brought us a victory. The podium picture at Miami is interesting. His firesuit is just plain white. It looks like he got it at a garage sale somewhere. It's pretty funny [laughs]. But as a result of what we'd done the Hollywood guys were on the phone the next day saying they'd made a mistake and they really wanted to support the program and they really liked Mauricio. They felt very bad. We had a handshake agreement with a senior executive of the company and they pulled the plug on us. They were quite embarrassed about it. They're very good people."

Paul: "How did you end up with Mark Blundell?"

Bruce: "When Danny [Sullivan] decided he wasn't going to drive again—I told Danny after '95 that I knew it had been a tough year and Danny was going through some personal problems—there was a lot of stuff going on with him personally. I told him that if he would put 100% of his energy into this program, I'd do another year. He's a very talented driver, but half Danny's problem is he doesn't want to put the effort in that it takes today. It's twice as much work as it used to be. Mauricio'd be out there with the engineers 'til 9 at night and Danny'd be at a dinner party.

"Some of that was starting to show and obviously we needed a better engineering situation. We would have brought someone else in the next year. I said give me 100% commitment and I'll go again. If not you've got a great offer from ABC-TV, and you're about to get married so maybe the TV thing is the right way to go. Danny and I are still good friends. I've got a lot of respect for Danny."

Paul: "So how did Blundell get into the picture?"

Bruce: "If we were going to run a two-car team we should have drivers who would complement each other. So we looked at a lot of people and tested a few. I missed all the testing. I was on my honeymoon sitting in a little grass shack in Fiji with my bride. Mark was head and shoulders above everybody else during the testing. He was everybody's pick. I had never even met him. So I got back from Fiji and I called him up in England and we talked for probably two hours. I just wanted to get to know him and I wanted to get to know his feel about the team and learn about him as a person.

"We talked some about money and I finally told him we were a ways apart and why don't we both think about it and talk again in a few days. I give Mark a lot of credit. He said, 'Look, I may get an offer. I may have a lot of things available, but I simply want to know where I'm going to be next year. Let's just talk it out now.' So we kept talking and we went back and forth and 20 minutes later we cut a deal.

"I felt like here's a guy who can help build the program and will help bring us sponsorship. And he has. He's likable. He's easy to work with. He goes out of his way to do things. He's got great feedback about the car. If you've listened in on the radio you've heard that."

Paul: "He talks about the car a lot."

Bruce: "Sometimes too much. Sometimes they have to slow him down and get him more focused, but he'll tell you anything that happened out there; you want to know about it and he can tell you."

Paul: "So, Bruce. What are you doing all this for? This is obviously a lot of energy and a lot of money you've put into this. What are you doing it for?"

Bruce: "Well, the fundamental decision I guess I made in '95 was... We'd come a long way. I liked what I saw in CART. I was largely without an occupation. Most everything I'd been working on had been sold for a variety of reasons, mostly not by choice. Our cellular communications company [McCaw Cellular] was sold. You know when you're a public company, and somebody wants to buy you and they put enough money on the table you have to go along with it or the shareholders turn around and sue you."

Paul: "So what are your goals now? What about this first race coming up? What do you expect?"

Bruce: "The first race, I think we're gonna be strong. I feel good about it. I think everybody's got a little apprehension 'cause of this race and the racetrack. Everybody is holding their breath a little bit about Homestead. [The square corners are considered dangerous and CART has implemented some special aerodynamic rules.] And rightfully so. I think what we need to do is to try to go into this race with a certain amount of caution and try and be sensible and have a really good race. I think it will be a good race, and I think we'll be in contention.

"Last year Mauricio ran solidly. It was Mark's first Indy car race and he'll never forget his first lap. [We both laugh. Blundell got on the throttle at the green flag and spun out in Turn 4, causing an early yellow flag.] We need to run smart and try to be at the front end of the pack when it comes to the end. Both drivers have run some good speeds there and now we need to focus on having two good racecars and be there at the end."

Paul: "What about the season? What's your expectations for the season?"

Bruce: "My gut feeling is that the engines will all be closer to parity than they were last year. Honda may still have a bit of an edge, but some of the Honda cars have taken themselves out of contention early on because the teams have made a lot of changes a little late, and probably Walker and Green will struggle a little bit. They're both very capable competitors. A year ago I thought both those teams had an edge on us and this year I think it's the other way around.

"Ganassi has a lot going. He's going to be hard to beat. They could have some internal unrest too, depending on what happens. Zanardi is looking awfully promising. But I've seen some promising combinations shoot themselves in the foot. We're trying not to be one of those. Fundamentally we're sitting here saying, 'Let's just be smart about what we do.' Let's be disciplined, let's don't kid ourselves, let's don't do 99% of everything really well, and then try to get that other 1% on a crap shoot. That's some of what we were doing last year from a decision-making process. We were so focused on that extra edge but we never got the basics. It's a fundamental discipline. Sometimes you have to say we're better off to do this really well and not try to take on the extra edge. Penske has done that well for a long time. Those are guys that no matter where their car is, by the time the flag drops at the end of the race, those guys are in there. They get into it and they race.

"I think that the bottom line here is we've got two very good drivers who have different strengths, which is good. I think they tend to elevate each other. They support each other but they compete. There's a good balance to that, an important balance. We've got a team that's got a lot clearer picture. It would be good if we had a few more weeks to let everybody get settled in. Allen McDonald [technical director newly hired from the Arrows Formula 1 team] brings a lot of sensible engineering discipline to the organization. He's very focused. And he's practical. And he's got a comfortable air about him, and I think that's good. He'll help the rest of the engineering people, including Galmer, get the most out of what they've got. So I think we've got a lot of strength there.

"John Anderson is a very solid, practical-thinking guy. He's shown a lot of growth, a lot of strength over the last year. In particular it was a tough transition for him to go from a hands-on, chief mechanic/team manager of a one-car program to being a vice president of a serious racing organization. It's a big transition, especially if you consider the complexities of a two-car team.

"We've got equipment we all feel confident about in chassis, tires, and engines. For the first time in the history of the team we've got the depth of engineering that's required for both cars. Jim Hamilton [Coming from Dan Gurney's All American Racers, Jim will engineer Mark Blundell's car.] was clearly a big addition. At least half the success of a race engineer is the way he works with the driver. The chemistry is vitally important and when it's not there the best setup in the world won't make that package go fast.

"Tim Neff did a terrific job last year engineering Blundell. But actually, considering the shock absorber program he's doing for us now, we were hurting ourselves having him do that. He could have been doing other things we needed. John Anderson worked well with Mark on the radio. We found that out when we made that change. There were some times when Mark really had his hands full out on the track and John was able to keep his spirits up."

Paul: "So Russ Cameron and John Anderson are just thinking about strategy during races?"

Bruce: "Right. Russ has come a long way. He was an assistant crew chief at Ganassi's when Mauricio was there. We brought him in and he's done really well. I needed to get John out of the shop and back at his desk some of the time. We needed somebody that John had some faith in, and Russ was the right guy to do that.

"Most of our success is going to be how we work as an organization. Hopefully we'll have a few less challenges than we've had in the last couple of years. And we can just be focused on what we need to be doing."

Paul: "I'm excited about being along for the ride. Good luck. I'll see you in a few days at Homestead."

Bruce: "See ya, Paul."

CHAPTER 2

SPRING TRAINING

CART Spring Training is an attempt to establish an annual, pre-season event where fans can mingle with the teams in a more relaxed environment than on a race day. I've been to several and I think it's great. All the new cars are there in one place, and that helps me see the differences. The engine and chassis manufacturers' technical people are there, and the lesser-known techie guys are there also, from the shock absorber technicians to the data acquisition suppliers. The team engineers are available too, if you catch them when they're not busy. For me it's a great chance to talk to all the right people.

For the fans it's the best chance they'll ever have to see the drivers and crews and cars up close and personal. Racing fans living in the cold part of the country can schedule a vacation to sunny Florida at this time every winter. There are also NASCAR, Indy Racing League, and sports car events in the state during this time, so you can see a lot of racing in a few weeks.

My arrangement with PacWest isn't a done deal yet, so I'm trying not to count my chickens. I know Bruce wants it to happen and everyone I've talked to seems positive. He told me PacWest has a two-day management meeting scheduled after Spring Training, and he will pitch the project to all the people there.

Colleen Howerton, PacWest office manager and travel coordinator, booked me into the Holiday Inn, Cutler Ridge — a strange name since there are no ridges in Florida, indeed no land much more than 20 feet above sea level. I fly on Wednesday, Jan. 29 from San Francisco International Airport (SFO) to Miami, arriving at 10 p.m. I take a wrong turn between the Hertz lot and the freeway and get lost. It takes almost an hour to get to the motel.

THURSDAY

On Thursday morning about 7:30 I go to the lobby for coffee on my way out to the car. Most of the PacWest team is sitting around on sofas and chairs. I only know a couple of them. I say hello to Trevor Jackson and Jim Hamilton, and then hit the road. I always get impatient to be at the track as soon as I'm dressed. I guess I'm afraid I'll miss something.

During the 15-minute drive from the motel to the track I'm thinking about what I should be doing today, and what I'll do if the PacWest thing doesn't work out. What if I piss some people off? Oh, well.

Homestead is a sleepy little town a half-hour down the turnpike from Miami. It was a military town built up to accommodate airmen stationed at Homestead Air Force Base. A recently built toll road and Miami expansion is converting Homestead into a bedroom community for Miami, but that trend was set back a few years ago by a terrible hurricane that ruined many of the houses. At the first race here in 1995 I saw some empty, unrepaired houses, but now I don't see anything like that.

If I take the first exit off the turnpike, the road to the Homestead Motorsports Complex is a straight, two-lane blacktop punctuated by a stop light and a couple of stop signs. I see acres and acres of what I think are tomatoes and strawberries. I also see rows and rows of exotic plants and trees that must be grown for nurseries.

The grandstands loom larger as I get closer. Some twists through the parking area get me to the back road that leads to the registration building. That's right. Registration is in a building — a nice, clean building, not some old trailer or tent like at the older tracks. This is the age of the motorsports complex.

PacWest sent me all the CART forms for an annual credential, called a "hardcard." I filled in the forms, mainly having to do with liability release and anti-drug rules, had them notarized as required, and put them in the mail. I'm supposed to get the hardcard at this event, but when I ask for it at registration I'm given an armband instead and told the hardcards will be ready at the first race here at Homestead a month from now.

Parking is restricted at most tracks. The teams, CART officials, and the media get to park in the infield. I haven't made arrangements for a parking pass, so I'm stopped at the entrance to the tunnel under the track and told to park outside. I get my stuff out of the car and hitch a ride in with the first car that has some room. It turns out to be the Lola guys: Chris Saunders, aerodynamicist, and Ben Bowlby, the chief designer. It's good to see them again. They drop me off in the middle of the infield.

It takes a few minutes to find the PacWest garage and hospitality areas. I stow my bag at the hospitality motor coach and meet a few of the PacWest people there. I spend the rest of the morning walking around talking to people. The first practice session is scheduled for 3 p.m.

The media center at Homestead is nice. The entire track is only a year old and it's a first-rate facility, putting most other American racetracks to shame. Each garage area is designed for two cars, and there is a television set mounted on each side of every dividing wall. These TVs have the same channels available as the ones in pit lane. You can choose several timing and scoring screens as well as a TV feed showing the cars on the track.

Mercedes-Benz Press Lunch

Press Conferences

My first official function is the Mercedes-Benz press conference and lunch at 11:45 a.m. The M-B hospitality area is about 30 feet by 30 feet under awnings hung from the sides of facing silver vehicles, a transporter and a motor coach. The silver side of the transporter behind the podium provides a striking backdrop. A magnificent black-on-silver mural depicts Mercedes-Benz racecars, past and present. Starting on the left is an exposed-radiator monster from the 1920s. The pre-World War II Grand Prix car is next, followed by the 300 SLR, a late '80s sports car, and a Marlboro-liveried Penske Indy car, probably the pushrod-engined 1994 Indy 500 winner.

Steve Potter is the manager, sports marketing, for Mercedes-Benz of North America. He introduces the drivers who will be using the Ilmor/M-B engine this year: Mark Blundell, Patrick Carpentier, Dario Franchitti, Mauricio Gugelmin, Greg Moore, Paul Tracy, and Al Unser Jr. Steve also introduces Hal Whiteford, vice president, operations, M-BNA, and Paul Ray, vice president, Ilmor Engineering Ltd.

It's sunny and warm with a nice breeze. It's very comfortable as we sit at round tables under an awning eating a very nice lunch. We're not roughing it here today. There's a pressed tablecloth, real silver, and an impressive floral centerpiece in the middle of each table.

Paul Ray talks to the group about the new Ilmor/M-B engine designated the IC108D. He says there were some reliability issues with the engine they ran last year, and this new engine has some design refinements to enhance reliability.

CART changed the rules to try to reduce horsepower and therefore speed on the tracks, so turbocharger boost is down from 45 to 40 inches of mercury (Hg.). Forty inches Hg. is the absolute pressure allowed in the intake plenum. At higher pressures a relief (pop-off) valve opens, venting the plenum to atmospheric pressure, which is roughly 30 inches Hg. The "boost," or excess pressure over atmospheric, is therefore only 10 inches of mercury, or about 5 pounds per square inch (psi).

The engine builders redesigned the intake systems and cylinder heads and the engines are turning more rpm. I'm hearing the new engines will have the same power as last year in spite of lower boost; my guess is about 900 hp. This is frustrating for the rules makers, but if they hadn't lowered the boost the engines might be at 950 hp.

Ray tells us Ilmor has built 44 engines for '97, up from 24 last year. Kits of engine parts go from Ilmor's plant in Brixworth, England, to two assembly facilities. Penske Racing in Reading, Pa., assembles its own engines. VDS Racing in Midland, Texas, assembles engines for the other teams. The initial assembly of each engine occurs at those facilities, as well as the rebuilds.

Each driver comments on the engines.

Greg Moore was a rookie last year, but he showed he could drive a car quickly. "I know what to expect this year. I was too aggressive a couple of times last year and it hurt me."

Al Unser Jr. was the victim of one of the most spectacular Ilmor/M-B engine failures last year, which occurred on the last lap while he was leading at Elkhart Lake, Wis. "You have to finish the race. Reliability is good," he says.

PacWest has switched from Cosworth/Ford to Ilmor/M-B for this season. Mark Blundell says, "My relationship with Mercedes-Benz started when I was driving for McLaren in Formula 1. I'm looking forward to continuing that relationship."

Mauricio Gugelmin: "We spent some time last year making decisions about the package we would race this year. Reynard is good. The Mercedes-Benz engine is good. We'll try to win some races this year."

My next stop is the Ford press conference, where Don Hayward, Ford Special Vehicle Operations (SVO), CART program manager, introduces Steve Miller of Cosworth Racing and drivers Bobby Rahal, Michael Andretti, Bryan Herta, Richie Hearn, and Christian Fittipaldi.

Miller says the XD design had some reliability problems last year and has been improved during the off season. "Lower boost and 35 gallons of fuel on board the car, down from 40, are the big rules changes. We've developed new cylinder heads, new parts in the valve gear, and a new plenum. The engine is turning about 500 rpm more than last year. We've been able to develop almost as much power as last year, even at the lower boost. We built 52 engines by the end of last season. There will be 86 total at the start of the '97 season."

First Practice Session

At 2:45 p.m. most of the cars are in the pit lane and engines are firing up so they'll be warm for the start of the session. This is my first chance to see the '97 machines.

The PacWest team is at the end of pit lane nearest Turn 4. At the other end is the Newman-Haas team, which has the new Swift chassis powered by the Cosworth/Ford engine. The Swift 007.i is here in public for the first time.

Wingless Swift

When I get down to that end I find Chris Saunders, the Lola aero guy, is there also. He's very interested in the Swift. We watch as the new car is rolled out onto pit lane. It doesn't have a front wing installed, so we think maybe they are being coy about showing it. Maybe they've got a super-trick front wing and they're going to put it on at the last minute before the car goes out so people like Chris won't get a good look at it.

The crew gets the car ready and Christian Fittipaldi gets in it. The car still doesn't have a front wing. They've got racer tape over the holes in the nose.

"They're not going to run that way, are they?" asks Chris. We watch as Christian pulls out on the track, and I look down pit lane to see a lot of people watching the car, just as we are.

Racing is a monkey-see, monkey-do culture, and I can almost see crew chiefs looking toward their tool chests to check if they have a hacksaw handy in case they have to remove the front wings on their own cars.

Fortunately for all those suddenly suspect front wings, Christian only turns some slow check-out laps before quitting for the day. I find out later that Swift has only made one front wing and it's late getting here.

I talk to David Bruns, the Swift designer, but I can't get him to tell me much. I can see he's done some interesting packaging at the rear of the car and I ask him about the transmission.

"It's in the back," he says with a bearded grin. I wonder if he's solved the ratio-change difficulties of a longitudinal gearbox in front of the rear axle. Bruns is a clever guy. Like Jeff Braun, my co-author on Inside Racing Technology, says, "How many BAD David Bruns cars have you ever seen?"

I have my scanner so I can listen to radio conversations as the practice session continues. I hear Andre Ribeiro complain about lack of grip. At 3:30 p.m. Jimmy Vasser has the best lap so far with a 29.335-seconds lap. Parker Johnstone, Paul Tracy, Gil de Ferran, and Bobby Rahal finish the top five.

An hour into the practice session I look at a monitor to see how the PacWest team is doing. Mauricio Gugelmin is seventh with a time of 30.078 seconds, and Mark Blundell is 16th with a 31.384. After the checkered flag at 4:30 p.m., Mauricio is sixth and Mark 13th.

After the session I talk with Steve Fusek about the team. "Bruce delegates the running of the team to Ando [John Anderson] and I. He doesn't micro manage us at all, but if we've got a problem with some guy and we need help, he's right on it."

The sun sets early in the winter months, even in Florida. I walk to my car as the sky darkens. My feet hurt, but I'm sure this is not the last time this year I'll experience that feeling. The track has some shuttles running people out to the parking lots but it's too late now, so I walk to my car.

South Florida is a wheeled culture and there are drive-in businesses of all sorts. As I turn under the freeway from the off-ramp I spot a drive-in liquor store across from the motel, so I pull in and buy a six-pack of beer. Right down the block is a McDonalds, and that determines my dinner. The time it takes to get service in these businesses reminds me of the "manana" nature of the area. There is no hurry here at all. People don't mind if you wait.

In the motel room, after the first Corona and half-way through the Big Mac, I'm reflecting on the day. Racing is a very complicated sport. I'm biting off a big chunk trying to explain it. The year looks like a very long jaunt into a big unknown.

FRIDAY

I get to the track at 7:30 a.m. It's overcast today and cool, about 65 degrees F. Both the drivers are here in the PacWest hospitality area. Mauricio Gugelmin is "Mo" to everyone. Mark Blundell is eating some frosted cereal and changing the battery in his cell phone. After he installs the new battery he puts the phone back in a scabbard on his belt. I leave my bag here and walk over to the PacWest garage.

I'm used to scrounging for food on my own at races, so it's nice to see a menu posted on one of the PacWest transporters announcing that lunch will be "Sliced Roast of Pork Loin with Cajun Mustard Sauce." That sounds better than a hot dog and fries.

At 8:30 a.m. I hear a few engines moan to life as the teams prepare for the 9 a.m. start of the first track session of the day. The cars go on the track on time and testing begins. I wander up and down the pit lane, watching the teams and catching glimpses of scoring monitors.

By 11 a.m. it's sunny, but still pretty cool. Several military jets fly over us, landing at Homestead Air Force base just a couple of miles away. One of the pilots decides to show us a little extra and accelerates into a tight turn, dragging snaky, white contrails off the ends of the wings. The roar of those engines momentarily drowns out the 15 or 20 engines at work down here.

A monitor shows me that Raul Boesel is quick on track right now with a 28.397-seconds lap. He's followed by Jimmy Vasser, Richie Hearn, Blundell, and Parker Johnstone.

Rick Gorne, managing director of Reynard, is here and I talk to him for a few minutes. I ask him how Reynard has earned the trust of the teams when Lola is so distrusted.

"We've built that trust," he says. "There's strength in numbers if you work together. The teams know we give everybody the same equipment. The teams need good engineers, but different teams need different kinds of people. We can help match up technical people with the teams, because we know all the people involved."

At 12:10 p.m. a monitor shows that Vasser has the fastest lap at 28.096 seconds ahead of Boesel, Hearn, Johnstone, Blundell, and Gugelmin. Vasser's time translates to an average speed of 194 mph, which is very fast for a 1.5-mile oval track. At 12:30 p.m., with 5 minutes to go in the session, Gugelmin pops up to third with a lap at 28.565 seconds. Vasser is still in first place, P1 to the crews, with Boesel in P2. Mark is seventh. Christian Fittipaldi takes the Swift out, but turns only a few slow, check-out laps. There is a front wing on the car, but I can't tell if it's trick or not. I'm just not that familiar with the aero details.

During the lunch break I talk to Ric Moore, Greg Moore's dad. He is fit to be tied. Greg's best lap is 30.263 seconds.

"My kid's not 2 seconds slow," he tells me.

Greg Moore drives for the Forsythe team, which is sponsored by Player's, a Canadian cigarette manufacturer. The team switched from Reynard to Lola chassis for this season, and the Lolas are slow.

The Tasman team, with drivers Andre Ribeiro and Adrian Fernandez, are also having problems with their Lolas. Rookie Richie Hearn, driving for John Della Penna, is the only Lola driver in the top five. Pat Patrick's team has already given up on the Lola chassis and came here with one new Reynard for drivers Raul Boesel and Scott Pruett. Boesel is in the car today and doing well so far. They'll take delivery of three more Reynard chassis soon.

Robert Clarke, who heads Honda Performance Development, tells me Honda's valve springs get special attention at its assembly facility in Southern California. "They're pretty small and could be easily put in someone's pocket. We put a serial number on each one and know where they are all the time. They're locked up when not in use."

All these engines, except for the Toyotas, are revving to almost 15,000 rpm, and those springs are what keeps the valves following the cam profile instead of hitting the top of the pistons. CART doesn't allow air-springs, as is used in Formula 1, so these steel-coil springs are a very critical part to each of the engine manufacturers, and they are improved constantly.

The cars are back on track again at 2:33 p.m. for the afternoon session, scheduled to end at 5:30. Al Unser Jr. and Paul Tracy are out first. A half-hour later Gugelmin is at the top of the list with a lap of 28.389 seconds. Boesel, Vasser, Hearn, and Unser Jr. follow.

At 4:20 p.m. Gugelmin goes faster, turning a lap at 28.268 seconds for an average speed of 193.220 mph. Blundell is 10th at 29.219 seconds.

Blundell's Big Crash

I'm in the PacWest pit when I see heads turn and hear on the scanner that Blundell hit the wall in Turn 2. He had just moved up on the monitor to fourth with a lap at 28.633 seconds, 190.757 mph, his best yet at this track.

I find a monitor tuned to a TV camera and it shows the car crunched up on the inside of Turn 2. I hear somebody on the radio say, "He's OK, but he's gonna have a headache."

Page Mader, one of the Firestone engineers, tells me, "I saw

The 18-Car on the Hook

him go into the corner and I heard him hit the wall. He was following Carpentier, maybe five or six car lengths back."

The car comes in on the hook with a big blue tarp, called a "diaper," strung underneath to keep the fluids from slicking up the track. All kinds of people converge on the car, for various reasons. The crew guys want to set it down and start to take it apart to repair it. They download the on-board computer and cover everything up as quickly as possible.

The Firestone engineers want to look at the tires to see if there was any tire problem that could have caused the crash. Bruce Ashmore of Reynard is right here to see how his product performed in this ultimate test of its ability to protect the driver. Wally Dallenbach, CART chief steward, comes up to look at the car. And competitors also arrive. Nick Goozee, Penske Racing, is here on the chance he can spot something revealed in the crash that he might not ordinarily get a peek at.

Jim Hamilton, Blundell's engineer, tells me, "He'd just made his best run and we made an adjustment to the rear sway bar."

By the time the debris is cleared it's too late to restart the session, so the track is closed for the day. The sun is dipping toward the horizon as a pair of F-14s scream overhead. I head back to the motel.

SATURDAY

At the PacWest hospitality area at 7:30 a.m. I meet Jeff Oster, the team's transportation manager and director of hospitality. More simply put, all the truck drivers and hospitality people work for him. Jeff used to be a mechanic and he knows the racing business from all angles.

I also meet Dave Loik, PacWest's full-time chef. Dave is European-trained and has been planning and preparing meals for large groups of people for almost 20 years.

Chris Woods and Don Mullins serve the people who enter the hospitality area. They also make sure that the crews get the food Dave prepares for them.

Mark Blundell is here also, eating some cereal. He says he's OK and jokes with people but he walks stiffly, and I'm sure he's in pain. That was a hard hit against the wall yesterday.

At 8:55 a.m. I'm on pit lane listening to warming engines and a blower truck on course. The pink, cottony clouds floating overhead when I first got here have blown away. It's sunny and clear now, with a cooling breeze. Cars roll out with the green flag at 9 a.m. sharp.

The crew of Blundell's No. 18 car pack up the pit equipment. Mark is OK but too sore to drive. His engineer, Jim Hamilton, and I talk about the rules for the upcoming race here which mandates speedway wings in order to lower downforce and reduce corner speeds.

"It's probably an inappropriate aero package for this track," Jim says. "You have to run the car really low to get the most out of the bottom of the car, but you can't go too low because bottoming upsets the car."

Scott Pruett is in Patrick's lone Reynard today. Michael Andretti is similarly driving the only Swift, since Christian Fittipaldi had it yesterday. It's cooler today and the denser air helps both the engine and the aerodynamics. Vasser quickly gets into the 27s. At 9:45 a.m. he's got the quick lap at 27.943-seconds. Mauricio, Michael, Parker, and Paul Tracy follow.

At 10 a.m. Patrick Carpentier scrapes the wall coming out of Turn 4. The black marks on the outer wall start right at the exit of the turn and go halfway down the straight. Track clean-up takes awhile, and Mauricio's car goes onto a setup pad in the garage area. A vacuum truck ambles down the track close to the outer wall, sucking up the carbon-fiber bits from Carpentier's crash.

Testing continues until the checkered flag at 12:30 p.m. Mauricio improves his time to a 28.031-seconds lap and ends up second quick in this session behind Vasser.

As the session ends Mark Blundell and John Anderson look over the stripped chassis Mark crashed yesterday. Mark is still moving stiffly. He's very thankful of the energy-absorbing seat fitted especially for him. "I don't think I would be standing here talking to you if I hadn't had that seat. The impact was extremely hard. The rear bulkhead has been bowed out by the force." I can see how the machined aluminum bulkhead at the rear of the chassis has been distorted by the weight of Mark and the fuel cell.

Just before the start of the last test session I notice Greg Moore's team loading up, getting ready to head back to the shop in Indianapolis. They had broken a differential case earlier, but I wonder if they've just decided to give up on the Lola.

At 2:30 p.m. the last test session of Spring Training begins with a green flag from starter Jim Swintal. It's warm, no clouds, a light breeze comes from the southeast — very pleasant.

Mauricio's car has an oil leak that has to be eliminated before he can go on track. He doesn't get in the car until almost 4:30, but quickly gets up to speed with a lap of 28.998 seconds, 188.330 mph.

Then Andre Ribeiro hits the wall in Turn 4. He's OK. Mauricio's car goes back into the garage area. It looks like he's done. Things are winding down now. Alex Zanardi has fast time in this session.

The combined time sheet with all the lap times for all sessions shows the Ganassi/Target team on top. Jimmy Vasser and Alex Zanardi have the fastest laps at 195.441 and 195.147 mph. Mauricio is third followed by Paul Tracy; Richie Hearn, surprisingly quick in a Lola; and Scott Pruett.

Blundell has the 13th-quickest time for the week. I have to wonder how that crash will affect his performance at the race here in a month. And what about the other oval-track races this year? Will he be spooked?

The checkered flag waves at 5:30 and Spring Training is over. Not quite, really. Both PacWest crews practice pit stops as the sun goes down. My flight back to San Francisco leaves early in the morning, so I go back to the motel for a couple of beers and some sleep.

Stagger

During Spring Training I noticed how careful the PacWest crew is with tire stagger. Scott Simpson, one of the truck drivers who's also the tire guy on the 17-car, was constantly measuring the circumference of the rear tires. He carefully wiped any dirt off the surface of the tire and placed the measuring tape just so to get a consistent and accurate measurement. He used a small stand with rollers so he could easily turn the tire.

The difference in the circumference of tires on the rear of a racecar is called stagger. On oval tracks CART cars use a locked rear axle — both rear tires rotate at the same speed. If the outside tire has a larger circumference, the car will tend to pull to the left, helping the driver turn the car. A typical stagger these days for CART cars is a few tenths of an inch. The cars are sensitive to stagger and the teams are very careful about measuring the tires and recording the measurements. The circumference of a tire can change slightly after it's stressed during a run on the track, so you'll see measurements being made on pit lane during practice sessions. Of course there are slight differences in tire circumference due to manufacturing tolerances so one set might feel a little better to a driver than another set that's supposed to be the same stagger. Those "sweet" sets get saved for qualifying or the last laps of a race.

Scott Simpson
Measures Stagger

It's a Start

For me Spring Training has been fun. I'm always happy at a racetrack watching cars and talking to racers about racing. I've met some of the PacWest people and they seem friendly and tolerant of my hanging around, watching, and asking questions. Bruce will pitch the book project to his managers at their meeting here during the next couple of days. Unless something weird happens, the project has started. I have no idea how it'll turn out, but it's started.

PacWest Shop Floor

Assembling the 17-Car

Tony Houk (Boomer) and Steve Ekeren
Work in the Subassembly Area

CHAPTER 3
THE SHOP

As I plan the book project and think about what it takes to tell the team's story, it seems logical to visit the PacWest shop so I can get to know the people and see the home base. The next opportunity is in late February when they're preparing the cars for the first race. So, on Thursday, Feb. 20 I'm on a flight from San Francisco International (SFO) to Indianapolis via Denver. I fly from sunny, clear, 70-degree weather in Redwood City, Calif., into the Midwestern winter.

FIRST DAY

I find the shop with directions faxed to me and arrive just after 8 a.m. Steve Fusek, VP business operations, introduces me around and Colleen Howerton, the office manager, makes some copies of their organization charts so I can tell who's who. I leave my shoulder bag and camera in a chair in the lunchroom. They're crowded, having outgrown the building, so the lunchroom will be my office. I've made myself some forms so I can get some information on each person, and I plan to do a quick interview with as many people as possible, take photos, and make notes about everything I see.

The PacWest Shop in Indianapolis

Stepping through the door from the front office into the shop, I see a large space that's bright and well lit. The floor has a gray epoxy coating, tough and oil proof. Four bays for the racecars occupy one side of the shop. Four new Reynards, a primary and T-car (back-up car) for each driver, sit on jacks in various stages of assembly. A fabrication shop, subassembly area, and paint shop are lined up front to rear on the other side of the building. The walls are a buff color and the cabinets are a medium blue.

They park the big transporters and motor homes in a big high-bay section at the back of the building. There is a transporter decked out in Hollywood graphics for Mauricio Gugelmin's car, the number 17, and another with Motorola logos for Mark Blundell's number 18 car. There's one more rig for the Indy Lights team. Parked outside on the asphalt are two motor coaches, around which the hospitality area will be arranged at each event. PacWest takes these two bus-sized motor coaches and a cooking trailer to all but the overseas races. At the races in Australia and Brazil they rely on local catering companies.

The two motor coaches are provided as a part of PacWest's agreements with Hollywood, Mauricio Gugelmin's Brazilian cigarette sponsor, and Motorola, the giant electronics company that sponsors Mark Blundell's car. Officially the cars are called the Hollywood PacWest Mercedes and the Motorola PacWest Mercedes.

Steve Fusek tells me he's negotiating to buy 5.1 acres adjacent to the shop property. The team is crowded now; two people work in a temporary building in the parking lot on the east side. About 60 people work in this building. More than 30 people travel to races regularly. Another 10 people work the motor coach and hospitality area. There are also shop-based people, office workers, fabricators, and subassembly technicians who don't travel to the races regularly.

I go outside and walk around the building to get an idea of the size of the place. A few hundred feet to the east is Walker Racing, and the building for the new Reynard wind tunnel is right next door. It's a dreary day outside, overcast with occasional rain, but not particularly cold.

I go back into the high-bay area and see they have a pit-stop practice area in one of the truck bays at the rear of the building. The layout is almost exactly as it would be on pit lane, with sections of concrete pit wall and a refueling rig.

I wander around, introducing myself and trying to fill out some interview forms. Everyone is busy. I watch what's going on and approach people only if they don't look too hassled. "Do you have a minute to talk?" is my lead-in. Some people look so busy I don't even ask. My strategy here is to avoid being pushy. If they don't want to be bothered, fine; I can't make them. Hopefully people will get curious about what I'm doing and maybe they won't want to be left out of a book about the team. I'm not going to get demanding and mess all this up right at the start.

Pit-Stop Practice

At 10:30 a.m. I see them start a pit-stop practice session. They open up one of the overhead doors to the outside so they can push the car into the pit box just as it would come in at a race. This is the crew of the 17-car. Mark Moore, the chief mechanic, and Jim Reid change the tires on the front end of the car. John Anderson, VP racing operations, called Ando by all, watches and talks over the results of each simulated stop. During one stop he disconnects an air hose to simulate a gun failure. They have a spare gun handy, so they don't lose much time.

The air wrenches they use are the best available, made by Metalor, an Italian company. But one fails, and Russ Cameron, the crew chief and race strategist for Mauricio, takes it apart to see what's gone wrong. There are four vanes inside that are made of a weak material, and they break often. Russ says they'll solve the problem by making some carbon-fiber vanes. While he's disassembling the air wrench Russ tells me the new rules for the 1997 season will make pit stops even more important during races. "They've reduced fuel volume in the fuel cells to 35 gallons instead of 40. We'll have to make more stops, and this makes it more dangerous."

As I talk to people during the morning I find out that most of the crew has the flu. "One of the Galmer guys brought it over from England," somebody says.

At 12:30 p.m. Fusek is back from the auction for the building and plot of ground next door. He signs some checks while we talk in his office. "I've never been in an auction like that before," he says. "There were 20 people from eight groups bidding, but only two real contenders. When we got to $425,000 it started to go up in $10,000 increments. We got it at $475,000. I wouldn't have gone that high on my own, but I had Bruce on the cell phone. It's his money. He kept telling me, 'Go more. Go more.' He says it's worth that because it's so convenient to our other property here."

Next I meet Ron Fusek, Steve's dad. Ron and his wife Mary run the suites that will cater to VIPs from the sponsors, mainly Motorola, the newly acquired sponsor of Mark Blundell's car. I go to lunch with Steve, Ron, and John Oreovicz, the PR guy, also new. They are all avid race fans, especially Indy cars and Formula 1. They buy and build model cars and discuss them at a level of detail that makes me feel left out. I think I'm an avid race fan, but these guys put me to shame.

Back at the shop I continue to watch what's going on and talk to people. It's almost 4 p.m. and raining. I've never before had the chance to spend this much time just looking at Indy cars up close. They're in various stages of assembly, so I can see a lot more than at a race.

The subassembly area is where components like wheel hubs, brake rotor and hat assemblies, and gearboxes are torn down and rebuilt. The guys working in the subassembly area are pretty much self-contained. They do their work in that area. In contrast, the people working on the cars walk quickly from one area of the shop to another, doing more than one thing at a time and continually talking to each other in the process. There's a lot of energy here.

Gavin Hamilton, lead mechanic on the 18-car, is a big, burly guy working on one of the fuel cells, preparing it for insertion into a chassis. Because the cells have come undersize from the manufacturer, the team has had to expand them by filling them with 200-degree water and pressurizing them slightly. Replacement fuel cells will come later.

Gavin is applying duct tape to the outside of the cell to prevent wear due to chaffing after assembly. He says the Reynard is pretty easy to work on compared to the Lola. "It's tough to get to the pedals with a Lola."

Gavin points out a plate on the right side of the Reynard chassis (called a tub) that provides an adjustment for the fuel cell capacity. A bolt on the outside of the tub reduces the volume when screwed in and increases when screwed out. Fuel cell capacity is specified by the rules, and this gives the teams a way to adjust it right to the limit.

The team fabricates a lot of its own pit equipment and also builds fixtures on the inside of the transporters. It's 4:20 p.m. and several people in the fabrication shop are working on these items. Randy Smay is the paint shop manager. He paints the pit equipment, as well as the car parts and bodywork.

At 5 p.m. Fusek takes me on a trip to check on the company that prints the graphics for the outside of the transporters and motor homes. These colorful designs are printed on 4.5-mil-thick, 3M-adhesive-backed vinyl material. They use Apple Macintosh computers to design the graphics to PacWest's specifications. It takes 15 panels 48 inches wide and 13 feet high to make up one side of a motor coach. These are the biggest panels used, but there are many smaller graphics applied to the racecars, motor coaches, transporters, and pit equipment. All the numbers and logos seen on a car are made this way, and there is a thriving graphic design industry in Indianapolis built on the unique requirements of the professional race teams.

After Steve is finished at the design house, we drive to 4A Gasoline Alley and Freelance Graphics, the company that applies the vinyl panels to the vehicles. Several guys are working on PacWest's Hollywood transporter when we arrive. They stand on ladders applying the vinyl material to the side of the massive transporter. It's difficult enough to lay the material on straight without ripples and bubbles, but they also have to heat it with a propane torch to get it to expand around rivets in the skin of the transporter. They use a round, stiff-bristled brush called a "rivet brush" to smooth the material. Bubbles of air that get under the vinyl are pushed to the outside or the vinyl is pierced with a pin to vent the bubble, allowing the material to lay smooth.

The rivets are bigger and spaced closer together along the bottom edge of the transporter. In this area the rivets are painted the same color as the design on the vinyl, and small holes in the vinyl allow the material to stretch enough to accommodate the rivet heads. Steve told me it costs about $26,000 to print and install the graphics for one transporter.

Lance Gibbs is the "lance" in Freelance Graphics. He's a bearded, balding Aussie in T-shirt, jeans, and shower clogs. I'm told he wears those clogs in all weather and his feet look the worse for it. Lance's feet are also very wide, so maybe he can't get shoes that fit. He's certainly a character, as is his dog, Toby, a big white shepherd of some kind. Toby enjoys attention and leans on my leg to let me know he wants to be petted. Lance tries to get Toby to do some trick he's famous for but Toby refuses to cooperate, and I never get to see the trick.

These people are working late on this Friday night, and Lance has ordered up some pizza, which he invites Steve and I to share. They take a break from work and we all munch on the pizza and talk. At 8 p.m. the shop begins to wind down. The transporter isn't finished, but they have applied all the vinyl available. More will be printed tomorrow.

I get back to the Hampton Inn about 8:30 p.m. I'm not hungry, but I have a beer at a bar/restaurant close by. At 9:15 p.m. I'm headed back to my room and I see Jeff Oster, the PacWest hospitality and transportation manager, in a fast-food place getting provisions for his ride home, a 1-hour drive.

"How's the battle going?" I ask. I had just met him earlier in the day, and I know that his crew is working hard to finish up the kitchen trailer and motor coaches in preparation for the first race at Homestead next week. They have to start the drive down there in a couple of days.

"It's been a long day," Jeff says, looking tired but still wired. "I was one of the last ones there and I'll probably be the first there in the morning. Steve was still there though."

SATURDAY

The weather was mild yesterday but the temperature dropped overnight and now it's in the 20s. I get to the shop at 8:15 a.m. and find about a third of the people I saw yesterday. I set my shoulder bag down in the lunchroom and go back into the shop. They're practicing pit stops again, but Russ is timing them now. They have a video camera set up so they can review and critique themselves.

They practice what they need to do if the driver stalls the engine after a stop. The guy on the inside rear tire doesn't have as far to go as the outside guy, and he'll get through changing his tire first. Then he grabs an electric starter off the pit wall and gets ready to stick it onto a shaft at the rear of the gearbox and turn the engine over. It's much easier to make up time, or lose it, in the pit lane than on the track.

This is the crew of the 18-car, Mark Blundell's car, practicing now. Butch Winkle, chief mechanic, works the outside front tire. Butch is the guy Mark keys on when he comes in for a stop. Mark is supposed to stop so the outside tire is just under Butch's outstretched hand. Daryl Fox is on the inside front, and Charlie Guilinger the inside rear. Gavin Hamilton changes the outside rear tire. Randy Smay is the fueler, while Tim Douthat, an expert fabricator, attaches the air hose that operates the jacks and also the vent hose.

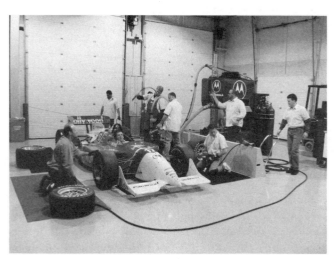

Pit Stop Practice

Mike Bauer, a transport driver, operates the "deadman valve," which is the main fuel valve. It's called that because if there is a fire and everybody has to run, the "deadman" lets go and the fuel flow is shut off. Stephen Kent is working behind the wall, holding a spare air gun to hand over if someone has a gun fail. John Roof is in the car acting as the driver.

Butch says, "Remember that stop at Nazareth [Pa.] when the jacks didn't go up all the way? We rocked the car back and forth to get the tires on." Everyone listens and some nod, remembering the event or filing it away for future use. This is a highly motivated group. You don't see anybody complaining or screwing off. I don't see anyone showing any less than complete concentration and 100% effort.

At 9 a.m. some other people rotate into the practice. John Anderson is here coaching, as he was yesterday. This is hard work. The guys wear gloves and knee pads to prevent scrapes and they get sweaty and out of breath.

The rest of the morning I watch what's going on, take photos, and make notes. Butch points toward what looks to me like a bare tub and says, "Mark's T-car is the one he crashed at Spring Training. It's waiting for a wire loom. Then the fuel cell will go in, then the aluminum bulkhead, and the motor and the wheels. That will all happen this afternoon. It looks worse than it is."

Sponsors: How They Landed Motorola

Steve Fusek is the vice president of business operations. He's been a serious racing fan all his life. In his mid-30s now, Steve is in a very high position given his age and experience. Bruce McCaw has given a lot of relatively inexperienced people a chance to shine. John Creak just moved from England to work for Fusek as marketing director. He's done similar jobs in the Formula 1 arena. I've got them both sitting in Fusek's office so we can talk about how they landed Motorola, the biggest sponsor yet for PacWest.

Paul: "So what's the Motorola story?"

Steve: "Are you asking questions or are we just talking?"

Paul: "How did it happen? The word got around that Parker Johnstone was leaving Comptech and Motorola was a big sponsor of theirs. All the teams must have heard about that and made a run at getting Motorola. You must have heard about it too."

Steve: "We had heard that Comptech was starting to crumble. The word on Parker going to KOOL and Team Green was starting to come out. We were in a position to offer Motorola a complete car, which we had heard was what they were looking for. But what we didn't have was any personal contact or knowledge of anybody at Motorola. We didn't know anybody there. So we were kinda at a loss as to where to go.

"Our photographer, Dan Boyd, gave us a name and we started calling. The problem was we were calling a general manager of a division and he didn't deal with our issues. We weren't getting anywhere and this was right at Thanksgiving of '96. We went to Denver to my folks' house for Thanksgiving. We knew that the Motorola sponsorship was in play and there were some people who had already gone to see them. As far as we knew it was only one or two teams. We found out later that everybody ran after them."

Paul: "It was Oct. 18 when Parker told Comptech he was quitting. I remember getting the fax announcement and calling Comptech to ask what was going on. They seemed shocked themselves."

Steve: "Yeah, and this was the end of November. So we went to Denver for Thanksgiving and spent most of that Friday at a Kinko's writing a letter and starting a proposal. I worked on the letter and John worked on the proposal. We faxed it to them from Denver and came back from Denver to Indianapolis, planning to leave Sunday night for Sebring [Fla.] for a Hollywood function. So we came back to town and left straightaway to go down there. That was Mo's first test in the '97 car and all the head Hollywood people plus a bunch of Brazilian media people came up for a ride-and-drive with the '96 car."

John: "The first day at the Hollywood press function we sat in the motor coach and tried to call the top guys at Motorola, and we couldn't get through to them. We were told they were out of town."

Steve: "And I was getting really sick."

John: "Steve had lost his voice. Eventually I got hold of Tom Crawford, the motorsports manager. I did the normal, 'Hello, we're PacWest, you've seen our fax.' Steve was sitting there opposite me and we were both listening to me talk..."

Paul: [laughs] "You were both listening to you talk?" John and Steve both laugh, maybe a little too loudly, perhaps remembering how uncomfortable they felt during this first contact, a potentially very important phone call.

John: "Crawford was sounding fairly lukewarm about us in terms of, 'Yes, Motorola is looking for another team; yes, they are going to stay in CART; they'd seen a lot of teams already, and they were very close to making a decision, etc.' They were going to make a decision within something like 48 or 76 hours. They were virtually there, and were questioning whether or not there was much of a point in PacWest putting a proposal in.

"But we kept talking and Tom started to ask a lot more questions, and then he asked some fairly specific questions about what we were doing with our cars and our drivers and our other sponsors.

"What I really wanted to do was to try and set a meeting up, to get Steve and me in front of Tom. And then come away from that meeting knowing exactly what they wanted so we could put a proposal together. Crawford was very clear there wasn't time to do that. We had to take a flyer and send a proposal to them."

Steve: "So the phone call we were on had to be the information gathering. It was all we would get."

John: "Yeah. At that stage it was very much, 'Send us something and we'll see about it.' We'd gleaned quite a lot of information during that 20-minute conversation about the types of things they were looking for. It was very obvious that the driver would be quite important, and the amount of exposure would be very important."

Steve: "Also the support that the team could give. I think that was the key — the support the team could give the sponsor. How were they going to be looked after? What kind of capabilities did the team have? What kind of vision did the team have as far as where it could go? Basically, how was Motorola going to be looked after?"

John: "It seemed to be quite important that, on the track, they were aligning themselves with a successful organization. Tom spent some time talking about the engines, the tires, the chassis, the overall technical direction the team was taking, and also our past performance."

Paul: "So he knew enough about the chassis and engines to talk about all that?"

John: "Yeah, he was very knowledgeable about CART and the packages and he knew about PacWest. We finished up the phone call on the basis that we were going to send him something. So we put the phone down in the motor home at Sebring, and Steve and I had a talk, very much deciding that we wouldn't send it; we would hand deliver it."

John: "We drove to Orlando to find a Kinko's. We had to do it two nights running actually, didn't we? We did Kinko's and then had to drive back to Sebring in the night, because that's where we were staying. We got back about midnight."

Steve: "And I'm dying."

John: "Each day he was getting worse and worse and worse. He'd come and sit in Kinko's with me and help, and then on the way back to the hotel I'd drive and Steve would crash and sleep in the car. We did this two nights running. [They both chuckle thinking about it now.]

"Then on Thursday we got a morning flight straight back to Indianapolis. We got in here about 1 o'clock in the afternoon and I had the discs from Kinko's, maybe about 25% of the proposal. At the same time we'd had a new computer installed here at the office.

"I came into the office and shut my door to get on with the proposal. I knew what I had to do. Steve went away to try to sort out the presentation of the proposal. He'd got a really good idea on one of the trips from Orlando to Sebring about how to present the proposal."

Steve: "We knew we were the last ones going into Motorola. On Wednesday I'd talked to Crawford from Sebring. My voice was starting to come back. I told him we had the proposal done, which we didn't. We thought we could get it done.

"I told him, 'The proposal's done. We'd like to bring it up, and maybe we can have lunch or something and talk about it. The other thing is that Mark is flying through Chicago on Friday, and this would be a good chance for you to meet him, if you're interested.' He said, 'Yeah, that would be fine. Why don't we have lunch?'

"So we had a meeting, which we didn't think we'd get. I had talked to Bruce on the phone about how we wanted to position ourselves with Motorola and bounced all the ideas off him. John and I had talked for hours and hours during the drives back and forth from the Kinko's in Orlando to Sebring.

"Bruce said, 'It sounds like something we can do. Let's go for it.' So we put it in proposal form then.

"On the flight back from Sebring we were talking about ways we could make a big impact when we walked in the door at Motorola. We just couldn't hand them a paper proposal and say, 'There you are.' We didn't want to look like everyone else. We needed to do something different. So we came up with the idea of putting them in steel briefcases. We'd put their names on the outside, and when they opened the briefcase the proposal would be mounted on the inside."

John: "While I got on with the proposal, Steve worked with some people here to get the briefcases and make some inserts molded to the inside to mount the proposals. Those are really top-quality briefcases. First we had to find them. So we sent Jeff Oster out to find three of them."

Steve: "He found them straightaway. But then, what are we going to do with them? How are we going to mount the proposal in there? Randy Smay, our painter, helped. We took a Styrofoam core and stuffed it into the bottom of the briefcase, and the proposal was held by a plastic picture frame. It ended up being a very nice presentation. It was something they didn't expect, and we got the impact we hoped it would."

Paul: "You gave them the briefcases?"

John: "Yeah. We made one each for Crawford, Bob Schaul [corporate VP and director of global markets], and Fred Tucker [executive VP/president and general manager of automotive, electronic, and computer systems]. While all this was going on with the briefcases, I was sitting in the office still, and it got to be 6 or 7 o'clock at night, and I'd got probably 50% of the text done. We're thinking, 'OK; the briefcases are in hand; it's looking reasonable. I knew it would be a late night getting it done. We'd booked flights to go to Chicago first thing in the morning.

"And all of a sudden my new computer seized. Completely seized. I couldn't extract anything out of the computer. I couldn't get the drawings or anything. I decided to use some old drawings I had and I went to another Kinko's to finish. The one on 38th Street. I'd been in there for about six weeks solidly while we waited for the computers to arrive here, so they'd got to know me quite well.

"The engineer who had supplied us our new computers tracked me down to the Kinko's, and we both came back up here to the shop. It's now 9 or 10 o'clock at night. He managed to rectify the problem on the computer, which was the CD player. We were able to extract all the information.

"So I went to another Kinko's up at Castleton, and I told Steve I just needed to get my head 'round it and get it done. So this is now 10 or 11 o'clock at night, and Steve is still ailing pretty badly. He headed home and I'm the only one in Kinko's that time of night. It was very quiet. It had started to snow as well. I had my papers all spread out over the floor. Time goes on, and it just took time to do it.

"I think I called Steve about 1 in the morning and told him I was close, and he should come on down in an hour or hour and a half. And then we could put it to bed. I called him again at 3 or 4 in the morning. He was still ill and had gone back to sleep. I'm saying 'You've got to come down here and see this, because we've only got a few hours to sort it out.' Steve comes down. It's now about 4:30 or 5:30 in the morning. We've got about 30 pages all over the floor at Kinko's."

Steve: "And about 3 inches of snow."

John: "Snow all outside. There's this guy in the background watching us in the Kinko's and wondering what was going on, because I don't think that was an average occurrence at Kinko's. Steve made some changes, I made some changes, and we come to the conclusion, 'Yeah; that's what we want to do.'

"We get the copies done. Steve goes back home. I wrapped it up and got them bound and I left Kinko's at about 6 in the morning, and we had a 9 o'clock flight. I figured I had time for a quick stop for breakfast, have a shower, put a suit and tie on, and then Steve and I can go.

"We do all that. We both get in the car and drive to the airport. The weather is getting really bad by then. We had the briefcases and we had them covered. We didn't want people on the plane to see what we were carrying, just in case. You know Indianapolis has obviously got a lot of racing people. We didn't want someone to walk up and say, 'Oh, you're going to see Motorola.'

"We get to the airport and get to the gate and there's no plane there at the gate. We've been up all night now and we're not feeling great, but we're still sort of psyched up about it. We've just got to get there and see them. The plane eventually comes and the people got off, but it doesn't look as if anyone was going to get on. They canceled the flight.

"Now it's 9 o'clock in the morning. We're due there at 11. There's an extra hour because of the time difference, so we have about three hours. So I say to Steve, 'How do we get there?' I didn't really want to drive. I'd been up all night. It had been snowing heavily. 'There must be a train,' I said sort of naively. Steve laughed. 'We'll drive,' he said.

"So we jumped in the car and I start driving. We get 5 miles out of Indianapolis and I'm nodding off and I have to pull into a rest stop. I just can't do this. I've been up all night, looking at a computer screen for about 10 hours. So Steve takes over and drives, at which point I called Crawford to tell him we'd be a bit late because our plane had been canceled, and he said, 'That's OK; you don't have to come up here.'"

Steve: "Yeah; he would have canceled the meeting, but we weren't about to do that. We said it really wasn't any trouble to get there; we'd just be a bit late. Meanwhile we were trying to keep the car on the road."

John: "Steve took over driving and we had to pick up Mark at O'Hare airport. We'd called him. He only had casual clothes at Sebring for that test. We told him to go out and buy some clothes, something smart. He had to put on a collar and tie and look the part. I slept all the way to Chicago. I woke up just before we got to O'Hare. I ran off and found Mark. He got in the car with us and we followed the map they'd kindly sent us. We called a couple of times for more directions. We got there just a little bit late.

"We signed in with the receptionist. She rings Crawford up and says there are three guys from PacWest down here to see you. We took a seat and waited. When Crawford comes down he's in his overcoat as if we're going to lunch. We introduced ourselves and he said, 'Let's go and talk over lunch.' Well, our presentation involves these three shiny metal briefcases. Steve's got one, Mark's carrying one, and I've got one.

"So I said, 'If you don't mind, can we go somewhere and do this properly, somewhere private and quiet so we can explain all this easily, rather than mess around over a dinner table?' He said fine and we went into the offices and went to a conference room. We sat down with Tom, and Steve leads it off and presented Tom with a briefcase. Tom opened it up and, bang, there's the proposal. It was beautiful. We put in some other touches as well; some business cards. It looked very PacWest. It was good.

"Tom opened up the proposal and started looking at it. He starts asking a couple of questions and I thought he was just going to flip it through to start and just listen and be polite about it. But he started reading the first page. That's always a good sign. We then sort of took him through it page by page, both Steve and myself explaining what was on each page and what we thought would be important to them, the way we thought the program with Motorola would work. Then he was firing questions back at us about some specific things. Between the three of us — myself, Steve, and Mark — we handled those questions as best we could. Mark was on show as well. He had to make a good impression. We were there for almost two hours. When we started to leave, Tom expressed a reservation about the briefcases."

Steve: "Those briefcases cost probably $500, and he asked us if we wanted them back, because they weren't allowed to keep anything like that. I guess it's a gift over some dollar level. I don't know what they did with them."

Paul: "What did Mark do during the presentation?"

John: "Tom asked Mark to tell his story. We had some time with Mark in the car coming from O'Hare and he was familiar with how the proposal read. He read it in the car, actually. Mark outlined to Tom his own track record and was also quite smart about including comments every now and then about how he'd been fairly well groomed in terms of commercial activities in the racing environment, having been with the Williams and McLaren Formula 1 teams."

Steve: "Mark fits in with us. We're a good match. Coming from McLaren, he knows how things should be done, and we'd like to be able to do things that well also. Mark knows that the way they do things is the way to do it."

John: "It was comforting to know we were putting Mark in and he would give a good accounting for himself. He's not big-headed in any way. He's very professional. He comes across well. Between the three of us we had a good meeting with Crawford. We came away from the meeting and we all got in the car and we drove to a local place to get a drink before taking Mark back to the airport. The first thing you ask each other when you get out of a situation like that is, 'Well, what do you think, how did it go?'

"I thought it went about as well as it could have gone. But I'm always fairly optimistic about things. I thought we'd done the best we could do. We got in front of them. There may still be things we can do. We'll have to play it by ear.

"They said to us that we would hear about it within 48 hours. It would be that quick."

Steve: "We talked about it all the way home. We talked ourselves in and out of it about five different times. [Both laugh.]"

John: "We called Bruce and talked it through with him."

John: "That was on a Friday. We were supposed to hear for sure on Tuesday. Didn't you get a call on Monday?"

Steve: "I got a call Monday morning from Tom. He asked a few more questions, clarifying things."

John: "Which is always a good sign."

Steve: "So we talked ourselves in and out of it a few more times. Then we were supposed to hear something Tuesday, but we never heard. I wanted to wait and not call him. I thought, 'He knows where we are. It's not like he was going to forget where we are.'

"He had plenty going on. I gave him some time and we waited. I think I called Tom on Thursday and asked if he needed any information. He said no; they were still in the evaluation process.

"Then Friday morning about 10 o'clock, I got a call from Tom. He asked a few more questions and he also asked what I had going on that afternoon. I told him I would be in the office. Then he said he'd like to come see us and take a look at the shop. We said that was no problem. He told us he had a flight booked already and would be in Indianapolis at 1 o'clock.

"So we had a quick clean-up in the shop. No one in the shop knew this was going on. We kept it secret between John and myself and Bruce. The guys who had worked on the briefcases knew there was a big proposal going out, but nobody really knew who it was."

John: "They got the shop looking all pristine. It didn't take much. Steve went off to pick up Tom at the airport. People were asking who's coming, but we just said don't worry about it and it will become clear later. Then Steve arrives at the shop with Tom, and when Tom takes off his coat, he's wearing a nice jeans shirt with a huge Motorola racing logo on it. Of course it took about 3 seconds for that to go straight away 'round the shop, and there's no secret now. We had a meeting in the conference room after the shop tour."

Steve: "Tom asked a lot of questions in the car, about how we would handle certain situations. I was driving and thinking and worrying about what we hadn't done or what else we could do. So we got to the shop here and gave him a tour.

"Then we went to the conference room and talked about some more specific details — hospitality needs and stuff like that. I think he had a 6 o'clock flight and it was getting toward 4 or 5 o'clock. We offered to take him to dinner, and we're starting to feel comfortable with Tom. It was getting to be a personal relationship instead of company to company. So we took him over to Union Jack's, John and myself. He delayed his flight, didn't he?"

John: "I had said to Steve when we knew Tom was coming to the shop that there was no way someone would make a decision without seeing what they're buying. So he almost had to come here before they could say yes or no. We were trying to talk ourselves into this as another positive sign. We had quite a good dinner, a couple of hours with Tom. No problems."

Steve: "Yeah, and he was getting more and more specific as we went along."

John: "Right. He said, 'How many of this? How many of that?' He was talking very specific details, rather than general, conceptual things. That was a good sign."

Steve: "It was getting to the end of the dinner and he was going to have to go and catch his flight. Their biggest concern at that point was our ability to compete on the track. He was starting to get very comfortable about our presence in the paddock and some of the new things we had planned for '97. We had not proved ourselves consistently on the track. So that started to be the key issue.

"He said they were concerned with that, and they had had some problems with that in the past with inconsistent results. They wanted to be involved with a competitive program.

"He asked if we would consider a contingency, some minimum-performance requirements. We were confident we would be competitive, and you always hope that you are. Tom was asking if we could live with some performance contingencies. We said 'Yes; we aren't afraid of that.' Then he said, 'If you're prepared to do that, we're prepared to offer you a long-term program, and I'll recommend that PacWest be the Motorola team.' "

John: "We dropped him at the airport, got out of the car and shook his hand. We took off and high-fived in the car. We went straight up to the north side to a bar for a quick drink, and it was almost like we didn't want to celebrate yet. We hadn't got it. We knew we were virtually there. We still had to get through the top level of management at Motorola. But we knew if we had the guy looking after the program recommending us, we thought we were probably there. It was a bit funny; we wanted to celebrate but we couldn't. Also, when you get into a position like that, you want to tell a lot of people, but again, you can't."

Steve: "So this was Friday. We were supposed to hear on Monday."

Paul: "That was Friday, Dec. 6?"

Steve: "Yeah. Then we didn't hear until Tuesday midday. Tom called me. He said they accepted his recommendation. I asked what his recommendation was. He said basically it was what we had talked about. I was in the shop on a phone, so I asked him to wait and I went into my office and we covered it enough to know we were basically talking about the same things.

"Then I said, 'That's fantastic; let's get it on paper.' And we got into how we wanted to announce the deal. The other part of this story is we had been interviewing for a PR person. We'd interviewed a lot and hadn't found the person we wanted. The day before Crawford came to visit, we'd interviewed John Oreovicz, and both John and I were impressed. We thought he was our guy. So I called John right after I talked to Tom and told him we'd like to offer him the job. He asked when he should start and I said by lunchtime if you can be here. His first day was when Tom was visiting the shop. It was a risk to do that before we knew we had the deal, but it worked out great.

"The best call I got to make was the one to Bruce. For all he had sunk into the team, to be able to call him and say 'We've got it!' was really great.

"The office didn't know and the team didn't know. This was Tuesday, and our Christmas party was Wednesday night. Tom said we could announce it at that party. He'd called all the other teams and told them about the decision. We'd do the press deal later.

"So, at the Christmas party, John Anderson and I got up in front of everybody and read a letter from Bruce that thanked everybody for a great year and looked forward to even better results in '97. The touring car team announced its PPG sponsorship, and then we announced the Motorola deal, which nobody knew about. The shocker part of that was fun.

"Everybody got up and cheered and clapped. We had all these pieces falling into place, with Mercedes and Firestone; Allen McDonald coming from Arrows; the drivers were signed; we had a major sponsor, Hollywood, on the other car; and now somebody else was buying into us. It gave everyone a little bit of a boost. I know John and I were buzzing, but everybody else was too now. There were a lot of excited questions about Motorola. It was a good start to '97 to be able to announce this deal and move forward."

Later I asked about the performance contingencies that Tom Crawford had brought up during the talks. Steve said it took two months to get the agreement on paper and the issue never really came up again. "Motorola just got more and more comfortable and confident in us, in PacWest. Performance wasn't an issue."

Talk with John Anderson

John "Ando" Anderson

About 1 p.m. John Anderson, Ando, and I go to lunch and I try to fit in an interview. Ando is 40ish, about 6 feet tall and fit looking, but somehow boyish. It's his energy and enthusiasm and optimism. He's obviously a natural leader.

Ando started in racing in Australia before coming to the States. He and his wife Lesley worked together; she'd do the books and travel and order parts while Ando worked on the cars. He came to work in Indy cars as a gearbox guy, and Lesley continued her work with whatever team Ando was with. Now he's vice president of operations and Lesley is successful selling real estate in Indianapolis.

We find a restaurant, but it's crowded so we sit at the bar and order some burgers. Like most of the PacWest people, John's story starts with the Rio race last year.

"Mark's crash there woke us up. We can't put new parts on a car and test them at the track during a race weekend. We're here to win first and evaluate development parts later.

"This year CART has lowered the maximum amount of fuel on board to 35 gallons from 40. That's going to make pit-stop strategy very important. Each car has an engineer; a back-up engineer, some teams call them junior engineers; and a DAG, data acquisition guy. They are going to have to keep up with the fuel calculations and the various strategies available to us as the race progresses. I work as race strategist for Mark and talk to him on the radio. Russ Cameron does the same with Mauricio.

"CART has tightened up the pit-stop rules. You can't just jump into the pits anytime. [Ando says 'time' as 'toime.' It's his Aussie accent. He also says 'bloody hell' a lot.]

"During an all-course yellow flag, the pits are closed until the leader has a chance to pit, and most of the time all the leaders will pit together. This means the teams are all competing directly against each other, and the quickest pit stop can get that driver out in first place."

Paul: "I'm impressed how hard everybody works on the pit stops."

Ando: "Yeah, everybody is involved in pit-stop practice. You have to listen to everybody. That gets them involved."

Paul: "Hiring the right people has to be important. The expansion of CART and Indy Lights and the new Indy Racing League [IRL] teams means good guys are in demand."

Ando: "First you get people you know you can work with. You can't have personalities that conflict. The environment of the team is important. It's a problem as we get bigger. But it comes down to individuals. You have to know the button to push on each individual to get his attention or make him see what you want.

"At first I was more interested in the job and how I should be doing it. The more people we hired and the more diverse the personalities got, I had to make more allowance for individuals. You have to be aware of the challenge of that. It can be a bit of a trick."

Paul: "Yeah; I don't think I did that very well when I was supervising people back when I had a real job. I think I was OK at telling people they did a good job and making sure they had the training and tools to do the job, but I wasn't good at the personal stuff. I'm too shy. I can see you're right out there in the middle with them. And then you have to do all the planning and paperwork. How do you find the time?"

Ando: "It can take over our lives. I've been doing it for 26 years. It's tough for a young guy. He might have a new wife or baby and he's at the shop until all hours. Sometimes you have to push them out the door. Other guys want to be home with the family, but they stick it out as a matter of pride."

Paul: "How do you hire the really key guys?"

Ando: "Money isn't the be-all and end-all for most guys [sounds like go-ees]. Money isn't high on the list. Here in Indy you have to make sure you're paying enough, but for most people, that won't be the reason they come to work for you or the reason they leave the team.

"You can tell when a team down the street is having problems because their best guys will be knockin' at your door. Number one, the environment has to be good. Two, the money has to be competitive, and three, the results have to be there. Excuses are OK for awhile, but you have to have the performance. These people want to win races and championships."

Paul: "People at PacWest seem pretty confident going to this first race. What if the team's performance down there is just so-so?"

Ando: "There'd have to be some reasons why that happened. It might be some stupid thing you can learn from, or it might be something out of your control."

Back at the Shop

At 3 p.m. we get back to the shop to find that Mark's primary car is almost ready to fire up. "We tried a while ago," Butch [Winkle] says, "but a starter wire was missing."

Casey Eason is the DAG on the 17-car. He's working with a laptop computer, changing the names of the sensor channels, for example, from Front Damper L to Damper FL. He's skeptical of the need. "It's a lot of trouble right in the middle of a thrash, and it obsoletes all the old data. And they [the engineers] don't look at the old data anyway. They keep adding sensors to the car, but nobody ever looks at the data."

Ron Endres is working on the 17-car, fitting a header box. This is a box made of thin stainless steel that insulates the exhaust headers so maximum energy gets to the turbocharger. The header box also prevents exhaust heat from burning the bodywork. Even with this insulation, you see the crew laying wet towels on the tops of the sidepods whenever a car comes to a stop. Heat soak will still blister the paint without those towels.

These new parts don't quite fit together, so Ron has to fit them, take them apart and work on them with an air grinder, and try to fit them up again. It looks frustrating, but he just keeps working on it.

At 4:25 the 18-car is getting closer to start up. The crew pushes the whole car, without wheels, on a wheeled dolly toward the back of the shop and out the overhead door into the high-bay area. They rotate the car on the dolly so the exhaust is just outside the partially raised door. It's cold out here, and everyone has on a jacket and gloves.

A splined shaft on the electric starter engages an internal spline in the gearbox and they bump the engine over a few seconds at a time until the oil pressure comes up. Then a longer burst on the starter, and it fires to life. They quickly look all over the engine and plumbing so they can spot leaks, but there are none.

Daryl [Fox] operates the throttle so the revs go up and down with a soft moan. I ask him what oil pressures they look for during the start-up process. "Every bump with the starter gives a couple of pounds of pressure," he says in his own Aussie accent. "It goes up 2, 4, 6, and so on until it gets to double figures. Then we can turn it over steady. After the engine starts, the fuel and oil pressures need to be in the 50 to 60 pound range."

An hour later Mauricio's primary car starts up also. Things are coming together, but they've got a ways to go. Some people clean up and leave, probably coming back in tomorrow, a Sunday. Others continue to work.

I invite Fusek and Creak to dinner. Steve can't go so John and I find a restaurant and have a good dinner. Then it's back to the motel for me and a short sleep before an early flight back home. This has been a great trip. I got to know a lot of the PacWest people and absorbed a bunch of information.

Starting a New Engine

CHAPTER 4
THE HOMESTEAD OVAL

The week before this first race I'm extremely frustrated and actually scared. I've sold people on this book concept, gotten commitments from companies to fund my expenses, and told everyone I know that I'm going to write and publish the best book ever on racing. Well, they believe me, and now I'm going to have to deliver.

There's one non-stop United Airlines flight a day from San Francisco to Miami. It gets in at 10 p.m. After getting a rental car, I find the hotel easily enough following the directions they faxed me a few days earlier. The Dadeland Marriott is an old hotel, but the rooms are nice and the service is a lot better than the cheaper places I usually stay. After check-in I have a couple of beers in the bar and some talk with a few PacWest people and then go to bed.

FRIDAY

My usual race weekend excitement wakes me at 5:30 a.m. I know it's a race weekend when I use sunblock for aftershave. I get some coffee from the lobby and have a look at the *USA Today* left outside my door.

Then down to the parking garage and out onto the toll road south to Homestead and the track, just as I did a month ago at CART Spring Training. It's all more familiar now.

I don't have to stop at registration this time, however, because Christy Clutter, PacWest sponsor coordinator, gave me my hardcard when I was at the PacWest shop last week. What a treat! No lines to stand in before being told to go stand in another one.

I can't, however, drive through the tunnel under the track without an infield parking pass, so I park right outside the tunnel and ride in on a shuttle bus. It's about 7:30 a.m. when I walk into the paddock. The PacWest garage area is near the Turn 4 end of pit lane.

There are four racecars arrayed in the PacWest garage bays, all in various stages of preparation for the first practice session of the season only 3 hours away. Most of the crew know me by now, because of my trip to the shop. I see nods and hear hellos and return them and shake some hands. The mood seems calm and busy. I try to keep out of the way while I watch and take notes.

Bruce and his wife, Jolene, come in greeting people, all smiles and pats and handshakes. Russ Cameron gets a sisterly hug from Jolene. Bruce has a wide smile beaming out of his round, bearded face. These people all like each other. They're working together energetically on something consuming and exciting.

At 9:30 a.m., still an hour before the first CART practice, the weather is balmy, probably about 75 degrees, with a 20 mph wind out of the east. A short-sleeve shirt is just fine.

Most of the crew are still working in the garage area, but some are setting up the pit areas and I chat with them. Ian Hawkins is a track support engineer for Ilmor. He baby-sits the Mercedes-Benz engine in the 18-car, actually designed and built by Ilmor Engineering in England. There's an Ilmor guy assigned to each driver using Ilmor/M-B engines.

Tire Guy

Scott Simpson is the tire guy for Mauricio's car and also drives the Holly-wood transporter with Tom Keene. I ask Scott what a tire guy does. "I chart the tire information and organize all the sets of tires we get from Firestone at every race or test. I work with Andy and Mo and the Firestone engineers. If I have ideas, I tell them what I think. The wheel sets have to go to Firestone to have the tires mounted and balanced or demounted. The tire pressure sensors have to work right. I bounce the tires to make sure the sensor is working. Setting cold pressures is important, and keeping records of the pressures and staggers."

Scott Simpson, Tire Guy, and
Brett Schilling, Firestone Engineer

"Do you suit up on race day?"

"Yeah, I do. I don't go over the wall though. I just do the deadman on the fuel rig. I don't have any desire to go over the wall."

Mark's Practice Session

The session starts at 10:30 sharp. The sun is getting warm, promising a sweaty day. Mark's car goes out as the green flag flies. Mauricio is in the second session. His car is still in the garage.

There really isn't much time on the track during a weekend and it takes awhile to sort through the many adjust-ments on a car while trying to make it

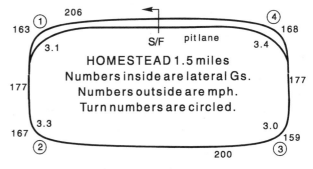

fast on the track and comfortable for the driver. Any glitch such as an oil leak or electrical problem detracts from the track time and crew focus needed to optimize the car's performance.

A yellow flag stops the session for a few minutes. Mark comes back into the pit lane for car adjustments. I'm listening in with my scanner as he talks to his engineer, Jim Hamilton. "The car feels a little bit hooky in Turns 2 and 4," Mark says. "I can't feel the entry real well. Maybe that's my inexperience. The car's just floating on me."

Jim tells the crew to put one flat of toe into the right-rear wheel, and he softens the front shocks as well. "It's not hitting on the bottom, so we'll lower the car too," Jim says.

Jim knows the bottom of the car isn't hitting the track because one of the guys has crawled under the car and looked at the skid plates on the underside. When the bottom of the car rubs on the track surface it grinds off some of the black paint on these skid plates, leaving marks that reveal where and how much the car bottom is touching. Driver feedback tells the engineer where on the track the car is bottoming.

Each PacWest crew has some pre-printed pads with a schematic of the car bottom. When the crew member looks at the bottom he marks up one of those sheets and gives it to the engi-neer. Then he sprays black paint over the old marks on the bottom.

These cars use ground-effects to produce downforce. The track surface speeds up the air under the car, reducing pressure there just as air speeds up over the top of an airplane wing. One of the critical tasks Jim Hamilton, and any other engineer here today, has is to set the car up so the bottom is very close to the track but not hitting it too much.

How much is too much? Well, you don't want so much weight on the bottom of the car that it takes weight off the tires. The result of that is loss of tire force and a spin. Just enough bottoming is great; too much bottoming is bad.

Mark replies to Jim's suggestion with one of his own. "Let's lower the car before we soften it up."

Jim tells the crew to lower the car two flats across the front and one at the rear. What that means is a rotation of an adjustment nut through the angle of two of the six flats on the nut. One flat is about 0.040 inch, or a little more that 1/32 of an inch. Six flats is one full rotation of the nut. When a car is near optimum setup a driver can feel a ride height change of one flat.

These photos show the front suspension. The close-up photo shows the pushrod between the rear leg of the upper A-arm and the steering arm. The middle nut turns the adjustment bolt which has left- and right-hand threads. Turning one way makes the pushrod longer and raises that corner of the car. Turning the other way lowers it. The other two nuts lock this adjustment bolt at both ends. Obviously there are four such adjustments on each car.

Right-Front Suspension

Close-Up of Ride Height Adjustment

Mark asks about the fuel load, saying he'd like it kept the same so he doesn't get confused by that variable. It's about 11 a.m. now and as Mark goes back on track, Mauricio's car is on pit lane warming the engine. Norbert Haug, Mercedes-Benz's worldwide motorsports manager, walks up to talk to Bruce. He looks very Germanic with his mustache and paunchy, no-neck build.

Mark comes back in after a few laps on the oval. "The rear is kissing on the straight now, so we need to go up a touch."

"What else?" Jim asks.

"I've got more feeling at the front," Mark responds. "More grip. The rear is a little uncomfortable though. Maybe we should get a read on the primary tires now."

PacWest uses Firestone tires. Both tire companies, Firestone and Goodyear, can bring two different tires to each race, called primary and optional. Every car must start the race on the same tires used to qualify. It's an important choice. You want to use the tire that makes your car and driver fast, but the tire also has to last between fuel stops during a race.

"We have a good reading on the tires," Jim says. "The spring rate's different on the primaries, so we'll need to raise the car. Let's work on the stagger now and get to the primaries later."

Mark goes back on track and works the lap times down over a few laps. I time him with my stopwatch at 35 seconds, 34, 32, 31.30, 30.91, 30.78, 30, 35. Then he comes back in.

When Mark is on the way in, Jim asks for telemetry data on tire pressures. Casey Eason, the DAG, data acquisition guy, on Mark's car, replies that there is no telemetry operating for this session.

Mark says there's more movement with the car now. "Longitudinally, front and rear. Also in Turn 2 and 4 there's no turn-in at the front. It's just pushing on through."

Jim: "Let's take pressures and amend them and get back out." There are 3 minutes to go in the session.

As the session winds down I realize all my nervousness and lack of confidence have gone away. People are talking to me. I'm seeing and hearing and writing down things that are significant and will be interesting for people to read.

Mark's final feedback to Jim: "The [tire] pressure change made a big difference. Turn 4 is the issue now. I've got understeer and lack of front grip. Turn 4 is the worst. I don't feel commitment yet. The car tracks about a lot."

Mauricio's First Practice Session

The green flag for the second group flies at 11:35 a.m. and Mauricio goes out on track right away. Navy jet fighters work in the sky overhead. I think they're F-18s. They fly in tight circles and the high angle of attack causes white sheets of condensation over the wings, and condensation trails slide off the wing tips in swirls. The guys flying those machines have much in common with the guys in the cars down here — fierce competitiveness and serious commitment.

Mauricio comes back in for some adjustments and goes right back out. He does some slow laps and then I clock him at 32.86 seconds, 31.50, 30.38, 30.53, and in. He radios to Andy Brown, his engineer, that he has a vibration — tires or engine. They make some adjustments and he goes back out.

Mo comes back down pit lane just as a yellow flag flies. The safety teams go out and look for debris on course. "It's not hitting at the back in Turn 1," Mauricio tells Andy. "It feels good on turn-in but light on the exit. In Turn 2 it's soft in the front. At Turn 3 it feels light on the exit with understeer and Turn 4 is the same. Maybe we just lower the back?"

"The weights are all good," Andy says. "If the understeer doesn't go away we should go to the primary tires after this run."

Andy pauses to look at data and adds, "The tire pressures are low." There are sensors on each wheel reading tire pressure and a radio signal transmits that data back to the engineer of each car. This is an expensive feature and the major justification is a safety-warning of a deflating tire, but the information is very useful to the engineers and drivers for other reasons.

Mauricio: "That's what it was then. Just forget what I said and we'll try again. I'd rather see the tires higher than lower. It's like a yo-yo when they're low."

Andy: "You used 6.4 gallons of fuel on that run." That figure also comes from data transmitted from the car. Each car has cockpit-adjustable front and rear antiroll bars also called sway bars.

Mauricio tells Andy how he has his set. "Is that what you want?"

Andy: "Yes; fine. Two clicks counterclockwise on the fuel mixture please."

Mauricio goes back out and does some slow laps before I clock a 29.64. Back in and stopped, he says, "The vibration is still there, but let's check the pressures as well." He goes through each corner describing in precise detail the behavior of the car.

At 11:59 a.m., on the way back out, Mo asks if fuel was added. "No," Andy replies. "You've used 9.5 gallons."

It's warmer now and I'm drinking water constantly, a half bottle at a time. But I don't have to pee, so I know I need to keep drinking. On this run Mauricio starts with a 32-seconds lap followed by 31.13, 30.03, 29.34, and another one I miss. He comes in, saying he doesn't like the car now.

Andy tells the crew to put on the finned engine cover and take some rear wing out. "For the record," Mo says, "If the car is like this in the race, we'll lose. I guess you've heard that before."

He asks for the monitor and they hand him an LCD monitor about 10 inches high by 12 inches wide and 2 inches thick. There is no cord attached. This is a system supplied by ARS, Advanced Racing Systems. The monitor runs on batteries and receives Timing and Scoring information via radio signals.

Mauricio goes back on track at 12:09 p.m. There are a few hundred people scattered through the stands. I time laps of 31.43 seconds, 29.71, 29.10, and 28.73. Mo comes back down the pit lane telling Andy about the car. They make some shock adjustments. Mo asks for the monitor and a drink.

Jim Hamilton, Mark's engineer, is listening to the radio also. He tells me that both drivers are saying similar things about the optional tires. He wants to see what Mo has to say about the primary tires. At 12:16 Mo is back out and I get times of 31.88 seconds, 29.70, 28.80, and 28.67. Mauricio is second quickest in the session, P2, at that point behind rookie Patrick Carpentier, who is surprisingly quick.

Mauricio is back out with 3 minutes to go in the session. I miss a couple of laps and then I see 30.06 seconds, 28.54, and 28.89. Coming back in, Mo says the car turns in slower and pushes at the exit. Andy tells Russ Grosshans, "Fill 'er up, Russ, and tell me how much it takes."

They're done for this session. Thirty-five cars ran in that session, with seven guys using both their primary and back-up cars. Alex Zanardi was quickest at 28.553, more than 191 mph, in a Reynard/Honda on Firestone tires. Next came Carpentier in a Reynard/Mercedes-Benz/Goodyear (28.608), and Mauricio with a Reynard/Mercedes-Benz/Firestone (28.640). Mark was 22nd quick in the session with a best lap of 29.902. Eighteen cars lapped within a second of Zanardi. This will be a very competitive season.

Tire-Pressure Sensors

The tire pressures must be very important or the drivers and engineers wouldn't talk about them so much. I ask Casey Eason about the sensors. "There is a tire-pressure sensor inside each wheel. A small battery powers the sensor and there's a radio transmitter in there too. You can see the antenna. The tires are tubeless so the antenna just sticks out inside the tire. Wheel rotation causes a force on a weight that starts the transmission. Fluctuating tire pressure can turn it on too. The transmitter broadcasts a signal carrying the pressure information.

Tire-Pressure Sensor with Transmitter

"A receiver on the car picks up the signal from each transmitter and knows which tire it comes from. All the right-rear wheels, for example, transmit on the same frequency. The receiver makes that reading available to the on-board computer system. The driver can view the values on his dash, and it's also transmitted to the engineering cart for display or recording there. If the pressure reading varies by 1 pound, the data-logging frequency speeds up. The PI system [the data logging and analysis software] also displays where on the track the pressure change happens, so if an object on the track causes a puncture, the safety team knows where to look for it."

Friday Afternoon Practice

Mark is out on track right with the green flag at 2:30 p.m. He's back in after a run of laps with a best time of 29.835. He tells Jim Hamilton how the car feels. "The car isn't stable. I'm getting no feedback under load."

Jim requests a shock change at the front. Mark asks for a reason for the damper change. Jim replies, "To give you more feel on the way into and out of the corner."

Mark continues to talk about the car. "Going into Turn 1 it feels like the rear is always on the edge."

Jim goes over the wall and looks closely at the tires on Mark's car, and then he tells Mark that the pattern he sees in the tire rubber "indicates just what you're saying." He tells the crew to make a specific change. Back on track, Mark turns a lap of 30 seconds flat and then 29.58, 29.36, 29.57, and comes in.

"I've got a softer front end now," he says on the radio. "It gives me more feedback. But the rear doesn't feel good; it wants to get away from me."

Jim: "Let's take some high-speed rebound out of the rear. The car seems to be responding to shocks. I'd like to know the effect of the rear bar too. I'll leave it up to you as to when to do it."

After the changes Mark runs some laps, with the best at 29.346 seconds. The sky is more cloudy now and the clouds are bigger and gray on the bottom. Rain? The wind is still from the east but seems a bit lighter.

After a few more laps Mark says, "No bar change yet. The car's got more sag in it now at the rear. It seems more comfortable, but it's not the support I need. The car's always talking to me at the rear."

Jim: "The tire temps are telling a good story now; they don't always. We'll talk among Tim [Neff, the shock specialist] and you and I to decide what to do next." This means Jim and Mark and Tim Neff will go off the radio to discuss shock absorber adjustments. You never know who's listening.

They make some shock changes and a ride height change. Jim tells Mark he will probably feel more push. Mark goes out and turns a 29.2-seconds lap. Mauricio's crew pushes the 17-car from the garage to the pit lane.

At 2:58 a yellow flag stops the session. Hiro Matshushita's car comes in on the hook, probably an engine failure. The Toyota engines are very fragile. At 3 p.m. Mark is out on track again and I get lap times of 30.50 seconds, 29.27, 29.11, and 29.16.

After he's back stopped in the pit lane, Mark describes the car behavior starting with, "It's a little better off now. The front is touching at speed. It's turning in too quickly." He goes on at length and in great detail.

At the end of the discussion Jim says, "We're going to reverse the strategy here. Let's pick up the front a little with the springs." He continues with quite a few spring and shock changes. After about 5 minutes in the pit lane Mark is back out with 3 minutes to go in the session.

After a few laps a yellow flag brings him back in and he describes the car to Jim. "It felt more stable, as you said it would, but the rear is still giving up on me. There's a little drift. The front goes a little bit and then the rear went."

"Any clean laps?" Jim asks. "When it was drifting, was that clean?"

"I think so," Mark says. "I think we should look at it." The checkered flag flies for that part of the session.

Mo's Practice Session

Now it's Mauricio's turn. After a green flag he works up to speed with laps of 35 seconds, 31.60, 30, 27, 29.62, and comes back in. "That's more like I had at Spring Training," he says, adding, "It's touching at the back."

Andy: "We've got a cut right-front tire. Let's change all four. Up 2 pounds on these. That last set had 35 laps." They put sticker tires on the car and Mo smokes the rears taking off down the pit lane. Several of the crew smile. Burning rubber is fun.

After a few laps in the 29s there's a yellow flag to let the safety team look for debris. Mo comes back into the pit box. "Looks like the pressures are OK," Andy says. "Let's go up on the high-speed bump all around."

As usual Jim Hamilton is watching and listening to what's going on with the other car. Anything he learns might help him make Mark's car faster, or Mark faster in his car. I've noticed that Mark's feedback seems unfocused and lengthy compared to Mauricio's. Mark says everything he can think of about the car, while Mauricio seems to filter his feedback for Andy, reporting only the highest-priority information.

"So how do you tell what really matters in all that information Mark gives you?" I ask Jim.

He laughs out loud. "Why did I know you were going to ask that?"

"Actually," he continues, "there is some consistency in what Mark says, and it's becoming clearer all the time. But I have to use all my tools to help me. I've got math channels to massage the data from the car, and the tire reads help me. He's a great driver. He's got the heart of a lion, and I think he's a good racer. The fine development of the car is not his strong suit. He's continuing to learn about oval tracks."

Mauricio goes back on track for a few laps at a time and continues to work on the car, telling Andy how it responds to changes. Every time he comes in he practices stopping his right front tire directly under Mark Moore's gloved hand. Bobby Rahal stalls on course, bringing out a yellow flag.

In the next run Mo turns laps at 30.66 seconds, 29.53, 28.92, 30.30, 29.23, and 29.49. He comes in at 4:07 p.m. "Twenty minutes to go," Andy says. "Do you want to go softer still? We were up 2 or 2.5 pounds on the right front [tire pressure]."

They make some shock changes and Mo starts the engine. The clouds of smoke that used to blossom from the turbocharger as the engine starts up are gone now. Paul Ray told me a month ago at the test at Laguna Seca they had the fix for that problem, and I see he was right.

Mo puts in some good laps: 28.60 and 28.87 seconds. I see Paul Tracy slap the wall at the exit of Turn 4 with his right-rear tire. There are several black smudges on the white paint in that location. Tracy's brush with the wall didn't seem to hurt the car, and he continues to circulate.

Mo comes back in and then goes out again. They make some ride-height changes because he says the car is touching down in the bumps. Then he turns the fast time of the session with a 28.305 seconds, almost 193 mph.

When he comes back in Andy says they should scuff tire set number two after this run so it will be ready later. "Did you try fifth gear?" Andy asks Mauricio. That's probably a lower gear than sixth and the engine will rev higher and produce more power.

"No," comes the answer. "I don't have the balls to do it."

It's now 4:27 p.m.; 6 minutes to go in the session. Mauricio is still at the top of the list on the monitor. Jimmy Vasser and Alex Zanardi are on track right up to the checkered flag. All these drivers are very competitive; they want to have the fast time in every session. But at the checkered flag ending the session, Mo's 28.305 holds for P1. That's an average speed of 193 mph. Mark's earlier best lap of 29.084 puts him in P16. The crews roll the cars back into the garage and start the preparation and adjustments for tomorrow's sessions.

A couple of hours later, after their technical debriefs, Mark and Mauricio come back into the garage area to talk to their crews. The sun has set and the light is almost gone. Some high cloud layers in the west show pink above fluffy, grayer clouds nearer the earth.

The concrete garages become islands of light and activity in the darkness. There are about 30 PacWest and Ilmor people working on the four cars. A couple of guys are polishing wheels. John Anderson and Russ Cameron talk seriously about gearboxes with Tim Love, the gearbox guy on Mark's car.

Relaxing Hospitality

Back at the PacWest hospitality compound, activity is also winding down. Chef Dave Loik has finished the crew dinner and also the dinner laid out here in the carpeted hospitality enclosure.

It's getting dark and I'm thinking about asking around to see if someone wants to have dinner at some local restaurant. But they all seem pretty busy, and I'm about to go back over to the garage area when Chris Woods, hospitality supervisor, tells me dinner is ready. Sure enough, under the bright silver covers of the warming trays is a wonderful dinner. I choose some salad with fresh quartered tomatoes, roasted potatoes, green beans, and a couple of slices of filet mignon that is pink in the middle just as I like it. This is a lot better than during Spring Training when I ate burgers and beer by myself in the motel room.

Bruce comes out of one of the motor coaches later, and we talk while he eats his own dinner. Bruce asks Greg Watson if there's some wine available and asks me if I'd like a red or white wine. I say I'll drink either and Bruce chooses red. This is the way to go racing!

At 8 p.m. I gather up my stuff and walk in the dark back over to the garage area, where the activity is calm and focused. I can see they're going to be here a couple more hours, but I'm tired and need to make some notes about what I've seen. I head back for the hotel.

GREG MOORE'S TEAM SWITCHES TO REYNARDS

Steve Challis, Greg Moore's engineer through Formula Ford 2000, Indy Lights, and last year, Greg's rookie season in Indy car racing, told me earlier today how they were forced to switch from a '97 Lola chassis to a '97 Reynard. They won't take delivery of the new chassis until late March, so they're actually using a '96 Reynard at this first race. Greg is 15th and 10th in the two sessions in the year-old car — a great showing so far.

Steve, like Greg, is Canadian and a really great guy. He works hard and smart and laughs easily, even if it's at himself. "I dunno, Paul," he explained, an open, earnest look on his face. "I guess I just couldn't make the Lola work. I tried real hard, but I just ran out of time. We tried some of our own stuff and some things Lola told us to try, but we just couldn't get it comfortable for Greg."

"When I saw you guys loading up before lunch that last day of Spring Training, I knew you were going to switch," I say.

"We had to," Steve says. "Greg's a good driver and there was no way he was that slow. Actually there's a competitive streak in me that makes me want to work on the car and turn it into an advantage. Maybe we'll regret our decision, but I don't really think so."

"The Lola suspension is very different," I say. "Does the shuttle bar work? Do those little coil springs act like a sway bar? Does the roll damper work?"

Steve screws up his face, probably remembering the frustration he's been trying to forget. "That part of the car is fine. When you put the numbers from that suspension into your simulation program, it acts just like it's supposed to. There might be some advantages there, but we ran out of time. We want to have a go at the championship and that means we have to be in the top five consistently.

"The Lola guys are great. They tried hard to help us and I wish them the best. We don't want a one-make series here. We wanted to make the Lola work, but we had to make the change."

I have one other question. "People talk about driver confidence being important, especially on an oval. There's got to be an engineer confidence factor also. Did all that frustration hurt your confidence?"

"It sure did," Steve admits. "That's why it feels so good now. Everything makes sense again."

SATURDAY

After a decent sleep, the morning shower and shave go quickly. On the drive south to the track I see some rain showers to the east, and when I get to the track puddles are everywhere. I stow my stuff at the hospitality area about 7:30. CART practice is at 8:30, so I walk over to the garage area quickly. The guys are swarming all over the cars and a few engines can be heard groaning and moaning through their warm-up.

Practice

The green flag waves promptly at 8:30 a.m. and Mark is on track immediately. Mauricio's car is being pushed onto pit lane. The wind is cooler, and stronger than yesterday. The gusty east wind goes the same direction as the cars through Turns 3 and 4, lowering the downforce they produce and destabilizing the cars. There is also a bump in Turn 4 that unsettles the cars, especially if they bottom out there.

Mark comes back in at 8:37 after a best lap of 29.50, saying, "I'm on the rev limiter into Turn 1 and also Turn 3. The rear wants to drift out. It just gives up."

Jim Hamilton's calm voice comes into my headphones. "The wind direction is consistent with what you're saying."

"It might be touching down a little bit," Mark says. "So we should check the bottom of the car."

"I'll look at the data for a minute," Jim says. And then, "I'm not sure I like what I did with the tilt."

"Turn 3 has the tightest radius," says Mark. "So maybe the tilt is a problem."

These are ground-effects cars, as I mentioned before. The bottoms of these cars, called underwings, are sculpted, within the rules, to use the close proximity with the track surface to accelerate the air under the car. When the air speeds up, its pressure goes down, and that low pressure under the car adds to the forces on the tires and increases the grip the tires produce.

Special rules for this race at Homestead mandate the use of small wings meant for high-speed tracks like Michigan. The resultant lower downforce is meant to slow the cars in the corners. Trying to regain as much downforce as possible, the teams are running the bottoms of their cars as low as they can. The cars roll in a corner just like our street cars, but not as much. The car is set up with some "tilt" when it's sitting still. The right side is higher than the left side, so when the car rolls in a corner, the bottom is flat to the track and as close to the track as possible.

A shriek of tires gets my attention and I look up in time to see a car sliding lazily (but still going over 100 mph) out of Turn 4 toward the inside pit wall. It hits the wall a glancing blow, sending up a cloud of dust, and skids to a stop near the start/finish line. Roberto Moreno is the driver. He moves around right away, so he's OK. The safety trucks speed quickly to him and a yellow flag stops the session until after the cleanup.

I walk across the pit lane to the wall to have a look. Black stripes snake out of Turn 4 right toward me and there are tracks across the grass, showing Moreno hit only yards down the straight from where Mike Bauer has been standing, tending Mark Blundell's pit board. Mike grins at me and shakes his head in comic relief. "He tried to get me."

As I walk back across the pit lane, Mark and Jim are still talking about tilt and cross weight. "Let's go up one flat at the left front and a half-flat at the left rear," Jim says. "We'll take out some tilt and reduce the oversteer."

At 8:53 the track is clear and a green flag flies. After a few laps Mark is back in, talking about the car on the radio. "It's nervous now. It's a handful; no comfort there. I'm constantly fighting it all the way through the turn. I can't lean on the car at all. It's going to let go. It's scaring me at all times."

Another car comes spinning out of Turn 4. It's Dennis Vitolo, a rent-a-racer whose main claim to fame is climbing up over the back of Nigel Mansell's car during an Indy 500. There are now more snaky black streaks on the pavement and another black smear on the wall at the exit to Turn 4. A few people brushed the outer wall yesterday, but it started off clean this morning. I guess they repaint the walls every night.

Jim makes some camber changes at the rear, reversing some previous changes. During the yellow flag to clean up after Vitolo, Mike Bauer walks across the pit lane to get a drink of water. "All those cars spinning at me," he says, laughing.

It's still windy and I can see fluffs of carbon bits from the bodywork of the two crashes blowing down the track along the wall on the far side of the track. Sweepers and the jet truck orbit the track trying to clean the stuff up and prevent tire damage when the session restarts.

At oval-track CART races qualifying is always scheduled for Saturday afternoon, so the morning session is the time for teams to try out qualifying setups, running the cars a little lower, lighter, and stiffer than for a race setup. That and the wind may be the reason for the spins.

Jim says now that he doesn't like the look of the left-rear tire. "I think we've got too much camber in it. Let's take out one of the shims. There's a ride-height correction for that. Let me see if I want to do that."

On road courses with both left- and right-hand corners, the usual setup includes negative camber — that is the tires at front and rear lean in so the tops of the tires are closer together than the bottoms.

A cambered tire produces extra forces in the direction it's leaning, in addition to the normal grip of an uncambered tire. In a corner, weight transfers to the outside tires and the car rolls trying to lean the outside tire into positive camber. The engineers would like those tires to have optimum camber in the corners where they're doing their work. On oval tracks they set up a car so inside and outside tires lean into the

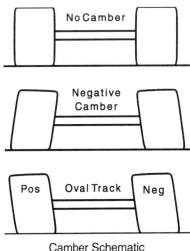

Camber Schematic

corner; the outside tires have negative camber and the insides have positive camber. It looks funny but it works.

At this point in the practice session Jim thinks he has too much positive camber in the left-rear tire. When he reduces that camber he also reduces the ride height of the car at that corner, because the tire will rotate down off its outside corner. He has to jack up the suspension to regain the lost ride height. "Let's go up half a flat at the left rear to compensate for that camber change," he says.

At 9:10 a.m. the green flag is out, but they're still working on Mark's car. Christian Fittipaldi, driving the debuting Swift car, is quick in this session so far with a 28.956-seconds lap. Mark is sixth with a 29.9.

At 9:14 Mark comes back in asking about lap times. He has improved to P3 with a 29.2. He says, "It's better on entry. I have some rear to work with now. It needs some more of that same dose."

Jim: "We're headed in the direction of PIR [Phoenix International Raceway] here. Let's do the rest of it. Let's raise it some more."

Mark asks about "the boost," wanting to know that he's as close as possible to the 40 inches of mercury limit without blowing off the valve. Someone says "up two" on the radio, telling Mark to turn the knob on his dash to a higher boost. Each increment of adjustment is one-tenth of an inch of boost.

As the crew is nearing completion of the new changes to the setup, Jim tells Mark, "You need to keep in mind what we're doing and let me know what happens on entry and sorta mid-corner to late in the corner. Soften the rear bar now also so we can go stiffer if we want." Mark goes back out on track.

The monitor now shows Christian Fittipaldi, Richie Hearn, Gualter Salles, and Mark in that order. At 9:23 Mark comes back in saying, "It's loose off the corner."

Jim: "Did that help or hurt?"

Mark: "Hurt. It's loose on me again."

Jim: "Let's change the tires and the valve. We'll go back squarer."

Mark: "What about the bar?"

Jim: "Bring it back to where it was. This is the qualifying program, so you know what gear to use." They make some shock and spring changes at the front and Mark goes back out at 9:27 with 3 minutes to go in the session.

At 9:31 there's a yellow flag. Mark comes in saying, "I can't get a clean lap. It feels like it turns in better. The platform feels more stable."

Jim: "No surprise there."

Mark goes back on track again, but there's another yellow flag and he comes right back in, asking about top speeds. He's told he's now at 204 mph going into Turn 1 where he had been turning a maximum of 201 on previous laps.

"The lead-in is better," Mark says. "But the rear end is floating around in a nervous manner." The checkered flag flies, ending the session.

Mo's Turn

At 9:41 Mauricio's car fires up in the pit lane. A minute later he's on track with the green flag. His back-up car is fully prepared and carefully covered, just behind the pit wall. After some laps Mo comes back in and says the car is loose everywhere. "Let's see where the pressures are."

They check tire pressures and Mauricio goes on track again. At 10 a.m. Mo comes back in and Andy asks if the car is bottoming.

"It was hitting a little," Mo says. "That's why I think the pressures are low." While tire temps and pressures get checked again all around, a yellow flag stops the session to allow a check for debris.

Andy reports on the radio to Mo, "We're 2 pounds down at the right front and also at the rear. We may be back to the same pressures as yesterday morning."

Mo: "There's a yellow?"

Andy: "Rahal [he pronounces it Ray-Hal] stopped somewhere."

It's 10:03 a.m. when the track goes green again. Thirty-five minutes remain in this session. It's warm, but the wind is blowing hard enough, so I'm comfortable. Mauricio is still circulating in the 30s. Christian Fittipaldi has the best time so far, 28.918 seconds. And then Parker Johnstone goes even faster. Mauricio comes back in, saying something isn't right. "Let's look at the pressures again."

Andy: "That could be it, but it rained quite a bit last night so the track's going to be green and that makes us loose."

A minute later Andy adds, "The pressures are still low. We're not gaining on it."

At 10:15 Al Unser Jr. goes to the top of the list with a 28.553-seconds lap. Mauricio isn't in the top 20. Then he turns a 29.2 and goes to 18th. Then he improves further to 29.189 and comes in. Andy asks him how the car feels on exit. "It's all there," Mo replies. "The turn-in is OK too. Don't go by the lap times. We're getting there."

Andy gives the crew some changes and tells Mauricio, "These tires have 60 laps on them now. The temperatures are down 30 degrees." Mo goes back on course to check these changes before going to new tires. After a few laps he comes back in for a new set of tires. Immediately on returning to the oval he jumps to P3 with a lap of 28.690 seconds.

Mauricio comes in for some adjustments and goes back on course, lapping at 35 seconds, then 31, 28.810, and 28.144. Mo is at the top of the list on the monitor now with about 10 minutes to go in the session. He comes back in and Andy suggests they change tires and put a few laps on the qualifying set of tires, "to take the sheen off."

Mo comes back in with about a minute to go and Andy asks him if he wants to change tires and have a last try for a fast lap. "No," he says. "That's OK. I know where I am." And he gets out of the car. He ended up in P1 with his 28.144 lap, an average speed of 194.045 mph. Mark is P18 at a 29.220 and 186.899 mph.

Jeff Oster Sewing This Year's Patches
On Last Year's Firesuits

Glitches Happen

At 11:30 a.m. I go to the hospitality area. Jeff Oster, the hospitality manager, and Don Mullins, a motor coach driver, are taking care of a major glitch.

On race day the entire pit crew is attired in Nomex firesuits because of the dangers of refueling the cars in a busy pit lane. These firesuits are billboards for sponsors just like the drivers' suits and the racecars. But the new firesuits for the '97 season haven't arrived.

Hollywood made a last-minute change to its logo and Sparco, the Italian manufacturer of the suits, wasn't able to get the new suits to Homestead in time. As a result, Michele Molin, part-time receptionist at the shop in Indianapolis, flew down here last night with last year's suits as excess baggage. She arrived at 1 a.m. and was met at the airport by Mary and Ron Fusek, Steve's parents, who also manage the sponsor VIP suites.

So Jeff and Don are sitting here among piles of firesuits, attaching the new Firestone patches over the Goodyear patches on the old suits. They tried staples but that didn't work, so they're sewing them with a needle and thread. It's a hassle and not needed with so many other normal things he has to do, but Jeff is amazingly calm and uncomplaining.

"This kind of stuff happens," he says. "I didn't sign up for this, but somebody's got to do it."

Competition Among Engine Manufacturers

During the '96 season almost everyone thought the Honda engines had a power advantage. Cosworth and Ilmor both stepped up the development pace, and at this first race of the '97 season, all three engines seem to be pretty equal. The Honda-powered cars still have the highest speeds on the straights, 211 mph vs. 204 for Ilmor/Mercedes-Benz and Cosworth/Ford-powered cars. But no one is dominating.

In the Saturday morning practice just completed, the top 10 times were set by four Cosworth/Fords, three Ilmor/Mercedes, and three Hondas. A dozen drivers have a chance to win the race. Only new-guy Toyota seems down on power, and it's only its second year of competition. Probably the best gauge of engine parity is what the drivers have to say, and here at Homestead, the Ilmor and Cosworth drivers aren't whining like they were last year.

Don Norton, Ilmor engineer, says, "I can hear the Cosworths coming off Turn 4 and it sounds like 14-2 [14,200 rpm] by my ear." Someone told me the Ilmors are turning a maximum of 14,400 rpm.

Butch Winkle, chief mechanic on Blundell's car, says the Cosworth engines' poor reliability is one reason he is at PacWest this season. "I was at Patrick Racing last year and I like all the people, but I want to win and I don't think the Cosworth engines will be reliable. They've got a bottom-end problem they just won't fix. I hear Rahal has blown three motors this weekend." The mechanics know a lot about what's going on.

This weekend the engines in the PacWest cars get changed after Saturday morning practice so they'll be fresh for qualifying later in the afternoon. I notice these new engines come out of the transporter with covers over them and someone tells me the Ilmor guys asked them to keep them under wraps. When I get a look I don't see anything I can identify as trick. I think the engine guys just try to hide things from each other.

Qualifying

For me qualifying is more exciting than the race. A lot can happen during the 75 to 200 laps of a race and luck creeps in there. In oval-track qualifying the driver gets three warm-up and two timed laps. The car has to be perfect and the driver can make no mistakes. He has to drive the car at the limit but no further. The qualifying order is determined by a drawing. The cars line up in order in the pit lane and peel off as their turns come. The session begins at 1 p.m. and I find myself walking back and forth between Mauricio's car and Mark's further back in line.

Early in the order Richie Hearn blows a constant-velocity joint in a driveshaft. Qualifying is delayed while the safety team looks for the scattered parts. Mauricio's crew constantly wipe and polish the car. Photographers elbow their way among the crowd and crew. TV teams move down the line as the cars go on track one by one. One of the TV announcers, Gary Gerould, has on a firesuit and he's attached to two other guys by his microphone cord. One guy shoulders the TV camera and the other has a battery backpack and a sound console. He also carries the microwave antenna that transmits their signal to the production trailer.

Stella, Mauricio's wife, is here. She's a small woman, pretty in a girlish way but not fragile at all. Her auburn hair is long enough to reach her freckled shoulders. We talked in the hospitality area earlier. She's curious about the book and doesn't seem put out at all by the idea. I watch her now, looking for signs of worry or nervousness and see none of that. She is intense, but not nervous. I guess if she's out here in the pit lane at this moment, she couldn't be afraid of anything bad that could happen.

Mauricio gets into his car about 1:30 and sets about getting belted in and comfortable. Alex Zanardi drives his Reynard/Honda/Firestone car to a 28.000-seconds lap, best of the weekend. That's 195.043 mph average!

This gives Mauricio something to shoot at. After every session so far either Mauricio or Zanardi have been at the top of the list. The sky looks about half full of white, fluffy clouds. It's warm but breezy and comfortable.

After Mauricio pulls out for his warm-up laps, I quickly walk back down to the PacWest pits and watch the monitors. I can see the lap times as they're posted by Timing and Scoring and also a video monitor showing the car on track. His timed laps are 28.112 and 28.025. He missed beating Zanardi by 25 thousands of a second, but he'll start the race on the outside of the front row. That's a good start for a team that was mid-pack last year.

Greg Moore drives his year-old Reynard to the third-quick spot, which is a great performance in a year-old car. At 2 p.m. the qualifying order is Zanardi, Mauricio, Greg Moore, Al Unser Jr., Scott Pruett, and Bobby Rahal.

I stand with Mark's crew and a crowd of photographers as he starts his qualifying run at 2:02. I hear Jim tell him "up two on the boost" on the radio. I'm not expecting Mark to get into the top 10. He really hasn't been comfortable in the car and has posted no decent times.

I use my watch to time him: 32.52, 29.11, 28.37, and 30.13. We all hear the PA announcer say "fourth place." The lap I timed at 28.37 seconds was really 28.27 and 193.132 mph. It's an amazing performance. Mauricio is on the first row with Zanardi, and Mark is in the third row next to Vasser.

Chip Ganassi, owner of the team Zanardi and Vasser drive for, leans toward Bruce. "You can win with two cars up that close." Of course his guys are right there too.

Back in the PacWest pits a few minutes later I hear Mark tell Bruce he got the car sideways in Turn 2 and again in Turn 3. "I had to back off the last lap."

A few minutes later when Mark is talking to some reporters, Bruce tells me he told Mark to take it easy before he went out to qualify. "I don't think he knows how," Bruce says, smiling.

Gil de Ferran drives a lap good enough for third spot on his first timed lap and then crashes in Turn 2 on his second lap. We all go to the monitors to see if he's OK and we see him move and start to get out of the car. Relief floods through everyone. This group of people is excited about their sport, but they are not immune to the prospects of tragedy. There's not much talk about it but everyone knows what can happen at a track where a solid concrete wall is 20 feet from a car going 180 mph.

We see de Ferran's crash replay on the monitor. He slides high going into Turn 1 and hits the wall a glancing blow. They replay it from another angle. Mark laughs softly as he talks to Jim Hamilton and Allen McDonald, and he sounds to me a little bit nervous, maybe in relief at how well he had qualified and how he had escaped crashing, as de Ferran had not.

Most of the PacWest people walk into the covered garage area or back to the transporter or hospitality area. Casey Eason, Mark's DAG, is packing up his gear in the engineering cart that is the pit-lane office for the people who engineer Mark's car and tend data coming from the engine and chassis sensors. Casey is a tall, skinny guy with black hair above a long face. He has a lot of energy he directs at whatever he's doing.

"That's an amazing qualifying effort from Mark, huh?" I say to Casey.

"Yeah; that is great," comes the reply.

"It seems that Jim Hamilton is doing a great job engineering the car," I say. "It seems to me it helps that he can use the data so well and read the tires too. Do you think so?"

"Oh, yeah; you bet," Casey beams. "Let me tell you. Things have changed a lot in this cart since last year. The data used to be a crutch and now it's a tool. Jim knows how to talk to a driver and use the data and look at the tires."

"Right," I say. "Reading the tires seems to be special. I don't see many engineers doing that."

"I think you're right," Casey says as he gathers his stuff up in his arms and heads for the garage.

Andy Brown is pleased with Mauricio's front-row qualifying effort. "If you look at his straight-line speed vs. the Honda-powered cars, his lap time is even more impressive," Andy explains. "Zanardi's turning 211 mph at the end of the frontstraight where Mo's doing 203 mph. I reckon he's a quarter-second faster than the field in race trim."

Post-Qualifying Press Conference

When I walk into the conference room at 1:55, Gil de Ferran is there on the dais by himself talking about his accident. His first qualifying lap earned him third on the grid even though he crashed at the start of his second lap.

"That's a helluva way to get out of tech inspection," is a comment from one cynical observer. That's an interesting point. I wonder how they perform post-qualifying tech inspection on a wrecked car?

Alex Zanardi and Mauricio Gugelmin
Talk at the Post-Qualifying Press Conference

De Ferran says his engine misfired as he drove into Turn 1 and the car just didn't want to turn in. "It slid toward the wall and I had to decide whether to brake or not. [He didn't brake.] I tried to keep the car turning so it would hit at a shallow angle. It worked. I'm OK. If it had been a hard hit I would have a ringing in my ears and a headache. I have none of that. The new seats and headrests are really working well."

A few minutes later other people dribble into the room and Gil tells his story all over again. He is a personable guy who comes across as bright; a real person.

At 3:15 the room is almost full of journalists and team PR people. We're getting impatient now. Some of us have heard Gil's story three times. Mauricio comes in and sits next to de Ferran. We're waiting on Mike Zizzo, the CART PR director, now. A few minutes later Zizzo arrives followed by Alex Zanardi, the pole winner, and his PR guy, Michael Knight. Gil excuses himself.

After some leading questions, Zanardi tells about having boost problems during his run and how he is fortunate to have found the right boost setting for his timed runs.

Someone asks Mauricio about losing weight during the off-season. He says he made some big changes, "not just in my weight but in my workouts and my focus. I had some personal problems last year, but now I'm completely focused on the team and my racing."

Car Prep for Race Day

The Formula Atlantic race starts at 5:30 and the buzzing drone of the four-cylinder engines fills the complex. In the PacWest garage area the cars go through a detailed tear-down and rebuild procedure. Monitors on the walls show the TV feed and scoring information of the race on the track, but they go largely unnoticed by the people at work in the area.

Certain components, such as the constant-velocity joints in the driveshafts, get a lot of attention. They are disassembled, inspected, and reassembled, some with new parts. Richie Hearn's CV failure during qualifying underlines the need.

I ask Mark Moore, chief mechanic on Gugelmin's car, about the CVs. "Ovals are especially hard on the CVs because of the funny angles an oval setup puts on them."

Steve Fusek comes into the garage and we talk about the race strategy for Mauricio and Mark. "We have to keep track of the fuel numbers, laps on this tank, yellow-flag laps, who each guy is racing with, who has pitted, and we have to look for opportunities. As I say that it sounds complicated, and I wonder if anyone can really do it. But Russ [Cameron] and John [Anderson] are very bright, very energetic people. They thrive on this stuff."

Jim Swintal: Starter

I see Jim Swintal and he waves and walks over to the PacWest garage. Jim is the official CART starter. He controls the race with the flags. Jim is tall and slim, and he thinks and talks quickly, with a lot of enthusiasm. He pays attention to what he's doing and he's good at it. Jim's wife, Diana, travels to some races. "I talked to Gugelmin and Zanardi about the start tomorrow," Jim says.

"Great," I reply. "If you can tell me something about that at every race, that's just what people would like to know more about. I'd like to know how things go from your perspective."

"Sure; we can do that," Jim says. "I think these two guys are the kind I can depend on to listen and do what they say, not game players. At every race I get the guys on the front row together and we talk about what I want to see at the start. Sometimes I'm the one doing all the talking and sometimes it's just one of the guys doing the talking. But these guys both did a lot of talking. They want to make sure it's a good start. Alex is concerned. He remembers last year."

"I guess last year Paul Tracy played a lot of slow/fast games with de Ferran," I say.

"Right. Tracy was too slow at the start and it caused some problems. I don't think Gugelmin and Zanardi will do that," predicts Jim.

"Well, good luck and I'll talk to you after the race," I say. "We'll try to do this at every race."

"Great!" Jim says. "Take it easy."

After the drive back to the Dadeland Marriott I find the maid has turned down the covers and placed chocolates on the pillow. Tonight the chocolates are racecar-shaped. This year it looks like I'll be staying in better places than in the past.

RACE DAY AT HOMESTEAD

Traffic can be a problem on race day, and the best strategy is to get there early. At 7 a.m. driving south down the toll road, a spectacular sunrise shows off to the left. The sun glows orange and yellow rays shoot through the dark clouds. Rain showers off in the west produce a perfect, complete rainbow. At the track there are puddles everywhere. That same rainbow shower may have passed through here earlier.

At 7:30 in the Hollywood hospitality area I ask Mauricio about the start. "I'm just going to try to roll parallel out of Turn 4 before I accelerate," he says. "I reckon some people might spin coming out of 4." Of course he's referring to some spins that happened last year when drivers got on the throttle too soon. Mark Blundell was one of those.

The Indy Lights cars go on track for their warm-up session at 8:05. I walk down onto pit lane to watch the Lights cars and to find Wally Dallenbach.

Pace-Car Ride with Wally Dallenbach

Wally Dallenbach competed in 180 Indy car races as a driver and has worked for CART since 1980. For 11 years he has been competition director and chief steward, and he's trying to retire. He's got the title special assistant to the president now, and he drives the PPG pace car and works with the safety team. Early in the week I asked Wally about getting a ride around each of the tracks this season and he says sure; just find him early in the morning when he makes his track check.

At 8:15 a.m., while a warm wind pushes some puffy clouds out of the east, the pace car, a Mercedes-Benz C36 with AMG aero and big-wheel additions, and I wait for Wally at pit out near Turn 1. The car is a four-door with avocado-green paint that has an orange tinge showing through where the sunlight shines on it. Metallic exorcist sunset?

Wally, in his trademark Western boots and hat, ambles up at 8:30, motions me in, and we roll onto the warm-up lane. He stops near Turn 1 to talk with members of the safety team. They have some questions about what they should do if and when, and Wally discusses all that with them and talks on a two-way radio with other officials until everyone is comfortable. Sitting there, I have time to notice the car has a very nice leather interior and a full roll cage.

He drives out on the track at about 60 mph, and we ride along past the jet truck blowing the line clean. "Do you have any questions?" Wally asks.

"Why are all the spins out of Turn 4?" is my first question.

"There's a bump there that upsets the cars," Wally replies, and sure enough, as he drives through Turn 4, I see a black patch with shiny areas where the cars are bottoming and polishing the surface. Skid marks start right at this point and snake down the course before intersecting the walls.

"Why are all these banked ovals getting built?" is my next question. "They're obviously dangerous for these cars. Why don't they build more flat ovals like Milwaukee?"

"The problem is the tires tear up the asphalt when there's no bank," Wally explains. "The NASCAR cars do it worse than we do."

"So NASCAR requirements are dictating track design?" I ask.

"If I had a hundred million dollars to build a track, I'd want a NASCAR date," Wally says matter of factly. "I'd want a CART date too, but I'd definitely want a NASCAR date."

That sums it all up for me pretty simply. Wally didn't blame anybody for the copycat oval tracks being built that are great for NASCAR but dangerous for Indy cars. He states it as an economic necessity. I know some important, powerful people have explained all that, but when Wally says it I believe it because I trust him.

Warm-Up

In the PacWest pits at 9:15 a.m., I ask Andy Brown if they will try any changes on Mauricio's car during the warm-up session. "We're pretty happy where we are, actually," Andy says. "We might try to get a read on the pressures on cold tires. It might help us this afternoon."

Mauricio is there among his crew, joking with Trevor Jackson and Ron Endres.

Jim Hamilton walks up and I tell him about the bump I saw in Turn 4. "Yeah; that's a good one," he says. "Did you notice the washboard surface in the corners?" Now that he mentions it I had noticed ripples in the asphalt through the corners.

"That's caused by the wheel hop of the NASCAR cars," Jim says. "The tire, wheel, spring, and shock absorber have a natural frequency and they pound those ripples into the pavement. It's about 35 or 40 hertz [cycles per second], about double the frequency of an Indy car. It rattles these cars pretty good. You can see it in the data off the car."

The engines in Mark's car and Mauricio's car were started earlier and they fall silent now as the temperatures have risen into the proper range. At 9:30 a green flag sends the cars on the track for the last check-out before the race. I turn on my scanner and hear race control say, "Tail lights on the rookies."

Mauricio comes back into the pit box and the crew runs a practice pit stop. He asks about an orange light on the dash. Mark is in also and the sidepods come off his car. For a moment the activity level rises to an intense peak as momentary problems pop up that need to be solved before the race.

A few minutes later Mo is P3, but complaining of boost problems and a slight push. Mark comes in for a practice pit stop. Several drivers exceed the pit lane speed and get black flagged, losing important time on the track. With 5 minutes to go Mauricio says he can't see his dash; the electronics aren't working. The checkered flag ends the session promptly at 10 a.m.

A pair of Navy F-14 jet fighters fly overhead in close formation. Their ripping noise screams power and speed. Down here on Earth the CART cars are actually not very loud. The turbochargers use energy in the exhaust to pack air and fuel into the engine, lowering sound levels. The stands are about 10% full. Is no one coming, or do people around here just show up late?

The Indy Lights race is green-flagged shortly after 11 a.m. After too many spins and wrecks the race ends under a yellow flag. Hopefully the CART race won't be so bad.

I see some PacWest guys eating in between the transporters, and I go over to join them. Foil-covered oven pans 1-foot wide by 2-feet long hold several steamy, good-smelling dishes. One pan is filled with meat- and veggie-stuffed burritos. A pan of pasta sits next to another pan full of baked potato quarters with a tasty, crumbly coating.

The guys are engaged in stuffing their faces, sipping cold drinks from cans, and talking about various women of their intimate acquaintance. The food is hot, plentiful, and tasty. It occurs to me I haven't talked to the PacWest chef yet.

Dave Loik: PacWest Chef

Behind the hospitality enclosure, Dave Loik leans against a counter in his kitchen, actually a spiffy-looking trailer hauled all over the country behind one of the motor coaches. Winding down from his last meal of the weekend, he has time to talk about how he got started cooking for a race team.

"I've always been a race fan," Dave begins. "I grew up in Columbus, Ohio, and I went to races at Mid-Ohio. I remember going to Can-Am races there starting in the early '70s.

"I was at a race at Mid-Ohio with some friends last year and Steve Fusek was out at the Carousel spotting for the team. I got to talking to him about my experience cooking, and he told me they might need a full-time chef. I was working as corporate chef for The Limited at the time. He gave me a card and I faxed him a resume. I visited the shop, and they made me an offer. I love it. I get to do what I do best and I get to be involved in racing. It's like I go to the races and cook for 50 friends."

Chef Dave Loik at Work in the Kitchen Trailer

"How do you get all the raw materials you need at the various locations?" I ask.

"I shop at the big, full-service grocery stores wherever we happen to be," Dave explains. "Winn-Dixie is good. I need a store that has fresh produce, a fish monger, and a good meat selection."

"Can you call in an order or do you just go to the store like any other shopper?"

"I just go solo. I get a couple of shopping carts and fill them up with what I need."

"The meals start early and go late. You must work long hours."

"Yeah, but 14-hour days are normal in the food-service business. I don't do that every day. I don't go to the shop in Indianapolis. I fly to the races. That's when I organize my menus. I'm continually developing menus. You have to be able to adapt to the situation at each track. You don't have a lot of space, and the water is limited. But none of that is any surprise if you have a catering background. It's the same at parties and weddings."

"How did you get into cooking?"

"Just cooking around the family when I was 14 or 15 years old. I liked to cook, so I went to the CIA [Cooking Institute of America] in New York. Then I worked for some European chefs in Columbus. I learn by doing. I worked for country clubs and hotels. It's great preparation for this."

Pre-Grid at Homestead

At a CART race on an oval track the pre-grid is staged on pit lane. Each car's crew pushes the car to the pre-grid or tows it behind a tugger. Even though the cars are spaced out 20 feet between rows, there are so many people milling around that it seems a solid crowd the length of pit lane.

At 12:55 p.m. someone sings the national anthem. I'm thinking about what I need to do and where I need to be to see what goes on and take notes and photos during the race. I walk back and forth between Mauricio's car on the front row and Mark's on the third, taking photos. The drivers get into the cars and get belted in and comfortable.

17-Car Crew on Pre-Grid

It's 1:10 and I ask Russ Cameron if he gets nervous.

"No. Not really; not usually," he says, "but I guess I'm a little nervous for this one because we're doing so well. It's also the first time we've had this amount of fuel on board. We're set to do the race in two pit stops if the right window happens."

Allen McDonald has only been with PacWest for a month or so. He was working with the Arrows Formula 1 team and now he's PacWest's new technical director. I ask him what a technical director does. "Well, I'm not really sure," he says with a mischievous grin. "I guess we'll find out sooner or later."

Standing there in the pit lane minutes before the race starts, Allen tells me his first job in racing was working for Gordon Murray, the Formula 1 racecar designer who came up with some brilliant cars at Brabham and then McLaren. "Not technically trained," Allen says about Murray. "Had a marvelous feel for it though. Lots of people in racing like that."

18-Car Crew on Pre-Grid

THE RACE

The cars move off onto the track for the pace laps at 1:38. I go back to the PacWest pits where I can see the pit stops and watch the TV monitors.

Mauricio and Zanardi start the race in a very orderly manner. Mo tucks in behind Alex in the first corner, but de Ferran passes him a few laps later. Mark is passed by car after car as he falls back in the field. I watch the TV feed and the Timing and Scoring information in a garage near the PacWest pit location. Norbert Haug, Mercedes-Benz worldwide racing manager, and Mario Illien, Ilmor founder with Paul Morgan, stare at the same monitor as the cars roar down the straight 100 feet away.

This is not a good way to watch a race. I want to keep track of what the crews on both cars are doing, but I can't be both places at once. I end up walking back and forth between the garage monitors and the pits. I'm never really confident I can tell what's going on. I comfort myself that my wife Pat is taping the race at home and I'll watch it in my own living room tomorrow night.

I can hear the voice of CART Race Control saying, "Tell car 34 [Roberto Moreno] to pick it up or pull out of the race." On lap 27 Al Unser Jr. comes in smoking. It's obviously an engine problem, but the official reason for retirement I hear on the scanner is electrical. A lot of teams cover up engine problems that way.

The first pit stops happen as a result of Dario Franchitti's crash on lap 44. Mauricio and then Mark come in for what looks to me like perfect stops. During the yellow-flag laps after the pit stops Mo reports on the radio that his weight jacker is maxed out, his sway bar on full soft, and he is having trouble shifting gears.

But 10 laps later Mauricio begins to feel comfortable racing the car. "We're moving," he says on the radio.

Russ comes back, "Great job, Mo. Get after 'em." Mauricio passes Vasser for fifth spot and Russ tells him, "You're faster than any other car on the track by a second."

Then de Ferran crashes, bringing out another yellow flag. Mark is in 12th place.

At 2:45 I notice the stands are full now. Maybe they all showed up during the first few laps when I was so excited. The weather is very comfortable; a few clouds and a nice breeze. The race goes toward 100 laps of a scheduled 148. Mauricio works hard in fifth place. I hear Russ say, "The fuel window is open." Both Mark and Mauricio pit for fuel and tires. The stops again look great.

A few laps later another yellow flag flies. Max Papis has run out of fuel on course. After they tow his car off the course it takes quite a few laps to align the cars the way CART officials want them. Mo says he doesn't think he's in the right spot. Evidently the cars that waited and pitted under yellow are now a lap ahead of those who pitted under the green flag. Confusion reigns as the drivers want to maintain a good position or move into a better position and the

CART officials try to get them in the proper order. The race goes green again, but Mauricio is a lap down now.

The excitement is gone now for me. With 10 laps to go Mauricio is seventh behind Zanardi, then he gets by and finishes sixth. Mark is 14th. The teams are talking protest because of the messed-up lineup during that last yellow flag. Some of the PacWest guys think Zanardi passed Mauricio under a yellow flag and should be penalized.

The drivers get out of the cars and talk to their crews. I hear Mo say, "Small things make a big difference. Zanardi comes out of the pit lane and jumped right in front of me. There is nothing I could do."

He's asked if he had seen what happened to de Ferran, who had made contact with Dennis Vitolo and crashed. "Gil takes big chances," Mauricio says with a knowing grin. "I discount him. The car got good after a while. At the start we were chasing the setup."

Steve Fusek says, "Maybe we should be more aggressive about getting our place in line before restarts?"

At 3:35 the cars are back in the garage and all the equipment is getting packed up and put away. John Anderson answers my question about how he feels after the race. "Bloody disappointed, really. Bloody bad start to the season. It's not like you bloody did it to yourself. It's really a rules thing out of your control."

Michael Andretti Wins

So who won the race? Michael Andretti drove a brand-new car, the Swift 007i, to a victory in its maiden outing, repeating what he did in a Reynard in 1994. It's still a surprise considering the level of competition in the series. The consensus is that the combination of David Bruns' mechanical packaging genius, the Swift wind tunnel, and the knowledge of Newman-Haas engineers Peter Gibbons and Brian Lisles adds up to an extraordinarily capable team.

Michael himself gets a lot of credit for this victory. He won five races and finished second in the championship in 1996 only to the formidable Reynard/Honda/Firestone package of Jimmy Vasser. Michael always gets the most out of a car, and that means Peter Gibbons has the data from the on-board computer and feedback from the driver under conditions of maximum performance. Christian Fittipaldi also drove the new car during development testing. In the race his Swift dropped out with an oil leak.

I stay one more night in Miami and then get up early to catch the 7 a.m. United flight (there's only one nonstop each day) back to SFO.

Steve Fusek, Post-Race Thoughts

A few days after the race I call Steve Fusek and record this conversation.
Paul: "So how did the weekend go?"
Steve: "Uuhmm, disappointing in the end, extremely disappointing. It goes back to something that sticks in my mind, something that Alex Cross [Swift Engineering VP] said to me. We were talking about their working with Newman-Haas and he said, 'The nice thing about Newman-Haas is they go to a race expecting to win.' I guess from that standpoint I'm happy to say we're bitterly disappointed over not winning that race, and especially not having a couple of guys on the podium."
Paul: "Boy; that's big expectations [laughing]."
Steve: "Well, we're capable of doing that. And something has to go wrong for that not to happen. For the overall weekend we had one of the best cars there — Mo's car. For us not to win the race or especially not to have a podium is really disappointing. We lost points there from my perspective."
Paul: [laughs]
Steve. "On the other hand, we're a team that finished 14th and 16th in the points last year, and now we put a guy on the front row and another guy in the third row. Yeah, that's pretty satisfying. It is nice to back up our testing and be competitive. At the same time we need to put

that exclamation point on it and win the race. The car wasn't the best on race day. It went away and we got it back and got it competitive again and there was a mess-up with scoring that didn't help.

"On the other side, the marketing side, I thought we looked pretty good. We looked like we knew what we were doing, but we were very much shooting from the hip on the whole marketing end of things. It was such a scramble just to get down there that we didn't have the planning that I would have liked to see.

"It was John Oreovicz's first week as a PR guy so there were some holes there. There were some things that would seem really obvious, but no one told him and he didn't know. Something simple like when Mark finished his qualifying run, he didn't have a hat. It was live on ESPN2. There were some things like that. I'll guarantee that'll never happen again. As soon as Mark got out of the car John realized he didn't have a hat for him. He knew straightaway. That's the kind of stuff that will be second nature by the time we get to the next race.

"We had a lot of new people. The motor home deal came together pretty good. It looked fantastic. I was really pleased about that. We got the right kind of impressions.

"I guess one of the proudest moments of the weekend was when Norbert Haug [Mercedes-Benz worldwide motorsports manager] came in on Saturday night to say good-bye to Bruce. I happened to be standing next to Bruce at the time and heard Norbert say, 'Bruce, you've got the best hospitality in the paddock, and your cars are the best on the track at the moment. You should be very proud.'

"Coming from him, that's a big deal. I know it made Bruce feel good, especially coming from that source. He's used to hanging around with McLaren at Formula 1 races."

Paul: "I was impressed by the lack of drama in the garage area among the crew. Everybody knew what they were doing, but nobody was uptight, nobody snapped at me or each other. I was just hanging around trying to keep out of the way, but someone could have shown some irritation and they didn't."

Steve: "I think that's what we didn't have on the marketing side. There was a bit of a panic mode all weekend. I'd like to see it more relaxed and everything is just second nature and we can relax because it's all sorted, an, if anyone has a question, we already know the answer. Ultimately that's where we want to get to and I don't think it's very far off, but we have some work to do to get there."

Paul: "Well, that was the first time under fire and you've got some very high expectations. But there's also some things that happened that you're proud of."

Steve: "Yes, we are proud. From the Motorola side, I had 10 voice mails this morning just from yesterday when I was out. I think six of them were from Motorola people saying, 'Hey, thanks very much. We've never been at this level before.' That makes us feel good. It's something I don't think they expected. The cars are doing well and the kind of service and client care that we give them is good. That makes us feel pretty good that we're getting that kind of feedback from somebody we just signed up a couple of months ago. From that standpoint everything went real well."

CHAPTER 5
THE ENGINEERS

When PacWest began, Bruce McCaw bought Rick Galles' interest in Galmer Engineering in England, acquiring its design, engineering, and fabrication capabilities. Allen Mertens came along with Galmer (Galles was the *Gal* and Mertens the *mer* in Galmer), and he became the PacWest engineering leader.

Almost every story of PacWest takes a turn at the 1996 race at Rio de Janeiro, and this one is no different. It was a Galmer-designed and built brake hat that failed and put Mark Blundell into the wall at a very high speed. Galmer leadership waned after that as the stateside engineering department became stronger.

Today the PacWest technical organization is headed by Allen McDonald, who came from the Arrows Formula 1 team. Allen reports to John Anderson, vice president of operations, and has about a half-dozen guys working with him.

Jim Hamilton was hired to engineer Mark Blundell's car. Jim has a unique combination of hands-on skills as well as analytical training. He lives and breathes racing, having driven himself in club racing and go-karts. Jim is extremely curious about technical matters, and he writes software programs that describe and simulate various tire, suspension, and chassis interactions. He came from Dan Gurney's All American Racers, where he contributed to that team's extremely successful IMSA GTP Toyota and its not-so-successful Eagle Indy car program.

Also working in Blundell's engineering team is Al Bodey, who has an off-road racing background and worked for Ganassi Racing before coming to PacWest.

Andy Brown has been engineering racecars for 14 years. He was with Galmer Engineering when Rick Galles and Mertens were partners. Andy and Mauricio worked together in F3000 and Formula 1 before being reunited at PacWest. They make a formidable team.

Patrick Beaumier is a French-Canadian engineer backing up Andy on the 17-car. Patrick is an experienced computer-aided-design (CAD) engineer.

Julian Karras came from Reynard in mid-season to be responsible for design and development projects. Julian is shop-based and only rarely travels to races, but when he does he's in the thick of things.

Tim Neff is the PacWest shock absorber guru. His title is shock engineer, but he has no formal technical degree. Shock absorber technology is shrouded in myth and mystery, so I prefer the title of guru. Tim has educated himself and uses his short but intense experience with racing shocks to come up with some unique and

Patrick Beaumier

innovative ways to keep the tires on the ground and the driver in control of them. Tim came to PacWest from Penske Racing Shocks. Before that he worked at Bobby Rahal's team.

Working with Tim on the shocks is Trevor Jackson, also from Penske Racing Shocks. Trevor assembles all of PacWest's shocks and calibrates them on a shock dynamometer as needed. During practice or test sessions, Trevor is the guy running from Mark's car to Mauricio's making shock adjustments. He has to keep both mental and paper records of exactly what he's done.

An extra explanation is needed here so Trevor's job can be appreciated. To adjust a shock you need to turn a bolt head from the side of the bolt. That means inserting a piece of wire into a hole drilled in the side of the bolt head and turning the bolt through an arc to the next flat of the bolt head where there is another hole. That is called one sweep, and there are six sweeps to one full turn of adjustment because there are six flats on a hex-headed bolt. Turning the bolt moves something inside the shock that adjusts the forces the shock generates.

Al Bodey

The point I'm trying to make is these adjustments are relative, and Trevor has to know how each shock was adjusted at the start of the session, how many flats from full open or full closed, and, as the session and the adjustments build up, exactly what the settings are on each shock at any time. Trevor does this very well or he wouldn't be given the responsibility.

After the first race of the season I catch the two race engineers at home base in Indianapolis and record phone conversations with them. I want to know about the testing done in the so-called off-season.

Left to Right: Andy Brown, Allen McDonald, Tim Neff, Mauricio Gugelmin, and Trevor Jackson

Allen McDonald and Mark Blundell

CONVERSATION WITH ANDY BROWN

Paul: "Do you always concentrate on Mauricio when you're at a test?"

Andy: "Yes, if he's running. We had a couple of tests where we just had the one car, and Mark would start off and Mo would take over later or visa versa. And then the engineers would all be there en masse. That's what we tend to do when we've just got one of the new cars delivered, and the second one hasn't turned up yet. We'll all try and learn as much as we can about that car and give our own input about the car."

Paul: "When you first get a new car, you really need to baseline that car against the setups and data of the old car."

Andy: "Yes, absolutely."

Paul: "What do you do when you get a new car?"

Andy: "We take it apart and put it back together again." (We both laugh.)

Paul: "You get some basic information about the car from Reynard?"

Andy: "And we also have our own wind-tunnel program. So the work starts before we get the car. We look at the suspension geometries, and try to compare that to the

The Dynamic Duo:
Mauricio and Andy

previous year's. We look at the spring/velocity ratios and compare that to previous years'. We've started our own wind-tunnel program prior to the car arriving, so we're comparing that data to what Reynard sends us also."

Paul: "That's a scale model that Galmer builds for you?"

Andy: "Right."

Paul: "Is that still a quarter-scale model?"

Andy: "It's one-third scale now."

Paul: "What tunnel does that run in?"

Andy: "Southampton University."

Paul: "That's not the one Lola uses; that's the one Reynard uses."

Andy: "That's the one Reynard used to use until they built their own facility at Shrivenham. They didn't actually build the new one. They took over an old Ministry of Defense wind tunnel and upgraded it to racecar spec, put a rolling road in it, and what have you. When they moved out of Southampton, it freed some time up for us. Jordan uses it still for their F1 program, but they're going to move to Brackley.

"We analyze all that data and come up with a starting setup which we think will apply to the car, and one of the benefits for us of sticking with Reynard is there was obviously a great deal of continuity with what we'd learned last year. The two big new things were the tires and the engines. To that end we did do some testing with the '96 car to try and evaluate the tires first and foremost so we didn't have three unknowns on our plate."

Paul: "So the first thing you did after the last race of the year at Laguna was go and test the Firestones on the '96 car?"

Andy: "Right. We did that at Milwaukee. It was Oct. 13, I think."

Paul: "So that was to evaluate the Firestones and see what the differences were that the car and the driver could feel."

Andy: "It was so the driver could evaluate the tires having the car and the engine as a known package at the time. This 40-day test rule we've got now inhibits you from running the old cars much at the end of the season. You tend to try and wait until the new car arrives. You don't really want to burn up test days that you're going to need to evaluate the car you're going to be racing. But, in this instance, because we were going to be faced with three unknowns — the car, the engine, and the tires - we decided we should do some evaluation work beforehand. That went very well, in fact."

Paul: "Is there anything you can tell me about the differences you found between the Goodyears and the Firestones?"

Andy: "Consistency was the biggest thing that struck us about the Firestones. Between the start and the end of a run the Firestones were more consistent. The Goodyears could do the times, there was no doubt about that. But with the Firestones it was easier to do the times more consistently, and maintain that time over a full-tank run."

Paul: "Yeah; Firestone seems to have something there. Right out of the box two years ago that was what I was hearing. The Firestones don't give up as much as the Goodyears over 20 or 30 laps. My guess is it's a construction thing, maybe a materials thing, having to do with the textiles in the construction or the bonding of the textiles to the rubber matrix."

Andy: "I think it's a compound thing. But there is a difference in the construction that gives the driver a better feeling of security. The Goodyears would have to take a set on the back end. The side wall would give a wobble which unsettled the drivers. If they could accept that wobble and drive through it, then, like we said, they would do the time. But the Firestone gives that feeling of security at the rear, which is the construction effect. But then I think there's a compound effect that gives them that consistency."

Paul: "That's interesting."

Andy: "Now explain Homestead." (We both laugh. Michael Andretti had won the first race of the year on the 1.5-mile oval at Homestead in the brand-new Swift chassis with Ford/Cosworth power and Goodyear tires.)

Paul: "Right. So the next test after Milwaukee was with the new '97 Reynard?"

Andy: "That was at Sebring. Mauricio did that one. We've got data from that track from previous years, so it's a good comparison. That was Dec. 3. Mauricio was in the car on Dec. 3 and Mark was in the car on Dec. 4."

Paul: "What happened at that test?"

Andy: "That was basically a shakedown test. The very first time you run a car you're looking to see... well, you primarily just watch it burn up [laughs]. The back of these cars gets incredibly hot and the manufacturers obviously aren't involved with running the cars. So normally there's inadequate heat shielding around the back. They don't want to send the car with more than necessary shielding because that adds weight. So one of the main things we do on the first run is find out what bit is going to burn up and which bits have the necessary heat shield and survive."

Paul: "Is there also some validation of the analytical work that you've done?"

Andy: "A little. It takes some time to get up to speed. I don't think we had too many mechanical problems at this particular test. That's always a danger with running a new car. Looking at my notes, Mauricio was quickly on the pace. There's a 55.1. It was pretty good."

Paul: "That would have been with the Ilmor/Mercedes engine for the first time?"

Andy: "Exactly. And 40 inches of boost."

Paul: "How did that go?"

Andy: "Mo was very impressed with the engine. We'd suspected from dyno figures we'd seen that we'd have more horsepower, even at 40 inches of boost, than we had last year with 45 inches. We were running the XB Ford/Cosworth engine in '96, an old design, not the latest spec. This test proved the point that indeed we had more horsepower. Perhaps slightly worse at the bottom end than we were used to, but we put that down to the lack of boost."

Paul: "What was the next test?"

Andy: "I think we came back to the shop and stripped the whole car to look for wear and tear. It was a brand-new gearbox as well from Reynard, their new transverse box. There were a few things in there that needed attention, and then we were back at Sebring on Dec. 11. That's really when the serious work began. My notes show us getting into shocks for the first time. Penske had pulled out as a shock supplier. [Starting in 1997, Penske Racing Shocks supplied parts to Team Penske only, ending support of other CART and IRL teams.] It put the teams in a bit of a hole, but we're more fortunate than most, having Tim Neff with us. We bit the bullet and decided to develop our own shocks, which wasn't the cheapest option by any means."

Paul: "When was that decision made?"

Andy: "It was whenever Penske pulled the plug last fall."

Paul: "So you got into some serious stuff at this Sebring test?"

Andy: "Right. Mo got down to a low 54 at that test. Maybe into the 53s already."

Paul: "How much better was that than with the '96 car? How do you compare something like that?"

Andy: "Right. Well one of the problems at Sebring is they have that movable chicane which seems to change from visit to visit, and it seems to change depending on who's renting the track. Whenever they have a tight chicane or a slightly quicker chicane it makes for a different lap. Mo would prefer not to use it because it adds some inconsistency, and cones get thrown across the track. But I think, compared to the last test we did at Sebring with the '96 car back in May as a part of the Detroit prep, our quickest then was in the 56s."

Paul: "Wow. The car was 3 seconds quicker?"

Andy: "Yeah. Mo put most of that down to the tires. He said they were very, very good as a street-course tire. We'd seen that last year, that Firestone had a better street-course tire than Goodyear. But in Goodyear's defense, that test was in May '96, and we saw how superior the Firestones were to Goodyear at Toronto, but by Vancouver, Goodyear had certainly closed the gap. Really, comparing May Sebring to the January Sebring wasn't perhaps fair, but it just confirmed what we'd already suspected from the Toronto performance, that the Firestone street-course tire was a very good tire.

"But at this Sebring test, the car was beginning to respond to changes as well. We made a fairly major shock change based on some of the work that Jim's simulation showed us. That was already beginning to pay dividends. Once we got the shocks in their working range, the car would then react to 100-pound spring changes and small ride-height changes. I guess what we went down there to sort out at that test was just how responsive the car was, and we came away very happy with its responsiveness to changes. If we raced at Sebring we think we'd do well, but unfortunately we don't [laughs].

"It's difficult to draw too many conclusions at Sebring. They've also destroyed the two most informative corners on the track when they rerouted the road to the airport. That corner by the pits is now full throttle for the driver with no effort, where before it was a quite good combination of tight corners and some high-speed sweepers with some interesting bumps in the middle. Really you just go down there for library information rather than specific setup information. We came away from that test very encouraged."

Paul: "Where next?"

Andy: "I think I went home for Christmas. And after that, I'm pretty sure we went across to Firebird. Hang on while I get those notes. We did a double-header at Phoenix. On the 11th of January we ran at Firebird, and we did the oval on the 14th and 15th.

"Firebird didn't go particularly well. The Firestones aren't suited to that track. We had a lot of understeer which we weren't able to dial out, but we also cut the test short because of some engine-related problems. We threw that back in Ilmor's court to sort out before the next road-course test. We went to the oval then."

Paul: "Does the 40-day test rule apply to tracks where you don't race?"

Andy: "Oh, yes. The only way you can get around it is if you're invited by the tire companies to do a tire test. That's why a team like Patrick has a great advantage, doing Firestone's testing. I hear they've done some horrendous number of test days. I think we're up to about 17 right now."

Paul: "So how did the oval test go at Phoenix?"

Andy: "Initially it went very well. Mauricio was ecstatic about the car on the mile oval. He was comfortable straightaway and did a 21 on his second outing. The car wasn't touching, which is why we weren't going quicker, and he just said this car is going to be great on short ovals.

"Then we had a gearbox problem which stopped his running. We only had the two cars at that stage. That gearbox had to come back and have some major surgery done to it. Mark carried on and got into the low 20s on the next day. We didn't learn much from Morris [Andy's anglicised nickname for Mauricio] apart from the fact that the basic car wasn't too bad. Mark ran both days. We had two cars. But Morris had to stop after the first morning. Mark carried on.

"Our next test was the Homestead road course on the 27th and 28th of January. I think we just had the one car there. We ran Morris the first day and Mark the second. We came away very happy from that test.

"One of the problems we had last year was brake cooling. The 4-inch bodywork clearance rule that was introduced last year gave a lot of people problems with the brakes. Previously the bodywork would guide the air into the brake ducts, but now the bodywork isn't around that area, and the air has plenty of escape routes rather than go down the brake duct. So the rear brakes especially were giving us a lot of problems.

"The Homestead road course is fairly flat and has fairly good grip. It has fairly long straights with 180-degree hairpins, so it was very good for sorting the brake package out. We came up with some solutions there which we then tried at the Laguna test. I think we've got that under control. I guess we'll find that out at Surfers. The other thing Homestead is good for is differential work and steering geometry work. That's basically what we concentrated on there."

Paul: "The new Reynard has an externally adjustable differential. Is that something you can use?"

Andy: "Yes. It's something you could only do during an overnight change before. There are still internal adjustments we do, the ramps and what have you."

Paul: "So that screw on the outside of the case adjusts the spring pressure on the friction discs? I assume that's a Salisbury-type diff."

Andy: "It's based on Salisbury internals. That external adjustment is the preload on the clutch pack. That's different than a standard Salisbury, that relies on ramp-separating loads to cause the clutch plates in the diff to lock. This system can work against the ramp-separating forces. So you can tune the point at which the ramps separate."

Paul: "OK; I see. That's always been the problem, the ramp angle determines the locking and unlocking characteristics. It's been difficult to make it so the diff goes free easily and doesn't lock up too abruptly.

"So the next thing was Spring Training. That was the 30th and 31st of January and February 1st."

Andy: "Right. I think we just had a half-hour shake-down on the 30th. And then we got into the serious stuff on the next two days. Obviously, there the aim was to come up with a race setup for the first race of the season. We had a fairly unique set of rules for that race that we'd never encountered before. Using speedway wings but being able to keep all the brake ducts on meant that it was significantly higher downforce level than a superspeedway, but the track has significantly tighter turns than a superspeedway. Having said that, it was significantly less downforce and less drag than a standard short-oval setup. There were some fairly new problems to solve."

Paul: "So were they braking hard into Turn 1 and Turn 3?"

Andy: "No, not really. The downforce level wouldn't allow it. They did have to slow the cars down, but they couldn't brake particularly hard. The cars were a bit too light to do that. We initially thought we'd be changing gears down into the corners, but that didn't turn out to be the case either. Those hands were needed on the wheel."

Paul: "Really? [laughs]"

Andy: "Yeah. As a short-term solution, that rules package might have achieved its aim, but as a long-term solution it's not the way to go. When you reduce downforce alone it turns the track into a one-lane racetrack, and it takes the racing element away. You need to have adequate grip in terms of the amount of horsepower you've got, so that you can choose your line come race day, so you can have the side-by-side and wheel-to-wheel racing that the fans come to see. I think what the rules achieved was a rather processional race, really. The drivers complained they couldn't overtake. A couple of people managed it, but they had something special going."

Paul: "So was the Laguna test next?"

Andy: "We stopped at Firebird on the way to Laguna because we had our third and fourth chassis by then. We shook those down at Firebird on the way to Laguna. We were at Firebird on the 11th and 12th of February. We had a lot of understeer again.

"The big benefit of the Laguna test was we had data from a race not too long ago, so it was a good chance to evaluate the '97 package to some fairly recent '96 data. That went very well for Morris. He was a match for [Alex] Zanardi. And, if we'd concentrated on more low-fuel running, he would have beaten Zanardi's time, but that wasn't really the object of the exercise. We also got into a tire-test program for Firestone on the last afternoon. So we stopped our chassis development at lunchtime of the last day."

Paul: "I remember Mauricio was quicker than Zanardi that morning, and Zanardi went out and pounded around for a long time in the afternoon before he ran a quicker time. It took him a while. So that had to be a pretty successful test?"

Andy: "Very. We were very happy with the outcome of that test."

Paul: "Then the first race of the season at Homestead came up pretty quick. Did you guys test anywhere else?"

Andy: "No; we decided to come back and spend some time in the shop concentrating on the race setup."

Paul: "Right. That's when I visited the shop. So how did the Homestead race turn out from an engineering point of view?"

Andy: "Very, very well for us. That was the most competitive we've been on an oval other than a superspeedway. Being on the front row was almost disappointing; we felt we should have been on the pole three-tenths clear of the field after the practice times were added up. I guess there was a lesson learned there. We'd got a little bit, I wouldn't say complacent, we were anxious to get the pole, but we were anxious not to blow it. And we'd got good boost in the morning, so we cranked that down a bit for the qualifying run thinking we definitely didn't want to blow the valve. We had enough in hand to perhaps drop the boost two- or three-tenths of a pound, which is what we did.

"Zanardi set his time just as Mo went out. I'm sure if Mo had known Zanardi's time he would have beaten it. But he didn't know the time at the start of his run, despite what he said in the press. He said all the right things then."

Paul: "Yeah, but he told me the next morning that he was pissed he didn't get the pole." [Andy laughs.]

Andy: "We coulda done it. The timing wasn't quite right. If Zanardi had been a couple of runs before us, and had we not, had so much in hand after the practice runs, I think we would have hung it out a little more. It was there for the grabbing really."

Paul: "What about the race?"

Andy: "We were a little concerned going into the race because there was one bad thing about the qualifying. We noticed that set of tires grew in stagger more than any of the others that we'd had. We wondered whether we should change the car or not and we decided not to because the next two sets we had looked fine. We'd been doing such quick times that we decided to leave the car alone and hang on for the first stint, which it turned out he had to do. I think he dropped down to 11th fighting the loose condition in the car. He had his bars maxed out. Mo is very intelligent working with the car and telling us what's going on. He had his weight jacker all the way to the right and his front bar full stiff and rear bar full soft and it was still loose. He stayed on the lead lap and I think he was 11th coming in for the first pit stop.

"I was a bit worried that the amount of looseness that he had was a little bit more than the stagger itself, so we did drop the tire pressures at the rear on the next set of tires. When we measured the first set of tires, sure enough, the stagger was, in fact, up. We also took a bit of front wing out at the pit stop because we felt if we sent it more towards a push with those changes, had it not just been a stagger effect, he did still have the roll bars and the weight jacker to get the push out of the car.

"With those changes he really did start to fly. He set his fastest race lap fairly soon after the pit stop. And his pass on [Jimmy] Vasser was fairly spectacular. They caught that on the TV. He went very deep into the corner and Vasser had to lock up, thinking he could go into the corner as deep as Morris, and wasn't able to.

"I think he set fastest lap of the race at that stage. He was only beaten by Michael at the end when Michael had a clear track ahead of him in the sprint for the end after the last yellow flag. Mo got all the way back up to fourth when all that nonsense happened. And there you go. It was looking good in the middle of the race."

Paul: "To a lot of teams I talked to down there, it was a throwaway race because of the rules. People were just hoping to not hurt anybody or lose any cars there."

Andy: "Especially for us; after Spring Training [Blundell's crash], it was gratifying to come away with both cars running strong at the end."

Paul: "So where did you test after the first race?"

Andy: "We did a test at Big Spring in Texas on March 13 and 14 as a prelude to Surfers and Long Beach. That's something we've done each year, is go down there and set up for the two street tracks. I think Morris actually holds the track record at Big Spring from 1995, which was a 61.5-seconds lap. He came within a tenth of that during this test. And since '95 the underwing exit has been reduced and the boost has been reduced, and he's still able to get within a tenth of that time."

Paul: "And then Nazareth. Didn't you guys test at Nazareth too?"

Andy: "Yeah; we went to Nazareth, but we just sat in the transporter and froze our asses off, basically [laughs]. Not good. It hardly got above 30 degrees the whole time we were there, and Firestone advised us not to run below 35 degrees with that compound."

Paul: "When was that test?"

Andy: "The 15th and 16th of March, I believe. Yeah; we had a day to get from Big Spring to Nazareth."

Paul: "OK; you had two cars both places?"

Andy: "We had two cars at Big Spring and just one at Nazareth."

Paul: "That's right. They both tested at Big Spring and then Mark had a Motorola appearance at New Orleans. So Mo did the Nazareth test alone."

Andy: "The transporters went in different directions, one of the advantages of the testing personnel that we have. We're able to have the race crews at Big Spring and the test team people were at Nazareth waiting for us."

Paul: "So that brings us up to the race at Surfers. The truck left for Los Angeles when?"

Andy: "The 24th; yesterday? Sometimes it's tough to keep track."

Paul: "So I'll see you on the charter next Monday in L.A."

Andy: "Right. That's a long flight."

CONVERSATION WITH JIM HAMILTON

Paul: "When did you actually go to work for PacWest?"

Jim: "I started Dec. 1, 1996."

Paul: "They had already done their Firestone evaluation test at the Milwaukee oval in October. They used the '96 Reynard with the Cosworth/Ford engine and just used Firestone tires instead of Goodyear. You weren't there for that. The next test was at Sebring on Dec. 3 and 4."

Jim: "The Milwaukee test was a fairly comprehensive test. I missed it. A lot was tried there and a lot was learned. The first Sebring test was, for us, just a shakedown for Mark. And it was a little bit more than that for Mauricio. Then the next one, if I recall, was Mauricio only again at Sebring. The shakedown went OK, but it was only a get-acquainted thing between Mark and myself, also between me and the Reynard, since I hadn't worked with one before.

"The second test, on Dec. 11 at Sebring, I participated to the extent of proposing some shock settings from my [software] simulations. We picked up some grip with those settings."

Paul: "So this was with Tim Neff's shocks?"

Jim: "Yes, that's right."

Paul: "You obviously have a bunch of knowledge and tools you've developed yourself. You've got some simulation software that you developed to help you understand what's going on with a racecar. When you come to a place like PacWest, how much do you show them?"

Jim: "That's a very good question, because it does inevitably become an issue. What I'm trying to do is make the

Jim Hamilton

best symbiotic use of what I've done and what they have here as well. There is some software I have that goes way, way back; it's not very user-friendly, because I've always been the only customer for it. But there is other software that's for sharing. Of course, nowadays you can protect software. You might give only a one-shot executable file or a protected executable file. But in the end there's a certain development of trust involved as well. So we're somewhere in between right now.

[I have to laugh at the timeliness of my question and the honesty of Jim's answer.]

"We have a very good working relationship here, and I'm working with Andy... [Noise in the background indicates some reaction from other people in the room with Jim who have overheard his side of the conversation.]

"Apparently I'm giving a speech which Andy and Allen have taken exception to. Maybe we don't have as good a relationship as I thought [laughs]. Actually they're a bunch of flatulent wankers. This is all on tape now. We're going to play it at the Christmas party [more laughter].

"There's a story to the simulations, of course. The story being how they get created and how they improve. They correlated well at Sebring with the new car. They did not correlate well at Laguna. What I found was that the aero model wasn't right. When you're running the car that close to the ground with that much downforce, particularly the front wing, it's difficult. And we needed better modeling for simulating the shocks. I did that and, once again, they correspond very well.

"At Sebring, Mauricio tried a setting that picked up grip but he didn't like the feel. He likes a certain feel to the car and, as you noticed at Homestead, he is very good analytically; he knows exactly what he wants. Andy gives him a great palate or menu to choose from and they've got great communication between the two of them. The result was we modified that setting for his style, I think at the expense of some grip, but with the gain of the good feeling that he wanted and the consistency he wanted as well. That was my only participation in that test. So that's the first two tests.

"That takes us to the Firebird [near Phoenix] tests in January. At Firebird I had used the shock simulation program with the track, giving quite a different input.

"Characterizing the track itself is one of the toughest parts of getting good results with a vertical-mode simulation program. Each track has its own different excitation and requires different shock settings. Firebird was quite different from Sebring.

"Also, at that test we had only last year's Firestone street-course tires, and there is a difference between last year's street-course tire construction, speaking generically, and this year's Akron road-course construction, which will also be the street-course construction. Although we learned some things during the test, we were learning on last year's tires. It wasn't 'till a later test that we got this year's tires to work with.

"At Firebird we did test some differential concepts. I think I overheard Andy telling you about the negative preloads that are adjustable now on the Reynard diffs. That is a clever thing and simple. It's not ideal. There's probably some magic blend of torque and side-to-side velocity-difference sensitivity which would be somewhat closer to the ideal, excepting of course, active control of the diff, which is beyond the rules.

"We were working on concepts like that in the Toyota GTP program at All American Racers. The rules were pretty much unconstrained in that series. We worked on active ride, traction control, and active differential as well. I think when you make an active effort to work on stuff like that, it helps you even when you have to go back to passive. Obviously Formula 1 is way ahead of us there because they've actually been through all those exercises and gone back to passive. It helped me to understand differentials, when I tried to make an active system."

Paul: "I guess when somebody goes through the process of actually writing the control software, then they get to know a lot about what's going on. Ian Reed [Paul Tracy's engineer at Penske Racing in 1997] said something about that when I interviewed him for that first book. I think he said, 'You can't put the genie back in the bottle.'

"When people learn about a new technology, a rules change can't erase that new knowledge. That's what you're saying, too."

Jim: "Definitely. It challenges you when you go back to a simpler car. And there's no such thing as a simpler car. If you make rules that restrict testing, then that enhances development of simulation software, which in F1 became quite expensive.

"In the aerospace business, where I first worked, simulation became extraordinarily expensive because it had to be 100% correct, it being the only way to predict what would happen with people out in space. And with our country's credibility at stake as well."

Paul: "So, at that first Firebird test, you guys worked on the shock simulation stuff and you also worked on the adjustable diff."

Jim: "We worked on aero things as well. It was still getting to know the driver and his style, for me. It's only recently I've learned some useful lessons about the differences in style. The driver and the car have responded. But I'm getting ahead of myself. Yeah, we went to PIR after Firebird.

"That was a good test at PIR. We traded some concepts from our collective experience about ovals. Our performance was somewhat understated there. We got down to a 20.2 or something. The only car quicker at that point was [Bryan] Herta, who was obviously running through a large assortment of Goodyear development tires. And we were still on last year's tires.

"We had only one day to work also. We left and the next day [Michael] Andretti got a little under our time in the new Swift. Of course that was a very auspicious debut to watch. Even if the Swift was a few tenths slower than us that first day, it came up to speed very quickly for a brand-new design.

"We were trying to get acquainted ourselves with the Reynard, the Firestone tires, PIR, and Mark and myself working together. One thing that was very evident in the very short time that we had to work with both drivers, since Mauricio had problems there, was the great difference in preference and certain areas of sensitivity which are quite different between the two drivers.

"There are some big differences in these two guys. One thing I found with Mark is that if he's outside of a realm of setup where he likes the car, then the feedback that he gives is, let's say, less useful, even contrary-seeming at some times. You give him a softer car and he reports it as a firmer car with better support. However, once you figure out what area he wants to work in and you get somewhere close, his feedback gets far better, far more precise, and he's able to report on sensitivities. By luck or whatever, those sensitivities agree closely with the simulations and they correlate well with improvements in performance.

"PIR was the first experience, for me, where aerodynamic pitch sensitivity was read quite differently between the two drivers. That should have given me a bigger clue, but it didn't then. Mauricio is very persuasive and very good. So one tends to look for the quarter under the light instead of in the dark alley [laughs]. I think that caught me out at the first part of the Homestead test at least, and perhaps in the race as well, but we've turned that corner now.

"Moving on, the next test was the Homestead road course right before Spring Training. We had some new-car, new-team start-up difficulties, but mostly we had engine installation problems that caused us to miss some track time. It was halfway through the second day before we got a good baseline. Mauricio had run the first day.

"We ran on a street-course tire made in Japan from last year that was hard enough that they had never used it in action. But it served quite well for that somewhat strange track. It's got little pieces of Elkhart and Mid-Ohio and it's got a couple of tight turns, but it's got some sweepers and carries quite a bit of speed. Of course, it uses some parts of the oval and frontstraight so it's hard to figure what that track correlates to, so we divided it up, analytically, into pieces and we worked with the pieces.

"We worked with suspension geometries and right away I found out that the Firestone tires respond in opposite ways, in some parameters, to the Goodyear tires. Let's say with regard to front-end geometries and front-end steer and camber-related angles. But we also learned that there were definite preferences that made the tires come to life. We worked most of the time with the obsolescent Japanese tires, but close to the end we got to the Akron road-course tires. And there we found some things.

"Goodyear has a great amount of data and Firestone a great lack of data. It's hard to get simple, first-order, linear compliance data out of them. When we did, we found the tires didn't match the data. For example, the fronts were softer than they were supposed to be and the rears were as stiff as the data showed. As a result we picked up rake and we picked up load transfer to the rear. We picked up a loose car. Just from incorrect tire compliances.

"This is just a feature of off-season testing. We were used to getting a lot more elaborate data from Goodyear, and although not all of it correlated well with our experience and regression results from track data, the radius data and spring rate data by which you do your basic aero setup was pretty good. It certainly was much more detailed than the data we're getting from Firestone.

"On the other hand, Firestone is pretty savvy. Lack of data hasn't kept them from winning poles and races. They're acutely aware of the need for better data. A lot of people have emphasized that need to them. We paid them a visit to Akron, and instead of beating them over the head with magic coefficients, we tried to help them come up with a simpler, entry-level program that would help everybody out.

"I also saw that preferences between the two drivers were quite divergent on the road course. Then we switched to the oval track at Homestead when Spring Training started."

Paul: "That was on Jan. 30."

Jim: "Right. That was an encouraging experience up to the point where we lost most of a car. Mark had set fourth-quick time of the day and was still out and improving the time when he got stuck behind Patrick Carpentier, who, despite his rookie status, was doing a pretty fair job. He didn't really do anything wrong in that particular instance except perhaps failing to move over, and he was out practicing as well.

"Mark had hung back for a lap or so trying to get a run around him, but he came up behind Patrick again and decided to at least show his nose and perhaps pass him on the next straight.

"I haven't seen the video, but from what I saw live and what people report from the video and what Mark reports, is that he came down across the line that Carpentier was on at a distance, closing between five and three car lengths, and he didn't feel much of anything except that the back was gone and he hit the wall. The car was a big mess. We did save the tub. The gearbox had come apart in an extreme way, but it seemed to do a pretty good job of absorbing energy.

"We have Trevor Powell seats in the cars, and they're plenty good. He's a perfectionist and he'll work all night. He'll have the driver in the seat all night if necessary during fitting. The seat seemed to deform in the perfect way, which isn't easy if one considers that there are loosely-coupled masses that are very important to a person, such as their head and torsos, for which the compliance of the foam have to be just right. And they seemed to be. That was very impressive.

"Mark went off to the hospital, got his CAT scan, and was back the next day. I learned that he's a pretty tough guy. He's got a lot of courage. He was hurtin' but he didn't show it. You had to look really carefully to see that he was hurting at all."

Paul: "That was extremely impressive."

Jim: "Yes, it was."

Paul: "I remember asking you a question about how the turbulence from the car ahead affects the following car. I expected that the front wing or the bottom of the car would be affected more, but you said it was the rear wing that was disturbed more."

Jim: "I suspect that it was. Based on Mark's report of what he felt, that's probably what happened. The testing that I've seen on traffic situations is fairly meager. Certainly he lost rear downforce, no question about that. And in such a sudden way that it was beyond any issue of car control. Nonetheless, Mark wasn't really unhappy about the test because we were showing well up to that point. His time didn't hold up near the top the next day but it was definitely promising for us and for our first pre-race testing experience. I was enjoying working with Mark. And as we got closer to what he likes, and it so happened that the track and tire conditions kind of led us in that direction, things went better. We were working on understeer, which allowed us to do some oval stuff that seemed to work reasonably well."

Paul: "The next test was at Firebird on the way to the Laguna test."

Jim: "At Firebird the layout of the track leads to understeer. It becomes, with those tires at least, quite difficult. The track is hard on tires, to some extent that's the temperature, and it's particularly hard on the left fronts. Although we were testing a number of developmental things, the understeer characteristic of the track limited the usefulness of that.

"Firebird is a good place to develop certain systems, but it's one of the few tracks that's even close to being representative, that's available in the off-season. If you look at the collection of tracks in California, where you can test in the winter, it's frustrating. Laguna is right there, but if you look at the others, the ones that have 'willows' in their name or their address [Willow Springs Motorsports Park and Buttonwillow Raceway Park], are, to me, fairly useless except for a basic shakedown."

Paul: "So you think Firebird is pretty representative of a street course?"

Jim: "It's the closest you're going to get. Even with the bumps, in the vertical mode, it's the lowest common denominator of appropriate test tracks."

Paul: "When you say vertical mode, that's what you're looking at with your simulations and data from the car. I assume this is what I've heard you get from tests on four-post shaker rigs, that, for maximum grip, you're trying for minimum change of tire-patch forces."

Jim: "That's one criteria. And you have to look at patterns and combinations of tire force. You can't keep them from changing. So if you look at patterns around the car, and if you have to accept the force variation, which ones are more disturbing to the car, which ones are less disturbing to the car. That leads you down certain paths for what you can do. You can't damp them all out. You obviously want to minimize them."

Paul: "Well, I'll want to pump you for some more of that about a year from now when I'm finishing up that shock book."

Jim: "Fair enough."

Paul: "The next test was the one at Laguna Seca, I think."

Jim: "Laguna was an uplifting test for Mauricio and for the team in general. It was a disappointing test for us. If I were to do that test again, I would ask for equipment that we have now, that I can't really describe [Tim Neff's "other" hydraulic systems]. And I would also use the better understanding that I have now about what the driver wants. We went with a stiff setup because the track was begging for it last year. All of us, including the Eagle I was working with, were set up very, very stiff — short-oval type stiffnesses — because the track had been paved. It had a lot of grip.

"What happened this year was, as with every track, Laguna began to pick up some bumps. The bumps are not random in terms of their placement and frequency. They're generated by cars. They just don't happen because of weather like they do at Lime Rock. [Jim laughs.] Every place you go you'll find the fundamental frequencies, of the cars and tires that run around there, are helping to create the track.

"The most common and obvious example of that is a dirt washboard road, which quickly assumes the wavelength of disturbance that corresponds to the average speed and average undamped wheel-hop frequency. It's usually a nasty frequency. It's the one that's most disturbing to the traffic. At a place like Laguna you have people going at quite different speeds with quite different suspensions. What happened there was that the entries to turns got fairly rough at frequencies that were quite disturbing to the cars. So this required a different approach. We had some equipment lacking there, especially on our side, because it was developmental and a team can only do so much to support a new project."

Paul: [laughing] "I talked to Tim Neff at that test and I knew he had some new stuff you guys were testing. What was funny was that he was all bent out of shape the first day worrying about whether his new toys would work or not, and then on the next day he was pissed because he didn't have enough parts to put on both cars."

Jim: "That's right. That's the way it goes. It doesn't work and everybody's pissed off, and if it does work the pressure's on to make more. That's the way it happens.

"But, taken as a whole, between the two cars and the tests we did for Firestone as well, we had a lot to do the second day. We needed a good result with Mark's car the second day. We failed to get it. We were missing some equipment, but I was missing some understanding about the realms where Mark likes to work. I just didn't understand that adequately.

"I did three countermeasures at the front of the car which made the car much more comfortable for Mark. It was probably only 50% of what was needed. Quickly we ran out of time. We had an opportunity to do some testing with Firestone, a great opportunity for us because we're a new team for them. Mo has been showing extraordinarily well. He's been dominating most of the pre-season testing and making the team look very good as a candidate for tire testing, which we really want to do.

"It's a huge difference when tires are being developed for your car and you get to do free testing. So when they asked us, we weren't about to turn them down. We did some compound testing with Mark on street-course construction which was not appropriate for Laguna, but he was able to get them a good result anyway. Mauricio did some construction testing, which we felt was quite useful. But that did constrain us as far as the tuning process was concerned, and we left off with Mark not really happy in the car. When Mauricio, who often tests with full tanks, got down to fighting weight, qualifying weight, he was a second and a half quicker than Mark, which was quite demoralizing for him. We learned a lot. We just didn't go as quick as we should have, for various reasons."

Paul: "On the way back to the shop you guys stopped at the Big Spring [West Texas] track for a test, I think."

Jim: "We did, and I'm hoping that was quite a big turnaround for us. I learned a lot there. I think I mentioned to you at Homestead on Saturday morning just before qualifying, when Mo had been at the top of the list in every session, that Mo is extremely articulate and persuasive and analytical, and that's a powerful combination with Andy. Although I was working with Mark on something a little bit more appropriate to him, I think that both of us were influenced by what Mo was saying.

"Just by coincidence, close to the end of the Saturday morning practice session these two comets crossed, and we had almost exactly the same setup with a very different result. That got me headed in a totally different direction.

"I realized that Mark needs his own car, and I made some big changes for qualifying and Mark responded, magnificently in fact. I only gave him 60% or 65% of what he really needed, but he picked up the car and put it fifth on the grid with quite a brave effort. But it still wasn't a happy car for him in Turn 3, and scared him to the point where he didn't really complete his second lap at speed. God knows what that would have been, because his first lap was one of the fastest first laps of any.

"I continued to make changes for the race, but I really started too late with this strategy of desperation, of realizing just how different his car has to be from Mo's.

"Everybody went somewhat loose in the race, but Mark wasn't really able to deal with it. Post-race analysis was very useful for me because at a place like Homestead where you have apex speeds above 180 mph, I would not have expected to find the differences in driving style that I did between our two drivers."

Paul: "You just didn't think it was possible to do the turns that differently?"

Jim: "I didn't think you could get away with it." [We both laugh.] But, if I just looked at steering and braking traces, I didn't see too much difference. But after some more in-depth analysis, I used my own experience as a driver, and I tried to put the thing together in vehicle dynamics terms. Then I found massive differences, which made me admire both drivers, really.

"Mark was able to take an approach to Turn 3 that put him in greater difficulties, but he was able to rescue the car during qualifying. That's what impressed me that he was able to save the car. I don't know that what I saw in the data was a big whoops or if he actually saved it. But there were two unmistakable big corrections there. After that I decided that Mark's got to have 95% his own setup. With the shocks and equipment we were working on becoming fully mature, then we went down to Big Spring with that in mind.

"We ended up with almost everything on the two cars opposite, almost all parameters opposite, things you wouldn't believe. Like geometry, maybe 11 or 12 geometric parameters, steering geometries, almost everything you could think of on the car, was preferred nearly 180 degrees out of phase between the two drivers. This makes for very, very different cars. But Mark was happier and happier and gave me better and better feedback. He read the shocks in a way that corresponded with lap times, with post-race analysis, including frequency-domain analysis and the simulations. Of course that makes him feel good, but you don't want to believe your driver or your simulator just because they agree with each other [laughs]. But in this case the lap times seemed to agree as well.

"We were about nine-tenths slower than Mo at the end of the Big Spring test; however, our times were done with more than 20 gallons of fuel vs. darn-near empty and in the heat of the day, when it was more than 20 degrees hotter. Looking at the data later, I'm really happy with Mark and I think Mark was happy too, not with the lap times but the approach and with the results of being able to work much more closely together.

"It doesn't sound like the same man reporting. For example, I didn't hear anything like, 'We need a more stable platform for the package' and things like that. I heard, 'This particular geometry works better from one-third to two-thirds of the turn, but I don't like the turn-in because it's not as crisp as it was.' That sort of thing, the kind of concrete feedback that's much easier to assimilate and much easier to respond to. So I was very much encouraged by the Big Spring test. And I'm looking forward to Surfers."

Paul: "What setup strategy will you use at Surfers?"

Jim: "I found that Mark likes a...If Mo likes a go-kart feel, then Mark definitely doesn't. He likes a car that he can feel. He doesn't like an oversteering car in nearly any circumstance. He has good car control, but an oversteering car just doesn't suit his style. Also, I had to come to grips with the fact that he could be very quick with a car that apparently had less downforce, particularly front downforce, than one would think was ideal. But as I dissected his driving style to the best of my ability with the data, I saw how he makes it work. So it's just accommodation to his style.

"At Surfers I want to continue to do that, obviously. I've got a couple of loops of aero, tires, suspension, and ride height, that I want to keep iterating on until the car really feels the best for him and it's consistent. At Surfers we have a fairly unique situation in that the prime tire and the optional tire from Firestone are made in two different countries with two different constructions. From what we've seen, the two tires may require different geometries. And I'm not just talking about simple static settings. So that'll be a challenge to adapt to, and we could have a Friday morning thrash.

"Big Spring has historically correlated with Surfers for a variety of people over the years, including little Al [Al Unser Jr.] and Mauricio. Surfers is a unique piece of road; it's very crowned. It reminds me of the country roads in Connecticut where I grew up. It's not exactly what an Indy car likes in transitions from the top of one cylinder to the top of another cylinder at a different angle, if you will. Those are some of the problems we'll have to deal with.

"Braking, turn-in, and traction are the issues. Mid-turn behavior is of less consequence there than it is at most places."

Paul: "Well, Surfers should be interesting. I'm certainly looking forward to it. It's my first trip down there. So I guess we're all on some big charter flight out of L.A.?"

Jim: "Last year I was lucky enough to ride upstairs in the business-class section. But still it's a long trip — 14 hours."

Paul: "Yeah; I'm not looking forward to the flight. I called for a seat and asked for an up-front window. They said 40K was up front. But K is a big number; that means it's a 747, 11 seats across. That's like a big bus. But for me it'll be time to talk to people and maybe record some conversations like this one. It's exciting. I'm already having trouble sleeping. That happens when I get excited. So I guess I'll see you guys in L.A."

Jim: "Right. Take it easy and we'll see you there."

CHAPTER 6

SURFERS PARADISE

For the overseas races, the ones in Australia and Brazil, the race promoter pays to transport the people and equipment. I'm scheduled on a charter flight leaving Los Angeles on Monday, March 31, arriving at Brisbane late the following night. The flight takes about 14 hours but we'll lose a day crossing the international dateline.

I've had morning flights from San Francisco to L.A. canceled because of fog and I have to make the charter flight or miss the whole trip. So I fly down Sunday afternoon, rent a car, and stay overnight with some friends. Monday morning I drive to the airport, return the car, and take the Hertz shuttle to the international terminal.

The PacWest guys have just arrived from Indianapolis, and I fall in line with them at the Quantas ticket counter. Their day started much earlier than mine. People from other teams are here also. Steve Challis, Greg Moore's engineer, tells me about their switch from a Lola to a Reynard chassis. He's just come from England where he supervised the final assembly of their car, and then they took it to Firebird Raceway near Phoenix for its initial shakedown. He's glad to be quit of the Lola and back on familiar ground.

After check-in, Stephen Kent, John Oreovicz, and I have lunch together. Stephen has some questions about book publishing. He'd like to write about high-end bicycle gear. He maintained tech equipment for the United States Bicycle Team before coming to PacWest. The flight is scheduled to leave at 3 p.m., and people begin to gather in the boarding area about 2 o'clock.

On board, Charlie Guilinger and I have the last two seats at the back on the right side. I'm in the window seat and only have one person to crawl over when I have to pee. Charlie is a nice guy and easy to talk to. Jim Hamilton is right in front of me. A guy in front of Jim bought a bottle of duty-free rum and extols the virtue of this particular brand to Jim. I didn't know it at the time, but this was an omen of bad things to come.

The plane is a Series 400 747 that can carry about 400 people. There are first-class and business-class sections in the front of the plane. Most of us are back here in economy.

GLOBAL POSITIONING

We're still preparing for push-back a little before 3 p.m. The television projection at the front of our section alternates between several images showing information from the aircraft's global positioning system (GPS). One screen tells us the temperature outside, now 17 degrees C; our altitude, 50 feet above sea level; our speed, 0 miles per hour; and our distance from departure, 12,037 kilometers. I assume the kilometers are from Brisbane, our destination on the east coast of Australia. The system cycles through a series of maps of the Western United States, the Eastern Pacific Ocean, and the entire Pacific Ocean, showing the United States on the far right and Australia down on the far left.

The noise gets pretty loud before push-back as people yak it up with friends. There might also be some locker-room nervousness about the flight. Fourteen hours is a long time to be cooped up on a plane, even one as big as this.

At 3:30 we roar into the clouds at 516 kph or 356 mph and 1,800 meters altitude or 6,800 feet. One screen says it's 13 hours and 32 minutes to our destination. We get a good view of Catalina Island in the Pacific Ocean off the Palos Verdes Peninsula south of L.A.

My fellow passengers are mostly CART team members and officials. The few women on board attract lots of eyes when they get up and move around. One of the Quantas flight attendants is very attractive, and she gets the eyes also. Some guys have brought cards and a game of 31 starts behind us. It gets loud and goes on for a long time.

I can see puffy white clouds below us and the rich blue ocean between them. At 4 p.m. the GPS screen says 873 kph and 8,841 miles to destination. Alcoholic drinks are free. I have a Fosters beer to help me get into an Aussie mood.

Three hours into the flight people are getting pretty rowdy. The last of the beer disappeared a while ago, and people are drinking wine and hard stuff. At least a third of the people are out of their seats. I try to sleep with no luck.

At 10 p.m. L.A. time, about halfway, I talk to Allen McDonald for a while. Allen had his engineering education paid for by the British Navy. He joined the Brabham Formula 1 team in 1985, working with its designer, Gordon Murray. We talk about the relationship between PacWest and Reynard, the chassis manufacturer. "Malcolm [Oastler, Reynard designer] sees most of what we do," Allen says. "We show him our setup sheets and the aero data we get from our Galmer model. He debriefs with us after sessions when he's around."

I know the teams never trusted Lola enough to share that kind of information, so I ask Allen about the trust Malcolm Oastler and Reynard have established among the CART teams. Allen says they trust Malcolm not to spread the information around.

"So the teams must believe that the information they share with Reynard is like the tide that raises all boats," I say.

"The teams don't believe in rising tides," Allen says. "They believe in tsunamis and hurricanes." We both laugh.

There are a lot of smart technical people working at the teams, and some teams have their own aero programs and build car parts of their own, as PacWest does. It seems to me that Malcolm has to have a hell of a lot of confidence in himself as an engineer and designer that he can leapfrog them with a new design every year.

At 10:20 p.m. L.A. time we have 6:37 to go. We're at 35,000 feet and 551 mph and still shy of the international dateline. About an hour later they serve us our second meal, some mystery beef and veggies. Not good. I shouldn't have eaten it, but I'm massively bored. It's quieter now and I try to get some sleep. Things got pretty drunk earlier.

About 5 a.m. Tuesday our time we're descending into Brisbane, where it's 11 p.m. Tuesday. I took my contact lenses out to sleep and now I go into one of the heads to put them back in. I feel tired and weak, but not horribly uncomfortable.

Since we're in the back of the bus we're also at the tail-end of the customs line, and it takes 30 minutes to get through. After a short walk outside the terminal we climb into whatever bus has our hotel's name on the front. I find the one for the Mercure Resort, leave my roller bag out for the driver to load, and get on. Most of the other people on board are guys on the Penske team. We're all pretty tired so there isn't much talk during the hour drive from the Brisbane airport to the beach-resort town of Surfers Paradise.

WEDNESDAY

I wake at 6 a.m. Wednesday morning. The Mercure resort is a nice place with a big pool. Someone told me it used to be called the Ocean Blue and most of the teams stayed here. I use the English-style hot-water pot in the room to make some instant coffee. Ater a shower and shave I walk across the street and a quarter of a mile north to the blocked-off streets that make up the racecourse.

The sun is barely up over the trees in back of the garage area. This is a pretty lush environment. The plants are tropical and it's almost 70 degrees at 7 in the morning. The racecars sit there, lined up neatly under covers on pit road. Containers full of team equipment and tools are stacked in each garage space.

There are very few people around, but I see Billy Kamphausen and I say hello. He looks at my white legs sticking out of my shorts. "Looks like you brought winter with you." Sticks and stones.

I've heard there's a fancy McDonald's restaurant right on the beach in the heart of Surfers Paradise, so I walk in that direction. When I get there I find Trevor Jackson, Daryl Fox, Mike Bauer, and Charlie Guilinger sitting outside, taking in the sun and eating breakfast.

The line inside is too long for me, so I visit with the guys for awhile and then eat breakfast at a small storefront restaurant a block away. At 9 a.m. the temperature is already above 80, and I'm sweating lightly in the shade of the beach umbrella protecting my table.

Later I walk back north along the strand, watching the offshore clouds and the breaking surf. I pass a few spectacularly beautiful young women barely dressed in scraps of cloth. The ocean is a deep blue out past the breakers, and the sun sparkles on the waves. White spray blows offshore, taking the tops of the waves with it. "Indy" signs are on every light post in several bright colors. That's what they call the race here, "the Indy."

A sign warns against skin damage from the sun. "Slip, Slap, Slop," the sign says. Slip on a shirt. Slap on a hat. Slop on sunscreen.

As I walk back to the CART pit area, I see that the backstretch of the track is the road that goes right next to the beach. It's closed for this week and turned into a racecourse. I notice that the road is crowned just as Jim Hamilton had said in the phone interview we had. I wonder how that will affect the racecars.

Without some chicanes to slow the cars, the turns at the end of the straights would be dangerous. I can see some guys building the chicanes. Workmen are laying curbing and gravel and green sod to form the chicanes and berms. It's all very tidy.

A Race Course on the Beach

Oz Is a Friendly Place

This is my first visit to Australia, and the people here seem very friendly and into doing things right. I find myself smiling at people because they're smiling at me. The standard greeting is "G'die" or "G'die ta ya."

It's after noon, and I'm sitting at a picnic table among some trees, eating a sandwich. The CART paddock and the Start/Finish straight are just in front of me and the backstraight behind me past a small lagoon. Two 11- or 12-year-old girls, tanned and slim and innocently pretty, ride up on their bicycles and shuck down to bathing suits, chattering and giggling. They lean their bikes up against a park bench and leave their towels, T-shirts, and shorts just lying there. Then they walk onto a suspension bridge over the lagoon and jump off the bridge into the water. They splash around for awhile, yelling and laughing, before they come back up the sandy bank to dry themselves, dress, and ride off.

The scene struck me. In many parts of our country their bikes and clothes would have been stolen in a few minutes. Barbed wire would be strung on that bridge because some kid got hurt jumping off and the parents sued. Someone told me Australia is similar to the United States in the '50s. I think that's true. We've lost a lot.

I spend the rest of the day hanging around watching the crews unpack and set up the garages. The PacWest crew is staying at a motel further away from the track than the Mercure Resort, so I don't see much of them in the evenings. Jim Swintal, the CART starter, asks me if I want to meet some of the CART people for dinner, and I join them at a good Italian restaurant on the main drag in downtown Surfers Paradise. It's a warm night and I walk to and from dinner.

Russ Grosshans Unwraps a Racecar

Stephen Kent Unpacks

THURSDAY

There's a media breakfast at the Conrad Casino and most of the CART drivers show up to talk to the local press and TV people. About 100 people are here at 7:30 a.m. and it's a good breakfast. Mark is here, but Mauricio doesn't arrive until tonight. The journalists know Mark from the Formula 1 races here, so he's asked to compare CART racing with Formula 1. "The attitude is the biggest difference. In CART everyone is open and friendly. It's the best racing in the world. There's not much racing in F1 anymore."

After the event winds down, I take a media shuttle back to the Mercure Resort and then walk to the garage area.

Update Kits

It's afternoon now and I'm watching the PacWest crew install some new brake ducts from Reynard. The ducts look like 1-inch aluminum tubing. They attach to the brake calipers and blow air onto the backs of the brake pads. I'm told the long straights here followed by slow corners are tough on brakes. Installation of these ducts takes a lot of hand fitting. They use air-powered grinders to remove material from the tubes. The up and down wailing of the air grinders is a constant noise coming from most of the garages.

The temperature is in the 80s and it's humid. I find I have to drink water constantly. Bob Varsha, the ESPN-TV announcer, is new to CART racing this year, and he walks through the garage area. I've known Bob for years, so I introduce him to John Oreovicz (Oreo) and Russ Cameron.

At 3:15 the PacWest guys are putting the Surfers setup on all four cars. The T-car [T for test] is prepared exactly like the primary car and has its settings updated constantly as the setup details change during a practice session. The goal is to be able to get into the T-car instantly if the primary is damaged. Track time is critical.

Thousands of local people are here wandering around, looking into the garages and watching the Aussie touring cars practicing on the track. Racing is popular down here, and the fans are knowledgeable.

A Beer at the Pool

The crews finish up around 5 p.m. and I go back to my hotel. I see some of the Reynard people at the pool and join them. Bruce Ashmore, technical director for Reynard North America, tells me he was going to be a farmer, but his dad's farm was struck with a sickness and all the animals had to be killed. He had to choose another career and he chose engineering because he liked to fiddle with the farm machinery.

He quotes the founder, Adrian Reynard, on hiring engineers. "Adrian hires engineers because he says you can train an engineer to be a businessman, but you can't train a business graduate to be an engineer."

I'm introduced to Barry Ward, a Reynard engineer who designs gearboxes. Barry is a friendly Brit, in his late 20s I'd guess. I ask him about the longitudinal gearbox in the new Swift that looks to be in front of the rear axle. Barry tells me about some tradeoffs between the Swift design and a transverse box as used in the Reynard. "The turbo has to be higher [in the Swift] which gives a higher CG [center of gravity], but the gears can be smaller because the step down is after the gears. But they turn faster, so there could be more oil drag."

Barry says Reynard gets a steady stream of resumes from people who want to work there. "But we only look at the ones with racing or hands-on experience. When they first come to Reynard they work a trial period for very low wages." I think that's smart.

Generally, everyone in racing starts out working for free. Behind each of us making a living in racing are a dozen people waving their arms and shouting, "I'll do it for free." This competition for jobs means only the best people and most committed actually get to work for the top-level teams. It also keeps wages and benefits low, but in recent years salaries and benefits have gone up.

Also here at the table are Derrick and Sandy Houk. They both work for Reynard North America in Indianapolis. They're a husband/wife team and drive the Reynard truck that takes spare parts to every race. Derek and Sandy first met when she was in high school and he drove her school bus. They didn't like each other then, but clicked when they met later. These are nice people.

FRIDAY

At 9:40 a.m. in the garage area it's warm and humid again. I guess that's just the way it is here. I can hear the whir and whine of the air grinders as the PacWest guys are still fitting the new brake ducts. The Aussie touring cars are on course, and they're noisy also.

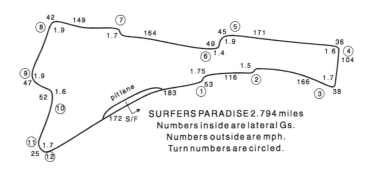

SURFERS PARADISE 2.794 miles
Numbers inside are lateral Gs.
Numbers outside are mph.
Turn numbers are circled.

A local TV crew is here interviewing crew members. They put the camera on Charlie Guilingerand ask him some questions. "They were asking about going over the wall, how it feels and stuff like that," he tells me.

An hour later all the cars and most of the drivers are in the pit lane waiting for the first practice session. I ask Andy Brown what he hopes to accomplish in the first practice. "Last year max downforce was the way to go to stabilize the car in the braking areas. With the smaller fuel cells this year, we might want to take some wing off to reduce drag and save fuel. We'll see in this first session."

Paul: "Do you plan changes in different directions based on what might happen?"

Andy: "Yes. You have to plan changes ahead of time, even though the odds are things will go differently."

At 10:50 motors are warming. The pits are filled with fans and this is only Friday. There are so many people here you have to swim through them to get from the pit box to the garage. Jim Hamilton tells me he thinks the most downforce for the least drag is the key here. "Traction, braking, and turn-in are very critical."

Nigel Bloom is the parts guy at the PacWest shop. He doesn't go to many races, but he's here in charge of the tires on Mark's car.

Morning Practice

The green flag starts a 1-hour practice session at 11:09. I listen to the radio conversations using a PacWest scanner. Both PacWest cars go out on rain tires for two reasons. The course will be very dirty so there's no reason to use slicks, and they need to scuff a set of rains anyway. When the cars come back in they both get a thorough check for leaks, as the sidepods come off and the crews look everything over completely. This "installation check" happens at the beginning of every session. It's called that because they've probably installed something since the last session. Sticker slick tires go on and both cars return to the track.

I can't see much of the course here, just the rear wing going by very fast on the straight and the cars braking hard for the chicane to my left. Both cars are set too low, so ride height is increased when they come in again. A red flag, caused by a crash somewhere, stops the session for awhile. At 11:35 the green flag waves again.

Mauricio comes back in saying the bottom of the car is still hitting hard. Andy tells the crew to raise it two more flats. Mauricio also tells Andy the fuel cutoff is too abrupt. "It's viscous," he says. Ilmor has a valve that cuts off all fuel when the driver gets off the throttle. This means the engine uses less fuel, but it makes the car more difficult to drive.

The monitor shows Scott Pruett has the top time right now followed by Michael Andretti, Parker Johnstone, and Greg Moore. Mark tells Jim the gearshift is messed up and the car is still hitting. Jim raises the rear of the car two more flats.

A yellow flag stops the session at 11:42, and it resumes 5 minutes later. Mark goes right out but there's smoke at the rear of Mauricio's car and his crew is looking for a leak.

Another red flag brings Mark back in at 11:53. Pruett is still P1 with a 1-minute, 39-seconds lap. "The car pitches forward in braking," Mark says to Jim. "It just goes solid and the rear kicks up." At the next green flag, both cars go out. Mark is in P17.

Mauricio is back in saying the shocks at the rear feel like they've lost pressure. He's in P5 with a 70.573-seconds lap. Alex Zanardi is in P1 now, and there's 21 minutes to go.

The next time Mark is in he says the car won't turn in for him. "The front is too compliant."

Jim: "The car and the tires tell me the car needs more mid-shock at the rear and less camber in the rear."

Mark: "Camber won't help."

Jim: "Raise the front three flats and back off on the mid on the front shocks." It seems to me Mark won't let him do what he wants, so he does something he hopes will help.

Mauricio's car has a leaky fitting on one of the new hydraulic systems at the rear. I'm not supposed to know about that so I don't ask. Mauricio is in the 17x car, the T-car, and he's third in the session now. He lost some track time because of the leak.

Mark is back in on another red flag, saying "The car is touching down on the straights."

Jim: "What about the curbs?"

Mark: "I can go over them but the car jumps about 2 feet in the air. The headrest just kicks the shit out of my head."

Alison Hill, a pretty English woman with curly blond hair, works media relations for Mark. I call her Mark's handler. She's on the cell phone a lot talking to writers in the Olde Country. She's listening to Mark on the radio also and says to me, "When he gets frustrated or impatient his speech slows down, like you do when you talk to someone who can't speak your language."

When the course goes green again most of the drivers rush to get back on the track with 6 minutes to go in the session. It's like a 20-car drag race out of the pit lane. The dust is blown off now and there's some rubber getting ground into the track surface. They could turn some good times.

I'm writing furiously in my notebook, trying to get the most out of what I'm seeing and hearing. Chris Jaynes and Dave Jacobs stare at the notebook until I notice them and then laugh. That starts a year-long running joke about how they don't see how anyone could ever read my notes. The checkered flag waves at noon. Mark's last comment is, "The car's too soft for me."

Alex Zanardi earns P1 in the session, turning a lap of 1 minute, 38.240 seconds. The rest of the top five is Michael Andretti, Jimmy Vasser, Christian Fittipaldi, and Scott Pruett. The PacWest cars didn't do so well. Mo is P8 and Mark P19.

The Swift chassis continues to look good, with both Michael and Christian in the top five. Andre Ribeiro is sixth in a Lola, so maybe that chassis isn't so bad. Paul Tracy is seventh in a Penske chassis. All the chassis manufacturers have at least one example in the top 10. This could be a very competitive year among those companies.

Back in the garage Tim Neff and the 17-crew look at the rear of Mauricio's car to find out what caused the leak that cost them valuable track time during that session. Tim tells me. "It's some new fitting we had made and they're not quite right. We can fix it but we lost some time, and it just pisses me off."

Friday Qualifying

Road-course qualifying is always divided into two groups. The fast half of the race field at the last street- or road-course race, I call them the fast guys, go first on Friday. Today's groups are made up from the qualifying times from the '96 race at Laguna Seca (Calif.). Saturday's qualifying groups are determined by the Friday qualifying times, and the slow guys go first.

The 17-crew is still working on Mauricio's car when the green flag starts the Friday qualifying session for the fast group. The crews lost some time between sessions because that first practice session ran 45 minutes late and qualifying started only 10 minutes late. Mauricio goes out on track with 22 minutes left in the session. Christian Fittipaldi is P1 for a while.

Jim increases the rear toe-in on Mark's car, and he goes back out. Zanardi turns a lap of 1 minute, 37.5 seconds to lead the session, bumping Christian to second. Mauricio makes up for lost time by driving his car to third quick with 7 minutes to go.

At the checkered flag Zanardi has gone even faster, 1:36.156. He's followed by Christian, Scott Pruett, Mauricio, and Michael Andretti. Mark is 14th, almost 3 seconds slower than Zanardi. Mark is not happy with the car.

The slow guys are on course now, and I walk out the back of the garage area, across the suspended foot bridge and take a look at the cars going through the chicane on the backstraight. They come from my right and brake from 180 mph into a snaky chicane that also has some serious elevation changes due to the crown in the road. The cars turn in to the left and go down, then turn back to the right and come back up, finally accelerating out while turning back to the left out of the chicane.

It looks to me like being quick through here takes some very precise car placement and just the right speed. Too quick into the chicane and the driver has to jump the curb, upsetting the car. Too much throttle coming out and the car slides wide into a barrier. Bumps in the road at the exit bounce the car up and down violently.

There are too many people here for me to get close to the fence, so I have to stand back about 6 feet where I can step up slightly onto some tree roots and look over some of the heads in front. People are constantly walking in front of me, including some beautiful young women showing a lot of tanned skin. They are very distracting.

Back in the garage area I see Mark's gearbox is apart. Tim Love, the gearbox guy on the 18-car, is changing ratios. I stand around and watch everybody work for a couple of hours.

At 6 p.m. the sun is getting low. It's late fall down here, after all. The 17-crew is finishing up with Mauricio's car, but Mark's crew is still busy. I head back to the hotel.

Too tired to go out and sight see, I order some pizza and a couple of beers from room service and watch a movie in my room. Later, a sit in the hot tub by the pool relaxes me and I go to bed.

SATURDAY

Waking up early and not getting back to sleep is the bane of trans-time zone travelers. This time when I wake up at 5:30 a.m. I remember to call my wife, Pat, at home. It's evening the next day there, I think.

After a shower and shave I'm walking to the track at 7 a.m. A high tide has caused water in the lagoon to rise up over the sidewalk under the road, blocking one route to pit lane, but I find another. It's cloudy today and I brought my rain gear, a coated nylon jacket with a hood, because the weather forecast includes the possibility of showers.

Mauricio is in the garage watching his guys prepare the car for morning practice, scheduled for 9 a.m. I want to get a ride around the track so I go looking for Wally Dallenbach. He and Gary Barnard, the chief course observer, are in the front seats of the pace car, and they talk about possible improvements and potential problems as we drive around. We don't go very fast but it gives me an impression of the circuit. It's narrow with tight corners, long straights and twisty chicanes.

The severe crown in the road can cause problems that result in setup compromises. For one thing, the outside tire can see more camber than the inside tire. And, if the ride height of the car is too low, the crown can rub on the bottom of the car hard enough to lift the weight off the tires and spin the car.

Morning Practice

The practice session starts on time. The sun is high now and, with a cloudless sky, it could get hot and muggy again today. Mauricio comes in after his first run saying, "The engine is running rough down low."

Andy: "Go fully clockwise on the fuel control."

Mauricio is saying the car is rolling too much so Andy has the crew change to stiffer springs at the rear and lower the ride height two flats.

Mark comes in saying, "The front won't bite. There's just no precision on turn-in. The rear is OK at the moment, but it's touching down at the front and the rear."

Jim: "I like the looks of the front tires in camber, but I think we should close the toe. Two flats less toe-in at the front, please."

After another run on course, Mark says "The car pushes like a pig. It turns in too late for the chicanes." He wants to make a spring change. "How many laps on the tires?"

Jim: "They've got 16 on them. We've got a red flag. Let me look at the data. We've got the time to make a more aggressive change at the front."

Both PacWest cars go out on track, but the session is interrupted again by a red flag. One of the Toyota-engined cars is dead on course. That's a consistent problem with street courses; when a driver stalls or makes a mistake and hits a wall, the car is in the way. Then the session has to be stopped so the car can be moved, towed back, or the barriers repaired, or all of the above.

Andy asks Mauricio how the car feels. Mauricio answers, "It's OK, Andy. Now we have a lot of grip. I'll turn some times now. How fast are they going?"

One of the crew hands the little ARS monitor to Mauricio, and he studies it intently. Mauricio has been complaining that the engine is running rough so the sidepods come off and some of the black boxes get changed. At 9:28 the session goes green again and the PacWest cars go back out. Mauricio is P16 and Mark is P18.

Mark is back in quickly, saying the clutch is going. "The car is just too stiff. I've got wheelspin and oversteer everywhere. It's too stiff."

Mauricio comes in saying the car is banging down under braking at the front and rear. Jim Reid goes under the car to look at the skid plates and then sprays them with black paint. He marks on the skid plate schematic and hands that to Andy.

Andy: "I want to take out some low-speed rebound and some high-speed bump at the front."

Mauricio: "Can we lower the car at the front?"

Andy: "Yes, I think we can. Let's lower the front one flat, please, guys."

Mauricio is ready to make another run, but a red flag stops the session at 9:41 a.m. Michael Andretti has slid down an escape road without hitting anything. The top five in the session are Scott Pruett, Alex Zanardi, Dario Franchitti, Jimmy Vasser, and Raul Boesel.

Mark tells Jim, "The gearbox is a little bit better today than yesterday, but the brakes are off. Every time I approach that second chicane on the backstraight, it's a bit of an issue."

At 9:46 the course goes green and both cars go out. As Mark moves out of the pit box, Jim says, "Sticker tires." That's so Mark will know they made a tire change.

A few minutes later there's another red flag and Mark comes in saying, "The car's too stiff." Jim softens the shocks at the rear and makes an adjustment to the limited-slip differential.

Most people know that the outside tires go farther in a turn than the inside tires. Road cars have a device in the rear axle called a differential that allows the wheels to turn at different speeds. It directs the power to the faster-turning wheel. Unfortunately for a racecar, that's often the unloaded inside tire, and it just spins. So racing differentials have ways to limit that difference in wheel speeds and direct power to both wheels. The new Reynards have a patented system that allows an external adjustment on the limited-slip differential.

During this red flag I walk over to the backstraight and watch at the second chicane. I can still hear the talk on the scanner. The cars go out again at 9:55. They look much smoother through here than they did yesterday. Most drivers are on the throttle earlier coming out, and the acceleration and bouncing over the bumps is even more violent. Some cars take big leaps sideways at full throttle toward the barriers on the exit. Mauricio's engine sounds rough. He goes in for tires. Mark is still saying the car is too stiff. They both return to the course with 10 minutes to go in the session.

Mauricio ends up P7 in this session with Mark P19. The three quickest are Scott Pruett, Jimmy Vasser, and Christian Fittipaldi. There aren't as many fans in the paddock area today, so it's easier to get around. Maybe they have to buy tickets to get into the paddock today. At noon both the 17- and 18-cars are on the setup pads getting the final touches for qualifying.

Fuel Slots

During that session I heard Andy telling Mauricio to select a new set of engine control parameters, the one that's fully clockwise on the switch. Each setting, also called a slot, chooses a set of control values for spark timing and the amount of fuel injected based on throttle position, engine rpm, and other values read by the engine management system. One slot might be for lean running during a race, another for max power and rpm for qualifying, etc. When the car is in the pits and a laptop computer connected by an electronic cable to the engine, the Ilmor engineers can alter values in the different slots. These slots will be much more important this year than last because of the smaller fuel tanks. The teams need to stretch fuel mileage as much as possible to avoid extra pit stops during races.

A new set of calibrations for these slots has recently been developed by "Dyno" Don Norton, Ilmor's calibration specialist and a senior trackside support engineer.

"The engine was already optimized for full-throttle, top-end performance, such as was required at Homestead, using our regular dynamometer," says Norton, who has been working in racing for more than 25 years.

"What we still needed to do, however, was make sure the engine was being fueled consistently in the slow corners, where the car is in first gear, at low rpm, when the driver goes to full throttle to accelerate away. For that we needed Mercedes-Benz's transient dyno in Stuttgart.

"The transient dyno gives you much better control of your experiments. You can simulate an entire race, avoiding all the variables introduced through driver input and changing track conditions, while logging much more data than you could in an actual track test. You can do in a day on the transient dyno what would take you a year to do on the track."

I've known "Dyno" Don for several years. I'll see him standing outside the Ilmor transporter, smoking a cigarette. He's got a mustache and glasses, and is usually wearing a black Mercedes cap. When he can, he answers my questions, and I enjoy talking to him.

Actually it took Don about two weeks to come up with the new calibration in use here at Surfers. He broke that dyno in Stuttgart this last winter, and he's pretty proud of it.

"I was talking to some German lady journalist," Don tells me, "and she was saying that someone had broken the transient dyno at Stuttgart. 'Yep; that's me,' I told her. There was a fire and everything. It was pretty spectacular." Don was calm and matter-of-fact as he told me the story, but I had to laugh.

Saturday Qualifying

The course goes green for the slow guys at 12:50 p.m., only 20 minutes late. I couldn't hear the CART officials earlier, but Casey Eason has put that frequency into my scanner, so now I hear the reason for the first red flag of the session. Water is running across the track somewhere. They find a way to stop the water and the course goes green again. I see some dark clouds in the south that seem to be spreading north toward us. The look like they have some rain in them.

At 1:24 it's 5 minutes until the fast-guys' session, and the engines in the PacWest cars are warming up. Mauricio says his engine cleared up in the practice session after they changed the ECM, the engine control module.

At 1:44 the fast guys get the green. Almost immediately Scott Pruett blows a motor and causes a red flag. When the course goes back green, Andy tells Mauricio, "OK Morris; let's give it a go."

Mark quickly turns a 1:38.056, a second quicker than this morning. Then he goes even faster with a 1:37.422 lap and is quickest in the session. Alison tells me that Dario Franchitti doing well is good motivation for Mark. He wants to be the quickest Brit.

Mauricio moves up to P4 and comes in. "I think we need more high-speed shock control, Andy."

Andy: "OK, Morris. Two sweeps of high-speed bump and high-speed rebound all 'round, please, guys, and up a flat all 'round."

Jimmy Vasser is at the top of the monitor now. Both PacWest cars are in and out a couple of times. With 8 minutes to go Mauricio is P4 and Mark P7. Then they both improve. Mo to P3 and Mark is P6. The track is getting quicker and all the drivers are trying harder.

The times tumble on the last couple of laps and Alex Zanardi jumps to P1 with a lap of 1 minute, 35.940 seconds. Paul Tracy, Jimmy Vasser, Greg Moore, and Mark round out the top five. Mauricio is P8, almost a second slower than Zanardi. It turns out Greg Moore and Mark had identical lap times, 1:36.754. Greg gets fourth because his second-fast lap is quicker than Mark's.

It seems to me that Mark has repeated what he did at Homestead. He wasn't comfortable in the car, but when it came time to qualify, he gutted it up and cut a good time. I ask Jim Hamilton about that. "I have to agree that's what it looks like," he says. "I made some big changes in the car. I looked at the roll rates, the wheel-movement frequencies, and I guessed at what I thought Mark was trying to tell me about the car. Maybe it felt better to him."

After only two races it's obvious to me that there's a big difference in the way the two driver/engineer teams communicate. Andy and Mauricio have worked together in Formula 1 and Formula 3000 years ago and now are in their third year at PacWest. They march toward a good setup with a minimum of discussion. They must do a lot of planning before the track sessions. Mauricio seems to have a good technical understanding of the car and what it takes to make it handle. He only tells Andy the highest-priority information.

On the other hand, Mark and Jim have only worked together for a few months. Last year Mark had two engineers; first Mark Heard and then Tim Neff. Mark seems to tell Jim everything he can think of about the car and leaves it to Jim to sort out what's important. It's obvious this is a frustrating situation for both Mark and Jim, but Mark is qualifying well, and if he can win some races, well that's what counts.

Race Prep

It's almost 4 p.m. and the PacWest crews are installing race engines to go in both the primary cars. The transmissions are getting some attention too. I can smell that unique aroma of gear oil. The exhaust systems have to come out with an engine change and several guys spend a lot of time carefully examining the headers, waste-gate pipes, and turbine inlet and exhaust pipes. They're looking for cracks that can blossom into leaks and sideline the car during the race. Tim Douthat is a master fabricator and welder, so he gets the job of rewelding cracks that can be repaired.

Mark Moore, Mo's chief mechanic, tells me the new brake kit will stay on for the race. "It's working. The brakes are no problem this year."

RACE DAY

As usual I wake at 4:30 a.m. and can't get back to sleep. So up and at it. I check my e-mail on CompuServe and visit the motorsports forum to check on what's going on in the rest of racing. After a shower and shave I go to the dining room for breakfast. An Aussie breakfast is similar to an English breakfast without the kippers. They make their scrambled eggs watery, but the fruit, particularly the tomatoes, are bursting with flavor.

Mark "Billy" Blundell and Steve Fusek

The tunnel under Ferny Avenue is blocked again by a high tide. I retreat a couple of blocks and cross the street with the help of a friendly police person. The walk to pit lane and the warm sun puts me straight into a sweat.

It's 8 a.m. and the PacWest guys have the primary cars on pit lane and the T-cars on the pads in the garage. They practice pit stops with the racecars in the pit lane, ignoring the start of the first race of the day. Supercars, called "tin-tops" here, are similar to early Trans-Am cars — big engines and tires — but they still look like production cars.

Warm-Up

The 3-minute signal comes at 10:05 and the green flag at 10:08. Both cars go right out and Russ Cameron asks Mo for a radio check. No answer. Finally Mauricio does answer, but there are parts of the course where he can't hear Russ, although Russ can hear him. Radios help racers tremendously, but they are also a constant problem, requiring intense maintenance. It wouldn't be so troubling if they weren't so useful.

When Mark comes in he overshoots the pit box with the engine revving up. The 18-crew pushes him back into place and he says the brake pedal doesn't feel right, causing him to get on the throttle and the brake at the same time. "The pedal is taut," he says. "But it doesn't feel right."

One reason that open-wheel racing is not more popular is the fan can't see what the driver is doing, especially with his feet. The 18-crew worries with the various parts of the throttle in the foot box, driver's compartment, and engine bay. Ando gets into the discussion with Mark. They're losing track time. At 10:18 Mark roars off full throttle and goes quickly up through the gearbox before he brakes for the Turn 1 chicane, barely 150 yards from the pit box where he was stationary just a few seconds earlier.

The sky is bright and blue. It's hot and I feel the first stream of sweat run down the middle of my back. Alison and Mark's wife, Deborah, who I haven't met yet, talk together behind me.

A red flag stops the session at 10:25. I hear Mauricio on the radio. "Ribeiro just ran out of talent at the chicane." I laugh and look around to see who else is laughing at his remark. Quite a few people are at least smiling. Mo is 11th quick and Mark 13th.

During the red flag both cars are in their pit boxes and the drivers talk to the engineers about their cars. Mark says, "The front grip is poor. There's a lack of turn-in and it just pushes straight through the chicane."

Jim: "We'll do the shock change we talked about. If the car isn't loose we might pull the rear

Deborah Blundell and Alison Hill

wicker so we can lower the drag." They talk some more and the guys slide the wicker, also called a Gurney flap or wickerbill, out of the rear wing.

Then Jim says, "No aero change. Let's make the shock change, front and rear." Noticing the rear wicker is gone, Jim corrects himself. "Sorry guys; the wicker goes back in."

Mark goes back on track with 12 minutes to go. The monitor shows Zanardi and Ribeiro at the top of the list. Mauricio is P11 and Mark P17. Mark comes in, saying "It jumped out of gear again." He's 12th fast.

Mauricio improves to third and comes in. Andy tells him the tire pressures are too high. He asks the crew to do a shock and a diff change. Mo says the brakes are stiff, but feel like they're going away.

Mark goes back on track, and with 2 and a half minutes to go in the warm-up, Mo goes on course for one more lap. The checkered flag waves at 10:42. Mauricio is fifth and Mark 12th. The top of the list is Pruett, Zanardi, Christian Fittipaldi, Jimmy Vasser, Mauricio, and Greg Moore. As soon as the drivers get out of the cars they huddle with their engineers and the crews quickly wheel the cars away to the garage. Other teams have assembled setup pads right on pit lane and some have portable tents to shade the pads.

In the garage I ask Mark Moore what's going on now. He tells me they push the cars to the fuel area and fill them up. "Then they go on the pads and we do the numbers. We give the numbers to the war room and they do their dance."

"How close do you duplicate the primary-car setup on the T-cars?" I ask.

Mark explains, "They should be good enough that the drivers can jump in and race them, but during a session the primary cars are changing constantly. Really, you just keep them as close as you can."

The noise goes up again at 11:40 a.m. when another touring car race starts. Lunch arrives about noon: a veggie plate, buns, a cheese and meat plate, and some fried stuff.

Neil Atterbury is the new DAG, just hired from the Arrows F1 team. I ask him how the food here compares. "A bit basic," he replies, being kind. I tell him it will be better at the U.S. races, where we'll get Dave Loik's cooking.

Neil tells me people are leaving Arrows now that Tom Walkinshaw has taken over. "It used to be a tight-knit little group, but now it's more like working for a big company. They'll come 'round and make it right eventually, but I decided I'd give it a try over here."

The War Room

I had asked to be in on the pre-race meeting. At 12:20 p.m. Steve Fusek finds me and says, "Come on." I follow him into a white, 15-foot-square tent on the grass behind the garages. A weak portable air conditioner makes it barely habitable. Fifteen guys, including the two drivers and myself, crowd around the central table. Bruce comes in last. This is the war room.

The issue at Surfers is fuel. Last year it was brakes, but the Reynard update kits work fine and CART has changed the rules so the cars can only carry 35 gallons on board. Andy is holding a piece of paper showing a diagram of the eight positions for the rotary switch in the cockpit that control the different fuel calibrations or "slots." The positions are labeled with various combinations of fuel percentage and whether that position has the fuel cut-off feature. Each position has a number and the driver will be told, "Go to slot number three."

Ando starts the meeting talking about the rules for realignment after yellow flags. These procedures have been changing as CART tries to figure out how to make things fair for all while running a clean and quick race. Unfortunately the complications confuse the drivers. If there were no radios in the cars things would have to be much more simple.

Al Bodey, the second engineer to Jim Hamilton on Mark's car, sets the tone on fuel. "If it stays green, we'll have to coast a couple of laps. We do have plenty of tires though." There is some laughter, but not from everyone.

Andy talks about tire stints and choices of primary (softer) or optional (harder) tires. It's confusing for me to keep up with the tire choices. The Firestone primary is softer but the Goodyear primary is harder, I think. The teams know precisely the tradeoffs, however, and make their choice for qualifying carefully. They have to start the race with the tires they qualify on, so if they choose the softer one and then in the race it goes off before the first pit stop, they're in trouble.

Because of the scarcity of fuel the green-flag window for a pit stop is one lap for a two-stop race. If they come in earlier, too many laps remain in the race to make it on a full load of fuel. The driver can't come in later or he'll run out of fuel. It's a long lap here with no chance of coasting into the pit lane.

This means both PacWest drivers have to pit on the same lap, clogging the pit spaces. They talk at length about cooperation from the Patrick team pitted in the next pit box upstream from Mark. A guy there is friendly and will not get in the way if their car isn't in the pit box. At 12:32 Bruce's cell phone rings and he steps out of the tent to talk.

The next subject is spotters. The team tries to have a couple of people in position around the track during the race to alert the people on pit lane when something happens at their location. This allows the team to make a quick move or alert the driver to a problem. Today Steve Fusek will go into one of the grandstands and Tim Neff will be in another.

Ando tells the drivers to save fuel on the pace laps. "Just lug it around easy like. And we don't want to lose a lap if there's a yellow flag."

"It's a long lap," says Mauricio. The meeting ends at 12:26.

Back in the garage area, pack-up has started already. All the tools and equipment have to go back in boxes and into an airplane that will take everything, cars and all, back to Los Angeles so the cars can race again at Long Beach next weekend. That hardly seems possible.

Right in the middle of the bustle and excitement of race-day morning, Malcolm Oastler and Bruce Ashmore lean on stacked Ilmor engine crates and talk intently over a sketch Malcolm is drawing.

About 1 p.m. the PacWest crews begin to get into their firesuits. The less modest ones just take off their shorts in the open on the grass back of the garages, not worrying about the people walking by. Others get behind crates or go to nearby restrooms. After they have the firesuits on everyone seems more serious, thinking about the race coming up and the jobs they need to do without error.

Bruce Ashmore and Macolm Oastler of Reynard

Pre-Grid

A half-hour later we're all out on the frontstraight forming up the pre-grid. A blast of noise from above has all of us flinching and looking into the sky. It's an over flight of F-18 fighters and an F-111 bomber. One F-18 goes straight up into the air right over us and spirals at the top of the climb before leveling off. The F-111 swing-wing bomber does the same thing, afterburners glowing down at us. That's the most impressive aircraft demonstration flight I've ever seen. It gives me goose bumps.

Bruce comes around, shaking hands and wishing the crews good luck. At 1:56 the command to start engines comes, and I go back to the PacWest pit. It's warm, but there are some clouds and a cool breeze off the ocean.

During the pace laps I try to figure out how to position myself so I can see what's going on. I'll be able to see the pit stops fine, and I have a good view of a TV monitor so I should be able to see what happens on the track.

THE RACE

The cars roar out of the last turn toward the green flag and then bunch up as they slow for the first chicane. Everybody gets through OK. We can hear the cars on the backstraight, and then

The 17-Crew Completes a Pit Stop

they come screaming down to Start/ Finish to start the second lap. The leaders go by, but Gil de Ferran and Christian Fittipaldi come together and slide by in front of us, all tangled together. They hit barriers off to our left. It's a very bad wreck.

The track is completely blocked near the chicane so the cars at the back of the field can't get by, but the front of the field is still racing on course. It seems to take awhile but a red flag from the starter's stand stops the race.

On the TV monitor I can see Christian moving, so maybe he's OK. Then as he tries to get out of the car he winces with pain and I can see him realize he's hurt. The medics arrive then and after a while they lift Christian from the demolished Swift. He grimaces and grabs onto the shoulder of one of the guys holding him.

I see de Ferran behind me, walking quickly from the crash scene toward his pits, head down. The other drivers come onto pit lane and get out of their cars. The cleanup starts.

I hear Mark say he has a gearbox problem. All the cars still in the race get topped up with fuel. I walk out to the wall on the other side of pit lane and look down to the left where the wrecked cars finally stopped. To the right I can see the black streaks they left as they slid by.

Neil Atterbury, fresh from F1, is working a pit board today with Stephen Kent. They were right out here when the cars slid by. Neil tells me he dove for the ground, protecting himself with the pit board.

Stephen says he saw it all. "The red car [Christian's] pinned the blue car [Gil's] against the wall here and they slid along locked together. They went by us right on the other side of this wall. I hit the deck. All these carbon-fiber pieces rained down on us." Now I notice the ground is covered with bits of bodywork.

After about 45 minutes the cars go out to start the race again, in their original positions except for Christian. De Ferran and Paul Tracy, who had a crash on his own during that uncompleted first lap, were able to restart the race in back-up cars. This time the crew guys working pit boards come back across pit lane to the pit boxes for the start.

The restart is fine and the pit-board guys go back across pit lane to take up their positions. The racing doesn't last long, however, as the first of many yellow flags flies a few laps later.

After that restart the drivers have a few green-flag laps, with Zanardi leading. Mauricio is fifth and Mark eighth. During the next caution period the cars come in for pit stops, where the PacWest cars lose ground, dropping to seventh and ninth. Mauricio's and Mark's pit stops looked good to me, but other cars got out ahead of them.

Paul Tracy is in the lead now just ahead of Zanardi. On lap 30 Parker Johnstone tries to out-brake Mark and Bryan Herta at the same time going into the Turn 1 chicane. Parker goes wide, his car gets high-centered on the crown of the road, and the three cars come together. Herta is out, Parker continues, and Mark ends up running in P19.

After two more yellow flags and a round of pit stops, Mauricio is third behind Pruett and Vasser. Mark soldiers back to tenth. I hear Butch Winkle, Mark's chief mechanic, say his car is OK except for a hole in the sidepod.

We see some good racing for a few laps. Mauricio is pressuring Vasser for second place and tries to out-brake Jimmy into a corner. He gets his car inside and it looks like a great pass, but then the rear comes out, hits Jimmy's car and both of them spin before getting going again at the back of the pack.

Here in the PacWest pits the anticipation of a podium finish or better quickly dissolves. Jolene looks upset and Bruce rubs her back. She's been cheerleading hard and her disappointment is strong also. The race has gone so long the sun is actually getting low in the sky. CART officials declare the race a timed event, and it comes down to a 10-minute sprint race after one last pit stop. Mark picks up a couple more spots to finish eighth. Mauricio is the last finisher still running, in 17th.

The Aftermath

After the checkered flag I ask Bruce how he felt about the race.

"Shit," he says with a grin. "What else can you say? Mo was running great and the whole team is disappointed. Mark came back great. At least we're running at the pointy end of the grid."

As Jimmy Vasser swings through the PacWest pit to stop in his own pit box right next door, he flashes a raised middle finger to show his non-approval of Mauricio's pass attempt. I guess I can't blame him.

Shadows are getting long as Mark tells me, "I had gearbox problems that hurt me on restarts. It was a long race. I was waiting for the right time to pass Herta when Johnstone went out wide and tried an impossible pass. I also had an unfortunate scuffle with Michael [Andretti]."

Several writers come by to talk to Mauricio about his try at Vasser. "I messed up," he admits. "I had him on straight-line braking, but then I had to turn and the back of the car came around."

I ask Mauricio if he has time in a moment like that to weigh the relative merits of a safe podium finish vs. a possible win.

"I'm going for the win all the time. I been second and third before, and I'm tired of that. I'm paid to win, and that's what I want."

A small group forms to debrief: Tim Neff, Mauricio, Mark, Allen, and Al Bodey. Tim says to Mauricio, "You and Zanardi were the most aggressive on the course."

Malcolm Oastler comes up to Mauricio, puts his hand on his shoulder, smiling. "Not to worry."

"The mistake was not running on Friday," Mauricio says, referring to track time lost because of the hydraulic leaks. I write that down carefully because that's one of the story lines I've decided I want to follow. Does the technical development PacWest is doing, mainly shocks and other hydraulic doo-dads, help them or hurt them? Today Mauricio is voting hurt.

I walk to the garage and the crews are packing up furiously. Further down the paddock the CART officials are also packing up all their inspection equipment. I ask some of the PacWest guys how they saw the day. Dave Jacobs comments on Mauricio's try at Vasser saying, "You got to go for the win."

Butch says, "The guys who stayed out of trouble finished one, two, three."

At 6 p.m. Mauricio comes into the garage to talk to his crew. "Thanks, guys," he says, smiling and looking them in the eyes. No one is critical. There ain't no way you're gonna blame a guy who's done his best and knows you've done your best in the same fight.

THE FLIGHT BACK: DRUNK CITY

People got pretty drunk on the way to Surfers, but that was nothing compared to the return flight on Monday afternoon. Once again the booze is free and some guys open up the duty-free bottles they bought at the Brisbane airport. It starts off pretty sedate, but after dinner things get rowdy.

I'm sitting in the back of the bus again, in an aisle seat this time. The area around the bathrooms in the back is filled with laughing, hooting, jeering drunks. There are some women back there also and I wonder if I'm missing a strip-tease or something even more prurient, but I'm too tired to go look.

As I get more tired and irritable the constant traffic in the aisle hitting my elbow and bumping against my seat back gets almost unbearable. Butch is sitting in front of me, and I manage to strike up a conversation by asking him how he manages to prepare the car perfectly without doing it all himself. That's the problem with supervision of any kind.

Butch laughs. "That is tough. Especially when you've got some young guys like Blake [Hamilton] and Stephen [Kent]. You really have to watch them. I could do it better and quicker, but I'm not supposed to work on the car. I can't tell them how to do every little thing, so you have to let them go. They'll make mistakes as they learn, and you can't let that get by or something could happen on the track. When they do make a mistake you really can't yell at them either. They have to learn on their own. You're right; it's tough."

In any other situation you couldn't pay me to watch a silly movie like *101 Dalmatians*, but with all these drunks I'm glad to have a distraction and a chance to hide in these earphones. At 3 a.m. our time we're finally only an hour from Los Angeles. The GPS says 37,000 feet altitude, -60 C, and 564 mph.

Chris Griffis is sitting near me, but he's been sleeping most of the flight. Now he has a suggestion for Butch that might help them find the problem with the gearbox on the primary car that Mark was complaining about. "I think we should think about switching the gearboxes car to car and see if the problem follows the gearbox," Chris says.

Butch looks off into the air for a considerable time and then says, "That's a good idea."

Russ Cameron is returning from the bathroom, and he stops to talk to Butch. They're already making plans for projects coming up in the next few days and weeks. It dawns on me that the next race weekend starts on Friday, four days away.

The plane lands about noon Monday L.A. time, and those of us at the back of the bus stand numbly while the front empties out slowly. "Wasn't that fun?" I say to one of the flight attendants. Her badge says her name is Annie.

"Not particularly," Annie says in a soft, down-under accent. "But we were warned. We know about these flights."

"Was this a bad one?" I ask.

"Pretty bad," she answers. "We had to clean out the lavatories several times. People were throwing up all over in there. I guess someone couldn't get in there in time and threw up in our coat closet."

Victoria Vanderwell is standing nearby listening. She says, "Well, I'll apologize for our colleagues." Annie just smiles.

It's amazing to me that the teams would allow their guys (male and female) to cause all this ruckus among the CART officials. How smart is it to be hassling the same people who run the races and inspect your cars? It comes to me that there are owners up front in first-class seats. I could have gone up there and told them about what their guys were doing back here. Instead I just sat here and took it. Not next time.

Off the plane at LAX and through customs, I board a shuttle bus for the United terminal and a 1-hour flight back home.

Charlie Guilinger Grabs Chris Griffis
After a Blundell Pit Stop

CHAPTER 7

LONG BEACH

The shuttle flight on Thursday, April 10, from SFO to LAX is the same one I took 10 days ago when I was on my way to Australia, but I'm a lot more relaxed today. This is one of those sunny days when the San Francisco Bay Area is really beautiful. The Golden Gate Bridge is clearly visible as we lift off east across the bay, turn north and circle back for the trip south. The coastal hills haven't turned brown yet, so there is a spectacular gradient from light green hills and rich green forests on shore, to foam green ocean near shore and dark blue deeper water. You have to look way out on the ocean to see any fog.

Long Beach is a 20-minute freeway drive from LAX. The room at the Renaissance Hotel in Long Beach is nice. After stowing my stuff, I walk out the door and across the street to the race-track. What a treat. I check out the Indy Lights and Indy car garage areas, talking to various people.

The bar at the Renaissance is very comfortable and I have a beer before bed. I don't get to sleep, however, due to a band playing rock music in a park behind the hotel. I'm on the 10th floor but they might as well be in the room with me. I complain to the front desk and call the Long Beach police. The band stops at 12:30 a.m., and I finally get to sleep.

FRIDAY

A 10-minute walk across the street and I'm in the CART paddock at 7:15 a.m. The sun is up and warm, but the air is still chilly. I stop at the hospitality area first to store my bag. Christy Clutter is there setting up for the Hollywood and Motorola VIPs expected later.

Mauricio is having some breakfast. I ask if he has a lot of sponsor commitments during the Brazil trip coming up. "Yes, and it's not being planned very well," he says. "It's the same here. I was lying there asleep this morning and Oreo [John Oreovicz, director of public relations] called to say he had forgotten about a photo shoot at 7:30."

A hundred yards from the hospitality area, the PacWest transporters are parked parallel about 40 feet apart. The space in between is covered by awnings that protect the cars, equipment, and crews from the elements, probably only sunshine at this race.

The guys are hard at work. Blake Hamilton dresses all the engines. He shows Russ Cameron a sheet from Ilmor that lists which engines should be used in what track session. Ilmor has just given Blake the information and he's concerned because he doesn't have the right engines dressed and ready for the first session. Russ tells him it's not that big a deal, but he'll go to the Reynard trailer and get the parts so that Blake can dress the one engine he doesn't have done yet. At 9 a.m. the Formula Atlantic cars go on course to practice. Their four-cylinder engines are extremely noisy, making conversation difficult.

I find a spot out of the way and watch people come and go, working and talking. I really enjoy being here in the middle of things. Noticing a front wing and nose laying on the setup pad, I spot what seems to be a new addition, a curved fence on the outside of the front wing end-plate. Russ Cameron tells me it's a new Reynard mod, another update kit, and it's supposed to lower aero drag. Allen McDonald says they're calling them ski jumps. According to Reynard the ski jumps increase front downforce, but Allen says they didn't see much difference when they tested it on the Galmer model in a wind tunnel. The ski jumps will be on Mauricio's car during the first practice session but not Mark's.

Later Andy Brown puts the ski jump in perspective. "It increases the downforce from the front wing, but what we do is lower the angle of attack of the wing flaps so we have the same downforce as before. The lower flaps let more air get into the radiator inlet. The final result of the ski jumps is better cooling and no loss of downforce."

This is a good example of how each component of the car is interrelated to many other components in sometimes confusing ways.

First Practice

Starting at 11 a.m., both drivers go out for an installation lap and radio check. The sidepods came off both cars when they come back in. Mo is back on course after a few minutes. Mark complains of a sticking throttle, so the 18-crew works with the linkage in the engine compartment and in the pedal box. It takes awhile.

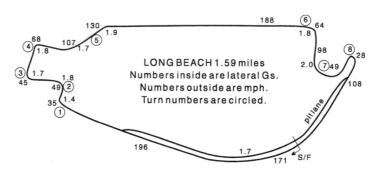

Alex Zanardi is quick early in the session, turning a lap of 53.960 seconds. Mo is fifth at 54.844 seconds. He's back in at 11:28 and Andy asks how the car feels.

"Pretty good," comes the reply. "I'm not touching much, the ground."

Andy proposes lowering the car and softening the shocks. "Sounds good," says Mauricio.

As Mark finally drives the 18-car out on track, Andy tells the 17-crew, "Tire pressures are up, so we just have to bleed a half-pound out of the rears." Mauricio returns to the track just as Al Unser Jr. goes off into the runoff area at Turn 1. I hear race control tell the starter to black-flag No. 99, Greg Moore, for leaking oil, and ask the crew to tell him to stay off the racing line as he returns to pit lane.

At 11:34 Mark comes in after his first laps at speed. Jim hands him a track map to use while giving his feedback about the car. This is an attempt to focus Mark's reports about the car's handling. Mark tends to scattershoot his feedback, and Jim needs to home in quicker on the higher-priority problems. To this end, the map has areas marked in colors and labeled A, B, C, etc. Area A is the braking area and entry into the first turn, the most important passing spot on the course. Area B is a similar section at the end of the backstraight before Turn 6. Mark seems to struggle to keep his comments focused.

After hearing what Mark has to say, Jim wants to lower the car but the tire pressures and temperatures are too low. Mark returns to the course and Mauricio goes out also. With 37 minutes left in the session, car 16, driven by Patrick Carpentier, hits the wall somewhere, causing a red flag. Mauricio comes in saying the car crashed right in front of him.

Mark brings his car in also. He's pitted directly in front of Mauricio and has to steer the car hard right and then hard left to get into the pit spot, almost running over Trevor Jackson's toes as he does. Trev looks back at me and raises his eyebrows. I'm glad I'm on the safe side of the wall.

The monitor shows Zanardi is fast now at a 53.040, followed by Herta, Vasser, and Boesel. Mo is 11th and Mark further back, still learning the track. He missed this race last year because of his broken foot in the crash at Rio.

Mark reports on the car, "The turn-in isn't precise; maybe even a little lazy." Jim asks him if he feels the different grip on the different surfaces.

"Yes, but at the moment I'm trying to find the bumps and braking points."

The green flag waves at 11:47 a.m.; 35 minutes to go in the session. I notice a guy standing behind me with Alison. His credential says Danny Blundell. I assume that's Mark's dad. He's a stocky guy with curly brown hair.

The stands across pit lane and the frontstraight from us are almost a third full. Already there are tens of thousands of people here. This race is a genuine L.A. happening, a great party in a party town. More than 300,000 will be here during the weekend. The sun is warm, and a light breeze off the water feels great.

Mark is not happy with the car. "Braking stability is a big issue now. The rear comes out really quite aggressively. The turn-in is weak, but when it does turn in the back comes out."

Jim asks him what areas on the map he's referring to, suggesting that they concentrate on areas A and B for now. The constriction of talking about that specific area seems to frustrate Mark, but he works at it.

Jim tells the crew to close the gap at the front by 4 mils. I assume he's talking about the free play in the hydraulic third spring at the front. This is a device that acts as a stop to limit suspension movement when aero forces build as the car increases in speed. The front wing and the underside of the car need to be at a specific ride height to generate maximum downforce.

At 11:58 Mauricio comes back in. He is seventh quick. Mark comes in just after Mauricio. "The car's gone a bit harsh and dead in its response; there's no grip. It's too tail-happy everywhere, Jim. The rear of the car lifts under braking."

Jim asks about the grip in areas E and F. "The car's too aggressive," is the reply. "It's lost grip all around."

"Reverse the last changes," Jim tells the crew. "Back out the mid [the third spring], raise the front [ride height], and change the front springs."

Mauricio comes in and tells Andy they should go back on the springs and the wing. Andy follows up with instructions to the crew to change the rear wing and make some spring changes. At this point there's 15 minutes to go in the session. The monitor shows Zanardi still quick followed by de Ferran, Tracy, Rahal, Pruett, and Moore. Mo is ninth and Mark off the screen on the monitor, which means slower than 18th.

Mark is still saying he's having braking problems. Jim asks him to compare the car's grip in sections D and F before and after the change they just made. He's looking for specific information instead of the general comments Mark tends to produce. But this time it doesn't help, as Mark makes some general statements that are hard to understand.

Next Jim asks what Mark thinks about the general damping support the car has. Mark says overall it's OK. Jim continues to try to use the map to focus the conversation and tries to get Mark's feedback about whether the car is better or worse before or after the changes they're making. Mark seems to resist, just wanting to say what he wants to say.

At 12:16 p.m. Mark brings the 18-car in for new tires. They change from the primary Firestones tire to the optionals. Mauricio comes in also. He now has the best lap time in the session with 5 minutes to go, 52.451 seconds. Tracy, Zanardi, Rahal, and de Ferran follow him on the monitor. Andy congratulates "Morris" on his quick lap and Mauricio says, "And it was a bad lap, too." Mauricio goes back out with 3 minutes to go.

Most of the drivers are on track during the last few minutes of the session, but they get in each other's way, making it tough to get a clear lap. Daryl Fox says, "Mo will post another fast lap right now." But he doesn't. Michael Andretti goes to P1 and then Zanardi tops him with a 52.076 lap. The checkered flag waves at 12:23 p.m. Mauricio ends up in P3.

After the session Jim asks Mark about the optional tires. "They seem to provide more grip and better braking in A section. They have more lateral grip but a lot of push. The car isn't square beneath me."

"There's a lot of clues here," Jim says. "There's going to be quite a different setup for qualifying."

Clues? I guess I thought finding an optimum setup was a more straightforward procedure than what I'm seeing. Before this season I just assumed the driver could feel exactly what's going on with the car's balance and grip level and report that fairly accurately to the engineer, who would then prescribe specific changes that would increase grip and make the driver more comfortable and the car faster. Maybe I underestimated the complexity of the problem and the subjective nature of driver feedback.

What can the drivers really feel, anyway? It's not like they've got a tire slip angle or side force gauge in their heads. What I'm hearing is they mainly feel balance — understeer (push) or oversteer (loose) — and movement. I wonder how many drivers can recognize different kinds of movement, such as sliding, chassis roll, or tire deflection?

Friday Qualifying

Just before the qualifying session I ask Andy if he made any big changes in the 17-car setup. "No, only small ones. Morris would kill me if I made any big changes. Actually I'd like to frame the setup sheet from this morning. It was just about perfect."

"Is that how you get ahead on a weekend, starting out with a good setup?" I ask.

"Yes. It really helps if you get it right straightaway. We had to slow work on some of our development systems. The gizmos didn't work."

The fast-guys' qualifying session starts at 2:32, 2 minutes late. Not bad for a street course running four race series on the same weekend. About 5 minutes later the first red flag flies when Paul Tracy spins and stalls on course. Mark comes in, saying "The car is softer in front. There's lots of amplitude in the car into the braking area of sections B and A. It's loose through D and F."

Jim says, "There's two or three things to address at the rear. I'd like to make it stiffer at the rear at low speeds. One flat down at the rear and add some low-speed compression in the rear."

I haven't asked about the shocks that Tim Neff has designed and built, but when I hear them talking about low-, medium-, and high-speed adjustments in both bump and rebound I can tell they've gone way past the usual three-way adjustable shocks available to most racers. Most racers think four-way adjustable shocks are exotic. These guys have six adjustments.

When the course goes green Mauricio drives off, but Mark stays while the changes are completed. Bruce and Jolene arrive and take up their usual stations in the scoring cart. That makes it more difficult for me to see the monitors, so I pace around trying to get a look between them or a peek at a monitor inside one of the engineering carts.

Mauricio jumps to P1 on the monitor with a lap of 52 seconds flat. When he comes in he says, "The car is touching less but the valve is blowing more and I can't be sure about traction." Andy suggests changing the waste-gate preload and reducing the low-speed rebound in the shocks.

Mark comes in and Jim decides to change springs. "Back off the rear tim," he tells Mark. The "tim" is some hydraulic device they've named after Tim Neff. I think that was what leaked at Surfers.

Andy tells Mauricio he has fuel enough for four laps. He's in fourth spot when he reenters the fray. Mark goes out on course also. He's in P10. Then Andre Ribeiro crashes, causing a red flag at 2:53 p.m..

When Mark's back in he tells Jim, "The other rear wing must work. Mo went by me easily." Again, not knowing the details of the development parts they have in their arsenal, I have to speculate they have a low-drag rear wing that Mauricio has tried on his car. Next, Mark asks about his damper forces vs. Mauricio's. Jim tells him the back is different and the front almost the same.

With 12 minutes to go in the session, the green flag comes out but the session is quickly canceled by a red flag caused by a Dario Franchitti crash at Turn 1. Andy tells Mauricio he has fuel for eight laps. Mark would like to change to a new set of tires, but Jim wants to make some adjustments and see how they affect the car before they try new tires. Among other things he suggests a change in the rear toe-in.

Mauricio is in fifth spot, Mark 10th. De Ferran is quicker than everybody by a second. The stands are about half full. It's getting warmer, but the on-shore breeze keeps the sun at bay.

Mauricio drives a quick lap and leaps to P2 with a 51.745, still a half-second arrears of de Ferran. Mauricio comes into his pit space, and Andy tells him there's only 2 minutes left, so there's no point in going out again. Mo nods his head solemnly and begins to get out of the car. His P2 stands. Mark is 16th with a lap of 52.909.

Shock Adjustments

Shock-absorber adjustments are mentioned frequently so some explanation is needed. The shocks, also called dampers, are not externally adjustable on street cars and, as such, represent a huge compromise in performance. Your car would handle better if the shocks weren't so biased toward ride quality. Racing shocks are not only externally adjustable but there several adjustments.

Springs are needed to isolate the driver and passengers from road irregularities and chassis movements caused by acceleration, cornering, and braking. But springs store energy when compressed, rebound when released, and tend to oscillate back and forth unless something absorbs that energy. A shock absorber absorbs energy and generates forces depending on the speed of movement of the suspension. A well-designed spring/damper system allows the chassis to remain relatively steady, and keeps the tires in contact with the ground despite bumps in the road and forces caused by cornering or changes in the car's speed.

Shocks on a road car are important because they damp (absorb) suspension movements, improve passenger comfort, and provide a way to control the driver "feel" of the car. The racecar driver also reacts to car movements and the shocks control how that happens. That's why shocks are so important when you're trying to make a car go quickly. Shocks give the race engineer a great way to control what the driver feels.

A bump compresses a shock and spring, so movement in that direction is called bump. When the spring pushes the suspension back down that's called rebound. A high-speed adjustment controls how the chassis reacts to quick (high-speed) suspension movements caused when the tire hits a bump. Low-speed adjustments control what the driver feels as the chassis rolls on the suspension in and out of a corner. Most racing shocks have two or three external adjustments, usually low-speed bump and rebound and high-speed bump. This is a "three-way" adjustable shock or a "triple clicker."

A "four-way" adjustable shock has external adjustments of both low- and high-speed damping in both bump and rebound. Shocks like this are not commercially available, but some teams make their own. I hear the PacWest guys talk on the radio about adjusting not only high- and low-speeds but also mid-speeds. Tim Neff has designed and built some unique six-way adjustable shocks. And they must work or the team wouldn't be using them.

Qualifying Press Conference

The top three drivers in the qualifying sessions go to a post-qualifying press conference where they answer questions posed by local and national print press. To start things off, Mike Zizzo, the CART director of public relations, introduces each driver and asks him a question. He asks Mauricio how the long trip back from Australia to his home in Florida affected him. "I feel good," Mauricio replies. "There's nothing different. No problems. I've slept well."

Someone asks each driver to comment on the competitiveness of the engines. Mauricio says except for the Toyotas, the engines are very equal, and this allows the teams and drivers to make more difference in the races. When asked about his car, Mo says, "It was a trouble-free day. I got a lot of laps and I'm happy with the balance of the car. I was surprised by how quick Gil went. I think I know what we have to do to make the car better. We can go faster tomorrow."

After this, most of the questions are directed at Gil de Ferran and Alex Zanardi. Mauricio slouches in his chair and glares slit-eyed at de Ferran to his left and the press people arrayed in folding chairs in front of the raised dais where the drivers sit. When de Ferran speaks Mauricio watches him with a tiny smile, as if observing a friend's favorite pet try to perform a trick too complicated for his skills. His preoccupied gaze floats around the room as the other two drivers field questions with long, folksy answers that charm the journalists and make them laugh.

On the way out I tell Mauricio maybe he needs to crash and spin more so the writers will have some questions for him. "I'll get the pole tomorrow," he says. "That will get their attention."

Friday Night Prep

Back in the garage area after the press conference, the T-cars are stowed in the top of the transporters and the primary cars are on the setup pads. The measurements that come off the cars go to the engineers, who compare the actual numbers with what they expect them to be and make appropriate adjustments for tomorrow morning's practice session. I hang around until about 5:45 and then go back to the room to change clothes for the fifth-annual *Racer* magazine party.

The *Racer* party is just across the street from the hotel. Knowing I can walk to my bed gives me some extra freedom, so I enjoy myself. As usual, anybody who's anybody is here and I have a great time talking to people, some of whom I only see here once a year. I make it back to the room OK, and the band isn't booming out back of the hotel so I sleep well.

SATURDAY

Saturday is the early day; practice at 9 a.m. I leave the hotel at 7:30 and walk across the street to the racetrack. It's sunny again. The early morning haze is already beginning to disappear. It's going to be another beautiful day, unless a cold wind blows in off the water in the afternoon.

At 8:55 I'm in the pit lane watching Paul Newman, Hollywood actor and co-owner of Newman/Haas Racing, push a dead scooter on the sidewalk behind the PacWest pits. He's headed toward the Newman-Haas pits further up the pit lane toward the hairpin. Even Paul Newman can run out of gas, I guess.

The drivers climb into their cars and go through their personal rituals of preparation. Mark has his helmet on when he gets into the car; Mo pulls his on after getting comfortable in the seat.

Saturday Practice

A green flag starts the 1-hour practice session, and the 17- and 18-cars both pull out right away. I finish my first roll of film of the weekend, and open up the camera to put in the next roll. I've been shooting four or five rolls and getting four or five good shots each weekend. I don't know if that's good or bad. I don't even know if the photos I think are best are really any good. They look OK to me.

Mark comes back in, saying "It's touching down pretty aggressively." Jim has the crew raise the car two flats at the rear. Mark has a full load of fuel, so they're working on a race setup. De Ferran hits a slower car, causing a red flag. Andy describes seeing it on the monitor to Mauricio as he's coming into the pits. Zanardi and Pruett are already in the 52s.

Mauricio says, "I'm catching Michael at the end of the straight. I don't know how much fuel he's carrying, but it looks like we've got as much horsepower as he does." At 9:25 a green flag resumes the session but another red flag stops it right away when somebody spins and stalls on course.

When Mauricio comes back into the pit box Andy says, "Let's add some more rear wing and more front wing to balance it. Up one flat at the rear to compensate for more downforce." With a green flag at 9:31, there are 50 minutes to go in the session.

You really can't see anything from the pits at Long Beach. You can hear the cars go by and make the last shift on the straight, but you see only the top element of the rear wing above the wall. My scanner is my major source of information. I have CART communications on one band, the 17-car on another, and the 18-car on a third band. I have all three on sometimes, but when I want to listen to the PacWest cars during a session, I just turn on those two channels. I don't listen to any other teams.

Another red flag stops the session at 9:36. Mark says, "The car feels a little aggressive at the rear, but not too bad. I can turn it in a bit sweeter."

Jim: "What about the mid-turn balance?" I don't hear the answer.

Jim: "Go up two flats at the front and put in two turns of front wing, please." The track goes green at 9:40.

Mauricio reports, "Coming out of the hairpin I'm lifting wheels. The car rolls too much." My guess is his car is rolling enough to engage the droop limiter at the front, lifting the inside front tire off the ground. With 39 minutes to go in the session, a green flag opens the track again for practice. Mauricio is sixth and Mark 15th. Andy specifies some shock changes and says to engage the "tim" another quarter turn.

Richie Hearn motors by slowly with a wheel bent up in the air. Zanardi, Boesel, and Pruett top the list on the monitor. Steve Fusek is nodding off sitting in the scoring cart. He and Bruce were still at the *Racer* party when I left near midnight. They must have had a good time.

Mark now has some serious complaints. "The car is hitting at the front. It's hitting so hard it's taking some weight off the front tires. The rear is picking up and moving out under braking. But it's a little bit better under braking." Jim suggests they change to the other rear wing.

Mauricio says he's got oversteer just about everywhere. "It's probably the tires," Andy says. "They're got almost half race distance on them." Both cars go back out with about 25 minutes to go.

When Mark comes in again he says, "We've got to get some front grip. It feels like it's overdamped." Jim asks for more front wing. With so many red flags the session has taken too long and will be checkered at 10:30 a.m. even if the teams don't get their full hour of track time.

With 10 minutes to go in the session Mauricio is fourth quick and comes in. He says he wants no changes on the car and then asks, "Can we go stiffer on the tim?"

Andy says no and tells the crew to add 3 gallons of fuel. Another red flag interrupts the session. Mauricio is now P4 and Mark P19. Bruce arrives and climbs into the scoring cart. With 5 minutes to go, a green flag resumes the practice session. With the scoring cart crowded, I have to find another means of figuring out what's going on out on the track. The laptops in the engineering carts are difficult to read but at least they show the times of that car. Mo is in P2. Mark is off the screen.

Mauricio ends up second in the session to Scott Pruett by less than a tenth of a second. Mark is 20th. Before he gets out of the car Mark says, "The car feels better under braking but isn't quite right in section B [at the end of the backstraight]. There may be too much roll."

Prep for Qualifying

Back in the garage area the cars go on the pads, the rain tires used to roll the car in come off, and the reference set of tires and wheels go on. This set of tires and wheels are used for the entire weekend, eliminating errors that might be caused if other wheels and tires aren't the same dimensions as these. Measurements on the setup pads are recorded to within one-thousands of an inch and are generally repeatable to 10 thousands.

At 11:15 Don Mullins brings some big pans of food covered with aluminum foil. Dave Loik's lunch today is rice, pasta in a meat sauce, baked zucchini, and spicy seafood burritos.

At lunch I talk to Casey Eason, who tells me how he got into racing. "I just dropped everything I had going in Denver and moved to Indianapolis with the goal of working for a team," he says. "I talked Ando [John Anderson] into trying me out. And it worked. Ando's great about letting people have a chance."

Casey is in his third full season with PacWest. He obviously loves what he's doing, but grouses about being responsible for so many different things. In addition to being the DAG in the 18-car engineering cart, he's in charge of all the radios. It can be a tough job to keep all those radios going reliably. People take the radios and the instant communications they produce for granted. When they crap out it's a surprise and a problem. Casey is glad Neil (Atterbury) is here, saying "He'll be good."

Saturday Qualifying Session

At 12:30 p.m. the Saturday qualifying session gets underway. The slow guys go first as usual on Saturday, and Mark is in that group because of his slow time in qualifying yesterday. He's still learning the course. A few minutes later a red flag interrupts the session. Mark pulls in and asks Charlie to put some tape on his helmet pad on the right side. "It's turning sticky-side up and catching the helmet."

At every race there are always volunteer firemen in each pit space, so they become invisible to us. The fireman in the 18-pit today has on a yellow slicker and hood. It's getting warmer and he strips open the Velcro front of his slicker and waves it a little to cool himself. He sees me watching and smiles. They do a good job without being in the way. I can see this guy become alert and move toward the wall when the cars come into the pit box or whenever the crew puts fuel in the car.

Mark goes back on track with a green flag at 12:48, but comes back a few minutes later when Ribeiro slides into the tire barrier just before the hairpin. Mark tells Jim, "The rear is popping up. The tim device might help." Jim asks the crew to lower the car at the front one flat and add more tim at the rear.

Jim asks Mark if a turn more front flap will help. Mark grudgingly agrees. Mark returns to the racetrack with the green flag and is the fast car in the session after a few laps. When Mark came in next time he says, "The tim might be working, but it's not giving me the control I need. I need the damping to keep the tires in contact with the ground." Jim tells the crew to add more bump damping at the rear and take out some low-speed rebound.

Then Jim tells Mark he's losing a half-second a lap with the rear wing on the car now, implying they should switch to the low-drag wing. "If it's there on paper we have to try it and see if I can cope with it on the track," is Mark's reply.

Jim says it's worth a half-second due to higher speeds on the straights, but Mark doesn't want to give up the rear downforce in the corners. He doesn't like the rear of the car at all twitchy. A typical trade-off: With less downforce and drag can the driver cope with less grip braking and cornering and get an overall quicker lap time with higher speeds on the straights?

Shortly after Mark leaves the pits I hear Control say there's a pit-lane violation on car-18 for 67 mph in the pit lane. He orders a black flag for a stop-and-go penalty. Mark drives in for the penalty, and Jim asks for a half-turn change in the differential adjustment and a half-pound increase in tire pressure at the front.

Mark returns to the track with 6 minutes to go in the session, but goes off into the runoff area at Turn 1. He gets the car going again but isn't able to improve his time. He ends up P12 in the slow-guy session. The fast guys will likely leapfrog him, bumping him down to a starting spot well back on the grid. Before he gets out of the car he tells Jim on the radio, "I have no control. It just doesn't feel right. I can't describe it." He's very frustrated.

At the first two races Mark complained about the car every session, seemingly making very little progress toward a faster, more comfortable setup. But at Homestead and again at Surfers he qualified well, surprising and delighting Jim and the crew. Today broke that pattern. The car didn't suit him and he couldn't drive it quickly.

Mo's Turn

At 1:30 Jim Swintal's green flag starts the fast-guy qualifying session. Phil Hill, the first successful American Formula 1 driver, is standing back of our pit with his son, Derek, a newly-professional driver himself.

Mark Blundell, Jim Hamilton, and Allen McDonald stay behind in their engineering cart after the crew takes the 18-car back to the paddock. They have a serious conversation with a lot of hand movements helping to describe the behavior of the car. Jim leaves after a few minutes while Allen and Mark continue to talk and watch the monitor showing the lap times of the fast guys.

At 1:37 Mauricio is in P3, and he brings his car back onto pit lane. "The back is ahead of me everywhere. There's lots of oversteer."

Andy asks him if less front wing would help. "I've got some understeer too. There's not enough grip. I need some downforce." Andy calls for the other rear wing and one flat more ride height all around to compensate for the increase in downforce. Mauricio adds the comment that the bottom is barely touching. Zanardi is quick in the session so far.

When he comes in next time, Mauricio says, "This guy is not the same as this morning. We should put the front shocks back." Andy says "go" to a switch to the other wing and changing the shocks back. He asks Roscoe (that's Russell Grosshans' nickname), to put 3 gallons of fuel in the car.

At 1:46 Mo is on course again with 12 minutes to go in qualifying, but he's back in right away due to a red flag caused by Alex Zanardi's crash. Would that stall Zanardi's qualifying effort?

The monitor shows the current qualifying order is de Ferran, Zanardi, Gugelmin, Herta, and Rahal. De Ferran had a crash in morning practice and didn't want to risk damaging another car in the qualifying session. He decides not to defend his time so he's not running this session. It's warmer today, and few cars will improve their times from Friday. The stands are more than half full. It seems to me that Mauricio has a chance at the pole position. He only needs a half-second improvement. Easy for me to say.

Andy summarizes the changes they made to the car as Mauricio sits quietly, waiting for the session to resume. "We changed to the low-drag rear wing, went down on the front wing flaps five and a half turns, and lowered the car one flat all around."

At 1:58 p.m., with 10 minutes to go, the session restarts. Mauricio's best lap so far is a 51.745 in yesterday's session. Try as he might, he can't get the car to go any faster. He has to settle for the third qualifying spot, inside the second row. Gil de Ferran's time from Saturday is good enough for the pole. Zanardi improves his time slightly, enough to beat out Mo for second.

In the press conference de Ferran talks about how difficult it was sitting in the car while Mauricio and Alex tried to beat his time. Again de Ferran and Zanardi joke easily with the journalists while Mauricio sits and watches them all, looking disdainful and bored.

As de Ferran describes his crash yesterday with the almost-stopped car of Gaulter Salles that happened when he was passing Hiro Matsushita, Mauricio looks at him like he's a jester performing for a court of fools.

When someone says, "A question for Mauricio," Mo feigns surprise at the attention and everyone laughs. The question is about Mauricio saying the day before that the qualifying speeds would be faster on the second day. "I was wrong," says Mauricio with a straight face, bringing on another round of laughter. He's intense, but he's got a sense of humor.

He continues, "Well, normally on street courses the lap times get better on the second day. If you look at the records, that's the way it is most of the time. Today I don't know what happened. It's a little warmer. I lost a little traction on my car. I think generally the circuit was just slower, and we didn't get the right setup for those conditions. Let's see what's going to happen tomorrow."

After the open-question session the drivers split up for one-on-one interviews. The bigger crowds are around Zanardi and de Ferran, but several people are talking to Mauricio. It occurs to me that these drivers are very competitive people. They know that the competition is not just on the racetrack. Mauricio wants these questions and the attention, but he's not willing to perform like a trained seal. As he earns their attention, he'll amuse and charm the writers like he did on this day. But he'll do it his way.

Measuring Toe

The wheels on a car aren't just pointing straight ahead. For street cars the front wheels point in a small amount — they have some toe-in. If the wheels get toed out the car can be darty under braking, so a little toe-in prevents this. Racecars sometimes run toe-out on the front, but mainly have toe-in at the rear. Adjustable links in the suspension makes precise settings relatively simple.

In the photo Ron Endres is measuring the distance from a thin nylon line to a flat surface on the wheel. He'll make another measurement on the side nearer the camera and the difference is toe-in if the front measurement is larger. A tube bolted to the front of the car and another at the rear holds this line a consistant distance from and parallel to the centerline of the car. The calipers Ron is using measure accurately to one one-thousands of an inch.

Ron Endres Measures Toe

One of Those Jobs

Back in the CART paddock at 4:45 p.m., I see Randy Smay is still hard at work on a job I saw him start hours earlier. As the photo shows, Randy is using a heat gun and a putty knife to remove rubber buildup from the tires.

Randy Smay Removes Build-Up

The team only gets so many sets of tires for a weekend. When the tires are hot they pick up blobs of rubber on the track called "marbles." This layer of rubber shears off easily as soon as the driver tries to corner hard, reducing grip. During yellow-flag laps prior to a race restart, the drivers weave the cars back and forth to generate heat in the tires and also to remove this excess rubber. Someone has to scrape the rubber off the tires so they can be used again. Some of these tires may be destined for use in the race.

Randy's job is not easy, especially when it takes hours. I see him shake his hands every now and then to loosen them up. "It's not a fun job," Randy says. "But somebody's got to do it. Only one set to go."

Back at the shop Randy manages the paint shop. He's a craftsman there but just another crew member on the road. On race day Randy dons a firesuit and helmet and fuels Mark's car during pit stops.

Saturday Night

The PacWest guys are still working when I leave the garage area to go to the hotel about 6:30 p.m. I shower and change clothes, planning to buy the crew some beers in the bar and maybe tag along for dinner with somebody. But they aren't in the bar when I look, so I walk out on the streets looking for a place to eat.

After a hamburger I go back to the hotel for a beer. Neil Atterbury is sitting by himself and I join him. We talk racing, of course. Since he just came from Formula 1, I'm interested in what he thinks about the CART series. "These cars seem to be very reliable," says Neil. "The teams don't work much on reliability problems and spend more time working on the setup."

That's a very interesting comment. Since the F1 teams build their own cars, including the electronic hardware and software and the gearbox and its actuation system, they would be responsible for all the debugging and development. CART teams, except for Penske and Newman-Haas, buy Reynard or Lola chassis with the engine installation included in the design. They expect the critical systems like the electronics and gearbox to work when they get the car, and mostly that's what happens. The result is what Neil observes: CART team have more time to develop the grip and balance of the car. That work is more necessary also, since over here we race on different types of tracks: short ovals, superspeedways, road courses and street courses. F1 teams race on smooth, flat road courses, all very similar to each other.

SUNDAY: RACE DAY

I go looking for and find Jim Swintal, the CART starter. "Last year we had a good start here," he tells me. "It's the same front row this year [de Ferran and Zanardi], so I assume the start will go well again. The problem here is a very tight urban circuit and the very slow hairpin leading onto the Start/Finish straight. The cars are single file on the pace laps but have to get side by side for the start. Gil has to be a good man and come onto the straight slow enough to let Alex get alongside him. He shouldn't accelerate before the green flag. If it's done right by the guys in front, we'll be all right."

At 8:30 a.m. the 18-crew is practicing pit stops in pit lane as the 17-car rolls up into its spot. I ask Mark Moore about the late night last evening. "We worked till 9 o'clock on Mo's car. It was mostly gearbox stuff. Something broke in there and we had to strip it all apart, even the drop gears, and clean out the pieces. The other crew worked till about 8 o'clock. We don't pay that much attention to which crew gets through at what time. We do our own thing and they do theirs. These guys are so competitive that if they start trying to beat each other, something might not get done right. We just focus on what we have to do. We weren't that late last night. I don't consider it a late night until it gets to be the next day."

Ben Bowlby, the Lola head designer, walks along pit lane, staring intently at each car. Ben is a good guy, young and intense. He's about 5 feet, 10 inches and slim. His hair is curly and dark red, auburn probably.

Ben is very intelligent with an interesting twist. He's dyslexic, meaning his brain doesn't process written material the same as most of us. He earned his engineering degree in England by building a Formula Ford and racing it himself. Written tests are very difficult for a dyslexic, so he devised his own program of study and the Formula Ford project was his final exam.

Eric Broadley, the Lola founder, likes Ben and has formed his design team around the young engineer. The '97 Lola Indy car has some radical features, but it is not performing up to its rivals. I can only guess at the detail he can recognize as he examines each car. I only manage to see the most obvious changes.

At 8:45 Mark Blundell comes onto pit lane to prepare for the warm-up session. I ask him what advice he has for Mauricio on the start and the first turn. "Just get through it as clean as he can. It's the same for me."

8:53. Mauricio walks onto pit lane. He looks very intense as usual, but he smiles as he talks to Russ Cameron and Mark Moore.

Warm-Up

8:58. The engines roar to life. Drivers are in the cars ready for the warm-up session. Right at 9 o'clock the green flag drops and both PacWest cars go on course. The sun is warm, but the air is still cool. The flags hang limp. Will it get hot like last year? Along the California coast it's tough to tell what the weather is going to do. With no breeze it could be hot, but an on-shore wind off the 60-degree water can turn it chilly in minutes.

This is L.A. and there are a lot of celebs and freaks roaming the narrow passage behind the pit spaces. I see movie star Geena Davis walk by wearing a baseball cap, long-sleeve shirt, shorts, and ugly work boots. Under all that she's still pretty. Other folks are sporting tattoos, but not as many as in Australia. Lots of pink and purple hair here also. The guys in the crew are watching too. Long Beach is one of the best stops for watching female skin, and the action is pretty good for so early in the day.

Mauricio brings his car into the pit box and the crew does a pit stop rehearsal. On race day Ando replaces Jim Hamilton on Mark's radio and Russ Cameron talks to Mauricio instead of Andy Brown. Ando and Russ are the race strategists, in charge of fuel strategy and pit-stop timing.

Mark comes off track still complaining about the rear end popping up, but his voice is not as strident as it was yesterday. "Can we add some tim?" he asks. "The brake pedal feels sloppy."

With 10 minutes to go, Mauricio escapes into a runoff area but gets going again. Another car stalls, causing a red flag. Mark is 10th quick and Mauricio 11th. They both come in and Mark asks how many laps on a tire stint today.

"Thirty-five laps," is the answer from Jim Hamilton. A green flag restarts the session with 7 minutes to go. Boesel, Pruett, and Tracy top the list. Their times are about a second and a half slower than qualifying.

Brake Bleeding

An hour after the warm-up, the crews are preparing the cars for the race, which will start in a few hours. The 17-crew is busy bleeding the brakes on the primary car. The object of brake bleeding is to move some brake fluid through the master cylinders, hydraulic lines, slave cylin-

Chris Jaynes Bleeds Brakes

ders in the calipers, and out of the system. Any moisture or air bubbles go with the displaced fluid. Moisture turns to steam at operating temperatures, so this and any air in the system has to be compressed before the pedal pressure exerted by the driver can act on the brake pads. A driver needs complete confidence in and control over the brakes on his racecar. He needs a firm pedal, and that means no air or moisture in the system.

Jim Reid sits in the 17-car while Ron Endres and Dave Jacobs man the bleed nuts on the front and rear calipers. Jimmy's legs are shorter than Mauricio's and he has to lie down in the seat to get his foot on the pedal. This job requires some coordination and communication. Jim yells "pressure" to signal he has his foot pressing on the brake pedal. Hearing that, Ron and Dave can crack their bleed screw and allow the fluid to flow through a plastic tube into a catch bottle. If they open the bleed nuts before Jimmy pressurizes the system, air can get in.

To make it more difficult for air to get into the lines, they drain the brake fluid into bottles through a plastic tube. The tube has one end in the bottle under the surface of the brake fluid. When the bleed screws open, Jim's foot moves down on the pedal, pumping fluid through the tubing into the catch bottle. As soon as Jim feels his foot stop at the end of the pedal travel, he shouts "down" and the guys know they can close the bleed screws. The operation continues until the crew is satisfied that the system is filled with fresh, dry, non-aerated fluid.

The front and rear brakes get bled at the same time because there are two master cylinders operated by the brake pedal, one for the front brakes and one for the rear. A proportioning mechanism between them allows for a driver-operated adjustment for brake balance, the proportion of braking on the front brakes vs. the rear brakes. If there's too much force on the front tires, they lock up first under hard braking and the driver can't steer the car. Too much bias toward the rear and the back of the car will come around under braking. It has to be right, and the driver might need to make adjustments as the car uses fuel between pit stops. All this brake bleeding and balance stuff is generally taken for granted, but it has to be perfect for the driver to have a chance to set a fast lap time or win a race.

Jim Hamilton tells me Mark has a better car today. "He's much more comfortable with it now."

"I can tell," I say. "I heard him say 'the rear is popping up' only once during the session."

Jim laughs. "The urgency in his voice says a lot. He was less concerned with that today than he was yesterday. This will be an interesting race for Mark. Parker [Johnstone] and Raul [Boesel] are gridded right with Mark. They have good cars. It will be interesting to see what happens."

I can hear the start of the Indy Lights race. A wreck and a red flag stops it after a lap or two. Street courses are difficult. The barriers mean the slightest mistake or contact between two cars results in a crash, and then the cars have to be moved and the debris and/or fluids cleaned up. The tight spaces between walls are dangerous and a long yellow-flag period can be a boring interlude in what should be an exciting event. The potential ticket buyers are concentrated in the cities, however, and street courses are a necessity.

Lunch arrives in the garage area about 11:15 a.m.: curried rice, chicken salad, pasta salad, baked veggies, and mixed fruit. I realize I haven't talked to Chef Dave this weekend. After I eat I walk over to the hospitality area and go through the covered areas to the kitchen trailer. Dave comes out onto the tailgate, leans down, and shakes my hand. "You can put me in the back pages of the book because that's where I always am, in the back."

Pre-Grid

At the motor coaches Steve Fusek gives me the two stickers that get me into the victory circle area after the race. One has the number 17 and the other 18. They don't want anybody in there except photographers and team members.

I ask Mauricio about his plans for the first turn. He pauses a second to think, then smiles and says, "I just want to get through clean."

Going from the motor coaches to the garage area is difficult now because of the press of people. People amble along, looking around, and then stop and change direction. Getting through them is like broken-field

Mark Moore and Russ Cameron
On Pre-Grid

walking. I try not to get impatient or annoyed. They're paying to see all this. Well, I am too, actually.

At noon the crew is already loading the disassembled setup pads into lockers in the bellies of the transporters. The race is an hour away and the packing has already started.

Most of the cars have been in the pit lane for a while. The 18-car is in its space. The 17-car is just arriving. The crew hooks up the 18-car to tow it onto the mainstraight to its pre-grid spot. There's room on the tugger, so I sit right on the front next to the driver, Randy Smay. We move in fits and starts backward up pit lane among other cars and throngs of people. It's a good time to people watch and I see Genna Davis again as she stands in the crowd just ahead to our left. She's obviously excited about being here in the middle of the action.

When the 18-car gets to its grid spot I get off the tugger and walk up to the front of the grid to Mauricio's crew and the 17-car. Mo and Russ Cameron talk leaning up against the wall, so I take a couple of snapshots.

Iain Watt, who engineers Max Papis' car for the Arciero-Wells team, walks by and I give him a gruff look and a hooked thumb toward the back of the grid where the Toyota-powered (under-powered) cars are gridded. Iain smiles wanly, puts his open hands up at shoulder height and says, "I'm goin'. I'm goin'."

We both laugh. Everybody works hard here, and if your car can't get to the pointy end of the grid, you might as well show some humor at the situation.

I see David Bruns standing by himself a few yards away from the Swift 007.i he designed last year using the wind tunnel he spent three years designing and building. He once told me the wind-tunnel project was "Deciding to build a house and then spending three years making a hammer."

"How's it going?" I ask.

"Oh, all right I guess," Bruns drawls. He's a tall, tanned, fit-looking guy. His full beard and dark glasses make it difficult to see what's really going on with him. I think he likes it that way, not wanting to give away any tidbit of the knowledge and experience he's built up over the years. I like David and enjoy talking to him, but I don't learn much. "The car's not as good as I'd like on street courses yet," he says. "We're working on it though." That's a lot of information, coming from David.

Back in the seventh row, Bob Schaul of Motorola is standing with Mark during the invocation. Bruce comes by to say something encouraging to Mark. Bruce grins at me and says, "Two good cars, two good drivers."

At 10 minutes to 1, after the invocation, Mark Blundell sits against the outside wall near his car and Parker Johnstone, gridded on the inside of the seventh row next to Mark, comes over to shake Mark's hand. Parker is smiling and talking, but Mark doesn't say anything or change his expression. He's got his game face on and this is one of the guys he wants to beat.

THE RACE

It's time for my game face also. I try to switch into an information-gathering/storing mode for the race. I know I'll have a tape of the race to watch when I get home, so I don't have to see everything here. It's a good thing, because it's very difficult to see anything from the pits here, even less than at Surfers. You can't see the cars because of the walls between pit lane and the frontstraight, and there is no big-screen TV visible from the pit lane as there is at some tracks.

Bruce and Jolene are in the scoring cart and I can't always see around or in between them. There are monitors in the engineering carts, but the guys get crowded there and I don't want to bother anyone. My major tool is my scanner, set to listen in on both the PacWest cars plus the CART and pace-car radios. So, I tell myself, it'll be enough to listen to the radio conversations, watch the monitors when I can, and watch the crew. I scribble notes constantly in my notebook. Sometimes those notes are a challenge to read, but they just need to record highlights that will jog my memory later.

The cars are on their pace laps and I hear Control say, "Green next time around." I ease into the back of the 18-engineering cart. Ian Hawkins, the Ilmor engineer, is right in front of me watching his laptop carefully. I wear contact lenses and would need reading glasses to see the small characters on the screen, so I have no idea what data he's looking at. Paul Ray, Ilmor vice president, would be happy to know that, being so paranoid about me seeing any of their magic. Casey, Al, and Jim are to my right. Ando, John Anderson, stands up on the top of the pit wall outside the cart. He's on the radio to Mark during the races, providing coaching and encouragement and relaying instructions. Russ Cameron is his counterpart for Mauricio.

Near the end of the last pace lap, I hear Control, I think it's Jack Hodge, say to all the corner workers, "Watch your butts out there."

The cars roar out of the hairpin toward the green flag. All kinds of bad things can happen. If even one of the drivers makes a mistake or succumbs to impatience going into the first turn and the slow corners right after it, a lot of cars could be eliminated on the first lap.

Fortunately the start is uneventful, and Mauricio settles into the third spot behind de Ferran and Zanardi. I can see on a monitor that Mark is 12th.

The top five cars don't get any passing chances during the first part of the race. Michael Andretti is right behind Mauricio, but blows a rear tire about lap 14. Jimmy Vasser has a similar tire problem. Getting the power to the track out of the slow corners is critical at a track like this. Michael blows several rear tires during the race, leading to speculation that some of the teams are using low rear tire pressures to help get the power to the track off the corners. The tire guys hate it when the teams abuse their product in search of performance. It always looks like the tire's fault.

On lap 16 of 105 we get a yellow flag. Roberto Moreno, driving a Swift and filling in for the injured Christian Fittipaldi, shreds a rear tire. Ian and Al talk and point to their laptop screens. De Ferran is still in the lead followed by Zanardi, Mauricio, and Pruett. All those cars except for the leader are on Firestone tires.

On the scanner I can hear the CART officials talking about debris on the track. They think that's what's causing the tire problems, and they want to find any foreign material on the track. Ando tells Mark to stay in high gear and conserve fuel during the yellow flag. Mark comes back with a complaint about understeer. Twenty laps are done and there's another seven or eight laps until the first pit stop.

Immediately after the restart, Paul Tracy punts Greg Moore at Turn 6, causing another yellow flag. (After the race Wally Dallenbach fines Tracy $25,000 for unsafe driving.)

The 17- and 18-cars come in for fuel and tires during the yellow-flag period. I get some good photos, I think. Raul Boesel stays out, so he's the leader after the pit stops. After him it's Zanardi, de Ferran, Mauricio, Pruett, Rahal, and Blundell.

Forty-five minutes and 35 laps into the race Michael Andretti has another flat tire. Boesel pits for fuel, moving the leaders up a notch. Ando tells Mark to go to position seven on the fuel. Mo is still P3 behind Zanardi and de Ferran. Mark is P7, having moved up from 14th on the grid.

One of the Toyota engines blows up in front of the home crowd, bringing out another yellow flag. Control says, "Car-24 out, electrical." They don't want to say it's the engine because, after all, this is the Toyota Grand Prix of Long Beach.

There's another round of pit stops starting at lap 42. Jim wants to make some changes to Mark's car: lower tire pressures and two turns up on the front wing. "That's one degree," he says. The PacWest cars are P3 and P6. Looking good.

At lap 50, almost halfway, there's little change. The order is Zanardi, de Ferran, Mauricio, Pruett, Rahal, and Mark. Al Bodey has several signs he's prepared ahead of time to let Ando know what to tell Mark about the fuel settings. Ando is still standing up on the pit wall, making it difficult to get his attention. Al reaches out to punch Ando's leg and flashes a sign when he thinks a change should be made.

Then Roberto Moreno hits the wall coming out of Turn 3. Too bad; he was doing well and everyone was rooting for him. He's a good driver, but has had to contend with marginal equipment driving for Dale Coyne. Subbing for Christian Fittipaldi is a big opportunity for him. Another yellow flag and Ando tells Mark, "It's not a roller. It'll be a while. Watch yourself."

After the restart the order is Zanardi, de Ferran, Mauricio, Pruett, Rahal, and Blundell. About 10 laps later we get another round of pit stops. Mauricio's stop is quick, getting him out in front of de Ferran for second spot. But Mark loses several positions to 12th. Mark came into that pit stop sixth and came out 12th. Ando coaches his driver, giving him encouragement and a goal. "That's Herta in front of you for position. Parker is in front of you." Ando knows Mark doesn't like Parker.

Mark needs a splash of fuel to make it to the end of the race. When he makes his pit stop on lap 97, he stalls the car, and although the starter was right there ready and the engine fires up right away, he goes a lap down.

Mauricio can't gain on the race leader Zanardi, but he's able to hold off Scott Pruett behind him in third. At 2:52 p.m. the checkered flag flies, giving the PacWest team its first podium finish in '97. Fusek's stickers get me into victory circle, and I take a bunch of photos.

"That's a relief," Fusek says, looking, indeed, relieved. "It would have been nice to get that one last week. This would be two in a row. The top guys from Hollywood are here and it's great that Mauricio did this in front of them."

Podium Shot of Scott Pruett, Alex Zanardi, and Mauricio Gugelmin

Press Conference

Mike Zizzo announces the top three finishers to the room full of journalists. "Finishing third was Scott Pruett in the Brahma Reynard Ford on Firestones. He is now the PPG points leader with 44. Runner-up was Mo Gugelmin in the Hollywood PacWest Mercedes on Firestones, matching his career best, '95 Miami, '96 U.S. 500. Alex Zanardi is our Toyota Long Beach GP champion. A 3.820-seconds victory in a Target Reynard Honda on Firestones. This is the first sweep for Firestone since Australia in '96. Three different engine manufacturers on the podium; second time it happened this season. The other time was Homestead. We'll get started with questions right away."

The first questions are for winner Zanardi, who continues to charm and amuse the assembly. Then Pruett talks about how they had to catch up after giving up on the '97 Lola chassis and switching to the Reynard in January. He praises the Ford/Cosworth engine for its performance and reliability (both lacking last year, which he leaves unsaid).

David Phillips of *Indy Car* magazine has a question for Mauricio: "You were right there all day in striking distance of Alex, but just couldn't reel him in close enough to take a run at him. Could you tell us about your race?"

Bruce and Jolene McCaw with the
First Trophy of the Year

"Basically, in the beginning, we were concerned about the fuel," Mauricio responds. "We ran very lean to make sure we had enough at the end. We deliberately pitted one lap early just to get a clean shot at the pits. When Alex did his pit stop I didn't believe it. I thought he didn't pit because it was so quick. Nevertheless, I just push as hard as I could. Gil was running very well. We were having trouble with the backmarkers. Then he went out. I think he must have hit the wall. Then it was up to Alex and myself.

"We seemed to be catching Hiro [Matsushita] every five laps [laughter]. It's tough to go around some of those guys. That's just racing, I guess. It seemed to be tough to get around them on the straights, and I seemed all the time to be behind them in the corners. Alex did super today and in the end I couldn't do anything."

Another question for Mauricio: "This year you've qualified well and you've run well. How is your team handling this pressure of being so close?"

Mauricio: "Well, we've handled it well. The main thing, we've pushed really hard to get a win, but at the same time to keep ourselves under control. At Surfers, of course, I was going very hard and I made a mistake when I tried to pass Jimmy and, I guess, that's just racing. It's nice to have a competitive car with a competitive engine. We have a great sponsor, that today has announced they will sponsor the Hollywood 400 in Rio. We gonna have the Motorola 300 after that so PacWest is gonna have, in the month of May, the PacWest 700 [laughter]."

The next question is for all the drivers, asking whether there was concern for the tires when all the flats indicated some debris on course.

Scott Pruett answers, "Michael let go right in front of me and it wasn't just a flat tire, it looked like it exploded. Michael did a superb job keeping the car under control at those speeds. We had our hands full weaving our way through it."

Mauricio: "There was a lot of debris and dust and everything, so it was difficult to see and your first reaction is to see where you can go to get through it. At the same time you don't want to go over anything that can damage your car, so it's not an ideal situation."

Long Beach is a Big Party

The Grand Prix Association of Long Beach announces a record total three-day paid attendance of 215,000 people. Its press release includes an estimated total on-site viewing audience of 300,000. This number comes from an estimate of how many people get to watch for free from hotel rooms or apartments in buildings inside and near the racecourse. It said 90,000 paid to watch the race Sunday. Friday's number was 48,500 and Saturday attendance was 75,000. All these numbers were up slightly from 1996.

CHAPTER 8

NAZARETH

There is a turning point in the book project on the flight from San Francisco to Washington-Dulles airport when I have time to put the race and interview files all together in my laptop computer. The resulting file has more than 50,000 words, and it makes me feel like I have a head start on the project, or at least I'm not as far behind as I thought. Maybe I can have some fun at this race instead of sweating the book.

The flight is pleasant until the plane begins circling near Washington. The captain announces there's been a lightening strike at the airport, knocking out one of the landing systems. I guess they got it going again, because we continue on to land only 15 minutes late.

On the turboprop flight to the airport in Allentown, Pa., I sit next to Sharon Johnstone. Her husband, Parker, drives for Barry Green's Team KOOL Green. Sharon and I talk about the pressure Parker is feeling this year. He's got a good team, a great engineer in Tony Cicale, and good equipment — Honda/Reynard/Firestone. If the team doesn't do well this year Parker could be blamed for it.

Crisis Planning

Sharon and I are able to catch up on a lot of subjects. I see her and Parker at almost every race, but we seldom have time to talk for long. One subject that comes up is what happens when a driver gets hurt, or more tragically, killed. At Toronto in 1996 Jeff Krosnoff was killed in a freak incident. His car rode up over the tires of Stefan Johansson's car, launching into the air and over a fence where it collided with a large tree, killing Jeff instantly.

At that time, like most teams, Arciero-Wells had no plan for this kind of incident but they rose to the occasion. Parker had dropped out of the race, and he immediately volunteered to take Jeff's parents to the hospital. Parker and Hunter Floyd also performed the sad job of clearing Jeff's hotel room of his personal effects.

"There wasn't any plan for what happened," Sharon tells me. "The team and CART hadn't planned for something like that. Cal Wells [the team co-owner] is a real gentleman. It was handled well, but there was a lot of confusion. Parker thinks it was providential that he was there ready to help. If there's anything good that can come out of something like that, maybe it's the plans that each team has now for situations like that."

Later, I ask John Anderson if PacWest had a crisis plan last year in Rio when Mark Blundell was hurt. "No, we didn't then," he says. "We handled it OK because some people stepped in and did the job. We have a more complete plan now."

Racing is based on reducing a very dangerous activity to a reasonable level of risk. For many years deaths in racing were rare. Then, in 1994 at a Formula 1 race at Imola, Italy, Ayrton Senna and Roland Ratzenberger died and started a fit of changes to tracks and cars in that series. In 1996 Krosnoff's death and the crash during practice for the Indy 500 that killed Scott Brayton shocked the U.S. racing community and forced racing organizations to plan for things nobody really even wants to think about.

Bar Talk

When I get to the Comfort Suites motel in Bethlehem, Pa., PacWest people are gathered in the bar. I fall in with a group going to the Tally-Ho, a nearby restaurant with a game room. We're the only people in the game room so we just take it over. Several of us play pool and others attack the basketball free-throw game. Just making free throws is too simple. Very quickly the tiny balls are ricocheting off the ceiling and walls from all over the room.

I keep pointing out what a competitive group of people this is, but it can't be overemphasized. From receptionists to drivers, winning is extremely important to them all. Having said how competitive everyone is, I also need to describe how much everyone pulls for members of the community who aren't doing well. Paul Tracy, a driver who gets more out of a car than almost anyone, has been crashing lately when he should be winning races, and people all over the paddock are pulling for him.

Lola Cars, a manufacturer of Indy cars off and on since 1965, is in real trouble this year. The cars are at least a second slower than the Reynards and Swifts. Teams with these other chassis want to beat the Lola teams, but they don't want Lola to fall behind and disappear.

Malcolm Oastler, technical director and chief designer at Reynard, is having a beer in the motel bar this evening and the Lola subject comes up. "Bit of a shame about Lola," Malcolm says in his clipped Aussie accent. "We're all in the same boat."

Allen McDonald, the PacWest technical director, is having a glass here also. He just moved from England to the U.S. Malcolm is an Australian living in England. They talk some English politics, saying the Tories aren't in as much trouble as the press is making out. We're all speaking English, but in three different accents. Malcolm often speaks in staccato bursts that defy understanding.

Allen asks Malcolm when he'll start designing the new car for 1998. "May," is Malcolm's answer. "We try to get wish lists from the teams, the 20 things they like or don't like about the current cars. When we see the same item on three or four lists, then we need to look at it. But sometimes you see the same thing on the 'love-it' list as you do on the 'hate-it' list."

During a conversation among us on the drivers and their basic racing abilities, Malcolm says, "Michael [Andretti] can move through the field. If he qualifies sixth you pretty well know he can win the race. He would have won that first race of the year at Homestead in our car too."

"So," I say, "you don't think the Swift is superior to your car at all?"

"No. It's a good car. But the Newman-Haas team knows what they're doing."

"I heard you sent Bruns [David, the Swift designer] a fax congratulating him on the new Swift."

"Yes. After their first test on the oval at Phoenix, I sent him a congratulatory fax. He's done a good job."

Allen McDonald and Malcolm Oastler

FRIDAY

At 7:30 a.m. I'm on my way from downtown Bethlehem to the Nazareth Speedway. You get off I-22 onto the Nazareth Pike, a rural, two-lane road. Monocacy Creek crosses the pike near the interstate, and I've seen someone fishing there every time I've driven by. Next comes Hecktown, where the landmarks are the Hecktown Cemetery and the Trinity Lutheran Church, which looks very clean and well maintained. Race traffic can be horrible through here because of the cross streets, stoplights, and lack of left-turn lanes, but this early there's no problem.

There are plowed fields and boxy, two-story houses on both sides of the road. I see corn stalks in the fields, but never any corn. The race here is always either too early or too late in the year. The last weekend in April is definitely too early for corn. The temperature is in the low 40s this time of day.

Motorola Hauler and 18-Car Garage Area

PacWest Garage Area

The crews are busy getting the cars ready for the first practice session. I notice a white board on the Motorola transporter door that shows a list of times for significant events today. Practice is at 10:30, lunch at 12:30, afternoon practice at 2:15, and dinner at 6:30. I hang around talking to people and watching what's going on for a while. I'm trying to get a ride around each track, so I go looking for the PPG pace cars.

A Lap on the Track

At 10 a.m. pace cars are going out on the track. Ken Lowe, the PPG pace car coordinator, has me fill out a liability release form and points me toward a red BMW. I get in and buckle up the four-point harness.

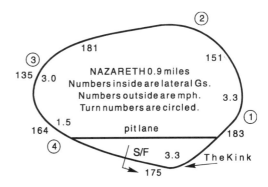

At the wheel is Gail Truess, a Pro-Rally driver. I ask her about the car. "It's a 325 M-model with some modifications. You'll have to ask the mechanic for the details."

This is Gail's first time at Nazareth, and she drives a few shakedown laps. What surprises me is how short and tight the track is. It's bumpy too. Gail brings the car back onto the pit lane, saying, "After a few minutes we'll go back out for a real ride." Great!

Back on track I ask Gail what gear she's in. "Third," she says. "I could use fourth in this car, but in third I can go right up to the red line and feather it in the corners."

In Turn 1 I can see shiny areas where the CART cars bottom out. There is a big triangular patch in Turn 4 that is darker and fresher than the surrounding asphalt. I ask Gail if she can feel the tires heat up and give more grip.

"Yes," she says. She's busy dialing steering into the corners and left-foot braking. I see 90 mph and 7,000 rpm on the tach.

TV does not do this track credit, making it look longer, wider, and flatter than it really is. This is a tight, narrow, bumpy track with 30 feet of elevation change. The cars have to brake hard going downhill into Turn 3 at very high speed. Nazareth is called a 1-mile oval, but really it's 0.925 miles in length. Track management calculates the average speeds using a full mile, jacking up the speeds by almost 8%. That's typical racetrack-promoter hype.

As Gail brings the BMW back into the paddock I see Mark Blundell out here in pit lane also. He's a rookie at this track so he's waiting to take a few familiarization laps around the track with Wally Dallenbach.

Friday Morning Practice

The slow guys are first in this session, but here today that includes Paul Tracy, Andre Ribeiro, Richie Hearn, and Bryan Herta. I decide to watch the session out at the corners, so I walk up out of pit lane and through the Indy Lights paddock toward Turn 2.

I'm listening on the scanner as the session begins, and I hear Control define "the kink" as the turn after Start/Finish but before Turn 1. This is important for accurate communications and dispatching of safety trucks.

I climb up into the wooden photo stand just inside the fence at the apex of Turn 2. Three pro photographers are working here among a bunch of amateurs. The three pros have 18-inch-long lenses on their cameras. They stand in a row in front of me and swivel in perfect unison as they track the cars going by.

Control says Tracy is quick in the session with a lap of 19.338 seconds, about 185 mph. He comes very close to the wall across the track from us as he exits Turn 2. The other drivers are a second slower. Tracy has thousands of miles on this track due to the testing Penske Racing does here. The track is owned by Roger Penske, and the team used Nazareth to secretly test the pushrod V-8 engine they used to win the '94 Indy 500. Back then Paul Tracy spent weeks in a motel in Allentown waiting through weather delays and engine modifications so he could track-test the engine on short notice. The most precious commodity in racing is track time.

Control says, "Tell the 24-car [Hiro Matsushita] to use the warm-up lane, because he's in the way."

I decide to walk down to the photo stand at Turn 4, and when I get there, I find more drivers and race engineers than photographers. I like to watch here because you can hear the driver get on the throttle. The earlier the better of course, and the smoothness or lack of it is what I try to catch. Tracy is on the throttle early and decisively. Others coast another 100 feet and come on it more tentatively.

At 11:30 a.m. the fast-guys' session begins. The sky is blue above some puffy clouds. The light breeze is cool, but the sun keeps me warm in a shirt and overshirt. On the radio I hear that Blundell missed his pit box when he came in after the installation laps. The crew razzes him about it. I hear Daryl Fox tell him, "Look for the Motorola signs."

When Blundell finds the pit box, I hear him say, "Tight little place, isn't it?"

Mauricio Gugelmin comes on the track and I clock him for several laps: 25 seconds, 23.28, 22.15, 21.19, and 20.68. He comes into the pits and goes back out again turning laps of 21.88, 21.01, 20.62, and 20.88. That's about 175-mph average.

Blundell reports an engine problem. "On the last lap my engine response fell down. The response was poor. I'm still getting used to the place. There's a bump in Turn 2 where the car feels quite harsh."

Jim Hamilton responds, "Change to the other wing position, please. The pressures look good and the temp spread is OK." Butch Winkle tells the crew to change the wing.

A yellow flag stops the session while the safety team looks for fluid on the track. Jim says add two turns of front wing to balance the new rear wing. They've gone to a higher-downforce wing.

Control hears a worker report that a PacWest car ran over a screw on the track, and tells a pit-lane steward to pass that on to the crew. As usual on ovals all four tires get a thorough inspection every time the car comes off the track. A blown tire at these corner speeds could be disastrous.

Mark asks about the engine problem. Jim reports he sees in the data that the engine lost a lot of boost. They change one of the electronic boxes. The green flag waves again at 11:50 a.m. Mauricio goes out and laps in the low 20s. Mark gets into the 20s also.

Mark comes in. "The front gives me a feeling of stiffness in Turn 2. The front grip just goes away in T3." Jim says he can lower the car quite a bit and tells the crew to come down three flats in the front and two at the rear.

Mark goes out and comes back in. "It's a bit stiff in 2. It's touchin' down in the kink, but not bad. We could come down a little bit more." Jim suggests some more left-rear camber and some shock changes.

After a few more laps Mark comes in again, saying "I'm still getting used to the place. It's a bit unique." Rookie Patrick Carpentier; Michael Andretti, who lives just down the road; and Al Unser Jr. are quick in this session so far.

The session ends with Mauricio fourth quick in the combined session behind Tracy, Carpentier, and Michael Andretti. Tracy turned a 19.198, Mo a 19.824, and Mark was 18th with a 20.712. That's not that bad for Mark considering this was his first session on the track. He's one place behind Alex Zanardi and faster than 10 other drivers.

Hollywood Hauler and 17-Car Garage Area

I eat lunch with the crew in the garage area, skipping the grilled, medium-rare steak for a chicken fajita, parsley potatoes, green beans, and fruit salad. I remember somebody requesting red meat at Long Beach. Dave Loik responded right away with today's steak.

There are several thousand fans wandering around the paddock and a few in the stands. The crowd today is 10% of a Friday at Long Beach or Surfers. This is a more intimate, regional event. The stands will be empty all weekend, but they'll be full when the race starts.

Mark comes out of the engineering room in the front of the Motorola transporter, and I ask him about the track. "It's a tricky little track. It's difficult to learn with the other cars out there. You're passing some of them and trying to stay out of the way of others."

"I was surprised when I got my pace car ride, how tight and short it is," I note.

"Yes," he agrees. "The TV doesn't do it justice."

Afternoon Practice

The green flag starts this session at 2:17 p.m. I've decided to stay in the pit lane. The overcast conditions have increased and rain is a possibility. It wouldn't be Nazareth without some rain. A minute after the green a yellow flag for debris stops the session. Control says something came off a Target car.

When Mark comes in Butch says on the radio, "It's the pit with the Motorola shirts." The crew won't let Mark forget his earlier mistake.

Mark acknowledges the teasing, groaning, "You guys."

A few minutes later I hear a report of rain in Turn 2. Control says, "No problem; we're watching it." But a minute later, at 2:24, a yellow flag stops the session because of moisture.

Mark tells Jim, "The car is touching down in Turn 2. It's still nervous. We might want to look at the pressures to see if they're up to standard."

I can feel some raindrops in pit lane, but at 2:39 a green flag restarts the session with 39 minutes left. Tom Keene and Scott Simpson uncover the stacks of tires they had covered up when it started sprinkling. Like everything else, the tire covers are specially made with PacWest logos. Five minutes after the green we see another yellow flag for moisture. Mark says, "It feels fine, but it's going to touch down when I get going faster."

Jim: "These tires are getting long in the tooth, so we just want to do a baseline with the latest changes when you go back out."

Mark: "Maybe we should change tires now."

Jim agrees and tells the crew to change to the other set. "These are harder and have more stagger. I don't think we should change the ride height much. Up a half flat at the pushrod at the rear."

At 2:46 the session resumes. It's windier now. The big flag at Start/Finish is standing straight out. Mark goes out on track and back in after a few laps. "It's a bit more comfortable,

Jim. It's softer and that gives me some feel. It's a little nervous into Turn 2. It somewhat destabilizes me. There's still a degree of roll in the car, and it feels like it wants to break away."

Jim suggests shock changes at the rear. Then Jim asks a specific question. "What do you feel mid-turn to exit in Turn 3?"

Mark: "The rear is a bit nervous, maybe due to roll."

The monitor shows who's quick in this session: Zanardi, Ribeiro, Vasser, Parker, and Mark. We have another yellow flag at 2:51 p.m. I feel sprinkles of rain. The clouds are darker but don't look like storm clouds. We're not going to have a frog-strangler here. A half-hour later the session goes green again. Due to the delays, Control informs everyone that this session and the next will only get 30 minutes of green-flag time.

Mark goes out and comes in again and tells Jim, "It's softer in the rear in terms of roll, but it still feels a bit nervous. There's too much powerboat effect."

Jim says, "We can do more or less of the same changes. I'll talk to Tim."

Jim again. "Is it better or worse after the last changes?"

Mark: "It is better, but the car is squatting too much. I'm concerned about nailing the rear and having it right come the race." Jim suggests some ride height and shock changes at the rear.

Mark goes back out with 3 minutes to go. Ribeiro is quick in the session at a 19.858 followed by Zanardi, Vasser, Franchitti, and Parker.

Fast Guys

The fast half of the cars start their session at 3:40 p.m. I had Mauricio's channel locked out on my scanner by mistake this morning, but I can hear him now. When he comes in the first time he says, "The car is not touching, but it is going to go loose."

Andy Brown: "Shall we go right to the springs?"

Mo: "Yes."

Andy: "Change the springs and come up two flats all around."

They don't mention spring rates

Jim Reid Belts Mauricio into his Car

on the radio, but you can guess that if they raised the car, they went to softer springs. The aero loads will push the car down more at speed, so they need a higher static ride height to keep from bottoming.

It's windier now, cloudy and cool. At 2:47 we get a yellow flag for moisture and the session stops. When Mo comes in they continue to work on the setup. "It's still going to go loose."

Andy: "Can we bring the rear ride-height down?"

Mo: "Let's do that."

Andy: "Two flats down at the rear. Up a flat at the front."

Jim Hamilton, Mark Blundell's engineer, walks over to Mauricio's car and looks carefully at the right-rear tire and then the right front, pursing his lips and shaking his head. The tires are very important here, and the Goodyears are faster than the Firestones so far today.

Mauricio continues to work on the setup. He's in P16, a whole second slower than Paul Tracy. Next time in he says, "If I use the brakes deeper I have some push in Turn 3. In Turn 2 I'm loose a little at the exit, but not too bad."

Andy: "Let's take some rebound out of the front shocks. We'll go down on the rear ride-height and lift the front. We've got 10 minutes left. We'll put the sticker tires on next time you come in."

Paul Tracy is quick in this session with a lap of 19.024 seconds. Mauricio's best is a 20.378. He comes in for tires. "The rebound helps in the corners. Funny thing, I still feel it touching in the kink."

Andy: "Let's see what new tires do for it." Mauricio is out on track at 4:12 with 5 minutes to go. He's P17 on the monitor. I time his laps with my stopwatch as he goes by Start/Finish: 25

seconds, 23, 22, 20.56, 24, 22, and 20.78. With one minute to go I see a 20.784 for him on the monitor. Then Mauricio's name pops up to P7 and the time is 19.846 seconds. When he comes in, I hear him say, "I just wanted to make sure we're in the first session tomorrow."

The rain starts out as a sprinkle and increases to a steady, light rain, ending the session. I walk to the motor coach and get my rain jacket.

As usual after Friday practice, the crews make an engine change. The car goes on the setup pad first and the numbers are recorded for the engineers. Then the cars go up on jackstands and the transaxle, suspension, and gearbox comes off the back of the engine. The engine comes off the back of the tub. With all the bodywork off, the fact that the engine is a structural member becomes apparent. All of the bending and twisting loads from the rear of the car have to go through the engine to get to the chassis (called the tub), which ends right behind the fuel cell at the driver's back.

At 7 p.m., after dinner, the engine changes are winding down. The 18-crew is changing springs and shocks on the T-car, bringing it up to current specs in case it has to be pressed into service. I ask Ando, "How did the team react to Mo's podium finish at Long Beach?"

"It was very positive," he says. "They see the potential."

Later, in the motel bar, Butch, chief mechanic on the 18-car, and I talk over a beer. "There's got to be a lot of stress in a family because of the travel," I say. "How many of your kids' birthdays and anniversaries have you missed?"

"Being gone from your family is a part of the commitment," Butch says. "But the teams use it too. You feel like you can't leave the shop. It's tough to get time off."

"Can't you guys cover for each other?"

"We try, but everybody is so busy, and the pressure is always there."

"As a chief mechanic, you're responsible for what the crew does whether you're there are not."

"Exactly," Butch says. "You have to make sure the car gets prepared perfectly, but you can't do the work yourself. And we've got some guys that are new to racing. They're learning, and you have to let them go on their own but catch it when they screw up so nobody gets hurt. And you have to do it so it doesn't hurt their confidence.

"I'll give you an example. Stephen [Kent] wanted to build the front end of the car by himself, so I let him. When I checked it out it wasn't right. I asked him how he picked the shims he used. 'I got them out of the shim drawer,' he said. I had to show him how to measure them and use the right parts. He learned it, but it took a lot of time, and we don't always have that."

Randy Smay Coils a Hose

SATURDAY

At 8 a.m. John Creak and Steve Fusek are checking out the placement of the decals that will show up in the in-car camera shots on Mauricio's car this weekend. There is a camera on the roll hoop looking forward and a rear-facing camera also. They've made a sticker to go on the bodywork in front of the rear-facing camera. To look right on screen, the Hollywood logo is very tiny, about a 16th of an inch high, so it's difficult to place just right. "Some people go way overboard with these things," Fusek says. "Too many decals and it ruins the shot and looks bad for the sponsors. You need to keep it simple and not get too greedy."

A couple of minutes before 9 o'clock I'm in the pit lane waiting for the start of practice. The wind is light from the west and it's cool, maybe 60 degrees, but the sky is clear and the sun warm.

Tire Stuff

Dwayne Joyner, a Firestone engineer and rubber compounder, and I have one of our normal conversations. We talk about many different subjects, but I usually have some tire questions and sometimes Dwayne will answer them and sometimes he won't. It's frustrating for both of us, but that's the way it is. Dwayne handles the frustration better than I do. Slowly I'm learning more about the tires, but then I just have more questions.

This time I ask Dwayne about how they get the fabric in the tire carcass to adhere to the rubber. "You have the same problem in racing tires that you have in street tires," Dwayne says, meaning he can explain this topic to me because it's not a racing-tire secret. "Some street radials use steel belts, but rubber doesn't stick to steel. They plate the steel with brass so the rubber has something to stick to. In racing tires we use light, strong textiles that start out as single filaments and get woven into threads. We coat those threads — it's like a sheath — and then they're dipped into an adhesive so they'll bond to the rubber."

This is an important point. Some of the tire guys throw out the phrase, "It's only rubber and string" to emphasize the contrast between how simple tires are as a concept and how complicated they are to design and manufacture. Sure, a tire is only rubber and string, but the way it's made and the thought put into the design can hardly be overemphasized. Those round, black things are extremely important.

Somebody walks up and asks Dwayne, "Can you run these things on the wrong side?"

"Only if you want to run the track backwards," is the reply.

The tires are designed for each corner of the car and the construction is not necessarily symmetrical. One sidewall might be stiffer than the sidewall on the other side of the tire. The right-rear tire might be stiffer overall than the left rear, especially on an oval where the right-side tires do most of the work.

Saturday Practice

Mark Blundell is in the first practice session that starts at 9 a.m. Shortly after the green flag they throw a yellow for debris. I hear Control say to have the 18-car, that's Mark's, look at the tires. A corner worker thinks he ran over something. Mark is running his T-car because they want to try something that takes awhile to change. He switches to the primary car after a few laps.

Paul Jasper crashes about 10 minutes into the session. I hear somebody say "code 1" on the radio, meaning he's OK. You don't want to hear "code 3."

Mark says, "There's some push in the car. It comes in quickly and is quite strong. The rear feels stable, but there is an increment of nervousness, but there's not much depth to it."

This statement is the least helpful I've heard yet. I really don't know how Jim Hamilton figures out what to change on the car with that kind of feedback from the driver.

They put new tires on Mark's car. Mauricio is here looking at the tires very carefully. He examines Mark's tires as he walks around the car, and he peers at the tires on other cars that are pitted adjacent to the PacWest pit boxes. Jim says they'll run enough on the primary tires to get a baseline and then switch to the optionals. The session goes green again at 9:27.

I time Mark for a few laps and get a 24-second lap and then 21.91, 21.50, 21.00, and 21.5. He comes back in, and they switch tires. "It feels better," Mark says, "I'm more comfortable with the rear. It feels more stable at the rear." Jim says he'd like a long run on the optional tires. Mark goes out on the new tires and gets down to some laps in the 20-second area. They call him in after a number of laps.

Mark: "The times are better. Lateral grip is improved. There's still quite a bit of push, but I can predict it. It's still a bit nervous in the kink, just a bit. And still a little harsh in Turn 2. That's the biggest issue with me. How are the pressures?"

Jim says the right front is a little high. Mauricio walks around the 18-car, looking at the tires again. He examines the right front longer than the rest. Greg Moore is P1 in the session with a lap of 19.902 seconds. Mark is P10.

Mark goes out on track again, and I time some laps: 22.06, 21.50, 20.67, 20.26, 20.44, and 20.93. They call him in to take some tape off the radiator inlet. Mark says, "It's gone neutral now.

I'd like a little bit of push. The steering load is not there in the corners. I need some feedback from the steering. It goes light on me." Jim tells the crew to go up one flat at the front.

Mark spins the rear tires and slews the car sideways going out of the pit box. There are 10 minutes to go in the session. Mark has a best lap of 20.08 seconds. He's been complaining of harshness in Turn 2 and saying the tires seem to be skipping over the bumps. When he comes back in Jim asks him if that was any better.

"Yes," comes the answer. "But it went neutral. Maybe the rear is getting too confident. I don't seem to be carrying enough load across the front. I need more grip." Jim says we can go back on the bump adjustment on the shocks and try it again. Mark goes back out on track with 3 minutes to go.

A checkered flag ends the session. Mark's best time on the monitor is a 20.233. When he comes in, Mark says "The changes were a little bit negative to the car. It's still skipping with harshness in Turn 2."

Mo's Turn

Mark Moore, Mauricio's chief mechanic, tells him, "Four laps on installation" as Mauricio takes the car out onto the track for his final practice session before qualifying this afternoon. Starting at 10:05, this is a scheduled 45-minute practice session.

When Mauricio comes back in for his installation check, he says, "Everything feels fine."

Andy: "Change tires. These are the primes from yesterday morning." Mo returns to the track.

As Scott Simpson lays out a set of sticker tires for the next change, I time some of Mauricio's laps: 23.26, 21.72, 21.47, 23.74, 21.00, 20.50, and 22.62. He says on the radio, "Lot of traffic."

Andy answers, "Understood. Good for tomorrow." More laps: 20.69, 20.31, 20.47, and in.

Mauricio: "Over the bumps in Turn 2 the car is still upsetting a lot. I have too much pitch in Turn 3. I tried the roll bar and it just pushed worse."

Andy: "Is it worse than yesterday?"

Mo: "The same." Andy calls for some tire-pressure changes and some rebound out of the front and rear shocks. Mo goes out for another run, but a yellow flag stops the session while the safety crews look for debris.

Mauricio reports, "The front of the car is washing out too much in turns 2 and 3."

Andy: "There's still 15 gallons of fuel on board. Let's get that down below 10 and do a dummy qualifying run. In Turn 2 is it roll or a flat slide?"

Mauricio: "It rolls and goes into a slide at the rear."

Andy: "While we're stopped for this yellow let's change rear springs." The crew removes the coilover units from the rear of the 17-car and takes them over to the spring tester. They replace the coil spring and test the unit to make sure they know the exact spring rate and preload before the units go back in the car.

I hear Control say, "The 5-car has a puncture, so there's something out there." A green flag restarts the session at 10:29. Work continues on Mauricio's car and he's out on track a minute later. There's 25 minutes left in the session. Mauricio turns some laps around 20.5 seconds. Paul Tracy is still fast in this session.

When Mo comes back in he says, "That helped the rear a lot, but the push is too bad. It washes out when I get on the throttle."

Andy: "Let's stay with these springs and get rid of the push in other ways." Tom Keene takes a stagger measurement on the rear tires while the car is up on the air jacks. The track goes green again and Mo goes out a minute later.

He gets into the 19-second area and then comes in, saying, "That helped but there's still too much push in Turn 3. I couldn't feel any change there."

Andy suggest some changes and says, "We'll switch to optional tires now. Just give me one lap to scuff them for qualifying."

When Mauricio comes back in to change the tires Andy says, "We'll put some front wing in now for the dummy qualifying run. One degree per side; that's the same as Milwaukee [when they tested there]." Back on track Mo turns a 19.38 after a few laps, jumping up to P5. Paul Tracy drives a lap in 18.769 seconds, a new lap record for Nazareth. That's 191.806 mph using the bogus track length.

Control keeps getting reports from corner workers about spray from the back of Michael Andretti's Swift, but when pit lane stewards check it out it's clean and dry. Andy tells Mauricio to try sixth gear as he goes back out for more laps.

"I have to come in," Mo says on the radio. "The weight jacker isn't working the way it should. The right-front tire pressure is too high also."

When he comes into the pit box and stops the car, he says, "I'm getting out. I have to think about it. I went the wrong way on the weight jacker, but when I came back it still pushed too much." At the checkered flag Mauricio ends up in P6 behind Paul Tracy, Patrick Carpentier, Gil de Ferran, Michael Andretti, and Jimmy Vasser.

Qualifying

17-Crew on the Qualifying Grid

The qualifying order is determined by a drawing, so earlier today team representatives gathered outside the media center and drew numbers. As the 17-car gets into position for qualifying, Jim Hamilton tells me Mauricio is on optional tires and Mark on primaries.

The 18x-car, Mark's T-car, had Mauricio's setup on it in morning practice, but it didn't work for Mark. The issue is somewhat clouded, Jim says, "Because the setup wasn't properly executed." I think they installed the wrong springs.

This brings up the point that changes to a racecar have to be made very carefully. One change at a time is the best way to do it because everything is so interrelated, but time constraints usually force the engineers to make multiple changes. Obviously, if you think you have 1,200-pound-per inch springs at the front and they are actually 1,400, the driver is evaluating an imaginary setup. That wastes time and effort.

Qualifying is scheduled to start at 1 p.m. At 1:20 they're blowing off the track with the jet truck.

Bobby Rahal is the first driver out for qualifying. Mark is about 12th in the order and posts a 19.868-seconds time that ends up 16th quick. Paul Tracy nails the pole position with a new qualifying record of 18.831 seconds, or 191.174 mph. Michael Andretti is second quick with a 19.193. Mauricio is the fastest driver on Firestone tires, in fifth spot with a 19.321.

The Skids

Every time Mauricio comes into the pit box during a practice session, Jim Reid goes under the 17-car to look at the pattern of marks on the skid plates, records the pattern on a piece of paper, and gives that sheet to Andy. Now, back in the garage area, Andy Brown gets on his hands and knees to take his own look at the skid plates on the bottom of the car. He and Jimmy talk about the pattern of marks that tells them whether the car is rubbing at the front or rear of the skids. This is important information that has to flow from Jim to Andy during practice sessions.

If the front of the skids is rubbing, the car has some rake in it; the front is lower than the back. If the skid is rubbing more rearward, there might be less rake. I say "might" because softer rear springs and/or shocks could also allow the rubbing at the rear. Or more rear wing could cause aero loads to push the rear down. Less front wing could do it too. So could low tire pressures at the rear. Like I said, everything is interrelated.

Andy tells me they have skid plates made from different materials, steel or brass, depending on how they want to move weight around. These cars generally weigh less than the minimum specified by the rules, so the teams can use ballast as they wish. Generally they want the weight as low as possible to lower the center of gravity of the car to minimize weight transfer during cornering. They might also want more weight toward the front or toward the rear, and they can use the skid plates and other ballast to do that.

Race Prep

At 4:20 p.m. in the garage area, it's engine change time for the PacWest guys. A new one is going in the 17-car, and the old one is coming out of the 18-car. I see a green fluid dripping out of a water pipe and ask Butch if they use antifreeze.

"Yeah," he answers. "Mostly as a water-pump lubricant."

"About 50/50 with water as usual?"

"Right."

Two hours later, after dinner, the 17-crew fires the new engine. A couple of minutes later the 18-crew starts theirs for the first time. They carefully check both new installations for leaks.

Jim Hamilton comes out of the engineering office in the front of the Motorola transporter. He's looking for something to eat, and finds a plate of brownies. I've already had my share of these treats, so we talk while he enjoys one brownie and then another.

The subject of our conversation is the vastly different driving and feedback styles of Gugelmin and Blundell. "Mo is more adaptive than Mark," Jim says. "He drives around problems, but Mark will stop you with the detail of his comments."

"But some of the things Mark says sound so off the wall," I say. "Today I heard him say something about 'a degree of nervousness with no depth to it' and 'skipping with harshness' and 'the rear getting too confident.' How do you make any sense out of that?"

Jim laughs. "I hope I can get a job after you write this book."

I have to laugh too. "But you have to be learning a lot. You are managing to improve the car for him. He's not doing badly considering his lack of experience in these cars and on oval tracks. I'm hoping there's a positive story here; that he'll improve and both of you look good."

"You're right," Jim says, reaching for an apple from the sack on the folding table at the end of the covered tent. "I am learning a lot. He's describing what he feels and I have to look at the data and the tires and listen to him and do whatever I can to figure out how to make him more comfortable in the car. He needs the rear end of the car nailed. He doesn't like to feel any movement back there. He's making me look into this stuff deeper than I ever have, and some of the classical fixes seem to work backwards from how it's supposed to work."

It's almost 7 p.m. I see the brains of the 17-car talking among themselves, standing in the door to the Hollywood transporter: Mark Moore, the chief mechanic; Andy Brown, the engineer; and Russ Cameron, the race strategist. They'll go over the issues of tomorrow's race and decide on a plan and contingencies.

I'm tired. I head for the car and drive toward a beer in the motel bar. They've got some kind of lager on tap that goes down very well. In the motel bar, John Oreovicz and I talk about racing.

Steve Fusek had told me earlier in the day that Mauricio was much better with his crew than Mark is with his. "We're talking to him about how to do that better. Mo is really good, but Mark doesn't seem to have time for you unless you're doing something for him."

It occurs to me that Gugelmin is bringing the sponsorship money with him (Hollywood, the Brazilian cigarette), while Mark is a PacWest employee. I'd love to know more about the difference in the team/driver relationship depending on whether or not the driver is bringing the money or he's a paid employee. I have to assume a driver who has control of a sponsor would have a stronger position with the team. He could take the money somewhere else.

SUNDAY: RACE DAY

At 6:55 a.m. I'm stopped in traffic a mile short of the gate. There was indeed a fisherman on the creek as I drove by this sunny Sunday morning. It's supposed to cloud up and rain later this afternoon, hopefully after the race.

At 7:30 I'm in the garage area watching the crews getting the cars ready for the day. The usual breakfast cereals and fruit choices are there but I need a chocolate doughnut, so I go up the hill toward Turn 2 to the Indy Lights hospitality area. Somebody has

Dave Jacobs, Mark Moore, and Chris Jaynes

already munched the chocolate doughnuts so I settle for a glazed unit. As usual there are several people to talk to, so I hang around a while.

More Tire Stuff

While talking to Indy Lights people, someone tells me the tire problem Michael Andretti had at Long Beach turned out to be a tire gauge reading too high. That would cause the tires to be at an actual pressure lower than the value on the gauge. I'll try to verify that with Goodyear or the Newman-Haas team.

I get to the Hollywood hospitality area in time to see the last few minutes of Saturday's F1 qualifying session from Imola, Italy. Then the live F1 race starts and I watch the start before I go looking for a Goodyear guy to ask about the tire gauge story.

First I go to the Goodyear trailer looking for Steve Meyers. Steve used to be the chief compounder for Goodyear Racing but is now the marketing manager. I find Steve in the conference room built into the front of the Goodyear transporter watching the F1 race with the other engineers. They are in competition with Bridgestone/Firestone in F1, as they are here at this race. When I tell him what I had heard he says he can't verify that, but it wasn't a tire problem. He suggests I talk to the team.

Just before the warm-up session I find Peter Gibbons, Michael Andretti's engineer, in the pit lane, and ask him about the Long Beach tire problem. "It was a team problem," Peter says and I think that's all he is going to say, but then he adds, "a tire gauge."

So why would a couple of pounds less tire pressure cause the tires to fail? The tire guys specify a pressure range for their tires at each race. Let's say it's 20 to 30 pounds per square inch (psi) for road courses, 25 to 35 psi for short ovals, and 35 to 45 for superspeedways. The higher pressures are needed to keep the contact patch roughly the same area, when the tire sees higher aerodynamic loads at the higher speeds of the faster tracks.

The Long Beach track can be described as two drag strips connected at each end by some squiggly bits. Braking into the slow corners at the end of the straights and getting the power down to the road out of the slow corners is crucial to a fast lap. Low tire pressure helps get the power to the road so the teams tend to use a pressure toward the low end of the range specified by the tire companies.

The lower the pressure the less stiff the tire and the more the tire flexes under load. The longitudinal acceleration loads transfer from the tread area to the sidewall at the shoulder. Lower pressures concentrate these forces into a smaller area of the shoulder, the corner where the tread and sidewall come together, actually called "the apex." Evidently, the lower pressures in the Newman-Haas rear tires structurally overloaded the tire at the apex, and caused the failures we saw.

If you look at camber on Michael's Swift when it's set up for a road or street course, you'll probably see more negative camber on the rear than most of the cars. I've been told Michael likes to toss the car, and the extra rear camber helps him catch it. Maybe this extra camber also put more load on the inside tire shoulder. As usual it takes more than one problem to cause a failure.

This tire gauge story could also be a scam to deflect attention away from a Goodyear design or manufacturing problem. I remember David Bruns telling me on the pre-grid at Long Beach that his car wasn't good enough on street courses. Maybe the team went too low on the pressures trying to get that little bit more power down out of the hairpin, and the tires didn't like it. The tire guys don't want the blame and the team doesn't want it either. It's that damn tire gauge's fault.

Warm-Up

At 10 a.m. a 30-minute session starts for the CART cars. Indy Lights had their warm-up an hour earlier. The flags are limp today. It's sunny, but high clouds keep the temperature cool. The PacWest cars are both out on track at the flag. They do radio checks and Mauricio comes in for a practice pit stop and an installation check before going back out. Mark does the same.

Ten minutes later Mauricio is in, complaining of a push. "The bumps in Turn 2 upset the car and it looses front grip."

Mark has a similar problem. "Just too much push; I can't get low enough in the corner."

Jim: "Let's look at the skids real quick and we'll try to lower the car."

After gauging the marks on the skids, Jim says, "Three flats down at the front and one at the rear."

After another stint on course both drivers still complain of understeer. Jim asks for a spring change on Mark's car and the crew does the work very quickly. "Great work, guys," Jim says as Mark returns to the track.

Mauricio tries the weight jacker but says it doesn't work. Andy asks him if he wants to soften the rear bar. "No," is the answer.

At the end of the session Mauricio is P11 and Mark P15. Paul Tracy continues to dominate. His best lap is 19.163 seconds, with Richie Hearn second with a 19.751. Six-tenths of a second is an eternity on a short oval with a 19-second lap.

After the session Mark tells me, "The car is good on its own, but when I try to stay with the other cars the rear pops out. The car is too neutral. This is my first time here, and it's very busy in traffic. I'm just hoping to finish as well as possible and pass some people and get some track time. Some of these guys have been doing ovals all their lives."

Daryl Fox Tapes Extra Padding
On a Blundell Knee

THE RACE

At 1:25 the cars are all lined up on pre-grid in pit lane. The photo shows Bruce and Mark talking while Daryl Fox and Gavin Hamilton add some padding to the inside of Mark's left knee. Earlier I had asked Steve Fusek if I could go with him to his spotting station to watch the race. After the invocation and national anthem I get on a scooter behind Steve and we go out of the paddock and through the tunnel. The scooter is pretty ungainly with both of us on it. We stop at the bottom of some stairs in back of the grandstands at Turn 4. Steve hauls the scooter onto its stand, and we climb the stairs. Our spotter passes get us right in.

We climb a long way up the stairs to the top row. There's about 4 feet of platform behind the last row of seats, and since we don't have tickets, that's where we stand. It's a shirt-sleeve crowd so we stand out, Steve in his Sparco PacWest jacket and me in a blue oxford-cloth shirt with my name and TV MOTORSPORTS logo on the right breast. The stands looked half-full 30 minutes ago, but now I can't see an empty seat. It's windy up here and thickening clouds are filtering the warmth out of the sun.

We have a magnificent view. The entire track is in sight except for the apex of Turn 2. I've never had a seat this good at any racetrack. It's a perfect place for a spotter. Tim Neff is spotting at Turn 2, where our view is blocked, and I hear him on the scanner saying, "These dinky stands are about to fall down."

As they drive their pace laps, the cars get tiny going into Turn 2 and big again in Turn 4 right below us. Here comes the start, but I can hear on the scanner there's a problem. I look up and see a large dust devil swirling across the infield toward Turn 1. It blows over a big tent. Control tells the starter, Jim Swintal, "No start. We'll do a track inspection to make sure there's no debris on course." The race starts under yellow and the laps count.

Russ Cameron and John Anderson (Ando) wear two radios, one to talk with the crew and the driver, and the other to listen to the spotters. Fusek talks on the radio periodically, informing Russ and Ando of the goings on here in Turn 4 that they can't see from the pit lane. I can hear them all.

The Start at Nazareth

The green flag starts the race for real on lap three, and Michael Andretti tries to pass Tracy with no luck. Andre Ribeiro blows a half-shaft on lap six, causing another yellow-flag period for track cleanup.

The track goes green again for one lap, but coolant from his own water pump failure gets Greg Moore sideways and causes another yellow flag. I hear Control say something about antifreeze on the track.

The race restarts again on lap 18 with Tracy, Andretti, and Carpentier up front. Mauricio is still fifth and Mark 14th. Unser Jr. lays back, gets a run on Mauricio, and passes him cleanly. Raul Boesel gets by too, and Mauricio is now in P7. This is a good race now after the early yellow flags. The fans are into it and there's a lot of excitement in the stands. This is why short-oval tracks make such good racing. I can see almost all the track, and there's action everywhere.

Mauricio tells Andy he has a push and his tire pressures are low. Control has been warning the crew of car-24, driven by Hiro Matsushita, to tell him to get onto the pace or they will black flag him. On lap 23 they do that and Hiro retires. He's just too slow on a dangerous track like this.

Michael Andretti finally passes Tracy on lap 35. Then Gualter Salles brushes the wall in Turn 4, causing another yellow flag. During the caution period Mauricio says his car was too pointy at first and just pushing now. Russ says to try the swaybar, but Mauricio says the car is moving too much.

Mark tells Ando his car is pushing in Turn 2 and bottoming in Turn 3. Ando comes back to Mark saying there's some telemetry problems, and he needs to know the fuel usage numbers off Mark's dash.

After the green flag, Michael Andretti continues to lead Tracy and Carpentier until lap 53, when he pits to change a tire that's going down. The tire sensors and telemetry allow the team to diagnose the problem, averting a crash.

Adrian Fernandez's Lola breaks a half-shaft, same as his teammate's, and hits the wall in Turn 3 to bring out another yellow flag on lap 59. There is a reason for those half-shaft failures. Maybe the team isn't maintaining them, but I doubt that. Maybe they're dialing in more camber trying to produce mechanical grip to make up for the lack of downforce. That could produce extreme CV-joint angles and cause failures.

Russ tells Mauricio to pit with the leaders. He's fifth now behind Tracy, Carpentier, Unser Jr., and de Ferran. Ando also tells Mark to pit. Mauricio's crew cuts a great pit stop and he beats de Ferran out onto the track. Mo asked for a turn of left front-wing. The race restarts on lap 70 with Boesel in the lead followed by Dario Franchitti, Tracy, and Mauricio. Mark is 12th. Both Boesel and Franchitti pitted earlier and are out of sequence on their stops.

The Toyota-powered cars continue to expire, with Max Papis causing the next yellow flag at lap 82. Russ tells Mauricio he's doing good. Mo comes back saying, "The clutch is going down, but I still got it."

Ando cheers Mark on. "When it goes green, put some pressure on those weasels in front of ya'!" The race starts again on lap 89. Boesel pits, so Mauricio is now third behind Tracy and Franchitti, who will have to pit soon. Then Mauricio passes Franchitti for second spot into Turn 3 on lap 102. Control's gravelly voice says, "Nice pass."

Mark is 11th now but Michael Andretti is moving up, passing people every six or eight laps. He goes by Mark on lap 104 and gets to 10th on lap 114. De Ferran passes Mauricio for second and Unser Jr. goes by him some laps later.

Mauricio says, "The vibration is unbelievable. I can't see." Russ tells him to hang on for 10 laps, and he can pit for tires. He's in fourth, running with the leaders; not bad. It could be a podium or maybe a win.

Michael Andretti has continued to pass people and he's fifth behind Mauricio on lap 140. But the realities of the new, smaller fuel tank come into play. Mauricio has to pit on lap 141 or run out of fuel. The pit stop is slow, and to make it worse, the leaders pit a few laps later under a yellow flag caused by Parker Johnstone's spin out of Turn 4.

"Mo got screwed," says Fusek.

Mauricio says, "The race is not over yet, guys. Who am I racing with?"

Ando tells Mark, "Your little Scotch friend [Dario Franchitti] is right ahead of ya'."

A green flag restarts the race on lap 153 but Mauricio is now in 10th, a lap down. Mark is in the same situation four places farther back. Tracy continues to lead, but Michael Andretti passes Junior for second on lap 177. There's less than 50 laps to go now of the 225-lap total race distance.

On lap 180 Mark's race ends with a bang as he hits the wall in Turn 2, causing another yellow flag. He's not injured, but he wanted to finish this race. I hear him on the radio. "I'm OK. Just got up in the gray. Wouldn't recover. Went straight in. Sorry, guys."

Ando says, "Great job anyway, mate."

A restart on lap 180 doesn't last long. Parker Johnstone has been holding up a long train of guys and the mirror on the left side of his car has loosened and turned down. Raul Boesel bumps him trying to pass and Parker goes into the wall just below us in Turn 4. Richie Hearn T-bones Parker's car, punching a hole through the tub and bruising Parker's hip. The front wing actually stopped the Lola's nose from poking further into Parker's car, saving him from serious injury.

During the yellow flag, Mauricio describes the racecourse. "Very difficult, a single line, lots of marbles. Lots of fluid from Parker's car."

After the restart, Michael Andretti presses Tracy for all he is worth. The crowd is thrilled by the sight of these two young drivers going head to head in every corner, running away from the rest of the field.

Unfortunately, with three laps to go Juan Fangio's Toyota engine lets go, belching all kinds of smoke and flame. The race ends under yellow, cheating us all out of a racing finish. Paul Tracy wins, giving Team Penske its first race victory since 1995. Michael is second and Unser Jr. third. Mauricio finishes ninth.

Post-Race

Afterward Mark tells me, "It wasn't too bad. I'm pretty satisfied. The crew nailed the first pit stop. I'd rather finish. It was just too much push. We made some tire pressure changes, and I used the weight jacker and bars. I wanted to try a higher line to pass Franchitti, but just 3 feet higher and the marbles just drew me into the wall. It takes forever to get to that wall, and while you're getting there you're frustrated as hell. It was a great experience for me on this track, but it's still frustrating not to finish."

Mauricio says, "Franchitti came out of the pits and pulled right out in front of me. I got pushed up high and had to get out of the throttle. I lost a couple of spots then. The second set of tires rotated on the rim, unbalancing the tire. I had a big vibration. Then we pitted at the wrong time. Parker's spin shouldn't have caused a yellow. That really screwed us."

Bruce is the team owner and he takes a larger view. "Mark was conservative in traffic, but both guys drove well. We're going to work real hard on fuel management. We need to improve. We had to pit for fuel; Tracy didn't. If it had stayed green it wouldn't matter. They're just doing it better. They could run at a harder pace using less fuel. This is a big setback for us."

Jim Swintal says it was a good start. "I told them to start pairing up on the backstraight and they did, both times. I didn't see that dust devil but I guess Wally did, because he stood right up and said, 'We're not going green. We need to take a look at that thing.' Both starts were good, so we must be doing something right."

We talk about Hiro, and how he's so slow and gets in the way. Jim thinks he's hanging on until the race in Motegi, Japan, next year. But what if they have to black flag him there? That would be very embarrassing.

The two themes I heard from Race Control all weekend were cars should use the warm-up lane unless they're at full speed, and Hiro is too slow. I don't think anyone would miss Hiro on the track. He does, however, put a lot of money into the sport. He is the president and financial supporter of Swift Engineering. There would not be a Swift wind tunnel or the new Swift 007.i without Hiro.

At 6 p.m. I'm walking through a field to my car. Fifteen minutes later I've driven 200 yards and I'm almost to the road. A few sprinkles of rain streak the layer of dust on the windshield. I couldn't get a flight out of Allentown tonight, so I'll stay another night at the motel and get up early for a 6:15 flight to Dulles connecting back to SFO. A week from now I start the trek to Rio.

Pit Stops During the Race at Nazareth

CHAPTER 9

RIO DE JANEIRO

This trip has been a source of fear and dread since January, when I knew I would go to every CART race this year. Horror stories from people about last year telling how hot it was, the primitive conditions at the track, lack of bottled water, muggings, and diarrhea has me scared.

The week before the trip I go to a camping store and get educated on water purification, buying a collapsible gallon jug and an inexpensive kit of chlorine crystals and hydrogen peroxide. This solves one problem, but I am still unenthusiastic about the travel involved. It takes me all day Monday, May 5 to get to Miami, where I meet the PacWest guys for an all-night flight to Rio de Janeiro, Brazil.

The Varig Airline flight crew has an air about them of aristocrats volunteering to serve meals to homeless people. Even the captain's voice over the PA drones lackadaisically. After some delays we take off at 10 o'clock in the evening Eastern time.

I manage to sleep some during the flight. We land in Sao Paulo at 5:30 a.m. Eastern or 6:30 a.m. local time on May 6. It's foggy here and on the way down I get to see a beautiful pink sunrise above the overcast. We can't get off the plane here in Sao Paulo; we just mill around waiting for some passengers to get off and others to board. It takes about an hour before we take off for the half-hour trip to Rio.

TUESDAY

When we get off the plane in Rio, some people collect our passports and process them all together before passing them out again. Giving up my passport to a strange person in a strange land is stressful.

As we walk out of baggage claim, there's a bearded guy standing there holding a sign with Dan Boyd's name on it. Dan's right behind me and the two of us meet Fred Raposo, our Hollywood-supplied driver. Hollywood is the best-selling cigarette in Brazil, and the sponsor of Mauricio Gugelmin's PacWest car and this race, the Rio 400.

Fred describes our surroundings on the drive from the airport to the hotel. Rio is famous for spectacular, rounded-rock mountains, and a tall one right at the entrance to the bay is called the Sugarloaf. Fred says the reason there are so many good Brazilian drivers is the roads of Brazil are dangerous and drivers have to be skilled to survive. I notice the lane markers don't seem to be honored. If a driver wants to straddle one and block both lanes for a while, it's tolerated. Traffic moves swiftly and then comes to a dead halt.

Fred is a pleasant surprise. He's lived in the United States and Canada and follows racing, Formula 1 and Indy cars, closely. One of his first questions is about the CART/IRL split. We have to admit we're as puzzled about it as he is.

When we arrive at the Intercontinental Hotel, we don't have to check in. They herd us into a room and hand out our room keys. Dan and I room together, which turns out to be the battle of the monster snores.

The Sugarloaf

Our first event in Rio is a Hollywood press conference at noon Tuesday at the Sugarloaf where Mauricio Gugelmin; Steve Fusek, PacWest vice president; and Kirk Russell, CART vice president of competition, join Hollywood people in talking to the media about the Rio 400. We ride a gondola from the ground to the first level of the Sugarloaf. A PacWest Reynard show car is on display for photographs during the press conference. They moved it up here by hanging it from the bottom of the gondola, and pictures of the car dangling in mid-air make all the papers down here and some in the U.S.

Hollywood Press Conference at the Sugarloaf

The Brazilian people at the press conference speak Portuguese, of course, but I notice that Mauricio sounds different. He enunciates his words clearer and spaces the words out instead of running them together as the others do. I ask him about that after the formal proceedings are finished. "I try to speak slowly and clearly," he tells me. "I work on that whether I'm speaking English or Portuguese." Mauricio constantly impresses me with his depth and the analytical way he goes about everything he does.

Kirk Russell tells me he's impressed by the improvements made at the track here. "The people here are very creative," he says. "They engineered and built this track in only five months last year. This year they've repaved parts of it and it's as good a job as you're going to get with the equipment they have. When you dump asphalt into the paver right out of a truck you get variations in the density of the pavement. When it's rolled you get an uneven surface. The best equipment, not available here, has a shuttle buggy that travels across the hopper to evenly distribute the material going into the paver."

After the press conference we get in another tram that takes us to the higher peak. The view is spectacular, and everyone takes photos.

Fred on Brazilian Culture

On the way back to the hotel Fred explains Brazilian culture. "We don't fight; we find ways to work around problems. If you have a business and some government guy is making a problem, you don't denounce him. You make him a business partner. Brazil is an organized chaos, but we don't revolt. We don't go to war. We don't let things get that bad."

"How did that culture develop?" I ask.

"I don't know," Fred says. "But we're different because we were conquered by the Portuguese. The Spanish were killers. They made people hate them. The Portuguese brought slaves from Africa, and they had a lot of babies with the slaves and the natives. That's a big part of us, so many cultures mixed together. Maybe it's more difficult to revolt when all the people are the same, all mixed up."

He also talked about the late Ayrton Senna. "The 1980s were very bad for Brazil, with inflation and a bad economy. But there was Senna, the very best in a high-tech sport. You could turn on the TV at 9 a.m. on a Sunday, and he would be there winning and waving the Brazilian flag. He became everyone's brother and son. When he was killed, it got very quiet here. For weeks everyone was down. The country took that very hard."

Caipirinhas

That night Hollywood feeds us all at Porcao's (Porky's), where Brazilian beef is the specialty. There is a salad bar, and I eat some of the prepared salads and veggies, breaking my resolve to eat only cooked foods. They serve the beef on skewers, cutting off slices directly onto your plate. Mauricio tells us to go easy on the cheap meat coming around first, and wait until they bring out the good stuff. It was worth the wait. Although more fibrous and salty than U.S. beef and a little wild tasting, the meat is juicy and delicious.

At Porcao's we drink our first caipirinha of many on this trip. Pronounced cai-per-rain-ya, this drink is a mixture of a cheap local liquor called cachaca (ca-shash-ah) and sugar on top of lime slices that have been mashed in the bottom of the glass. It's a potent drink that goes down easy and causes next-day headaches among the undisciplined.

WEDNESDAY

This is a nice hotel. The restaurant next to the pool, called the Verandah Cafe, is open for breakfast at 7 a.m. The sun is coming up over the mountains. It's about 75 degrees and humid; comfortable as long as you're sitting still. The coffee is strong but a different taste than I'm used to. Even with ear plugs, I didn't get much sleep. Dan's snoring is very loud.

I continue to eat the fruit here with no problem, but I'm drinking only sterilized or bottled water. A flock of small birds swoops around on the verandah, devouring any crumbs on the ground. The bolder ones fly into the restaurant and perch on the table until shooed away.

THE TRACK

Fred drives us out to the track for the first time on Wednesday. On the way he tells us about the favelas, communities of shacks put together by poor people who live off the books, paying no taxes but getting no benefits of government either. He points out a small favela near the track called the Bernie Ecclestone [Formula 1 czar] favela. Fred laughs and says poverty and excess go well together.

Inside the Team Office at the Track

When we get to the track we have to go through several checkpoints, some manned by soldiers with automatic weapons. After a drive over a bridge that crosses the backstraight, Fred lets us off at a gate where our CART hardcards get us through into the paddock.

Dan was here last year and he's amazed at the improvements. The portable offices for each team are shaded by tents and air conditioned and have refrigerators, 110-volt power, and phones. Cases of bottled water are stacked high all over the paddock and in each team's garage area. The daily temperatures will reach the mid-80s instead of over 100 degrees like last year, when the race was a month earlier in the heat of their summer.

I decide to walk the course to get a look at the pavement and the new barriers, so I head out toward Turn 1 from the pit lane. The barriers are pretty simple really, tywrap-banded tires held together with wire mesh. The outside surface of the barrier is a vertical face 4 feet high made up of three layers of Goodyear Super Thor conveyor belting. Bolts through the belting anchor to steel cables that attach to the concrete wall. A blue plastic material lies on top of the tires and tucks in front and rear. The desired result is a barrier that will decelerate a crashing car without bouncing it back out into traffic. During the upcoming weekend a driver is bound to test the barriers, and if they work, this kind of system should be considered at all high-speed tracks, especially ovals. They do need some room however, so narrow tracks would have to be widened.

The Crash Barrier, a Great Idea

It's a 1.864-mile course in a D-shape, so Turns 1 and 4 are more acute than the relatively gentle Turns 2 and 3. The backstraight takes a long time to walk. Some media people are getting rides in a black Mercedes-Benz. Mauricio is driving it, and he waves at me as he speeds past.

When I get to Turn 4, I find about 40 people finishing up the last stretch of barriers. I talk to a supervisor named Nelson who tells me his company has been working on the track project since 1995. He grabs the outer layer of the barrier and shakes it, saying proudly, "Treeple protection." It's hot out here, high 80s at least, and I'm drinking water constantly.

Back in the paddock about 12:30 I find the PacWest crew is about to finish up and head back to the hotel. Some of the guys are talking about golf, others about a beer by the pool. Fred isn't in the parking lot so one of the other drivers calls him on a cell phone and he's here a half-hour later.

Going back to the hotel Dan gets some photos of some of the Hollywood signage along the roads. At a spot near the beach just short of the hotel we see some hang gliders landing in the sand. Fred points to some mile-high peaks toward the east where these guys launch into their glide, eventually landing right where we're standing. What a country of contrasts. People with cars and hang gliders living among people who have nothing.

The hang-glider guys are upset because they can't fly for the next four days. Helicopter traffic to and from the racetrack will be heavy, and the local authorities have banned their flights.

Go-Karts

On Wednesday evening Hollywood has another treat for the team. This time it's an evening at the Nelson Piquet indoor go-kart track. Some of the PacWest guys are very good karters, and the competition is intense.

My turn comes in the second group. Driving suits and helmets are provided. We lap the twisty track for 5 minutes, and then they form us into a grid and start a 20-minute race. I get going pretty quick, but the faster guys lap me easily. My concentration is fine at first, but after a while I start to get tired. I look at the scoreboard and see we're only on lap 18. I remember the first group had done 32 laps. I hang on until the end. Luckily I fit the seat pretty well or I wouldn't have had the strength in my arms and shoulders to finish.

For me it's just as much fun watching, so I concentrate on the food and beer and don't go out again. Mauricio and Mark drive one race with some of the better drivers, including Peter Schultz, one of the owners of the kart track, and Flavio de Andrade, president of Souza Cruz, manufacturer of Hollywood cigarettes. Chris Griffis, Tim Neff, Chris Jaynes, and Daryl Fox are the smoothest drivers among the crew. Mauricio wins the feature race.

Later in the Intercontinental Hotel bar Jim Hamilton tells me the Rio track is actually pretty bumpy. I didn't think so during my walk. He had a ride in that M-B I saw Mauricio driving. "The car was lowered and stiff-sprung. I could feel the bumps." We have a few more caipirinhas. They go down easily and help me get to sleep. I need some help, considering Dan's snoring.

THURSDAY

Sitting at a white-cloth-covered table having coffee in the Verandah Cafe, I have to admit this is a beautiful part of the world. The sky is as blue as it gets, and the breeze is sweet with flower blossoms. I feel tired from a lack of sleep, but still no diarrhea. My coffee cup never gets empty; the service here is exceptional. I don't want to know what the room costs. Oh well, I only have to pay half.

On the way to the track Fred tells us the story of how Rio came to be. God made Rio a perfect place: beautiful scenery, balmy climate, and no floods or earthquakes. People living elsewhere were upset and scolded God for being unfair. "Wait 'til you see the people I'm going to put there," he said.

"That might say something about our self image," is Fred's comment.

At the track, car preparations go on even though the drivers won't get on the track until tomorrow. The PacWest guys are all talking about the karting last night. On the road the crews don't often have time for fun outings, so this was a rare treat. They are all either sore or hungover or both. I'm a little sore.

In the media center I pick up a memo from the race organization providing the teams with the fax number of a florist in Miami so people can send flowers on Mother's Day, this coming Sunday. That's very thoughtful.

Goodyear has a logistics problem. A shipping mix-up caused its Formula 1 tires to come here and some of the CART tires arrived at Monaco. Some panicky air freight will solve it all.

It's almost 1 p.m. when one of the engines turns over for the first time. Chris Griffis and Gavin Hamilton spin over the 18-car engine with no spark plugs in it. When the oil pressure gets up they put the plugs in and fire it up.

I see one new techie trick on Mauricio's primary car. They've fabricated a different waste-gate exhaust pipe so it exits on top of the diffuser instead of at the side. This allows a stainless-steel panel inside the left rear tire that cleans up the airflow in this area.

This modification also allows a more narrow rear track. There has to be 4 inches between the tires and any bodywork, and the old waste-gate exhaust was in the way. I assume these are drag-reduction improvements. They only made enough parts to fit the two primary cars, so the T-cars don't have this new mod.

This is a high-speed track, so they've come up with some other aero mods also. The ski-jumps are on the front wings, but the fences on the bottom and rear of the front-wing endplate are only half-length. I'm told the rear wing is also a low-drag version of the regular Reynard parts.

Other team's cars have various combinations of these wing variables, but I don't see the waste-gate exhaust pipe on any but PacWest cars. That's an in-house part, not Reynard.

TALK WITH MARK BLUNDELL

Back at the hotel pool I ask Mark if he has time for a talk. He does, so we go to a quiet corner of the pool area and I set up my recorder. He's in khaki shorts and a blue polo shirt. Mark has brown eyes and short, dark brown hair.

Paul: "The conversations between you and Jim are a lot different than the ones between Mauricio and Andy. They've worked together for a long time. And the whole driver-engineer relationship must be very personal."

Mark: "Yeah, they're going to be different conversations anyway because me and Mauricio [sounds like muritzio] are very different in our descriptive way of transferring our information across about the car. We've also got a different situation. One, where you've got a guy who's worked with an engineer for a very long period of time, and another where you've got two people who are new to each other. They're got to get to know each other very quickly on a personal level and on a technical level. Those two points are the key elements between a driver and an engineer. You have to build up a personal relationship and each get the other's thought pattern and process in his head. In the future, hopefully, Jim will even know from my tone of voice or the expression on my face inside the crash helmet when things are good, bad, or indifferent. You know?"

Paul: "Right. I've already seen some of that. I can hear that myself. It's got to be tremendously difficult to be out there doing what you're doing and also feel what the car is doing. How do you go about that? What are you feeling?"

Mark: "That's part of being a race driver, I guess, is the capacity to take on board so much information over laps and laps. And at the same time you have to extract the maximum from the machine. There are two processes. There's one which is the pure driving element. You're physically and mentally optimizing yourself inside the car to drive. The process of when to brake and when to turn in. At the same time you're also taking in information as well. It's a natural process. It becomes easier with experience. A driver manufactures it over time. There's a difference in drivers. Some are sort of naturally gifted at trying to take that on board and explaining it and some have to work at it. It's difficult to explain."

Paul: "You're feeling several things, I guess, the varying forces from the steering wheel. What about tire deflection vs. chassis roll? Can you tell the difference?"

Mark: "Yeah. The whole aspect of the car, you're deciphering information what's comin' back to you all the time. You're feeling feedback from the steering wheel, whether that's motion or load; and you're feeling the seat of the pants, which is one of the best senses you got out there. There's audible tones. The car and you need to become as one. Then it becomes a lot easier. When things are not going well it's difficult to get there and then the handling problems get too great and you can't get your head around it and it comes to the point where you try to overdrive and maybe the engineer gets frustrated as well. But when it all gels together you can really use your senses to define the problems at the minutest point."

Paul: "Have you found there's one particular thing about the car that has to be right before you can get comfortable?"

Mark: "You go for your basics. You need to be in the ballpark on aerodynamics and ride-height wise you're in the ballpark. There's nothing worse than driving a car that's touching down every few seconds. And there's nothing worse than riding around in a car that's mighty high. You're losing efficiency from that point, increasing roll and so forth. There's probably a couple of key points to your diving style which you won't actually veer away from too much. It's a combination of learning a car with an engineer. Over a period of time you'll sort of build in those standardized issues for you as a driver.

"As an example, for me, I drive with quite a lot of low-speed bump in my dampers, which other guys don't like. My style of driving dictates that I need to have that for the balance of the car. I don't like too much front flap in the car. I can drive with a little bit less front flap than Mauricio does. There's a pattern of things like that."

Paul: "When did you start racing?"

Mark: "Racing full time was back in 1984 when I started in single-seaters in Formula Ford 1600. My bigger car days really started in '87 in Formula 3000 in Europe. Then I got into sports car racing in '89 and '90. And '89 was my breakthrough in becoming the test driver at Williams. I did quite a lot of miles and worked with a great bunch of guys. People like Patrick Head and other people with a wealth of experience. I learned a great deal.

"In Formula 1 I've got a hell of a lot of test miles. That's not actually appliable in certain areas to what I drive now. It's a learning period for me to adapt to an Indy car. Primarily, the Formula 1 car was a lot more efficient aerodynamically. It hid a lot of the problems. The Indy car is actually a lot more balanced mechanically. We didn't do near as much damper work in F1 as we do now with Indy cars. That takes a bit of getting used to."

Paul: "What other difference do you see between F1 and Indy cars?"

Mark: "From a driving standpoint, my style still needs to be adapted. I'm used to driving a very nimble, precise, light car with immediate power when I ask for it and immediate turn-in and pretty much no roll in comparison to what I've got now. The Indy car is a lot heavier. It doesn't stop as efficiently. It's on steel brakes, not carbon. It's a turbo, so there's a degree of lag there, not much, but it's there. It's a heavier, clumsier car in a way. It's got a quite different feel to it. It's taken me a while to adapt in style and evaluate what the best setup is for me."

Paul: "Are you learning in big leaps?"

Mark: "You never stop learning. I'm always learning."

Paul: "At Homestead and again at Surfers, it seemed that you weren't happy with the car all during practice, but when it came time for qualifying, you did very well."

Mark: "That's a clear factor of us not tuning the car in quickly enough. Some of that's just a case of me and Jim not gelling as a package. We're trying to feel each other out. But when it comes to qualifying it's a case of throwing caution to the wind and hanging everything out. It's not the best way to go about it."

Paul: "What else can you say about the engineer/driver relationship?"

Mark: "It needs to be a tight, close relationship. One of the problems is that my technical description or explanation of what's going on with the car is very different to what Jim's ever heard. Straightaway we have some differences there, which is kind of funny in a way, because we're talking about the same thing, but in fact we're talking two different languages. That's a big issue. It sounds crazy but it's a simple thing and it takes time to get that understood.

"The other point is the driver is quite a key guy in terms of motivation and focus for everybody around him. From Jim all the way down through the team they're all part of my team and you've got to keep yourself head-high and focused and draw everybody along with you. Whether you're having a good time or a bad time, it's something you've got to take on board."

Paul: "What did it mean to you to get Motorola as a sponsor?"

Mark: "For me it's a great situation to have a big corporate sponsor like that. The team has improved a great deal. It's a credit to Bruce and the whole team. I'm part of that team and I'm very happy about it. To a certain extent it's increased the level of pressure and awareness of what's going on with a team. It's not just on my shoulders. It's on everyone's shoulders. We all want to go out there and perform at our best. It's a business. It's run on a business basis."

Paul: "Do you think that Motorola is a good fit for you personally?"

Mark: "As a company and what they stand for, I hope I'm a good ambassador for them. I come from the U.K. but I'm driving in the U.S. and four other countries for the championship. Motorola has a presence in all those countries. Ultimately I'm going out there to do the best job I can for the team and the sponsor and that's inside the car and outside of it."

Paul: "What about your helmet design?"

Mark Blundell's
Helmet

Mark: "I requested this design when I went to a helmet painter early in my career. I wanted something that would be noticable. The colors are all my favorite colors: red, yellow, and blue. The big thing is the initials MB on the top which I actually wanted because of the dream that one day I would race at Monaco and the photographers take shots down on the Leow's hairpin. They can see the initials. There's some great action shots of people there. Sometimes the top of a helmet is space that's wasted anyhow. The other thing that came in years afterward is the words, 'The will to win,' which is a motto my late grandfather used to say to me, 'You must have the will to win.' When he passed away I put that on there to remember him. It'll always be on there."

More Caipirinhas

Jim Walsh, director of worldwide operations for Motorola, hosts a feed for the crew Thursday night. We eat at another beef place, Maurio's, consuming more caipirinhas and beef. To me it's pretty classy of the Motorola people to show this kind of appreciation for the crew. Jim is a fun guy, and he likes to be around racing and racing people the same as myself. The beef here is not as salty as at Porcao's. I like it better.

Since we're being driven to and from the restaurants, we don't have to worry about drinking and driving. Many caipirinhas are consumed. Somebody abstaining from a round was in danger of "going a lap down." Mark Blundell is good-natured about some teasing from his crew. Actually, he doesn't have much choice. On the drive back to the hotel our van driver is a small, smiling Oriental lady the crew has taken to calling "Mom."

FRIDAY

Another beautiful day in paradise. In the Verandah Cafe at 7 a.m. I watch one of the waitresses throw bread crumbs to the flock of birds to keep them from bothering the guests. A couple of guys clean the pool area. Surprise; it's supposed to be warm again today. Fred comes for us at 8 a.m. and drives Dan and myself to the track.

Pace-Car Ride

Ken Lowe, the PPG pace-car coordinator, puts me in the Corvette with Margy Eatwell driving. She drives us out onto the black asphalt and accelerates hard to Turn 1, slowing there and then getting on the throttle for the no-lift Turn 2. Jim is right; I can feel the bumps, especially in Turn 4 where Margy has to brake hard.

As we go down the long frontstraight I see 122 mph on the speedometer. The car feels very forgiving. She brakes very hard before turning in for Turn 1, and I can feel the slip angles increase when she gets back on the gas. "It goes into a drift easy," Margy says. "You can scrub speed or accelerate with no surprises." This is a fun ride.

First Practice

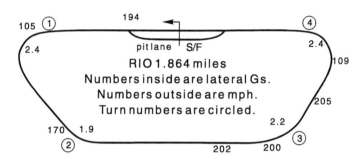

The first practice session starts promptly at 9:45 a.m. and is scheduled for two 1-hour sessions ending at noon. There are no support races here; the CART cars are the whole show. Nazareth qualifying times determine who's in the two practice sessions, so Mauricio is in the second, or fast-guy, group. His crew is practicing pit stops. They simulate an air-jack failure and Dave Jacobs uses a hand jack to raise the rear of the car.

As Mark heads out on track, Al Bodey tells him to bed in the new brake pads. Almost immediately, Andre Ribeiro hits the new barrier in Turn 1, causing a yellow flag. He's OK. When Mark comes in he says the track is dusty and bumpy into Turn 4. "The car is touching down hard and the ride is very harsh." Jim looks the tires over carefully and tells the crew to raise the car four flats at the rear and two at the front.

After some more laps in the car Mark says it's still touching down quite hard. Mark wants the tire pressures to show up on his dash. Casey says he'll fix it between sessions. Jim decides to go to stiffer springs at the rear. About 10:15 Mark goes out with a lot of wheelspin. The sky is hazy today, making it difficult to see the mountains that ring this valley.

A yellow flag for a track inspection brings Mark back in. He's still saying the car is touching down quite hard. He says the balance is good but there's a general lack of grip.

Jim makes another spring change and raises the car nine flats at the rear and four at the front. The starting setup must have been way off. Mark wants a gear-ratio change also because the car hits the rev limiter before he gets to top speed. Jim says they don't have time now.

Mark goes on course again and gets his lap times down into the 42-second area, about 160 mph average. Alex Zanardi and Parker Johnstone are fast in the session. Mark is P5. When Mark comes back in he says the car is more stable. "I'd like to drop the tire pressures and then try the other tires." Jim raises the car further, two flats at the rear and one at the front.

Mark goes back out with 18 minutes to go in the session. Zanardi is lapping in the 41s. After a couple more stints on the track interrupted by yellow flags, Mark has driven a lap of 41.89 seconds. After some more adjustments and a new set of tires, Mark turns a 41.36 and then a 41.26, which is his best lap of the session.

The session gets the checkered flag and Mark comes into the pit box saying, "No way I can keep up with that Honda [Zanardi]. I get a car length on him going into a corner and he gets a car and a half coming out. That's grunt!" Zanardi's best lap is a 40.783 for P1 followed by Adrian

Fernandez, Parker, Roberto Moreno subbing for Christian Fittipaldi, and Mark. The safety team goes to look at the tire barrier that Ribeiro hit, pronouncing it OK.

Mauricio's session gets a green flag at 11:30. He's out right away and Andy Brown does a radio check and then says, "Let's just do this slow and calm."

In reply Mauricio screams into the radio, "Ahhhhhhhhhiiii!"

After a few laps he comes in and switches cars. I don't know which one is the primary car. The back-up or T-car should have an "x" on the rear-wing endplate after the car number, but I don't see an "x" on either. A yellow flag stops the session. The safety crews go on course to inspect for fluids. I hear Control say, "The 99-car rear is wet. We're looking for gear oil."

Mauricio goes out again when the course goes back green. After a few laps he comes in, and Andy asks him how the car feels.

"Pretty good. I'm just touching on a few bumps."

Andy: "How's the traction out of the corners?"

Mauricio: "Good."

Andy: "Do you want to go for stiffer rear springs? That will give us a lower ride-height."

Mauricio: "Go for it."

Andy: "How are the skids, Jimmy?"

After getting the information about the skid plates, Andy tells the crew to come down five flats at the rear. Mauricio goes back out.

They go stiffer on the rear springs again later in the session and continue to fine-tune the ride height. With about 15 minutes to go in the session Mauricio is P13 with a lap of 41.02 seconds. Michael Andretti has the best time of 40.222 seconds.

Mauricio turns a 40.745 for P2 and comes in for new tires. Michael is still P1 followed by Mauricio, Paul Tracy, Zanardi, and Greg Moore. Mark has been bumped down to P18.

Andy says, "We're at a point where we should raise the rear one flat." Two gallons of fuel go in and Mauricio goes back out on track. He improves to 40.476 to hold P2 behind Michael. That's an average speed of 165 mph. They're hitting 195 top speed on the backstraight. On the way in to pit lane Mauricio runs the car out of fuel so they can fill up the fuel cell and see exactly how much fuel the car can draw from it. Russ Cameron says, "Good session."

Race Control

Two 45-minutes practice session are scheduled starting at 2:30. I had asked Wally Dallenbach if it would be OK for me to come to Race Control for this session so I could see how they do things. He said fine, so just before the session starts, I walk across the frontstraight and climb over a barrier and through the fence. After a climb up a lot of stairs I come to a small room at the top of the grandstands. This is where Race Control resides. Besides Wally, there's Kirk Russell, vice president of competition; Jack Hodge, operations coordinator; John Friede, safety coordinator; Gary Barnard, chief course observer; and Irene Chambers, recorder.

Jack Hodge is the voice of Control. He's the guy I hear on the scanner giving the primary instructions to the safety teams and worker chiefs at each corner. Jack has a cold and periodically pushes some kind of throat lozenge past his white mustache. He's trying not to lose his voice, which is even more growly today than usual. John Friede dispatches the safety trucks. We can see the entire track from here.

These people sit on office chairs along a desk-high shelf under a window that covers the entire front of this room. I'm standing behind them, looking out the window over their heads. To my right is a bank of TV monitors showing all the timing and scoring information plus the TV feed. The room itself is narrow, only about 8 feet deep from window to back wall, and about 20 feet wide from the entrance door on my right toward Turn 1 and the window at the other end looking toward Turn 4. Wally lounges nonchalantly on an office chair off to the left, reading. He, Gary, and Kirk talk together while the other three people are speaking into microphones.

At 2:40 p.m. the session goes green. Mark Blundell is in this first session so I hear the 18-car conversation on the scanner as well as the CART communications. The difference today is I can watch the CART people that I usually only hear. In addition to the corner workers and safety teams, there is a Timing and Scoring group in another room nearby and, down in the pit lane, pit marshals are the communications link between the teams and the people in this room. Running a race in a fair, safe, timely manner requires a lot of people communicating effectively and making quick decisions.

Mark is having problems with the electronic dash in the car. It sounds like it's actually loose and moving around. He also says he doesn't like the feel of the steering. At 3 o'clock Mark says, "Get the other car ready. I can't drive this one. It rattles the shit out of me." He switches cars as de Ferran turns a 40.289-seconds lap to go to P1.

Wally continues to sprawl in his chair and look around as if what's going on down on the track is the furthest thing from his mind. In reality he sees and hears every detail happening around him. Now and then he asks a specific question or gives a specific instruction.

Mark ends up P9 in the session with a lap of 41.040 seconds. Various mechanical and electronic gremlins limited him to eight laps total in those 45 minutes, which is not good. Just before the checkered flag Wally says, "We've got 15 minutes between sessions. I'd like a thorough track inspection."

The second practice session, the fast guys, starts at 3:51 p.m. Wally has been bothered by the number and position of some photographers in Turn 4. He calls Mike Zizzo and asks him to come to Race Control. When Mike gets here Wally points down to Turn 4 and says there's so many photographers down there that they're blocking the corner workers' line of sight. Mike says he'll take care of it and leaves.

Mauricio was out on track at the green flag and he comes back in, saying the car is better than this morning, "but it's touching down hard." Andy raises the rear two flats and lowers the front one flat.

Greg Moore is now under last year's track record with a lap at 39.897 seconds. Mauricio is in P19 with a time of 40.978. There's a yellow for a track inspection after Paul Tracy has a puncture. The pit marshal says it looks like the tire ran over a bolt. They find a bolt on the frontstraight near Turn 4.

Andy suggest a rear roll-center change, but the track goes green again and Mauricio goes out. He improves to P16 and comes back in. They make the roll-center change and some shock changes. Andy asks, "Is push our biggest problem?"

Mauricio: "Yes. It's better, but still too much."

At 4:31 Mauricio drives out of the pit box again. The monitor shows Greg Moore still in P1 followed by Michael Andretti, Richie Hearn, and Roberto Moreno. Mauricio comes in saying it's still pushing. Andy adds some low-speed bump to the outside rear shock and low-speed rebound at the inside rear. I don't understand how that change works, but I guess they do.

Here in Race Control, Gary Barnard is upset because one of his observers said "yellow, yellow, yellow" and scared everybody. That's the call if there's a crash, but there was no crash at that time.

Mauricio comes in for fresh tires. He's in P14 when he goes back out at 4:45 with 5 minutes to go in the session. I watch the monitor as he reels off the laps starting with a 43.062, then 40.707, 40.266, and 40.025. That gets him to P6. He turns a 40.144, then 39.929 for P5. He runs out of fuel as the session ends.

Michael Andretti jumped to P1 with a lap of 39.626. He's followed by Zanardi, Moreno, Bobby Rahal, and Al Unser Jr. Mauricio is pushed down to P8. Mark is P21, a second and a half off the pace.

After the session is over I thank the people in Race Control for letting me watch, and then go back down the stairs and across the track. The PacWest cars are back in the garage going on the setup pads. When the crew starts to wind down, Dan and I find Fred and he takes us back to the hotel.

Later in the bar at the Intercontinental, John Creak (we call him Creakie now) says that Mauricio is serious about getting the pole tomorrow. He wants to make a splash for the home crowd. They're going so far as to take the in-car camera out of the car to lower the weight; more likely to put the weight lower in the car. Hollywood is paying for that camera so the team had to ask them to forego the exposure during the qualifying broadcast. They agreed.

One of the Ilmor guys tells me they've got three special development engines here this weekend for qualifying. Two go to the Penske drivers, of course, but the third goes to Mauricio.

That's a big deal. They could have run it on Mercedes' transient dyno at Stuttgart, but decided to track test it here. To me that's a huge vote of confidence in Mauricio and the PacWest team.

SATURDAY

My shower and shave are done by 6 a.m., and Dan and I are in the car with Fred at 6:30. I tell Fred that the people here seem broad-shouldered and healthy. "That's South Rio people," he says. "The people in the favelas are scrawny and undernourished." Security is tighter at the track today. The car gets in the paddock gate only to let us off, and Fred has to go back out over the bridge.

We left the hotel too early for me to get coffee by the pool, but there is some good coffee in the team office and some squares of cake. We actually have a waiter-person who makes sure the coffee and cake are there, as well as the food later at lunch. I can feel the coffee hype me up, but the lack of sleep is telling. I feel tired, but have no stomach problems, thankfully.

In the PacWest garage I learn the over-and-under waste-gate exhaust modification isn't being used here. They think it's too fragile to take a chance. That makes me wonder if running at the pointy end of the field is pressuring the team toward conservatism.

Allen McDonald tells me they consider reliability to be a high priority. "I end up arbitrating between Jim and Andy. They want to make the cars faster, but track time and finishing the race is important. I'm really a race engineer so it's a step up for me to look at the bigger picture."

Martin Lewis, Mark's PR guy along with Alison Hill, makes sure I know about the problems they had with the setup yesterday. It seems to me there's a plot on to replace Jim with Allen. It's always disappointing to see politics get involved. Jim is trying hard and wants Mark to succeed. Chemistry, however, between a driver and his engineer is extremely important. I guess the pressure is on Jim now.

Steve Challis, Greg Moore's engineer, is upset they didn't get P1 in practice yesterday. "We had a few minutes to go and could have gotten P1, but Greg got caught behind Jimmy [Vasser]. We learned about how the car felt in traffic though, and that was probably more useful than P1."

At 8:05 a.m. engines are warming, a familiar sound now. It's cloudy and supposed to rain this afternoon or tomorrow. It would be very bad if it rained on race day. With all the flights back scheduled on Sunday night and Monday morning, they'd have to get the race in somehow.

Most of the cars are in the pit lane at 8:45. The stands across the straight are about 25% full. The music is very loud. The beat is so big I can feel it in my chest. People are dancing in the stands.

An engineer for one of the Toyota-powered teams comes by and tells me they blew six engines yesterday, all for different reasons. "Mechanical failures?" I ask.

"Some, yeah;" he says, "some not."

"Why would they want to do their basic development work at a race and blow them all up right in front of everybody?"

"We're still working that out for ourselves, at the moment," he says with a straight face. I have to laugh. The inscrutable Japanese. Who knows what lurks in the caverns at a big company like Toyota? It's an American failing that we believe everybody thinks like us. They're in the third year of a 20-year plan. What if a few motors blow up?

Practice

There is a group of Firestone engineers talking together so I join them, and we get to talking about how they came to work for the company. Dwayne Joyner, the Firestone compounder, tells me he has a degree in oceanography, but couldn't find a job doing that. So he got a chemistry degree and went to work in Akron at Firestone.

"Little Brett" Schilling has a chemistry degree and was recruited out of school by Firestone. Keith Shrieve is one of the few tire engineers who's switched companies, in his case from Goodyear to Firestone.

I can hear Control asking someone to get the promoter to turn the PA system down. It's interfering with normal conversation. This is probable evidence of a culture clash.

Mark's Group

Mark's in the first practice group. He seems much more in charge today, asking questions about the sequence of tire sets going on the car. The session starts promptly at 9 a.m. Dario Franchitti spins and hits a tire barrier, but not hard, causing a yellow flag. Mark comes in saying the course is very dusty. "We'll wait 'til some of that crap blows off."

There's a cut in the left-rear tire on Mark's car. "Big Bret" Hrivnak, the larger of the two Firestone engineers named Bret(t),

Pit Lane During First Practice Session

says it's too bad a cut to use, so they switch to a new set.

The course goes green again at 9:09. Mark comes back in after a few laps. "It's loose, and I can't downshift into fourth. The gearbox was fantastic yesterday. The track's slick; shitty really. The car turns in good but there's not enough grip."

Jim asks about the brakes, and Mark replies, "That's OK, except for the gears. It's not touching down. Can we lower the car?"

Jim: "I'd wait for better track conditions."

Mark insists, and Jim tells the crew to lower the car one flat all around. Jim seems less aggressive about making the car faster, taking cues from Mark instead of suggesting action. Tim Love, the gearbox guy also called "Dr. Love" or just "Doc," messes with the shift linkage. Mark goes out on track after a long yellow flag and spins in Turn 1, lightly contacting the barrier.

"Something is broken," Mark says on the radio. "There's a lot of fluid."

I hear Control say the car was losing fluid before impact. A wrecker comes motoring up the pit lane with the battered 18-car on the hook and the driver in the cab. Mark gets out and the wrecker goes off toward the garage with the car still on the hook.

Butch jogs toward the garage with several guys who will start repairing the primary car. Butch comes right back with the fitted seat and some of the cockpit pads. Mark gets in the 18x-car as soon as they have the seat installed. Someone says a coolant hose came loose in the right-hand sidepod, dumping fluid on the right-rear tire. A yellow flag stops the session, giving the 18-crew time to get Mark ready to go in the T-car.

Mark goes out but exceeds the pit lane speed limit, getting a black flag. Yellows continue to interrupt the track session and CART uses the two-thirds rule, saying this and the next group will only get 40 minutes instead of a full hour. When Mark returns to the track, there's 15 minutes left.

When he comes back in, Mark has a host of problems, including a loose dash unit. "There's too much front grip," he says. "I can't get on the throttle. I'm nervous the rear will get away from me."

Jim makes some changes and Mark goes back on track in P8 with 5 minutes to go. Scott Pruett is P1 with a lap of 39.800 seconds. One of the Toyota-engined cars blows up and causes another yellow flag. Mark comes in saying maybe the last changes had some benefit, "but the car is too pointy."

Jim: "Let's lift the front one flat."

Mark goes out again, but another spin stops the session. I can feel a few raindrops, and Control says, "Let's keep up on that moisture, guys."

Mark suggests they scuff tires. "There's too much traffic to get a time."

Jim: "Might as well." That's what they do with the remaining few minutes. The practice session ends at 10:24. Mark only had six timed laps, with a best of 41.104 seconds, 2 seconds off the pace.

A thorough track inspection between sessions takes a few minutes. I walk back to the garage area to see what's going on with the damaged 18-car. Allen McDonald and Russ Cameron have relinquished their management roles in favor of some hands-on work. They're removing the big pieces from the car and starting the tear-down that will be finished by the 18-crew when they return from pit lane. Russ tells me, "I saw some coolant dripping out of the sidepod before the car went out, but I thought it was just some that had puddled in the undertray."

Mauricio's Group

The session starts at 10:57. The sky is still cloudy, but the overcast seems lighter than when it was sprinkling. It's warm and humid, and there's no breeze. Mauricio goes out with Andy saying, "Can you warm up the oil a bit before we go to full throttle?"

Mauricio starts a series of laps on the track with adjustments in between. Mark Moore tells his guys, "Keep looking at those tires every time he comes in." They are very careful about punctures.

Mauricio comes in saying, "It feels pretty good, Andy, just a little loose and some mid-corner push."

Roscoe Changes Gears on Pit Lane

Andy: "We'll drop the rear and add some front rebound."

After another run on course Mauricio says, "I think I'm on the rev limiter too much."

Andy: "We could change gears but it would take 10 minutes. Let's work on the car as it is. We could make a shock change."

Mauricio: "Do it, Andy. The car is not far away. I get a flat drift now. I don't feel the roll."

A yellow for a track inspection gives them time to change gears, so Roscoe (Russell Grosshans) gets on his knees in front of the right-rear tire and opens up the access plate on the side of the transaxle. He's wearing gloves to keep from getting burned as he handles the hot gears. After changing out the sixth gear, he bolts the access hatch back on and moves his tools back to the pit wall.

A green flag restarts the session at 11:27 and Mauricio goes out to scuff a set of tires for qualifying with 10 minutes to go. Roberto Moreno is P1 in this session so far. Mauricio is seventh quick. He scuffs a couple of sets of tires and the crew practices pit stops when he comes back into the pit box. The session ends with Mauricio in P6. Mark is 29th. Mauricio drove 18 timed laps in contrast to Mark's six.

In the garage Mark's primary car is coming back together. The main problem was a broken transaxle tail case. The replacement was "painless," according to Russ Cameron. The tail case doesn't look like much but it's a magnesium casting with some significant machining. Its cost is $5,000, I'm told.

QUALIFYING: THE FIRST POLE

Qualifying starts about 1:45, only 15 minutes late. As usual all the cars are parked diagonally in pit lane, backed up against the wall next to the frontstraight. Michael Andretti's Swift is in line just ahead of Mauricio's car, so we get a good chance to look at it up close. David Bruns' design features some interesting packaging in the area just behind the engine. The in-line transmission allows everything to fit together very compactly. Maybe that allows cleaner airflow to the rear wing and the diffuser. The car seems to make a lot of downforce.

Adrian Reynard and his technical director, Bruce Ashmore, are here looking hard at the Swift themselves. I ask Bruce what he sees that impresses him, but he dodges the question amiably, which is one of his skills.

After about half of the field has had their runs, the order is Roberto Moreno, Bobby Rahal, Bryan Herta, and Paul Tracy. As the number of cars in line before Mauricio's dwindles, it's time to warm up the engine. It doesn't start on the first try so they check some switches and try again. It still won't start. I see some worried looks. On the third try the engine fires up, and the looks turn to relief.

As soon as Michael Andretti pulls away, Bruce Ashmore makes some notes on a pad. He must have seen something interesting. Bruce is a racecar designer so he can look at a car and know the specific purpose and trade-offs for every part down to each bolt and nut.

At 3:23 Mauricio pulls away. To get the pole he needs to beat Moreno's lap of 39.325 seconds. Moreno is Brazilian also, so he'd like some glory here at home himself.

I time Mauricio's laps with my stopwatch: 41.07, 39.60, 39.39, and 39.03. That should do it. "We've got Zanardi yet," Andy says. But Zanardi has an engine misfire and does not make a qualifying run. The pole belongs to Mauricio.

I congratulate Andy, who says, "Mo always has a lap in the bank."

Mauricio is mobbed by media people, mainly TV crews. Moreno comes to congratulate him, but I think Mauricio doesn't appreciate Moreno cutting in on his moment of glory. The rivalry continues in the press conference. Bobby Rahal is here by himself for a while during the time Mauricio and Moreno continue to talk to the TV people. Bobby tells us his story and leaves when Mo and Moreno get there. The two are a real contrast. Mo is handsome and aristocratic. Moreno is impish.

Mauricio is pleased with a new track record and his first pole, which is also the first pole for the PacWest team. He's grinning as he speaks to the media crowd over the noise of a nearby helicopter.

"I'm happy with the changes we made in our equipment. I've felt good since before Spring Training. I feel lucky to have these guys working on my car. Hollywood is a great sponsor."

Words from the Garage

Back in the PacWest garage, Martin tells me Mark is pissed about the hose clamp breaking and putting him into the barrier. I see Adrian Reynard talking to Blundell and then Bruce McCaw, the team owner. I guess he has to bear the brunt of their displeasure.

I ask several people how it feels to get their first pole position. "It's magic," Andy says. "The development motor was a big part of it."

Mark Moore says, "It's OK." An engine starts up, drowning out his voice. He stops and thinks until the noise subsides. "It's always good to get a pole, but it's better to do it here for Mo and the fans here. But it's just the pole, and only gives us a good starting position in the real war tomorrow."

"That motor was for qualifying only," Ando tells me. "It's a development piece, definitely not reliable enough for a race." The Penske drivers had those engines also. They qualified fifth and ninth.

I asked Ando how Mark feels about Mo's pole. "Left out, probably," is the answer.

Martin confirms that. "Mark is totally pissed off, completely knackered. Adrian Reynard said those hose clamps fail all the time. Bruce jumped all over him, but the team should be changing them."

"Pretty cool," Trevor Jackson says about the pole.

Chris Jaynes says, "It's all right. It's good to be up front to start the race."

At 5:10 p.m. Ando hands out the team's meal tickets for the food in the tent just outside of the paddock toward Turn 4. He tells the guys to stop what they're doing and go eat. The clouds are providing us with a beautiful sunset framed by the spectacular mountains toward the west. Tim Neff, Allen McDonald, Jim Hamilton, and Al Bodey are in a deep discussion. This is not a shining moment for the 18-car and Mark.

RACE DAY IN RIO

We were told yesterday that security would be tougher today, and Fred wouldn't be able to drive us into the paddock parking lot, leaving us with a half-mile walk from the lot outside the track. But one of the other Hollywood drivers had the right car pass, so Fred made a color copy of it and we have no problem this morning. Fred flashes the pass and smiles as the soldiers wave us through.

In the PacWest garage at about 7:30 a.m., I ask Mauricio about winning the pole. "To tell you the truth, I was expecting it from the test at Sebring last year. I knew it would happen. It's good timing that it happened here, and to be the first Mercedes and first Firestone car, that's really good for the team. They do all the work. They made this happen. I get to have all the fun."

Steve Fusek: "If we win today we can write our own ticket with Hollywood. A year ago Bruce told Flavio [de Andrade, of Hollywood] he'd make some changes and here we are on the pole. It couldn't be better timing for us. One of the Hollywood guys came down to pit lane after qualifying and gave me a big hug. He said, 'Should we write the check now?' "

John Creak says, "I heard what the Hollywood guy said and told him, 'Wait 'til tomorrow and we'll tell you how much.' "

Tim Neff, the PacWest shock guy, is pleased with the way his parts are performing. I don't know how any of his stuff works and I don't even ask. "It would be fine with me," Tim says, "if you don't put me in the book at all."

"Oh, I think you'll be in there, but I won't give away any of your secrets, if I ever figure out what they are."

"You should tell it like it is in this book," Tim says. "You'll probably get more respect for it that way. But you might not get back in here again."

I laugh. Tim knows a lot more about the team's warts than I do. "I'm going to record what I see and hear, and report on that," I tell Tim. "And I'll try to explain some things that fans might not understand. I'm not going to be mean, but I can't pull any punches either."

Tim shakes his head. "I don't envy you."

I ask Don Norton about the advantages of the developmental engine. Is the improvement a mechanical thing? "It's mechanical. We'll announce it at Portland. I was supposed to have Mo's engine on the Stuttgart dyno. We had three of them and we wanted somebody to run the third one. [It's understood that Penske Racing gets the first improvements. Roger Penske is a part owner of Ilmor.] The Firestone tires seem to be better than the Goodyears, so PacWest was an obvious choice.

"After the qualifying session I told Paul [Ray, Ilmor vp] I forgave Mo for taking my engine. But actually this is a better use of the engine. You get proof of concept where it counts — on the track. You can dyno them all day, but you don't really know 'til it gets in a car on the track."

Warm-Up

This session starts on time at 9 a.m. The whole team seems to emit a glow of energy. They seem more focused, more determined. After some laps on course both cars come back into their pit boxes. Mauricio says his car is lacking a little bit of support. Mark says his is too stiff. "There's some instability. The car is just too nervous for me on entry. It's not touching down much." Jim lowers the car one flat and takes out two turns of front wing.

There are only a few people in the stands. We've got a few clouds in the sky, but mainly it's sunny and warm with a nice breeze. After another turn on the track Mark is in for adjustments. He says he'll try the tim next time out. Maybe this is the magic doo-dad Tim Neff said is working well at this track. From the conversations it must be something that helps the car under braking. That would work at a track like this where the cars brake very hard from high speed.

I can hear cars shifting gears at different places on the frontstraight. Some guys shift about midway at Start/Finish and others make a shift further down the straight. This is a hybrid track. It looks like an oval, but drives somewhat like a road course.

I hear Andy tell Mark Moore, "Take the wickers off the fuglehorns." That might sound like doubletalk, but "fuglehorns" is what they call the extra airfoils on the outside corner of the sidepods just ahead of the rear tires. I look and yes, they do have wickers, also called Gurney flaps, on them.

Mark says, "Zanardi just pushed me up to the wall twice. Maybe he didn't see me, but I'm a bit pissed at him."

Mauricio gets out of his car with almost 10 minutes to go in the session. I guess he's happy with the car. Marty Reid, one of the TV pit announcers, comes over to talk to him. The session is over at 9:49. Moreno has the fast time of the session. Mark is in P11 and Mauricio P12.

The PA music is now an English-language ballad sung in harmony by a female group. It's got a big thunka-boom, boom, boom background. Even I could dance to that. It's a toe-tapper for sure.

Back in the garage, Butch says about Mark, "That boy is a racer. He'll go right to the front."

A few minutes later, about 11:15, a naked woman prances through the paddock. She's no beauty, but she draws a crowd. Colors of the Brazilian flag are painted across her behind around to her belly. A teeming horde of guys boils around her, fighting to get a glimpse. I push my way in to get a photo. I click off several shots, but don't get anything but the back of male heads and leering faces. Obviously a happening unique to this event.

Pre-Race Meeting

The regular pre-race meeting is in the team office with the usual crowd in attendance: Bruce, Mauricio, Jolene, Andy, Steve, Jim, Mark, Allen, Russ, Ando, Tim, Al, and Mark Moore. Butch is busy with his crew, working on Mark's car. Mark Moore will fill him in. Most of us are standing. A few sit in the cheap-looking office chairs that came with this portable building. Mauricio lays stretched out on the carpeting next to the back wall.

Ando starts the meeting. "The race is 133 laps, 238 miles. It'll take three stops, but could be done with two stops if there are enough yellow-flag laps. Fuel strategy is important. There were 11 yellow flags for 46 laps last year. The drivers need to pack up quickly for the restarts. And we need to be right-on with the calls to pit. This is a big track so we can't wait 'til the engine's sputtering. It won't make it to the pit lane."

Andy says it's possible to run the whole race full rich even if it goes green the whole way. "We'll start at 94% rich and go as lean as we can to maintain our track position. We'll stay out as long as we can." Al Bodey says the 18-car will start using a fuel slot that is 94% rich, and go to an 86% slot in traffic.

Steve Fusek and Tim Neff are going to the stands to spot. "Take some hats," Fusek says. "People have been begging for Hollywood hats all week. That'll help you get where you need to go." The meeting is over at 12:36 p.m.

In the garage they have the 17-car up on jacks, cycling it through the gears with the engine running. They installed a new gear position potentiometer, and they want to be sure it's reading correctly. Chris Jaynes is in the car operating the throttle and gearshift.

I haven't eaten anything so I go hunting in the office and find some breakfast cake and a Coke. Mark lies on the floor with a Sony Walkman on his chest and earphones on his head. His eyes are closed and he has his hands folded across his chest. He's singing softly to himself.

Back outside I talk to Jon Beekhuis, a TV pit reporter. Jon says he has a flight back to the U.S. tonight. "I've got a live show from Indy tomorrow." That reminds me there's a world there outside of this paddock. Practice for the Indy 500 starts tomorrow.

At the cars get towed down the pit lane for the pre-grid formation, some jet fighters, F5s I think, scream overhead at very low altitude, almost grandstand height. Jim Hamilton says, "They can do anything they want down here. They don't have safety regulations like we do."

Jim tells me the Goodyear-shod teams are having to scrape buildup off their tires. "They're a lot softer than the Firestones." He also admits he made a mistake on the initial setup for Friday practice. "I used a software program from outside the team. I won't make that mistake again."

THE RACE

The stands across from the pit lane are more than two-thirds full. Each stand shows a predominant color; one is red, another orange. The big sponsors down here must have bought large numbers of tickets for those grandstands and given the tickets, along with colorful T-shirts, to employees or customers.

The command to start engines comes at 12:58 p.m. After some pace laps the leaders are coming up the straight to the green flag, but some cars come together in Turn 4, causing the first yellow flag even before the start. I hear Mark say, "Maybe I'll be in the pool early."

Several cars are out of the race immediately. Andre Ribeiro comes into the pits for a new front wing. Parker Johnstone is involved in the crash but continues. The race restarts on lap four, with Mauricio leading Rahal and Moreno, but some contact among Tracy, Herta, and Moreno brings another caution period.

At the lap-10 restart Tracy spins all on his own, looking pretty silly. During the caution laps Ando cheers Mark on, "Get 'cher temps back up, pal. Use a lower gear." Two laps later the race starts again and Mauricio leads for a lap before Rahal passes him. Mauricio is having problems getting full boost.

Richie Hearn causes the next yellow flag, spinning in Turn 4 but not hitting anything. The race restarts on lap 28. The leaders are Rahal, Mauricio, Greg Moore, and de Ferran. Mark is up to 10th. During the yellow-flag laps the PacWest drivers are trying to conserve fuel. Al Bodey holds up a sign for Ando and he passes the word to Mark, "Fuel slot number five."

Russ tells Mauricio, "Get your nose up under Rahal's wing and get a tow."

Green-flag pit stops start about lap 40. Greg Moore and Mauricio pit together on lap 43 and have a drag race out of the pit lane. Greg wins and Mauricio loses several spots blending into traffic.

Mark spins on lap 49 trying to pass Zanardi, causing another yellow flag. He gets going again and stays on the lead lap. Ando tells him, "You're doing good. Lots of cars are out of sequence. Hang in there."

Mark says he might have flat-spotted a tire and that could cause some vibration at speed. Jim looks at the tire pressure data. "The pressures look OK. It looked to me like the tires were rolling through the spin."

On lap 55 the race restarts with Mauricio ninth and Mark 11th. Mo falls back and Mark passes him for 10th. Then

17-Car Pit Stop

Mauricio loses it going into Turn 1. On the monitor it looks like Roberto Moreno touches Mauricio, but there is actually no contact. The crash looks like a big one but Mauricio is all right. Mark pits during the yellow-flag period caused by Mauricio's crash.

Mark is 10th at the restart but drops back to 12th after a few laps. The race becomes one of attrition, with Bobby Rahal leading at the end by stretching his fuel. Rahal only made two pit stops. With 10 laps to go Ando tells Mark, "Get your boot in there, mate."

Rahal's gamble ends when he runs out of methanol on the next-to-last lap. Paul Tracy inherits the lead and wins the race. He and Greg Moore were the only finishers able to make it on only two pit stops. Several other front-runners run out of fuel, and Mark ends up in eighth, picking up three spots in the last four laps. Mark pitted for fuel on lap 97. Rahal pitted last on lap 84.

After the race the PacWest people are gathered around Mauricio's car, looking at the damage. The tub is punched in right in front of the left-front A-arm mount. It's repairable but they'll send it back to Reynard in Indy for repair, getting in return the chassis Parker Johnstone was in when he crashed at Nazareth.

18-Car Pit Stop

Russ tells me the boost control wasn't working right on Mauricio's car. He was loosing power because it was letting the pop-off valve unseat. That's why he had a problem keeping up. Andy is pissed, uttering a four-letter word over and over, but he's still smiling.

Bruce, as usual, is philosophical and positive. "It started right. We were excited by getting our first pole. It's a great milestone for the team. We have to keep doing things the way we're doing them. We were hoping for a win, but Mark had a good race. He just started from too far back."

Jim Swintal, the starter, tells me he talked to the front-row guys, Mo and Moreno, separately about the start. "They did it OK. I wanted them to get going before Turn 4, and they did it as we planned. The guys in back were probably going too fast and that caused the contact right before the start. The barriers did their job well. Look at how much money they saved PacWest alone this weekend."

Mark Moore agrees. "The barriers kept Mauricio from getting hurt."

"The barrier worked great," Mauricio says. "It was like sitting down in a chair."

Butch had this to say about the event: "It was an up-and-down week. We wasted a couple of days getting Mark comfortable in the car. The spin in the race and the tire vibration after that hurt some. We had excellent stops. Mark's third stop was for fuel only. If we hadn't stopped we would have run out like Rahal."

Sunday-Night Unwind

The Intercontinental Hotel is actually pretty ritzy as long as you don't look too close. The bar occupies half the lobby area and includes a piano and a lounge area with some nice sofas and granite-topped wrought-iron tables. This Sunday evening the bar is very busy. The Penske guys are yelling and toasting Paul Tracy's win. They've had a dry spell. Ian Reed, one of the engineers, tells me there was almost no fuel left in Tracy's car at the end.

Mark Blundell is having a few drinks with his crew, letting down his hair. Some local girls are here, young, dark beauties, and Trevor Jackson has latched onto one. They eventually leave together. Randy Smay is not functional. He just sits real still and smiles.

Mauricio is sitting on the floor with his back up against the wall, talking to Allen. He thinks there is "some instability" in the adjustable hydraulic system they have that's supposed to help braking. He says he braked at the same place as before and spun off into the barrier. He also talks about the boost control problems. He's not whining about it or upset, but just talking about it to make sure Allen knows what's going on so the problems can be addressed.

Jim Hamilton and I decide to go to the smaller, cheaper restaurant on the lobby level and have some dinner. Jim is usually very guarded in answering my technical questions, but tonight he's more forthcoming, prefacing his answers with, "After four caipirinhas I'll answer that."

He feels he's doing his best for Mark and thinks Mark is a skilled and courageous driver. He's disappointed that he's being blamed for Mark's poor performance. It seems to me that Mark has brought some Formula 1-type politics across the water. Martin Lewis, his PR guy, acts like a paid apologist and rabble rouser. Maybe you need that in F1, but over here it sticks out like a sore thumb.

Monday Tourists

Our flight leaves at 10 tonight, so we have all day to play tourist. Fred tells me about the Brazilian gem industry, and I get him to take me downtown to the offices of H. Stern. They have a tour that gives me a short education on the types of semi-precious Brazilian gems available and how they're processed. After the tour I'm herded into a very richly-furnished room and given a sales pitch. I'm a little put off by the pressure. I am shopping for a gift for my wife, Pat, but I don't see anything here that I really like.

Statue of Christ the Redeemer

Fred tells me about a similar company right next door to H. Stern, so I go looking there and find an earring set I like. Then we go back to the hotel to pick up Dan and my bags. We check out of the hotel, and begin a day-long tour of the area orchestrated by Fred.

First he takes us up into the mountains to the famous statue of Christ the Redeemer overlooking the entire Rio area. The views are spectacular. It's a beautiful, sunny day with only a little haze over the city. Then we drive around the west side of that mountain through some parks in the rain forest and some posh residential areas. We come across a peaceful creek with a small waterfall and stop to take some photos. Dan uses my camera to take a picture of Fred and myself with a waterfall behind us, and Fred says, "Show that one to the U.S. Immigration Service with my regards, Paul."

We skirt the fringes of some of the famous favelas, outlaw communities on the sides of the mountains where people build their own houses from scraps and pay no taxes. Fred says poverty is not a problem in most of the favelas; the people have jobs and work hard. Deadly punishments dealt quickly from powerful men provide order in these places. Fred sees freedom in the favelas.

Fred and Paul

He drives us back south past the Intercontinental and farther, past where we had been turning off to go to the track. He pulls onto a road that runs south, and we drive about 20 miles along the beautiful coastal beaches, then through some hills to a small stone restaurant on a look-out point over some lush swamps and meadows. We had to drive through a small forest fire coming up toward the restaurant. This is wild country.

Drinking a soda at that lookout, we sit looking at the sun getting low over the green wetlands and forests. It's almost 5 o'clock, so we head back toward the city. Fred drops us off at the airport and we say good-bye. He added an amazing amount of insight and information to this trip. If I ever make this trip again I'm going to contact Fred first.

In the airport building we hook up with the PacWest guys and a group of us find a corner in a restaurant. Trevor is looking sad and I ask him what's going on. Trev hands me a small, colored piece of paper folded twice down to a square about an inch on a side. I open it up to find a note inside:

"If one day in your mind pass my image, try do me real, because I exist when you still thinkin me. I love you."

It's signed "Soraya." That must be the local girl he met.

I copy it down in my notebook and give it back to Trev. "That's poetry."

"Yep," he says, quietly.

We hang around for hours. I'm bored and hungry, ready to get out of here, so I risk eating some last food, ordering a plate of french fries that turn out to be greasy. Everyone is pretty tired and subdued, but when we go through security and get to the waiting area next to the departure gate, the mood improves and the joking resumes.

This trip is a unique opportunity to go to a race in a city I would never visit on my own, but like any race weekend, I want to be home as soon as it's over. At 11 o'clock, when I walk through the door of the plane to start my 20-hour journey home, I depart Rio in a flash. After takeoff we're climbing up over the city. I look up from the book I'm reading and wonder what are those lights down there. Oh. That's Rio. I'm gone.

LOGISTICS

Moving all the team equipment, racecars, and spare parts from Indianapolis to Brazil is no small feat. Two specifically-modified Boeing 747s based in Long Beach, Calif., started loading in Columbus, Ohio, on Thursday, May 1 and departed for Brazil at 8 p.m. on May 4. It took 12 hours to fly the 5,500 miles, including a fuel stop in Port of Spain, Trinidad. The cargo is 56 racecars and equipment totaling 450,000 pounds and valued at more than $45 million. The airplanes burn 320,000 gallons of fuel on the round trip.

Billy Kamphausen is the CART director of logistics and assistant technical director. He says a typical two-car team will take the following:

4 racecars

16,500 pounds of equipment

2 engineering carts

2 tuggers

10 tool boxes

2 folding tents

2 pit boards

50 sets of springs

4 additional engines

260 spare gears

1 scoring cart

2 fueling rigs

14 sets of wheels

25 firesuits

40 two-way radios

200 hats

The Sugarloaf from the Redeemer Statue

CHAPTER 10

GATEWAY

The Motorola 300 at Gateway International Raceway creates a race event full of firsts. This brand-new, 1.25-mile oval track built in Madison, Ill., across the Mississippi River from St. Louis, delivers what CART thinks it needs to compete with the Indy Racing League, a race on an oval track located right in the heart of America. This track also serves a new market here in the Midwest, and the town seems to have welcomed the race as a first-class happening. Motorola is a Midwest company, based in the Chicago area a short drive away, and is the sponsor of this race, as well as being the sponsor of Mark Blundell's car.

The Saturday race means my travel starts on Wednesday this week, so I fly from SFO to St. Louis via Denver on May 22. When I get to St. Louis, road repairs turn a 15-minute drive from the airport to downtown into an hour. Then the hotel, the Regal Riverfront, has no reservation in my name. They have plenty of rooms though, so there's no problem. The hotel is newly built and right on the river, and I have a nice room with a good view.

THURSDAY

The track is in Illinois just on the other side of the river, taking all of 15 minutes at 7 a.m. My first stop is the PacWest hospitality area, where I discover I've left my camera in the hotel room. That's just less to carry around today. The temperature is in the 60s this morning with some high clouds and a light breeze. On my walk toward the garage area I have to put on my sunglasses because of the dust stirred up by cars in the unpaved parts of the infield. The facility has an unfinished look. If it rains it'll be very muddy.

Since the track is brand new, CART scheduled a special practice yesterday. The PacWest guys tell me the track still had a dusting of lime on the fresh asphalt and it took a while for the cars to blow away all the white stuff. Alex Zanardi, third in CART points so far this season behind Paul Tracy and Scott Pruett, turned fast time yesterday with a lap of 25.244 seconds and an average of 181.112 mph.

Pace-Car Ride

My driver in a PPG pace car is Gail Truess again, this time in a modified pickup truck that will be the actual on-track pace car for the weekend. I can definitely feel some bumps, especially in Turns 3 and 4. In Turn 2 I feel some undulations that could upset a car. These defects in the track seem dangerous to me.

Morning Practice

The session starts at 10:42 and the PacWest drivers go right out on track. They're in the slow-guys' session because of their times in practice yesterday. The cars still throw a lot of lime dust into the air. After some laps on track and their installation checks, Mark and Mauricio go

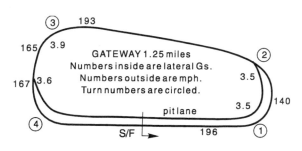

GATEWAY 1.25 miles
Numbers inside are lateral Gs.
Numbers outside are mph.
Turn numbers are circled.

back out and turn laps in the 26s. Coming back into the pit lane, Mauricio reports to Andy, "The car is pushing a little bit in Turn 2 and hitting hard in Turn 4."

Andy: "We've lost the right-front tire-pressure sensor. Let's go up a flat at the rear and down a flat at the front. That should help the push."

Mauricio: "That will help, Andy, but the bumps are quite bad."

Mark says to Jim: "There's not a great deal of push in the car; it's very neutral. I'm concerned that I don't have enough support at the rear. It feels like it's bouncing on the tires, not touching down."

Jim: "We'll give you less front wing and re-baseline the car. Then we'll look at changing springs. We've got a puncture, so let's switch to the prime tires."

Both cars go back out. Bryan Herta has the fastest lap so far with a 25.649. Mauricio is second fast. When he comes back in Andy says he'd like to go to stiffer springs and the softer tires. Mo agrees. Andy also lowers the car all around.

CART throws a yellow flag for a track inspection. Mark is up to P5. The spring change on the 17-car takes only 5 minutes. Mark says the understeer is a funny feeling, like the car is still moving. Jim changes the inside rear spring. "The car is flat 1,800 across the rear." On ovals it's common to use a different spring rate at each wheel. Jim is saying the spring rate at each rear wheel is 1,800 pounds per inch.

Actually I said that wrong. The spring rate at the wheel depends on suspension geometry such as the movement ratio of the rocker between the pushrod and the spring, and also the angle of the pushrod. What I should have said is Jim is using springs rated at 1,800 pounds per inch, meaning compressing them 1 inch takes a force of 1,800 pounds.

The session restarts at 11:08. I hear Control say, "They've been two abreast through Turn 4." A few minutes later car-25, driven by Max Papis, goes too low in Turn 2 and drops a tire off the track, kicking some dirt on course. The session stops for a cleanup.

I decide to walk down to Turn 4 and see how the cars look over the bumps there. It really thumps them good! The whole car jumps in the air. Controls calls a yellow flag for another cleanup and penalizes the 25-car 8 minutes of track time.

Mark comes in, saying to Jim, "The car is better, but the front is loading and unloading. Maybe it needs more wing."

Jim Smith, a technical support guy for Öhlins shocks, is in the photographers' stand at Turn 2. He says the PacWest cars look good over the bumps. He's using his stopwatch to get section times in Turn 4, and tells me the 17- and 18-cars are the quickest. He's right; they seem to be very smooth and fast through here.

I see Parker Johnstone go a half-car-width higher in Turn 4 and his car is smooth, no bump. Now I notice more cars do that, but it might not be the quick line. There's another yellow flag for a track inspection, and they penalize car-25 again for kicking rocks on course at Turn 2. I hear Mauricio say the car is touching down, and Andy asks him if he wants to raise the car at the pushrods or do it with tire pressures.

"Tire pressures won't do it, Andy," Mo answers.

The session ends at 12:04 p.m., and Andy says, "Good session, guys." Mauricio has the best time with a lap of 24.550 seconds, 186 mph.

I watch the fast-guys' group on the monitor in the press tent. Early in the session Paul Tracy and Michael Andretti march up the list, but Mauricio's name stays in P1.

Then I decide to walk to Turn 1 and see how the cars look there. The barriers are close enough that the speed of the cars is apparent. I've been told the key to a fast lap on an oval is to carry speed into a corner and maintain maximum speed all the way around, in contrast to the classic road course line which is slow in and full throttle out.

Greg Moore seems fast so I pay attention to him and watch his car. Entering the corner the rear of his car seems to make a big wiggle before it takes a set. It looks scary. Then I see him come into the corner much faster than before. The engine is noticeably louder and at higher revs. I'm amazed at the difference. He might have been coasting those other laps!

At the end of the session I walk back to pit lane and look at a monitor. Greg Moore is P1; he has the fastest combined time of the two groups. Mauricio's time holds for second. His and Greg's lap times are very close, 24.489 and 24.550. That's an average of 186 mph. Other drivers at the top of the list are Michael Andretti, Bryan Herta, Raul Boesel, and Paul Tracy. Mark is P17 with a 25.086.

Afternoon Practice

At 3:40 p.m. the 17- and 18-crews are practicing pit stops in their pit boxes as Indy Lights practice ends. Mark is in the slow-guys' group that starts at 4:04. After a few laps on track he says, "The car feels looser, a little bit more nervous at the rear, a bit high, maybe, at the rear." Jim makes some changes and Mark goes back out.

Control says the 25-car is still kicking dirt on the track again. Mark comes in off the track saying, "There's more push, but it feels more stable."

Jim: "What about we drop the front and raise the rear?"

Mark: "OK, but maybe up only a little at the rear."

Jim: "Let's go down a flat at the front and up a half-flat at the rear. "Mark goes back out and improves to P3 in this group. A TV guy from the local Channel 5 interviews John Anderson.

Malcolm Oastler, Reynard chief designer, is here looking at the monitors in the Motorola engineering cart. It's warm so he's got on shorts, loafers with no socks, and an Aussie hat. I ask him about a rumor that Reynard is getting involved in Formula 1 with Jacques Villeneuve, and the speculation that Malcolm will move on to the bigger challenge in F1 soon, whether Reynard enters that arena or not.

"They don't know me very well if they think that," Malcolm tells me. "I've had offers to go do things like that for a lot of money. I have environmental concerns. What matters to me is the people I work with."

At 4:24 Mark is still P3 in the session with a best lap of 25.391. With 15 minutes to go in the session Paul Jasper hits the wall in Turn 2, causing a yellow flag. After the cleanup Mark goes on track and comes back in. He's not happy with the car. "It's got a lot of push in 3 and 4. I used the weight jacker but the front tires are just scrubbing all through the turn."

Jim: "Reverse the last two changes. I want to make some tire pressure changes." When Mark comes back in they switch to a set of optional tires. This is the race set they'll scuff now.

"Let's get the pressures straight," Mark says. "We can't run the crap out of these." This group is through at 5:04. Parker Johnstone is the fast driver with a lap of 24.679 seconds. Mark is P4 at 25.190. He improved a few tenths late in the session.

The fast-guys' group starts at 5:18 p.m. The air temperature is cool, so the lap times could be fast in this session. Mauricio is out right away, and after a few laps, comes in saying, "The car is OK through Turn 1. The grip is down a little. It's a little light at the exit." Andy suggests they add some rebound at the front.

After his next stint on course Mauricio says, "The whole car feels bound-up. We need to free the car up." Dave Jacobs finds a cut right-rear tire so they change to another set.

"We need to free the car up," is a phrase heard often, especially at oval tracks. Understeer or push, when the front tires are at bigger slip angles than the rear tires, is safer than oversteer, where the rear slip angles are larger and the car wants to swap ends. Understeer is controllable; oversteer is not. For this reason most engineers approach an oval setup from a starting point of understeer. Larger slip angles produce more side force but also more tire drag forces. When the car is pretty close to a good setup but still pushing a little bit, what the driver feels when that last bit of push gets dialed out is less drag. The car feels more free.

Andy: "Did the rebound adjustment bind up the rear? Maybe we should take it out?"

Mauricio: "Try it." They also lower the car one flat at the rear.

Several cars have cut tires so they stop the session for a track inspection. Paul Tracy has the fast time so far, 24.478 seconds. Andy suggests to Mauricio, now in P18, that he try braking along with the throttle, entering the turns. "It might help settle the rear. You can use your bars, too."

With 20 minutes to go in the session Tracy is in P1 on the monitor followed by Boesel, Parker, Vasser, and Hearn. Mo is off the page. Next time in Mauricio says, "I reckon the car is too high. The front just washes out." Jim Reid climbs under the car to check the skids and then sprays them with black paint.

Andy: "What about the bump in Turn 4?"

Mauricio: "Fine. I don't think the car is low enough." Andy lowers the car one flat all around.

Mo goes out again and they continue to fine tune the car, scuffing a couple of sets of tires also. Then Michael Andretti blows an engine — a Cosworth/Ford. It's a whopper. I hear the safety teams talking about finding engine pieces all over the track. They diaper the car and bring it in on the hook.

It's a long cleanup, requiring 27 minutes. When the session restarts there's 5 minutes to go in the session. Mauricio is in P13 with a lap of 24.946 seconds. Tracy is in P1 with a best lap of 24.379 seconds and an average of 187 mph. Mauricio improves to a 24.608 for the fifth-fastest spot. Mark has been bumped down to P18.

At 7 p.m. we get served a good Dave Loik dinner. The 18-car gets a fresh engine, but the 17-car has a boroscope inspection that shows it's OK to run tomorrow. A boroscope is a fiber-optic device with a good light source that goes into the combustion chamber through the spark plug hole. Using this device, an engineer can take a good look around and see if there is any obvious damage or wear.

FRIDAY

The hotel has a nice coffee lounge in the lobby in the mornings, so I'm there before 7 a.m. and read *USA Today* for a few minutes before the short drive over the river. The lobby is all windows on the east side and the sun shines in, brightening the room and making it easier to wake up. I'm at the track at 7:15 even though it takes awhile to find my rental car in the huge parking lot across the street from the hotel. Half the cars in there look alike, so even if I remember the color it doesn't help.

As I'm walking through the paddock I see Ric Moore, Greg's dad, and Greg's engineer, Steve Challis. "I was standing down at Turn 1 yesterday," I tell them. "I saw what must have been that P1 lap Greg cut. That's impressive. He was obviously on the throttle much more on that lap. Are they full throttle in any of the corners yet?"

"No," Steve says, smiling. "They're lifting some. But partial lift doesn't slow these cars that much. We don't tell them that." We all laugh.

"Those fast laps must not be much fun," Ric says. "He doesn't do 'em very often."

Steve smiles, "It's probably scaring the shit out of 'im."

Friday Practice

At 10:13 a.m. it's 2 minutes until the start of CART practice. The sky is full of high clouds, and there's a warm wind from the south. At the races in Australia and Brazil it was a breeze. Here in the Midwest it's a wind.

Mark comes in after a few laps and says, "The car is sitting down a little at the right rear. It's got a little bit of push, not too much. Trevor, will you take that stone off the right-front tire for me?" Trevor Jackson steps over to that tire and picks off a sub-pea-sized rock. He looks at it hard and then puts it in his pants pocket.

Jim summarizes the changes before Mark goes back on track. "We went up on the front flaps, and changed to a higher-downforce rear wing. You've got a higher-downforce car now. We raised the ride height to compensate."

At 10:30 Mark is P3 in the slow-guys' group. Bobby Rahal and Richie Hearn are ahead of him on the monitor. I hear Control say, "Car-27 [Parker Johnstone] lost a screw about 1 inch long on the frontstraight."

During a yellow flag for a track inspection, Mark says, "The car feels better. It turns in better, but some understeer is creeping in. I tried to make a bar change, but I couldn't finish that last lap because of the yellow flag. I still get the feeling that the right front isn't working right."

Jim: "Let's go up on the springs 100 pounds front and rear. From the looks of the skids, that might help you run more aggressively." With 8 minutes left Mark is P6. The next time in he's upset someone cut him off into a corner. They're scrubbing sets of tires as they work on the setup.

After another stint on course Mark says, "Something's not right. The car just gives up at the front in the transition between Turns 1 and 2. Turn 4 is the same; it just gives up at mid-corner."

Jim makes some front wing and shock changes. They put on a set of sticker optional tires. At the checkered flag at 11:04 a.m. Mark is in P6 for this group with a best lap of 25.240. Bobby Rahal is in P1 with a 24.657. That's 185-mph average.

The fast-guys' session goes green at 11:18 a.m. Andy tells Mauricio, "Let BOSS look at this valve and then we'll try the other one."

OK, now I know that the BOSS system pinpoints the maximum boost that each CART-supplied pop-off valve allows. I still don't know exactly how it does that. Maybe it uses the ninth butterfly in the intake system to control plenum pressure. All V-8s have eight throttle butterflies, but most CART engines have another one in the turbocharger compressor exit manifold just before the boosted flow goes into the intake plenum. The Ilmor guys are very hush-hush about BOSS, which probably means 'Boost Optimization Software System.' Anyone listening to the radio conversations can hear what I'm hearing.

Mauricio comes in after a stint on course saying, "It's more stable in the bumps, Andy."

Andy: "Was it the rebound changes or the sway bar?"

Mauricio: "It was the rebound. I didn't touch the bar yet. I'm not really pushing yet."

Andy: "Is it bottoming?"

Mauricio: "Not bad. Would somebody please wipe this bug off my visor?"

Andy: "Could you do with some more rebound on the front?"

Mauricio: "Maybe I could." He goes back out at 11:35.

Later in the session Greg Moore blows a motor right at Start/Finish, causing a yellow flag.

Andy tells the crew to change the pop-off valve. To Mauricio he says, "We've got some softer springs mounted [meaning there is a complete set of coil-over units with softer springs mounted on shocks identical to the ones on the car, for quick change-out] if you want to try them, but we need to evaluate this rebound change first."

Messages to and from the safety teams cleaning up the track walk on Mauricio's reply so I don't hear him. I hike to Turn 2, where I climb up onto a photographers' stand to watch the rest of the session. This is great. I'm about 40 feet in the air, so I can see the entire track. The stand is made from standard industrial scaffolding. The weather is perfect, with only a few huge puffy clouds in the sky and a light breeze from the south. Behind me in the infield are some ritzy-looking motor coaches.

The course goes green again and after Mauricio drives away on pit lane I hear his chief mechanic, Mark Moore, say, "Look at Carl Hogan [owner of Hogan Racing, pitted next to PacWest this week] order people around in their pit box. I'm sure glad Bruce doesn't do that." I laugh out loud and then look around sheepishly to see if anyone notices. They don't.

When Mauricio comes back in he says, "That's better, but the tires are going off."

Andy: "OK. Let's scuff our qualifying set. Let's just check the balance with these." Mauricio goes out for a couple of slow laps to take the gloss off that set of tires and check the balance. There's about 11 minutes to go in the session, and most of the drivers in the group are on course trying to get that last little bit out of their setup.

When Mauricio comes back in, Andy asks about the balance. "Not bad in 3 and 4," says Mauricio. "It's a little bit loose in Turns 1 and 2."

Andy: "Let's go up a pound in the right-side tires. We'll make a shock change also."

Bryan Herta looks quick as he goes by my perch, but I can't see a monitor from here. With a few minutes to go in the session I climb down and walk back to pit lane. Paul Tracy is, once again, the fast guy in the session. His time is a 24.265 seconds, 188.420 mph. The other leaders are Raul Boesel, Bryan Herta, Alex Zanardi, and Jimmy Vasser. Mauricio and Mark are ninth and 19th.

Lunch is shrimp and pasta, stuffed green peppers, veggies, and salad. Ron Fusek, Steve's dad, comes through with a bunch of Motorola VIPs on a tour of the garage area. Ron does a great job describing things so people can tell what's going on here.

Gavin Hamilton asks me where my Rio photos are, so I go back to hospitality and get them out of my bag. The naked-woman photos get passed around and the guys have fun remembering the trip. The memory of the experience gets better as time passes. If I make that trip again I'll do it a lot differently.

QUALIFYING

The cars are all lined up against the pit wall and qualifying starts at 2:50. Once again I walk to Turn 2 and my perch. It's just too good a spot to watch from anywhere else.

Mark is second in line. His time is a 25.241, 181 mph, not good. Paul Tracy is fifth in line and turns a 24.353, 187 mph, which could be the pole time. It doesn't last long, however, as Raul Boesel goes on track next and beats Tracy's time by a hair, driving a lap in only 24.324 seconds and 187.96 mph. I hear Control say Boesel's speed on the backstretch is 6 mph faster than Tracy's. I'd guess that means the Penske chassis has too much drag for the downforce it produces.

Mauricio is the 14th driver to qualify. He seems smooth and fast as I watch him go by. And he is, turning a lap time of 24.374 or 187.57 mph for third place on the grid.

After the session I walk to the conference room for the pole press conference. Mauricio says, "We are very happy with the balance of the car. This place is new to everybody. Who knows how many miles the engineers did in computer simulations? It was a good lap; we just lacked a little speed."

Raul Boesel came to CART from Formula 1, but he has always been strong on oval tracks. When he's asked to explain this, he says, "I can't. It just feels good when you have the confidence to go fast through the corners."

Mauricio is asked to comment on the forces in the corners. "It's tough. Your eyeballs get stuck on the side of the car [laughter]. It's a lot. We get used to it, and the car supports us, but I'm not sure about some of the bearings and other things on the car."

Another question for Mauricio is about how well he's been qualifying and when he thinks he'll win a race. "Races are being won because of fuel and how you stretch your window. The team has stepped up, but it's time to work harder than ever."

Paul Tracy answers questions with corporate phrases using all the sponsor names. His words could have come from a tape recorder. I think about the race at Long Beach when de Ferran and Zanardi charmed the journalists while Mauricio watched. Now he's the guy that comes off charming compared to Tracy and Boesel.

Race Prep

At 5:30 Saturday afternoon the PacWest crews are installing the race engines and getting the cars ready for tomorrow. Mark Moore is changing out the brake rotors on the 17-car from the lightweight qualifying rotors to more durable parts for the race. The lighter rotors have thinner webs cast in between the surfaces, and save 1 pound per wheel.

"The old rule of thumb was 20 pounds of weight on a car was worth a tenth of a second on the track," Mark tells me. "If you look at the grids today and the qualifying times, you can see that a few pounds might make a difference. We run closer to the weight limit than most teams."

I look at the qualifying times and there's less than a tenth of a second between the first three cars.

RACE DAY

Usually I check out of the hotel on race morning, but the last flight out tonight is too early. I'll stay in the hotel tonight and leave early tomorrow morning. I have to remind myself this is Saturday. I'm used to race day being Sunday.

When I get to the PacWest hospitality area about 7 a.m. Mauricio is there having some cereal. One of the stories I've decided to follow for the book is whether PacWest's technical developments help or hurt results on the track. I ask Mauricio about that.

"You have to know when to use it and how. So far this year it's an advantage — everywhere but Australia, where we had a leak that cost us some track time. I qualified eighth there."

"What about BOSS?" I ask.

"It's a good system," Mo says. "But it doesn't work at all tracks. I can do better myself at some tracks."

"It looks to me like the driver is the only one who can make the final evaluation of technical benefits," I say.

"Yes, that's right," Mauricio says. "The engineers try real hard to make some advantages and usually they work, but they only see numbers. I can use all my senses."

Warm-Up

This 30-minute session starts at 8:15. Two Toyota-engined cars blow up early in the session, causing lengthy clean-ups which last almost 30 minutes. After the green flag, Mo goes on course. When he comes in he says he wants to try another pop-off valve.

Mark says, "The car just lacks lateral grip. In Turns 1 and 2 it pushes with a load-unload situation. It's on the loose side at turn-in, but it pushes in mid-turn. It feels like only half the tire is on the road. It goes into the corner and then just gives up."

Jim adds some toe-in at the left-rear wheel. Mauricio is in P9 and Mark P10. Arnd Meier hits the wall in Turn 2, causing another yellow flag and long cleanup. He won't start the race.

Jim says "There's 11 minutes to go, but I don't think we'll get all of it."

Mark reports on the effect of the changes. "It's not bad, but it's still a little bit nervous at turn-in. The mid to exit is OK. I have to keep a low line."

Mauricio is scuffing sets of tires that will be used in the race. His crew practices pit stops, simulating race conditions. When they're through Mark Moore says, "Take off the knee pads. That's it for the hot stops."

Mark Blundell is still not happy with his car. "The Turn 1-2 transition to mid 2 is not good. It transfers load across the front. There's a lot of push that's not good in traffic." Mark then asks for one turn of left-front wing, and they do that. Jim also drops the front tire pressures by 2 pounds.

After one more yellow-flag period for a track inspection, the course goes green with a couple of minutes to go. Greg Moore has the fast lap and Mauricio is second quick. Mark is P10. The session ends at 9:17.

I've heard there is some concern among the drivers about another driver blocking them as they're trying to pass into a corner. That can get very dangerous on an oval, where the slightest contact between cars can cause a crash and hurt somebody. I'm told that in the drivers' meeting on Friday, Wally Dallenbach told the drivers, "We don't drive these cars; you do. There wasn't much blocking at Rio, but we looked like idiots at the start."

Jim Swintal, the starter, tells me Al Unser Jr. had a good idea that will help the starts. "The cars will form up into double file a full lap before the start instead of on the backstraight just before the start. That will eliminate the rear of the pack having to speed up just before the green flag. Junior [Al Unser Jr.] seems to be taking a leadership position among the drivers. He sits in the front row and, when he speaks, he turns around and addresses them all."

"You've got Boesel and Tracy in the front row," I say to Jim. "What kind of start do you expect?"

"They've made good starts before," he says. "I have high hopes."

Pre-Race Problems

Mark Blundell's car has been spitting oil at the back and the crew is now taking the turbocharger out to change an O-ring seal. It's almost 10 o'clock and it's getting cooler. There's some clouds coming from the south that could mean rain during the race.

18-Crew Thrashes to Repair a Turbo Seal

At 11 a.m. the 18-crew has finished the turbo repair, and they're getting into their firesuits. The teams are towing the cars onto pit lane, so I walk there myself and start thinking about the race. The Budweiser Clydesdale horses are pulling a beer wagon down the frontstraight. The animals are huge, much bigger in person than on TV. A guy runs along behind them cleaning up the inevitable droppings.

Right at noon we're all on the frontstraight as the pre-race ceremonies continue. I feel a few raindrops. The national anthem is sung, worse than any rendition I've ever heard. Al Unser Jr. is gridded in the row behind Mauricio. Just before getting into his car Mo walks over and has a chat with Roger Penske. Roger is a part owner of Ilmor, and Mauricio drove a Formula 1 car that was Ilmor-powered. I see them talk on almost every pre-grid.

The drivers get into the cars, and I start to think about going to Turn 2 and watching the race from that photographers' stand. Mark Moore turns to me and says, smiling, "We prepare for war."

THE RACE

The race starts just as I get up into my perch. I don't have a jacket or an umbrella so I hope it doesn't rain. Raul Boesel starts well from his outside front-row position and passes Paul Tracy for the lead. Roberto Moreno causes the first yellow flag when he slows on course during lap eight. The order is Boesel, Tracy, Moore, Unser Jr., and Mauricio. During the caution period Mo tells Andy his tire pressures are too high, and they'll have to lower the cold pressures in the next set of tires. Unser Jr. has to make a pit stop to repair a problem with his rear wing.

After the restart Zanardi and then Vasser pass Mauricio, leaving him in sixth. Mark moves up to 17th from his 20th starting position, but then I hear his engine running badly and he pits on lap 29. It's some electrical problem they can't fix, so he retires. Mark's slow-down on course causes a yellow flag, and Mauricio pits for tires and fuel on lap 32. Some cars don't pit and Mo is in P8 after his stop. The leaders are now Boesel, Tracy, rookies Patrick Carpentier and Dario Franchitti, and Zanardi.

The First Lap of the Race in Turn 2

Five laps later the Toyota engine in Juan Fangio's car lets go and the track goes yellow again. I hear Mauricio say, "He blew up right when I was on his gearbox. Shit!" Mo was about to pass the slower car coming out of Turn 4, and now his helmet and visor are covered with oil. Boesel, Franchitti, and Carpentier pit but Tracy stays out on course.

We have a green flag on lap 46 with Tracy leading followed by Zanardi, Vasser, Moore, and Mauricio. Tracy makes a green-flag pit stop on lap 65 that puts him a lap down. Zanardi is the leader but he's soon passed by Greg Moore, who's been moving up through the field. Mauricio is fourth.

The passing I'm seeing is impressive. It was hoped this track would develop a groove wide enough to allow passing on the outside, but that's not happening. Maybe there's a groove and a half. The way I'm seeing it happen is a guy gets a drive off Turn 4 and pulls up inside the passee going into Turn 1. Sometimes the cars go side-by-side for a while before the outside driver has to back off. He just doesn't have room at the exit to get on the throttle as hard as the inside guy.

Boesel and Herta stop on course on lap 74, bringing out another yellow flag. Most of the field stops for fuel and tires, leaving the lead to Dario Franchitti. I hear Russ tell Mauricio, "BOSS off. Down two on the boost."

Tracy moves back onto the lead lap, and at the restart begins to move up. Pruett passes Mauricio for fifth. Franchitti leads for about 15 laps but has to pit, giving the lead to Vasser.

By 103 laps into this 236-lap race Bobby Rahal slows as he goes by me in Turn 2 and stops the car on the backstretch. He struggles to get out of the car quickly and rubs his arm like he's been burned. A yellow flag slows the field.

Russ asks Mauricio about the car. "It's still pushing," Mo answers. "I did all I could with the weight jacker. At the next stop maybe we can put in some right-front wing and I'll go back on the weight jacker."

At the restart on lap 110 the leaders are Vasser, Moore, Zanardi, Pruett, and Mauricio. Al Unser Jr. and Paul Tracy have been moving up and now they're running seventh and eighth. Tracy is right on Junior's gearbox for a couple of laps and them goes under him into Turn 1. They drive side-by-side through the entire turn before Tracy accelerates away. It's a beautiful pass and wonderful discipline and control by two good drivers.

At lap 120 CART calls a yellow flag for rain. It's been sprinkling off and on since the start, but the track is beginning to get wet now. There's some confusion in the PacWest pits as to whether Mauricio should pit. The leaders come in and he follows them onto pit lane.

Back out on course, Mauricio tells Russ, "The valve is still popping; I don't know what to do." The jet blower, a jet engine mounted in a Toyota pickup truck, goes on course and begins to lap slowly, blowing moisture off the racing line. The racecars circulate slowly behind the pace car, that same modified pickup truck I rode in and still being driven by Gail Truess.

As the cars come back on course and line up, there's some confusion about who pitted when, so Wally Dallenbach makes a decision to realign the cars that are still on the lead lap. The rain slacks off, the track dries, and we get a restart on lap 135. Michael Andretti is the new leader followed by Vasser and Zanardi. Mo is seventh.

Less than 10 laps later Scott Pruett crashes right in front of me. He's running in sixth spot just ahead of Mauricio. I watch him come into Turn 2 and the car twitches, barely, and it looks like he's OK. Then the back end comes around and he's in the wall at the exit of Turn 2 with a loud bang and a flash of fire. Pieces of the car go everywhere. It's scary to watch, but I see him move in the car right away and then he gets out.

The rain comes back during the cleanup so the blower truck comes out and begins to circle methodically around the track, trying to keep the racing line dry. The yellow-flag period lasts almost 40 laps. Russ says to Mauricio, "The restarts are killing us. What can we do?"

Mauricio sounds upset. "The valve is blowing. This car is eating me up."

In addition to the blower, they've got all the wreckers on course also, but the track gets good and wet. I can hear the radio conversation between Ken Lowe and Gail. As she goes around the track she reports on how wet the track looks and how much she needs to run the windshield wipers. After a while Control begins to worry about how much fuel is in these vehicles, but the reports come back that the pace car and the blower truck, the two most critical units, have enough fuel for now.

Russ comes back to Mauricio with the suggestion from Mark McArdle, one of the Ilmor engineers, that he not saw at the throttle. "That confuses the plenum pressure sensor."

"I appreciate the suggestion," Mauricio says. I can't tell if he's being sarcastic or serious.

At 2 o'clock it's raining lightly on me. My shirt is getting wet and I'm thinking about going down under the stand, but it's warm and I'm not really uncomfortable.

Russ tells Mauricio, "If this goes green, we can make it to the end with one stop and we've saved the highest-stagger tires for last."

Five laps later Mo says, "I'm getting tired of this. It's raining just enough to keep us from going green."

On lap 163 after 20 laps on the track, I hear Gail say she's down to a quarter tank of gas. The rain is easing up and the PacWest guys are trying to figure out if they should pit now before the course goes green again.

"It's a difficult call," Mo says. If there's another long yellow the cars might be able to run to the end of the race without another stop if they come in just before the green flag. Risky business!

At lap 176 Mauricio says the track is dry. The blower truck driver reports he's about out of fuel for the jet engine. Some cars peel off into pit lane. Russ tells Mauricio to pit if the leaders go in. Zanardi is the only one in the top eight to pit.

The green flag restarts the race on lap 180. The race order is Michael Andretti, Vasser, Moore, Mauricio, and Tracy. Tracy immediately passes Mauricio into Turn 1 and gets by Greg Moore on the next lap.

Tracy is looking good. He pressures Jimmy Vasser and tries to pass, but gets the door slammed in his face. Andretti falls back and Vasser is the new race leader followed by Tracy, Moore, and Mauricio. Mo still has a chance for a win or podium finish here.

Another yellow flag comes out at lap 196 while the safety team picks some debris off the track. Mauricio pits but a lot of guys don't, so when the race resumes, Dario Franchitti is the leader followed by Carpentier and Zanardi.

Now the race will be determined by how much fuel each car has and how the driver can conserve what he has and still get to the front. It's difficult to believe everyone ahead of Mauricio will run out of fuel.

Tracy moves up consistently. Franchitti falls out of the lead to be replaced by Carpentier. Will this be a rookie's race? Two laps short of the checkered flag the order is Carpentier, Tracy, Zanardi, de Ferran, Vasser, and Mauricio. Carpentier must be running on fumes. He offers no resistance when Tracy passes him on the next lap. Tracy holds on to win his third race in a row. Maybe the Penske team is back. Will they be able to win another CART championship?

Mauricio is disappointed when I find him in the pit box. "I had a push all day. We lost places at every restart because of boost problems. We're knocking on the door. We're competitive. We'll keep running hard. You can't chase a win. It will come to us."

The 18-crew has already cleared their equipment out of pit lane. When I get to the transporters, they're getting ready to leave the track to drive back to Indianapolis. The 17-crew is not far behind. Everyone is busy and I can't find anyone to talk to, so I go to the hospitality area and pick up my bag. It's still windy and looking like rain.

I'm in no hurry to leave the track because I don't have a flight out until tomorrow, but after looking around again I don't see anyone to talk to. The road across the backstraight is open, and it will close again soon for a support race yet to run. There is no tunnel under the track like at most ovals. To hell with it; I'm getting out of here. By 3:30 p.m. I'm back at the hotel making some notes and thinking about dinner.

After dinner and a few beers, I'm watching the 10 o'clock news on TV and see a story about how much money and jobs the new racetrack will bring to the St. Louis area. They say, "Downtown business owners will put millions of dollars in their pockets. Twenty-nine hotels are completely sold out this weekend. Fifty thousand out-of-towners will spend $715 each."

That's all nice to hear. I'd say this has been a very succesful first race and I'll look forward to coming here again.

CHAPTER 11

MILWAUKEE

This is the start of a long trip for me. I'm flying on Thursday, May 29 from SFO to Chicago and then a short hop on a turboprop up the west shore of Lake Michigan to Milwaukee. After the race on Sunday I'll drive the rental car to Indianapolis and visit the PacWest shop for a few days before driving to the race at Detroit. I'll fly home from there on Sunday, June 8.

Everyone seems to enjoy the race at Milwaukee. This used to be the first race after the Indy 500, and its casual atmosphere was a welcome relief from the "spectacle" of Indy.

The Milwaukee Mile is actually on the Wisconsin State Fairgrounds in West Allis, a blue-collar town a few miles from downtown Milwaukee. Just behind the grandstands are the buildings where pigs and cows get judged during the State Fair. Across the street from the backstretch is a row of modest, two-story homes. The whole event is charmingly low key.

FRIDAY

The track is only a 10-minutes drive from the motel where the team is staying. It's cool this morning, about 60 degrees, and overcast. There have been some sprinkles of rain. On the way in from the parking lot I stop at the Indy Lights tent for some coffee and a chocolate doughnut. Then it's on to the PacWest hospitality area to store my stuff before going to the garage area.

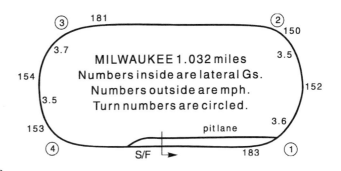

CART practice starts at 10:30 this morning. The team drives to this race, so the guys have been here since yesterday and they're winding up the preparation of the racecars.

Randy Smay tells me he won a tire-changing contest last night at a sports bar called "Rumors."

"The Penske guys were there, and I really enjoyed beating them. They had an electric lug wrench and the lug nuts weren't glued on the wheels like they are when the NASCAR guys do pit stops. I did it slow the first time, but then I figured out how to handle the nuts. You've got to hold each one as it comes off, set them all down together, pick them all up together, and start them on the studs so the wrench can run them on tight. The tire and wheel were heavy. That surprised me the first time. We're used to aluminum wheels."

This is another example of how competitive these people are and how thoughtful they are about what they do.

First Practice Session

There's a delay starting the practice session because of a weeper in Turn 3, some water coming through the track surface. The session was about to start, but then the word came to shut the engines down. It's about 65 degrees and overcast, but it's getting lighter. There's a light wind from the south.

Allen McDonald has replaced Jim Hamilton engineering Mark Blundell's car. Of course Andy Brown remains as Mauricio's engineer. No one told me about the change. I just see Allen talking on the radio to Mark, and Jim just standing there. I talk to Jim about it, and he puts a positive face on it, but there has to be some grief involved. The relationship between a driver and engineer is intimate, and a failed relationship is always a hurtful experience. Jim tells me Allen will engineer the car for two races, and then they hope to have someone more permanent.

We get a green flag for the slow-guys' group at 10:38. Mark goes out and comes back in for the installation-lap check. I now have a way to tape the conversations I hear on the scanner, and this will be the first time I'll use it. Before I start the tape I hear Allen tell Mark, "All right, mate, you know what tires you've got and how much fuel, so just go out and see what you think about this great setup." Mark drives off down the pit lane and does about eight laps, turning a 22.68-seconds best time. Then he comes back in.

Mark: "The tire pressures have risen up a little bit high. Overall balance of the car, the rear of the car, is really quite stable at this point. Turn-in is just fine. Turn 2, it wants to exit with a bit of push and also with 3 and 4 as well, push from mid to exit there."

Allen: "Was the car touching?"

Mark: "Just touching coming down on this frontstraight. There's a couple of high spots there. Under braking it's not touching down. And elsewhere on the circuit it's fine as well, so it's probably still a bit on the high side. You can check the skids, but it feels OK."

Allen: "The car's hitting at the rear and not at all in the front, so we'll come down half a flat at the front and one flat up on the rear."

After a pause, Allen says, "The tire pressures we've got here are basically spot-on on the right front; a pound up on the right rear; and uh … Jesus Christ! … I just misread Randy's writin' there. [He was looking at tire temperatures as recorded by Randy Smay.] OK on the left front and a couple of pounds high on the left rear. So we've just gone a bit higher on the rears, basically. So we're correcting those."

After a yellow flag that stopped the session Mark goes back on track at 10:54. He is back in after a few laps. He's P2 with a lap of 21.989. Pruett is P1 at 21.680. This is about 171-mph average.

Mark: "Actually, I've just gone out on that run and suddenly there's a lot more push being produced in the car. I just went down like 10 or 11 pounds left-front weight, trying to see if that would reduce it. It's not making any inroads after that. At the turn-in the car feels a bit shallow at this point. When I go into the turn the grip level at the front isn't quite as precise as what we need it. The push in 1 and 2 is very excessive, pouring in lock from mid to exit especially. And, uh, way too much push, just a lack of front grip in general."

Allen: "The front weight didn't make any difference?"

Mark: "Going down like 11 or 12 pounds on the front-left weight didn't seem to put anything in there at all; didn't give me any improvement in front grip. Which is kinda surprising."

Allen. "OK. Let's try going a bit softer on the front springs, eh?"

Mark: "Current situation is that we're in fifth gear running out of rpm very quickly. Going to sixth gear is a little too long when you're in the turn, especially with the balance we've got at the moment. We've got to keep the rpm up higher in top gear."

Mark goes out at 11:03 and he's back in at 11:07. He's P6 now. When Mark comes back in Allen asks, "Better?"

Mark: "I think it's a little bit better in that it's not touching down as harshly as the previous run. At the rear it's still touching a little bit, but doesn't seem to be that aggressive."

Allen goes 100 pounds softer on the rear springs. Mark makes another run and then comes in, saying on the radio as he comes down pit lane, "It's touching down at the front more than it was. And it's got a big degree of understeer in the car."

Allen: "So maybe that's because we went softer at the front without making a ride-height change."

Mark: "I think going softer helped to get turn-in grip. It seems like there's a bit of front roll coming into the car now, which is a bit disconcerting because with the roll there's a loss of grip. So we're just very short of front grip at this point. The rear of the car doesn't seem to be any issue."

Allen: "Let's go 100 pounds stiffer at the rear, all right?" Mark nods affirmative.

Allen [to the crew]: "Up 100 pounds at the rear, please."

Mark: "You might need to just go up on the ride height about a half a turn, just to stop the front touching down, because on a couple of the bumps mid corner it's just touching down midway through."

Mark, after another stint on course: "We definitely need to address the gearing, since we're a little bit out on gearing. Sixth gear is really a little bit too long for the turns, especially with the grip level at the moment."

They make some changes. There's about 18 minutes to go in this group. Mauricio is in the next group, and he's getting ready to get into his car. Mark returns to the track at 11:17 in P4 at 21.716 seconds. Next time in he starts talking while he's slowing to turn into the pit box. "The car's touching down all over the place, [especially] going into 3. Got to get a bit more support, more stability. I can go in harder. But it's just kicking up underneath the car at that point."

Allen: "All right guys, sticker tires please. And, uh, we'll go up half a flat all around. All right? Unfortunately, as much as it hurts to do it." A pause. "All right, we've corrected the pressures in these tires, and if they don't come out right I'll buy you a beer tonight. All right?"

Well, the atmosphere is certainly more upbeat. Maybe I didn't realize just how strained the relationship was between Mark and Jim. Mark goes back out with about 10 minutes to go in the session. He's P4 at a 21.715; Scott Pruett is still quick in the session at a 21.138.

Allen tells the 18-crew, "Let's get set three ready; probably no fuel."

Next time in Mark says, "It's better with the stagger. Still lacking front-end grip, 1 transition, 2 exit. But I'm still touching down a little bit under braking, especially when I go into Turn 3. The front end of the car's just touching, and it's just unsettling the car as I turn in. Turns 3 and 4 are not too bad as a series, but 1 and 2 are losing time. I have to just back out from mid-1 to exit-2."

Allen: "Up half a flat all around, please."

Mark: "You want to just go up a bit more at the rear, Al? To put a bit more rake in?"

Allen: "Yeah, bloody good idea. All right. Go up a half a flat at the front and one and a half at the rear, all right?"

Butch repeats for the crew, "One and a half at the rear."

Mark: "This engine is definitely gone. I've got to scream about this one, because it's what we said in St. Louis. Here today, it's got no punch. Something is wrong."

Mark's out on track again with 3 minutes to go. He pops up to P2 with a 21:225 and comes back in with seconds left. Allen asks him, "All right, how'd it go?"

Mark: "A lot more lateral grip, obviously, with the tires. Because we've got an increase in grip now, when the car's loaded up from mid to exit, especially in 3 where the corners [are] a little bit shallower, I've got an extra bit of grip, and the car's loading and unloading on the front end. The front's still the weak point. The rear is OK; it's fine. But I haven't got a constant front end at this point, constant with load. [Turn] 1 and 2 it really gives up on me and I have to just back out. It's costing me a lot of time there, I know that for sure. Then I've got nothing underneath me to punch out of the corner. Very weak at this stage, engine-wise. That's holding me back. But it feels definitely better."

Allen: "Well. Well done."

Fast Guys

This group gets a green flag at 11:39 a.m., starting the second 45-minute session. Mauricio asks about the fuel mixture, and Andy says use slot zero. Mark Morris tells Mo two laps and in for an installation check. The sun is out now and the clouds are thinning.

When Mauricio comes in for the installation check, there's some smoke and the engine cover comes off, but there is no problem and he goes back on track.

Mauricio shows up on the monitor with a lap of 22.239 in P16. He comes in asking, "Tire pressures, Andy?"

Andy: "They've climbed a lot. I think we should just set those down because of that, and you are touchin' a little right now already and we don't want to be touchin.' We should be pulling the car up some."

Mauricio: "It's too early. Not too quick. That's not a problem."

Andy: "Let me know about the skids as soon as you can, Jimmy."

Andy, after a pause to study the piece of paper: "Up a flat both ends, guys. I want to try this run and see if the pressures repeat like they did at the test. [The team tested here a few weeks ago.] The high stagger was definitely a gain for Mark, so I think we should go for that early and work with that high stagger."

Mauricio: "Ten-four, I agree with that." He goes on track at 11:49 in P18 and improves to P15 with a lap of 22.008 and heads back onto pit lane. The crew lays out the high-stagger set of tires.

Mauricio: "For more control we need a bigger stagger."

Mark Morris: "Change all four tires."

Andy: "The tires pressures are still up a fraction, 2 pounds all 'round."

Mauricio: "It's pushing more through 2; that's the problem. Turns 3 and 4 pushes, but not too bad."

After a track inspection a green flag restarts the session at 11:59. Mauricio goes out in P12 on the monitor at a 21.756. During this run he improves to a 21.516 for P5. When comes back in the crew measures stagger on all the tires while the car is up on its air jacks.

Mauricio: "Two is the worst corner. Once I tried to open the gas too soon. With the brake or without the brakes, the thing just washes out. Four is starting to feel like this. It seems as the speed increases, the center [of pressure] moves further back. The front tires just can't take it."

Mauricio goes back on track at 12:06 p.m. in P7. Paul Tracy is P1 with a 20.802. Mark is still P3; his time in the first half of the session is holding up. Mauricio comes back in at 12:08 in P6 with a lap of 21.382. There's 20 minutes to go in the session.

Mauricio: "It's better but still not enough. Can we just raise it a flat on the back?"

Andy: "Yes, that's just under one and a half mil."

After a pause: "OK, Morris, that's an avenue we can pursue. You know I'm a little unhappy with our spring rate for the race. So I'd like to come stiffer on the front springs, because that's going to allow me to drop the front two flats, if I come up 200 pounds on the front springs. The other gain from that will be that the front will come up less as you get after the throttle. It'll react less to the weight transfer to the rear."

Mauricio: "Let's go for it." The crew changes springs, checks tire stagger, and takes tire pressures and temperatures.

Mauricio: "When I get out of the turns I feel some hesitation in the engine. I don't feel the valve popping. Does Charlie [Charlie Harris, the Ilmor engineer] see anything there?"

Andy: "He's seeing a few pops when that's happening."

Mauricio is out on track again at 12:12 p.m.

Mark Morris: "What about the front pushrod change?"

They hadn't completed all the changes necessary and Mauricio has to come back in. He's back on course in a couple of minutes. At an oval track, where the laps take little time and the in- and out-time for the pit lane is also quick, a mistake like this doesn't cost much track time. On a road course it would be worse. That's the first time this year I've noticed a mistake like that. Mauricio isn't able to get up to speed and turn a hot lap before a yellow flag stops the session for a track inspection.

Andy: "Did you feel much of a change in the car with this stagger change?"

Mauricio: "Not really; just small."

Andy: "It's a low stagger set. There's only two counts difference between the two sets we've tried." The Firestone tires come with stagger numbers from 0.20 to 0.30 inch. Two counts means two hundreds of an inch, 0.22 to 0.24 inch, for example.

Mauricio goes back on track with 14 minutes to go in the session. On the monitor the order is Paul Tracy with a 20.710, Patrick Carpentier, Scott Pruett, Raul Boesel, Mark Blundell, and Mauricio with a 21.357.

Then Al Unser Jr. jumps up to P5. Mauricio turns a 21.417, then a 21.205 for P6 ahead of Mark, and he comes back in.

Andy steps out of the engineering cart to go over the wall and take a long look at the tires on the car, especially the right front.

Mo's out on track again at 12:25 p.m. He turns a 21.083 for P5 and then 21.020 for P3.

As he comes in he says the car needs more rake. "We need to go up a half flat at the front, and at the rear, one flat."

Andy: "Did you catch that, Mark?" The crew goes to work on the changes.

Andy: "We've got 10 minutes of green left, Morris. I would like to try the optionals to get a feel for them. We'll evaluate this rake change and make sure we've got the ride height where we need them, and then go to our first set of optionals."

Mauricio: "Ten-four."

Mark Morris: "Tires at the next stop, guys." Mauricio goes back on track for a few more laps and comes back in.

Andy: "How's the front ride height? Is it OK to just raise the rear when we put these tires on?"

Mauricio: "No; the front's still touching a little bit, Andy. We have to get it up and more rake."

Andy: "OK; we'll figure these pressures will be a little bit low. We'll come up a flat at the front and a flat and a half at the rear."

Mauricio: "I'm having a tough time getting into this [pit] box here."

After a pause: "So we're going up a flat and a half at the rear and one at the front?"

Andy: "That is, effectively, twice as much at the back."

Mauricio goes back on track with 4 minutes to go. He's still in P3. After four or five laps he improves to 20.922, 20.916, and then 20.903, but gets bumped down to P4 before the end of the session. Paul Tracy is P1 with a best lap of 20.710, followed by Boesel, Carpentier, and Mauricio. Mark Blundell ends up in P9 with a time of 21.225.

Friday Afternoon Practice

Mark and Mauricio are both in the fast-guys' session due to their times this morning. The slow guys are first and they start at 2:33. The fast-guys' session starts at 3:37, and I'm watching from the middle of Turns 1 and 2.

This track is unique in the way you can get so close to the cars on course. The bumps in the track used to be the story here, and I first noticed tire bounce here three years ago. Today I see another tire/car/driver phenomenon — yaw oscillation.

The first thing I notice is Paul Tracy's car twitching at the rear entering the corner, but as I stand here longer and watch all the cars, I see something similar going on with Greg Moore's car and then Michael Andretti's.

I first noticed something like this at Homestead in 1996. Paul Tracy's car took a big wiggle at the rear going into Turn 1. I couldn't imagine the car moving that much without scaring the driver out of his wits. I just thought it was Tracy's courage; it's what he's famous for. I decided that was him oversteering and catching the car before it spun.

Now I'm seeing more detail the longer I stand here. It looks like the rear of the car yaws out in a big movement, comes back in too far and moves out again but not as far. Maybe there's one more smaller oscillation before the car settles to steady state in the middle of the turn. It looks like a yaw oscillation that decays toward steady state just as an undampened spring behaves after an initial deflection.

I don't hear the big changes in throttle that impressed me the first time I was here 3 years ago. Back then Mario Andretti and Jimmy Vasser were off and on the throttle in huge bursts. I don't hear that now.

I'm also listening to and recording Mark and Mauricio's radio conversations and the CART channel also. The scanner picks up one transmission at a time. When there are several people talking at the same time I can get pieces of each conversation.

Mark says, "Just on entry to the corner it's still acting like I've got a little more front grip available to me at turn-in, but it's making the car a little bit nervous. And it doesn't seem to be generatin' the roll sensation like what we incurred in this morning's session."

Mauricio: "Traffic's a bitch. It's starting to go predictably to oversteer. It moves right coming out, when I'm really leaning on it. The understeer wasn't too much of a problem."

Mark: "The car also feels like it could use a little bit more front grip, and I feel also through the steering load that there's a bit more grip being produced. But I can't seem to maximize it because the entry's slightly more nervous. That's pertaining to Turn 3 as well. It feels like we've got the entry a bit sharper and it's actually a bit off-putting because I can't get into the car early enough because the car's not setting early enough for me to get into it and get on it harder at the exit."

Mauricio: "The rear didn't feel that planted. That could be a factor."

Mark: "We need to try to kill the turn-in just a little bit and also try to get the car to take a bit of a set a bit earlier on. Definitely with the primes as well, the car feels a little bit more nervy than what it did with the optionals."

Andy to Mauricio: "How's the turn-in? Any change since this morning?"

Mauricio: "Turn-in is fine. It's no quicker. It's about the same."

Out here in the corner I can't see a monitor to tell me who's going fast, but I can see what the drivers are doing. I'm standing right in the middle of the corner. Michael Andretti drives lower in the corner earlier than most drivers. It seems most of them come in high on entry and drive a late apex line, not coming down to the white line until the last third of the turn, about 50 feet to my left.

Mark: "Under braking it's no big effect. The front end is more stable for turn-in and the car seems to be a little bit more stable throughout the whole turn."

Allen: "Good. OK. What's your biggest problem now?"

Mark: "Still feels like the car's not going into a set early enough. I can't read the car as well as this morning. It's not as predictable. And I don't get any sensation that it is taking a set. It's still push mid to exit. On the entry I need to get a bit more reading or feel from the car earlier on. It feels like it's still quite high, and I don't feel it touching down at all."

Allen: "All right; let's go down a half a flat all around, please. Is it a better ride on bumps?"

Mark: "It doesn't feel like anything at all underneath the car. And there's no reading and no sensation of it touching down. It doesn't feel like it's taking a set early enough, you know, by far I don't feel like there's any roll in the car. It gives me that impression. I feel the roll's still there but because I can't get any feeling or feedback on it, it doesn't give me a good car to predict when I'm into the turn." He goes back on track.

Coming back onto pit lane, Mark talks on the radio while he's still driving toward the pit box. I can hear the engine revs decrease as he talks. "Take that bump out. It causes too much understeer in the car. [Turn] 1 and 2 is a big problem."

Allen: "OK; good. So should we go the other way there, the other direction?"

Mark: "Could be a direction, but I'm still not happy with the car in terms of I can't feel it going into the turns. It still feels up very high and there doesn't seem to be any set there. I can't feel it going into the set with some roll, to get on it and make it predictable."

Allen: "Can we go four sweeps softer on the right-front low-speed bump? Yeah, four sweeps softer."

Mauricio comes in off the track saying, "It's lacking grip out there, basically. I think we should do a shock change."

Mark Moore: "Let's take the rear cover off."

Andy: "What we were going to do was put more bump into the rear, which would help the corner when you don't go for the throttle. 'Cause the exit is more like a steady state. If I do that I'm just worried that it might upset the rear a fraction, and we should do a little bit at the front to help that, so maybe we should put the front rebound in at the same time?"

Mauricio: "Let's try it and see and just do the bump if it's worse."

Andy: "I'm just going to put rear bump in the car, guys."

Mauricio: "You should look at these tires, Andy. They're wearing pretty good."

Andy: "This set of tires is up to 55 laps. Obviously, a third race distance is 66."

Mark comes off the track after a few laps. "A little bit better," he reports. "It's making the car slightly loose. It's giving me a slightly loose feeling because it's sticking the front a bit better in the mid-corner, and it's giving the sensation that the rear wants to come a little bit loose. It doesn't, but again there's no feedback. Still I get the impression when I turn in, I can really lean on it and get the car to give me some feedback instead of being in a set. It still feels numb."

Allen: "OK; let's give it a half a flat lower all 'round, please. This feeling of not taking a set, did this happen since we did the geometry change, or has it been there since the first thing?"

Mark: "One, you don't get that sensation of that roll going in with the set. Two, it does still feel quite high on the circuit. It's not touching down, which was an immediate response back to me when we were running. And the speed at which it turns in at the moment is actually a little bit quicker than where we were. The push has actually slightly increased from where we were also, but it's swapped ends. It's too nervous on entry, and then I can't maximize the corner anyway."

Allen: "What do you think a bit of tim will do? Will that help?"

Mark: "Yeah; it's possible. Maybe we can just do a run with these tires and get a feel for it and then maybe put some tim in. Maybe we need to come back down on the rear ride height again? Maybe that will make the difference?"

Allen: "Don't forget that ol' tim is now cockpit adjustable, so that you can uh, you can do it from there."

Mark comes back in after a few laps on track. "Instead of the front grip, it's got a big slip now on the front, and the front end is also feeling very heavy in load. It turns in too quickly and the front end of the car feels very heavy all the way through the first part of the turn. The car now feels loose. Somewhere along the line we just dropped off from where we were this morning, because it's totally changed ends in terms of balance."

Allen: "All right. Well, there's, I guess, a number of options, a number of things we could do to fix that. We could go back softer on the rear springs, up 100 pounds on the right front, that's another one. What's the car like touching down now?"

Mark: "Oh, just feels like it's touching down into the Turn 1 here about 25% or 30% in. So it's touching down like vertically. It's not like it's touching down with roll in the car. Definitely the front end now has got too much of a slip to it. Far too much. The steering is really heavy. And it's very quick to turn in and it keeps that weight all through the corner and the rear just feels nervous as hell."

Allen: "We're going to go 100 pounds softer on the rear springs, please."

After a pause, "What is your weight on the right front?"

Mark: "I just did that on that run there. It's about 6 pounds across; 6 or 7. Maybe I should go a little bit more to try and get the car to have a little bit of push on it. There wasn't much push on it and it felt very loose. Way too neutral on turn-in and carrying the front end far too efficiently around the turn and making the rear too nervous and loose."

Andy: "Give me a C shutter on the left please, Mark [Moore]."

The "shutters" are carbon-fiber blanking pieces that partially cover the cooling-air exits on the top of the sidepods. Fewer shutters installed opens up the cooling-duct exits, flowing more air but increasing aero drag. For that reason all the teams want to run with more shutters, a smaller opening, resulting in less drag.

The Toyota-powered cars always have bigger cooling-duct exits than cars using the other engines. Not only are the Toyota engines 100-horsepower short of the competition, but they blow up frequently, they use more fuel than the other engines, and they are inefficient, requiring more cooling.

Mark: "The turn-in feels better, but to be honest with you, it actually feels like the car is still loose. It's giving me that feeling, the feedback, that the rear end's not happy, it's not stable. It's still not stable on entry. It's soft now and it rolls onto that right-rear corner, and just carries the nervousness all through the turn. It feels like it's touchin' down slightly in the 1-2 transition."

Allen: "Did you try the weight jacker that time?"

Mark: "Yeah; I went to more right-front weight just to try to get some push into it."

This is the first race Allen and Mark have worked together, and they're having trouble getting the car comfortable for Mark. To me there is a difference in the conversation from when it was

Mark and Jim. There's less tension now and the problems seem to be mutual, not just Jim's problem, as it seemed before. But even though they're working well together, they seem confused.

After another run on course Mauricio comes in, saying, "I stopped using the brakes through 4 to get more rake middle corner. That helped."

Andy: "OK. What I want to try is another rear-bump adjustment. I do want to be sure that last change is better, so I want to come up one more sweep on the rear bump."

Mauricio: "Ten-four."

Mauricio: "Andy, the way these primes are looking I'm a little bit concerned how the optionals are going to take."

Bret Hrivnak and Tim Douthat
Check for Punctures

Andy: "Let me grab Bret [Big Bret, a Firestone engineer whose last name is Hrivnak] and I'll see if anyone else is sharing those concerns before we do the optional run, then."

Mark comes in, saying, "The car feels better on entry, but it seems to me it still gives me the sensation of, when I get in about 20%, the rear feels a little bit nervous, more than we had this morning. Now, when I get to the mid-corner in 1 and 2, we got a push comin' back in the car. Comin' in quite heavily. Same with 3 and 4; we got a push comin' back into the car now. It still feels a bit unnervin' on entry because of the rear, but at least when we get to the mid we got the push element comin' back." After some changes Mark goes back out.

Andy says to Mauricio, "Speaking to Bret, he's not too concerned about the wear on the optionals."

With 4 minutes to go in the session Mark comes back in after trying some changes. "It just doesn't feel right, Al. I mean you can feel the grip generating from the tires, but I can't use it. This car just feels like it's just straight down on its right-rear corner. The front's up and I feel like I'm steering the car on the right-rear wheel. It's lost a bunch of stability on entry. Now I'm shit-scared of the rear. It feels like it's goin' to come 'round on me, 'cause it's got no feeling to it. Then in the middle of the corner it picks up a bunch of push."

Allen: "All right. Well, let's do a sit-down on it and go and scratch our heads, eh?"

I guess there's no use flogging the car and driver when you don't know what to do to improve things. Given the differences in the two driver/engineer conversations, it's no surprise when I walk back and look at a monitor to find that Mark is in P16 and Mauricio is P2. Patrick Carpentier has the best time in the session with a lap of 20.397 seconds and 182 mph.

Fuel Valves

I see a CART guy checking out the team's refueling equipment so I take some photos and ask him a few questions. Paul Leyton is a member of the CART technical committee and a Burger King-franchise owner in real life.

"I go from team to team testing the fuel and vent nozzles and the hoses. It's mandatory that we do an inspection each weekend, and we do rechecks on request. The most critical part of a pit stop is the refueling because of the danger of fire."

Paul Leyton Tests
Fuel Valves

Engine Changes

Back in the garage, engine changes are in progress. A new exhaust header design has come from Ilmor. The new headers are made from Inconel, a steel alloy with a high percentage of nickel. Russ Cameron tells me these headers give about 10 extra horsepower and are made from thinner tubing than if they used stainless steel. The Inconel is heavier than stainless but much more durable; more expensive too. A set costs about $6,000. After a header set has 1,500 miles on it they don't race them anymore, but they're good for testing up to 2,500 miles.

The 18-crew is in the middle of an engine change. Daryl Fox, John Roof, and Gavin Hamilton pull the old engine out while Blake Hamilton wheels a new engine into place.

The 17-engine gets a boroscope inspection after which Mark Moore asks the Ilmor engineer, "Clean bill of health, guys?"

John Roof Inspects an Exhaust Part for Cracks

Mo's a Wank

Andy, Mauricio, and Russ are talking casually, and I want to know what they have to say about the yaw oscillations I saw at Turn 1.

"A lot of cars are going in there with a big twitch, but you look smooth, Mauricio. I couldn't tell you were going that fast. I was surprised when I walked back and saw you in P2 on a monitor. You're making it look too easy."

"So you thought I was wanking, eh?" Mauricio says with a sly smile.

"I couldn't see the times," I say, defensively.

"Andy," Mauricio says, "you'll have to dial some twitch in it."

"I can do that easily," says Andy with a big grin in the middle of his beard.

Mauricio turns back to me, "Actually, I'm flat on the throttle deep into the corner. I only lift when I feel the front wash out."

A bit later Russ tells me, "Mauricio has a studied smoothness. He thinks about it a lot. His throttle trace [throttle position vs. time on a graph from the data-acquisition system] is very smooth. He carries a lot of speed into Turn 1, and he's still on the throttle but he's left-foot braking to stabilize the car."

Jim Hamilton comes out of the engineering office in the front of the 18-transporter.

"I know you like engineering a car and driver," I say. "Do you miss it?"

"I'm having a lot less negative fun," Jim says with a wry grin.

SATURDAY

At 7 a.m. I'm in the garage area. It's going to be sunny and warm today. Low clouds are burning off rapidly. The PacWest cars are on the setup pads and some guys are eating breakfast cereal out of plastic bowls using plastic spoons.

Practice

The weather fools me. It's clouded up again by 8:45 and getting cooler. I'm in the pit lane waiting for the start of morning practice. Mark is in the slow-guys' group and will go out for a 45-minute session at 9.

Back in after his first stint on course, Mark asks if there is anything that can be done to make his steering lighter. Allen says he'll have a chat with Malcolm Oastler and Jim Hamilton about it. They have some time to talk, because Adrian Fernandez backed his car into the wall at Turn 4.

Mark explains, "The pure weight of the steering is quite significant, holding against it, and actually, when it leads you into the turn. The car just seems to want to turn in too quick."

Allen: "Does it actually pull to the left?"

Mark: "Yeah. It pulls to the left. You have to hold it straight down the straight." A radio station is blaring in on my scanner, drowning out some of the conversations. It comes and goes.

Allen suggests a front-caster change. "This will do two things. First of all it will lighten the steering. Second, it will stop the steering pulling in so much. We can do that now while this yellow's out."

Charlie changes shims in the rear, upper A-arm mount of the front suspension. Jim Hamilton tells me, "Drivers who grow up on ovals like to feel the car want to turn in, but Mark and Mo don't like to have to hold the car straight while they're on the straights."

After the change and a few laps on course, Mark comes back in.

"OK; how's the car?" Allen asks.

Mark: "It feels a little bit better than what we finished up with yesterday afternoon. It still seems to be turning in a bit too quick and the rear still seems to be a little on the nervous side. Not a lot of push to talk about at this point." Allen increases the camber on the right rear. This also requires a toe-in and ride-height change.

Mark goes out and comes back in to report on the changes. "That seems to have stabilized the car on entry and the rear of the car is more stable into the first 20% of the turn. Now I'm picking up more of the understeer transition. More like what we were achieving yesterday morning. From mid to exit, pure push. Coming off of 4 it's at a level of 3.5; coming out of 2, a level 3. It's still a bit nervous takin' it in, but it's a lot better than what we had." He emphasizes the word "lot."

Allen: "Now, on the basis that we should always try to work from the start of the corner 'round, should we try to address the rear first or should we try to get onto the push?"

It sounds like they've been talking about a procedure to help them get more organized in developing the car. Mark used a number to quantify the level of understeer, and now Allen talks about working on a corner from entry to exit. I wonder if this will be any more successful than Jim's efforts. Mark just doesn't seem to be able to talk about how the car feels in any way other than his unique way.

Mark: "I still feel that the rear of the car could be improved. If we can still achieve a better entry, that would give me a better trajectory around the rest of the corner."

Allen: "OK. Let's do one of two things: either softer on the rear springs or up 100 pounds in the right front. What do you think?"

Mark: "I'd like to try both. Whatever you want to try — both. The rear I'd like to try because it might take a set a bit earlier. The front I'd like to try because I think it might transfer some weight to the rear of the car as well. The car still feels like it's not taking as quite as good a set as what we achieved yesterday morning, but it feels a hell of a lot better."

Allen: "All right, go 100 pounds softer on the rear springs, please."

After trying that change Mark drives back in, saying there's too much push. Allen asks, "Are you now totally happy with the car on turn-in?" It's another attempt to isolate a problem and solve it.

Mark: "It's better. I don't have to worry about the rear of the car at this point. The limiting factor now is the push mid-to-exit." Allen asks for a change to the rear toe-in. Mark is P6 in this group with about 20 minutes to go.

When Mark comes back in he says, "It moved the understeer to later in the corner. Then when it comes in, it comes in with a big hole. It gets me another 10% or 15% into the corner. Then it's a big loss of grip. When I have to back out for traffic and then get back on it, the engine doesn't pick up smoothly. It's got really poor response."

Allen adds some front rebound, high-speed and low-speed. Mark tries that on course, comes in and reports, "That's a lot better. It just cuts down the understeer. The car's a little bit reactive on turn-in, just a little bit quicker. The front jacks down slightly. I can cope with that, but I prefer to make it a bit quieter. It's got more front grip and that carries all the way to the end of the turn."

They scuff a race set of tires and another set also. There are 10 minutes to go in the session. Mark is P4 with a best lap of 21.157. Roberto Moreno is P1.

Mark describes how the car feels on the fresh tires: "With the extra grip from the tires there's a little bit more lateral load being created. I can go in a bit deeper and turn the car in more efficiently, but it's balanced front and rear. If anything, with the extra grip it's causing the rear-right corner to sit down quickly. It's a bit too quick, and if we could slow the action up I think that might help me."

Allen: "The pressures are a little off; that might be why you're feeling that."

Mark: "Maybe we should leave it then." Allen increases the pressure in the right rear by 3 pounds. The radio station in my scanner is playing country music. I hear a Lyle Lovett song.

After the checkered flag Mark comes in and says, "I've got more front grip. Now I've got a bit more precision to go in. It holds me longer in the radius. The front right feels like there could be a bit more weight in there, just to give me a bit more support, some more mechanical grip so that the load would be more constant. The load is wandering as I get to the middle; it's uneven. It needs to be a bit more constant so one steady angle on the wheel will carry me through."

Allen: "All right. Good session. Well done." A lot different from yesterday, that's for sure.

Steering Forces

Malcolm Oastler, Reynard chief designer, has been here in the PacWest pit the entire session, and he grills Mark now about what he was feeling before and after the caster-angle change. This is where I should insert a clear and easy-to-read explanation of how a change in caster effects steering forces. Since I don't understand it completely myself that's not going to happen.

I will make a very simple effort to explain why Allen suggested that change and why Malcolm is so interested. Caster angle has to do with the location of the center of the tire contact patch vs. the front-wheel steering axis, the line about which the wheel and tire rotates in steering. A caster on your chair has the steering axis ahead of the contact patch, so the forces on the wheel make it trail the steering axis. The forces the driver feels on the steering wheel come from forces trying to rotate the tire, the wheel, and therefore, the steering wheel. These forces change with slip angle, caster angle, camber angle, and maybe other things for all I know.

Steering force is one thing a driver uses to feel where he is vs. the ultimate grip of the car, so it's not surprising that a small change in these forces can make a big difference to a driver. If the steering and suspension geometry is such that the steering forces fall off predictably as the tires reach their limit of adhesion, that gives the driver some useful feedback. Malcolm wants to design a car that behaves predictably and promotes driver confidence when operating at the limit.

During this session Mark complained about the way the steering felt, changes were made, and Mark reported the car felt better. He also went half a second faster than in yesterday afternoon's session.

Mauricio's Practice Session

Right after the slow-guys' group ends I hear Control say, "I'd like a quick turn-around, guys." He'd like a quick track inspection and cleanup so he can get back on schedule. That 45-minute session took an hour and a half.

The green flag flies at 10:29 and Mauricio is out on track right away. When he comes in he's asking about the tire pressures.

Andy: "I don't think they're far off. Another couple of laps and they would have been at our intended pressures. Is that going to be a problem for the race, being as low as they were at the start?"

Mauricio: "Yes." Mauricio speaks no word before its time.

CART rules prohibit any warming of tires before they go on a car. The air pressure in the tires when the car first goes on track is called the cold pressure, but the tires can actually be hot to the touch if they've been in the sun. In use on the track, the tires are doing a lot of work and heat builds up. The pressure in the tires goes up with temperature, and there is an optimum tire pressure for a particular setup.

During a race a car goes back on track after a pit stop with cold tires. Cold rubber doesn't have as much grip, and the handling will be off until each tire comes up to the right pressure. If the cold pressures were wrong, the hot pressures will be wrong. All this is the reason for the tire-pressure guessing game that goes on during practice sessions and a race. Mistakes are costly.

Andy: "OK; we'll help them [add some pressure] a little and we'll have to work around the slightly higher pressure. Any feel for that spring change, or do you need to evaluate that once the pressures are up?"

Mauricio: "Yeah; I'd rather see the pressures up and then evaluate that. The balance is pretty good. With the low pressures the car walks too much."

Andy: "Okey doak, let's put 2 pounds in the right-side tires, please, Scott; 1 pound in the left." A yellow flag stops the session while the CART officials look for a car dropping oil. The pit marshals check all the cars for drips. The course goes green again at 10:40. When the 17-car fires up, a gout of smoke rolls out of the exhaust.

"We should get a blanket and send smoke signals," Mark Moore says. So far he's the one-liner king of the book project.

When he comes back in, Mauricio says, "I feel the front springs are probably helping, because the car is just a little bit freer than yesterday." His voice rises with "little bit" to denote a very small amount.

Andy: "What do we need to improve now?"

Mauricio: "The entry of 3 is just becoming a little bit on the light side. Two is better than yesterday but I don't seem to be able to carry the same speed into 3 as I did yesterday. We should do some things now to see if we can improve that."

Andy: "What I was going to suggest was front bump, because that helped yesterday and it'll help slow the turn-in down, and I'm going to put a bit more in the right front than in the left front."

Mauricio: "You're only doing a front change, not at the back?"

Andy: "I think so, right now."

Mauricio goes back out. He's in P14. Paul Tracy has gone to P1 in this session with a lap at 20.568 seconds. Mauricio improves to P5. When he comes back in, he asks to have his visor cleaned. "Rahal was throwing some oil." Indeed, Bobby Rahal has blown an engine, causing a yellow flag for a cleanup.

Mauricio: "I like the bump change, but I'm getting a little bit tail happy, so we could start taking some rake off or just do a shock change at the back."

Andy: "From what the skids look like, I'd actually like to come up on the front because they are kissing there, and the rear skid, if I lower it, we're going to be touching too much. So I'd like to come up a flat on the front."

Mauricio: "We have to find a way of getting rear grip again. I think what you're doing is going to take front grip away, and I'm not gaining any rear."

After another stint on course Mauricio says, "It's a little bit tail-happy. Sometimes it's very knife-edge with the steering wheel. If I'm not really smooth with it, the back end slides."

Andy: "And is that just right on the turn-in?"

Mauricio: "In the middle of the turn when I'm full gas. It's not on the turn-in. It's the middle of the turn to exit."

Andy: "What really helped that at Nazareth was pulling rear bump out of the shocks. Yesterday though, when we put high-speed in it was giving more understeer, so I'm gonna do a shock change, and I'm gonna come off the bump because it's a gas thing now rather than what it was yesterday. Take four sweeps of low-speed bump out of it. It was the high-speed bump that was helping yesterday, in terms of the balance. I'm going to take the low-speed out to try to get the car to squat a little as you're on the gas."

Mauricio: "It should be running better without the BOSS off."

Andy: "Yeah; I think BOSS just takes the valve too close to the limit. If we can use BOSS to find the limit and then come off a coupla clicks."

Mauricio: "Which map should we use?"

Andy: "We want to go back to zero while we evaluate this valve. We have a yellow for a track inspection. We'll go back to slot zero and turn BOSS on until it's found the limit of this valve and then turn BOSS off and go down two clicks." That pretty much explains what BOSS is for, and how they're using it.

The track inspection continues, so Andy says, "If you still have that problem [tail-happy], I'd like to look at front rebound, but on both sides. We put rebound on the right yesterday to help the front mid-corner and on out. I think it'll help front grip and it'll help as well in a race situation not to have as much rebound in there. It'll look after the tires a bit better."

Bleeding Brakes on Pit Lane

Mauricio: "For a race situation we're gonna have to take some rake out."

Andy: "With the race pace from previous years compared to qualifying, I'm confident we can lower the rear-ride height for the race. We've got it set now for the speeds we're doing now. We're going to end up with a car that's too high for the race."

"That was all Rahal," Mark Moore says about the long time it took for the track cleanup.

The track goes green again at 11:04 with 21 minutes to go. The monitor shows Carpentier has the fastest time followed by Tracy, Franchitti, Moreno, and Mauricio.

When Mauricio comes back in he reports the car is balanced but lacking grip. He's getting a "flat slide" or "a four-wheel slide," which are the terms he and Andy use when the car has reached the limit of its grip.

Andy says, "So it's an overall grip problem we're lookin' at now. We could try going stiffer and lower, but I think it's a little bit late in the session to be going to that now. We could try pulling the rebound out of the front, and doing a little bit more on that rear bump. Maybe we can pick up a bit more mechanical grip all 'round."

Mauricio: "Let's try that, Andy."

They also change the pop-off valve to the one that's giving the most boost. They get two pop-off valves from CART to use in each session. They pick one for the race.

Andy: "OK Morris; let's scuff our qualifying set and then we'll do a dummy qualifying run."

Then Andy summarizes the changes: "We took four sweeps of low-speed rebound out of the front, and took four sweeps of low-speed bump out of the rear."

Mauricio goes out for a few laps, but he doesn't like the shock changes and says so as he drives into the pit box. "It's too soft, Andy."

Andy: "Let's go back on those low-speed changes. How 'bout putting some high-speed in, continuing what we were doing yesterday? Is that something you want to try?"

Mauricio: "Let's try that." He's in P7 now. Tracy is still P1.

After trying those new changes, Mauricio says, "It's a little bit light at the back. I think it will be better with new tires."

Andy: "Understood." They scuff the set of tires they'll use for qualifying later today. Mauricio likes the balance with them. He's now P8 with a best lap of 20.691 seconds.

During the dummy qualifying run he improves to P4 with a lap of 20.557 seconds. Paul Tracy continues his domination, ending this session with the best lap time, 20.225 seconds or 183 mph. Patrick Carpentier and Gil de Ferran are P2 and 3. Mark

Butch Winkle and the 18-Car and Crew
On the Qualifying Line

ended up 15th in the combined times for this morning practice session.

Qualifying

The first car goes out to qualify at 1:30 p.m. Mauricio drew the 19th spot and Mark will make his run 28th, the last driver in line. The weather is great. It's warm with a cool breeze. The sky is full of puffy clouds.

Paul Tracy sets a new track record with his qualifying lap of 20.160 seconds and 184 mph. When Mauricio goes out I time his laps with my stopwatch: 22.39, 21.17, 20.52, and 20.40. Timing and Scoring says his best lap is 20.385 seconds, 182 mph. That puts him in the front row next to Tracy.

Allen talks to Andy after Mo's run and adjusts the tire pressures on Mark's car in an attempt to fine-tune the balance with some feedback from Mauricio about how the car felt. Mark's laps are 23.26, 21.64, 20.63, and 20.82. He goes a little slower on his second timed lap, but the first one earns him 11th on the grid. That's not bad, considering the confusion on Friday. To put his qualifying spot in perspective, he'll start the race ahead of Jimmy Vasser, Bobby Rahal, Michael Andretti, Gil de Ferran, Alex Zanardi, and Bryan Herta.

Mauricio and the 17-Car Crew
In the Qualifying Line

The post-qualifying press conference starts at 3:10. I've been to a lot of these because Mauricio is qualifying so well. He's been in the top three at five of the seven races and on the front row at Homestead, Rio (pole), and here, Milwaukee.

Boesel is the third-quick qualifier. "The weather changed; the car was looser."

Mauricio says, "It was a decent run. I ran hard on the second lap, but I had a little bit of push and I was loose coming out of Turn 4. That hurt my time. We're up front and we have a stable car."

Someone asks Mauricio what he could do to end Paul Tracy's run of race victories.

"Paul is on a high right now. We have to do our best on the car and the pit stops and hope for the best. We're doing well on the ovals, but I'm more comfortable on the road courses coming up."

Asked to comment on the track, Mauricio says, "It's a great track. The fans are close and they can see the cars moving around. Most ovals we can't get away with that. It's exciting racing here."

Back in the PacWest garage area I ask Mark Moore if Mauricio's car was good in qualifying.

"Yeah, he was happy with it. This morning it was loose and it hurt his confidence a little, but it was planted this afternoon."

Carbon Fiber Repair

Randy Smay is repairing some damage to the roll-hoop on the 18x-car, Mark's back-up car. The guys store the cars up high in the transporters at night. Everything is in the hauler and locked up. They were rolling this car off the power lift into its bay and didn't notice they still had the TV camera mounted on the roll-hoop. The camera mount broke and Randy is repairing

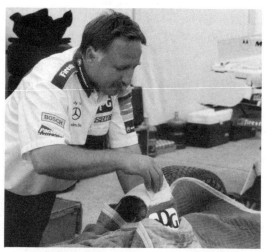
Randy Smay Repairs the Camera Mount

it. He sands the surface, smoothes on some epoxy, and lays in the cloth. After it sets up Randy sands it down smooth and paints it. It's as good as new.

Race Prep

The 17-car has an oil leak in a turbocharger seal similar to the one the 18-car had in St. Louis. The crew see it before it becomes a problem and replace the seal. Mauricio's car gets an engine change but Mark's passes a boroscope inspection and will run the race tomorrow.

The 17-crew also switches the transmission from the T-car to the primary car because the drive and drop gears on the primary car are lifed-out — have too many operating hours on them.

At 6:30 out in pit lane the 18-crew is practicing pit stops. Russ Cameron has made a modification to a manual jack they use if the on-board pneumatic jacks fail. Charlie tries it out. About 10 minutes later they finish up and push the car back to the garage.

SUNDAY

At 6:45 a.m. I'm sitting outside the fairgrounds waiting in a long line of traffic. The gates don't open until 7. Then I figure out I can bypass the line and go around to the back gate, where my hardcard gets me in. The traffic here is handled very casually, or sloppily depending on how you look at it.

In the PacWest hospitality area Mauricio introduces me to Zeca, his father's cousin. "He taught me to drive," Mauricio says of Zeca. "I was 6 and he was 19. He had a go-kart he let me drive."

"He got better than me real quick," Zeca says, smiling. Zeca works for Mauricio and comes to most of the races. He's a nice guy and we manage to talk often although his English is rough. We talk racing. His real name is Jose Mello, but I only hear his nickname, Zeca.

Later Zeca tells me that he and Mauricio were roommates with Ayrton Senna when Mauricio first moved to England to race. Just thinking about Senna makes me feel like crying. These guys lived with him. I can't imagine the loss they felt.

At 7:50 the 17-car is on the setup pad. Neil Atterbury watches and Mark Moore writes numbers on a setup sheet as Jim Reid and Dave Jacobs take measurements. A few feet away the 18x car is also on the pad next to the Motorola hauler.

Tim Douthat tells me he did some welding repair on some exhaust components last night. This team doesn't seem to suffer the exhaust problems that I see at some teams. A cracked header can put a car out of a race just like a crash.

It's 8:15 and I'm in the pit lane watching Mike Bauer, Trevor Jackson, and Tom Keene lay down strips of colored duct tape to guide the drivers into the pit boxes during pit stops. The warm-up session starts at 9 a.m.

Russ Cameron tells me about the pit stops. "Fuel isn't a big problem here. Only 10 laps of yellow will save us enough fuel to go the distance. But the laps are only 20 seconds, so you can go a lap down easily if you mess up a stop. That means we have to come in at the right time and the stops have to be perfect. We did 10 or 15 practice stops yesterday and we'll do more this morning, maybe 25 or 30 total."

Warm-Up

I walk to Turn 1 for this session, just down the pit lane and through a gap between the concrete wall and a chain-link fence. There's no one there to check my credentials. It's all grass between the barriers near the track and the fence behind me. Fans are beginning to line the fence as they set up their campers and pickups and barbecues.

Some guys are already drinking beer. It's getting warm, but there's a nice breeze. The cars go out right on time and, once again, I notice some big yaw oscillations. The tires are probably cold and not up to pressure — that might make it worse. I hear Mauricio talking to Andy about needing some more rear grip.

After a few more laps on course Mauricio says, "Down one flat, Andy." Andy asks the crew to lower the car one flat at the rear.

"The right rear is getting a little thin on the gauge," Andy says, "but my only option is the primaries, and I'd just as soon stay on these."

Mauricio: "That's OK, Andy, I'm only going to do one more run."

Andy: "Have you tried the throttle response like on a restart?"

Mauricio: "Not yet. I'll do it."

"We're going to do a hot stop," says Mark Moore to his guys. "Get ready."

The session ends at 9:34. As he comes in off the track Mauricio says, "The car is getting loose but it's just tire wear."

Lola Problems

Peter Spruce is the sales manager at Lola Cars Ltd. I see him in the paddock and ask him if he's going to have to give some cars away next year to overcome the sales resistance created by the Lolas' lack of performance this season.

"We wouldn't do that," he says. "But we might have to scale back the operation, maybe work with only one team. The best thing that could happen, of course, is to get the cars going at a competitive pace. We're working on that. We've shipped a car back to the factory and we think we have the fix. We're working very hard on that. And we think we'll have an investor in about six weeks."

The company is now "in administration," which is the equivalent of our Chapter 11. A court-appointed administrator controls the company financials and protects it from creditor lawsuits. It looks like Eric Broadley, the founder, will have to sell a portion of his company to an outside investor just to have a chance to stay in business. A bitter pill!

Six months ago the company was thought to be successful, having sold almost $10 million worth of '97 Indy cars. In the last year it also sold 40 Indy Lights cars for about $160,000 each. Allowing for Carl Haas' distributor commission, this would generate more than 5 million additional dollars for Lola.

Unfortunately Mr. Broadley had a yen to field a Formula 1 car. That program was an embarrassing disaster, but worse, it must have strained Lola's resources and crippled its Indy car development. Reynard, Swift, and Penske aren't standing around doing nothing, so Lola has fallen behind.

The rumors say there is a lack of stiffness in the engine mount area that allows some uncontrolled flexing at the rear of the car. The result is a lack of stable and repeatable response to suspension forces that confuses the drivers and engineers. I'm guessing there is an aero problem to boot, either a simple lack of downforce or extreme sensitivity to changes of pitch and roll. It would be a shame to see Lola go away!

Pre-Grid

The race is scheduled to start at 1 p.m. At noon I'm in the garage watching the PacWest crew finish up the cars. Mark Moore tells me, "The race today could come down to how well Mo gets into the pit box. There's not much room in the pits at this racetrack."

Fifteen minutes later the 17-crew is done and ready to go to pit lane. "What did we forget?" Chris Jaynes says. "We're done too early."

"Shall we go?" Mark Moore asks. "Let's be one of the first cars out there for a change."

The pre-grid activities are exciting, as usual. We listen to the invocation and the national anthem. The stands are filling up.

Bruce McCaw is here, and I tell him about my conversation with Peter Spruce. "They asked me if I wanted to look at their financial package," Bruce says. "I told them I wasn't interested."

At 12:50 the drivers get into the cars and start the engines. I walk toward Turn 1. Out on the grass in between Turns 1 and 2, I get all my gear together. I make notes in a small notebook and listen to the radio conversations on the scanner and record them with a microcassette recorder. As the cars start their pace laps I hear Control growl, "You guys watch your butts out there."

THE RACE

At the start Tracy surges ahead and Mauricio tucks in behind him. Michel Jourdain crashes in Turn 4 on lap three. Mark has slipped from 12th to 15th. During the caution period Russ tells Mauricio, "Let's just hold station until after the last stop."

Mauricio asks about tire pressures and Russ says, "Two pounds down."

On lap 10, still under yellow, Russ says, "Mo, from what we've seen on the consumption, we may have to run 90%. That's slot two."

Ando tells Mark, "Work on that fuel."

The race restarts on lap 13 and the cars roar by me lap after lap. It's very exciting being this close to the cars during a race. I'm really only about 20 feet closer than the fans standing along the fence behind me, but the cars seem very near. This will definitely spoil me!

Greg Moore is moving up. After starting fifth, he passes Raul Boesel for fourth on lap 25. A few laps later he gets by Carpentier for third. Now he passes Mauricio and begins to challenge Paul Tracy.

Parker Johnstone spins into the wall at the exit of Turn 2, just outside of my line of sight. It takes almost 10 yellow-flag laps to clean up the track.

Russ tells Mauricio, "The fuel is good. You can use push-to-pass any time you want."

"Push-to-pass" is a button on the steering wheel that tells the engine management system to add extra fuel into the intake, giving a burst of power.

Russ tells Mauricio, "We will pit with the leaders. Pack up. Hustle it in and hit the marks."

When the pit lane goes green, Greg Moore drives onto pit lane and the pack follows him. Paul Tracy gets his stop done first and comes by me back out onto the track in front of Greg and Mauricio. Jimmy Vasser and Al Unser Jr. are fourth and fifth.

Mark improves to 11th with his stop. Ando yells, "Good goin'; picked up a spot."

Mauricio tells Russ, "Too much stagger."

A green flag restarts the race on lap 61, and I get to watch another long period of intense racing. Carpentier gets into Turn 1 side-by-side with Unser Jr. and they come by me in formation smooth as glass two laps in a row before the rookie surges ahead out of Turn 2. About 15 laps later Mauricio is still third, but he has a tough time getting by Bryan Herta, who's a lap down.

Greg Moore is pressing Tracy for the lead and I hear Mark Moore say, "Maybe these two brave young lions will get stupid." Greg makes the pass for the lead on lap 86. Twenty laps later Juan Fangio spins and collects Gualter Salles in Turn 4, bringing out another yellow flag.

Mauricio tells Russ, "The car is better, but it goes loose in traffic." That explains why he's had trouble passing.

On lap 108 Russ says, "The Penske guys are ready; follow Tracy in. Pit. Pit. Pit."

The leaders charge in for tires and fuel. Greg Moore and Bobby Rahal crash together in the pit lane and Greg loses two spots. Tracy motors by me out of the pit lane followed by Mauricio, Greg, Vasser, and Michael Andretti, who has been passing cars steadily and moving up the order. Mark improves to ninth. "Good job," Ando says.

Another great one-liner from Mark Moore: "Great stop guys; they're cheerin' for us at home."

After a green flag on lap 125 the cars run in that order for less than 10 laps before another crash; Max Papis this time. Most of the leaders, including Mauricio, pit again, but Moore, Vasser, Rahal, and Boesel stay out on course, playing their fuel mileage card. Mauricio emerges in fifth spot and Russ tells him, "That's 140 laps. You can go all the way — 100% on fuel. Moore didn't pit and you're the leader of the group that did."

A green flag restarts the race on lap 145 with 55 laps to go. Michael Andretti passes Mauricio right in front of me and Tracy gets by him a lap later. Mauricio looks loose; the rear of the car is wiggling in Turn 1. He's fighting the car. Mark is in ninth spot running a conservative but steady race. Ando tells him, "Play with that jacker."

The order is Moore, Vasser, Boesel, Rahal, Andretti, Tracy, and Mauricio. Andretti moves past Boesel on lap 168 and passes Vasser on lap 181. Greg Moore looks very fast and comfortable. Will he win his first CART race today? That would be fine with me. I like Greg, his dad Ric, and Steve Challis, Greg's engineer. They deserve it. But he could just run out of fuel!

Mauricio is really pressing Tracy, and he finally gets by about 10 laps from the end. He immediately starts to gain on Rahal, who is in fifth place and nursing his fuel.

It's an exciting race right to the end. Andretti is pressing Moore, who could run out of fuel at any moment. Rahal slows on the next-to-last lap, running out of fuel as he did at Rio. Mauricio passes him and then he passes Paul Tracy also. Greg Moore wins and runs out of fuel on the cool-off lap. Michael Andretti gets second and Vasser third, followed by Boesel and Mauricio. Mark finishes 11th and gets the last CART point.

I hurry back to pit lane, where Russ tells me, "There were 92 laps on that load of fuel for Greg." He's shaking his head in wonder.

Mauricio is not a good loser. He's a competitive guy. "I'm disappointed. Three guys took the risk. It was a hard race. It's hard to take a risk like that. Some you win and some you lose."

Russ says, "We didn't race as hard as I'd like. Michael went through the entire field."

Standing here among the team I feel that at this moment, Mauricio wishes the team had been more aggressive on the fuel strategy. Maybe they hadn't thought about doing what Greg did. At the same time, Russ wishes Mauricio had passed some people on the track.

It looks to me like you can win races if you can pass people on the track. You can only depend on the strategy and the pit work for so much. The driver has to be able to pass people.

Mark says, "We got a bad start because of a gear-change problem. We lost four of five spots. We suffered some boost problems. The balance of the car was good the last part of the race."

Good for Greg Moore. His first CART win!

CHAPTER 12

MIDSEASON AT THE SHOP

After the race at Milwaukee I hang around in the paddock talking to people before getting on the road to Indianapolis. The guys on the crews have to drive the team vans back to Indianapolis tonight, so I ask what route they suggest. Several people say it's best to go right through Chicago so that's what I do, starting out from the track at 4:15 p.m. Except for 45 minutes of stop-and-go traffic going into Chicago, it's a quick trip. The drivers in Chicago are the most reckless I've ever seen. As I get near Indianapolis I run into some rain, and I get to the motel about 9:30 p.m.

MONDAY

Monday morning the weather is overcast and foggy, and the roads are wet. I set up my stuff in the lunchroom at PacWest. There's a refrigerator, soft-drink vending machines, a double sink, and cabinets for cups and glasses. In one corner of the room is a rack of cubbyholes with employee names over each one. Today a lot of these have paychecks in them. In another corner is a big-screen TV and VCR.

I ask Mark Moore what he has to say about the Milwaukee race. "We might have been able to go the distance with the fuel Mo had, but I'm saying that we shouldn't do that kind of stuff just because those other guys did it. Our numbers at the time said we couldn't. Do you change the way you're doing things? I told them we should keep doing the same things. We're knocking on the door every weekend. Sooner or later we'll win one. I'd rather we do things right and finish rather than gamble and lose."

At 10:30 a truck comes to the back door and a lot of the people buy a snack. The lunchroom fills up then, and someone turns on the TV and puts a videotape in the VCR. The 18-crew watches their Milwaukee pit stops and talk among themselves about their performance, trying to see how to do the stops better.

I've still got a cough left over from Rio and I find out a lot of people came back with the same thing. We compare prescription antibiotics and decongestants. Some people developed sinus infections and others have chest symptoms.

Subassembly

The PacWest shop includes a subassembly section where three full-time guys work on components such as drive shafts, A-arms, hubs, calipers, and rotor assemblies. The car mechanics seldom work on these parts; they take them off the car and put them back on after they've been rebuilt. Jeff Horton, also known as Fuzzy, is the subassembly supervisor. "It's a full-time job for one guy just working on brake pads and rotors."

Many racecar parts are checked for cracks after use and reinstalled if there are no cracks. "The hubs get crack-checked after every race," Fuzzy tells me. "We polish the ends of the vanes where they meet the outer ring so we can see cracks easier. Steve Ekeren is the crack expert. He's been to classes on that stuff."

Tony Houk, known as Boomer, also works in subassembly. He and Steve Ekeren are shop-based; they don't go to the races regularly. Boomer does fill in for a race mechanic now and then, but Steve works full-time at the shop.

Boomer is assembling brake rotors and brake hats. He uses a special anti-seize compound. "It's got nickel in it," he tells me. These guys work on batches of parts, four to 10 units, taking them apart, cleaning, and inspecting them, and putting the assembly back together. When they're done with a batch there is a drawer or cabinet where the parts belong. They carefully fill out the proper paperwork for each critical operation on each part.

Engines

Blake Hamilton is the engine technician. He came to PacWest from VDS, the Ilmor/Mercedes-rebuild facility in Midland, Texas. "I have to keep track of 15 motors," Blake explains. "I keep records for the life-critical components and work up an engine usage plan for each weekend. Mark McArdle at Ilmor directs that program, and we modify it as needed."

At each race Blake dresses every engine as it comes out of the shipping box from Ilmor and releases it to the racecar mechanics.

Details

I see three transaxle assemblies, with gearboxes attached, lined up waiting for rebuild and decide to take some photos. As I'm focusing the camera and scoping out the right shot, Fuzzy says, "Wait a minute." He walks over and takes a shop towel out of a turbocharger compressor exit and replaces the towel with the proper red-plastic plug. These guys like doing things the right way.

Transaxles Lined Up for Rebuilds

At 5 p.m. some people are cleaning up and leaving for the day. About an hour later I go back to the motel to make some phone calls. After dinner I'm driving back past the shop and decide to stop and see who's there. It's 8:15 and there are about 20 people still working. Steve Fusek; Mary and Ron Fusek, Steve's parents; and some of the engineering and shop people are still busy.

TEAM MEETING

Every week, usually on Tuesday, PacWest has a team meeting in the lunchroom. Ando starts this one at 8:05 a.m. with a critique of the Milwaukee race. "We qualified well and the race was good until the last yellow flag," he summarizes. "Basically we made a cockup of our bloody fuel stop. We're going to address the fuel situation with individual team brainstorming meetings.

"On the bright side, our oval-track setup works. Mo passed Tracy late in the race. It's frustrating. We're bloody close. I'm pissed Greg Moore got his first win before we did, but they did a good job and we need to do better."

Ando sums up, "We're knockin' on the door. Be hard on yourselves. Think about organizing your stuff in the pits. Coil up the hoses and have everything tidied up."

Other people have comments. Russ Cameron says, "We're building good cars, but there are some small things we can do better."

Daryl Fox mentions security: "The front of the car gets covered up, but not the back."

Ando agrees. "Yeah, the covers get forgotten."

Allen McDonald: "We'll look at the fuel mixtures and do some more planning."

Butch Winkle: "We had some good pit stops. We passed people in the pits."

Ando: "Gavin [Hamilton] did a good job; bloody good."

Dave Jacobs: "What about trying to lower the weight of the car for the road courses?"

Ando: "We need to look at that, and see if we can save some weight. Also, Fuzzy said he saw a scavenge pump with a cracked fitting. Somebody used a skid-plate bolt that was too long and it stuck too far up. We need to look at that."

After some more announcements and suggestions, Ando ends the meeting on an upbeat note. "We're goin' to win some races this year. Let's bloody kick some ass in Detroit."

Gearboxes

In the subassembly area, Roscoe (Russell Grosshans) and Dr. (Tim) Love are rebuilding gearboxes. At 8:40 a.m. Roscoe takes the final drive gear out of one transaxle casing while Tim is putting a gearbox back together.

The gearbox is a special Reynard-design, a six-speed transverse box, meaning the gears are on a shaft that goes across the car instead of on the same line as the engine crankshaft. Transverse gearboxes can be lower, and their weight is more in the middle of the car. A lower center of gravity (CG) uses the tires better, and less weight at the ends of the car reduces the polar moment of inertia, allowing the car to change directions better.

Roscoe Heats the Case

"The Reynard gearbox is a good piece," Roscoe says. "You can loosen these seven nuts, take that side-plate off, and change third through sixth gears. With the old longitudinal Reynard box you had a nut on the back of the shaft you had to break with 250 ft.-lb. These cars are easy to work on. They've put some thought into some little things that make a difference."

Roscoe needs to remove some parts that are interference-fit in the case so he has to expand the case with heat from a torch and use a slide hammer to get them out. He sprays the disassembled parts with brake cleaner and carefully inspects everything, especially the bearings. It takes two guys to break loose the nuts on the final drive gear. Boomer comes over to help.

At one point Roscoe finds a slim sliver of metal in a filter housing. He holds it up for Tim Love to see. Tim frowns at it. When Roscoe pulls the oil pump out of the case he turns to me and says, "This is its heart." Roscoe places all the parts in plastic bins and wheels the bins into the cleaning room on a cart.

Barry Ward, a gearbox designer for Reynard, comes into the shop about 9:30 a.m. and spends some time with Allen McDonald and Tim. PacWest has had some pits and scratches develop on bevel gears. Barry would like to get examples of those parts back to the factory in England for inspection.

At 10:50 a.m. the food truck comes. Roscoe eats at his bench, looking over blueprints and numbers from his measurements. Some of the tapered bearings require a precise preload during assembly, so Roscoe uses his measurements and calculations to select the proper shim that will give that preload when everything is bolted up. At noon Roscoe and Tim go over the numbers one last time before assembly begins.

Tim has a transmission going together, and he uses an assembly lube on all the rotating parts. "It mixes with the oil eventually."

Later in the afternoon Roscoe is putting his gearbox back together also. At 5 p.m. he heats the case so he can fit the drop-shaft bearing. He taps it in and torques it down. He also uses pre-lube on all the parts. He checks the bevel lash, the clearance between driving and driven gears, with a dial gauge. This measurement has to be right on. It is, of course.

Tim has finished assembling one gearbox, and it will now go on Mark Blundell's T-car. Tim begins to rebuild the gearbox that will go on Mark's Detroit racecar. "It's not a complete rebuild," Tim says, "just the gears and diff."

I ask how much time it takes them to rebuild a gearbox. Roscoe says, "It'll take me about 25 hours on this one. Steve cleaned the parts. That cut maybe four or five hours off my time."

Tim says, "The one I just did for Mark's car took about 30 hours for a total teardown and rebuild."

At 6:30 p.m. Mauricio is in the conference room signing hero cards. That's what they call the promotional give-away cards. He's just started, and he's got 300 to do. He's methodical about it. He and John Oreovicz and I talk for a while. Then it's dinner and back to the motel.

WEDNESDAY

At the shop at 8 the next morning, Roscoe tells me he finished that gearbox last night about 9:30. He came in today at 6:30 to start another one.

Danny Jenkins is a fabricator. He starts with stainless steel or Inconel sheets and makes an exhaust header, turbo crossover pipe, or waste-gate exhaust pipe. In this photo Danny is standing by his workbench, where you see some work in progress.

The first step is to make wood tooling the exact size and shape needed so he can form the metal shapes. Then he cuts the sheet metal, forms the compo-

Danny Jenkins at his Workbench

nents, and welds everything together. Usually there's some cutting and fitting to make the part fit the car. "There's lots of fab work on a race team," Danny tells me. "They're making constant changes on the cars. We made the fueling rigs also. We tried to make 'em look nice, with rounded corners."

FAMILY LIFE IS DIFFICULT

You have to be impressed by the dedication and hard work of the people working in racing. The travel and long hours cuts into family life. Early in the project I decided to talk with some of the wives to get their perspective.

Kasey Winkle

Butch Winkle, Mark Blundell's crew chief, told me how he met his wife, Kasey.

"I was at a race in Portland and a bunch of us were at a bar. She caught my eye and I was watching her turn guys down when they asked her to dance. I didn't think I had a chance. Finally, I just went over and sat down and started talking to her. Then a slow dance came up and I said, 'Sure you don't want to dance?' We fit together like two spoons and that was it. If there was ever love at first sight, that was it. I know I'm lucky. She's a great wife."

Kasey looks like the California girl she is, tall and athletic and pretty. They have two boys: Zachary, 11, and Blake, 8. Kasey is open and straightforward, completely comfortable talking to me about her life as a racing wife and mother.

Paul: "Where were you born?"

Kasey: "Santa Monica."

Paul: "Were you a race fan?"

Kasey: "Yes. It was when I moved to Oregon. I was 10 years old. When I was a kid we all went to the racetrack to watch the drags and hang out. I met Butch in Portland. Not at a race. He was there for a race. It was around midnight at the Red Lion Inn near the track. He finally got up the nerve to ask me to dance. The rest is history I guess you could say. That was 12 years ago, 1985."

Paul: "That's a great story."

Kasey: "It worked out. So we lived in Indy for a while and then in North Carolina and then Michigan, when Butch worked on GTP cars. Back to Indiana and then to New Mexico where Butch worked for Rick Galles. We were there five years. Then back to Indy to the Patrick team and now we're here with PacWest."

Paul: "This job was an opportunity for Butch, wasn't it?"

Kasey: "Yes, it was. He hoped he would get to be the the crew chief for Raul Boesel at Patrick, but it didn't work out. Along came this offer and he took it."

Paul: "Are you mainly a mom?"

Kasey: "Yes. Before I met Butch I was trying to get a nursing degree. When we first got together money was a factor and all the moving and then I got pregnant. I put the nursing on the back burner. Now I work as a waitress part time in Nobleville, in a little ice cream store. But mainly I deal with my kids."

Paul: "The salaries for the crews seem to have gone up the last few years."

Kasey: "It's a lot better. Butch got almost $13,000 more a year to come to work for this team. Salary-wise I've seen it get better. Back when he first worked as a number one mechanic it was right at $35,000 to $38,000 a year. Now it's $60,000. It's a huge difference."

Paul: "What are the pluses and minuses of a racing family?"

Kasey: "It's a real individual thing. It starts with the type of person the wife is. Myself I like time alone. I like to not have to worry about dinner or a routine with Butch all the time. He knows I like some of that. I don't always tell him how much I like to be by myself at home [laughs]. We've been together a long, long time so something's working. I love the sport, as well. I don't get discouraged when he's not home when he says he's going to be home or there's a test that's popped up and we can't go to Six Flags or whatever. You have to just take all that in stride. Things change a lot.

"When my boys were real little, it was hard because I was stuck at home a lot. I couldn't go to the races regularly. We didn't have family around home. It's only been the last few years that I've been able to go. That's made it better for us. We can be with him a little more that way.

"The positives are, I'd say, it's something Butch can do that he enjoys so much. Some people think it's real glamorous, but he works his butt off. I know how hard they work and they put up with a lot of BS too. But he's able to travel and I hope some year we can go with him to the race in Australia.

"The kids have perfect attendance at school all year. I don't start taking them to races till May. Their teachers consider the travel good life experience for the kids. Most cities we go to I take them somewhere. Thursday or Friday we go sight-seeing. We get out. We don't just hang out at the race the whole time."

Paul: "How do you like living in the Midwest?"

Kasey: "I love the Midwest. I like the farm land and the whole thing in Indiana. They have great schools. I've been real happy. I remember when I came to Indianapolis to visit Butch right after we met. He said to come and just see how it works. I wound up going home just to get my personal belongings and we got together. I never went back to Portland after that."

Paul: "Did you know what you were getting into then?"

Kasey: "No, I really didn't. Gosh, I'm 35, so I was pretty young. I was more concerned with being in love and didn't really think much about the details. It was really rough at first. Some of the jobs he had in the beginning were terrible. They'd put those guys in terrible hotels sometimes. We've come a long way in that. It just gradually got better."

Paul: "What advice would you give to a young racing couple?" We both laugh at the thought.

Kasey: "It would mainly be for the woman. You need to be confident of yourself. You need to be pretty independent. I can't depend on Butch for a lot of things. If you start letting the business get in the way of the relationship that you have it's not going to work. They ARE gone a lot. They keep adding more races. If you don't like to be left alone it's probably not going to work out. That's the main thing. And trust. You have to trust each other too. There's a lot of women walking around at the tracks. And these guys are in the limelight all the time.

"You can't just sit around and wonder when he's going to make it home. There's times when it's hard for me to adjust the things I'm doing. When he comes home and we've been in a routine of our own and then suddenly I have to jump into his deal, his laundry and all his stuff. That's what I hate about saying good-bye when he leaves for races. At that point I'm used to having him home. I'm going to miss him I know, but then I get to where I'm not missing him and we're into our stuff. When he comes back, getting into the swing of things is tough. That's when we argue, right when he comes home. [She laughs again.]

"So I think you have to be a real easy-going person. That's the whole heart of it. I don't think I could be a driver's wife. I would worry way too much. That scares me. Butch has been run over before but I don't worry like I'm sure the driver's wives do.

"In a nutshell, I think you have to be able to trust him and you need to be self-confident and you have to like being alone and going with the flow, being easy-going and don't let things get to you. Things just go along good for us. They really do."

Paul: "I'm glad to hear that. Butch is a great guy. Thanks Kasey, for taking the time to talk to me."

Kasey: "You're welcome."

Lesley Anderson

Lesley and John started out in Australia and worked together in racing for years. Now Lesley has a successful business selling real estate in Indianapolis. She has bright eyes, a girlish laugh, and a lilting trace of Down Under accent.

Paul: "How did you and John meet?"

Lesley: "I'm from New Zealand and I was on a holiday in Australia with a group of girl-friends. We went out to a dinner and dance place. He was there with all his buddies. We talked and danced and had lots of laughs. He took my number and said, 'I'd like to ask you out some-time.' And he did. He called up and we started going out. At that time he was about to leave to go overseas on a trip. That was about 1966 or 1967 [laughs]. I was only 5 at the time."

Both of us laugh. "Weren't we all?" I say.

Lesley: "I thought he was just wonderful. I liked him. I simply fell in love. He went over-seas for two or three years. We corresponded a little bit. He'd occasionally call. He was always in the back of my mind. I thought he was the one. But he was an adventurer and he had a lot to do and see. I wasn't ready to rush around and get married. I wanted to travel a lot myself. We're very much alike, really.

"Then he came back and we dated for a while, on and off. We knew each other probably seven years before we actually got serious and decided to get married. We were really good friends for a long time. We got married in 1972."

Paul: "Was he in racing then?"

Lesley: "He wasn't in racing when I first met him, but he was a couple of years before we got married. He was a mechanic on a team. We got married on a Friday and had a Saturday and Sunday for a honeymoon, and he left on Monday for three months. He did the Tasman series in Australia and New Zealand.

"So we got married and...three months later [laughs] we saw each other again. And that's the way it's been on and off ever since. I worked with him on teams for years and years. At one stage I traveled and worked beside him for the team."

Paul: "What did you do?"

Lesley: "I did all the coordinating — the travel, the bookkeeping, the expenses, all the timing and scoring, looked after all the uniforms. I used to make lunches for all the guys. We didn't even have a refrigerator in the truck, let alone a gourmet meal like we have now. I used to get up at the hotel at 5 or 6 o'clock and go to the grocery store and make all the sandwiches in the truck in between practice and qualifying so the guys could have a sandwich."

Paul: "How did you get over here?"

Lesley: "We came over here in '73. He came over here with a driver to compete in the Formula 5000 series. I came over with him and we liked it. He kept getting offers from teams that would come down and do the Tasman series. Eight years later he said, 'What do you think?' It seemed like a good idea to both of us. We sold our house and came for a year or two to try it out. We're still here 17 years later [laughs merrily at the idea]. It has been wonderful and it still is."

Paul: "Did you continue to work with John over here?"

Lesley: "I did all the travel. We were in California for about five years. Mike Curb Motorsports was an Indy car team. Tom Sneva and John Andretti were the drivers at one point. We lived in Thousand Oaks north of Los Angeles. John was crew chief and team manager. I used to do all the team arrangements. It was a two-car team. I had a girl that answered the phone, but I did everything else.

"We'd get back from a race on Sunday night, 3 in the morning, go back to work at 8 and get ready for the next race. There was a lot to do in a three-day period. We had to leave again on Wednesday for the next race. We weren't a team with a big budget so you couldn't afford to have a lot of staff."

Paul: "Marriage is difficult anyway. Is it better or worse to be working together?"

Lesley: "For us it was better. People tell us, 'Our marriage wouldn't last five minutes.' We both had exactly the same interests. I used to do stuff for him before he'd even ask me. I knew him so well and I knew what he wanted. We just got on really well when we work together. It's amazing really with all that traveling day and night six days a week next to each other. I guess I've always had a lot of respect for what he had to do, the pressures and stress. I'm very understanding about it I suppose. I know what he's going through. I know what sort of a day these guys have.

"Now that we don't work together, it's still fine. I just had a hard time adjusting to not having him around. But I'm very independent anyway. I like my space. I kind of enjoy sometimes, being able to make my own decisions and not having to rely on somebody and being in control, I suppose [laughs]."

Paul: "It sounds like racing has been a very positive thing in your marriage. I don't hear anything negative."

Lesley: "I do miss him now that I don't work with him all day. We got on so well. When we were first married I was an administrative assistant for an engineering company and I didn't travel with him when he'd be gone for three months at a time. I missed him terribly then. I found it harder when I was younger. Now I'm much more accepting. But I never complained. You can't try to change somebody. That's what he did. That's what he does. I married him because I liked him the way he was."

Paul: "Does he bring the pressures of the job home at all?"

Lesley: "Not really. I know when he's had a bad time. He'll be a grump and I won't push it. I just leave him alone. He needs to just go read a book or watch TV. He doesn't need me asking a bunch of questions. I've always got plenty of things to take care of."

Paul: "You don't have any kids, do you?"

Lesley: "No, we wanted to have children when we were younger but we said let's get all the traveling over. It's not fair to have children when he's gone all the time. The responsibility should be on both, not just one. We planned to do it, but it was past us before we realized it. Which is sad, really."

Paul: "Do you feel the loss? Do you think you've missed anything?"

Lesley: "No. Not really. We've missed that type of life. But we couldn't have had the kind of life we've had. We've lived in so many cities and countries. We've traveled together and really enjoyed life together doing what we enjoy doing. I don't have any regrets."

Paul: "Was it easy to get into the real estate business?"

Lesley: "I've been doing it four years. It was something I've always been interested in. Since we've moved so much I knew what was involved {laughs]. I thought it would leave me flexible to travel with John, but I've become so involved and it's doing so well I don't do that much. I used to help John out in the office on weekends and after work I'd come here and do things for him. I miss that. I don't have the time. But I enjoy what I'm doing. It is a little bit difficult though. I'd like to be with him more, but neither of us have the time [laughs again]."

Paul: "I've run out of questions. Thanks, Lesley."

Lesley: "All right. That was fun. But you will let me see it before you put it in the book. No telling what I said."

Paul: "No problem."

Here's what Ando had to say. "It wasn't fair to her to take care of kids. We always worked as a team anyway. I'd run the crew or manage the team and Leslie would do the travel and uniforms, and manage the business. For me it was like having another pair of hands. I knew all that stuff would get handled. Now she's selling real estate in Indianapolis and working as long hours as myself."

Christine Brown

Earlier in the year I told Lesley I wanted to interview a wife who is critical of racing life. She suggested Andy Brown's wife, Christine. I talked to her on the phone and she came to the shop. Christine is slim and pretty. She talks with a soft British accent. She tells me the Brown children are: Laura, 10; Jessica, 8; and Sean, 1.

We went outside and sat in my rental car so we could have a quiet, private place to talk and I taped a conversation. She didn't sound that negative to me, but later Andy gave me a letter Christine wrote to me:

Dear Paul,

Further to our conversation today in your "office," I think that while trying not to be too negative, I was actually too positive. I think I have added in this letter comments to make a more balanced view of being married to a racing man and living in a foreign country.

I especially wish I had told you how much we do miss our families. Last year was especially hard, as my youngest brother was diagnosed with cancer in March. I did fly over in June, with my two girls and pregnant with Sean, when my brother had extensive surgery — for just three weeks. My brother died at Christmas. I had a new baby and was unable to be with my family at this terribly sad time. We have actually missed four funerals and maybe one wedding this fall while living in the U.S.A. At Christmas we make sure we are with family. Twice we have flown family here and we spent one Christmas in England.

In England I can work as a registered general and pediatric nurse. I would have to retake all my exams to be able to work as a nurse here, and so have for the moment put my nursing behind me.

This year there are two times when the race meetings are scheduled every weekend for three weekends. This is very hard on my children, who miss their dad, and on Andy. There are no days off to make up for the weekends missed, so he works three weeks without a break. When he is at home, Andy generally falls asleep on the couch.

All three of our babies have not accidentally been born out of the racing season to ensure Dad's presence at the birth. We decided to avoid all the worrying associated with a spring or summer delivery.

On the positive side again, there is one way in which a "motor racing marriage" benefits. All the traveling means that there is no chance for life to get boring and routine.

Sincerely,

Christine Brown

That certainly sums up the sacrifices necessary when a career decision takes a couple away from family support. The woman often has to give up everything and deal with the children full time. These are three strong, intelligent women doing all they can for their families. The difference is that Kasey and Lesley are in comfortable, stable situations. Christine's level of discomfort is higher. Something will probably change.

About 3 o'clock Wednesday afternoon I say good-bye to everyone and hit the road for Detroit.

CHAPTER 13

DETROIT

The drive on Wednesday from Indianapolis to Detroit is without drama. The team is staying at the Westin Hotel in the Renaissance Center right on the Detroit River in the middle of downtown. This building complex is only a few years old, but it already looks rundown. Does anyone who runs a hotel ever actually stay in one of the rooms? The air-conditioning control in my room has a big red light on it, and I have to cover up to go to sleep. The vending refrigerator seems to have been stolen; there is a space for it but it isn't there. The elevators are slow and the people at the front desk are too.

I've heard the Greek Town section of downtown Detroit has some good food so I go out to walk in the direction I was told. Unfortunately I get a few streets off on the way there, and some guys are lurking around looking at me like I'm fresh meat. I make a turn in the right direction and find a more friendly street. I pick a restaurant named Pegasus and have a good meal and a few beers. I find a better route to walk back to the hotel.

THURSDAY

There's a media lunch at the Detroit Yacht Club on Belle Isle near the track. I sit down at a table with Chris Economaki, editor of *National Speed Sport News*, and two Indy Lights drivers, Chris Simmons and Mark Hotchkis. We have a good discussion. Chris is always good for some stories. He knows everybody in racing.

Some guy from the promoting organization speaks to us, telling about how they've made some improvements because his wife lost her shoes in the mud last year. My shoes didn't dry out until I got off the plane at home last year. God forbid they should think ahead. I'm glad some big guy's wife lost her shoes, or they wouldn't have improved the track at all. As far as I'm concerned this city and this racetrack are shameful. The big car companies and Detroit community leaders need to get to work. CART has a lot better places to race than this.

About 1 p.m. I find the PacWest garage area and say hello to the guys. The paddock isn't paved. They've driven sections of plastic pipe into the ground and this supports the trucks and equipment but allows grass to grow up through the pipe sections. Sections of plywood are laid down in the PacWest area to give the guys something solid to work on.

Working on the Grass

Peter Gibbons is Michael Andretti's engineer. I see him on pit lane and ask about the yaw oscillations I saw at Milwaukee.

"Does the driver feel that?" I ask.

"Oh, yeah," Peter says, grinning. "They feel it. It's a form of oversteer. It depends on tire pressure, tire condition, and fuel load."

As usual I walk around and talk to people and take photos. Later I walk from the hotel to Pegasus again for dinner. The Detroit Red Wings hockey team is in town and they're playing downtown. Greek Town is crowded, so I go back to the hotel.

FRIDAY

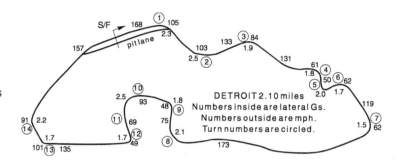

CART practice starts at 11 a.m. The 18-car has a problem when the engine starts up at about 10:30. The crew begins a quick tear down to replace a turbocharger. The turbo sits under a cast part called "the toilet seat" that has to be removed to get to the turbo. They don't want to lose any track time, so as many guys help as can get hands on. John Roof, Gavin Hamilton, Tim Love, Daryl Fox, Butch Winkle, and Russ Cameron are working on the car. At 10:55 they're safety wiring nuts and bolts as the car goes back together.

The session starts late, typical of a street circuit. The weather is nice; it's sunny with some high clouds. The track here on Belle Isle has always been very bumpy. Sections of the track have been ground down this year to try to eliminate the bumps. Unfortunately this leaves some very rough and abrasive patches of concrete. The green flag starts the session at 11:19. Both the PacWest cars go out for a lap and come back in for installation checks.

Mauricio: "It's quite tail happy right now."

Andy: "Down eight flats on the rear rods, please."

Mauricio: "The whole car could be lowered, I think."

Andy: "Lowering the rear as much as we are will bring the front contact point down as well." Andy adds, "After checking the skids, let's put some high-speed bump in the car to decrease the amplitude." A yellow flag stops the session and then a green flag reopens the track at 11:28.

At 11:43 Mauricio comes in, saying, "Something's not right at the rear. It's touching down and rolling side to side; it takes a long time. The cruise control is not working. Can we work on that?"

At 11:50 p.m. Michael Andretti is P1 and Mark is in P2, but a few minutes later Mark moves up to P1 with a lap of 1:12.632. He comes in and Allen says, "Take me through your least-favorite corner."

Mark: "It's that high-speed, fourth-gear right-hander onto the backstraight. [Turn 7 on the map.] The car crashes down and then the rear falls over."

At noon Scott Pruett blows a motor and crashes, causing a yellow flag. Mark is still P1 followed by Paul Tracy, Raul Boesel, Michael, and Mauricio. Mark comes in saying, "The gearbox is giving me some trouble on downshifts. The car's a bit pitchy. It turns in too quick and the rear feels unstable. The car is lazy on response; not the front, but the rear. I could carry some more speed through here [Turn 1], but the car is lazy changing directions."

Allen is on his knees, leaning into the cockpit, looking at a map Mark is using to talk about the car's behavior at specific parts of the course. Allen says, "No need to try the other tires right now. There's oil from Turn 8 through Turn 13." A green flag restarts the session with 20 minutes to go.

When Mauricio comes in after a run, Andy says, "Let's go softer on the bump at the rear. Then we may have to change springs." Another red flag waves.

Mark is now P6. He tells Allen, "I couldn't get a clear lap. We're getting some push and the gearshift is keeping me from coming down."

Mauricio is having problems with his dashboard readout. The session restarts at 12:25. I walk a couple of hundred feet around the corner to Turn 2. It's fun to watch here because you can see the cars come out of Turn 1, a fast right-hand turn, into Turn 2, a very quick left turn ending in a big hump over a bridge that spans a dirty little creek. You can stand within 30 feet of the cars as they go through Turn 2 at full throttle. They jump up over the bridge, heaving sideways, and then squat back down as they squirt off to Turn 3.

The violence in the motion and the noise the cars make adds up to an impressive amount of energy input to the senses. It's rare to be able to stand this close, and that adds to the excitement and illustrates the commitment the drivers make going into the corners and the confidence they have in the car and their own skills.

Ric Moore, Greg Moore's dad, is at Turn 2 as I walk up. "I don't like coming down here," he says. "It scares the shit out of me." He grins and I laugh but we both know he's serious.

It seems to me that Mark is on the throttle earlier in Turn 2 than most drivers. At 12:35 both PacWest drivers come in for changes, and when they go out there's 4 minutes left in the session. Allen tells Mark, "All right then, this will be your last run, so make it a good one." Mauricio is P2 with Mark P4.

After the checkered flag Mauricio says, "Clean those tires and save them." Paul Tracy is P1 with a 71.012-seconds lap. Mo is eight-tenths back followed by Bobby Rahal and Mark.

Both PacWest crews build setup pads right on pit lane. They'd rather not have to do that but there isn't any solid, level ground in the garage area. That's another serious deficiency at this racetrack. The garage area gets muddy or dusty depending on whether there's rain or not. The pads are assembled in minutes, and the cars are rolled on and measured.

Setup Pad in Pit Lane

Friday Qualifying

Mauricio and Mark are in the fast-guys' qualifying session due to their performance at the last street course, Long Beach. That seems like years in the past, but it was only two months ago. The session starts at 3:54 p.m. It's warm with high clouds and a wind from the northeast.

As Mauricio pulls out of pit lane, Andy says, "Don't forget the brake bias."

Mauricio: "I did that already."

A red flag stops the session after a few laps. Andy tells Mauricio, "That was a good time but you got the red flag, so it won't count." The monitor shows Tracy, Herta, and Blundell in the top spots. Mo is P12. He's having dash problems.

Mark comes in complaining about shifting gears. Tim Love makes some adjustments to the shift mechanism.

There's a green flag at 4:15. Mark Moore says, "Well, let's see if we can find a clear piece of racetrack again." Getting a clear lap without being balked by another car is a problem here. Evidently Mo finds some space. He goes to P3 with a 71.008-seconds lap.

Mark is now P8. The monitor shows the fast three are Greg Moore, Rahal, and Mauricio. Then Michael Andretti takes over P1, dropping Mo to P4, and Mark improves to seventh quick. The PacWest drivers come in for adjustments and return to the track with 12 minutes to go.

Mauricio improves to P2 behind Greg Moore. Then Mo spins into a tire barrier, knocking a wheel completely off the car. It happens on the right-hand corner going onto the backstraight. We can see the replay on the big TV screen across pit lane. The car goes on the hook and a guy in scuba gear wades into a pond to retrieve one of the wheels. It's floating in the water with parts of the suspension links still attached. Mauricio is out of the car unhurt.

The 17-crew packs up and moves back to the garage area to repair the car. The session restarts at 4:48 with 6 minutes left. Scott Pruett jumps up to P1 with a new lap record of 69.572

Andy, Mauricio, and Jimmy
Assess the Damage

seconds. This time holds until the end of the session. Greg Moore is P2. Mauricio's time holds also and he's P3. Mark qualifies 11th.

Back in the garage area Mauricio tells me what happened. "I was getting away with a lot of stuff, and I was thinking this lap might be a good one. Then it pushed into that tire wall. The wall should have stepped back a little. [He's smiling at the thought.] The wheel and tire went over my head and flew over the wall. I was a little worried when I saw the A-arms still attached, and it was coming toward me. I did a 360 about 4 feet in the air and that wheel flew past me into the water. It was just floating there smoking." To illustrate the steam rising off the hot tire and wheel, Mauricio has both hands in front of him, palms down, and he wiggles his fingers.

Friday night I walk to Greek Town again and eat at Fishbone's, a big, noisy restaurant. The hockey crowd is out again and I talk to a lady named Sue who has a wingnut on a string around her neck. Detroit Red Wings, wing nut, get it?

SATURDAY

I wake up early and instead of trying to get back to sleep, I just get ready and leave, arriving at the track at 6:30 a.m. This gets me a good parking spot and cuts down the walking. In the PacWest garage area there's a M.A.D. meeting announcement on the door of the Hollywood transporter. That's "Mechanics Against Detroit." It sounds good to me but I assume it's a joke.

As usual Saturday sessions are early, with CART practice scheduled for 9 a.m. There's not enough pit space for the T-cars so they're left in the garage area, but they're hooked to tuggers all ready to be towed to pit lane if the primary car is put out of action.

Saturday Practice

The session starts on time but Adrian Fernandez crashes immediately, causing a red flag. Mauricio says the rear of his car is too low. "Even when I change gears, the back hits the ground." His cruise control isn't working either.

Andy tells Mauricio the tire pressures are still 3 to 4 pounds low. "Do you want to help these pressures [add air pressure], Morris, or just leave them?"

Mauricio: "Leave them for now. The back is going like a yo-yo now."

Andy: "Well, I mean, that's not a usual feeling, is it?"

Mauricio: "I was talking about the pressures, plus the grip level I was getting. The movement is not a pressure thing." Andy talks to Trevor Jackson about shock changes.

Allen asks Mark, "How's the car on entry?"

Mark: "It still needs to be a bit better than what we have it, but it feels a bit more encouraging. The car's got mid-corner, increasing grip but it's making the car a little bit snap oversteer on exit at this point. It's still unsettled on entry because it's still a bit too stiff on this right corner especially. It just locks, like every turn."

Allen: "All right, the options are to soften the front springs, or the front bump that we put in yesterday, or the front rebound that we put in yesterday."

Mark: "Let's try the springs just very quickly to see if that gives us a bit more benefit in terms of going in and holding a bit more front grip more consistently into the turn."

The session restarts and both cars go out. When he comes in, Mauricio complains about locking front brakes. "I didn't have that yesterday. We shouldn't be locking that right front."

Andy: "OK; soon as I've got some data I'm going to have a look at it. I can compare our shock offsets in the pit lane compared to yesterday, which will give me corner-weight indication."

Mauricio: "Also, I have to sort out those lights and the cruise control. Otherwise it's going to be really shitty in the race."

Mark: "It's a little bit more secure under braking, but it's still not as good as what we need it, basically. The right front just locks up consistently and I go in on a tripod effect, three wheels. We picked up a bit of mid-corner grip, but it's a little bit of a deficit to us as we come off the turn because we come off with flick oversteer."

Allen: "So if this works shall we go softer on the rear springs?"

Mark: "Yeah, I think we can try that."

After a run on the shock changes Mauricio comes back in. Scott Pruett is P1, Mark is P4, and Mo is P16. There are 41 minutes left in the session. "That was better, Andy," Mauricio says, "but it's still not the answer. We've got a lot of amplitude on the back of the car."

Andy: "OK. Let's not forget that these tires now have 43 laps. I would actually like to go to the other set of tires now for the rest of the session, and see what's it's like on those new tires before I make a change. We've got a red flag, guys. The other alternative is to just come up 100 on the rear springs and to come down on that shock setting."

Mauricio: "We talked about changing the roll center?"

Andy: "We could change the roll center under the red flag and do another run on these tires."

Mauricio agrees, so Andy says to Mark Moore: "OK, Mark, please, mate, we're just going to reverse the box on the rear uprights." That changes the angle of the upper A-arm, changing the roll center and affecting the way tire forces feed into the chassis.

There's a green flag at 9:31. Mark, in P3, is out immediately, as is Mauricio, still off the monitor. Both PacWest cars come back on pit lane after a couple of laps.

Andy: "How's the right-front wheel now?"

Mauricio: "Still very light, but under power it squats so bad off the turn with the left rear or right rear it just picks up the inside wheel."

Allen: "Was that a big improvement or what?"

Mark: "I went a little bit stiffer on the rear tim just to quiet the rear of the car down, Allen. But that quiet-down is just slight on entry, but at the same point we're still sufferin' a little bit of nervousness on entry on the front end as we go into the initial turn-in. At that point the car feels like it's got a bit too much flap, especially at high speed. It's got a little, like there's more push in the mid-range. We need to settle the car down a bit in traction. I have to wait for a hell of a long time to get on the gas hard. It could put the power down a bit smoover and a bit quicker."

I ask Alison, his handler, about his accent, using "v"s for "th"s as he does here, saying "smoover" instead of "smoother." She tells me it's a North London accent that gets corrected if you go to private school. It's a British class thing.

Andy: "I'm going to change tires this time. Do you want to back off half of that bump change at the same time? Or should we just try another set of tires to see if they can handle that bump change?"

Mauricio: "Let's change the tires and back off a bit on that. There's definitely not enough grip at the back in traction yet. Also, through Turn 3, the front is bouncing a lot. I don't know if the shocktopussy is too stiff on the front. It's possible I can hear the end plates rubbing."

The shocktopussy is what they call the hydraulic third spring. There are a lot of hoses going into it; like octopus tentacles, I guess.

Andy: "Red flag, guys. [Paul Tracy is into a tire barrier somewhere on course at 9:38.] I want to change the ECU, Mark, to see if that's anything to do with these lights. They seem to have a connection. How did the roll-center change help, Morris?"

Mauricio: "It helped the change of direction. The car was just sharper. Therefore I could be sooner on to the gas."

Allen asks Mark about the car, and he says, "I actually didn't get a clean lap out there because Andre [Ribeiro] was friggin' about. But the car feels slightly better on the rear from the point of view that it takes a little bit more of a compliance. It's got more compliance and it's settled down on the rear. At the same point it is touching down too much. It touches down quite harshly here on the frontstraight, and on the backstraight as well. It goes into a set no problem; you can cope with that. There's more push in the mid-speed corner at this point."

Allen: "All right. Something we've been wanting to try is lowering the rear roll center. We've got a red flag and this is a good time to do it."

Mark: "I think this is a good time to do it. We should be careful we don't get a little bit lost."

They talk themselves out of the roll-center change and go softer on the rear springs instead. At 9:50 both cars are back in pit lane after a run on track. Mo has improved to P7; Mark is in P8. Zanardi is P1 at 70.451 seconds.

Andy to Mauricio: "How's the car, Morris?"

Mauricio: "I've got some middle-corner understeer. I'm going stiffer on the rear bar now. I want to try a bit more of that."

Mauricio goes back on course at 9:49 with 20 minutes to go. The 18-crew is still changing the rear roll center. Mark is on course again at 10:01 a.m. just as Mauricio comes back in. Dario Franchitti is P1 now with Mauricio P9 and Mark P10.

Andy and Mauricio decide to go stiffer on the rear springs. With about 10 minutes to go Allen has the 18-crew change to sticker tires and asks Mark, "Before we go out, is there anything else you think we can do to the car?"

Mark: "I just really could do with a little more front grip somehow. I don't know if you want to put it in aero 'cause it's going to be too much on the high speed. I just need a bit more from the actual turn-in to the mid, just in between that gray area of 25% or 30%."

Allen: "What if we use a little bit of front rebound, eh?"

Mark: "Just a small change, like a sweep or somfing, Al."

Allen: "Extra sweep of high-speed, low-speed front rebound, please."

Mauricio comes in and Andy says, "OK, Morris, there's just about 6 minutes to go. I'm just going to put these tires on and make sure the pressures are right for this afternoon."

Mark still doesn't like the way his gearbox is shifting. "I just want to get on the brakes and shift. I want to shift. That's me. I want to shift. It just won't let me. I just screw myself every corner. I've got no drive and I've got no retardation. I'm just nowhere. And then I have to gaver [gather] it up and turn in."

His accent gets worse when he gets excited.

Mark and Mauricio both go out on new tires with about 5 minutes to go. Mark improves to P2. Traffic on course makes it difficult to get a clear lap. The track is so narrow and bumpy it's difficult to pass. The session ends with Scott Pruett in P1, Dario Franchitti P2, Mark third, and Mauricio P8.

Conversation with a Formula 1 Engineer

During the CART Indy car race at Detroit there are always visitors from the sister series, Formula 1, whose only North American race date is the weekend after Detroit at Montreal. I take this opportunity to talk with Rod Nelson, Gerhard Berger's engineer at Benetton. Rod is in his 30s, tall and slim. He engineered racecars in F3000 before going "to university," earning a Ph.D. in hydraulics. That was the perfect entree into Formula 1, what with all the hydraulic systems on board.

I ask Rod about the difference between F1 and Indy cars.

"The big difference, of course, is that F1 teams make the cars while over here they buy them. And our rules are much less restrictive. That changes the emphasis. F1 teams spend a lot of time and effort to make the car reliable, test teams and all. They've spent large sums of money on state-of-the-art wind tunnels and are constantly making new aero bits. The engine is a means to drive the car through the air, and the power output is very important because the more drag you can overcome, the more downforce you can produce.

"We don't spend as much time on mechanical grip as the Indy car teams. I couldn't tell you anything about the roll centers, for instance. Dampers aren't as important with us. We tend to use software simulations and a seven-post shaker to dial in our setups at the factory before we go to the race. We don't adjust the dampers much, where over here that's one of the most critical components because it's not restricted by the rules."

"Do you make frequency sweeps or input road data to the shaker?"

"I'd rather not talk about that. We do simulate aero loads."

OK; fair enough, but at least I asked the right question. The object of the perfect setup is to maximize aero downforce, minimize aero drag, and minimize changes in tire-patch forces caused by the tire and wheel failing to follow the road. You can input a wheel movement at varying frequency to a four-post shaker (a hydraulic ram under each wheel) and measure tire patch forces. Bungee cords holding the chassis down can simulate static aero loads that the car would see through one corner at a specific speed. With a seven-post shaker (three additional rams hooked to the chassis), you can input dynamic aero downforce and the rams at each wheel simulate road irregularities recorded by the on-board systems during a real lap on a racecourse. Adjustments to tire pressures, shocks, and springs optimize the setup.

"What about driver feedback?" I ask Rod.

"Sure; that matters. If the driver's not comfortable in the car he can't drive it quickly. We have several versions of the factory setups and we try to sell one to the driver with as few tweaks as possible. Every change has some combination of gains and losses, but as you deviate from the optimum the car won't go as well."

"I read that Benetton had trouble adapting their cars from Schumacher's style to something drivable by Berger and Alesi."

"That's right," Rod confirms. "Michael likes a stiffly-sprung, skaty car with oversteer. He drives the car through the usual mid-corner understeer and uses the throttle to control it on exit. Ferrari must not be able to make that happen. He's been complaining of understeer in the press. Our new guys found that setup undrivable. Most drivers don't like oversteer. You can't really argue with someone who's won F1 races when he says he's not comfortable in the car."

Saturday Qualifying Session

The 30-minute qualifying session for the slow guys gets the green flag at 12:52 p.m., only 42 minutes late. An hour later there's been a lot of red flags and nobody does any great times. Like all street courses, this track gets faster as more rubber is laid down. It's an advantage for the fast guys to be second on Saturday afternoon.

At 1:45 p.m. the fast guys get a green flag. Mauricio is P3 and Mark P15 at the start of the session, set by yesterday's qualifying session. The stands are about half full, a good turnout for a Saturday. The weather is nice; partly cloudy and warm with a cool breeze.

Mauricio is back in at 1:52. Andy asks, "How's the ride height, Morris?"

Mauricio: "Seems to be fine. I'm just crashing [bottoming] a bit, but no more than this morning."

Andy: "Do you want to drop the bump out of the shocks like we were talking about, or try softer springs?"

Mauricio: "We could do both."

Andy: "Go back down 100 or 200?"

Mauricio: "200; go two."

Andy: "We need to come up three flats on the rear pushrod, please."

Mark comes in complaining of push. "It's pushing even in the high speed coming onto the last straight; lot of push there. The car's also a little bit lively on the rear in terms of lack of grip; the rear's coming out."

Allen: "So you reckon we could take a turn of front wing?"

Mark: "We have to try it because we've got too much push in the car at present. I'm also concerned that the rear of the car seems to be a little bit lively. Some of that just could be because there's more push, and that push is inducin' oversteer."

Control has a report that the 18-car touched a wall somewhere, but the CART pit marshal looks the car over and reports, "18-car shows no damage." Mauricio goes back on course in P11.

Allen tries to nail down Mark's report of understeer. "The push is like everywhere, in all parts of the corner at all speeds?"

Mark: "I got a lot of push even through that last one, more than we had before."

Allen: "How much do you reckon you could take, one or two turns?"

Mark: "Just a degree, OK? Maybe just one and a half turns, just under a degree. A degree might be a bit too fierce."

Allen: "OK; two on the right and one on the left, please."

Bruce and Jolene climb down from the scoring cart. He's driving in the Neon Challenge race this weekend with a bunch of other business guys and some media people. His qualifying session is on track next.

Mark goes back out. Mauricio comes in, complaining of understeer. I turn off the CART channel so I can concentrate on the driver/engineer conversations.

Andy says, "We can soften the front springs to help that. We've got 13 minutes left. Or we can try some low-speed rear bump?"

Mauricio: "Low-speed rear bump. The back is quite good, but not the front."

Mark is on course and he comes on the radio saying, "I just clipped the left-hand corner."

Al Bodey: "Ten-four."

Mark, coming down pit lane toward his pit box: "This car is shit. I'd really like to get rid of this gearshift problem. There's no friggin' way I can drive like that. I just locked up the rears and slid through the corner."

Allen: "OK; does the car feel OK?"

Mark: "It's fine other than the left-hand corner."

Andy: "Red flag right now, guys. I don't think it's going to be long. Mark just knocked some tires out onto the track. Should we try any other changes, Morris, or leave it at this for now?"

Mauricio: "Are you lowering the front? And then the bump change at the back?"

Andy: "Yes; I put some low-speed rear bump into it. Your complaint, is it just about like a pendulum now, it's rolled over and then it takes too long to come back?"

Mauricio: "Exactly, and I keep locking front tires because of it."

Mark asks about the car: "Is it repairable?"

Allen: "Yeah; we'll have a go for it, yeah."

John Roof is working on the left rear of the 18-car, replacing some suspension pieces. It helps that the crew has on hand at all times replacement A-arms and tie rods adjusted to the exact lengths of the parts that are on the car.

Allen: "OK; how was the car with more front wing?"

Mark: "It feels like it's going to be OK to carry with new tires. I never got a clean lap. I was just trying to experiment — to downshift early to try and settle the car, but I can't work it like that."

Andy: "OK, Morris, I don't think this yellow is going to take long so I don't want to get into a major change and get caught out. There's just under 12 minutes of green left to evaluate this change, and then we'll go to fresh rubber."

Mauricio: "Why don't we go for the fresh rubber now?"

Andy: "You don't think it's worth evaluating this now? It's just one or two laps and then a set of tires?"

Mauricio: "Yeah; let's do that." This is about as contentious as their discussions get.

Andy: "Did you play with the rear bar adjuster at all?"

Mauricio: "No, I haven't. I was already locking the fronts, so I didn't want to do that."

Andy: "Do you want us to back that out a couple of sweeps? Cause that seemed to lock the fronts this morning when you went softer with it."

Mauricio: "Let's do that." I think they're talking about something else and just calling it "the rear bar."

Allen: "How many minutes to green, then?"

Al Bodey: "There's 11:53 left and we'll serve an 8-minute penalty, so there'll be about 4 minutes to go when we go out."

Mark: "What's the penalty for? Because the tires came out on the track?"

Al Bodey: "Because we caused the red flag."

The session fires up again at 2:08. Mauricio goes out in P10; Mark is still in P11. Mauricio radios he's coming in and says, "I don't like that. In the high-speed corners, it's just like a big oversteer."

Andy: "Understood, Morris. We'll back that change out."

Mauricio: "I'm still struggling with the same thing, traction and the middle-corner push. The problem is the tires are so soft it's very difficult to read the car too."

Mauricio goes out on new tires with about 6 minutes to go in the session. Gil de Ferran has gone to P1. The checkered flag flies at 2:20. Mo improves slightly to P8, a half-second slower than the pole. Mark ends up in 10th. They're not making a lot of headway on the setup.

Before Mark gets out of the car he says, "Good job putting the car back together, guys. That was good. I needed one more lap. I shouldn't have gone off in the first place. Thanks for gettin' it back together."

After the session I talk to Allen McDonald, asking how he thought qualifying went. "It wasn't really very good, was it? It seemed like there was a good time ready to leap out there, but it never happened. It's a difficult place, this. It's low grip and it's bumpy, so the setup is very knife-edge. Mark's trying hard and he's good at racing, so we should be all right for tomorrow."

Mauricio is in the garage area talking to the 17-crew so I tell him, "You've been at the front of the starting grid so much, it's a surprise you're not at the front of this one."

"That's OK," he says, smiling. "I know why we're not there. We went the wrong way on a suspension change. We'll be better tomorrow."

The Trans-Am race starts an hour and a half late at 5:30. The big cars pound around making a lot of noise. I watch for a while in Turn 2, but can't get interested. They have the same problem with this track the CART cars do; no room to pass. I'm always worried I'll miss something if I'm not right there with the PacWest guys, so I go back to the garage area.

Back at the hotel I decide to stay in and avoid the hockey crazies. I order up a room-service burger and a couple of beers and watch the game on TV. The Red Wings win the game and the Whatever Cup. After the game I can hear the noise even though I'm on the 31st floor.

RACE DAY

I wake up at 4:30 a.m. and can't go back to sleep. I'm still worrying about getting a parking spot that will allow me to see all the race and still make the plane.

The sun is barely up when I get to the track at 6 a.m. There isn't any guard to prevent me from parking in a lot just on the island side of the bridge. This afternoon I can walk to the car and boogie right on out of here. If Mark or Mauricio win I can get photos and quotes from somebody later. They're starting in the fourth and fifth rows and you can't pass here, so fat chance of them winning anyway.

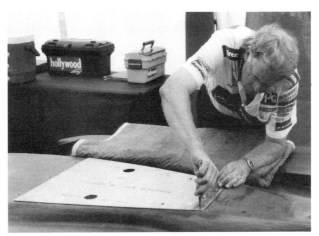
Tim Douthat Installs a New Skid Plate

The CART teams are just getting here; this is a rare instance of me at the track before them. It's cool and the sky is clear. It could get hot today. Indy Lights are on track before the CART teams, so I head for the Indy Lights hospitality area where I know I can get some coffee and a chocolate doughnut. After that I walk to the PacWest hospitality area. I'm the first one there, so I sit down to finish my doughnut and I hear a burst of laughter from the KOOL tent across the way. TV highlights of last night's IRL race show A. J. Foyt slapping Arie Luyendyk like some fat little girl angry at a playmate.

Over in the PacWest garage area I ask Roscoe how late they stayed changing engines last night. "Eight o'clock," he says, "not bad."

"Anybody go out in that hockey mess?"

"No," he says, grinning and shaking his head. "We just hid out and ordered room service. We were all too scared." Same as me! I feel better now.

Walking over to the Media Center for a copy of the starting grid, I see Bob Raschke, the guy who drives the jet truck. I tell him I was listening in and watching at Gateway when he was out there for so long trying to dry the track.

"We used 700 gallons of jet fuel at St. Louis," he says. "Sometimes it's difficult getting fuel at the tracks. It's done differently at different tracks. Some places they bring in 55-gallon drums and others have standing tanks. Here at Detroit we have to go outside the track for gasoline for the trucks. They have license plates so we can do that, but we really don't like to risk them on the street."

"How well does that jet dry a wet track?"

"It will dry moisture off the track if you go slow, but what it mainly does is maintain the heat already in the track."

The Boss Gets to Drive

At 9:15 I'm at Turn 2 watching the Neon Challenge race. Bruce qualified on the pole and is leading the race, building a lead slowly. The cars look very slow droning by on tiny, squealing tires, but I know they're fun to drive. Bruce has some very fast vintage cars he races often enough that he is a fast, smooth driver.

On lap five Bruce gets his car a little too sideways in Turn 1 and does a long, lazy spin, almost, but not quite, hitting the barrier at Pit Out. He gets it going again, losing a few places, but I can almost see the grin through his helmet.

Silly Season

I ask Steve Fusek about Silly Season, that time from the middle of the season on when there's lots of talk about who's going to do what next season. "What about Mauricio's and Mark's contracts?"

"I think they'll both be back," Steve says. "We want to maintain the continuity."

"I assume you're happy with the Ilmor engines and the Firestone tires. Will you look at the Swift chassis?"

"This is the time to look at everything, and we will."

In the pit lane I see Julian Robertson, Jimmy Vasser's engineer. There's been rumors Jimmy will switch from Ganassi Racing to another team.

"If Jimmy switches teams, would you go with him?"

"Don't know," Julian says, all teeth and spectacles. "I'm not in on any of that. The relationship is working well. Drivers are very different and you need some time to figure out what they want and what they mean when they say a particular thing."

If I was a team owner I'd pay more attention to keeping the driver and engineer together if they're successful.

Warm-Up

In the pit lane waiting for the warm-up to start, John Anderson tells me Charlie Guilinger had a call from his wife last night saying she was having a baby. They sent him back to Indianapolis in a rental car, and he made it in time to see the birth of his son.

The green flag is at 10:55 a.m. Mauricio stalls the engine on his first attempt to pull out into the pit lane, saying, "Nice beginning."

Russ asks Mauricio about the clutch. "It's OK," he answers, "but it feels a bit thin."

He and Mark go out and do some radio checks before coming in for the installation check.

Allen: "The first run will be about six to eight laps, Mark. Then you come in and we'll do a sort of practice stop and change to the fresher tires. All right? The other thing to remember is these tires have race pressures in them, so it'll take a few laps for them to come in. You'll probably be touching a bit more to start."

Mark: "With all the fuel on board and the low pressures it doesn't feel too good, so we'll give it a good three laps before we get on it then."

When Mauricio comes in after his first long run he says, "The steering is almost coming off in my hands on the slow corners under braking. It vibrates left to right and I'm locking a little bit the front wheels so could be the shocktopussy is little bit too stiff. I need more traction on the rear but the car doesn't feel bad."

Andy: "I'd put your brake balance a bit, just a turn, one turn to the rear. That was looking too much to the front. How 'bout the ride height right now?"

Mauricio: "Just touching. Touching a little bit on the front approaching Turn 1. The back is just at the end of that backstraight; I'm hitting a little bit. I guess under braking it's the slow stuff, not the fast stuff. The steering wheel is doing this." He saws the steering wheel from side to side.

Andy: "OK; you don't feel it through the pedal then? It's actually a chassis reaction to the braking?"

Mauricio: "It's a chassis reaction. The pedal is steady."

Andy: "You don't feel the front rocking at all? It's just a reaction to the steering?"

Mauricio: "It's a reaction to the steering, but I locked one wheel rather easily, so it could be that we are too stiff on the shocktopussy."

Andy: "Well, let's try it. Let's come out 12 clicks, please, Trev. The pressures climbed up a little, Morris. We were up two at the front. We were pretty close at the rear. Should we keep it that way for the balance? Otherwise we're going to have to start a bit softer in the race."

Mauricio: "Let's keep it like this. If we were to do a change, I'd want it at the back to improve traction."

Andy: "Do you have any falling-over feeling at the rear?"

Mauricio: "No, not at all."

Andy: "That's a flat slide back there?"

Mauricio: "Flat slide and inside wheelspin a little bit, but it's better than yesterday."

Andy: "OK; let's take the high-speed bump out of the shocks like we were doing on Friday with this setup."

At 10:11 Mark comes in after his run and Ando talks him into the pit box as they do a practice race stop. "Down the middle, down the middle, that's it, on the mark. Stop!"

Mark: "OK; the engine is like gutless in this configuration, slot four and five. No guts whatsoever. [They are trying a very lean fuel map and one of them has a fuel cutout feature that eliminates all fuel on closed throttle. It makes the car more difficult to drive.] Anyway, basically the car is, Allen, high-speed understeer, push, but also, with the fuel on board and the weight of the car, it's got a little roll in the car and that roll is going across the rear and makes the rear nervous and start to fall over. But there's a lot of push mid to exit with the car. That also just characterizes the mid-speed corners. The same basic balance. Entry into the corners is not too good also with the weight. The car is a bit unstable. There's a bit of pitch in it. When you've got to turn, the car, it takes one big, umph [he grunts to indicate the severity of the action], a real big set. And when it sets in, it kicks the ass out."

Allen: "All right, was it better with tim?"

Mark: "It was slightly better with the tim with the rear on entry, but it just promotes more understeer, it's just usin' up the front tires too much at that point. It gives me more rear set on entry to the corner, but it promotes too much push mid to exit. So we have to come back.

"I'm gettin' some vibration under braking as well, Allen. I don't know whether it's the pads and the disks not comin' in very cleanly, but under heavy brakin' there's a lot of vibration at the front end of the car."

Allen: "Yeah; Mo's complainin' of the same thing. Strange. You can actually feel it through the steering, yeah?"

Mark: "I can feel it through the steerin' really prominent. I mean, it's big."

Allen: "OK; what's the car like for touchin'?"

Mark: "Touchin' down slightly into one and into that backstraight there, into Turn 8. Basically it's just the fuel on board, the mass. But it's not too bad."

Allen: "OK; give it two sweeps of high-speed and low-speed rear bump, please."

Mauricio comes back in from a run and Andy says: "We've just got 7 minutes of green. Give me a rundown on the car."

Mauricio: "It's better. I've still got the push."

Andy: "OK; I'm going to pull out some rear bump again, and I'm gonna add a bit of front rebound. How's the braking now, Morris?"

I can barely hear Mo over the roar of his engine because he's talking into the radio as he comes in for the stop. "The brakes are better. It's softer at the back. I like it. I think we should take some rebound out of the rear. I'm still lifting the inside rear. And what about rebound on the front because it's starting to push out of the corners, like the middle of the corners?"

Andy: "Understood, Mo. I want to take another sweep of high-speed bump out. I'll take out five sweeps of low-speed rebound at the back as well, and I was going to add four sweeps of low-speed to the front. How was the decel? Did you feel it?"

Mauricio: "I hate it. Between 1 and 2, it's really bad. I go for the gas and there is a hole there."

Andy: "OK, Mo. Only one more lap at this fuel setting and then go to slot four. That should put the fuel cut back into it, but it should be better."

Mauricio goes back on course but the engine dies, stranding him out there. "The throttle cable broke, Andy," he says.

Andy: "Understood, Morris. How was the car on the last run?"

Mauricio: "Pushing too much."

Andy: "Understood, mate."

Mark comes back in also complaining about the engine response with the special fuel settings. He ends up the session in P14, with Mo in P8.

After the warm-up Bruce tells me he had a great time in the Neon race. "I didn't mean to spin the car, but it was more fun passing some guys while I was catching up than when I was running out front."

Race Prep

At 11 a.m. in the garage area Dave Jacobs and Jim Reid replace the throttle cable on the 17-car. It's a big job and requires removal of some of the cockpit components. Dave removes the "buckeye," which is the round opening that mates with the refueling valve, so he can thread the throttle cable from the engine compartment through the cockpit to the foot box. I get a look at the failed cable, and it's very frayed right at the end where it attached to the pedal.

While I'm standing here watching I see Roscoe talking to Ron Endres, probably telling him a joke. Ron's nickname is Toby. Of course Rocoe's real name is Russell Grosshans and I know him as Roscoe, but he's also called Toby II.

When he talks to someone, Roscoe looks like he's dancing out parts of the tale. He smiles and laughs, using his whole body — shuffling his feet, nodding his head

Tom Keene Works on a Rotor

and making faces, shifting his weight from one foot to the other, and flapping his arms around. Now that's communication.

The 18-crew has the bottom of Mark's primary car off to clean out the oil that accumulated there when someone left the oil tank cap loose before the warm-up. That caused a minor flap on pit lane because it looked like an oil leak and took some time to clean up that could have been spent on track.

At 1 p.m. some of the crew are suiting up and getting their game faces on. Others are finishing up the cars. The 17-car has a new throttle cable and the brakes are bled. After the brake-bleeding operation, Ron goes around to each caliper and carefully sprays brake clean into the bleed fittings and wipes each one off, one on each side of every caliper.

Fuel Strategy

I see John Anderson (Ando) eating some lunch, and I ask him about the race strategy. "The race is 77 laps," he says. "We get enough fuel to go all the way on a green flag, but in the last five years there's an average here of 21.5 laps under a full-course yellow. If there's a yellow flag in the first 13 to 17 laps, we'll pit for fuel and tires. It depends on track position.

"There's a possibility we could do the race on one pit stop. If we have a lot of yellow flags early in the race and then get a yellow flag with 42 laps to go, we figure we can go all the way to the end, but we need some yellow-flag laps at the end to do that."

This is the year of the fuel gamble. The gamble paid off for Paul Tracy at Rio and Greg Moore at Milwaukee. Bobby Rahal lost both places. Competition is so close this year, just running up front doesn't work. Maybe you have to gamble to have a chance to win?

Ando also tells me they've talked to Mauricio about being more

Al, Allen, and Ando Plot Race Strategy

aggressive on the short ovals, passing cars like Michael Andretti and Paul Tracy do. "Mo doesn't like risking the car, but sometimes you have to."

At 1:55, only an hour before the start, the 17-car is still on the setup pad on pit lane. As I watch, the crew finishes up. They roll the car off and start to disassemble the pad. Pack-up has already started back in the garage area.

I've got all my stuff stowed here in pit lane for a hasty exit. All I have to do is grab my black shoulder bag and run. I reassure myself that I won't miss anything because the PacWest cars are starting eighth and tenth and passing is difficult here. There's so many wrecks on street courses they might both be out of the race early, and I can leave with a clear conscience.

The Race

The excitement generated on pre-grid is always a surprise to me. I'm right here in the middle of all the best teams at the top of the sport. I like these people — who they are and what they do and how they do it. At 2:28 the PA announcer, Chris McClure, dramatically gives the "Drivers to your cars!" call.

I ask Mark Morris, Mauricio's crew chief, about the throttle cable. "I can't believe how lucky we are that it broke on the last lap of warm-up instead of the first lap of the race. It probably broke because Mo has been on the gas so hard this year."

The engines start up and I go over to the PacWest pits. This is a pretty good situation. I've got a big-screen TV I can see and there are monitors I can get a glimpse of to see the order on course. The view of the cars from the pits is meager; all you can see is the top of the rear wings.

At 2:40 the cars are on their second pace lap and Ando is telling Mark, "Slot zero on the fuel. Position zero for the start." That's the deal today. It seems they have a fuel slot programmed to do everything but make a banzai pass. That's still up to the drivers.

Russ warns Mauricio, "No passing before the green flag."

The cars roar down the straight toward us but it's a no-start; the yellow flag flies, not the green. Ando immediately tells Mark, "Position four on the fuel."

Russ says to Mauricio, "Zanardi lost a nose. The Mexican is in the fence." The field circulates while the wreck gets cleaned up. Zanardi is out of the race.

Ando continues to talk to Mark: "No matter where you are, when I say it's green, you go racing. Back to zero on the fuel. Warm it up; let's go."

Russ to Mauricio: "Green this time by." That will start lap four. De Ferran leads; Mo is seventh; Mark ninth. The race restarts as Mark complains of vibration and Vasser gets by him. After a couple of laps there's another yellow for debris on course. "The radio is shit," says Mauricio, managing to sound disgusted even through all the noise on my scanner and all around me.

I decide to walk to Turn 2, and I'm there at 2:59 as the race restarts the second time on lap eight. But three laps later there's another all-course yellow flag. Mauricio says he's guessing on the radio messages. This could be a very boring race. Maybe I should leave now.

Mark says, "The car has a lot of push entry to mid and oversteer out of the corners." Ando suggests he go up on the tim. Andre Ribeiro crashed, causing the yellow flag.

The race goes green once again on lap 14. Bobby Rahal begins to press Mark for 10th and passes him on lap 16. Rahal just gets through Turn 2 better, maybe because of Mark's push, and squirts inside of him going to Turn 3. "Stay with 'im," Ando says.

The cars roar by with no change in order for another 10 laps, and then Scott Pruett disappears from second spot. I hear Control say it's an engine. The order on track is Gil de Ferran, Scott Pruett, Christian Fittipaldi, Dario Franchitti, Michael Andretti, Greg Moore, Mauricio, Vasser, and Mark. The first pit stops begin. Greg Moore stays out as do Mo and Mark. They move up toward the front as the leaders pit.

On lap 28 Ando tells Mark, "Six laps before your pit stop." On lap 32 the order is Greg Moore, Mo, and Mark. But Richie Hearn hits a barrier somewhere, causing another yellow flag.

Ando to Mark: "Pit next lap. We'll put some front wing in to help the push."

The pit lane gets very crowded and confusing as all the cars which haven't pitted come in at the same time. When it's all over the order is Moore, de Ferran, Christian Fittipaldi, Michael Andretti, Mo, and Mark.

During the yellow-flag laps the drivers aren't working so hard and they talk some on the radio. Mark says the car is touching down in Turn 1.

Andy tells Mauricio, "We've been conservative on the tire pressures [lower, probably, but they'll rise as they heat up] and that's going to hurt you now, but it'll be better on the long stint."

Ando to Mark: "The three cars in front of you are on Goodyears and they have some problems. The more yellow laps we have the better we look for a one-job." That tells me they're thinking about going to the checkered flag without stopping again.

The race goes green on lap 41. There's 36 laps to go. Can the PacWest cars go that far on fuel? They went 34 laps on the first tank, but there were nine yellow-flag laps during that time.

On lap 43 Michel Jourdain Jr. crashes at Turn 12. Is this the yellow flag that could make the difference? But the CART officials choose to handle this with a local yellow. Mo and Mark are fifth and sixth.

The course goes full yellow on lap 51 and almost everyone comes in for a pit stop. The PacWest drivers stay out, and after only two yellow laps, the course goes green with Mauricio in the lead and Mark second followed by Patrick Carpentier and Greg Moore. The PacWest guys know they don't have enough fuel to go all the way, but right now they're happy to be in the lead. Mark Moore, the 17-car crew chief, says, "Oh, does the God of racing smile on us?"

No, she didn't. In THE most exciting finish of the season so far, the PacWest pair manages to hold first and second spots in spite of lean fuel maps, fuel cut-off valves, and short-shifting. It looks like an unprecedented one-two finish for a team that was mid-pack just last season. Then, on the last lap, Mauricio's fuel runs out, giving the lead to Mark.

Mark rounds the last corner and can see the checkered flag for his first win and PacWest's first win. Then he too runs out of fuel. Greg Moore surges past for his second win ever and second in a row. Mo and Mark end up 16th and 17th, a lap down.

I miss the end of the race. I'm walking toward the gate when Mark Moore pleaded to the deity, feeling stupid and guilty that I won't be with the team for the first win. I can talk to people at the next race. That's how I rationalize it as I flee the scene.

Thanks to the parking spot, my exit is clean. I try to find the race on the radio, almost rear-ending a car in the process. I can't find it and finally give up. I get to the airport just in time. A guy on the Hertz bus heard on the radio that both cars ran out of fuel on the last lap. Well, that's not so bad after all. I just missed witnessing massive disappointment, not an historic first win or one-two finish.

On the plane I wonder about the no-pit, go-slow, hope-for-yellow strategy. That would only work at Detroit because passing is so difficult, another reason why this racecourse should not be used unless it's changed drastically. But did the slow pace prevent the spins and crashes that would have caused the badly-needed yellow flags? If so, the original strategy was flawed.

CHAPTER 14

PORTLAND

This is Thursday, June 19 and my 8:35 a.m. flight up the West Coast from SFO to Portland is great. My view out the plane window looks east and I watch the snow-capped peaks slide by for an hour and a quarter. I wonder just how disappointed the PacWest guys are about the Detroit race.

The pilot eases us down through scattered clouds to the Portland airport, which lies right next to the banks of the mighty Columbia River. After a short ride to the Hertz lot in a crowded bus I find my car and drive north over the Columbia into Washington state, west to Interstate 5, south back over the river to West Delta Park, and enter the Portland International Raceway.

My hardcard gets me past the gate and I follow the "Press Lunch" signs to a grass parking lot. Local media people, drivers, and PR people mill around outside of the tent where the event is almost underway. The drivers are more relaxed at these events because their racecars and fans aren't here. I would attend more Thursday media events, but I'm usually traveling.

Going to a race is like traveling to see friends that I've been away from for a while. Bryan Herta (Team Rahal) and Richie Hearn (Della Penna Motorsports) are talking golf when I walk up. Bryan tells me about his quick times at the Mid-Ohio test the week before and Richie talks about how fed up he is flogging the doggy Lola chassis he's stuck with.

"I'm working my butt off putting on a show for the corner workers and I'm still a second slow," Richie says. "There wasn't any reason to test after the first day at Mid-Ohio. I'm glad we left early. It's not any fun driving your heart out and ending up a second and a half off the pace. The Lola guys don't have any idea what's wrong with the car."

PacWest Garage Area

After the free lunch I walk over the bridge that spans the frontstraight to the CART paddock. The PacWest guys are hard at work on the cars. I hang around the garage area saying hello to everybody and watching what's going on. Someone notices I had my hair cut. I look around and see a lot of fresh haircuts. When you have a week without a race in the middle of the season, you better take care of some of the necessities while you have the chance.

There are some personnel changes. Boomer and John Roof are shop-based, but they're here filling in for Charlie Guilinger, whose wife had a baby during the Detroit race, and Blake Hamilton, whose wife is due to give birth soon. Daryl Fox says, "I didn't know guys were supposed to get maternity leave." Chris Griffis is back on shop duty. Russ Cameron's dad died, so he'll miss this race.

Detroit Negatives?

At the hospitality area at the east end of the paddock I run into Steve Fusek and ask him if he thought there was anything negative about the Detroit result.

"I don't think so. After the Milwaukee race the Motorola guys asked us why Greg Moore won. [Fred] Tucker and [Bob] Schaul wanted to know more about the fuel strategy stuff and how much time we spend looking at that and planning race strategy. They sat in on our pre-race meeting at Detroit, and they knew exactly what we were planning.

"The way it worked out at Detroit we had to make that last pit stop two laps before optimum, and historically there are two yellow-flag periods of eight to 10 laps total late in the race. This year it didn't happen. We were five yellow laps short of having enough fuel per our plan. I was spotting in the grandstands on the backstraight and a couple of fans figured out who I was. One asked, 'Are you going to pit?' I told him, 'no.' Later he asked, 'Can you make it?' I had to say 'no' again.

"But the cars kept running and on the last lap I thought maybe we had a chance. Then I heard Mo's sad voice say, 'I'm out of fuel, guys.' But Mark came by me at full song so I was excited again. I got on the scooter to head for pit lane and I heard the PA say, 'We have a new leader.'

"There were some tears on pit lane. It brought the team together. It took lots of working together to get that chance to win that race. We got 20% of the TV coverage and a lot of positive feedback from Motorola and Hollywood. We adapted our strategy for that specific track. That particular strategy only works at Detroit because you can't pass there.

"Anything negative? Only that we didn't win. We're all pleased with what happened and our sponsors are pleased and we got a ton of attention. But next year if someone looks at the statistics it won't matter. We finished 16th and 17th. They won't know how close we came to a one-two finish."

"Why go with the same strategy on both cars?" I ask. "Why not be conservative with one?"

"Well, the strategy is either right or wrong," Fusek answers. "If Mo had won, how would we justify to Motorola using a different strategy with Mark?"

Back in the garage area Butch Winkle, Mark Blundell's crew chief, says he wasn't bummed by the Detroit race. "I knew we were four or five yellow laps short. I was surprised Mark kept going as long as he did. I called my wife and the boys later and they were much more disappointed than I was."

About 5:30 in the afternoon work is wrapping up in the paddock, so I find the Sheraton at the airport and check in. For once I'm not staying at the same hotel as the crew, but the CART officials and other series regulars are housed here and I have people to talk with in the bar each evening.

At 7 p.m. I meet some of the PacWest guys at Who Songs and Larry's, a Mexican restaurant on the Washington side of the river. We have a few pitchers of margaritas, eat too much, and watch the drawbridge go up and down.

FRIDAY

About 7 a.m. I'm talking to Tom Keene, one of the PacWest truck drivers. Keeping the equipment clean and polished is one of the truckie duties when the team is at a race, so I ask Tom how they go about that.

"There's a company that follows the series just to clean the haulers. They come around and wash the tractors and trailers at the tracks. But we got here at 6 o'clock Tuesday morning, and there's a truck stop with a wash station right across the freeway from the track. We washed the haulers there, and when we got in here and parked, we polished the chrome wheels and wiped silicone on the tire sidewalls. After that we just use some spray cleaner to keep everything wiped off during the weekend. The mechanics wipe off the racecar all the time, but the truckies keep everything else clean, all the racecar wheels, the haulers and tuggers, and the pit equipment."

They work especially hard on the wheels for the racecar. Several sets of tires might go on the car during a track session, and the bright wheels get covered with rubber from the tires and dust from the brake pads. After every session you'll see guys in each pit, usually truckies, carefully polishing each wheel until it's sparkling.

Pace-Car Ride

Today the PPG Pace Car Team is staging at the inside of Turn 9 and Ken Lowe tells me to be there at 9:30. They put me in the black V-8 Lotus Esprit with Margy Eatwell driving. These are small cars on the inside made tighter by a full roll cage. I hit my head twice getting in the seat and buckled up.

Margy accelerates out onto the frontstraight past Start/Finish and gets on the brakes hard for the Festival Curves, a slow, switch-back chicane labled 11 and 12 on the track map, that was added a few years ago to prevent the cars from going over 200 mph. Turn 1 is a large-radius sweeper to the right that Margy takes in one big drift before slowing for the tighter Turn 2. She describes the course in a steady voice as we continue the lap. Turn 3 is back to the left and Turn 4 is another right opening out onto the backstraight that is not straight at all. I know a snow-capped Mt. Hood dominates the distant view, but clouds are in the way today and I don't have time to look for it. Turns 7 and 8 are a left/right chicane at the end of the straight that Margy takes very fast. The Lotus handles the transitions well and Margy brakes while heading the car to the right into a surprisingly slow Turn 9.

"Slowest corner on the course," Margy says. She's on the throttle early and the V-8 sounds great pushing us into our seats as we slide left out to the concrete barrier, whip under the foot bridge, and speed toward Start/Finish and another lap. We come to a stop again in Turn 9 and I only bump my head once on the way out. A great road course!

Back in the Garage Area

The pace in the paddock is stepping up in preparation for the 11 o'clock practice session. Mark Blundell is in his driving suit foraging the breakfast table for a bite to eat. I ask him about the Detroit finish.

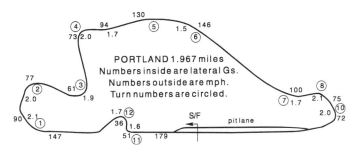

"When I was in Montreal at the F1 race people were talking about it a lot. They all said they wished we'd won, but they were glad to see us running up front."

"Anything negative about it?"

"No, I don't think so. It wouldn't be good if we'd made the same mistake before."

"How did it feel leading the race?"

"It felt good," he says, his mouth curling slightly into a wan smile. "What was really tough was those 40 laps trying to keep those people behind me."

Pit Lane

At 10:35 I'm in the pit lane watching the teams get ready for the first practice session of the weekend. Allen McDonald, PacWest technical director and acting engineer on Blundell's car, is there. I ask him how things went at the test at Mid-Ohio last week.

"It was good. We tested some setup variables and some engine stuff."

"Will you continue to engineer Mark's car?"

"Yeah, but I don't want to. I like doing that sort of thing, but that's not what they hired me to do. Roberto Trevisan worked with Mark some at the Mid-Ohio test, but it's not fair to ask him to leave the Indy Lights team when they're doing well."

"That wouldn't really be a good career move for Roberto, would it?" I smile. I had heard that Roberto and Mark hadn't worked well together at the test. Just not the right chemistry, I guess.

Allen smiles and shakes his head. "It's a difficult situation."

"It sure is. A good race engineer's got a job right now in the middle of the season, so you don't have a good pool to choose from. And if the right guy was loose and took a look at the situation, why would he want to jump in and risk being Blundell engineer number five?"

"It's difficult," Allen repeats. "But I'm not going to make the decision."

"Who is?"

"Bruce and Ando, I guess."

"After the Detroit race I spent some time transcribing some of the tapes off the scanner, and you certainly maintain your good humor during the sessions." He smiles again.

"It sounded like you guys got a little lost in the second Friday session at Milwaukee."

"Big time," Allen admits through his fingers. His chin rests on one hand and that elbow is resting on the other arm wrapped across his chest. He's thinking about the upcoming session probably, but also listening to me.

The Indy Lights session goes green flag after a crash. The noise level goes up. I continue to probe what I know is a delicate subject. "It seems when Mark gets lost on the setup, his feedback becomes even more desperately unfocused."

Allen laughs with a long series of hearty "Ha, ha, ha's." They die down to chuckles and he grins at me over his sunglasses.

"You like that, do you?" I say, smiling. "Desperately unfocused?" He laughs some more.

"Well, I'm supposed to be a writer. I'm supposed to have a way with words."

His chuckles finally run down. "I'll try to be kinder than that in the book," I tell him. He laughs some more, maybe a little nervously at the mention of the book. I'm sure they all wonder how much to tell me and how it will come out in print. Right now, I don't really know those answers myself.

"I'd like to show how complicated all this is, especially the driver/engineer relationship," I say. "Before I got more involved in this stuff, I assumed the driver was able to feel, quantify, and accurately report grip levels, and understeer/oversteer levels. But what do they really feel, anyway? Mark's obviously a good driver and racer, but he's never won at the top levels."

"Andy's worked with him in F1," Allen says. "He said Mark's feedback wasn't that great then either, but he was blindingly quick as a driver. Then he went to McLaren at a time when they seemed to be lost. Maybe that's where he learned to give the feedback we hear now."

We also talk about the lateral compliance and yaw oscillations I saw at Milwaukee. Allen says when he was at the Arrows Formula 1 team, they tested Bridgestone tires at the same time they ran Goodyears at the races. "We experienced something similar to what you're describing, and the drivers hated it."

Friday Practice Session

It's sunny with hardly any clouds in the sky. It's hot in the sun, but there's a cool breeze. Mauricio and Mark are both in the first session which starts at 11:15 a.m., 15 minutes late.

They both storm out of the pit lane at the green flag, and come in after one lap for a look-over. I see smoke at the rear of Mo's car. They take off the engine cover and wipe around with paper towels.

Mark says, "It sounds like something rubbing underneath the car. Maybe someone can have a look underneath. The noise is kinda strange." Mauricio goes out again while Mark's crew looks for the source of the noise. When Mauricio comes in he says he has a huge vibration and bad brakes.

Andy says, "OK, Morris. Umm. The pressures were up at the end of that run. Based on what you're feeling maybe we should put some rebound into the car, or maybe we can drop the car a little."

Mauricio: "The brakes are just junk. When I go to brake for that fast chicane on the back of the course, the pedal is soft."

Andy: "How is the balance through the long corners?"

Mauricio: "A little bit of push, but I wasn't attacking it because I can't stop the car." Mark Moore, Mo's chief mechanic, sends some guys back to the garage area to take the brake rotors off the T-car so they can install them on the primary car during the practice session.

Allen to Mark Blundell: "OK; what's the worst problem now?"

Mark: "The car's horrible right now. Second gear, third, fourth gear, I get up to fourth and fifth and it won't let you shift. It just sits there at full revs. It's blocking you for changing. And again, it feels like it registers fourth, but it goes from fourth straight into sixth on the register on the dash. When you try to change up it's definitely in sixth because it won't let you go up another gear. So you sit there at full throttle, and it should be lettin' us change and it won't let us do it."

Mauricio is having some handling problems and Andy asks, "Then when we get the over-steer, I take it it's a flat slide rather than the thing rolling over into oversteer?"

Mauricio: "Definitely a flat slide."

Andy: "I want to come down a flat on each front pushrod, please, and I want to come up one flat on the rear rods, please."

Later in the session Mauricio says, "It don't feel bad in the quick chicanes, a bit heavy on the front, but it's not loose or anything."

Still later Andy summarizes some changes for Mauricio. "We came down two on the rear springs, went up one flat on the rear rods, and from the skid we came down one flat, front rods. So more rake should help the push." More rake moved the aerodynamic center of pressure (CP) forward, putting more force on the front tires which increases their grip.

Mark tells Allen about the car: "The car just feels like it's touchin' down way too much at this point, at the rear of the car especially. And also it's too pointy at this stage. Not that it feels like there's too much frontal grip, but the split between front and rear feels too severe. The front goes in, it gets too pointy, and it kicks the rear and the rear's very light all the way through the turn at that point."

Allen: "OK; up 200 pounds on the front springs. We'll pick the rear ride height up as well."

Mark: "We should go one turn to the rear on brakes because it's locking up the right-front wheel pretty easily, Allen, as well."

"The engine just blew up," we hear Mauricio say on the radio out on course.

Andy: "Understood, Morris."

Mark Moore: "Bring the T-car."

Mauricio: "We going to use the other car?"

Andy: "It's on its way, mate." With 34 minutes to go Mauricio is in P14, Mark P15, and a red flag has stopped the session. Mauricio's Ilmor/Mercedes-Benz engine has expired. His crew brings the T-car onto pit lane and starts to transfer some components from the primary car to the T-car.

At 11:49 a green flag restarts the session. Mark goes out on course but Mauricio is just getting into his backup car. He starts the engine at 11:50, waits for the temperatures to come up, and returns to the course 2 minutes later with 30 minutes to go. They've lost some time that could have been used to dial in the setup, but they could have lost much more time if they had been less well prepared. To me, this is a remarkable demonstration of the value of a properly prepared backup car and a crew ready to make quick changes.

Mark comes in to report on his car's handling. "Well then, not much change in the actual quality of the ride, but the thing just gets into a pattern; it's just pumping itself down the straight like that. [His gloved hand porpoises through the air.] It gives it an exaggerated effect."

Allen: "Given the bump rubber systems that we're running, I think it's going to be pretty uncomfortable down the straight. I think you're just going to have to grin and bear it, mate. But we'll take a flat out of the rear anyway, OK? One flat out at the rear, please."

Later Mark has this to say: "On the front just as I turn in for the fifth-gear chicane the car goes a little bit soft when you turn in. I reckon you could carry it through there if the rear had a little more support. When you come off the chicane on the exit the rear's very light and just falls over."

Allen: "Yeah, when we walked around yesterday evening, it's there you're gonna need a really good front end, good and stiff to make it good at changin' direction and stable for you."

Andy to Mauricio: "We've got the rotors off the racecar and we're going to put them back on this car. There's no one running the ski ramps out there, and from what we tried at Mid-Ohio I think that's one test we don't have to do now."

Allen to Mark after a run on course: "How's the car?"

Mark: "It feels like it's got a little more support. The actual car across the rear, slip-wise it's still pretty big. It feels like there's too much front downforce at this point as well. The car feels too pointy and the center of pressure is just too far forward."

Allen: "Butch, are we ready to change the rear wing? Can we do that quickly?"

Butch nods and Allen says, "Let's change the rear wing."

Mauricio: "I don't know how long to go, but I want to do the bars."

Andy: "OK. Tell me what you want to do with the rear springs after this run. Do you want to go softer? That last run was a little harsher feel. On the TV the only one I can reach any conclusion about is Rahal looks really soft at the back. He's P6 right now and Herta's second. I would imagine their cars are the same. De Ferran is quickest with this rear wing. Herta is second quickest with the rear wing we have on this racecar. So that's one test we do need to do. Could we switch BOSS off, please?"

Allen to Mark: "What's the car like on touching down?"

Mark: "It's touching down a fair amount, but again some of it's just a pumping effect as it travels down the straight. To be fair, you look at the track and it's bloody bumpy and full of undulations. Carrying it down the straight is not a big issue at the moment. We can look at that later. We should look at the corner weights when we get on the pad again because this right-front wheel's got a real tendency to lock up even though we've got a turn to the rear on braking."

At 12:02 p.m. Mark is in P11 with a lap of 61.789 seconds. "The car is a little better; it's increased a little bit in push once the car's got stable in mid-corner. The car's very reactive in ride, very reactive. Under braking? A massive pitch problem. The rear comes up very high, very light, and quick and then when you turn in, the rear is always there. I'm catching lock everywhere, Allen."

Andy to Mauricio: "What about the rear springs? Do we want to try the softer ones?"

Mauricio: "Yes. Let's do that."

Allen to Mark: "Couple hundred pounds softer on the rear springs, then?"

Mark: "We got to try it. The very basic read of the car is that the ride quality is very poor. It's having a vast effect on the car under braking. When we go under braking the car's got a lot of pitch and the rear comes up very high, quick, and light. As I turn in the front's got good turn-in just in terms of strong grip, but the rear's got no grip whatsoever and it's also got no support. But the car just slides; I mean just the rear of the car out, but I can't feel whever ['whever' is his North London accent coming through] it's too stiff and sliding or whever it's too soft and falling over, then sliding."

Mauricio: "Can somebody get a rag for me for the visor?"

Andy: "Come up three flats on the rear rods please, guys."

Mark: "Coming off this last turn onto the pit straight the rear kicks on a bump and it completely kicks it out of line. And also when I want to apply the throttle, I have to wait until the car's basically in a straight line."

Allen: "OK. We're going to go 200 down on the rear springs."

Andy: "Trevor, can you hear me? I want to come out eight clicks on the front, please."

Mark Morris, finishing up a change on Mauricio's car: "OK; watch yourselves, guys. We're coming down. Stands are out." Mauricio goes out for an installation lap in the T-car.

Andy to Mauricio back on pit lane: "Eleven minutes to go, Morris. That gives us two runs, one of which is the tires. Was that rear spring change positive?"

Mauricio: "Ten-four, ten-four. I want to do the tire change."

Andy: "Understood. Give me another eight clicks out, please, Trev."

Mark to Allen; "Two things. The ride is better with the springs and the car is a little bit more stable under braking because of that. It's not quite so reactive. I feel I want to drive the car into the corner a bit harder but there's nothing there on the rear to let me do it. There's nothing there to give any reading."

Mauricio says his dash reading went away. Andy answers, "Understood, Morris; it's a problem with Pi. [Pi Research supplies the on-board computer system.] It's crashing."

There's about 6 minutes to go in the session. Scott Pruett is quick with a 1:00.357 lap. Mark is P11 and Mauricio is off the bottom of the monitor. That means he's slower than 18th quick.

Mark Moore tells the 17-crew, "The next time in, we need to take the left-hand sidepod off the car. And we're going to change all the tires."

Andy tells Mauricio: "These are the options [tires] going on now. Try slot zero again on this run." Mark jumps to P5 and then P4 with a 1:00.575. Then Dario Franchitti pops up to P2, dropping Mark to P5, where he is at the end of the session.

With a few minutes to go Mauricio is still off the monitor. Andy consoles him. "So we'll get together with them [Allen and Mark on the 18-car] and see what they tried. And we'll take it from there. I don't think they were too far from what we were doing either [the setup]. So the time's there."

A little later in the garage area I ask Mauricio what happened. "Everything happened, with both cars. Nothing happened good."

Besides the engine "blowing up," the computer display in the car, the dash, crapped out several times, and the brakes had a huge vibration early in the session necessitating a change of rotors. The 17-crew learned almost nothing about the course or the car in this session. Mauricio ended up 29th and 39th in the two cars he drove, 2 seconds off the pace.

I'm told the Ilmor development engines that powered Mauricio to the pole in Rio have a problem dropping valves, but if they go past 30 miles they're usually good for 300 miles. They'll install another development engine now and race with it, if it lasts past the 30 miles.

Friday Qualifying Session

At 2:40 p.m. the green flag starts this half-hour fast-guys' qualifying session. Both PacWest cars are in this first session, and Mark Blundell is out on track immediately. Mauricio waits until his oil temperature gets to 140 degrees F and then motors down the pit lane. There is some pressure on the drivers to do well in today's qualifying because the weather reports say tomorrow will be rainy. If that happens, this will end up being the only qualifying session for the race.

Several of us in the PacWest pit stand and watch the Timing and Scoring monitor instead of the cars. From here the only part of the cars we can see as they whiz by on the frontstraight is the rear wings. Since that's meaningless, we watch the times changing on the monitor.

Scott Pruett quickly gets his lap time down to 1:00.306 for P1. Then, about 5 minutes into the session, Gil de Ferran goes under a minute with a 59.922-seconds lap. Mark is P5 and Mauricio P9.

Andy to Mauricio: "The tire pressures are a little bit high all 'round but the split's OK. Did you say oversteering or understeering? I lost the start of the message."

Mauricio: "Over, over, over."

Andy: "Understood, over." A car stalls on course causing a red flag that stops the session at 2:48 p.m.

Andy: "All right, Mark [Moore], we have a red flag; I need to go to a B shutter on the left-hand sidepod, please." This is a cooling flow adjustment. Andy has seen a high or low temperature somewhere in the data transmitted from the on-board sensors.

Mauricio comes in saying, "It's still oversteering in braking, and then when I try to go to the gas on the exit, it goes to oversteer."

Andy: "Have you tried the rear bar setting?"

Mauricio: "No I didn't, because it's only happening in some places."

Andy: "What do you think about coming up slightly on the rear springs? It seems that by coming up on the front spring and dropping the front ride height we've given more front grip. We need to come up just a fraction on the rear spring now. Just one or two, to bring the rear ride height down?"

Mauricio: "Let's do that. Let's go two. The key will be to get the ride height down."

The course goes green at 2:52 p.m. Bruce arrives in pit lane. He climbs into the scoring cart and turns the monitor to the video signal. I have to look for another place to get the times. My only other choices are to the engineering carts, but they have vinyl curtains hanging down in back so I have to peer around that and the other people to try to catch a glimpse of a monitor. At 2:57 there is another spin and stall that causes a red flag. It's Greg Moore.

Andy to the crew: "Can you connect the rake control on the gearbox, guys, so we can put two sweeps in?"

This a rare mention of one of the techie tricks Tim Neff has developed. I think the "tim" control they refer to is a cockpit-adjustable rake control. If you hydraulically connect the front and rear shocks, you can conceivably control how much the car dives under braking or squats during acceleration. Check valves and adjustable restrictions are the control possibilities. This could be the "rake control" Andy just mentioned. I guess they aren't as secretive as they have been. But nobody has explained it to me yet!

With about 5 minutes to go in the session Mark and Mauricio are ninth and 10th on the monitor. As he comes into the pit lane I hear Mauricio say, "Andy, leave it like it is."

Andy: "Understood, Morris. I hope that means it's better."

Mauricio: "It is better. It's still not right, but we don't have time to change it."

Andy: "We're making a change to the engine calibration. We want you to go to slot one. That should help the boost."

Andy: "Make sure we don't unplug, Roscoe, until we tell you." That's so the connection doesn't get unplugged while the new calibration is loading into the on-board system.

Andy: "We can unplug, thanks."

Mauricio has trouble with the cockpit-adjustable rear swaybar right at the end of the session. He moves up to P10 and then to P7, but Paul Tracy moves up the list and others jump up also. The checkered flag waves at 3:15 p.m. Blundell finishes the session in provisional qualifying spot number eight with Mauricio 12th. Scott Pruett has the provisional pole with Dario Franchitti second, and Gil de Ferran third. If it rains tomorrow, this could be the starting grid.

Debriefs

It seems to me the debrief groups are fairly intense. Andy, Mauricio, and Zeca huddle in the 17-car transporter talking over some printouts. Outside, sitting in folding chairs at a table, are Mark Blundell, Allen McDonald, Al Bodey, and Malcolm Oastler, the Reynard chief designer.

This table is also the eating area and fans amble by a few feet away, staring at everyone and everything. That's what the price of a paddock pass gets them. There are light tubular barriers between the fans and the garage area that are generally honored, but in a rare display of cheek, two young women in shorts scoot right past the barriers and ask to have a picture with Mark. They smile and hand their little camera across the table to Malcolm and ask him to take the picture. Then they both squat down behind Mark, lean forward to put their heads on either side of his, and beam photo-smiles across at Malcolm. Mark flashes a smile, Malcolm snaps the photo, the ladies chatter their gratitude and depart. The meeting resumes as if never interrupted. What strikes me is the politeness with which these very serious and busy men accommodate those fans and then get right back to work without any show of irritation at all. To me this is professionalism and common courtesy. Can you see that happening in any other sport?

Back at the Sheraton I have a few beers and talk to some of the CART people who are also staying there. Jim Swintal, the CART starter; his wife, Diane; and I talk about Ayrton Senna. Each of us tells how we found out about his death at the Imola track in Italy in 1994. I was watching the race live. It's difficult for me to even think about Senna without getting teary. I never got closer than 20 feet to him, but he is a very special person to me even now. It's comforting to hear that they have similar feelings.

SATURDAY

After a 10-minute walk from the parking lot I'm at the Indy Lights hospitality tent for my morning coffee and chocolate doughnut. The weather is not as good as yesterday. We have intermittent showers and it's cool, about 65 degrees.

I get to the PacWest garage area about 7:45 a.m. On Saturdays CART practice is early, 9 a.m. Both the 17- and 18-crews have one car finishing up on the setup pad and the other warming its engine. Butch Winkle, Blundell's crew chief, says they will also run the development engine this race. "The new 08 motor is probably worth three-tenths of a second a lap," Butch says. "We've been changing a lot of motors. Just the logistics of dressing and changing motors and having the right one in the right chassis at the right time is tough. It keeps us on our toes. Every time we've been at the shop we've had the back end off both cars."

It's showering off and on and the Indy Lights cars are supposed to be done with their practice at 8:45, but they're still out there. The CART practice will be late.

At 8:50 a.m. in the pit lane I ask Andy Brown what they do to the setup to optimize it for a wet track. "It's just our dry setup with rain tires installed. You seldom have a completely wet session, and our dry setup's good enough."

"You don't soften the springs and shocks and add negative camber like I've been told you're supposed to do in the wet?"

"The tires would like it, but you can do without all that, and then if it gets dry we don't lose time changing back."

Saturday Morning Practice

It's not raining anymore and the track is drying. I decide to watch this session from the pit-board signaling area between the mainstraight wall and the outer pit lane wall. I'm standing right across from the starter's stand so I can see Jim Swintal and Gordon Ensing clearly. Tom Keene and Mike Todd are handling the pit boards for PacWest today.

The session starts at 9:07. Some cars are on slicks but most are on rain tires. The PacWest cars go out, come in for their installation checks, and go back out on track. I can't see a monitor so I don't know what the times are. I am listening to my scanner, so maybe I can hear Control say who is fast.

A Wet Pit Lane

When Mark comes in he says the car has a lot of push and it affects the braking. "The front feels nervous," he says, and complains about some gearbox problems also. From out here I can see what the other teams are doing when they come in for pit stops. Christian Fittipaldi switches from rains to slicks.

Mauricio comes in and Andy asks about slicks. Mauricio says yes, so the 17-crew changes tires and also makes a shutter change. I assume the car was cooling too much and they installed another shutter that gives a smaller duct exit.

Mauricio: "These tires [rains] are not lasting when the track dries. They are going off quickly."

Andy asks him about the ride height and he answers, "It's OK. It's touching on the backstraight a little but the track is changing quickly so there's no reason to go out again now."

Andy: "What about balance?"

Mauricio: "It's pushing but going to oversteer. The tires just went away really quick."

Mark started the session in the T-car. At 9:26 the crew pushes the primary car onto pit lane and Mark makes the switch. The sky is lighter now and some teasing sunlight plays around with us. At 9:32 a red flag stops the session. A car is dead on course and has to be towed in.

The guys manning the pit boards out here where I'm standing are mostly truck drivers doing one of their other jobs as are Mike and Tom. They all know each other and one of them has some smoked salmon and crackers he's passing around. It was a big decision for me to watch from the pit wall because of the cars going by at 70 mph on the pit-lane side and 180 mph on the frontstraight. I don't want to screw up and look silly or hurt myself. Here I am taking all this stuff seriously and these guys are having a picnic. The truckies definitely have a sub-culture all their own.

At 9:34 a.m. a green flag restarts the session. Most of the cars are on slicks now as the track continues to dry. Paul Tracy is still on wets, however, and he uses the track close to my pit wall looking for what water remains on the track to cool his tires. Mauricio goes out at the green flag, but Mark is not in the primary car yet. Fernandez and Ribeiro flash by in their doggy Lolas. At least they have each other to race with.

Another red flag at 9:38. Mauricio tells Andy, "The car feels about right, so don't touch it." The Safety Team bump starts Parker Johnstone, who stalled to cause the red flag, and he motors into pit lane. We get a green flag at 9:42.

Allen tells Mark as he goes out, "Take it easy. It'll take a while for the tire temperatures to come up."

I hear Control say, "The line is dry, so smoke is smoke." That's a significant call. When the track was wet, oil smoke or a spray of coolant was not easy to detect what with all the rooster tails of water off the tires. So he's announcing to all the corner workers that if they see something that looks like smoke, now it probably is smoke.

With 30 minutes to go Control says that the fast drivers in the session are Mauricio, Andre Ribeiro, Christian Fittipaldi, Greg Moore, and Raul Boesel. At 9:48 the track is getting drier and a cold breeze is coming from the south.

I can see the Festival Curves from here and I watch as Mark dives underneath Michael Andretti going in the turn. That's the main place to pass on this course. The cars are hitting 180 or so on the straight and have to slow to 35 or 40 for this slow switch-back chicane. The entrance to these curves is wide, so if a car gets a good drive off Turn 9 a pass can be made on the straight or under braking.

Michel Jourdain Jr. spins, causing a red flag. Mauricio is in P1. He comes in at 9:51 saying the pop-off valve is causing him some trouble. He's not stopped in the pit box yet but he continues, "Let's do a valve change and also shocks."

Andy: "I'm thinking rear rebound. Do you agree?"

Mauricio: "Ten-four." They really know and trust each other.

Mark comes in after a quick lap that moved him up to P4. "Fair go," Allen says.

Mark: "It's better on entry but mid to exit the car is developing push. It's too reactive under braking. I feel it's slightly under-aero, but I don't want more wing. I'd like to find some mechanical grip. We should look at the rake."

The green flag waves again at 9:57. Control says, "Under 20 minutes."

With 17 minutes to go I feel a few sprinkles. Mauricio goes out after a red flag.

Mark's car is still in the pit box. "I don't have big enough balls to go out there now," Mark says. Mauricio comes in for rain tires. At 10:09 the rain gets harder. I have on a coated nylon rain jacket. I pull the hood up over my cap and headphones. Mauricio goes out for a few exploratory laps on his rains.

The 64-car, Arnd Meier, goes hard into the tires at Turn 8. I was told later he slithered across the wet grass like it was ice. Mauricio comes in saying, "It was good to have a look at where the puddles are."

I hear Mark Moore say, "Can I have my jet ski?"

Control says, "We've met the guaranteed time. Let's let the clock run and let it run out." A few minutes later the rain lets up and some cars go back on course, but most crews pack up and move back to the garage areas.

Saturday Qualifying Session

It's 12:30 p.m. in the pit lane. The track is still wet and the slow guys are first today, so they get to dry the track for the rest of the cars. If, that is, no more rain falls. Blundell is eighth and Mauricio 12th from yesterday's qualifying session, so both would like to improve. It's still overcast but there is blue sky to the west. A cold wind blows from the southwest.

I talk to Bernie Meyers, team manager and chief mechanic for Payton-Coyne Racing. They recently bought a '97 Reynard chassis for their driver, Michel Jourdain Jr., from Bobby Rahal.

Bernie says the Lola didn't give the driver any feedback about how close he was to the edge of adhesion. "The rear doesn't follow the front," Bernie tells me. "Christian Danner drove for us at Detroit. He'd never been in the car before, and after five laps he confirmed all the same stuff we'd learned with Michel. The Reynard is much better."

This makes me feel even worse for Richie Hearn, still stuck with his Lola. Oh, well.

At 12:44 the Saturday qualifying session begins. I hear someone on the radio saying "98-car short cut the chicane and did not follow the procedure."

The Festival Curves are very slow and require precise braking. Drivers who brake too late can just go straight through, but that could confuse the Timing and Scoring system and might get in the way of someone who had been in front of them going into the corner. "The procedure" is that the car has to stop before returning to the track and proceed only when a corner worker tells the driver the track is clear. The penalty for not following the procedure is a loss of the previous lap time.

At 1:05 about halfway through the session the sky is mostly clear. The fast guys are warming engines in pit lane. The noise of cars going by on the straight is a constant, but the noise and energy level of teams preparing for the next session ramps up sporadically, like increasingly higher waves breaking on a beach.

At 1:30 the fast-guys' qualifying session begins. I hear on the scanner as Allen asks Mark if he wants to hang back a minute while the other guys "blow the shit off the track."

Mark says, "No; I'll go slow and bring the tire pressures up."

A minute later Mark comes back in saying, "I don't think anybody's going to do anything for a while at this point, because the chicane is still fairly greasy and damp going in. And also the fifth-gear chicane as well. So maybe we'll just sit around for a bit and see what they do." But he can't stand it and a few minutes later he goes back on track.

Mauricio comes in and Andy says, "Give me eight clicks on the mid-front please, Trev [Trevor Jackson]. I want the fronts [tires] to be 1 pound below our intended hot."

Andy asks Mauricio: "Flat sliding or rolling?"

Mauricio: "It is a flat sliding, Andy. It rolls and sticks in there and then right at the end I gotta flat slide."

Andy: "Do you want to pull some of that rebound out at the back?"

Mauricio: "Let's try that."

Andy: "On the [tire pressure] sensors we were 2 pounds up all 'round but the split [tire pressure difference front to rear] was what we wanted. I'm going to drop the split by 1 pound to try and help the mid corner and we've done the rebound change to try and help the exit."

Mauricio: "Well, that's good news to try and help the exit. But the rebound, we been there. Wasn't perfect. I need something else."

Andy: "OK; give it a run like this and I'll get that change prepared. You've all but equaled the time from yesterday, which is more than other people are doing right now, so we're within a shout of going quicker."

Both cars are in and out of the pit lane tweaking their setups and waiting for the right time to cut a good lap. Tim Neff is not at this race, remaining back at the shop designing next year's shocks. This makes Trevor Jackson the lone "shock guy" here.

Trev is a tall, broad-shouldered kid, and I can see him taking up a lot of space as he bends down over the nose of the 17-car, carefully turning knobs. They keep him hopping making changes. Later he told me, "They tell me how many sweeps to change on a certain adjustment on a particular shock on either Mark's or Mo's car. I have to concentrate to know what I'm doing and make the right change in the right direction."

Mauricio, coming in off the track: "More oversteer coming out from the turns."

Mark has the same problem. "The car's got more oversteer in it presently. It just feels like I've got a pendulum-effect on the car again. Just swingin' from side to side."

Allen: "OK. One thing we can do is to wind some more shock in at the front. Do you feel that the car's connected at all under braking?"

Mark: "It still feels like the car's split because the front still feels quite harsh, but as soon as you go on the brake the rear just steps out of line. That lap especially just trying to get into the corners, it feels like it's got a bigger split front to rear."

Mark and Mauricio go out again with about 6 minutes left in the session. De Ferran is still the quickest. Then Scott Pruett jumps back up to P1 with a new track record of 59.383 seconds. Mauricio turns a 59.860 for P4.

Mark ends up in 11th spot on the grid. Mauricio's time holds up and he improves from 12th in yesterday's qualifying session to fourth on the grid for the race. This earns him the Budweiser Accelerator award for biggest improvement from one qualifying session to another. I follow him and Oreo to the victory circle where Pruett gets his pole qualifying check and Mauricio picks up a $1,000 check also. A few drops of rain begin to fall.

As I walk back to the garage area the rain begins to fall harder. Fifteen minutes later a strong wind is blowing hard rain. By 2:30 p.m. the drains fill up and puddles begin to form.

Tech Inspection Problems

The cars need to go to tech inspection after qualifying. Mark Morris and some of the 17-crew have taken the car to tech, but now I see Mark walk back in a hurry and go into the garage area to find Ando. They talk a little more urgently than usual, and it gets my attention. I follow them back to the tech tent where the 17x car is up on stands being measured.

It turns out that the "2-inch" measurement between the bottom of the car and the bottom of the sidepods is very close. This is a critical measurement because it is one of the ways the rules makers limit the amount of downforce the bottom of the car can generate. If the entire bottom was flat and the "tunnels" were unlimited, these cars could generate 4,000 or 5,000 pounds of downforce just with the bottom of the car, not counting the wings.

Rain water is running in from outside the tent and wetting the area under the car where people are lying. There is a man and a woman from the tech inspection crew, and now Ando is on his belly under there. I ask Mark Moore if it's OK.

Problems in Tech Inspection

"Yeah, it is, but it's too close for me." In the end they get a provisional pass, and are told to bring the car back in tomorrow for another check before it goes on course.

Working in the Wet

It was the 17x-car, the backup car, that Mauricio qualified today, so that's what he has to race tomorrow. But they want to race the development engine with the bigger headers, so they have to take that out of the primary car now and install it for the race. They end up switching a lot of parts between the two cars.

Working conditions are not enhanced by the hard rain. Puddles form and water depth in some places is a couple of inches. Dr. Love (Tim Love, the 18-car gearbox guy) puts some plastic bags over his shoes but one leaks and it becomes a little bag of water for his foot.

Tim Love Works in the Wet

The 18-car brain trust, Al Bodey and Allen McDonald, are talking to Mark Blundell at a table in the back of the garage area. Malcolm Oastler joins them and I notice him jabbing a finger hard into the table to emphasize a point while talking straight at Mark.

Later at the hotel I drink a beer out of the fridge in my room and watch TV. All of a sudden there's Dr. Love being interviewed on the tube. It's a nice piece, really, with him talking about the effect of the wet weather. He's standing in the rain with a blue hood over his head and they zoom in so you can see his day-old beard and calm eyes. Tim sounds honest and knowledgeable and comes off great. The entire piece on the races is several minutes in length and very enthusiastic and positive.

RACE DAY

I'm at the track about 7 a.m., and stop again at the Lights hospitality tent for my first coffee at the track. The sky is overcast and it's sprinkling off and on.

When I go to the PacWest garage area this morning I ask Andy Brown if this year's Reynard is stiffer at the rear than last year's. He says, "Yes, but neither is as stiff as the '95."

"Lola's saying that's the problem with their car and all cars had the same problem last year."

"I doubt it's that simple," Andy says. "They were saying it was a rear-bulkhead stiffness problem as long ago as Long Beach, and they still aren't going faster on the track. If it was simple they would have already fixed it."

At 8:15 the 17x-car is back in tech inspection and it gets approval this time with no problem. I didn't ask what it took to fix it. Obviously they have ways to shim the skid plates so the bottom of the car is just a hair more than 2 inches lower than the bottom of the sidepods.

At 8:35 a.m. the 18-car is warming up for the 10 o'clock warm-up session. The engine exhaust makes my nose and eyes burn more than usual. I wonder if it's the humidity. It's still sprinkling rain.

At 9:15 in the garage area, both the 18-cars are gone and the 17-car is on the setup pad. Indy Lights cars are on course. The sky looks lighter to the south and west.

In pit lane the 18-crew is practicing pit stops in the wet. Ando is timing them with a stopwatch. Butch stretches and moves around to warm up and loosen his body as would any professional athlete preparing for a training session. At 10 minutes until 10 the sprinkles have stopped and the sky is definitely lighter. But any minute rain clouds could rise out from behind the grandstands on the other side of the straight.

Warm-Up

The green flag starts the session right at 10 a.m. Light rain is dripping down. Both PacWest cars go out on slicks. A few minutes later Greg Moore is dead stick at the chicane. His crew tells CART that there's no oil pressure. They throw a red flag and tow him back into the pit lane in counter-course direction.

Mauricio is still having problems with his brakes. "It's the same problem that I had with the other car. It's shaking all over the place."

Mark to Allen, "I'm not sure about the shift. It feels stiffer, but it's sticking in the gate. It's more the effort and then it's difficult to select the gear very smoothly. Balance-wise, just under braking, it feels OK at this point into the chicane, but again we're brakin' very early because it's a little bit slick down there."

Mauricio: "The car was touching a little bit, but I wasn't at full speed yet. The brakes, Andy, the steering wheel comes out of my hands, that's how bad it is."

Andy has some radio problems and changes out his transmitter. It's raining harder now.

Mark and Allen talk about switching to rain tires. Mark resists. "If it stops raining it's not going to take too long to dry back out again."

Mauricio: "I think what happened to these discs, Andy, they cool down. You heat them up too much and then they cool down." They're changing the brake rotors on pit lane. One or two guys work very intensely at each corner of the racecar.

Andy to Mauricio: "I'm watching the monitor. There's hardly any spray out there if any. But the final turn looks a bit greasy." Parker Johnstone spins at Turn 5 and gets going again.

Andy: "We've got a red flag, guys. Where are we with the other car's brakes, Mark?"

Mark Moore: "Chris and Ron, go back and start pulling the brakes and the pads out of your car." They've decided to change rotors on the 17-car, so those guys go back to the garage area and take the rotors off the other car and bring them to pit lane. The wet track is causing some spins and red flags that allow time to make the change.

Andy: "We've got 10 minutes of green left, Morris, and I don't think this is going to be a long yellow. They've just got to give Carpentier a bump start. Is there any point in our going out again with these brakes as they are? What I'm doing at the moment is getting the discs off the other car."

Mauricio: "Well, there is no point with these brakes; they're no good at all. I mean the whole car shakes every time I touch the brake pedal. I can feel the rear wheels shaking."

Mark Moore: "Start taking off all the wheels and the brakes."

Andy to Mauricio: "It takes about 5 minutes to change these. We should go for it just in case there's a red flag. I want to check to see if these are OK for this afternoon."

Mark Moore: "We're going to leave these pads. We're just going to change the discs."

Blundell goes out on track at 10:37, when the session restarts. Mauricio goes out with about 6 minutes to go in the session. Mark Moore says, "Good job guys. I woulda never thought we'd get that done in time."

Chris Jaynes comes back, "We had practice with that shit yesterday."

Mark is back in with 5 minutes to go. "The car's not too bad and the grip level doesn't feel too bad, but the surface water's not there so the tires are just tearing up. Too much roll in the car, too much movement. You want me to go back to the other fuel position or leave it on this one?"

Al Bodey says, "Come back to position three." The crew changes from wet tires to slicks.

Mark: "In top gear we seem to be at terminal speed pretty easily with the revs."

Mark goes back out as Mauricio comes in for slicks also.

Andy: "OK; there'll just be a couple of minutes left. I want to get as much of a scuff on these as I can, but the other thing to try is the yellow calibration on your in-lap."

The 17-crew practices a hot pit stop when Mauricio comes in for the last time. The session was trouble-filled for Mauricio and his time shows that, 26th fast. Mark, on the other hand, ends up fourth quick behind Christian Fittipaldi, Alex Zanardi, and Michael Andretti.

Back in the garage area, Mark Moore tells me Mauricio's brake problem was caused by some problems with the rotors they get from a company in North Carolina that pre-beds rotors and pads for the NASCAR teams. "The last three sets were shit: the ones in the Detroit warm-up, Friday, and again today."

For some reason brand-new brake rotors and brake pads don't work well. Teams spend valuable track time "bedding in" pads and rotors. There is a specific procedure for warming them up and applying the brakes hard that gets the components comfortable with each other. Pre-bedding is a way to eliminate the on-track procedure, but it's not working for PacWest.

Pre-Grid

Around noon, after they've had their race-planning meeting, I ask Ando to tell me about the race strategy. "It's a 98-lap race, but you can't go 98 green-flag laps without some fuel conservation. We can do about 4.4 miles per gallon during the yellow flags. We'll run the development engine because it's a lot stronger. It has a problem though and that's what happened to Greg Moore just now in the last session. But if you get past 30 miles, it doesn't seem to break. It's a calculated risk."

Firestone Rain Tires

Goodyear Rain Tires

"Do you have a fuel slot for a wet track? A softer throttle response?"

"Yes, but the driver still has to be easy on and off the throttle."

About 45 minutes before the race the cars take their places in the starting grid on the frontstraight. I ask Allen McDonald about the Firestone rain tires. "They seem to be pretty good, but they aren't worth much as soon as it gets dry. We stand them up a bit because we've been knocking the corners off."

"Stand them up" means less negative camber. As we speak, a light but steady sprinkling of rain keeps the track wet. Everyone wears some kind of rain jacket or carries an umbrella.

Christian Fittipaldi is in the second row next to Mauricio. He's on Goodyears and Mo is on Firestones, so I take some pictures of a rear tire on each car. The photos show the Firestone tread pattern is more open and the rubber blocks are smaller and taller, so it should push the water away better but also deteriorate quicker on a dry track. I fondle blocks of rubber on both tires. The Goodyear rubber feels softer and stickier than the Firestone stuff. Who knows which will be better? Tires are a black art, and weather conditions will certainly change during the race.

THE RACE

The cars start their pace laps right about 2 p.m. and the rain is getting harder. Bruce, Jolene, and Al Gugelmin, Mauricio's brother, are in the scoring cart. The team has put up a folding awning to keep the stacks of tires and the tool boxes out of the rain. That makes the pit area behind the wall more crowded than usual. I have to keep moving around to see what's going on and keep out of the way. My rain jacket keeps me dry but I'm holding a scanner, a tape recorder, and a notebook, and I need to keep them all dry. When drops fall on my notebook I have to rewrite things.

During the pace laps the PacWest drivers do a radio check around the course. It's still light sprinkles, but there are some very dark clouds looming in the south. I can hear Jack Hodge, the voice of Control, say, "This will be a 98-lap race. You guys watch your butts out there."

Andy talks on the radio to Mauricio: "If there's an incident at the chicane the yellow flag will be shown by the blend line, not at the Start/Finish line."

I can also hear on the scanner Ken Lowe giving precise instructions to the pace-car driver: "Give me 65 [mph] on the mainstretch from Turn 4 on down to 8."

Control: "OK, radio people, let's remind the drivers, no passing 'til you pass the Start/Finish on the start. Let's everybody watch everybody and everybody take care of everybody, and let's get through that first turn."

Mark Moore: "Everybody be ready. We'll probably go to drys before too long at this rate."

Andy: "Lights out on the pace car, Morris." His voice sounds a little tighter than in the practice sessions.

Control: "Packin' up at 8."

Andy: "Pace car onto pit lane." Then: "Green flag, green flag."

The green flag flies at 2:07 p.m. The cars generate a huge cloud of spray, and the field spreads out on the straight as the drivers try to get a clear view of what's in front of them. For the ones in the middle of the cloud of water, it must be an act of faith and will for each driver to keep his foot down on the throttle in the face of such uncertainty. The Festival Curves have a transition from asphalt to concrete in the chicane and back to asphalt at the exit. This is an added difficulty for the drivers in the wet.

Pruett leads that first time into the Festival Curves followed closely by de Ferran. Mauricio gets by Christian Fittipaldi for third. On the second lap de Ferran spins and Mauricio comes by in second spot. I can't see a monitor, so I try to watch as the cars come by on the straight. All I can see there is spray. Finally I notice a big-screen TV past the Timing and Scoring building further down the straight. Watching that I can see the cars going around on the track.

On the fifth lap Mauricio passes Pruett late on the straight just before the chicane and takes first place in the race. Next time by he's stretched out a lead of six or eight car lengths. Pruett is on Firestones same as Mauricio, so it's not just the tires. Mauricio said later that he thought he had the fastest car in the wet. It sure looks that way.

As Mauricio puts more distance between himself and Pruett, Jim Reid looks around at me and raises an eyebrow. A couple of laps later Trevor also gives me a look, rolls his eyes, and smiles. The hoping and waiting for that first win has begun. Blundell is in eighth up from 11th on the starting grid. Bobby Elrod, the relief truck driver, comes up from the garage area to grin at everyone and pat butts in encouragement.

I hear Andy tell Mauricio about hard rain at Turn 3. Shortly after that we get a heavy shower on pit lane. The rooster tails kicked up by the cars on the straight in front of us are even thicker now. Andy tells Mauricio to turn BOSS off and go down two clicks on the boost.

Mo is still leading, still pulling away on lap 11, when a yellow flag comes out for the removal of a plastic cone on the racing line. Andy to Mauricio: "You had 12 seconds on Pruett in second place. Next time we'll lean it out and save some fuel."

At the restart Mauricio pulls away again. Mark is up to fifth. On lap 18 Chief Steward Wally Dallenbach decides it's too dangerous to race with this much standing water on the course. They wave a yellow flag and dispatch the blower truck to get rid of the puddles. Almost immediately the rain starts to slack up.

Mark Moore says, "The rain is letting up. If they'd let the cars run they would have pumped the water off the course quicker than that blower truck." Good point.

I'm standing under the cover at the front of the 17-car engineering cart, close enough during the quiet time when the cars are on the back side of the course to hear Andy say, "A few cars are pitting, mostly the ones on Goodyears."

Ron Endres, one of the mechanics on the 17-car and the outside-rear-tire changer at pit stops, jokes nervously about a wet stop. "When I run around that rear wing carrying a tire, I'm gonna look like a scared dog on tile."

I hear "one finger next time by" on the scanner at the same time I hear Andy say Mo is getting 5.5 miles per gallon and Mark 5.1 during this yellow-flag run. On lap 24 of 98 scheduled, the race restarts. Mauricio makes a great start and lengthens out another lead. Zanardi passes Pruett for second place on lap 28.

A couple of laps later Christian Danner stalls on course, causing another yellow flag. Immediately people around me start getting into position for a pit stop. I just try to take some photos of Mauricio's stop but not get in the way. The result is bad pictures.

Zanardi beat Mauricio out of the pits for the lead. Trevor tells me Mauricio didn't get going right when the car came down off the jacks. Now Mauricio is second and Mark sixth. The Firestone rain tires that came off the two PacWest cars sit in stacks steaming with moist heat. They look great, however, with no visible wear or chunking. They certainly did a great job for this team.

After one green-flag lap, Al Unser Jr. and Dario Franchitti get tangled at the Festival Curves causing another yellow flag, the fourth, on lap 35. The order is Zanardi, Mauricio, Vasser, Tracy, Michael Andretti, and Mark. Just before the restart Billy Kamphausen comes over to Andy and says, grinning, "Be cool."

"Tell that to Zanardi," Andy growls.

Andy thinks it's going to be a timed event for sure now. There have been too many yellow-flag laps and the remaining laps can't be completed in the allotted 2 hours. The sprinkles are very light and the track is drying out on the racing line. The cars swerve toward the pit wall as they come by in front of us looking for water to cool their tires. Andy asks about slick tires, "What's the best set?" Then he tells Scott to get set number three ready.

On the radio Andy tells Mauricio to say when he's ready for slicks. Ando says to Mark, "Go to slot one on fuel for the restart."

Mark gets by Michael Andretti on the lap-38 restart and a lap later he passes Paul Tracy for fourth. He goes around Vasser on lap 41 for third behind Zanardi and Mauricio. Scott Pruett spins out of Turn 9 for the second time today and stalls, causing another yellow flag on lap 45.

Andy to Mauricio: "I suggest we stay out. I think there'll be more yellows, and maybe we'll stop on the next one and switch to slicks. I can't see wets lasting 'til the end of the race. There's probably 45 minutes left in the race. We need another 15 minutes on these tires."

A few laps after the restart at 3:25 p.m. another yellow flag flies caused by Herta, Ribeiro, and Salles getting together in the Festival Curves. After the cars are queued up behind the pace car, I hear Mauricio saying, "I'm bored." And then, "It's no good for slicks yet."

At the restart the order is the same, but when P.J. Jones spins causing another yellow on lap 53, Zanardi pits for fuel only, electing to stay on wet tires. This puts Mauricio in the lead followed by Mark and Greg Moore. This is the same order as the last laps at Detroit!

Mauricio radios to Andy: "No slicks! It's too wet for slicks."

Ando to Mark: "Slot two on the fuel."

Andy to Mauricio: "Stay out. Do not pit." And later, "Good call on the tires." Then, "We've got 17 or 18 laps worth of fuel."

On lap 56 of 98 a green flag restarts the race. The order is Mauricio, Mark, Moore, Johnstone, Tracy, Boesel, and de Ferran. Mark Moore groans into the radio, "This is just like Detroit. We're one, two and there's Moore behind us. They're even pitted next to us again."

Control says, "10 minutes to a timed-race decision."

Andy to Mauricio: "The Goodyears are beginning to get an advantage in these conditions."

With the track drying out the Goodyear rain tires, with more rubber area in the tread, come into their own, and the Firestones get too hot for lack of water to cool them. Paul Tracy, on Goodyears, passes Greg Moore (Firestones) for third on lap 62. But before he can gain on Mark, Tracy pits for slicks and then spins off course before he can get them up to temperature. If he had taken his time warming up those tires it might have been a very different finish.

On lap 66 Mo pits for slick tires, leaving Mark in first place ahead of Greg Moore. A lap later Mark comes in for slicks also and Moore follows, but the 18-crew work a great pit stop and Mark gets out ahead of Moore.

The order now is de Ferran, Zanardi, Christian Fittipaldi, Michael Andretti, Adrian Fernandez, and Mark. Mo drops to ninth. He tried too hard on cold slicks and spun off course, losing several spots.

At 3:57 they declare a 2-hour timed event. By my watch that leaves 11 minutes, about six laps. The leaders are on wet tires that are giving up on a drying track. Mark and Mauricio are on slicks and moving up but it's difficult passing off line due to lingering moisture. It's very easy in these conditions to make a mistake. Most racing fans think guys go fast because they've got more courage than the next guy, more "balls." But at times like these, patience and judgment are much more valuable than raw courage.

Mark is in sixth and Mauricio in eighth with six laps to go. They're moving up in the order, passing cars almost every lap. Mark goes to fifth, then on lap 75 he's third behind Christian Fittipaldi, who's on Goodyear wets like the leader de Ferran. After two laps worrying Fittipaldi, Mark passes him and starts his run for the leader on the last lap. Raul Boesel, also on slicks and overlooked completely by everyone, is also on slicks and coming up hot on Mark's tail.

In one of the most exciting finishes in racing history and the absolute closest finish in CART history, 0.027 seconds between the first two cars, Mark noses out de Ferran for his first CART win and the first for PacWest.

Everyone around me jumps out onto pit lane and pounds backs and hugs each other. I start taking pictures, but there is only one left on that roll. I should have changed that earlier. By the time I put in a new roll of film, everyone is running down pit lane to the victory circle, and I follow them.

In victory circle I snap some pictures during the yelling and screaming. Bruce pushes past me to hug Mark. Deborah, Mark's wife, is on the outside of the crush of people and just kind of prances around looking for a way into the mass, grinning and crying and wiping her eyes. Then the mob relaxes and Mark, Bruce, and Jolene come through and climb into a convertible for a victory lap of the course.

It'll be a while before they show up at the post-race press conference, so I walk back to the garage area to ask the obvious question, "How does it feel?"

Allen McDonald seems to be in shock. We had been talking about Mark's feedback woes only that morning. "Well, it feels pretty good. It was a matter of staying out and then coming in at the right time for the dry tires. We did the same as Andy."

Andy is pleased and says it's a team effort. "We had to pit first and then Mo made a mistake and went off in the grass. It shows the team can do it."

Everyone is happy at the win, but they're also beginning to pack up for the trip back to the shop. Two important tests, one over the July Fourth weekend, lie ahead of them. In this business they don't get much time to think about the victories. They think about that while they work toward the next one.

Mark Blundell and Crew in Victory Lane

Press Conference

Raul Boesel, third place, comes in first, then Gil de Ferran, runner-up. It's almost a half-hour after the race before a tired-but-smiling Mark Blundell climbs up into the narrow portable building and Mike Zizzo, CART director of public relations, starts the press conference. Mike summarizes each driver's significant accomplishments and asks for comments on today's race.

Boesel says, "The whole race I was counting how many Firestone-tired cars were ahead of me. Mine was so great that I was hoping there wasn't many. I'd like to thank Firestone; they really did their homework. It really made a difference today."

De Ferran talks about the last couple of laps when he was on Goodyear rain tires and Mark was on Firestone slicks: "We knew it was going to be tough, and I was just waiting because it was a matter of time before anybody with slicks was going to catch us up. With three laps to go, Derrick [Walker, team owner] came on the radio and he said, 'Mark is right behind Christian.' I hoped Christian [Fittipaldi, on Goodyear rains also] would make it tough to pass. And I think Christian held him up for a lap, so that helped. Then on the last lap I was getting a lot of wheelspin. I thought I had it made coming out of the last corner. I tried to stop the car going in so I would have good traction, but Mark was able to go underneath me. I thought I won the race because I thought I crossed the line just before, but I guess not."

Then it's Mark's turn to talk about his first CART victory ['92 Le Mans was his last win] and the first ever for PacWest. Zizzo asks Mark, "Can you talk about the gamut of emotions you've gone through in the last two races, the gamble with the fuel at Detroit and now the situation with the tires? Just talk about the last two races; it's been unbelievable."

"It has been an unbelievable couple of weeks," Mark says, beaming tiredly. "In Detroit it was a fantastic high for us, and then one of the biggest lows of my life. It was a blow for us, for me and Mauricio, failing to get to the finish. This weekend things seemed to be going pretty good for us. Conditions were going to be variable and I was looking at the sky and thinking it won't be any problem at all, it suits me fine. The car was great. The team gave me a good car for the race, on wets or slicks. It was good all the way to the end of the race."

Bruce had come into the room and is sitting at the head table with the drivers. Zizzo asks Bruce to comment. "Well, it had been raining all day and obviously, right at the end, you could see the track drying quickly. We made the call to switch to slicks at just the right time."

Someone asks Mark to describe the last lap. "Well, when I was out there at the end on slicks we ran into a bit of a problem with traffic, with Matsushita, a couple of laps from the end. He came down across my nose at one corner and I had to slam on the brakes and a few other people got around me. That gave me a bit of excitement. [Actually, Mark made some very nasty comments on the radio about Hiro Matsushita, as all the drivers have at one time or another.] Then I was chasing Zanardi and Greg Moore. But Zanardi went off course. That was a bit of luck.

"Then the race was on. John Anderson was on the radio to me, telling me that the leader was only 6 seconds in front and the guys ahead of me were all guys that I needed to pass. Christian made it a little bit difficult but we were on slicks and I put the car alongside him a few times and eventually I got him coming down the backstraight into the chicane.

"I caught up to Gil fairly quickly, and then tried to go around Gil in several places and I was out in the grass at one point. I thought, well, we're gonna end it here, but I managed to collect it. And he came into that last corner, and in fact I pretty much knew what he was going to do because I would have done exactly the same thing. He got off the gas a bit earlier and slowed the pace down, but I was able to jump out of line and get on the gas and went through the gears as we dragged down to the line. And it worked. [Mark grins, and everyone laughs.]

Bruce McCaw, Raul Boesel, Mark Blundell, and Gil de Ferran

"It was just sheer traction at that point. He was on worn-out wets and I was on slicks. If you see the lap times we were running at the end, we were running a whole bunch faster. We came off the corner just a whole bunch faster. If we had come around at the same pace as a lap before, the win would have been easier, but Gil slowed the pace and that evened things up."

Answering another question about working his way up from the 11th starting spot, Mark says, "Well, basically we had a very good start. The conditions were great for us at the beginning of the race. The visibility was very bad there in the middle of the pack. We just chipped away at people. The Firestones were working very well. I was a little bit apprehensive when the track started to dry out. The tires are a bit on the soft side, but they kept going OK. As the race went on we just kept catching people and going by. We picked up some spots during the pit stops. The team did a very good job. Then when we got out on slicks late in the race and we moved very quick then compared to other teams, but it was tough to get around people because it was wet off line."

The questions are winding down and I feel myself start to worry about getting to the airport for my flight home. I shut off the recorder, pick up my bag, and head for the door.

Coming out of the press compound, I see Butch Winkle and some of the 18-car guys waiting to push the winning car in for tech inspection. People from other teams have come to offer congratulations. I say congrats to Butch and shake his hand. I feel the emotion then, just the gladness that all of them are getting to feel good about the great job they've done. I don't remember anything about the conversations that happened then. I was trying not to cry. I really felt great for the guys.

Reactions

A week after the race I call John Oreovicz to see what's going on at the shop. The crews are testing at Elkhart Lake, Wis. They'll be back for a couple of days before a Fourth of July weekend test at Michigan.

John tells me about the team meeting on the Wednesday after the win. "It was one of our more mellow team meetings. Fuzzy [Jeff Horton] had told everybody he would shave his hair into a mohawk if the team won a race. Colleen had some clippers and did it right in the meeting. When we win the next one she has to dye her hair. We've had calls and faxes from all over the world. I'd say it's pretty positive."

Oreo switches me to Colleen and she confirms she shaved Fuzzy's hair, "Right there in front of everybody. The next win I have to dye my hair, red if Mo wins, blue if Mark wins, and purple if it's one-two. Jeff and I had been trading races. Detroit was my race and I was thinking about mixing the colors as I watched the race on TV. We all knew it was going to happen some-time. We've got some spirit going here, so what the heck."

When I call Jeff Oster, the hospitality and transportation manager, to talk about a trip with the truckies, he tells me he's seen a higher level of commitment from everyone since the win. "Mark's win lifted a big load from our shoulders, but added some pressure too. The door is opened to even think about a championship. Zanardi really didn't get started 'til this time last year and he almost won. I see a change in the attitudes here. People seem to be willing to work harder and later. It takes a relentless pursuit of winning to make it happen. They've had a bite of the carrot now, and it's still dangling out there in front of us. Everybody feels it."

Jeff hadn't been at Portland, and when I say I'll see him at Cleveland, he tells me maybe not. "I'm working on some projects for '98 now and won't travel as much. My department got started late because the Motorola deal came through late, and we didn't know before that what to plan for. We want to get ahead for next year. This is really a very busy time with so many races in a row, but we have to start looking at next year."

On another phone call I talk to Steve Fusek and ask, "How does this first win change things?"

"It legitimizes everything," is Steve's answer. "And we don't have to wait anymore. It totally changes our attitude. We were gonna do it and we all knew it, but now we've done it. The Motorola people are pleased, of course. They kinda took a flyer with us. We made some pretty bold statements, and this backs it all up. Creak and I are flying to Brazil this afternoon to sign the new Hollywood deal. It's all coming together now."

I actually got phone calls and e-mail messages of congratulations myself, like this was somehow a victory of mine. I certainly didn't feel that I contributed in any way, but it was great to be that close to the people responsible for it. I think the people congratulating me were acknowledging what it meant to my book project that the team had won a race.

This probably won't be the last win in '97 for PacWest.

Mark Blundell with the Winner's Trophy and Roses
(Dan Boyd Photo)

CHAPTER 15
THE GUGELMINS

Mark Blundell's wife, Deborah, doesn't go to many races so I never got a chance to talk to her. During the Portland weekend I did record conversations with both Mauricio and Stella Gugelmin. The two interviews make a good chapter.

Thursday afternoon at Portland I go to the hospitality area looking for Mauricio. We had talked about scheduling an interview several weeks before and he said that Thursdays were a good time. When I find him he says we can do it now, but he has one of his twin sons with him. "Wait until Zeca [Mauricio's cousin, Jose Mello] gets back and we'll do it while he watches Bernardo."

Stella, Bernardo, and Mauricio

While I wait I jot down some questions to ask. A few minutes later Zeca hasn't returned so Mauricio suggests we start anyway, and we go into the Hollywood motor coach. He takes Bernardo into the front of the motor coach so he can play there.

In the middle of the vehicle there is a kitchen area with a small table, big enough to seat four tightly, and we sit there. I set up my recorder and we start the interview.

Mauricio Gugelmin is a native of Brazil, but he now lives in Fort Lauderdale, Fla. He's 34 years old. Mauricio is a handsome man, in the movie-star sense even. He's about my height, just under 6 feet tall. He works out and his body is fit and slim. His skin is brown and taut over strong cheekbones, and his chin is square under a straight nose and generous mouth. Short, dark-brown hair, very conservatively cut, frames a broad forehead.

I've heard the phrase "gun-fighter eyes" but only seen it a few times. Mauricio reminds me of Pancho Gonzales, the best tennis player in the world in the '50s. They both have a mixture of European and New World blood, but it's the eyes I notice. They look at you soft and steady and open, but intensity beams out of the apparent calm. I'm guessing there's a very strong, very emotional man here with big dreams and big drives, but he's learned self control and applies himself in an orderly manner with discipline and intelligence.

Paul: "What's your background? How far did you go in school? Did you have a job before you got into racing?"

Mauricio: "Well, before I started to race it was even difficult to get a job because I was 6 years old." His grin says "Gotcha."

I have to laugh. Mauricio's native language is Portuguese. Speaking English, he has a slight accent that I will reproduce faithfully where I can. But his speech is careful and articulate. There is never a problem understanding him.

Mauricio, continuing: "I was fortunate enough that I had a father that supported me on that, and he pushed me to the go-kart along with my brother Al. So I was driving, at the same time, I started driving when I was 6, even road cars, with a clutch and everything. I started driving on my own when I was 6. So that was the same time as when I went to school and those things just moved parallel — go-karts, school, and basketball, if you believe that."

Paul: "Basketball? Really?"

Mauricio: "Yeah. Then at one point I was on the county of Paranan official basketball junior team. I was really good at basketball. I'm not tall but at that stage, for my age, I was average height or average-to-higher."

Paul: "How old were you?"

Mauricio: "Then I was about 12. And my coach said to me one day, 'You either going to have to play basketball or race go-karts.' And I said to him, 'Good-bye.' [We both laugh.] I always felt that a sport with something pushing me, some kind of a motor, was more pleasant than sweating around in a small square trying to reach that basket. [He laughs again.]

"Now I know I would never have made professional with my height, but those guys do pretty well. Then I carry on with my studies until I was racing professionally already; I was in Formula Fiat in 1981. That was the first single-seater that I drove after go-karts.

"The first year that I drove Formula Fiat that was the same year that I went to university, which is college here, right? I went to college in business management. Actually, in Brazil you got to have an exam to go to college. Maybe there is a hundred places and you have to fight over them. I passed into two different places in business management, two different universities, and one in attorney, how you say?"

Paul: "Lawyer, a law degree."

Mauricio: "Right, a law degree. And I started to go for the business management, but I only did one year and really not focusing a lot into that because I knew, at least my plans..."

Mauricio has to stop to answer a ringing phone. "I have to get it; there's nobody else here."

There was no one on the line so he continues. "I already had my mind set to go to England, because [Ayrton] Senna had gone in '81, and I kept in touch with him and he was doing FF1600.

"It was a matter of finding the right timing to sit down with my dad and say, 'Look, can I go to England?' And that's what I really wanted to do and see his reaction, because that was my biggest question mark. I had made up my own mind. I had made calculations that if I sold my motorcycle, which I had a nice motorcycle at the time, and my car and my Formula Fiat which he gave me, I could probably raise half the budget I needed for the following year in England.

"I used to study in the morning, and in the afternoon I used to go to his office. He was always involved in the timber business. We still got farms and the cattle business. I used to go there and show my face and learn all the time. He brought us, my brother and I, we used to do different levels of work through the company to learn everything.

"So I said to him, 'How would you feel if I go to England next year? Would you help me?' And he just stopped. It was one of those big, long pauses and he said, 'Look, if that's what you really want to do, I'll support you.' I was kind of surprised. Where do I go from here?

"I asked him, 'How did you decide that really quick?' He just said, 'Well, last year when you asked me to race Formula Fiat, I said I would support you, but I thought you would do two or three races and see you're not gonna like this and you would be back home. But it surprised me because you did so well and you are doing well.' And I actually won the Brazilian championship in that.

"So he said, 'If that's what you want.... Your mom is not here and I know she would be against it.' Because I lost my mom when I was 8 years old. He said, 'You've proved to me that you have your head on your shoulders and I'm going to support you,' which was very nice."

Paul: "That's impressive."

Mauricio: "And he did support me. And then after that...Zeca's here; can we just...?"

Paul: "Sure."

I stop the recorder while Mauricio asks Zeca to watch Bernardo. The little boy has been so quiet I had forgotten about him but Mauricio hadn't, and it was probably bothering him that no one was watching his son.

He resumes his story. "So by doing that I had to stop the business management that I was doing for the one year. In Brazil you have eight years to finish your four years, but I just stopped. That's gone, and I don't regret it one little bit. That was it. I went to England."

Paul: "And you hooked up with Senna over there?"

Mauricio: "Well, I knew Senna from days in go-karts. In '78 the Brazilian championship was in Porto Allegre in the south of Brazil. He came there with a little station wagon with his kart on top and the engine and tires all in the car.

"We had a nice team. Zeca and myself used to drive for a proper go-kart team with a bus and go-

Mauricio, Steve Fusek, and Bruce McCaw

karts all inside and everything. Because we were racing different levels, I asked him if he wanted to leave his go-kart with us and he laughed, so he had to use his own car to go back and forth to the hotel.

"One day he actually borrowed my car. How it happened was that he was in his car and he forgot his helmet in the hotel. He asked to borrow my car and he went back, got a ticket and crashed my car on that trip to get the helmet. So when he came back I told him don't worry, if you want you can leave your go-kart in our transporter so you can use your car. And he said, 'Fine.'

"Our relationship started like this because he thought I was going to just be really mad. But I didn't even charge him for the ticket or to fix the car. In Brazil the ticket goes against the car license plate rather than the driver's license. So I guess we had a smooth start to our relationship. Since then we had always been in touch and he was in England a year before I went, so I asked him if he could arrange to get me a test with Van Diemen. He said, 'No, you don't need a test. I just mention who you are and you go straight to the works team.' "

Paul: "Really? So you went to England just after Senna and then, I think Zeca told me, the three of you roomed together?"

Mauricio, laughing: "We used to rent this little house in Norwhich. It was 60 pounds a month and that was a lot of money for us."

Paul: "When was that?"

Mauricio: "That was 1982."

Paul: "You raced Formula Ford over there?"

Mauricio: "Formula Ford 1600 and Senna was Formula Ford 2000. I won the 1600 and he won the 2000."

Paul: "Where did you go from there?"

Mauricio: "I went to the 2000 and he went to Formula 3. I won the 2000 and he won the Formula 3. From there I went to Formula 3 and did the same thing. He went to Formula 1."

Paul: "When you're saying Formula 3 you don't mean Formula 3000?"

Mauricio: "Formula 3. Formula 3000 only came the year I was in Formula 3, which was '85. And then Formula 1 was turbo so they felt all the new guys should really go to 3000 rather than go from Formula 3 to Formula 1. And Senna was really the last one, him and Brundle, to make that jump. Although some of the guys later, Hakkinen did. But not very successful. So I did Formula 3000 and then Formula 1."

Paul: "So what was your first Formula 1 drive?"

Mauricio: "Uuum. When I first test it was....Hah! It was Williams; it was a secret test. At Fuji. I used to drive Formula 3000 for Honda. So they had me test the new engine developed for Williams at Fuji in 1987. It was a secret test. Even Frank Williams didn't know about it. [We both laugh.] He found out later and he wasn't too happy about it because I was so close to Ayrton Senna and Senna had a Renault engine and he wanted to know how the Honda behaves. And then eventually he got a Honda in his car.

"Frank Williams saw me at Detroit 'cause I went to Fuji, did the test, and came back through Detroit, because of the Detroit Grand Prix, before I went to Europe."

Paul: "What year was that?"

Mauricio: "That was '87. Frank said to me, 'Hey, Mauricio, how did the FW...I think it was the 11 at the time, feel?' like joking. But he only found out after the test had happened."

Paul: "So that was when Senna was with McLaren with Prost?"

Mauricio: "No, that was when Senna was with Lotus with Renault engines. '87 was the yellow car; the Camel car."

Paul: "Right. I was at the Detroit GP for several years there, and I remember that yellow Lotus. It must have been the next year he was at McLaren with Prost. I have a picture above my desk at home that I took of Senna and Prost standing and talking to each other, civilly, maybe the last time."

Mauricio: "Well, in public they always talk civilly. Between four walls maybe not. That's the way professionals do it."

Paul: "Oh, OK. [Both of us chuckle at that statement.] That's interesting. So then, that was your first...." The thoughts about Senna and Prost distract me and I stumble around trying to come up with the next question.

"So how did that turbo engine feel, compared to what you were driving in Formula 3000?"

Mauricio: "It was unbelievable. First of all the amount of tires we had to go through just to do a test. And Honda used to keep steel brakes instead of carbon because of cost. But they weren't strong enough for the car. It had over 1,000 horsepower. So it was just ridiculous."

Paul: "There had to be some throttle lag."

Mauricio: "Yeah, there was some lag, but not bad. But when it hit your back it felt like, whoa."

Paul: "So you had to be going straight when you got on it."

Mauricio: "Oh yeah. Pretty much. It was one of those things like flat out [he puts his hands out in front like holding a steering wheel], then big brakes, and du, du, du around the corner and then boooom. It was impressive.

"The impressive thing was, I started on low boost. That year it was four bar maximum you could run. [That's four times atmospheric pressure, which is 15 pounds per square inch, 60 psi total. CART cars now run with a plenum pressure of 40 inches of mercury where 30 inches is one bar. That's 0.33 bar boost today or 5 psi vs. 4.0 bar then, or 60 psi.] I started at 3.6 bar and every click was .2 of a bar more. But then the last click it went from full lean to full rich on the fuel, they said. So one click more and full rich and you're going to gain 169 horsepower just with that little change you make."

Paul: "Wow."

Mauricio: "That change was as much as a Formula 3 engine had total."

Paul: "That is impressive. And here we're talking only a fraction of a bar in these cars today."

Mauricio: "And then after that I tested for March. And then they signed me for '88. So I drove for them in '88, '89, '90, and '91."

Paul: "March? That wasn't the name of the team. I don't recognize that."

Mauricio: "It was Leyton House. It was March but became Leyton House in '89. '88 it was still March. I was there 'til '91 and then I did one year with Jordon/Yamaha. And then '93, early in the year, I started looking around here. I spoke with Galles quite a bit, and quite a few different teams.

"In the end I decided to do three races with Dick Simon, which was the guy that had the capability for putting another car on the road for me to drive. So I did that. And then I signed for Chip Ganassi for '94. That was the wrong move."

Paul: "Why so?"

Mauricio: "Because....he told me one thing and delivered another and sold something to Michael [Andretti] and delivered another for him too."

Paul: "Actually I did an interview with Bruce that will be early in the book where he talks about this, and you and Michael getting together later and talking about it [laughing]."

Mauricio: "Yeah. In '95 when I just signed with Bruce, Michael came up and we talked and we just touched on that. We're both mad for different reasons, but he was right. Michael was right and I was right. And he [Ganassi] basically screwed both of us."

Paul: "And then what? That was '94. Then in '95..."

Mauricio: "In '95 I got together with Bruce. I wasn't signed yet. He told me to come to Sebring and do the testing. I did the test. They had been there once with the new car and then I joined them. After that test we sat down and agreed that I would drive for him."

Paul: "This was with Hollywood support?"

Mauricio: "At the time we were working on Hollywood. They were a little bit concerned. There was some TV problems in Brazil. There was a bad network that was producing the race. They were just seeing how we were going to do it. We kept working on it and they weren't sure they were going to be in racing, but in Miami our performance made them come back pretty quick. We qualified second and we led for a long time before finishing second."

Mauricio in his Office

Paul: "So after the Miami race Hollywood came back?"

Mauricio: "More [other] people were prepared to join us too, so they came back."

Paul: "Then in '96 you did the whole season with PacWest?"

Mauricio: " '95 and '96."

Paul: "At the first of this season you talked in a press conference at Spring Training about having more focus and how you'd lost a bunch of weight. What was going on before and what caused the changes, and what changes did you make?"

Mauricio: "Well, before, when I came in.…'94 was a tough year for me, for different reasons. First, we came to this country, which I wanted to do; Stella was pregnant; and the twins were born and one [Giuliano] had severe problems during birth; and Senna died. So it was a combination of facts that made me…I wouldn't say that I lost focus, but it made me a very busy person just to keep everything alive. And that goes from home to racing to fighting with Chip Ganassi, to getting him to pay me, and just a bunch of things that I don't really like to even think about.

"And then in '95…plus, you know, even in Brazil, Hollywood doubted what they wanted to do. The best thing that happened in '95, I joined Bruce and he's a great person. Even besides racing, I mean, just as a human being, it's hard to find anybody the same as him.

"Everything just came together nice, but I was still going through some process of making my life really stable, you can understand with the problem I had at home. There's a lot of things that goes on and, you know, you're always the phone waking you and sometimes you have to rush to the hospital to do stuff, but that's normal life for me. It doesn't bother me, but it's not as simple as if you didn't have all that. I had to change the structure of the house. I had to bring more people to help me and all that. It was difficult for me to have the time that I really need to devote to my profession, which now I have it. But it literally took two years to get that organized. Plus having the funding to do that.

"So it's not that I want to do that; I was a lot better prepared like I am now when I was in Formula 1; it's just that I was hit with quite a few things at the same time that made this be late. And this year I'm not as sharp as I'm going to get. I'm still planning. Between '97 and '98 I'm going another step with my training. We live in a competitive world over here, and I feel I've got as much as anyone else out there. And my team has also made a step."

Paul: "In what way?"

Mauricio: "In…probably maturity. Being able to plan long term. In this business you don't plan short term. If you do that, you're dead."

Paul: "Umm. What about the engineer/driver relationship? Maybe you can talk from a driver's viewpoint. What about the engineers you've worked with, and how that's led to what's going on now?"

Mauricio: "Well, I'm lucky because I've mainly worked with one guy. Andy Brown has been my engineer in Formula 1. I had two years without him in Formula 1 because he moved to a different team. First in Indy cars I had John Bright, which was at Ganassi. He was very good but the poor guy had to almost polish the car as well as drive the truck and organize everybody and engineer the car. I mean we had seven guys on that team. That was one of the jokes. So that didn't make life easy.

"Then I joined PacWest and Andy has been with me since and he's just great. I mean he deserves a lot of credit for what has been going on. Because he's a very smart guy. In a way he's shy. Not a lot of people know him. There's a guy who can probably read my mind and I can probably read his mind. That's ultimately where you want to get, when you have 45-minute sessions."

Paul: "I've listened to almost every minute of every track session the whole year, and you guys just seem to kind of march toward some setup every session. There's only been a couple of times I've heard you get lost. There was one time you got out of the car [laughing] a few minutes before the end of a session. It was an oval, I think. You'd been messing with the weight jacker and you said 'I've got to think about this,' and got out of the car. Most of the time you guys seem to consistently march toward where you want to go."

Mauricio: "Yeah. Probably what I did that time, is that something was going wrong with the system and there wasn't any point in us to carry on. It wasn't the nice way. Don't even run because it's gonna lead us in the wrong direction. A lot of the time that happens.

"But people tell me that when they listen to us it's like when we have a conversation here. And other drivers are very different. Although with Mark I know it's completely different. But I don't listen too much to that.

"I just like to be as clear as I can and as positive as I can and give Andy just the information that he needs without creating stuff that doesn't exist. I'm not driving a space shuttle. It's a goddamn car with four wheels and a steering wheel. And the corner has certain parameters. There is different corners too with an entry and a middle and an exit. I just split the corner the way it is, and I have a good feel for what the car is doing and what I need too. There's no point if you don't know what you need. I can give suggestions what I want to do, but Andy, he knows how I like the car. I particularly like a car that's neutral or loose. I don't like a car that pushes."

Paul: "What else about your driving style? Do you know, can you describe your driving style compared to other drivers, what you like and don't like?"

Mauricio: "I've seen a few drivers who seem to be like my driving style, like Gil [de Ferran]. He's similar in the way he moves the car, the way he moves the steering wheel. I don't like to jerk my car. I'm not a hacker. You probably look at me going around and say, 'Jeez, he's going slow,' and then you put the watch on and go, 'Where did that come from?' "

Paul: "That's exactly what's happened a few times."

Mauricio: "Yeah; and that saves equipment and you save everything and you don't even break a sweat."

Paul: "Do you go into a session with a plan? I know you and Andy have a plan, but yourself as a driver, how do you go into a session and decide for yourself what you're going to do? Is it separate from Andy?"

Mauricio: "No; it's all together. For tomorrow, for example, we've already sat down, we know where we are. We have a few things we think are pretty smart to try here. We've gone through those things. What's different with Andy is, for every problem that we may face, we already agree from what happened before what's the fix for those problems. And we attack it the same way and we keep reminding each other because sometimes you forget that another click of rebound in this particular place helps you coming out of Turn 7, for example; I'm just throwing out an example. That's the secret. You do a lot in a short time.

"The secret about engineer and driver is to keep the focus and be positive about it even when you do things that go backward. 'Cause sometimes you do things that go backward, but you learn from that. On the whole picture, that's a gain. The stupid thing is touch the area again."

Paul: "So what about Detroit? What about all the fuel stuff going on?"

Mauricio: "It's quite clear. I mean, we could tell on Saturday night there was a possibility. I made a decision with Andy that we're going to do that. And we took the risk. I think the other team just followed us, basically. I don't know if they were planning that."

Paul: "So how do you feel about the way that came out?"

Mauricio: "I feel fine. I was disappointed 13 laps from the end when I knew I wasn't going to make it unless I got a yellow. I had 9 gallons to do 13 laps, and even if I pissed in the tank I wasn't gonna make it. But at the same time the feedback I got worldwide from that was just tremendous. I think I'd rather see us doing that, especially at Detroit, because nobody can pass. So you have to be creative and we were. And we just didn't get the break.

"All those other guys, they're shitting themselves if we'd got a yellow. They knew it was on the cards. Some of the teams thought we were going to run out of fuel four laps from the end and we didn't; it was half a lap. Not even that."

Paul: "So what's going to happen the rest of the season? What would you like to happen and what do you really think will happen?"

Mauricio: "What's going to happen is exactly what's been happening in the beginning of the season, in my case. I'm going to be competitive everywhere I go. What I'd like to happen is for me to get some of the lucky breaks that I didn't get yet. And then I should get a couple of wins by the end of the season. That will be a really nice reward for all these guys I have here that support me."

Paul: "And next year? What do you see happening?"

Mauricio: "We have a really bright future together. I want to see this team at the top of it and the way things are going I think we're going to be involved together for a long time. That, at least, is my plans. And I think that Bruce shares that plan too."

Paul: "I think I heard you say you've applied for U.S. citizenship?"

Mauricio: "Oh, yeah. For residence, not citizenship. I need to wait another five years for that. I may do that later, but my green card is on its way. I really enjoy this country, after I've been around the world. You guys take it for granted what you have here."

Paul: "Yes. You're right about that. We do. The Rio trip was a great opportunity for me. I was scared to death about that trip. I just knew I would get the runs."

Mauricio [laughing]: "It's not that bad."

Paul: "I didn't have any problem at all. We had a great driver that Hollywood provided. I would do it again. But I also see where, if you had an opportunity, that you might want to live somewhere more stable. Why are you thinking about moving here?"

Mauricio [pointing to his son Bernardo, playing with Zeca behind me]: "That's one of the reasons there, that little guy. And his brother Giuliano. They'll be 3 in July."

Paul: "That's all I can think of to ask. Anything else you can think of?"

Mauricio: "That covers pretty much what I've done. A lot of the stuff you know because you've been here all this year."

I turn off the recorder but we continue to talk like any two race fans about various things. Then the subject of tires comes up. I know he has a page on the electronic dash that shows him the tire pressures, so I ask about that. Mauricio says it's not just the absolute value of the pressures but the rate of change of pressures that's important to him. I turn the recorder back on and ask another question.

Paul: "Do you go out there during a practice session looking at the tire pressures to see the rate of change knowing you'll need to know that during qualifying?"

Mauricio: "Yes, that's something I work with, but ultimately you want to achieve three things for qualifying, actually four things: the right tire pressure with the right temperature on the tire; a clean lap, which is traffic, you have to work with it; and the least amount of fuel in the car, a light car. So by doing that on all the sessions I work it out how long it takes me, the way I like to do it, to bring the tires to where I want them, pressure and temperature. Because you can bring up the temperature very fast but the pressure will be low and the car will be bumping. [He bangs his hand on the table and his ring makes a harsh sound.] There's a technique for that. That's how you get the best out of the tires."

Paul: "A big part of that must be the clear lap."

Mauricio: "That's the variable. That's the one you can't control. You have to be prepared to give one lap away or whatever."

Paul: "But on an oval you don't have to worry about that because you're the only one on the track."

Mauricio: "No, on an oval you don't. An oval is straightforward."

Paul: "Is it easier to qualify on an oval?"

Mauricio: "In that respect, yes. But to bring all four tires the way you want them, pressure-wise is OK. Temperature you can't really do it that well. And then it's more on the knife-edge. 'Cause everything is more on the limit. On ovals you work on individual corners. On road courses and street courses you work the front and rear tires, work on each end. The car is not as efficient on the road course as it would be on the ovals. On the ovals, if you have the ability, you can make the car really perfect for those corners on that circuit you're gonna run. The road course is always a compromise because the corners are so different and you can't pick and choose what you're gonna do."

Paul: "How much has the engine contributed this year? How much of the success is due to the [Ilmor/Mercedes-Benz] engines?"

Mauricio: "A ton. It's hard to quantify percentage-wise but the engine and tires, they both made a step forward. Performance-wise it's the quality, the reliability. The tires [Firestone] and the engine they seem to be very consistent. And then the team, Andy, myself, we all step up a bit."

Paul: "There's a game people play about what's important in the 'package.' You've got the chassis, the tires, the engine, the driver, that's four things you could talk about. How would you rank those in importance?"

Mauricio: "You know the most important thing? What is the easiest thing that will make a car go quick? Tires!"

Paul: "And after that?"

Mauricio: "If you quantify dollars for performance it's tires. To have a significant gain on an engine you have to just throw money and time at it. It's unbelievable. And all these guys they have six, seven teams, so multiply that by how many engines per team and politically they have to be correct and give everybody the same engine. It just takes forever.

"Tires, it's just they have a batch of glue here and different temperature there and they just grip like crazy and the times just come down. Most important thing is tires for lap times."

Paul: "How about the other things? How do they rank?" I wasn't going to let him off the hook.

Mauricio: "I'll go tires, drivers, chassis, engines."

Paul: "Great interview. Thanks."

Mauricio: "No problem."

TALK WITH STELLA GUGELMIN

Stella and Bernardo

At the PacWest hospitality area, some Motorola VIPs are having a breakfast with Mark Blundell on one side, and on the Hollywood side, Stella Gugelmin is here with her son Bernardo. I ask her if this would be a good time to talk and she says yes. We start to go into the motor coach but there are too many people in there, so we sit at a table. Bernardo plays nearby.

Stella is a small woman, 5 feet and 3 or 4 inches tall. She has shoulder-length, auburn hair and she's very pretty in a wholesome, girlish way. She seems comfortable talking to me and answers questions in an open, honest manner. She speaks excellent English with only a slight accent.

As we start talking, a practice session for one of the support series starts, and I'm worried about the recorder picking up our voices. I speak a little louder than normal and Stella must notice because she does the same thing.

Paul: "Maybe you could give me some background. What you did before you and Mauricio met, and how you met?"

Stella: "I met Mauricio when I was very young. I was like 16 and he was 18, so I was studying. Then we got married two years after. I was 18 and he was 20, and I at that time I had just finished my first year in university. I was studying to be a speech therapist. I left everything when we got married. We met through a common friend in a restaurant. We are from the same town in Brazil, so that's how we met."

Paul: "What town was that?"

Stella: "Curitiba. [She spells it for me.] It's in the south of Brazil."

Paul: "Was he involved in racing then?"

Stella: "Oh, yeah. He was racing already. I met him a few months before he moved to England to start his international career."

Paul: "Was that a plus or minus for you that he was involved in racing?"

Stella [laughs softly]: "At the time I didn't really realize much because...I mean I watched my first race after I got married. I was studying so I was involved with my own things. I didn't get involved at all in his racing career until we got married. It was a minus to be so far away from your boyfriend because I was in Brazil and he was in Europe, so we only saw each other on vacation. But we made a good choice. We've been together for 13 years now."

Paul: "Was it difficult for you to pick up and move with him to England?"

Stella: "No. I was very young, so for me it was exciting. It was difficult to leave all my family behind. In Brazil we are very tied to our families. We live in our parents' home for a long time. So in a way if was difficult to leave my family behind, but at the same time it was very exciting. It was something new. I was looking forward to that."

Paul: "Senna's death was something...even for me and I never knew him, I was never closer than 20 feet to him, but for me still, it's still very emotional. How did that affect you?"

Stella: "Oh, for us it was devastating. It was an awful year for us. I was pregnant with my twins so I was 7 months pregnant by then, and it was very hard. I had to go to bed. We were very close. We lived together for a year. He was a close friend to us, so it was devastating. It was a terrible year for us, '94 was just, we had too many bad things happen in our lives."

Paul: "Do you think a racing marriage is a lot different from another marriage? You've never been in a different situation so maybe you can't answer that. What difference do you think there is?"

Stella: "I think the difference is the traveling, because they always traveling, so if you don't go with them sometimes you never see them, so you have to sort of follow them around or try to, to be together the most you can in their careers. I think that's the difference because a normal marriage, they have jobs from 9 to 5 so they are home every night and that's the difference. I cannot complain. I think it's exciting to live the life we live. It's not boring at all. So [laughing] you never get bored. You're always doing something different."

Paul: "How has it been different since you came to PacWest?"

Stella: "We were living in Europe before. Living in the States is nice and we had our first children so everything the last few years for us, we've had many new experiences."

Paul: "What do you think will happen in the future? Do you ever let yourself think about what would happen if Mauricio gets hurt?"

Stella: "No, I never. I only live the present. We've had to secure ourselves after we had the children. You think more about what if bad things happen so we have insurance and wills and things like that normal parents will do after they have children to make sure they will be all right. So we have done that which we hadn't even thought about before we had the children. But I always live the present; like, if I come to a race, I never worry. We just take things as they are and try to think for the best, not for the worst."

Paul: "So you don't worry when he's on the track in the car?"

Stella: "No, I do worry. I get anxious. I worry that he will not get a good result. I want him to have a good race. But it's not a worry that he's gonna get....It's not scary. It's just a normal worry. You get anxious; you want him to do well, during the race or wherever, you know. It's just a different feeling. It's not that I have in the back of my mind that he's going to get hurt. It's not like that. You know that the danger is there and there is a chance of something happening, but you don't think that way."

Paul: "If there are some racing wives out there who are worried, what advice would you give them?"

Stella: "Just to relax and enjoy life, otherwise your life is gonna be miserable [laughing]. I mean if you're worried the whole day, you gonna have a miserable life. You might as well enjoy it."

Later, I think about our talk and decide I'm extremely impressed with Stella. Besides being pretty she's also intelligent, positive, lively, and open minded. Mauricio is lucky to have that kind of partner. He might not be able to do what he's doing if he didn't have Stella.

Mo Is in the Shadows, but this Is a
Great Photo of Stella

CHAPTER 16

CLEVELAND

The time since Portland seems like months, but it's only two-and-a-half weeks. I'm getting on a plane again on July 10, heading to Cleveland, the start of the second half of the season — nine races down, eight to go. We've got three in a row now: the airport course here, a street course in Toronto, and the fast, 2-mile oval at Michigan. Will the PacWest guys win another one? A few of them have tentatively broached the championship subject. For that to be a possibility they have to win some more races right now. Paul Tracy is still the CART points leader with Greg Moore and Michael Andretti close behind.

From the Cleveland Airport I drive to Burke Lakefront Airport and find the PacWest garage area. Everybody is ready to leave for the day and some say they're going to "The Flats," a downtown restaurant area. I join them in the lobby of the hotel where we're staying, and we crowd 16 people into a van for the short drive. Mark Blundell is in the group along with a pair of English guys he introduces as sponsors and his brother, Colin. It's a lot of fun to watch the kidding and horseplay going on between Mark and his crew. One of the benefits I get out of this project is to participate in the adolescent atmosphere, but I don't have to work the long, hard hours these guys put in. The team didn't have time off between events like I did. There were two tests, including one at Michigan over the July Fourth weekend.

FRIDAY

I'm at the Burke Lakefront Airport building at 7:30 a.m. to pick up my parking pass. Surprise! They find it easily and hand over a nice package of maps and info. Some races this works and some it doesn't.

Indy Lights isn't here but Formula Atlantic, Super Touring, and Trans-Am races crowd the schedule, and there is something called the Electric Formula Classic. As a result, CART practice and qualifying don't happen until afternoon.

At 11 a.m. a lot of fans are already here in the paddock. It's sunny and hot as usual, and the fans are in shorts and T-shirts. If the cooling breeze off the lake dies down it can be brutally hot here.

Pace-Car Ride

At 1:30 p.m. I'm in line for a ride in a PPG pace car. The schedule is an hour behind. Quite a few drivers are here for a familiarization ride on course with Wally Dallenbach, including Dario Franchitti, Arnd Meier, Max Papis, and Greg Moore.

When my turn comes I get in the V-8 Lotus Esprit driven by Jennifer Tumminelli. Jennifer is a tiny woman, and obviously a good driver. She talks about the car and the course during the run, accelerating, braking, and turning with speed and confidence. Mismatches between the big concrete blocks that make up airport runways make this a bumpy track, but over the years they've ground down some of the worst spots and used asphalt to smooth others. My big surprise here is how the runways are crowned for drainage, and the dipsy-doodle effect that has when the

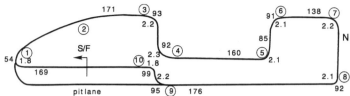

car goes from the outside of one runway to the inside, runs on a crossover to another runway, and then goes from inside to outside again. We go up and over, bump, bump, up and over again. Once again the pace-car ride reveals a surprise about the track although I've been watching races here on TV for 15 years, and this is my fourth race here in person.

Practice

The session starts at 2:25, an hour late. Both PacWest cars go out right away. The pit lane is on an access road to the main runway, where the cars speed by us going right to left. The approach to Turn 1 is extremely wide, creating good passing opportunities. It's beyond me why this type of corner is not recreated at other tracks. The cars brake hard here and accelerate out onto the backstraight where we can see them brake for Turn 3 onto a crossover road and accelerate again through Turn 4 back onto the main runway, going away from us to the right. We can barely see them going clockwise around a square during Turns 6 through 8. Then they accelerate down the same access road that pit lane occupies, but they jog to the right through a chicane onto the main runway again before coming back toward us from the right. Start/Finish sits just in front of the pits. The benefit of this track is the unobstructed view the fans have from the grandstands behind us.

Both cars come in for an installation check and go back out. Next time in Mark says, "It feels like the car is scrubbing on the end plate like it's done before. It's pretty reactive over the bumps at this point. It feels quite stiff. It's got some push in the front."

Mauricio is in also: "When I get to the apex, the car just bounces like it is too stiff. The back has a huge amplitude like the air spring is just throwing me up." This is the first mention I've heard of an air spring.

Allen tells Mark, "There's two options. The first one is just to go soft on your front roll bar now. The second one is do a front wing change. What do you fancy?"

Mark: "Let's do the bar for the moment and I'll do a quick scan."

A red flag stops the session. When the course goes green again, Mark says, "Tell Mark [Moore] to get out of the way. I'm going to lay some rubber." He does.

After another run on track Mauricio says the car is too stiff over the bumps. Andy asks, "Does it feel like the skid hits and it launches at the front, or is it coming through the wheels?"

Mauricio: "It's coming through the wheels, and it's only one place that's really bad. It's probably still the back. The air spring is just too stiff."

After some changes and another run on course Andy asks, "Do we need more of the same, Morris?"

Mauricio says, "It was a big improvement, Andy, big improvement. It's still bouncing a little bit on the front. I think we should be taking some more out of the front."

Andy: "How are the ride heights?"

Mauricio: "Touching at the front, still. But I think we could be more aggressive in the rear setup."

Jim Reid goes under the car to look at the skids, and Andy goes over the wall to talk to Mauricio off the radio. It's about 10 minutes to 3 o'clock, and Paul Tracy is in P1 with a lap of 100.711 seconds. Mark is P2, but he improves to P1 with a lap of 100.614. Mauricio is P18, 2 seconds slower.

Mark describes the car: "I've got some increased understeer, just because of increased stiffness. I've got more of a car to turn in with, support wise. There's some stick coming in but it's leveled off the rear; the rear of the car is not so washy. It doesn't have this big hook-effect. I went up full-stiff on the rear bar; that's no good whatsoever. It just makes the car slide; it's too nervous. The crossover transitions, where the car goes up and comes back down again, still feels a bit harsh in those areas. We're running out of revs big time down here, into 1. The car's also quite stiff on braking and the wheels are off the ground, even the front wheels, under braking into 1. It's not touching down at this point."

Allen: "First thing is to take out some front mid-speed, which will help stabilize the car under braking. That will help us lower the front ride height and give you more grip. Try that, then we'll look at the front bump as a next change, and then start talking about the rear spring stuff."

While the change is being made Mark complains about the gearbox. His driving style is to go into a corner very late, brake extremely hard, and go down through the gearbox as quickly as possible. The surface here is very grippy because it's an airport. He can brake really hard, and the gearbox just can't react as quickly as he needs.

Allen: "In the mid-front we've gone 15 clicks softer. All right?" Mark goes back on course.

Mauricio comes in and Andy asks, "What's the basic balance of the car?"

Mauricio: "Power understeer. Off the gas it's a little bit oversteery but not that much. The ride is a lot better now. It's still crashing down too much at the back and too much amplitude at the back too."

Andy: "The way the rear's moving, Morris, is it one big reaction after the bump or is it bouncing a lot after the first initial reaction?"

Mauricio: "It's not a big reaction."

Mark comes in off course and Allen asks, "How goes it, mate?"

Mark: "First, it's a bit scratchy with traffic and stuff, but the car's not braking comfortably into 1 and also into the chicane. The car's got a little bit more pitch in it and it's acceleratin' the rear movement in amplitude. But it's slightly more forgiving when it crosses the camber in the road. It's lost a bit of bite on turn-in. It's lost a bit of stiffness when it goes into its roll. Understeer levels are quite high still."

Allen: "OK, let's go back in the 15 clicks. What we're going to do is go to damping now. On the low-speed bump we'll go six softer."

Al Bodey: "Mark, keep your eyes peeled out there. There's a lot of cars out there. You passed on the yellow flag out there somewhere. Keep your eyes open on the flags."

Mark: "I don't recall doing that. Was it Salles? I just backed off when we got into the yellow situation. I didn't overtake the guy."

Ando jumps into the conversation: "They gave us a warning. What they may do, if they spot us again, they may give us a penalty."

Mark: "OK, John, we can argue that. The way they left the car out there was pretty danger-ous as well."

Mark is still having gearbox problems. "The gearbox, Allen, that's holdin' me back a bit, as I want to go quicker and deeper into a couple of the corners. We still need to work a bit more on that."

Allen: "We've backed out on that mid, and we've gone softer on the low-speed bump. All right, mate?"

Mark goes back out as Al Bodey says, "24 minutes left." Mark is in P7. The monitor shows Alex Zanardi has the fast lap followed by Michael Andretti and Gil de Ferran.

Mauricio, in P15, describes the car: "It's still coming in high and crashing it and bouncing back."

Andy: "OK, I've got a solution for that for the rear. I'd like to try a stiffer front spring for the oversteer in and understeer out. I think we've just got too much amplitude in the front. So I'm gonna come up four on the front springs."

Mauricio: "Ten-four." Then he asks for the monitor and an umbrella for some shade.

Andy summarizes the changes: "We went up four [400 lb.-in] on the front springs and lower on the front ride height two flats. I'll put 10 sweeps of high-speed bump into the rear, which repeats the thing we did earlier which you found positive."

Mauricio is on course at 3:13 with 18 minutes to go. Mark is P10 and Mo P14. Then Mark improves to P6 with a lap of 1:00.273. Mauricio is back on pit lane and Andy says, "10 and a half minutes, Mo. After this run we'll do the sticker run." They make some shock changes and he goes back out.

Mark drives a lap at 59.720 seconds and improves to P3. As he comes in Allen asks about the changes.

Mark: "It feels a little better with the tim and wing. It made the car a little bit pointy on the front. It's kicking the rear out. We need to hook up the front and rear together again. It's gettin' better grip. It's just more pitch-sensitive."

Allen: "Take me through a lap."

Mark: "Braking into 1 the front wheels are off the ground. The rear's got a lot of amplitude in it, vertical movement. Turn-in OK, but traction still not great. We can improve that. Turn-in to the first change, that's OK, but downshift is really difficult. Push mid to exit. Rear of the car slightly unbalanced. Next one, turn-in is OK, mid to exit oversteer. Turn-in for 6 and 7, rear stable, but just a big push all the way through, but the rear's on the edge, nervous. The chicane, amplitude up in the braking, rear gets loose, mid-corner push. That's causing the car to be loose."

Al Bodey says, "Go to slot seven, Mark. That will be your qualifying rev limit." With about 4 minutes to go Mark is fifth-quick and Mo eighth.

Andy adds some rear rebound and Mauricio goes out again. A red flag flies and CART decides to end the session at 3:30 to preserve the schedule. Zanardi has the quick time of 59.073 seconds or 128 mph. De Ferran, Christian Fittipaldi, Bryan Herta, and Bobby Rahal follow. Mark is seventh and Mo 10th, a second slower than Zanardi.

Ando Talks About the First Win

When I get back to the paddock Ando is here, and I ask him if I could record a short interview. We sit down on a tugger and I say, "Tell me about the Portland race."

Ando: "We knew straight away from the weather forecast it was gonna be a major crapshoot. The big trick in wet races is stay out of everyone else's accident and be there at the finish. Experience at Portland told us that the possibility of changing to dry tires was always there, and we were very pleasantly surprised at the performance of the Firestone wets. They've really done their homework.

"It was obvious half-way through that race that the Goodyears were comin' good. It was a very interesting race, I thought. It's funny, we've had people congratulate us on the win, but it wasn't a matter of doing things right, it was a matter of doing the least things wrong. It was our turn.

"I think Mark drove a hell of a bloody race. He likes someone in the pits. He likes to feel there's someone there for him, sorta givin' him a helpin' hand when he needs it. Givin' him a bit of a gee-up when he slows down, and givin' him a thumbs-up when the time's right. I enjoy doing it with him too. It's a good give-and-take situation with the pair of us.

"It was one of those deals, the drying track, the 2-hour time limit, when to go to slicks, the teammate is in the next pits. There were so many things to look at and we just happened to make the right decision, and a lot of it you gotta shoot from the hip. That happens so many times in those sorta situations.

"You saw Herta come in early. They had nothing to loose. They tried slicks, he loses five spots and goes off course. You see the situation with Little Al; it's like a plane crash. There's so many contributing factors. We just had more pluses than minuses.

"I was real happy for the team, and I really felt for Mo. But I think the best situation happened. That's really given Mo a leg up. He's givin' it everything. His win is not too far away. But Mark needed the lift more than Mo. His team did as well. It all fit. The whole situation, not only what happened, but who it happened to. It was a good weekend all around, I thought, lookin' back on it now."

Paul: "What really determined what happened when you came into the pits for that last time?"

Ando: "You're very aware of what the other guys are doing. The TV makes it so much easier where you can look around the track and see if it's drying here or wet there. We started to see the ol' gray line appearing, so things were drying out. I was still a bit concerned. Really, I wanted to keep him on the wets as long as possible and not lose too much time on the drying track, and give him that chance when it looked good to go to drys.

"Mo came in a lap before us. We could have come in at the same time. I looked at that and I thought, the one thing we don't want is a shit-fight in the pit. That was really the deciding factor, not what the time was. Obviously we're aware of that. I wanted to give Mo a clean pit in and out and Mark the same situation. That worked perfectly for Mark. We had a clean pit coming in. We were by ourselves. I won't say it was a lucky call, but my main consideration was not interfering with each other, given a tire change where anything could happen. I thought there was a chance at that stage where we were lookin' pretty good.

"The interesting thing about it — it was obviously great to win the race, but there were so many strategies. I knew from the way that Zanardi jumped in front of Mo at one of the stops there that they must have short-fueled. That's what it turned out to be. They had a different strategy to play than us. We'd looked at what we could do and talked about the different scenarios. We decided the way to go. The other guys shot a little bit from the hip and unfortunately that didn't work. It was a great race strategy-wise, and obviously a great result for us."

Paul: "Mark said after the race he didn't know who the leader was right there at the end."

Ando [chuckles]: "I think deep down he must have. I got on the radio to him a couple of laps previous when Mark came up behind Christian. I said, 'The two leaders are in front of ya. You're in third place. It's 6 seconds to the leader. Christian is the one you want now.' I didn't tell him who was actually leading the race. When he took Christian and then he was on Gil's behind, the way Gil was driving, Mark didn't need me to tell him, 'Hey; nail this guy.'

"We could see it on the television, and Gil was protecting his line and makin' it hard for him. That was like waving a red flag to Mark. He might not have known that this guy's in the lead, but deep down he had to know. The best thing I could have done was let him get on with it without any distractions from me. And he got it done."

Paul: "So you didn't say anything to him because you thought that was best?"

Ando: "That last lap, no. We were right across from Start/Finish so we saw he'd won. Pandemonium. My little umbilical got pulled out. I felt the radio get pulled. We erupted in the pits. By that time it didn't make any difference to him. He'd won the race. It was a funny sort of after scene. He said, 'Where'd we finish?' And there was no reply from anyone [laughing]. I think it was Daryl came on and said, 'You won it, pal.' There it was."

Paul: "How did the win affect the team? Have you seen any changes?"

Ando: "The big thing I've seen is Mo has really got a spur in 'em. That's the big one. And Mark knows he can do it now. I'm a realist. You've gotta be there at the right time. The winner makes the least number of mistakes of the ones that's in there with the best chance. We did it that weekend, and we have to prove ourselves at the next one.

"Mo has been there consistently in qualifying, in practice, and in the race at different stages, but unfortunately not the last lap. That's really put the spur to him. As far as the guys are concerned, I haven't seen that great a difference. We sat down at our team meeting on the Tuesday after, and everyone was elated whether they wore red shirts [Hollywood, Mauricio] or blue shirts [Motorola, Mark]. We do make a policy of one team in the place. Mo's guys are disappointed for themselves and for their driver, but they did feel the lift. But you're only as good as your last race, arncha? We're gonna prove it all again."

Paul: "I watched the end of that race several times. I was impressed that Mark didn't screw up. There's so many ways to screw up there. How do you find that out about a driver before you hire him?"

Ando: "We've got two very different drivers. Mo, technically, is terrific. The guy could engineer the car himself. Mark needs a hand with his engineering. He needs to bounce things off someone with the engineering, or during a race, on the radio. But the guy is a helluva bloody race driver. Mo may be a little too calculating during a race. Mo will say, 'Well, there should be a spot appearing over here any minute.' By the time it appears, it's too late. Whereas Mark is more instinctive.

"That run in the wet there? That takes so much finesse and so much coolness and patience. That's what that takes. You've gotta be there at the end, so stay out of everybody else's accident. Look at Little Al and Franchitti's crash. The one thing where Mark lost his cool was when Hiro held him up going into the chicane and Greg Moore got 'round him. He comes screamin' on the radio. He's got to vent his frustration. It's not going to do anybody any good, but it helps Mark. I can come in then and say, 'Get on with the job. Put it behind ya.' And he did it. It was fantastic. He's a terrific racing driver. We had good pit stops obviously, but he did it on the track."

Prep for Qualifying

That was not a sterling practice session for the 17-car this morning. Back in the garage area, Mauricio, Andy, Tim Neff, Mark Moore, and Russ Cameron sit around one of the folding tables talking. Andy is making notes on a track map. Both the 17-cars are on the setup pads and the guys are taking measurements.

Mark is joking with his crew. I ask him about the crown in the runways. "It makes it difficult to balance the car. Those corners crossing over between the runways are 110- or 120-mph corners."

"Is the course any less bumpy than last year?" I ask.

"The same," is Mark's answer.

Roy Wilkerson has just rejoined the PacWest team from Della Penna Motorsports, where he had a chance to advance to crew chief. He's glad to be back here as a mechanic. He says to Mark, "I missed hearing you bitch about the gearbox."

Everyone laughs, including Mark, who sticks his chin out and comes back with, "Nofing's changed."

Mark walks over and sits down at a table with Al Bodey, Allen, and Ian Hawkins, the Ilmor guy. They begin their debrief. Andy and Mauricio are still talking at the other table.

Jeff Stafford is another new guy here. He's a truckie, replacing Mike Bauer. It takes at least two guys to drive a transporter. One drives and one sleeps, but they're still limited to how many hours they can stay behind the wheel, so they end up staying nights in motels on long runs.

Mike Todd and Jeff drive the Motorola hauler while Scott Simpson and Tom Keene man the Hollywood transporter. Scott is Mo's tire guy, and Tom mans the pit board. Mike Todd runs Mark's pit board sometimes, alternating with Stephen Dent. Jeff and Mike also keep the garage area clean and organized, including the eating area.

When Andy has finished his debrief with Mauricio, I ask him about the runway crown. "Runways are always crowned more than your average interstate, because they need to drain better. It gives you more exit oversteer because the road falls away."

Friday Qualifying

The tuggers are crowded, so I have a long walk to pit lane for qualifying about 5:40 p.m. My feet hurt. The schedule is still an hour late. There's more wind now, and it's still warm but not uncomfortable. Both PacWest cars are in the first session, the one for the fast guys, because of their Portland qualifying times. Three minutes before the session the 18-car is warming the engine, but the 17-car is just rolling into the pit box. I think Mark Moore, the chief mechanic, just likes to cut it close.

The session starts at 5:45. Both PacWest cars hold in their pit boxes until most cars are on track and then they go out, trying to create a clear track for themselves. In Mark's case it works, and when he comes in a few laps later he's in P1.

"It's a lot better car. The front-to-rear balance feels a lot more comfortable since that spring change. I'm coming through 6 and 7 a lot quicker, and I'm actually just touchin' down, ride-height-wise on the front of the car, 'cause I've just got a lot more speed through there. Maybe we can go a little bit more, another step again? It's such a good improvement."

Allen: "One softer on the rear springs, please."

Al Bodey: "Go to position six on the fuel, Mark. That might help you on your shift problem."

Mauricio comes in saying, "I need grip all around."

Andy: "Can we be lower?"

Mauricio: "Well, I am crashing down some."

Andy: "Up on the rear rods a flat and a half, please."

Allen tells Mark: "We've gone softer on the rear springs and up one and a half on the rear ride height. OK?"

Mark goes out on course again just before 6 p.m. The sun is getting low but this is mid-summer, and it's got a ways to go. Alex Zanardi has set the fast time so far. Mark is P5 and Mo P10.

Next time Mo comes in Andy says, "I'm going up again on the rear ride height, and to keep the aero balance I've put two turns of front wing into the car."

Mauricio: "I changed tim one; should I go more?"

Andy: "That's your feeling in the car, Morris. If it's loose on entry then try more. You've got enough fuel in the car for seven laps."

As Mark comes back in he talks as he's driving down pit lane, so it's hard to hear him over the engine noise. "There's too much roll in the car now, Allen. The rear of the car rolls and falls over. I also went up on the front bar the last two laps, but the car's too reactive, too stiff at the front."

Allen: "Do you want a change or just stick with it?"

Mark: "I'd like to stick with it and carry it on new tires. We can see if we can just get the best out of the car with the new rubber."

Mauricio comes in, saying "I've got a little bit more understeer. The car feels very harsh everywhere." He's in P6 with a lap of 58.898 seconds.

Andy: "The understeer, I can help you with more wing, and we can make the shock change to help the harshness."

Mauricio gets more fuel and fresh tires before returning to the track. When he comes back in he says, "That did induce a bit more understeer. It reduced the amplitude and the harshness there."

Andy: "We've got 7 minutes of green. There's enough fuel in the car to get you to the end."

Both PacWest cars go out on track. Zanardi is still the fastest qualifier, followed by Herta, de Ferran, and Pruett. Mo is P6; Mark P10. Mark goes quicker and earns P8 with a lap of 59.096 seconds. Mauricio improves to P4. A red flag flies with 3 minutes to go.

Andy says, "This isn't going to be a long red. They're just going to tow Scott Pruett out of there, so there's not much I can do. The pressures look like they were comin' in just fine. Aero balance? Anything we can change quickly?"

Mauricio: "It's a little bit of oversteer coming out, but the middle of the corner is less push, so we're about there."

Mark says, "That feels a little bit better than what we had for the last run. Unfortunately that last lap would have been a clean one to do a time. We're screwed [by the red flag]. The car is still rolling over, and also the car is bottoming on the right-hand front. That's upsetting me in 6 and 7."

Mo and Mark go out at the green but so do the rest of the drivers. It's one of those end-of-session drag races out of the pit lane. Mauricio goes to P3 and Mark to P5, but both get bumped down as other drivers are finishing laps started just before the checkered flag. I stand there and watch them go down the list on the monitor.

Alex Zanardi earns the provisional pole with an impressive 57.423-seconds lap. Bryan Herta is almost a second slower in P2 at 58.151 seconds. Mo is fifth with a lap of 58.407 and Mark is P10.

The slow guys go out for their qualifying session, and Andre Ribeiro drives Tasman's new Reynard chassis to P5, dropping Mo and Mark one spot. He's 2 seconds faster than his teammate, Adrian Fernandez, still driving a Lola. That's the nail in the coffin for the Lola.

This Friday is winding down even later than usual. We get some hamburgers for dinner about 6:40. At 7:30 I head for the hotel. After a few beers in the basement bar I'm in bed at 10 o'clock. A TV blaring across the hall wakes me at 4:30. I call the front desk and somebody comes and beats on that door. The sound goes away but I get up at 5:15 anyway.

SATURDAY

Downstairs at 6:15 I sit outside by the front door and talk to Tim Douthat for a few minutes. Soon some of the other guys begin to arrive and then Butch pulls up in a team van. When they leave I find my car and drive the half-dozen blocks to the airport parking lot.

I have to walk through the Trans-Am paddock on my way in, so I stop and talk to some of the people I know in that series. Tommy Kendall is winning all the races so far and he's pretty pleased. Tom Gloy is switching to NASCAR trucks, and we talk about some of what they've been learning running those races. His engineer, Chris Andrews, and I talk about the engineer/driver relationship. I've learned a lot listening to the PacWest radio conversations. The engineer/driver relationship is very complicated; there is a lot of subtleties involved.

At 7:30 in the PacWest garage the cars are on the setup pads. I notice the rear tires on both cars have a lot of negative camber at the rear. The cars are sitting up on the inside corners of the tires. Andy tells me the reason. "Cleveland has our highest-speed low-speed corners." He grins mischievously, enjoying saying that confusing sentence.

"Turn 1 is only 60 mph," Andy goes on. "The rest are 110-to-120 mph and bumpy. The track is pretty dirty so we need all the mechanical grip we can generate. The camber helps."

Computer Woes

At 8:45 Dyno Don Norton is here and that's unusual so I ask him why. "I'm watching Charlie [Harris] use my computer. He picked the wrong options to defrag [defragment, a consolidation of files] his hard disk. It's been cranking for 20 hours now and it's still going strong. He's not sure how long it'll take. I loaned him mine but I won't let it out of my sight."

I know this is serious, but I laugh anyway. To these guys their laptop computers are their profession, maybe their life. Charlie pulls a connector out of the 17-car and comes over to us, saying "It crashed. You have it backed up?"

Don nods, fingering his mustache.

"You guys must have a pretty good relationship," I say, grinning.

"With each other, not with the machines," says Charlie, looking resigned.

Talk with Mark Blundell

In the hospitality area I see Mark, and ask if we can talk about the win in Portland. He has time so we sit at a table on the Hollywood side, and I set up my recorder.

Paul: "Let's start with Detroit. Is there anything that could have been done better there? Could you have gone just a little slower and saved enough fuel to get to the finish line?"

Mark: "I suppose you could say that. It's very easy to say that after the event. I think at the time the way we ran was the right thing to do. From my side of things personally it was a close call, because I had to be aggressive to pressure Mauricio and be defensive because Greg Moore was behind me. And, in the middle of it all, try and save fuel. From our point of view we ran as well as what we could. Unfortunately we lacked a pint of fuel at the end of the race. That's the luck of the draw."

Paul: "Was there anything negative about the loss?"

Mark: "It wasn't a very nice feeling to get so close and be so far, but we knew we'd be strong at the next race. We knew we'd been strong from the beginning of the season. We came on strong, but the bad news came with the good news. We knew we could win races; that gave everybody in here some confidence. We walked away with our heads up high."

Paul: "I thought you came across great in the TV interviews at Detroit. You were very emotional, about to cry, but you were very positive about it. You seem to be very good in front of the cameras. Is that natural?"

Mark: "It's part of the modern-day racing driver's makeup. You have to be the diplomat, the commercial man, the TV-radio guy, the print guy, and the driver at the same time. I've vented my frustration on the steering wheel before I get out of the car and then, quickly, sort of got myself composed and took on board that the camera was going to be there soon and prepared myself for that. Although I did feel pretty down and felt like sort of, you know, squeakin' a few tears out my eye ducts, but there's still a job to do after that race and that's how I look at it."

Paul: "On to Portland. What about the setups there? How did that go?"

Mark: "It went reasonably well. We sort of chipped away at things. We've been trying to get these last few tenths out of the car with just a few little changes, and that's something which is coming along better the more Allen and I work together. It's so competitive here that you only have to be a sniff away and you're a league away. That's the problem. We were competitive in both dry and wet conditions. We were quite pleased with the progress through the weekend."

Paul: "What about the water spray at the start?"

Mark: "We were in P11 on the grid, right in the thick of things, and visibility was unbelievably bad."

Paul: "How in the hell do you keep your foot on the throttle, when you don't know what's in front of you?"

Mark chuckles: "You just have to hope that the people in front of you are OK, and that no one's going to collect you from behind as well. It really is a big element of luck. At the same time it's a little bit of a gut feel.... I don't know what it is; it's like another sense that comes around you, and you feel comfortable with it or you don't. Obviously you try to duck out into a pocket of vision as much as you can, and at the same time, you try to listen to the guys in front of you to hear when they back out of it and you back off, and it's a difficult situation for sure, but it's one where you have to deal with the conditions."

Paul: "You seemed to be able to pass people pretty easily."

Mark: "I capitalized on conditions. I feel very happy with the car in those conditions. I made up a lot of places in a short period of time. It is a very long race there, and I already had in my mind that we were going to just sit and wait for what developed. Even when we were still running wet tires we were second, and at one point, first. Our strategy in the race was good. The tire change at the end paid off."

Paul: "What about the pit stops?"

Mark: "Very good. We'd been working on that and they were good, clean stops. We'd been working on our entry and our exit. That was a big contribution."

Paul: "When the track was drying out at the end, what did the rain tires feel like?"

Mark: "With the wets we had a cut-off point, a lap time where the tires just give up and you start to go slower. The car becomes difficult to handle. I was aware of that, and actually we were on the radio calling for tires a bit earlier than we put them on. The call was good from John and the team, to keep me out there and monitor the progress of other people and look at their lap times. They timed it just about right and then it was just down to me, to make sure that I stayed on track. Most people got into trouble. We just did a good job by staying on the track and gettin' the tires up to temperature and pressure and reading the grip that was available and then heading on through the pack."

Paul: "When you got on dry tires there at the end it was still wet off-line, but you were still able to pass people."

Mark: "That was the only down side of going on slicks and trying to overtake people who were taking the dry line and leaving you the damp line on slicks. A couple of guys made it difficult, but fortunately we still got 'round them. Everything came together quite reasonable for us and we were able to make some very good, clean passes. Probably in a couple of areas where people were a little surprised."

Paul: "Like where?"

Mark: "Like goin' into the fourth-gear chicane."

Paul: "That's where you got Christian."

Mark: "He made sure I was on the wet line. It probably surprised him we managed to get down inside of him under those conditions, especially with the slick tires, but that's part of it."

Paul: "What was Ando saying?"

Mark: "He was just keeping me informed. He backed out of the radio at the end of the race because he knew I was very focused. I was pulling up to anybody in front of us and making sure we got by. When I wanted to come in for slicks he'd just calm me down and say 'No, just wait a little bit longer.' Towards the end he said the leader was 6 seconds in front. He didn't actually tell me who the leader was, but he did that from a point of view of not puttin' any more pressure on me, to let me run my own race and get by the guys. Sometimes that's better. He knows 100% that anybody in front of me, I'm goin' to try and get by anyway. I don't need any instructions on that."

Paul: "There in victory lane, things got pretty emotional. Bruce came over and hugged you. How did that feel?"

Mark: "It was great. It's been a long time since I've been on the podium with a win. I've been on the podium a lot with a second or a third, but to win the race and to win the first race for the team, to have the first win for Motorola, the closest finish in history, there were so many things — to have the race be Bruce's home race, to come back from Detroit, the big thing is my father was there, my brother was there, my wife was there. It was great to have my family around me, because I'm 5,000 miles away from everybody, from my family. It's part of my family make up; it's tough to carry on like that."

Paul: "What's changed? After all this time in racing with no victory?"

Mark: "I don't think anything's different, to be honest. You put a credit behind you, and go on. It might have taken a little bit of pressure out of the situation. We've delivered, but at the same time you don't give up trying to deliver again. We have a little bit more confidence because everybody knows it's a possibility to do the job. There's evidence to prove it now."

Paul: "What about the engineer changes? Is part of this win the relationship you've got with Allen? Or are you coming around more to Indy cars?"

Mark: "We had some changes made for the right reasons. People were better focused in different areas. They're doing a great job at that. That's definitely going to help us. I'm now working with Allen and we get along very well even though we've only had a short relationship. The changes made have benefited the whole team."

Paul: "That's all I can think of. Thanks."

Mark: "Sure."

Morning Practice

In the pit lane just before 10 a.m. there's still a cool breeze off the water, but the sun is beating down. A green flag starts the session at 9:55. After his first stint on course Mark says there's too much roll in the car.

Allen: "Roll or lack of grip?"

Mark: "The rear compared to the front has too much roll. It's a lack of grip too."

Allen: "Try the rear bar and see if that helps."

Mark returns to the course. Mauricio comes in and Andy makes a spring-rate change, going down 200 lb.-in. at both ends.

Mark Moore: "Take the shocks off the car." They remove the complete shock/spring coilover units, change out the springs, check the overall length of the unit and the spring rate, then reinstall the coilover.

Mauricio: "The front should help because in the hairpin it's still pushing too much, and in a few places in mid-corner it's still pushing. My apex is getting almost where I want it, but still I'm having to make an early apex."

At 10:26 I hear Al Bodey say, "Are you all right up there, Mark?"

Mark replies, "Yeah; I just slid it into the tires. It should be OK. It went in very soft."

He continues to talk while he sits in the stalled car. "Basically the car feels a little bit better with the rebound. That seems to make the rear a bit more quiet. It's that on-off gas that's catchin' me. I've gone up on the bar and that gave me more support at the rear. The car's pretty nervous though, and some understeer's coming in after that tire change."

A red flag stops the session so they can tow Mark into pit lane. Zanardi, Moore, and Christian Fittipaldi are fast in the session so far. Mark is 14th and Mo 18th. Mark's car has no damage. The crew checks it over and changes tires.

Both teams are struggling with the up-and-down nature of the crossover corners. Mark explains to Allen, "The problem is the corners are not flat. At Elkhart the corners are flat, and you have time to stabilize the car on the entry. Here you cross the camber in the road and it's uncomfortable. The whole car tends to looseness from turn-in and you carry that all the way through the corner. When you cross the camber it's not nice."

Mauricio says, "There's lots of roll at the back. Through the change in directions it's maybe that I have more grip, but it takes a long time from one side to another."

After another run on course Mauricio is still concerned with the roll. "I need less roll in the car. It's very difficult to control. We have to cut the roll somehow, but I don't think the bar is the right way."

Andy: "Is it worse when the ride height is high or when the ride height is low?"

Mauricio: "When the ride height is high."

Andy: "What I'm thinking of is to use the mid-rear perhaps a bit more aggressively, so we can get the ride height lower and put another softer rear spring in to help the rear grip, but still use the bar." This sentence ends up being a question, but I don't hear Mauricio's answer. I think the "mid-rear" is the hydraulic third spring that may have an air spring now. If they stiffen that they can lower the car without increasing the bottoming due to aero downforce and go softer on the main springs at the rear, gaining grip. Complicated, huh?

Mark comes in also complaining of too much roll at the rear. Allen asks, "When you went stiffer on the rear bar, what did that do?"

Mark: "It gives you the impression that you've got more support when you start to turn in, but you can't carry the speed because you don't have the grip. You're really just tip-toein' on the throttle pedal, waiting for the car to rebalance before you can get on the gas."

Allen: "Let's go 100 softer on the rear springs. And up a flat on the front ride height, please."

It sounds like both drivers are having similar problems with the cambered corners. On a level track the car is in transition during entry. Weight is transferring forward and to the outside. The middle of the corner allows some time at steady-state, and then weight transfers to the rear and inside as the car accelerates out. With the up-and-down movements due to the road crown there is no mid-corner. The engineers use the mid-corner to give them an idea about the basic balance of the car. They don't have that in the transitions at Cleveland.

At 10:55 there's a red flag caused by Max Papis spinning into a tire barrier. Alex Zanardi is P1 with a time of 58.711 seconds. Mauricio is P11 and Mark P16.

Andy sums up the problem: "The decision we need to make, Mo, is whether we really feel the car was that much of an improvement. Should we try to solve this problem with some shock changes, or maybe it's not worth giving up in those transitions what we're gaining with the rear bar elsewhere?"

On oval tracks the sway bars and weight jacker are used to balance the car as fuel load and tires and the track itself change during a race. At road courses a sway bar allows driver adjustment of balance but costs a little in grip.

Mauricio: "This is a difficult one. I feel in the short run, for qualifying, the bar'll be better, but then for the race it'll be worse."

Andy: "For now we need to think about qualifying, and we'll look at the bars again tomorrow morning in the warm-up. So what we'll do is make some shock changes back there and see if we can help that snap oversteer when you give it the power through the transitions."

Mark comes back in and reports, "It actually felt a little bit better on balance. I came down on that rear bar to halfway and the car feels slightly better. It's still got some roll in there, but with the bar up stiff it gets us in there but then it kicks out. Comin' back on the bar gives us more longevity into the corner. It allows me to balance the car out. But what we got is more push in it at the moment. It's even pushing coming into the chicane. When I turn in I haven't got a quick turn-in to the corner anymore. I've got push, hit the apex, and then I'm slow off the exit into the pit straight."

At the green flag after Papis' crash all the cars roar down the pit lane to start the last part of this final practice before afternoon qualifying. Mark Moore says, "The race to the first corner is on."

Both PacWest cars go on track to evaluate the changes just made to the cars. Then they need to change to new tires and do a simulated qualifying run, if they can get a clear lap. It seems to me the conversations during this session emphasize the complexity of the decisions and compromises these guys make.

Mark radios in, "I hit the wall with the left rear. Uum, scrubbed it pretty hard. I didn't get a run there because of the traffic. Everybody's prickin' about. We can just change tires and I'll go with it and try."

The crew checks out the car and changes tires. Zanardi is still P1. Mauricio is P11 and Mark P17.

Both cars do better on sticker tires. Raul Boesel jumps from nowhere into P1 at the end of the session with a lap of 58.131 seconds. Alex Zanardi is second quick but is a second off his time yesterday afternoon. Maybe the heat has slowed the cars? Mauricio is now sixth and Mark ninth.

When Mauricio gets out of the car he says, "The car is OK, but I have to think about it."

One of the differences I've observed between the two drivers is that Mauricio is more adaptive in the car. I'll bet that right now he's thinking about how he can modify the way he's driving the car to get more out of it in both the flat corners and the dipsy-doodle transitions. Mark is more likely to drive the track naturally and report the deficiencies in the car in detail.

Qualifying: The Starter's Stand

Jim Swintal has invited me to join him in the starter's stand for a session. Gordon Ensing, the assistant starter, is skipping this race so Jim Ohanesian is assisting today. We climb onto the scissors lift and they run it up about 8 feet. It's swaying in the wind a little, but that means it's cooler also.

This is a great view. We're about halfway from the chicane, Turns 9 and 10, to the hairpin Turn 1. The far end of the course is still a long way off, but the view is better from up here. With 5 minutes to go before qualifying the blower truck goes by right under us, sending hot air and dust swirling around.

Jim Ohanesian and Jim Swintal

The slow guys are first out to qualify. The top of this scissors lift is about 6 feet wide and 12 feet long. Jim Ohanesian will flag this session, so he's standing in the corner nearest the on-coming cars. Jim Swintal stands to my left leaning back against the railing. Past him is a tiny TV camera on a metal pole. That camera gives the TV audience a shot over the starter's shoulder.

At the end of their first lap the cars scream out of the chicane toward us up through the gears and then go back down through the gearbox and brake hard for the hairpin. They shift gears very quickly, and I can see why Mark Blundell is so picky about the gearbox. I see Unser Jr. slew sideways as he shifts and brakes at the same time into Turn 1. The Penske cars are really slow here.

Depending on the line they choose, the cars bounce and dart around on the frontstraight. Jim Swintal looks toward the far course with binoculars and says, "Richie [Hearn] did a triple-360 back there."

With 5 minutes to go in the session the order is Boesel, Vasser, Gualter Salles, and Unser Jr. Then Junior does a 58.612 and goes to P2, bumping Vasser down.

After that group, the blower truck goes by again. I hear Butch say they'll wait a little bit before they send Mo and Mark out. Jim Swintal starts the fast-guys' qualifying group at 3:05 p.m. Michael Andretti and Max Papis are the first two drivers to go by under us. Then Paul Tracy gets sideways accelerating out of Turn 10. On the radio I hear reports of smoke from Mark's car. Mauricio comes hot out of Turn 10 and screams past us.

Mark Moore, Mo's chief mechanic, says, "Don't you love the silence on the radio? We get to wonder whether he's got a good car or a bad car." They're probably all gathered around the monitor over there in the pit lane.

Ron Endres comes back, "We were enjoying the silence when somebody got on the radio." I hear Mauricio say he made a mistake. A few minutes later he says he did it again.

"Pit, Morris," Andy says.

Mark stays wide at the entrance to Turn 1 as Zanardi dives under him. Jim Swintal is watching also. He turns to me and grins. I could get used to the view from here. About 10 minutes into this 30-minute session the order is Zanardi, Herta, Andretti, Boesel, and Mauricio.

Jim Swintal has a habit of tapping a rolled flag on the rail of the lift. It's probably just nervous energy, because the taps come just before or after he waves a flag or responds to the radio.

Mark is in the pits telling Allen the car feels more stable at turn-in, but there's some oversteer and push as well. Mauricio flashes by us and his car looks smooth, not darty like most. Allen suggests some shock changes to Mark. I can hear Timing and Scoring relaying the current qualifying order to Jim. He writes it down on a white board fastened to the rail in front of him. With 14 minutes to go, the order is Zanardi, Herta, Fittipaldi, and Mauricio. Mark is in eighth.

Mark comes back in saying he can carry the car with a new set of tires. Allen suggests some changes anyway. As the session winds down Jim Swintal's rail-taps become more predictable. Control says, "1 minute."

Jim responds, "1 minute; course is clear." And two quick taps on the rail for punctuation.

He throws the checkered at 3:36 p.m. Zanardi is by far the best here. His pole lap of 56.984 is more than a half-second quicker than Gil de Ferran in second spot. Mark jumped up to third followed by Michael Andretti. Christian Fittipaldi and Mauricio will fill the third row.

Tech Problems

At 5 p.m. in the PacWest garage area I notice the 18-car isn't back from tech. I walk over to the CART inspection area in a big hanger building. The car is up on stands and the 18-crew and also Ando, Allen, and Russ are all standing looking at the right rear of the car. When I ask what gives, Butch says, "minor discrepancy."

The problem is the "2-inch rule." They had a similar problem at Portland. The undertray beneath the sidepods has to be at least 2 inches higher than the bottom of the car, the bottom of the skids. The 18-car has been measured in at less than that. Dr. Love tells me it's a heat thing, and they're waiting for the car to cool off. There are some support rods at the rear of the undertray that are very near the turbo waste gates. Eventually the parts cool, pulling the sidepods up, and CART passes the car.

At 6 p.m. Jim Walsh from Motorola presents a plaque to Mark Blundell and the crew commemorating the first win for the team and Motorola. Mark has a sunglass sponsor now and passes out free samples to the crew.

A fresh race engine is going on the 17-car at 6:15. The 18-crew is an hour behind due to their quarantine in tech.

Jim Walsh Presents a Plaque to Mark Blundell and his Crew

The new engine in Mauricio's car fires up at 7:10. Both Mark and Mauricio are here looking at a new steering wheel that could become available next season. It's got two small digital displays built in as well as several sets of warning lights. Some information that is displayed on the digital dashboard behind the steering wheel can be shown on the wheel itself and seen more easily. Both Mo and Mark are very interested.

I ask Charlie Harris how his computer problems worked out. "The defrag finally finished and the computer is well now."

Later, in the hotel bar, the PacWest guys have a good time and so do I. To bed at 11:30.

SUNDAY

With no coffee available in the hotel room or the lobby, I get ready very quickly. Indy Lights is not here, but I'm in for a pleasant surprise because there are some chocolate cookies along with the usual coffee at PacWest hospitality. In the garage area at 7:15 both cars are on the setup pads.

Mike Todd and Neil Atterbury are both limping. Mike's toes are painfully blue and swollen. "I was headed for pit lane," he tells me. "A guy driving a Ganassi tugger offered a ride but didn't come to a complete stop. When I sat down on the front my foot got caught and folded over under the tugger." Ouch!

Neil had a similar accident yesterday. They both were treated at CART Medical, as is anyone who has a hardcard. This is a service provided by CART. I hope I don't ever need it.

Stephen Kent is dressing engines this weekend. Blake Hamilton is on maternity leave; his wife had a baby. "I work with Blake some at the shop, but here I work on the front of Mark's car," Stephen tells me. "I like that better, but there's more pressure. You think you're done and the engineers change something. With the engine you have to plan the work and you know what you need to do. The guys working on the cars are more under fire."

At 9 a.m. in the PacWest hospitality area I watch the start of the Formula 1 race at Silverstone, England. Mauricio says, "I don't get to watch many F1 races anymore. The timing is usually wrong."

Mark is in the Hollywood motor coach on the telephone to the F1 announce booth. We can hear him on the TV. Of course they ask him whether he'd rather be driving in F1.

"I'd rather be in the front row there," he says diplomatically, "but the second row here isn't bad."

Warm-Up: More Brake Problems

The pit lane is already roasting hot at 9:30. There is no breeze at all as the session starts. Early-on Mark complains of brake vibration and a loose car. Mauricio and Andy decide to disconnect the rear sway bar. Both teams pay a lot of attention to the tires. I see a lot of pickup on the tires when the cars come onto pit lane. Rubber shreds off the tires in the corners and rolls into "marbles" which stick to hot tires, building up a thickness of old rubber on the surface.

An hour after the session I see Russ and Mauricio examining brake rotors. Do they have the same problem with brake vibration they had in Detroit and Portland?

Ando explains: "The manufacturer's changed something on the bloody pads. We pre-bed the discs, but there's some bloody something blochin' onto the rotors, and it sticks every time it goes by that spot. We've found we can bed our own. We sand them lightly and then bed them again. That works OK."

The Motorola guys, Fred Tucker and Bob Schaul, come out of the pre-race meeting in the engineering office at the front of the Motorola transporter. "How is that different from meetings at Motorola?" I ask.

Fred answers, "Well, it's not like a technical meeting. It's more of a review to make sure everyone knows what's going on."

"Do many sponsors get invited to meetings like this?" I ask.

"I don't think any do," Fred says. "Steve [Fusek] invited us and we go, but we keep our mouths shut and hope they keep asking us."

Tim Neff, the shock guy, is here and we talk some. "I'll be happy if my name is in your book but nothing else. Everything I say about shocks is bullshit anyway."

"I know," I say, grinning. "That's because you're smart enough to know that what you're messing with is extremely complicated."

"Exactly," Tim says.

Pre-Grid

The race is scheduled for a 2 p.m. start. I'm almost to pit lane before I have to hoof it back to hospitality to get my scanner and headphone. When I finally get to pre-grid I see the 18-crew has the bills of their hats turned up showing various messages for Mark.

I ask Russ Cameron about the race strategy. "It's pretty straightforward here. It's too easy to pass to control the pace. There's lots of lead changes. There's only one or two yellow flags historically. The race is 90 laps and the pit windows will be laps 28 and 29 for the first stop and 59 and 60 for the second one."

THE RACE

It's the usual excitement during the pre-grid ceremonies. Usual? Am I getting jaded? At 2:02 they start the engines, and I go to my station near the front of the 17-car engineering cart. I can look in over Andy's shoulder and see a monitor. During the pace laps everyone here gets set. Ando and Russ perform radio checks with Mark and Mauricio. I hear Control say, "Everybody take care of everybody and let's get through that first turn."

18-Crew Has Messages for Mark on the Caps

Christian Fittipaldi is gridded on the inside of the third row next to Mark. At the start Christian takes a chance down the inside, and he makes it through to third place. Mark Moore says, "Bad start."

Certainly for Mauricio it is. He's forced to the outside and drops from sixth on the grid to 10th at the end of the first lap. Mark only drops one spot to fourth at the start, but then people begin to go by him. Bryan Herta flies by Mark going into Turn 3. On lap four, Zanardi, de Ferran, and Michael Andretti are the leaders. Mark is seventh and Mauricio ninth.

The cars string out and roar around the course like a train. Mark Moore says, "The first seven guys are on Goodyears except for Zanardi."

The PacWest guys are struggling. Ando encourages Mark, "You're as quick as any of 'em. Just hang with 'em."

Butch Winkle and Bruce McCaw

I hear Al Bodey say, "20 laps. We could pit now if there's a yellow."

Richie Hearn blows a tire and crashes on lap 21, bringing out a yellow flag for track clean-up. I'm standing right in front of the engineering cart where Andy and Russ are talking about what they should tell Mauricio to do. I hear Control say the pit lane is closed because of debris. Russ calls Mauricio in. I start to say something to Andy and Russ, but quickly remind myself that I'm just reporting here. I don't know what's going on. It is, however, a good example of how involved I can get in all this. It's impossible to be around these people and not be pulling for them.

Some cars turn onto pit lane, including Mauricio, who follows the leaders. A few, also including Mauricio, drive through and are penalized for coming in while the pits are closed, even though they didn't stop.

Mark stays out. There's some confusion there also. What a screw-up! During the yellow period Russ tells Mauricio, "It was my fault. We pitted when the pits were closed. We have to go to the back of the line."

There's so much confusion and talk about what to do that nothing gets done. Bruce gets down from the scoring cart and walks over to Russ and suggests, "Why not bring Mo back in before this yellow is over and go for two stops?"

Russ looks astounded. "Good idea," he says.

"Pit next time by," he says to Mauricio. Some similar conversation must have been going on in the Ganassi pits, because Zanardi does the same thing.

Ando decides to stay on the pit-stop schedule, so Mark's in the lead on lap 32 when the course goes green, but he has a big problem. Since he was the only guy out there going slow on

Pit Stop for Mark Blundell

hot tires, he's picked up all the marbles and they're layering on his tires like snow on a snowball. He tries to save his position going into Turn 1, but slides wide on the old rubber and loses places to de Ferran and Fittipaldi.

Zanardi and Mauricio are 21st and 22nd at the restart. I hear Russ say, "What a pisser. It's not a good day for us, but it's worse for the polesitter. Zanardi got a blend-lane violation too."

Mark has to pit for tires and fuel on lap 34. He's 23rd after his stop. At midway in the race the leaders are de Ferran, Fittipaldi, and Herta. Mo is 17th and Mark 21st. Zanardi has improved to 18th.

The course stays green for the next round of pit stops. Zanardi has passed almost every other driver and actually leads on lap 60! He pits on the next lap. On lap 67 Mark is 17th with Mo 18th. Zanardi is third.

Mark improves a few spots. On lap 81 he passes Vasser for 13th. "Good move," Ando yells into the radio. Mark makes up three positions on the last two laps to finish ninth. Mauricio comes in 15th.

Zanardi wins the race with one of the most incredible exhibitions of passing I've ever seen. His car control and sheer speed during that drive have to be one for the record books. I'll keep the videotape of that race for a long time.

Mark looks very tired as he gets out of his car. He has a big blister in the palm of his left hand. He says, "There were big clumps of rubber flying off the pace car, and they built up on my tires. That's what messed up the restart. The car wouldn't turn. It took three or four laps to get that rubber off. I had a good racecar."

Mauricio looks less tired, just resigned.

Chris Jaynes says, "That sucks. This feels like last year. No matter the pit-stop mess-up. Look who won. You've got to pass people."

In the media center Alex Zanardi is ecstatic. He thanks Michael Knight, his PR guy, and says he's glad to have won Michael's 50th race victory. Michael has done PR previously for Mario Andretti, Michael Andretti, Nigel Mansell, and Jimmy Vasser.

He also reveals one of the reasons he looked so much faster than everybody else between the two pit stops. He pitted later than some of them on the first stop and didn't have to stretch his fuel. His stop at lap 30 was optimum for this 90-lap race. For that reason he could use full rich, full revs, and full throttle. Chris Jaynes is right too. Other guys, including Mauricio and Mark, had plenty of fuel also. It was still Zanardi who won the race, not his engine or fuel.

This was a bad race for PacWest. Besides the race-strategy confusion, two guys got hurt in paddock accidents. Up high in the race at Detroit, down low at the finish, way back up at Portland, way back down in Cleveland. What an amazing roller coaster.

CHAPTER 17
TORONTO

On a flight to Chicago on July 17 making connections to Toronto, I feel no excitement yet. I had three days at home but I needed most of that time to get my newsletter to the printer. The sinus infection from Brazil is hanging on, and I have some fluid sloshing around in my left ear.

In Toronto we're staying at the Skydome Hotel right downtown. After I check in it's only a short walk to the entertainment district where a block is roped off for a beer-sponsored party that's a part of the race promotion. There's some good food and a bunch of nice-looking women, standard for Toronto and Vancouver.

FRIDAY

The 17-crew has room for me in their rented van, so I ride with them this morning, leaving my rental car in the hotel parking lot. Mark Moore is driving and he laughs as his guys disassemble and reassemble various interior parts of the van. These people have boundless energy and enthusiasm. Mark lets us out right where I would have parked, so I didn't save myself any walking by riding with them.

We walk a section of the course on the way to the paddock, winding through the concrete barriers. I peel off and stop at the hospitality area to stow my gear. All the motor coaches are parked on the concrete playing area of an old arena. The empty stands rise all around the colorful coaches and tents.

At 9:45 in the PacWest garage both cars are on the setup pads as usual. Practice is scheduled for 11 a.m. Formula Atlantic was scheduled to start at 9, but trackside barriers are still being placed and manholes welded down. The schedule is slipping. Jim Swintal, the CART starter, tells me some water-filled barriers have been put on top of communications lines, cutting them. Race Control will start using radios. "We're an hour behind on a tight schedule," he says. Temporary courses are difficult.

Practice

Indy Lights practice is delayed until later in the day so CART practice can start on schedule. Standing in pit lane we can see a new building right across the frontstraight from us behind the grandstands. It's very modern, all tubing and glass in contrast to the older buildings here in Exposition Place. To our right is Turn 1, a 90-degree right

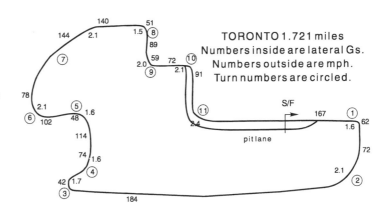

TORONTO 1.721 miles
Numbers inside are lateral Gs.
Numbers outside are mph.
Turn numbers are circled.

turn, not very far down-course from pit out, making it difficult for cars coming from the pits to blend in before the turn. The backstraight is long and bumpy. After that the course goes twisty until the pit straight. This track is a challenge, but the charm of the city and the enthusiasm of the fans here makes it a favorite stop.

We get a green flag at 11:08 starting an hour session for all CART cars. Both PacWest cars are out on course, but Mark comes back in saying his third and fourth gears feel the same. "If they're not the same, it's only a couple of hundred rpm. You go to peak revs and change and it's the same gear. You can't change down either, because there's too big a drop."

Mauricio says his car is crashing down on the backstraight. Andy raises the back of the car but it doesn't help. When he comes back in, I hear Mauricio say, "Let's go straight to the other shocks."

Mark Moore says, "We're swappin' rear shocks, guys. Just take 'em completely off."

Mauricio explains further, "The car, with the higher rear end, is still crashing some, but at the end of the straight the rear wheels are coming off of the ground. I'm having a middle-corner push with a slide still at the exit. It's just the concrete doesn't have any rubber at all now. The push is coming from the concrete." A red flag stops the session. Max Papis has slid into some tires.

"Perfect timing," Mauricio says. The shock change won't cost them any track time because of the red flag.

Andy: "What we need to start lookin' at, maybe, is some tim two as a way of not having to keep raising the car."

"Tim two" must be one of their hydraulic tricks, and I don't have a clue what it is.

Mauricio: "OK, let's back-to-back these shocks and see what's going to change on ride height too."

Tim Love is taking the gears out of Mark's car. Randy Smay has jogged back to the transporters to get a replacement gear. He's having trouble finding it, and Ando is on the radio to him about where to look and what to look for.

"Can you tell me what truck it's in?" Randy says on the radio.

Mauricio goes out to evaluate the shock change. When he comes in he says, "I prefer this; I've got more control of the back of the car."

Andy: "Any problems, power down?"

Mauricio: "No, not really. There's a little bit more wheel spin, but I'm not moving because of it."

Andy: "OK. Well, our next plan was to hook up the front bar. We can see if it helps the car on turn-in and power down."

Mauricio: "Let's try that. We could afford to lower the front, but leave it for now."

Andy: "How about the bottoming on these shocks? Was it improved at all?"

Mauricio: "Yes; it's just less amplitude. It doesn't hit as hard."

Roscoe has run back to the paddock to help Randy, but Randy jogs into the pit box with the gear so Mark Moore radios to Roscoe to stop running. Dr. Love installs the gear. Ando tells Mark, "We're just buttonin' up now. The cover's gettin' tightened up and the wheels are going on."

Mauricio wants to keep the car low. Andy says, "We're already using tim two quite a bit on the straights. I'm a little concerned about using it that much more."

Randy comes back huffing and puffing, and I hear a voice on the radio say something about "...coughing up a paint ball." That refers, of course, to Randy's spray-painting trade. Mark is back out on course with a new gear at 11:37.

Mauricio has tried the car with the front sway bar connected and comes back in saying it's bad everywhere. Andy says, "I suggest we disconnect that and try a stiffer spring on the front and lower the ride height." That's an interesting trade-off. Without the roll stiffness of the front sway bar they need stiffer springs to control roll. They'll probably stiffen the shocks in rebound also. Stiffer springs resist compression due to aero loads at high speed allowing them to lower the static ride height.

Mauricio: "Ten-four. We could lower the ride height anyway, even without the spring, but it's better to do the spring now." Halfway in the session Mauricio is in P17 and Mark P18. Alex Zanardi has the fastest lap so far.

Mark comes in and Allen asks, "How's the car?"

Mark: "Still having trouble with the gearbox. When we change down, the rear of the car locks up quite easily. There's a little too much roll in the car, but I can feel a flat slide. We need some more compliance. On entry and also on acceleration it just gives us a good, flat slide. Can't lay the power down. A lot of push in the car at high speed. Not enough aero in the car."

Allen: "Your flat slide, is that from the rear? Is it loose or what?"

Mark: "Basically it's very nervous on turn-in. Coming into the corner, the rear end of the car is coming up under braking. The rear is lockin' up easily. The gear shift is inteferin' with down-shifting and the up-shifting is not good. As you come in the rear floats up, starts to get light, starts to walk, and then as soon as you get into the corner the rear just slides off. I'm just carryin' the car with an oversteer all the way through the turn."

Allen: "OK, let's go 100 pounds softer on the rear springs, please."

Mark: "Also it feels like the car is poppin' down slightly down the straight, but it feels more like the mid to the front of the car than anything else."

After a run on the softer rear springs, Mark says, "I can't say it gave me any benefit, Allen, because under braking the car is still very weak. It didn't give me any improvement there. The rigidness of the bar on the rear end is making it nervous. Going into the corner it just slides out on me. There's no roll in the car; it won't allow it to roll, it just slides."

Allen: "OK, let's disconnect the rear bar, please."

Mark goes on course to evaluate the changes and comes in to report, "It just gets a little bit of roll in the car. Still got a problem going in under braking with the rear being too light and too responsive under braking. I went up on the [front] bar and that seemed to give a little bit of help and stabilize the rear of the car. Still feels like we need to get some more mechanical front grip. We need to tighten down the amplitude at the rear."

With 7 minutes to go Mauricio is 12th and Mark 14th. Both are struggling. Michael Andretti is now P1 with a lap of 59.122 seconds.

Andy says, "OK, Mo, I'm going to try some front rebound. Do you want some front wing at the same time?"

Mauricio: "Ten-four."

Andy: "Will one degree of front wing be enough or should we add more?"

Mauricio: "Just put one degree."

Andy: "Two full turns on the front wing, please, Mark. Any other comments on the tires?"

Mauricio: "The others are a bit more consistent. I don't know where the pressures are, but the car doesn't feel like I got the grip. In the middle corner I have to slow down too much because of the understeer." They're talking about the difference in the primary Firestone tires and the optionals, but they don't say which is which.

Mark improves to P3 with a 59.689-seconds lap. He comes back in saying, "That was a very nice lap because of traffic. The rear of the car, when I get on the brakes, it just lets go pretty quickly. The rear comes up high and jumps out sideways. Also push wise, I'm strugglin' with a little bit too much push."

The session ends at 12:10 p.m. Mauricio comes in saying, "The car is weird at the back, Andy. Even on the straights it's scary. Something is not right back there. It pulls when I brake."

Michael Andretti's fast lap held and he's still P1 followed by Raul Boesel and Mark, who improved slightly to a 59.563. Mauricio is 15th, a second and a half slow.

Early in this session my camera quit working, so I won't have any photos from this race except what I can get from other people.

Looking for Answers

In the garage area Mauricio and his crew are looking at the rear of the car. Something is wrong, but they're not sure what. Roscoe is also changing gears on the 17-car.

I ask Dr. Love about the gears in Mark's car. "I don't want to talk about it," he says, seriously. Then he grins and says, "Basically, I put the wrong gear in it. It's hard to see the number stamped on the gear because the material is so hard, but I should have counted the teeth to be sure. I'm kicking myself, but Mark did OK anyway. The red flag gave us time to change it."

John Anderson, Ando, is here also, so I ask him what happened in Cleveland.

"There was a bloody lot of confusion there. Mo came in behind Zanardi when the pits were closed. Next time by I called Mark in, but he'd already gone past the pit entrance. Then we decided to try and stretch the window, but I got distracted and the race went green again before we got Mark in. He had to make a green-flag pit stop. I just messed up the whole thing."

I ask Mauricio about the course here. "It's about the same as last year," he says.

"What about the pavement changes?"

"The cars are gonna push on those concrete patches until some rubber gets laid down."

Qualifying

The schedule is shuffled around to get the Indy Lights practice in, so CART qualifying isn't starting until 2:40 p.m. I walk toward Turn 1 to find a place to watch the cars going into that corner. Because of Jeff Krosnoff's death here last year they've added more fences to keep people back from the track. Instead of modifying the more dangerous locations they've put new fences everywhere, making it difficult to see anything.

After an early red flag, Mark is trying hard and hits a barrier. "I just hit the left rear on the curb, and something's given because it's not steering."

Butch says, "OK, guys, we've just got a bent toe-link. We're gonna go ahead and replace it off the T-car. OK?"

When he's in the pit lane, Mark says, "We're just not gettin' the grip level we were this morning. It's sheddin' a bit of grip."

Allen suggests going stiffer on the front springs. Mark says, "At the moment the car is just flat-slidin' everywhere. We can just go back on the changes and see if the car comes back to us a bit more."

Mauricio comes back in saying, "Middle-corner understeer. It's bouncing a little into a flick oversteer. The balance really hasn't changed from this morning. It's a little bit better on entry; a little bit less understeer on the entry. It's still very loose, that's the biggest thing. Turn 1, the middle-corner push is just...a lot. The front I don't feel touching. I feel the back crashing in the middle of the straight."

Andy: "Well, I would actually like to raise the rear because of the understeer and drop the front. What about a softer rear spring at the same time? Do you feel much roll in the car?"

Mauricio: "No, I don't feel the roll. You can do that."

Andy: "Does it feel like a harsh hit when you hit those bumps, or is it the reaction after it? Sounds like we've got too much rebound in there."

Mauricio: "Feels that way... on the front."

Andy: "We're going to come out on front rebound, Mark. Would you get the front hatch off, please?"

At 2:59 Mark is back on course for a lap to evaluate the car after the repairs, which only took about 7 minutes. As he drives out of the pit box Allen tells him, "Think about any changes you might want to do. If you want to do a rear spring change, we'll get straight onto it."

Mauricio comes back in. "On the slow stuff, I've got some more understeer. I'm just talking about the rebound change we did."

Andy: "Did we help that mid-corner with front wing or should we put that rebound back in?"

Mauricio: "I think we should put the rebound back in but also something else too. Where I brake I don't stop as good and I start locking the rears. Soft front springs don't seem to help the front grip."

Andy: "I don't have time for a front spring change right now. How's the front ride height? Is it hitting too hard now?"

Mauricio: "It's hitting, but not that hard."

Andy: "Can we come down some more?"

Mauricio: "We can come down one more."

Andy: "What would that do for the braking? 'Cause if it helps where you don't have to brake, look at using tim one. With that rake that we've put into the car with the changes that we need for the mid-corner balance from what you were saying, it's getting beyond that when you brake for the slow stuff."

Mauricio returns to the track. Michael Andretti has the fast time with a 59.448-seconds lap.

Mark says, "The rear is still the key point. It just keeps sliding out still. It feels better than what it did with the damper changes. It's a little evil under braking as we had this morning. It's still lackin' some grip at the rear."

Allen: "Give the front shocktopussy three clicks in, please. While you're there, Trev, give it some front low-speed bump as well."

Mark: "What was the actual last lap time?"

Al Bodey: "61.65."

Mark: "I'm surprised at that."

Mark goes back out as Al Bodey says, "6 minutes to go. You've got enough fuel to go to the end, Mark."

Greg Moore comes into Turn 1 a little hot, locks his brakes, and spins around to the left, scrapping his front wing along the barriers on driver's left. He gets going again. The cars seem to turn in very sharply. They feather the throttle through the apex and then increase the power smoothly. The drivers have to be careful or the cars slide out and brush the wall at the exit.

Mark goes by me a couple of times, looking smooth. At the checkered I hear Butch say, "I guess we're P2. Nice job everybody, nice job."

Michael Andretti has the provisional pole position with a time of 59.408 seconds. Mark is second at 59.894, and Dario Franchitti, a rookie, is third. Mauricio improved at the end of the session to seventh with a time of 60.361.

Press Conference

Dario Franchitti is a fresh face in the CART press conferences. He's still in his driver's suit but Michael and Mark have changed. Dario says his tires were only good for one lap. He's using Goodyears, and they always seem to go off more than the Firestones.

As Dario speaks, Mark and Michael talk and joke together. Mark is asked if he's on a roll since Portland. "We'd like to think so. I was trying a little too hard this morning and broke a toe-link against a barrier. I sat in the pits for a little while, but then I had a good car and got a clear lap." Mark seems confident here and very comfortable. He's a different guy since the win at Portland.

Michael, also on Goodyear tires, says, "This is a new qualifying setup because of the tire war. The race setup will have to be different. You can destroy tires here if you drive wrong."

The drivers all agree that one result of the tire war is more marbles on course during a race. Hunks of rubber pile up off line and make passing difficult.

When we come out of the press conference at 4:35, we find there's been a shower. The Indy Lights cars are qualifying on rain tires. Back in the PacWest garage area, engine changes are underway. The shower quits and things are wet, but not as bad as it got at Portland. Tom Keene is sweeping water away from the area under the tents.

Later I walk through an underground tunnel to the new building on the other side of the frontstraight so I can talk to the Indy Lights people I know. After a while there, I decide I'm ready to go back to the hotel, but since I didn't bring the car, I have no ride. Thinking the hotel is not that far, I start walking. An hour later I'm at the hotel and my feet hurt.

John Oreovicz, Victoria Vanderwell, and I have dinner in the Hard Rock Cafe that looks out on the Sky Dome playing field. After dinner Tim Love and I walk to a nearby Planet Hollywood for a beer. Tim, like most of the crew, is a racer himself. He has a Triumph and competes in autocrosses.

SATURDAY

Parking is easy this morning, making me think once again how stupid it was yesterday that I didn't drive. The crews got here about 6 a.m. At 7:30 they are all busy with preparations for this morning's practice at 9. It's sunny and cool, and the wind is light.

Mark Moore is about to install one of the pop-off valves CART has delivered to the 17-car. Each car gets two for each track session, and during the session they try to find out if one valve allows more boost than the other. "Pick the valve, Paul," Mark says.

The two valves are numbers 008 and 071. The chassis number of the 17-car is 08, so I pick the 008 valve. "Well, we'll see how good you are," Mark says, grinning.

Chris Jaynes says, "Yeah, and he can change the valve in the middle of the session."

"You don't want me working on the car," I say. They both roll their eyes and nod agreement.

"I saw Mauricio looking the car over yesterday afternoon," I say. "Does he do that a lot?"

"He's very aware of his car," Mark says. "He's got a good eye. In '95 here we were in the dungeon over there [the automobile building where the garage area used to be]. He looked at the rear suspension and said one of the springs was bigger than the other. I couldn't see any difference, but we put a caliper on it and he was right; that coil-over was 20-thou [.020-inch] bigger in diameter than the other one. We had the wrong spring in there."

Practice

At 8:50 a.m. in the pit lane, the Indy Lights teams are towing their cars and equipment back to the building on the other side of the track. I ask Allen McDonald what changes he sees in Mark since the win at Portland. "He's a bit more confident, isn't he? His feedback about the car seems to be better, more focused."

"I heard him use the term 'flat slide' yesterday," I say. "Andy and Mauricio use that a lot. Did you suggest that to Mark?"

"No; I guess he picked that up himself," Allen answers.

A green flag starts the session at 9 o'clock. Both driver/engineer teams battle with the severe compromises raised by this track. The slow corners and bumps demand some compliance in the suspension, but braking from high speed and grip in the quicker corners requires downforce. Aerodynamic drag goes along with high downforce from the wings, and that slows the car on the long straights. The answer is using the underwing better; getting max downforce from the bottom of the car helps everywhere. I think PacWest's hydraulic third springs (shocktopussies) in the front and rear suspensions and the tim device could give them an advantage here. But the low-grip concrete patches are still a problem.

About 15 minutes into the session Mark earns P1 with a lap of 59.692 seconds. Mark Moore, Mo's chief mechanic, says, "Our boy next door is in P1." Mauricio is off the monitor page.

Mark Blundell sounds much more positive and energetic on the radio. He also might be a bit more demanding. At one point he chides the crew for being slow getting the engine cover off, saying it's costing him track time. That's a turn-around. Early in the season the crew was goading him on.

Mauricio and Andy have been fighting a problem of lack of grip at the rear. After another try on a set of changes Mauricio says it didn't help. Andy asks, "Should we go all the way back to where we were before, or just half the changes?"

Mauricio: "All the way back. Then do a front change. Still middle-corner understeer; that's the problem." Andy reverses rear shock, spring, and ride-height changes. A red flag gives them the time.

Mark has been adjusting the tim from the cockpit. "If I stay on the brake pedal for a long period of time, it keeps it quiet. If I get on the pedal and get off of it again, the rear snaps back out. And it's pretty noticeable. It's a bit strange because you have to sorta drag the brake into the corner. If you do so it keeps the car flat and quiet, or quieter. If I get off the pedal because I want to start to turn the car in, which I need to do because I need some grip at the front, the rear pops. And the pedal is too soft now for the race. There's not enough pedal there."

After another stint on track Mark talks about the tim again. "It actually feels a bit better in terms of taking the car in under braking, but again, I have to stay on the pedal for a longer duration going into the corner. I can go in deeper and deeper, but I don't have enough front grip to take the corner itself, and the rear of the car is still light and drifting."

Allen: "Sticking to the program that we discussed, the next change we'd like to try is going a bit softer on the front shocktopussy to see if that helps the braking. Do you want to try that now or in a couple of laps?"

Mark: "Let's do a couple of laps first. That would be better." He's still in P1. Mauricio is P11 with 40 minutes to go in the session.

After another run Mark says, "That's a little bit better, but the rear is the problem. It's just getting looser and looser. It's like it's going to slide into the wall. Shall we do the shocktopussy?"

Allen: "Three turns softer on the shocktopussy, please."

Andy asks Mauricio, "Was that last change any improvement?"

Mauricio: "It did improve a little bit, but still, when I get to the concrete the car just goes straight."

Andy: "How's the turn-in now?"

Mauricio: "It's OK, but it could be better. I'm still not too loose. I'm also touching the limiter on the straight."

Andy: "When that happens you'll have to get out of the throttle because this is the race engine. I've taken some low-speed bump out of the front because of your comments from yesterday — how it's possible the concrete would affect the car in roll. After this run I'd like to try a tire-pressure change."

Christian Fittipaldi moves up to P1 with a lap at 59.494 seconds. Conditions are right for some fast laps. The air is cool, but the sun is heating the track surface. Mark is P2. Mauricio is P6, and he says he needs a higher top gear. With about 20 minutes to go in the session Alex Zanardi now has the fastest lap of 59.206 seconds. The order behind him is Fittipaldi, Herta, Mark, Andretti, Rahal, and Mauricio.

Mauricio comes in saying, "I can get into the corner but then it pushes. When I know it's concrete, I have to turn before and go through the concrete with the steering wheel straight. It's just lack of grip. As soon as I hit that concrete the front just washes out."

Andy: "How is the roll in the car right now?"

Mauricio: "The roll is not bad. It's just lack of grip, middle corner. There's no grip for the car to roll."

Andy: "Trev, let's have two sweeps of mid and another four sweeps of low-speed." A red flag for a crash by Paul Tracy gives the 17-crew time to change top gear. Roscoe is on his knees in front of the right-rear tire changing the parts.

Mark comes back in and Allen asks, "All right, so what's our biggest problem now?"

Mark: "I'm a little bit unsure of the car under braking. I'm still gettin' that lightness like the wheels are comin' off the ground. Then, as we turn in, the car feels light on the rear. We've got to improve the car on entry and try to improve the grip. The problem is these concrete patches. The grip drops off there. You get a little bit of feel when you turn in, then the car drifts across the concrete patch and then picks up the grip again. You have to recompose the car and get off again. Out of it all it's the tires and the life of the tires; the rear is the biggest issue. That's what's holding you back more and more, just trying to control the rear."

Allen: "The rear roll, is that still a problem?"

Mark: "When they grip it's no problem. When you've got grip there you can get off the turn. You place the car, you floor it, and you get off the turn. When the grip goes away you get sideways on the gas. Then there's roll. It's lack of grip that gives you a bigger impression of roll. It's still the same."

Allen: "Two sweeps softer on the rear bump, please, both high-speed and low-speed. We'll see what that does. This will be a reasonably short run and then we'll stop for tires."

The course is still under a red flag. Andy asks Mauricio, "Towards the end are we gonna need some rake? We're not? OK, so we got enough in it. We'll have 12 minutes of green, Morris. We may get another run in depending on our change, but you should consider the stickers."

Mauricio: "On this run?"

Andy: "Right. I pulled out 60 thou on the mid-front and raised the front a flat at the same time. We've upped the front-bump forces, especially the low-speed, to see if we can get more grip." At the green flag both cars are out on course. Mark is P3 and Mauricio P7.

After that run Mark says leave the changes and go to the fresh tires.

Mauricio reports those changes are "A little bit better. Still understeering too much. Especially Turn 1; that's the worst turn."

Andy: "OK, Mo, there's 5 minutes to go so we'll go for tires and I'd like to pull the rear wicker. I'd like to move the center of pressure forward and I'd like to do it that way to pick up some speed on the straights." Removing the wicker, also called a Gurney flap, from the rear wing will lower the downforce and drag generated by the rear wing. That moves the overall downforce distribution forward, which is what Andy wants. He's looking for front grip.

Mauricio: "Ten-four."

With 5 minutes to go the order on the monitor is Zanardi, Fittipaldi, Ribeiro, Herta, and Mark. Mo is eighth. Two laps later Mauricio has the fast lap at 59.027 seconds, and Mark is a close second. Zanardi, Rahal, and Fittipaldi round out the top five.

After a walk to the media center for a time sheet, I get back to the garage area at 11:05 to find Mark, Allen, and Al Bodey talking over a track map at one of the tables in the eating area. Mark is talking animatedly, using his hands to indicate car behavior.

Mark Moore tells me, "That's something to write about, first time our cars have been one-two in a session."

Blundell's crew crowds around me to look at the time sheet. "We would have been faster with sticker tires," Daryl says. Everybody's lining up for lunch. It's good, one of Dave Loik's best — steak, medium rare, with mushroom gravy and mashed potatoes.

Qualifying

In the pit lane at 1:15 Greg Moore and Mark are standing together talking. Greg's team is pitted next to PacWest again. Greg is Canadian, of course, and Mark is English, so the two of them together draw a huge crowd of photographers and autograph-seekers here in Toronto. This is one of the times for "pit walks," meaning people with a certain ticket can walk freely on pit lane. CART is much more open to fans that any other top racing series. Formula 1 goes to great lengths to keep the fans away from the teams, and you'd never get this close to the drivers at a NASCAR Winston Cup race.

The slow-guys' qualifying group goes on track. I ask Andy Brown what he did to solve the grip-on-concrete problem for qualifying. He grins and says, "Just handle it, Mo. You're fastest."

Mauricio is sitting in the scoring cart. Mark is here, talking to Allen. The grandstands across the straight from us are almost full, showing the sophistication of Canadian motorsports fans. They know the significance of qualifying.

With 3 minutes to go in the slow-guys' group, Andre Ribeiro jumps into P1 with a lap of 59.295 seconds. Bryan Herta is second. Just before the checkered flag the PacWest crews are warming the motors in their cars. Roy Wilkerson adds oil to the 18-car. Butch says, "What are you doing adding weight to that car?" Roy grins.

Ribeiro ends up with the fast lap in the first group, followed by Michael Andretti and Bryan Herta. The fast-guys' session starts at 2:12. Mark and Mo wait as the other drivers pound out of the pit lane. I hear Andy say, "40 seconds, Mo." Then Mauricio goes on course before the other cars complete their first lap. He'll have a clear course in front of him.

When Mauricio comes back in he says, "I lost traction from this morning."

Andy: "All right, let's pull that bump change out that we put in this morning and go the other way. What about the bottoming, because we did raise the car as well?"

Mauricio: "Yeah, I'm not bottoming. Just very high, higher than this morning for sure. We must be losing something there." Andy requests some changes from the crew.

Mauricio: "What are the changes, Andy?"

Andy: "I took four sweeps of low-speed rear bump out, so that's two less than this morning. I dropped the car a flat at the front and a flat-and-a-half at the rear."

Mark doesn't go any faster and returns to pit lane saying, "Basically the car has more of a rear problem again under braking. I don't seem to be able to slow the car down because the car has too much amplitude in it again. The grip level has gone away from the rear again."

Allen: "Three sweeps softer in high-speed and low-speed rear bump, please. You can also try a little bit more tim to see if that helps."

Mark: "I put more tim in it then as I was goin' around. Like a click. Feels OK, but once the tires go off you don't get a good read."

Al Bodey says, "14 and a half minutes." Allen makes some tire-pressure changes also. Mark goes out for another run.

Mauricio comes in saying, "The rear is not the same, because it's just sliding on the tires."

Andy: "OK, Mo. What about the ride height? Can you make a spot-on lap with the next set of tires?"

Mauricio: "I am touching; still not as hard as this morning, but I was blowing the valve a little bit. The car just doesn't seem to be as good through the turns as it was this morning."

Andy: "Well, I'll tell you what. Let's put it back the way we had it, because it was pretty good. We gotta choice. You can either baseline that with 13 minutes of green left and then we'll do a low-fuel run the last 5 minutes, or do the stickers now with a low-fuel run."

Mauricio: "Do the stickers now."

Andy: "Three gallons, please, Roscoe." Mauricio goes out at 2:31 p.m. Michael Andretti's time has held from the first group. Dario Franchitti is P2. Mark is P8 and Mauricio P11.

Mark drives down the pit lane into the pit box saying, "Still got the same problem under braking. The rear is jackin' up quick and coming around sideways. Two or three times going into the corner I'm going completely sideways, as we were yesterday. The car felt comfortable again this morning."

Allen: "Change the tires, please. How's the car for touch?"

Mark: "The car feels like it's touching down a little bit more than what it did this morning as well. Also we're under-geared. It's hittin' on the rev limiter too early."

Allen: "All right. Let's drop the rear a flat, please. Now what about this rear bump? Do you think we should go back to where we were before?"

Mark nods yes and then says, "Maybe I should try and get it on the first timed lap again, or should I do a slow lap and build on it?"

Allen: "I think it's best to go for it on the first lap, mate."

Mark pulls out of pit lane and Allen says, "7 to go; run 'til the end."

Dario Franchitti is in P1 now with a lap of 58.618 seconds. Mark gets into the 58s also, with a 58.926 for P2. Mauricio comes in for tires and is back out with 3 minutes to go. Mark Moore says, "Two timed laps."

Blundell can't improve his time. "I think the tires are gone," he says.

The checkered flag flies at 2:47. Franchitti has his first pole. Mark is P2 and Bobby Rahal is P3. Mauricio ends up 10th. As Mark drives back into pit lane, Butch says, "Hey, guys; make sure you whoop it up for him." They do.

Qualifying Press Conference

Rahal and Mark are here, taking questions. "We made some big changes," Rahal says. "We went better. The car likes this course, the tires too." He is the fastest driver on Goodyear tires.

Mark has a new toy he's playing with, a trick video camera. He turns it on the crowd of journalists, photographers, and video cameras in front of him, grinning and laughing. When he puts it down, Rahal is through talking so he picks up the camera and points it at Mark, who grins even wider for his own camera.

"We set a good time on old tires," Mark says. "I'm disappointed we didn't go quicker. We had good balance and the engine was good. We're doing well now because the PacWest team is gelling. We've got a lot of strength."

Dario comes in late because of all the hoopla associated with his first pole. Mark videos him also. "On the fast lap we'd made the time in the first part of the lap, so I took it easy then," Dario says. "I was surprised by it, actually."

He's asked about the emotional greeting from his burly car owner, Carl Hogan. "I was afraid of his hug," Dario says, "but I didn't feel it much, really."

Mark mentions some changes on the team as part of the reason he's doing better now than earlier in the season. After the formal questions, Tim Tuttle, writer for *On Track* magazine, talks with Mark one-on-one and asks about the changes.

Mark says, "Jim Hamilton was my engineer at the start of the year, but the chemistry was lacking. He's now doing data analysis and software development that's helping the team. Allen and I clicked, and we're working together well."

Pit-Stop Practice

At 3:40 a Canadian street-stock race is running on the track in front of grandstands 30% full. I'm back on pit lane watching the 18-crew practicing pit stops. It's the usual pit-stop assignments for the Motorola guys. Daryl Fox is changing the inside front. Butch, also the chief mechanic, is on the outside front. Gavin Hamilton changes the outside rear, and the inside rear is Charlie Guilinger. "Timmie D.," Tim Douthat, handles the vent and air-jack lines. Randy Smay is the fueler.

As they catch their breath between practice stops I says to Butch, "Your boy's looking pretty good."

"Yeah," Butch says, with an open-mouth grin. "Mark's really pumped up. It just happened."

They finish up, and as Butch, Daryl, and I walk back to the garage area, I ask, "Is there more pressure on the guys over the wall when the car qualifies on the front row?"

"The pressure's really on when your guy's in the lead," Butch says. "You just have to suck it up and do it just like practice. That's why we practice so much. During Sunday morning warm-up we do a full-on hot stop. It's different with the car coming in onto pit lane."

Race Prep

The 17x-car is getting an updated differential installed. The primary car is on the setup pad. It had its diff changed last night.

I tell Allen McDonald I thought he seemed nervous before that qualifying session. "I've been scared all weekend, really," he says. "I was sure we didn't have a very good car, and I've been absolutely astounded when Mark's gone quick."

"Hey, it's nice to be wrong that way," I say. We both laugh.

At 5:30 Neil Atterbury is repairing a thermocouple on a brake rotor. That's a rough environment for a temperature sensor so they have to be repaired often. Neil is still limping from his Cleveland accident. The underwing is going on the 17x-car as the diff change winds up.

A little later I go to the car and drive back to the hotel. For dinner I'm on my own so I go to a place called Montana's and have a pizza and some beer. Then it's a walk back to the hotel and bed.

SUNDAY

As usual, I pack my bag in the room and check out of the hotel on the way out. My flight out this afternoon isn't real early, but I need to get away quickly. When I get to the parking lot at the track I put the rental car in a space near the exit. One of the security guys tells me the route to take out of the lot that will get me onto the freeway toward the airport. Then I walk to the hospitality area and stow my gear. It's 7 a.m. and no one is here yet.

In the garage area, tear-down and pack-up have already started. There's a lot of activity and I have trouble staying out of the way. CART warm-up won't start until 10 a.m. Indy Lights have their warm-up at 8, so I walk to the pit lane at 7:45 looking for Jim Swintal, the starter. "What about the start?" I ask.

Jim says, "This is the first time I've had two neophytes on the front row [Franchitti and Blundell]. They've never given me any reason to doubt them, so I think they'll be OK. I've told them what's fair and foul. The rest is up to them."

Back in the garage area engines are firing up and warming, whooping up and down in rpm. The weather's going to be fine. It's sunny but cool now, and some high clouds show in the west.

Over the Wall

That's the expression used by the crew to describe working pit stops during a race. I started talking to some of the guys about it yesterday, and continue this morning. "So, Butch, what does it take to go over the wall?"

"You have to be quick. Basically, we have tryouts every year and the fastest ones get to do it. Just to look at him, Charlie [Guilinger] doesn't look like he'd be quick. Well, he is. He's almost always the first one done. At Detroit he stood up and the rest of us still had our guns on the nuts. He's a sleeper."

Butch is right; Charlie doesn't look like a fast guy. Charlie likes to eat and it shows, but Charlie also has an air of confidence about him. He's certainly not cocky, anything but. Charlie is a good guy. He's a competent athlete and he knows it.

Next I ask Gavin Hamilton, "You like going over the wall?"

"Oh, yeah," comes the answer. "That's the whole fun of it. If you're standin' around you're still part of the team, but over the wall, you're doing something that can make a difference."

"You talkin' about goin' over the wall?" Roy Wilkerson pushes Gavin with both hands.

Gavin laughs and explains, "Roy did it before, and when he left I took over. He's back now and he's pissed."

"It's worse than that," Roy explains to me. "I've only missed five pit stops in 10 years."

At 9:30 the PacWest crews have moved the cars to the pit lane for the warm-up. I continue to ask about going over the wall. "It's a big adrenaline rush at first," Daryl Fox says. "Then it becomes a part of the job. The worst pressure is on a timed pit stop. Most of the time we're through changing tires before the fuel is in, but on a timed stop [timed to take on a specific amount of fuel], you have to do it as fast as you can."

Tim Douthat handles the jack and vent hoses on Mark's car. He says, "It's the idea you can affect the outcome of the race, that and the adrenaline. You get used to the pressure. I've been doing it 14 years. You can get hurt. Last year at Cleveland I got run over. I saw the rear tires light up, but you're hung out there off balance. I broke my heel and tore some ligaments. There was a fire while I was under the car. They didn't get it on TV. Thank goodness my wife didn't see it."

Randy Smay, the fueler on the 18-car, tells me, "It's the best part of the whole deal. It makes the late nights worth it."

"What about the pressure?" I ask. "You're hugging that fuel hose and there's always leaks when the valve comes off the car."

Randy shrugs, "I don't think about it. You might choke."

Warm-Up

At 9:40 the primary cars are in the pit lane and the T-cars, 17x and 18x, are under cover behind the pits. I ask Allen McDonald if he made any big changes to Mark's car. "No big changes. I'm a bit paranoid about the tim device, though."

"I saw some pretty elaborate bleeding procedures going on this morning," I say.

"Yeah, we've been working on how to do that so it bleeds right."

While we're talking Butch is in the 18-car mashing on the brake pedal while Daryl has his hand stuck in under the wing feeling something. "It's working," Daryl says. Mauricio's crew is practicing pit stops.

The green flag flies at 10:05. The PacWest cars go out and the crews do a radio check. Mauricio can't hear Andy on the backstraight. When Mauricio comes in he says, "Everything is OK, apart from the radio and a small vibration on the disks. It's touching a little bit on the backstraight, but nothing dramatic."

Andy: "You're P7 right now, with that 61.29. Zanardi did a 60.25. You did that run on slot zero, which is giving some data for fuel consumption. I'd like to go to slot three for this next run, please. Do you want the front wing as well as the stiffer bar, Mo?"

Mauricio: "Hold the front wing." He goes back on course about midway in the session.

Mark comes in. "The car's got oversteer coming in, Allen. I've gone up one more click on the tim. I've gone up stiffer on the front bar and that gives me a lot, then it's puttin' too much load in the front tires. I've got to back off the bar. It needs some more rear grip. On entry the car is still poppin' up a bit. At the apex to exit it's still not clean enough. There's still too much over-steer. On the high speed, especially coming onto the frontstraight here, the front of the car is loading and unloading."

After a long discussion Allen sums the changes: "OK. So we've reset the rear pressures and we've gone softer on rear-bump damping." Mark returns to the track.

Mauricio comes in saying, "I'm lacking traction and middle-corner grip at the front. I went stiffer with tim but I couldn't really check it, that was on the last lap. I'm still locking the rear wheels. Maybe I have to go softer with it. On the straights it's fine; the problem is Turn 1 and Turn 8 where it's locking."

Andy: "What you said about the tim, maybe we're not using it enough. We're going to change the rear cover now so we can see if the antenna is our radio problem. Try slot two this time, please." Mauricio returns to the track.

The next time Mark comes in the crew simulates a pit-stop. Ando talks him in and the guys change tires. After the checkered flag Mauricio is the last driver in off the track. He says, "The radio didn't get any better, Andy."

Strategy

Back in the garage area the crews are still fiddling with the tim device. It must give an advantage here or they wouldn't use it. We can hear the Indy Lights race start and then stop. There must have been a crash somewhere.

The CART race will start at 2 p.m. I ask Russ Cameron about the race strategy. "Mark is starting on the primary tires, the softer ones. Mauricio is on the optionals. The softer ones might not last. It should be two pit stops, but depending on yellow flags we could take a partial load on one stop. That could give us track position. We need to go fast early in the race. The marbles will make it tough to pass later on."

At 1 p.m. I'm in the pit lane. The stands are about half-full. The sun shines through some high clouds. It's warm but there's a cool breeze. I ask Andy about the strategy. "We're on the harder tires. It's not as hot as I'd like to see it. We've got enough fuel here, so the pit-stop windows are big."

Pre-Grid

The drivers are getting in the parade cars for an introduction lap. Butch passes out the spare wheel nuts to his guys. If they drop the one that comes off the car they can use the spare. Each guy has a way to hook it on his uniform so he can grab it quickly.

When Mauricio is getting ready to put his helmet on, he takes his Hollywood cap off and puts it on Victoria Vanderwell's head. It fits down over her ears, and Mauricio says, "See how small her head is?"

Victoria laughs. She's a little embarrassed, but Mauricio doesn't kid anyone he doesn't like.

I walk up to the front of the grid where Mark is on the front row and ask Allen about race strategy. "We'll stay out and wait for yellows to pit."

"Will the tires last?" I ask.

"They're right on the edge," Allen says.

"Wear or going off?"

"Both."

"How much do they go off?"

"Three-quarters of a second."

THE RACE

The cars' engines start at 1:58. I walk back to the PacWest pits. The cars get rolling and I hear the teams doing radio checks. Roscoe is the fueler on Mauricio's car. His eyes grin at me out of the opening in his helmet. He pats the fuel hose as if to say, "It'll get the job done."

The excitement grows as Jim Swintal gives the drivers the one-finger sign telling them they'll get the green flag next time by.

At the start Dario Franchitti has the inside line to the first corner, but both Mark, on the outside of the front row, and Bobby Rahal, on the inside of the second row, get a jump on him, and they go three abreast on the frontstraight. Dario edges ahead into Turn 1, but Rahal decides to give it a try. They hit. Dario spins. Mark squeaks by on the outside and finds himself the race leader.

Franchitti and Fittipaldi stall their cars blocking the course so there's a full-course yellow to get them started. Ando says to Mark, "Nice job gettin' around there. Bloody Rahal should know better." The race restarts on lap three with Mark in the lead followed by Rahal, Scott Pruett, and Andre Ribeiro. Mauricio is 11th.

Mark drives steadily in the lead, denying Rahal any gain. Behind the leaders, however, Alex Zanardi is coming through the field. Starting sixth, he fell to eighth on the restart, but he's been passing people and gaining spots. On lap seven Mark has a seven- or eight-car-length lead on Rahal. Zanardi is fourth. Ando tells Mark, "Hold your position. Just hold it there. Back off a little on the pace."

On lap 11 Zanardi passes Scott Pruett for third spot, and on lap 18 he gets by Rahal. He's gaining on Mark. Ando tells Mark to pick up the pace and gives him the interval. "Back to Zanardi, three and a half [seconds]."

Mark Moore says, "Can you believe Fernandez won here last year, and now he's back there racing the Toyotas?" Adrian Fernandez is driving his Lola in 22nd spot.

At lap 20 Russ Cameron says, "The fuel window is open."

Ando tells Mark he has a 4-second cushion on Zanardi and 8 seconds on Rahal. "Let Zanardi come up to ya; we need to make some fuel here, mate."

Zanardi doesn't gain any ground, and I hear Mark Moore say, "I bet they had to turn the fuel down in that Honda." That sounds right to me. Zanardi probably used a bunch of fuel passing those cars the first 15 laps.

Ando and Russ start counting down the laps until pit stops for their drivers. Here's where the crews earn their money. I'm glad I asked those over-the-wall questions. I feel more excited with the pit stops coming up because I know more about what the guys are doing.

Mark pits on lap 34. Ando talks him in. "Keep it up on the limiter. That's it. Bring it down. Straight down the middle."

Zanardi pits at the same time but gains no ground. That means everybody did their jobs perfectly. Zanardi didn't gain coming in or going out of the pit lane, and both crews nailed the stop. The pits were crowded, making their jobs even more difficult.

Greg Moore and then Raul Boesel lead one lap each until they have to pit. Mauricio comes in a lap later and gains a couple of spots to ninth. On lap 36 Mark and Zanardi are once again one-two, with Ribeiro in third. Ando tells Mark to "make fuel."

Later Ando tells Mark, "You're holding a good 2 seconds there. Nice and steady. Ribeiro is third and Michael fourth."

Every time Mark comes by on the frontstraight, Ando gives him some information or instruction or encouragement. He's coaching Mark the same as any coach with an athlete in any professional sport.

On lap 62 Mark is gaining on Parker Johnstone and Al Unser Jr. Parker is on the lead lap, but Junior is a lap down. Mark yells into the radio that he wants them to get out of the way.

"Go on up there; you'll do good," Ando says.

Mauricio is also having passing problems. "I'm wasting time behind these guys and I can't pass." On the TV monitor, the rubber buildup off line is noticeable. Mauricio pits on lap 65.

Ando tells a pit marshal he wants the blue passing flag for Parker and the word makes its way to Jim Swintal, the starter. I hear him say, "We're working it." Zanardi gains some, but Mark gets by Parker with a good move.

Zanardi pits on lap 69. Mark has been saving fuel and can stay out on course. As Zanardi comes out from his pit stop, he slides wide into Turn 1 and collides with Greg Moore. That brings out a full-course yellow and allows Mark to make a yellow-flag pit stop. Butch tells his guys, "We're not going to put in all the fuel, so it's going to be a quick stop. Just be calm and let's do a good stop here, OK?"

Ando talks Mark into the pit box. "Watch for Butch. Down the center."

As Mark roars out of pit lane in a cloud of rubber dust and smoke, Al Bodey says, "slot seven, slot seven."

Wally Dallenbach makes the decision to send the sweepers and a blower out to clean up some of the marbles on course. Mark uses this time to warm his front tires. Ando tells him, "Give 'em a little bit more than you normally would to warm 'em up."

As the blower comes by on the straight in front of us, Stephen Kent and Blake Hamilton, working the PacWest pit boards, have to crouch down behind the wall to escape blowing debris. Mauricio says. "They're making it worse, just blowing it around."

Ando coaches Mark on the restart. "Don't crowd the pace car. Give 'im a bit of breathin' room as you come around and the lights go off. Go back to slot zero as you come around for the green. When you get down the backstraight, go to zero. Keep it off the marbles."

We go green again on lap 78. The leaders are now Mark, Zanardi, Ribeiro, Andretti, Pruett, and Mauricio. Mark continues to hold a lead on Zanardi. Ten laps later I hear Mauricio, still in sixth, say "We made a bad choice of tires."

Bruce is in the scoring cart and I see him start to smile. First and sixth isn't bad.

At the checkered flag the Motorola crew gives a loud yell. They all tumble into pit lane pumping hands and pounding backs. They run off toward the frontstraight, where Mark has stopped the car. After more yelling and back slapping with Mark they head toward victory circle.

I find Andy and he says, "Mo had trouble getting a clear lap in qualifying and it's tough to pass here. We had third-fast race lap though."

The victory-circle celebration is raucous and the PacWest people are just as excited as the first time. Maybe this one seems more real, less of a fluke.

It's time for me to head out. Some of the PacWest guys also have an early flight. We walk to the parking lot to our cars and start to inch our way out. A bus is clogging things up. Canadians are like the British in that they don't mind standing in line. I play the ugly American to my advantage, changing lanes and taking unorthodox routes around stopped cars. Sometimes the PacWest van is ahead of me and sometimes it's behind. When we get to the freeway they streak off into the distance.

Alex Zanardi, Mark Blundell, Bruce McCaw, and
Andre Ribeiro on the Podium
(Photo by Art Flores)

LOOKING BACK

Waiting at the airline gate after passing through customs, I think about the race. Like Andy said, it takes a good qualifying spot and perfect pit stops to win here. Mark and his guys made that happen. Their first pit stop was perfect, taking only 32.156 seconds. Mauricio's guys were only a second slower, but he lost three spots. The second stop for the 18-crew was a blistering 30.405 seconds. For comparison, Zanardi's stops were 32.257 and 30.868 seconds. That plus Mark's consistent driving and good fuel-mileage management made the day.

Butch is right about Charlie. I watched him during the stops. He had his tire on very quickly, then he would jump up and man the starter in case Mark stalled the car. He actually had time to move the starter shaft up close to the transaxle. As Mark started forward Charlie dropped the starter and pushed on the rear wing. It was like watching ballet for the big boys.

CHAPTER 18

MICHIGAN SPEEDWAY

The flights from SFO to Denver and Denver to Detroit on July 24 are uneventful. The team is staying in Ann Arbor, Mich., a short drive west of the Detroit airport. There wasn't room for me where the crew is staying, so I'm rooming at the same hotel as the PacWest hospitality staff.

The camera I've been using for three years crapped out at Toronto. Supposedly the warranty will repair it but it takes four weeks, so I bought another one. This new camera is a state-of-the-art single-lens-reflex body with a 200 mm zoom and auto everything. I've got to learn to use it, however.

Mark Blundell's win at Toronto earned him 21 championship points and moved him up to 10th overall. Mauricio Gugelmin's sixth-place finish added eight points to his total, and he's now in ninth place in the championship. Paul Tracy is still the championship points leader, but Alex Zanardi and Michael Andretti are within six points of him.

Michigan is the third race in as many weeks. We get a week off after this race and then go to Mid-Ohio. Michigan is one of only two 500-mile races on the schedule. The last race of the year at Fontana, Calif., a new track this year, is also 500 miles, and the track is supposed to be similar to Michigan. Both facilities are part of Roger Penske's empire.

FRIDAY

I leave the motel at 6 a.m. and drive through the rolling Irish Hills on a two-lane road with gentle curves. Lakes, planted fields, and wooded areas glide past me. There's some fog at first, but about halfway to the track that clears and the bright orange rising sun jumps into the rear-view mirror, looking like a big stop sign.

It's a 40-minute drive so I'm at the track before 7 o'clock. After going to the wrong gate I figure out I'm supposed to go to the administration building to pick up the parking pass I'd faxed ahead for. The window isn't supposed to be open yet, but a pretty blonde lady is there and the pass comes with a smile. It's not like that at all the tracks. At Toronto there was no acknowledgment of my parking request, but a lady slipped me one anyway.

After driving through a three-lane tunnel under the entrance to Turn 1, I get herded to the paddock parking lot. The security people won't let anyone walk the short way across the road, so it's a long walk down the fence to a gate and back down the other fence to the hospitality area and the PacWest motor coaches.

After I stow my stuff in one of the belly lockers of the Hollywood motor coach, I head toward the garage area. On the way I spot a couple of Lola guys standing in the back of their hauler. Since I'm curious about the Lola performance deficit and the announced management buyout, I stop and talk to them. Aerodynamicist Chris Saunders and Ben Bowlby, the designer, are two of the six people who've mortgaged their homes to participate in a management buyout of Lola Cars, Ltd. The founder, Eric Broadley, will not be involved in the new company, and the consensus is that's good for the company.

They say they still don't know exactly what part of their car is causing the problem, but they are concentrating on the aerodynamics. They've redesigned the gearbox to stiffen the rear of the car with no improvement. It's interesting to me that they are reduced to the serial replacement of components that I've often done myself when one of my own cars isn't running right. Even the experts get stumped now and then.

Chris and Ben are hopeful they'll be able to get enough money to develop the car and continue next year. They know that it will be almost impossible to sell cars, so they'll probably have to give some away. They'll try to find a team or two to work closely with while they catch up to Reynard. They've got a tough row to hoe.

Garage

About 8 a.m. I get to the PacWest garage area. The team is in two bays of the covered garages, and the haulers are parked just across the aisle. There's a space for the tables and a canopy between the big rigs. The air is thick and humid already, and the temperature is supposed to get in the 80s today and 90s tomorrow. Rain is also possible late today.

The PacWest Haulers

Butch Winkle, the 18-car chief mechanic, tells me Toronto was a perfect weekend. "Everything we did was perfect. You hope every weekend is like that, but it's one in a thousand."

Dyno Don Norton, Ilmor engineer, says the engines in the cars today and race day are race-spec 008 engines built for reliability, and are actually called 009 engines. The normal 008 engine will run in practice and qualifying on Saturday. He intimates that during qualifying the engines will be turning a new, higher-level of rpm.

"15 thou?" I ask, just guessing.

"I can't officially confirm that, but it's about right."

"Wow; that's a lot of little pieces jiggling up and down pretty fast."

"Yeah," he says and his chin goes up with pride. "These are very impressive engines."

Russ Cameron stops to talk, and I ask him about any new tricky bits. He says the primary cars have different rear-wing end plates for low drag, and they've spent some time adapting a big turning vane in front of the sidepods that was a '95 part, and is supposed to generate more downforce.

CART is concerned that the speeds at Michigan are over 230 mph and the cars are getting faster every year. As a result, all the cars here this weekend have to run a "blocker" in each side of the diffuser. The blockers are plugs that cut the diffuser exit area in half, reducing the airflow and lowering the amount of downforce produced by the underwing. They are set into the outer corners of the diffuser exits. They're hoping the cars will need to run their wings at a higher angle of attack and the resulting drag will slow the cars.

Pace-Car Ride

At 9:30 I walk down to Turn 1 where the PPG pace cars are staging for their laps. After about a 15-minute wait my turn comes for a ride, and I climb into the Corvette. We get up to speed very quickly heading down the long backstraight. The wind swirling around the inside of the car is so strong I don't take out my notebook, so I don't write down the driver's name, and I don't remember it later either. At 120 mph on the straights scrubbing to 100 in the corners, this is a quick ride.

The Michigan Speedway is a D-shaped, 2-mile track with the curved part of the D on the frontstraight. It's banked for very high speeds. The D shape lets the fans in the grandstands see about two-thirds of the track, and it also makes Turns 2 and 3 tighter than 1 and 4. The balance of the car is extremely important because for most of the lap the car is in a curve. At the speeds of the CART Indy cars — over 230 mph — the balance is mainly aerodynamic and changes require an angle-of-attack adjustment on the secondary elements on the top of the front wing. The crews turn a T-shaped bolt on the front-wing flap to adjust its angle of attack. The rear wing is adjusted by changing the angle of attack and using Gurney flaps of different heights.

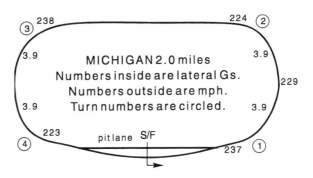

Tires

Traction characteristics of tires change constantly as the cars run on the track. Heat fluctuations and stress produce changes in the fabric construction and in the rubber tread compound, altering the shape and stiffness of the tire and the way the tread grips the track surface. After 10 hard laps a driver will feel the difference in the tire and usually a change in the balance of the car. Either the front or the rear tires go to a bigger slip angle than the car had when the tires were fresh. If a car is not balanced it's slower in the corner. When the tire changes and slows the car that's called "give up or" "going off."

Balance Adjustments

These cars have cockpit-adjustable devices so the drivers can make fine balance adjustments separate from the wings. This weekend the PacWest cars have cockpit-adjustable anti-roll bars in the front and rear suspension. There is also a weight jacker, a hydraulic cylinder at the right-front coil spring seat. This changes the static weight distribution across the front tires and alters balance. This is called diagonal weight transfer or cross weight. The NASCAR guys call it "wedge."

A short explanation of wedge: An increase in static weight (force on the tire patch when the car is sitting still) on the right front also increases weight on the left-rear tire and decreases weight on the left front and the right rear. The overall weight of the car does not change.

Think of the effect of sliding a wedge under one leg of a four-legged table. More of the table's weight is on that leg and the diagonal leg. And now there's less weight on the other two legs. Those legs are solid, of course, and the two light ones just come off the floor.

A racecar has springs, and as the springs compress or extend, they reduce or increase tire static force. I'm saying static because none of this alters dynamic weight transfer caused by turning corners, braking, or accelerating. What the weight jacker does is change the static weight distribution so when the dynamic changes occur, their result is different and the car's balance in a corner is different.

Confusing? You bet. It takes me five chapters to explain this whole thing completely in the book on racing shocks that Jeff Braun and I are working on.

For now just remember that upping the weight on the right front increases understeer by slightly decreasing grip at the front and slightly increasing grip at the rear. A decrease in weight on the right front has the opposite effect, a decrease in understeer coming from more grip at the front and less at the rear. In the following conversations you'll hear references to the weight jacker.

Practice

The first practice session is scheduled for 11 a.m. and I walk onto pit lane about 15 minutes early. The rookies, Dario Franchitti, Patrick Carpentier, Arnd Meier, and Gaulter Salles, are still on the track near the end of their special rookie practice session. I walk up to Ian Bisco, Cosworth vice president, who is standing and watching the cars, and he says, "Listen to the cars. Can you hear that rumble?"

Butch, Roy, and Gavin Get Mark
Ready for Practice

It takes me a minute of trying but then I hear it, a low, beating rumble underlying the screeching roar of the engine. "What the hell is that?" I say to Ian.

"I don't know. I haven't heard that before," comes the reply.

I walk on down the pit lane. The PacWest pit is the one closest to Turn 1 and it's a long walk. When I get there, I ask Gavin Hamilton about the rumble.

"Pretty neat, huh? It's not new."

The 18- and 17-cars are ready to go and the drivers about to get in. Russ Cameron walks around each one jerking on the rear wings and bending over to pull on the steering arms. I've never seen Russ do that before, and it shows how concerned everyone is about the very high speeds of this extremely dangerous track.

Allen McDonald tells me he's respectful of the track. "I'm very well aware that I have no experience with this kind of track. It's a bit scary really."

I smile at him. "I don't see how an intelligent person could think otherwise. What kind of setup are you starting with?"

"We've got a lot of aero and toe-in dialed in for Mark, more than Mo. He's running straighter with less scrub. We'll start off slow with Mark and try to get him comfortable."

"It's toe-in at the right rear that's important, isn't it?"

"Yeah."

It's warming up now, but there are some high, hazy clouds that might cut down the heat. A cool breeze blows for a while, and when it stops I get a hint of just how hot and clammy it can get here.

At 11:05 a.m. the green flag flies on the first practice session. Mauricio is out right away, but Mark has Charlie fussing with the mirrors on each side of the cockpit, making sure that each is just right. On the radio Mark is talking about some minor alterations he'd like for the guys to do that would make his seat more comfortable.

I put my headphones on and fire up the scanner. When I put my headphones on, the rumble of the cars is even more noticeable. The headphones reduce the overall noise level, but the low-frequency rumble comes right through. I'm guessing this rumble is a result of intense vortices swirling off the diagonal fences in the inlets to the underwings of all these cars. These vortices put a lot of energy into the flow under the car, and that retards the buildup of a boundary layer as the air slows down in the diffuser at the back of the underwing. I think all that roiling air at 240 mph beats against the bottom of the cars and produces this powerful rumble. Once you hear it, it gets your attention.

Both cars come back in after a couple of installation laps. Mark's car has a steering rack designed for superspeedways. The front wheels turn less for the same steering wheel input than with the standard rack. Small steering inputs can move the car around too quickly at 240 mph. But Mark doesn't like it.

Mark: "It feels OK. The steering wheel is actually quite a long way right-hand down. It's quite a big amount. I'm not sure what I'm gonna do with that much. It's quite a big angle. Also, as well, we need some pad in here because my head goes over far too much."

Dario Franchitti is already turning laps at 228-mph average. He was out during the rookie session and is obviously comfortable with his car at that speed. That's a 31.487-seconds lap on a 2-mile racetrack!

Mauricio comes in off the track and Andy asks, "Any traffic at all?"

Mauricio: "Yeah, plenty of grip, I just blow by them easily. The car feels very draggy. Maybe we could take out some more wing?" Andy gives some instructions to the 17-crew about checking the rear-wing angle with a digital readout inclinometer and adjusting the wing to the middle hole. Mauricio goes out again. When he comes back in he says, "That's better. The car is fractionally heavier but the car feels more stable, that's for sure."

There's a yellow flag to tow in a stalled car and Mark comes in saying, "OK, first things first. Still need a bit more padding in here because my head is just going over too far. It doesn't need a lot, but maybe just another 3 or 4 mils. It doesn't feel like the brakes are coming in that well when I'm gettin' on the pedal. The retardation level isn't building up quick enough. The car's got a little bit of vibration in it at high speed. Just, you know, a high-frequency vibration. This left-hand mirror, as well, it's impossible to see out. There's nothing at all you can see from it.

"Grip-wise, I'm just building up, but the grip doesn't feel very forthcoming to us at the moment. The steering weight is pretty light; there's not a lot of weight in the steering at this time. And that doesn't transcend to any grip as well at this point. If we've got some time I'd like to change this screen as quickly as possible. We need to get the other one because this screen is so big it's difficult to get a good line of sight into the corners. I'd like to run the short one to see if we can live with it or not."

Andy takes his headset off and climbs over the wall to look at the tires on the 17-car. Mauricio tells him, "It's not touching at all."

Andy: "OK. Let's come down a flat all round, please, Mark, and change the rear-wing end plates. At the end of this next run it'll be 50 miles on the engine. I'd like to check the oil. Do we have to do anything with the revs, just to check oil?"

After conferring with Ian Hawkins, the Ilmor guy, Andy tells Mauricio, "OK, when you come off at the end of this run, can you hold the rpm at 4,000 for a short while?" Mauricio goes out for a run on the big oval.

Butch has sent Stephen Kent back to the hauler to look for the shorter windscreen for Mark. He's having trouble finding it, and there are several radio conversations telling him which cabinet to look in and him coming back about not locating the part.

Mauricio comes back in. He's in P3 after turning a lap over 229 mph. "A bit more push, but I was faster too. I'm talking a small amount."

Andy asks the crew to lower the car one flat all around, "and take a half-turn out of each front wing as well, please. We've changed the rear-wing end plates."

Mark's back in: "The vibration's still there. It doesn't seem to be going away. The other thing is, usin' this rack, I don't seem to be able to get into the pits clean with the amount of lock. It's going to be a little bit tricky maybe, gettin' the car into position right." The 18-car now has a swath of blue duct tape on the right side of the cockpit holding the extra padding that's been added per Mark's request. Charlie Guilinger has been working on that all session.

Mark talks to Allen after another run on the track: "It feels better now. I put another 5 pounds of cross-weight in across the front, just to try to get a bit of push and get up to speed."

Allen: "Would you like it if we took out some more front wing? Would that help you?"

Mark: "No. I think we should leave it as it is at the moment. I've got to get up to speed a little more."

Mauricio has an engine problem. "It's dying on me, Andy." He comes in just as another red flag stops the session. He's P1 in the session with a 230.821-mph lap. The order on the monitor is Mauricio, Parker Johnstone, Michael Andretti, Dario Franchitti, and Bobby Rahal. Mark is not on the monitor page, which means he's slower than 18th.

Mark tells Allen: "There's a bit of vibration in there. I'm not sure I like the rack because it's too much feeling. It's too much movement. You go for the corner and you feel like you've got a dead wheel, because there's just too much play. And I can't actually decide to go into the corner with the level of steering effort and the level of grip. I'm fighting to get a clean line. The car, also, when I go into 3, on entry, the thing takes a big step in the front. It's got like a big lack of grip on initial turn-in. It doesn't feel that nice."

Mauricio is on the track and he radios in to Andy complaining about the pop-off valve blowing at part throttle. Andy tells him, "We think we should leave it like that rather than give up boost when you're running wide open. It does reseat itself quite quickly. Does it upset the car?"

Mauricio: "No, it doesn't." Mauricio says he doesn't think the engine is pulling as well as during the test they did here. He's in a lot of traffic and he says he's going to slow and get out of it.

Andy cautions, "All right, but think about race day." He knows Mauricio has to get the car dialed in and himself comfortable running in traffic and passing people easily even when the disturbed air behind cars degrades the aerodynamic performance.

Mark to Allen: "Going into the banking, you turn in and there's just a big steering movement with no front grip at that point. It's upsetting when you go into the turn."

Andy and Mauricio discuss some aero tradeoffs. "Yeah, I know where I want to be with those, Morris. It's more efficient to get the downforce from underneath."

Downforce from the bottom of the car due to ground effects might be 3,000 pounds or more at the speeds these cars are going. There is very little drag penalty from that. The tires are the main source of aerodynamic drag. Even the wings, trimmed out like they are, don't generate much drag.

Mauricio tells Andy the car is still pushing when he's lapping by himself. He says, "The car feels very draggy, Andy."

Andy responds by saying he can "trim it out." He lowers the car a flat all around. Mauricio goes back on the track. When he comes back in, Andy listens to his feedback and says, "I want to do one more run on these tires, Mo. And we've, perhaps, gone over the edge with these wing settings. Next run we'll put the optionals back on, and see if you get the grip back."

Mark is still unhappy with the steering. "It doesn't feel quite right in terms of feedback. It's not giving me a good feel out on the track, and even coming in, as well, it's like a pain in the ass. You can't get enough lock on to get into the pit box."

The crew finds a cut right-front tire on the 18-car. They change all four. A quick deflation of an outside tire here could cause a dangerous crash. Before this last run Allen had the crew change the front-caster angle by removing a 0.100-inch shim from the rear mounting point of the front upper A-arms. That moves the top of the hub carrier to the rear, increasing the caster angle.

Allen: "Can you feel it any better with the increased caster?"

Mark: "Feels like it might be a little bit better. I just have to get up to the right speed and we'll get better feedback from that change."

Allen: "When you come in after this run we're going to check the oil level. It's obviously very important to find out where that's at. What you need to do is rev it to 4,000 when you come in. Keep it at 4,000 and then shut it down."

It seems the Ilmor-Mercedes engines use a lot of oil at this track. I'm told it's mainly when the throttle is closed and the car is coasting. Low pressure in the cylinders during closed throttle can suck in oil past the valve-stem seals. That could be a result of low-friction seals. Generally for weight and volume reasons you'd like to run with a minimum of oil in the car, but you obviously can't get to a point where you run dry.

Mauricio comes in for tires and tells Andy, "The car is on the light side. Most of the time I was in traffic as well."

Mark comes in and talks to Allen: "There's still too much push in the car. I've gone back about 7 or 8 pounds on the weight jacker to try to see if that improves it, but it doesn't. It's just too much pure push, aerodynamically. Also the car has a bit too much roll in it. Gettin' into the corner it's too much roll, and push, especially mid to exit in 1 and 2. But also because of the turn-in issue, there's that pocket of no grip as I turn in. Then it picks up in grip, but whether that's caused by a lack of front aero and a bit of roll in the car I'm not too sure. And also I get some lack of rpm in fifth coming down into 1. I change to sixth but the engine doesn't really want to pull very well. The last 500 or 600 rpm it's not clean."

Allen: "All right. Let's try a bit more front wing then. Yeah?"

Mark: "Yeah; put some more front wing in. Also I'm not happy about the rack. I'm not sure it's the best way for us to go. There's too much movement. There's too much steering for the amount of push. Maybe that's exaggerating the push because of the amount of lock."

Allen: "What do you reckon, a turn or two of front wing? Half a degree or 1?"

Mark: "Let's put one in and try it out."

Allen: "One turn or 1 degree?"

Mark: "1 degree."

He goes back out for a run and comes back in with the report, "Still feels like it's short of grip, total grip. When I'm into the bankin' it still feels like it's not producing a great amount of grip at this point."

Allen: "What's the car like for touching down?"

Mark: "It's touching down really small towards the rear but really light."

Gavin climbs back up from looking at the bottom of the car and nods to Allen, verifying that what Mark has described is borne out by marks on the skid plates.

It's about 12:30 now, and even though the session started an hour and a half ago there is still almost a half-hour left of a 1-hour session. Engine expirations and track inspections for debris have lengthened the session. Mauricio is still P1 on the monitor, while Mark is off the page.

Mauricio comes in and they talk about tire pressures. Andy says, "I think we've lost all the sensors apart from the right rear, and that looks quite high. I thought that this rear wing would give us too much push. We'll put in some more front wing."

Mauricio: "On my own coming out of 4, I had to breath it a little bit. I don't like the look of the right-rear tire."

Andy: "OK. What I'd like to do with the tires, I'd like to run these a little bit longer to check durability. They're going to give us 'til 1:03, which is just under 30 minutes away."

Mauricio: "13 or 30?"

Andy: "OK. It's 26 minutes to go."

Mark is in again: "Still feels like there's too much push in the car, Allen. The grip level has definitely come up with the front end. But it still needs to have more grip. We need to make the car a little bit more harmonious between front and rear. With that turn of wing in, it starts to give you a hint that the front and rear are going to split slightly in balance. Also it still feels like there's a bit too much roll in the car. If we clean up that push then we'd pick up a bit more speed. Again, that last 400 or 500 rpm it just won't pull; it won't pull the skin off a rice pudding."

Mauricio comes in saying the car is still pushing slightly. Andy says, "What I'd like to do is a front-camber change on both sides." He explains the change to Mauricio off the radio.

Chief Steward Wally Dallenbach is here in the pit box looking things over.

Trevor Jackson cleans the black smears off the nose of the 17-car while the camber change is going on. Mauricio goes back on track at 12:48 p.m. with 16 minutes to go in this first session. Raul Boesel jumps up to P1 with a 31.089-seconds, 231.593-mph lap.

Mark comes in and Allen asks, "Well, what do you think?"

Mark: "I think there's probably a little more grip there with the pressures, but it's given it a bit more push. Just a little more grip coming off the turn is promoting a bit more push in the car. Along with the push we've got an increase in roll. I tried to go up stiffer on the front bar which helped a little bit, but there's still too much push in the car. I came back again on the front bar to see if I can get both the front and the rear to roll into a set, but it gives too much roll. I didn't like it. I'm currently back in the middle, but we've got to sort something out to cut a bit of the roll down and also utilize a bit of the grip it's given us."

Allen: "Is it roll or it just, uh, do you just feel the front doesn't have enough grip? Does it actually, physically roll?"

Mark: "It's a sensation of roll. I mean that's the only thing you can feel. You can feel the sensation of roll, but definitely the front's still lacking grip. If we can increase the front grip that will help me no end, but at this point in time it feels like when the front grip winds off, then the roll comes in. That's the feedback it gives ya. And when you go stiffer on the bar it tends to give a little bit of help, but it's still got a degree of understeer in there. It's not giving me any benefit there at all."

Allen: "What's the downside of the roll? Is it just your feeling?"

Mark: "Yeah, it's just my feeling at present. I mean, the priority would be to give me some more front grip, overall, at this point. That's what I want."

Wally Dallenbach,
CART Chief Steward

Allen: "What about going up on the rear-roll bar then? We can decrease the roll to, uh, to basically give you more front grip."

Mark: "Yeah, if you feel that's a logical step for us. I could try that, yeah. Do I keep the front bar at full stiff, do you think, or just leave it in the middle there where we had it to start with?"

Allen: "Just leave it in the middle, and then try going up to, uh what, say for a start, number three on the rear bar and work your way out."

My conclusion from this conversation is that Mark got confused on the effect of anti-roll bars. He had an understeer and stiffened the front bar, which would add to the understeer. Without pointing out the mistake, Allen steered him toward stiffening the rear bar, which promotes oversteer and would result in less understeer. This is a good example of a diplomatic engineer. Or I could be totally wrong.

It's getting a little cooler. Some high clouds drift in from the west. During a red flag Mark asks about the speeds and Al Bodey tells him, "We're P21 with a 225.9. Fast time is Boesel with a 231.5; Mo has a 231.1; Pruett a 230.9."

The track goes green again at 12:55 p.m. There's about 8 minutes to go in the session. Mauricio goes out. The 18-crew is changing Mark's tires, and then he's out on the track also.

Mark comes back in after a couple of laps. "There's a lot of push in the car, way too much, especially coming off of 4."

Allen: "Can we take any more front wing?"

Mark: "Give me half, Allen, half the last change. And I'm going to go back a little bit on the rear bar."

Allen to the crew: "Give me a turn of front wing, please." And to Mark: "What do you want to do with the rear bar? Full stiff?"

Mark: "I just want to trim back. If I get a bit more front grip I just want to trim back a little bit on the bar and make sure it's not too stiff vertically."

Mark goes back out. There's less than 5 minutes to go. Jimmy Vasser is P1 now followed by Boesel, Mauricio, Pruett, and Parker Johnstone. Mauricio comes in and Andy says, "We've got about 2 and half minutes to go. I can just get a set of tires on and put a lap on them for a balance check."

As Mauricio comes down the pit lane Mark Moore tells the crew, "Go to [set] 4B. We're going to put them straight on and leave. Don't check the bottom either, Jimmy."

Mauricio: "The push is still there, but I feel the car is bound up." He goes back out for the last couple of laps.

Mark comes in as the checkered flag flies. Alex Zanardi popped up to the top of the list briefly, but Raul Boesel topped him before the checkered. The top runners are: Boesel, 233.440; Zanardi, 232.829; Vasser, 232.333; Mauricio, 232.036; and Michael Andretti, 231.854. Boesel's lap time is 30.843 seconds and Mauricio's is 31.031 for a difference of 0.188 seconds. That's pretty close over a 2-mile track. Mark ended up in 16th with a 228.521 mph and 31.507 seconds.

Looking at the relative aero settings, I notice that the 17-car has a negative angle of attack on the rear wing. The 18-car is running bigger front- and rear-wing angles, and the Gurney flap on the back of the rear wing is also taller than the one on the 17-car. Mauricio is already trimming the car out for maximum qualifying speed. He'll have to go for more downforce for a race setup to prevent the car from going light when closing up behind another car.

Between Sessions

The cars are on the setup pads, and the crews are busy verifying measurements and getting ready to make corrections that will come from the engineers after the debrief. Daryl Fox sees me and says, in his Aussie drawl, "Was that pretty exciting there last weekend, Paul?"

"I'm supposed to be asking you that."

"It was a good feeling," he continues. "We had some great pit stops and Mark raced like a champion. I think the other team will be there this weekend."

Mark, Allen, Jim, Al, and Malcolm Oastler sit close together at one of the folding tables and talk while most of the rest of the two crews eat lunch all around them.

I see Jim Swintal, the CART starter, and talk to him about the Toronto race. I say, "It looked like the start went well; Mark let Dario lead a little past the line."

"Mark is that kind of guy," is Jim's answer. "And there's more of them like that now that do what they're supposed to do. I tell 'em what I expect and they do it."

Second Practice

At 3:04 p.m. the second practice session starts. Mark and Mo hold back while most of the drivers roar off onto the track right away. They're each going to scrub a couple of sets of tires early in the session. The sky is clear and it's hot and muggy. I'm drinking water constantly, but I never have to pee. The water just goes out through my skin.

After about 5 minutes Paul Tracy's car reports cut right-side tires. They throw a yellow flag for a track inspection. The green flag starts the session again at 3:16 p.m. Once again I notice the rumble from the cars. Jim Hamilton tells me it's a vortex-shedding phenomenon working on the bottom of the car. My guess was right. It's an awesome sound.

Mark says the right side of his seat has collapsed again, and he has boost problems. "The boost is up and down like a yo-yo. The car feels nervous in the front end. We've speeded up the rack sensation. [Gavin replaced the speedway steering rack between sessions.] All of a sudden it feels nervous at the front. So when it leads me in, there's a bit of nervousness and that gives a bit of a hesitant rear. Maybe we just have to drop a bit of flap out of it to calm it down."

Allen: "Yeah; let's take out a couple of turns just to get us on the other side of this."

Mauricio comes in saying, "It's pushing so bad I can't do it flat."

Andy: "The suggestion would be to take some incidence out of the rear wing." Then he says to Mark Moore, "Middle hole, please, Mark."

After another run Mark reports to Allen, "I don't like the way it feels presently, because the car, for one thing, has got more vibration in it. But also the car in general has got a lot of harsh movements in it. The thing is really harsh. It just doesn't fit into the banking. And it feels loose. It feels a bit more consistent around the turn, but the rear of the car just doesn't feel nice at all. I don't have any confidence whatsoever to go in and keep in it. I feel like I'm hangin' on, Allen. I feel like I'm pivoting about the steering wheel, pivoting about the front of the car. And also, engine-wise it's still not very consistent. It fluctuates a hell of a lot."

Allen: "We're going back on the springs, back to where we were this morning. And we'll have a talk with Ian [Hawkins] about the engine. What have you done to the bloody engine, Ian?"

I laugh out loud at this, and then look around sheepishly. "Little Brett" (Firestone engineer Brett Schilling, who is taller than me but smaller than "Big Bret" Hrivnak, another Firestone engineer) is smiling also, but I'm not sure if he's laughing at me or Allen's remark on the radio.

There must be 40 people within 20 feet of me and I'm shoulder to shoulder with at least three, but I laughed out loud like I was at home by myself. This makes me realize how intense I am in the middle of all this, and how that isolates me. I'm cut off from most outside sounds and all the people around me by the scanner headphones and the concentration I need to see and hear and record what I think is important. I'm starting and stopping the recorder to catch the radio conversations. I'm writing in a pocket notebook the time of day, remarks, lap times, and speeds, so I can recall later what happened when. I do all this hoping I'll be able to present a coherent story of the session.

The 18-car is pitted closest to Turn 1, with the 17-car in the next box up the pit lane to my right. The rest of the teams are strung out down the length of the pits. I'm standing about 8 feet from the 18-crew, and I can see just about everything they do. I'll get a blast of excitement being this close to a pit stop during the race.

It's about 85 degrees and very humid. I feel sweat running down my back and I've drunk a whole bottle of water the last half-hour. The front of my shirt is dark with sweat. An occasional breeze gives me a momentary cool feeling. I'm watching and listening to everything that's going on, trying to keep up and not miss anything. Every 10 minutes or so I walk over to look at a monitor so I can see lap times and average speeds. Sometimes I can watch a monitor long enough to see the quickly changing order as drivers try to set fast times at the end of a session.

I'm concentrating so hard it's like I'm in a phone booth. My laughter at Allen's joke with Ian brought me out of it all for a short time. I wouldn't want to be anywhere else. Back to work!

At 3:27 p.m. there's a yellow flag that stops the session. Andre Ribeiro is P1 with a lap at 230.703 mph. Mauricio is seventh and Mark 18th. During the yellow-flag period Mauricio says the car is still pushing, and Mark reports on the continuing boost problem. Andy suggests that Mauricio try a stiffer rear bar adjustment. Mark is also having radio problems and they change his transmitter. Allen tells Mark to turn off BOSS, the Ilmor boost optimization system. A green flag restarts the session, and the PacWest cars return to the track.

At 3:35 p.m. both cars are back in. Mauricio is still talking about the push. "The car is pushing. Are you sure the stagger is right?"

Andy: "This set of rubber has 41 laps on it. The grip's been hurt by the heat cycles."

Mauricio: "It's not the tires, Andy. Are you sure the stagger is where you want it? The tire has nothing to do with it. The car is pushing like a pig."

Andy: "Have you tried the rear bar yet?"

Mauricio: "... moved the rear bar and the weight jacker." He started talking before he pushed the button.

Andy: "Have done or will do?"

Mauricio: "Will do the rear bar and then the weight jacker."

He goes out for another run and comes back in reporting the same problem. "I used the weight jacker. I want to make sure that it's doing what you think it's doing because it pushes just terrible." His voice rises in frustration at the end of the sentence. This is about the most confusion and frustration I've ever heard from the Mo/Andy duo.

Andy: "Pull the front cover off guys, and measure that weight jacker."

Michael Andretti is fastest in the session now with a 231-mph lap speed. Mauricio is P15 with about 28 minutes to go in the session.

After a run on track Allen asks Mark, "Can you get any feeling for the car?"

Mark: "It feels like there is a bit more front grip, but also the ride quality just got a bit harsher on the front end and there's a bit of vibration. I can't get a clean run. I can't run with the engine like this."

Mauricio comes back in saying, "The car is just going straight up to the wall."

Andy: "The only thing I can think of really is front cambers. Everything else we've done in sequence. If it's anything, it's probably your left front that hurts." They make some changes and Mauricio goes back out.

When he comes back in he still has balance problems. Andy tells him, "The ride heights don't look that good. It looks like I've softened the rear too much relative to the front of the skids. We've raised the rear a flat, and I want to run that and then we'll go to the wings."

Mark is back in at 3:48. He asks, "Do you want to keep running on map one or zero?"

Al Bodey says, "Stay on map one."

Mark: "OK. The boost is more stable; still not strong but more stable. Basically, Allen, going in I got a bit more front grip, but we're still lackin' for grip in the front, especially from mid to exit of 2. When we go into the entry of 3, there's still that no-grip area right over that crest. The problem is at the moment that the rear of the car still feels a little bit nervous. I need that planted so I know the rear's going to stay with me. But there's definitely still too much push in it because that's scrubbing off speed."

Allen: "Where we're losing the most speed is, you know, by the fact that we're not quite flat [not full throttle all around the track], so is that because of the front or the rear?"

Mark: "Well, it's almost because the rear doesn't give me enough confidence to stay with it, but on the same point, there is still too much push in the car. I don't think it's too far away, but at the same point if I had more confidence in the rear to know it's not going to jump out of line on me, that would give me more, you know, more confidence to keep the thing flat and carry the understeer. It doesn't feel like it's touching down anywhere either [Mark pronounces that 'eever,' his North London accent again]."

Allen: "I've got a few choices for ya. How 'bout going softer on the rear springs, giving a bit more grip at the rear, or a damper change, softer on the rear bump? What do you reckon?"

Mark: "Any change that's gonna give me a car which is gonna give me a full sense of the bankin' and is gonna set with me. Whatever is gonna give me the confidence to just jam on the gas pedal and stay with it. And if there's push in it, I can carry that. The rear end still walks a little bit at the moment going into the turn. As soon as I get to the middle of the turn, it just doesn't feel good. And when I come up against traffic I'm still not in a comfortable position to place it and stay on line with the gas in." Allen's tactic of giving Mark choices doesn't work if he won't make a choice.

Allen: "OK; go one step softer on the rear springs, please. Come up a half a flat at the rear."

Mauricio comes back in. "Andy, I used the weight jacker but it's still pushing like a pig. I think we're better off putting the weight jacker back to the middle and try to do other things."

Andy: "OK; let's do it with the wings. Do you want to take some out at the rear or put some more front wing into it?"

Mauricio: "Whatever's easier for you. Right now I think we're just about there; we just need to change the balance."

Andy: "Put two turns of front wing in, please, Mark."

Mauricio: "I can't believe how bad the balance is. I cannot get this thing wide open."

There's a yellow flag for debris at 3:54. Mark comes back in and Allen says, "All right, take us through a lap then."

Mark sits in the cockpit with his visor up and uses his gloved hands to accent his report. They talk about it for a while and Mark finally agrees to a sequence of changes. Just before Mark goes out for another run, Allen sums up the changes. "All right, we went down one step [100 lb./in.] on the rear springs, and we added some rear ride height."

It's almost 4 p.m. I'm hot and sweaty and looking forward to a trip to the air-conditioned media center and filling up my water bottle. Both PacWest cars are running laps in the 227-mph area. Mauricio is P14 and Mark P16.

Mark reports after a run: "It feels like it's gonna be better when I just get a lap up to speed. The rear of the car feels like it's a little bit more stable. It doesn't feel like it's gonna touch down at this point, but we're 6 miles an hour off on speed but there's more push. The right-front weight — puttin' that cross weight in is just gonna promote more push."

Allen: "If you feel too much push, just come back on the front bar to start with."

Mark: "It's definitely an improvement over the last run. So maybe we can bring some front grip back in the car and link the front and rear up."

Allen: "So where are you on the bars now?"

Mark: "Uh, three, I think on the front. Yeah, three. And full stiff on the rear."

Allen: "How much time have we got, Al?"

Al Bodey: "17 minutes."

Allen: "Go down one step on the front springs, please."

A yellow flag at 4:01 p.m. stops the session, and it goes green again at 4:07. The 17-car is P14 and the 18-car P16. They're still lapping in the 227-mph area. Michael Andretti is P1 with a 31.037-seconds lap at 231.981 mph.

Mauricio improves to P10 and comes in wanting more front wing. Andy: "Understood, Morris; 1 degree or 2 degrees?"

Mauricio: "Let's do 2 degrees."

Andy: "Just keep the engine running, Morris. We'll just turn the wing up." Mauricio goes right back out.

Robby Gordon, a CART driver last year now driving in NASCAR, comes by and talks to Steve Fusek. They were together at Derrick Walker's team. Robby crashed a lot when he was driving a CART car, and now he's crashing a lot in NASCAR. He's here for an International Race of Champions (IROC) race Sunday morning.

Mark comes back in having improved to P12. "That feels better. It feels like there's a bit more front grip. I'm about halfway on the rear bar. The car's got some vibration. Maybe some pickup [on the tires] or something like that, but the front end vibrates quit a lot. We did a 228?"

Al Bodey: "228.3."

With about 12 minutes to go in the session the top five are Raul Boesel, Michael Andretti, Parker Johnstone, Scott Pruett, and Andre Ribeiro. Boesel's best lap is 233.971 mph.

Mauricio goes out and improves to P6, a 231-mph lap, then P2, at 232.799. He comes in saying, "The car is still not like I want it, but it's pretty close."

Andy: "OK, Mo, I'm going to put another set [of tires] on for scuffs. We'll do like a simulated qualifying run, and then use that set for tomorrow morning."

Mauricio: "It's still pushing just a little bit. Put another degree of front wing."

Andy asks for tire set 7B. "Where's 7B?" someone asks.

Andy: "Let's put 8B on. Sorry, 7B doesn't have sensors."

There's about 5 minutes to go in the session. Mark improves to P6 at 231.229 mph and comes in. "The rear feels better, Al. Still got a little bit of that walkin' sensation in there. There's still a little bit of push in the car, and I have to set the car up in the early stages of the turn to compensate for the push. We could take a little bit of that out, but I'm still nervous about that walk."

Allen: "Let's see if we can fix the walk."

Mark asks about the speeds. Al Bodey tells him, "Boesel's fast at a 233.9; Mo is second at a 232.7; Michael at a 231.9. You are P6 at 231.2."

Mark: "OK."

Mauricio comes back in for another set of sticker Firestones and returns to the track.

Mark improves to P5 with a 232.183. Coming in, he says there's some fluid in the foot well under his heel. "It's very slippery. The balance is good, Allen. I feel like I'm running out of gearing."

Mauricio pops up to P1 with 1 minute to go. His average speed is 234.283 mph and 30.732 seconds. The checkered flag flies at 4:34 p.m. Mauricio holds P1. Boesel is second followed by Scott Pruett, Alex Zanardi, and Mark.

In pit lane right after the session I talk with Allen McDonald. "I was afraid at one point in the session that neither you or Mark would make a decision about what change to make next."

Allen laughs and then says, "This place is bloody dangerous, and I'm very aware I don't know what I'm doing."

"Well, you seem to be doing pretty well. I think I can see a difference between the way you're handling Mark and the way Jim did it. You're giving Mark choices where Jim just made changes himself trying to make the car faster and more comfortable for Mark. Your way seems to get Mark more involved, and maybe makes him more vested in the change, and then more willing to make it work. Is that why you're doing it that way?"

"Yeah, partly. But that's always been my style, engineering a car and working with a driver."

Walking back toward the garage area I see Alex Zanardi and Greg Moore walk out toward the outer pit wall and stop to talk. Alex's conversation is animated, with a lot of hand gestures. Greg is standing with his feet widespread and his arms folded across his chest. Alex cost Greg a good finish at Toronto by running into him in Turn 1. I'm glad to see the drivers talking out their problems instead of giving paybacks on the track.

Back in the Garage Area

Looking at the times from that session, Michael Andretti's is the only car on Goodyears in the top 10. The Firestone tires are almost always better when it's hot, but they are simply dominating here so far.

Blake Hamilton says he's got a lot of work because of all the engine changes this weekend. "The engines that ran those first two sessions will come out now and the 008 engines go in for Saturday practice and qualifying. We'll see 15 thou in qualifying."

"Woo, that's a lot of revs," I say. "They're turning them loose tomorrow, huh?"

"That's right. And then the 009 motors go in for the race. That's a 500-mile race spec engine."

At 4:50 p.m. the 18-car is on the setup pad. The 17-car is still at tech.

Mark Blundell changes into shorts and goes into the garage to talk to his crew. He and Daryl Fox engage in some teasing banter. I can tell Mark enjoys this a lot. He enjoys everything more since that first win at Portland.

Mark has dark hair, cut conservatively short. He walks with his hips out front and his toes splayed out. He looks kind of nerdy. If you put him in an office with computers and partitioned cubicles, he'd look right at home. Today he's all smiles and has time to sign posters, caps, and photos for fans. But a few minutes later he, Al Bodey, and Allen McDonald are hard at work at a table between the haulers.

Ten minutes later the 17-car comes back from tech inspection. Malcolm Oastler, the Reynard technical director, and Ian Hawkins, Ilmor engineer, have joined Mark, Al, and Allen. The 18-car is well into the engine change while the 17-car is just going on the setup pad.

About 6 o'clock I decide to leave for the hotel. As I get in my car I can see through the bleachers into pit lane where the 18-crew practices pit stops with the T-car. That's why they're performing so well during races.

SATURDAY

I'm at the track at 6:30 a.m. A few high clouds in the east create a great sunrise, with streaks of orange and red bleeding into the purple. People are already at work in the hospitality area. Breakfast smells drift in the air. Dave Loik, the PacWest chef, chops vegetable 6 feet off the ground on the ramp sticking out the back of his cook trailer. I stow my stuff in the Hollywood motor coach and walk over to the garage area. The 18-car is at the fueling station, and when I get to the PacWest garage the 18x car is on the setup pad. The 17-crew hovers over their cars also. The air is already 75 degrees and muggy. It's supposed to be hotter today than it was yesterday.

This will be an early day, with practice at 8 a.m. and qualifying at 10:15. I ask Chris Jaynes how late they worked last night. "We were at the track here 'til 10 o'clock with the motor change. We got to the motel at 11 and left this morning at 4:15."

That conversation with Chris makes me look around to see if I can tell how tired the guys are. Everyone is busy and so intense that I don't really detect any serious fatigue. This is the third of three races on consecutive weekends.

Chris Mellon works for Doug Peterson on the Hogan Racing crew. He asks about the deadline for my book. "I need to have the masters to the printer right after the first of the year," I tell him. "I'll do all I can with it until the deadline, but I probably won't really be perfectly happy with it. I'll just have to button it up and send it off."

"Same as we do with the cars," is Chris' comment. I never thought about it that way before. Every test or practice session or race starts at some specific time, and the cars have to be ready — safe and performing perfectly — no excuses.

Saturday Practice

It's 7:45 and I'm in the pit lane. This is an unusually early practice session because of the IROC practice and Automobile Racing Club of America (ARCA) stock car race later in the afternoon. Mark gets in the car to try out his seat. There's been some modifications, and Butch Winkle, Mark's crew chief, makes some adjustments after Mark gets out.

There's a lot of joking going on. Mark is a happy camper these days. He picks up a big orange traffic cone, turns it around, and holds the small end to his mouth like it's a megaphone. "Helloo, race fans," he yells to the totally empty stands that start far to our left in Turn 1 and continue way off to the right toward Turn 4. "Everybody sit dooowwwnnn." More laughter.

At 8 a.m. the session starts. Mauricio goes right out. He's in the 17x-car because they're saving the qualifying engine in the primary car. Mark is settling into his new seat and asking what fuel slot he's supposed to be using.

When Mauricio comes back in after his first run he's already in P1 at 233.403. He tells Andy, "The balance is pretty good." It's amazing he's that fast that quickly.

Andy: "Since you're wide open already, do you want to take the wing out now?" Mauricio says yes and Andy has the crew adjust both the front and rear wings to a smaller angle of attack. This will reduce aero downforce and drag.

When Mark comes in Allen says, "All right, mate, let's see what you think of these soft springs, especially at the rear."

Mark: "There's definitely more front grip in the car. But the rear of the car doesn't feel solid. There's a lack of security."

Later Mauricio complains of pushing in traffic. Mark says his car has improved and pushes less. But the rear still feels insecure. Allen makes some shock changes at the rear. At 8:22 there's a yellow flag for a track inspection. Mark is P10. Mauricio is P2 behind Scott Pruett.

During the yellow-flag period Mark reports the car has more roll, but the rear is "still walkin'. "Allen makes some adjustments, including adding 1 pound of air pressure to the right-side tires. He asks Mark, "Is this a grip problem or a rolling problem, do you think?"

Mark: "When you go into the turn you can feel the rear go into much more roll than we had yesterday. As soon as I get it in the corner and it starts loading, it starts to slip. And then toward the exit it's still walkin' and that's why I'm lifting out."

At 8:29 the green flag restarts the session. Both cars go out. Mark is P10; Mauricio is still P2 behind Pruett. Mark immediately improves to P7 with a 231.3-mph lap. When Mark returns to pit lane he tells Allen the car is better. "It's [the walking rear] still there, but it's better."

Andy is changing the pop-off valves on the 17-car. Maurico says, "All those valves are terrible." Raul Boesel has gone to P1 with a lap at 235.664 mph, moving Mauricio down to third. Mark is P10. Andy sends one of the valves to the CART trailer to be recalibrated.

Both cars continue to improve in small increments. Mauricio ends the session in P1 at 236.453 mph, with Mark in P4, 234.765 mph. Allen tells me that Mark likes the primary tires while most drivers like the option. "The option has more grip, but Mark feels it binds the car up."

Gifts for Blundell

Jade Gurss of Cotter Communications, the public relations firm working for Mercedes-Benz of North America, has called a press conference during which M-BNA presents Blundell with a high-tech mountain bike and a set of photos taken by Jesse Alexander, one of the most famous racing photographers. Both gifts stem from the Portland race victory.

Chatting with journalists before the proceedings begin, Mark says, "You have to have a tow to do the fast times today."

Mark Blundell and Crew Lined Up for Qualifying

Qualifying

This is the earliest qualifying session in my memory. At 10 a.m. we're in the pit lane and the cars are getting lined up against the wall. Mark is ninth in line to qualify and Mauricio 19th. Mark's turn comes and he turns a best lap of 31.392 seconds or 229 mph.

Jon Beekhuis, pit announcer for ABC and ESPN, kneels down next to the 17-car to interview Mo for the qualifying show. When his turn comes, Scott Pruett has the best time so far and Mark is in P5. Mauricio looks intense, as usual. His crew seems solemn; maybe it's just determination. They think Mark has had his wins, and it should be Mauricio's turn. His warm-up laps go quickly and his best timed lap is 30.836 seconds, 233 mph. That's good for P2, only a tenth of a second slower than Pruett's best.

Trevor Jackson looks disgusted. "P2 sucks."

Mark gets bumped down to 11th spot on the starting grid.

Pole Press Conference

The media conference room is very small, but today it's welcome because it's air conditioned. Raul Boesel, third on the starting grid, comes into the room first followed after a few minutes by Mauricio. Boesel explains why he brought the car back in after only one timed lap. "I had a big push, so there was no reason to complete the last lap."

Mauricio is introduced as the runner-up in the race last year and is asked about track conditions. "The conditions change, but only very minor. I ran everything my car had. Scott just beat me and that's fair."

Scott Pruett, the pole winner, says his Cosworth/Ford engine has a lot of horsepower and reliability.

The drivers are asked to comment on the "blockers" in the diffusers.

Mauricio says, "We tested here. They are a good thing. We have to be careful with the car on the track." Boesel agrees, as does Pruett. All three drivers are on Firestone tires; in fact, the first five cars and seven of the top 10 are running Firestone tires.

Jon Beekhuis Interviews Mauricio
For the ESPN2 Qualifying Show

Asked about his car, Mauricio says, "We have a very reliable car; maybe not the fastest, but the most consistent. The Firestone tires are very consistent. Unfortunately, these guys [Pruett and Boesel] run the same tire. [He grins, and everybody laughs.] We have a good car and a good team. Mark's done a good job, especially at Toronto. The team has grown and improved tremendously."

In the Garage

At 1 p.m. some of the guys are taking a lunch break. Race engines are going into the cars. The air is hot and muggy. This is Midwest weather at its worst. The temperature is in the 90s and the humidity is about the same. I ask Russ Cameron if the crews get some time off after this race.

"No," Russ says. "We have a tire test coming up at Sebring. We'll drive back to Indianapolis Sunday night and prep the cars on Monday. We'll take one car each for Mark and Mo. The trucks will leave Monday night or Tuesday morning, and the crews will travel Tuesday. We test Wednesday, Thursday, and Friday. Having a test team helps, but some of us like Andy and myself go to all the tests."

"Well, you don't have a life anyway," I say, grinning. "What else would you do?"

"Exactly," Russ says, and he's serious.

I ask Allen McDonald about the importance of balance at a track like this. "You're in the turns for most of the lap," he says. "Mark's 'walking at the rear' problem is him correcting for oversteer and then turning again. He won't admit it but he really doesn't like an oversteering car. It gets into a feedback loop all through the corner. He says it's pushing, but the rear is walking. If he'd let the rear of the car take a set like Mo does, he'd be faster."

I try to explain what I think he's saying. "So if the car is balanced, then the front and rear tires are at about the same slip angle. In that condition there's less scrub than if that same car is pushing."

"Yes," Allen says.

In more detail, Mark is feeling the rear come out as the rear tires try to go to a slip angle that will produce the lateral force necessary to keep the car in the turn. Mark doesn't have the confidence there is a limit to the movement he feels. He calls it "nervous at the rear." Allen has to dial in some push to keep him from feeling the rear come out. Compared to Mauricio's car, Mark's front tires are at a higher slip angle and produce more drag for the same lateral grip. His rear tires are at a smaller slip angle and aren't generating as much lateral grip as Mauricio's. Mark's car also has bigger Gurney flaps and higher angles of attack on the wings. The result is slower lap times.

Extra Practice

The CART cars get an extra practice this afternoon after the ARCA race. The green flag starts the half-hour session at 2:57. Both the PacWest cars are mainly scrubbing sets of tires for the race, and using their T-cars to save the race engines.

After several runs on the track Mark asks, "How many sets to go, Allen?"

Allen: "We've agreed to scrub some of Mo's tires, so we have three more to do."

Mark: "In your dreams."

At 3:29 Mauricio is out of the car. Mark makes another couple of runs trying front-wing adjustments. He gets out of his car about a minute before the checkered flag at 3:43. The speeds in this session were 5 mph slower than qualifying.

The cars are towed back to the garage area. I ask Mauricio if he thinks it will be difficult to pass tomorrow.

"If it's hotter," he says, "the cars will be less stable because the air gets thinner. [He presses his thumb and forefinger together to illustrate thinner.] You just need to run more downforce."

The crews are changing engines, installing the fresh 500-mile spec race engines. They work in covered garages that are open on both sides, but there is no cooling breeze today. The team has a couple of fans with 2-foot diameter blades on stands and they help some. There's certainly less banter this afternoon. Instead there's a lot of pasty faces, serious looks, and slack-jawed stares. This is the first time I've ever noticed the guys looking tired. But there's no griping at all.

When I get back to Ann Arbor, I stop and get myself a six-pack of beer. Then I decide to get a burger and eat in the room. After that wonderful meal I go to the lobby to see if any of the PacWest hospitality people are in the bar. Dave Loik is having a beer and a smoke, so I sit down to talk. Several other people come in from the track and some join us.

Dave asks me some questions about the book; how I got the idea and how it's going. "Have you seen anything negative about the team?" he asks.

I have to think about that for a moment. "Not really," I tell him. "Nobody's gotten mad at me. I try to stay out of the way, but even so, everyone's been very friendly and patient. Now that you asked, that's pretty extraordinary, don't you think? As far as I'm concerned it's a great bunch of people."

"That it is," he agrees.

SUNDAY

I wake up early and don't have any luck going back to sleep, so I get up and get after it. Since I'm staying overnight and flying out Monday morning, I don't have to check out. I'm at the track at 6:30, in time to watch another magnificent sunrise. This morning there are some purple and gray clouds framing a big, red ball of a sun. The air is cool and moist, just getting us off guard with brief comfort before a baking day.

By 7:15 motors are groaning and whooping in the throes of warming. Chris Jaynes tells me they were through here at 7:30 last night but were here again at 5:30. I like to stay at the same motel as the crew so I can hang out with them in the evenings. I'm not at their motel this weekend, but it sounds like it's no loss.

At 7:45 I'm in the hospitality area just in time to see the end of a TV replay of Saturday qualifying for the German Grand Prix from Hockenheim. Gerhard Berger is announcing his retirement. Mark Blundell is here looking preppy in a white polo shirt, khaki shorts, and white tennis shoes. In contrast Mauricio is wearing a Hugo Boss shirt and jeans and soft, brown moccasins with no socks. Stella, his wife, is here looking very pretty in black pants and a white, sleeveless top. We all watch the start of the F1 race on one of the big-screen TVs hooked up to Speedvision through a dish on one of the motor coaches.

Warm-Up

At 8:45 I walk to the PacWest pit boxes for the 9 a.m. warm-up session. Jim Hamilton tells me the cars have gone up on downforce about 8% from the qualifying settings, so the cars will be better in traffic during the race. The session goes green right at 9 o'clock. When Mark comes back in off the track the first time the crew does a practice pit stop. The pit boxes here are short and the cars have problems turning in and getting straight in the box. Ando talks to Mark about how he has to be careful turning in during the race.

The sun is hot on my back, and I can feel that first drop of sweat running down my spine. The race-morning warm-up is a practice session for the CART race officials as well as for the teams. The pit stewards talk a lot to Control on the radio and also among themselves off the radio. They lean toward each other in pairs and each person pulls one earphone away from an ear so they can talk.

When the PacWest cars are in their pit boxes the talk between Mark and Allen and Andy and Mauricio is low key. There is an intermittent cut-out on the radio that is annoying, but it doesn't eat up much of the conversations.

After a run Mauricio says, "It hits and bounces back quite high like we're a lot softer than yesterday."

Andy: "It's probably the extra downforce, Morris."

Mauricio: "I have a little bit of push too. Coming out of 4 it just gets a bit light. But I don't feel the grip is the level that I would like to have, Andy. The car is hitting in 3 and 4, which it never did before. And a little bit at 2."

Andy: "We're going to put set 13 on for scuffing. We have a tire that was down close on 6 pounds, Morris. That's probably the soft feeling and the bottoming."

Al Bodey tells Mark, "P1 is Pruett with a 229.7."

Mark: "With the [wing] angles a bit more acute, at turn-in the rear of the car is just not comfortable."

Allen: "OK; we'll try going a little softer on the front bump."

Max Papis blows another Toyota engine in Turn 1, and a few minutes later he jogs past behind us going to his spare car. On the track I see Mark pull alongside one of the Penske cars going into Turn 1. He makes the pass on the inside before the middle of the corner. That's a good sign. The turbulence of the car in front can make the following car feel light. In that case Mark looked comfortable enough. Maybe he'll be able to pass some cars in the race.

Mark is out of the car before the end of the session. He talks to Allen about the difference in the concrete area where the pit boxes are and the asphalt pit lane, saying the concrete is slicker, and he'll need to get over onto the asphalt as soon as possible after a pit stop.

Andre Ribeiro ends up with the quickest lap in this session. He turns a best lap of 232 mph. Mauricio is P2 with a lap at 231-mph average. The stands are about 20% full.

At the end of the session I ask Allen McDonald about the big turning vanes they were planning to use earlier in the weekend. "We don't need them," Allen explains. "We were low on grip when we tested here, and we thought we'd need more so we brought those vanes. But we have more grip for some reason."

"Well, Allen," I say, "you can't just let grip come and go like that. You have to account for it."

He laughs. I'm sure there are a lot of things that happen that they just don't have time to analyze as well as they'd like. There's only so much time on the tracks, so they have to carefully prioritize what they do.

Getting Hotter

I go up on the media center roof to watch the start of the IROC race. It's starting an hour late because of a power failure here at the track earlier. The heat is very distracting. The metal rail around the roof viewing area is so hot I can't touch it. Al Unser Jr., Jimmy Vasser, and Alex Zanardi are in this race and the CART race also. I don't see how they could afford to try too hard in this race, since it's much less important to them. But they're competitive people and it's probably tough to back off.

THE RACE

The CART grid is a few minutes late because of the power failure and the IROC race. They have to keep to their schedule because the CART race is on live television starting at 1 p.m. At 12:15 the 17-car rolls up to the front row of the pre-grid.

I ask Andy about the race strategy. "We want to stay on the lead lap and wait for the 20-lap sprint to the finish. We'll pit on a yellow flag if we have less than a half-tank of fuel."

The drivers get into the cars and I go back to the pit box and take up my station. When I put on my headphones and turn on the scanner, I hear Control say, "If power goes out again, we'll have flags in the same places as the lights." The stands look like they're 90% full.

The cars roll out for the pace laps and form into two rows to avoid the huge crash last year in the U.S. 500, when they started three abreast. Jim Swintal waves the green flag and the race is on. Mauricio gets a great start, and it looks like he's going to lead Pruett into the first turn but Pruett takes advantage of the inside line and they go through Turn 1 side-by-side. Pruett holds on and leads the first lap, but Mauricio goes high and passes Pruett on the outside at the exit of Turn 2. The leaders are Mauricio, Pruett, Boesel, Parker Johnstone, and Zanardi. Mauricio creeps away from Pruett and builds a 3-second lead.

On lap 10 P.J. Jones' Toyota engine blows up catastrophically, complete with fire and smoke. At the same time CART loses power to the timing light at the Start/Finish line. During the yellow-flag laps, Billy Kamphausen runs up the steeply banked track and kneels down next to the outer wall. Control tells the teams to let their drivers know Billy is up there on the track working. I hear Ando tell Mark and Russ tell Mauricio. Billy manages to repair the damage, probably caused by debris from the blown engine. I think I hear on the radio he duct-tapes the light back in place.

Ando Standing on the Wall

Mark started 11th and lost a couple of spots in the early laps, but he regains them when a few cars stop for fuel during this caution period. Mauricio tells Russ Cameron, "The car is going loose, but I've got it handled. I moved the sway bar." Mark is also having handling problems, and Ando is coaching him on how to adjust the bars.

The race restarts on lap 21. Michael Andretti started 19th and improved to sixth on the restart. At lap 30 he's in third behind Mauricio and Pruett. Russ tells Mauricio, "Pick up the pace. Michael is passing people."

Paul Tracy is pressing Mark for 12th and Ando says, "Stay away from Tracy. Hang in there."

Another yellow flag for debris in Turn 3 slows the race on lap 34, just in time for a pit stop. Michael Andretti beats Mauricio out of the pits. I hear Mo say he messed up. Russ says, "Follow him awhile. No problem."

Andy says to Mauricio, "Your used tires look perfect."

Andre Ribeiro stopped during the earlier yellow-flag period and stayed out this time, moving to first place. The order at the restart on lap 40 is Ribeiro, Andretti, Mauricio, Pruett, and Boesel. Mark is ninth at the restart but falls back rapidly, complaining of a push. Ando tries to get him to work with the weight jacker and sway bars, but nothing seems to work. He's 12th on lap 54 when Parker Johnstone crashes heavily at the exit of Turn 2. Another yellow flag waves and the cars slow. I hear Mauricio say, "I ran over something." Most of the drivers pit.

Mauricio's engine stops running on the backstretch. He says he's running out of fuel but it turns out to be something electronic. He has to be pushed into the pit box, and he loses a lot of time. The crew takes the sidepods off, and as they're working on the car I hear Mauricio say, "Something is majorly wrong."

Finally the engine fires up and he gets away. At the restart he's four laps down in 20th spot. Mark restarts eighth. The leaders are Dario Franchitti, Bobby Rahal, Zanardi, Pruett, and Patrick Carpentier. Ando tells Mark to pull in closer to the wall on the next stop. Mark says, "The rear is still nervous."

Mauricio's chance at a win is over, but he's still running. Mark Moore says, "Mo's running 232s." Several cars are out with transmission problems, including Jimmy Vasser and Andre Ribeiro. Then the same thing happens to Michael Andretti. As a result, Mark moves up to sixth on lap 101.

Just before halfway, at lap 120, the cars begin to come in for green-flag pit stops. A small fire flares up during Mauricio's stop and Roscoe's leg is burned very slightly. His firesuit saves him a lot of pain. The water used to douse him wets the pit box enough that Mark has to be careful coming in for his stop a few laps later.

Then Bobby Rahal hits the wall at Turn 2 about the same place as Parker. At the restart Carpentier leads followed by Pruett, Tracy, Herta, and Zanardi, who begins to move up. He takes the lead on lap 153. Mark has kept pace with Zanardi, moving up to fourth as Zanardi takes the lead. Mauricio is 12th, five laps down, but Mark Moore says, "We're the fastest car in the race, guys."

Mauricio makes another pit stop on lap 164 because a tire exploded on the backstretch. Mark comes in on lap 171. Ando is saying, "Right down the middle." I'm so close I can see the pieces of paper and plastic fall out of the front of the cooling ducts as Mark stops the car.

Mark Blundell Stops Under Butch's Hand

Wheels Come Off and Fuel Goes In

Mauricio Out-Drags Michael Andretti

I hear Mauricio ask why the tire exploded. Russ says, "We're talking to Firestone about it. We'll give you an answer pretty quick."

A few minutes later Russ says, "It looks like maybe you ran over something and punctured it."

Scott Pruett crashes in Turn 2 on lap 174. It looks the same as what happened to Parker and Rahal. During the cleanup Mark tells Ando, "The car still has a bit of push even when the tires are fresh."

At the green flag on lap 183 Zanardi is still leading followed by Blundell, Tracy, de Ferran, and Bryan Herta. Mauricio is seventh, five laps down.

Al Speyer, Firestone director of motorsports, comes to talk to Allen McDonald about running out of tires. Allen tells me they qualified on the primary tires and are running quicker in the race on optionals, but Firestone didn't bring enough optional tires.

Ten laps after the restart Mark is within 2 seconds of Zanardi, but he's yelling "push; gotta push" into the radio. Ando tells him to hang in there and work with the bars. At lap 200 Mark is 4 seconds behind Zanardi and 8 seconds ahead of Paul Tracy.

Mauricio pits again on lap 204. Mark Moore says, "Let's have a good one this time."

Russ Cameron tells Mauricio, "When you leave the pits take it nice and easy. There's nobody else on the same lap. Let's save that gearbox. Everybody push on the rear wing."

It's a good stop, which makes Mo's earlier problems even worse. If he was among the leaders right now he could win this one. Mark is up there in the hunt but doesn't seem to have the car he can drive around Zanardi.

Mark comes in on lap 211. Ando talks him in: "Nice and easy. Steady now. Steady. Hold it. Hold it. Nice and easy."

Another great stop! Butch says, "Good job, fellas."

This is a 2-mile track so the race is 250 laps. At lap 220 Zanardi is leading with Mark a long way back but still on the same lap. Russ asks Mauricio to slow up and give Mark a tow. Fans are beginning to leave their seats and head for the parking lot.

Mark gains on Mauricio but he's still 200 yards back when he yells about a push. Russ tells Mo to pull away so Mark can speed up. Mauricio can't go to the end without another stop for fuel. There is some speculation among the team that Zanardi might also have to stop, while Mark has enough to go to the checkered flag. Some suspense develops, and Bruce comes down out of the scoring cart to talk to Allen and Ando. Mauricio pits for a splash of fuel on lap 238.

Ando is encouraging Mark on the radio every time he comes down the frontstraight. "Four laps to go. Hang in there."

I hear Control talking to Jim Swintal: "Two laps next time by, starter."

"Copy; two laps next time by," Jim answers. He's probably tapping the flag on the railing.

Ando says, "One to go, Mark. Only one."

Control says, "Checkered flag next time by."

Finally, Ando says, "Way to go, Billy, bring her home. Bring her home."

Zanardi wins. Mark is second and Gil de Ferran third. The 18-crew yells and heads off running toward Start/ Finish.

Mauricio finishes sixth, down six laps, and has the fastest lap of the race at 232.581 mph vs. 226.979 for the winner, Zanardi. Only 10 cars are running at the end of the race. Seven of the cars that fell out listed transmission as the reason for retirement.

The 18-Crew and Mark Blundell Celebrate

Press Conference

The conference room is cramped but it's cool. Gil de Ferran finished third. He talks about how the car had a lot of understeer at first but they kept working on it.

Mark is introduced by Mike Zizzo, CART director of public relations. Mike says this is Mark's third podium in the last four races, and it's his best career finish on an oval. Mike asks him if he switched from the hard-compound Firestone tires to the softer tires. Mark answers, "We actually had too much understeer at the beginning of the race. We went onto the options and the car balance came good. We had to go back out at the end on the harder tires because we ran out of the softer ones. That's why we dropped off a bit of speed at the end there. The tires overall worked very well and were very consistent."

Alex isn't here yet so Mike opens the floor for questions. Someone asks about the vibration Mark had during the race. "We got a lot of pick-up on the harder tires," Mark says.

Mark Blundell, Alex Zanardi, and Gil de Ferran

"We had a lot of vibration. I was hangin' on for dear life. My left hand went to sleep on me. It's OK now; it's still working."

Zanardi shows up about 4:45. Mike says this is his first victory on an oval and he's the new points leader over Paul Tracy in second. This is the sixth victory in a row for Firestone.

Alex says, "You have to be lucky to win a 500-mile race. I was trying to take care of my equipment. Other people throw their equipment into the walls. That's not a good idea. The car was running beautifully. Honda seems to need less fuel than the other engines. I have to thank them a lot.

"Also my engineer, Morris Nunn, has never won here before and I'm very proud to win for him. The car was pushing a little bit but it was OK. We have to thank Firestone too."

The drivers are asked about the track. Mark says, "Basically you have to drive to the limits of the car. You try to optimize it every time you go on the track. We got a lot of components inside we can adjust, with corner-weight jackers and roll bars. There's plenty of work goin' on inside the cockpit. At the same time you're in communications with the pits, so they're givin' you some ideas of what we can do when we come into the pits. You're tryin' to improve the performance every time you're out there. The object is to try to win with what you've got underneath you. If you do 500 miles like that and finish, then you can sit where we are [grinning]."

Paul Dana, writer for *AutoWeek*, asks if the drivers knew about the Reynard gearbox problems and what they did to keep that from happening to them.

Mark answers, "Yeah, I was aware, my team kept me informed about the transmission problems. Basically what we did, we just took it very easy on the transmission on downshifting, coming into the pits, and even short shifting somewhat going out, although you have to be careful because the gearing is so long here. It gives the transmission a bit of a thump. We were aware of it and we tried to drive accordingly."

David Phillips asks why the crashes happened at Turn 2. Was that a difficult corner?

Mark says, "I have to be perfectly honest and say there is no way the car was as stable as we had it at both the Michigan races last year. We could place the car wherever we wanted and it was stuck to the road. Today it was very tricky. Traffic was very hard. Even trying to come by a backmarker, you had to be in a real strong position on the road to make sure you could get by him. When I tried to come up behind Mauricio [sounds like Maritzio], I had to back off because I almost ended up in the wall comin' out of Turn 4. For no apparent reason, it's just a character of the car." The consensus among the drivers is that the aerodynamic blockers hurt the stability of the cars.

Alex Zanardi is asked if it bothers him that there are bad feelings about his aggressive driving style. He answers, "It's normal when you do well that people — they don't hate you — but they want to be in your position. That's normal. When I was second to Mark in Toronto, I said congratulations, but, uh...."

"You hated me," Mark says, grinning.

"No," Alex says and the whole room laughs. Mark is laughing too, but he blushes and wipes nervously at his chin.

"No," Alex repeats earnestly. "That's not true. He deserved the race. He drove well. I was driving hard, trying to push him into a mistake. But he didn't do a mistake. He had a good car, but he took advantage very well of that factor. But I would rather have been in his position. I'd rather be able to get in front of him."

The press conference winds down and I walk to the PacWest garage to talk to people about the race. As I'm walking I think about the genuine, human conversations that came out in that press conference and how different that is from just a few years ago, when Al Unser Jr. or Michael Andretti would mumble a few sponsor and team platitudes, just trying to get out of the room as soon as they could.

The worst I ever saw was at Loudon, N.H., a few years ago when Team Penske finished one, two, three and the drivers — Emerson Fittipaldi, Al Unser Jr., and Paul Tracy — bad-mouthed Goodyear, their tire manufacturer, saying there hadn't been enough engineers on hand to take tire temperatures. This new batch of drivers may have foreign accents, but they are decent, expressive human beings.

John Oreovicz Gathers Quotes

Garage Comments

I'm in no hurry to leave and it's a good thing, because the traffic getting out of here is a mess. In the garage area the guys are packing up for the trip back to Indianapolis. Russ Cameron says Mauricio's engine restarted as soon as they changed one of the black boxes in the engine management system. "He lost five laps while we figured out what was wrong. The blown tire wouldn't have been so bad by itself. The car was good. He set fast lap."

Steve Fusek says, "Mauricio is not happy."

I asked Roscoe how bad he got burned. "Aw, it wasn't that bad," he says. "My leg will be a little red. I got bumped and there was just a little fire."

At 5:15 I'm getting my stuff out of the belly locker of the Hollywood motor coach when Mark comes back from the media center. Everyone claps as he comes in and his pleasure shows. Bruce tells Greg Watson to break out some champagne and they all toast Mark's runner-up finish.

I congratulate Bruce on the good result and say, "You know, several people have told me I should point out to you that you guys weren't worth a shit until I got involved with the team."

Bruce grins broadly and says, "I was wondering when you were going to say that."

I meet up with Alex Cross, Swift Engineering vice president, and we decide to get in the traffic leaving the track and stop somewhere for some food. It takes us an hour to get out of the track, but then we find a great pizza and beer place called Kelly's. It's still hot and humid, but we sit outside on a deck in the shade and feel an occasional breeze. After an hour of conversation I'm wound down from the race and head back to the motel in Ann Arbor.

Up at 4:30 a.m. to make the drive to the Detroit airport, it's still dark when I leave the motel. I'm on my way home.

CHAPTER 19

MID-OHIO

On a plane again August 7 I'm flying from SFO to Denver and then on to Columbus, Ohio. Mid-Ohio, along with Elkhart Lake, Road Atlanta, and Laguna Seca, is a classic natural-terrain road-racing course. People come from all over the Midwest and camp here for days to revel in racing.

We're staying at the Knights Inn in Mansfield, Ohio, which is about an hour drive north of Columbus. The Knights Inn is a modest but clean old motel. A restaurant across the street called Damon's is full of race fans. That's where I find most of the PacWest crew at dinner time. After a few beers with them I'm in bed early.

FRIDAY

To get to the track from Mansfield you drive about 15 miles south through some small towns on twisty two-lane roads. The track is bordered by fields and woods. Everything is very green, which means it will probably rain sometime during the weekend.

CART practice is not until 11 a.m. today. At 9 a.m. in the PacWest hospitality area, Mauricio tells me about the tire problem at Michigan. "It must have been a puncture. The car started pulling to the left, so I knew something was wrong. I started to slow and the left-front tire just exploded. I turned a little to the left to get the weight on the corner that still had a tire. I probably lost a lap because I had to go slow through 3 and 4 so I could get to the pits. I was already five laps down."

Mark joins the conversation, and they start talking about the near-misses they survived during the race. "I would have gotten a tow from Mauricio late in the race," Mark says, "but the car pushed terribly. And I was a long way back from him, too."

"I almost hit the wall in Turn 4," Mauricio says. "When I passed Franchitti, it slid up toward the wall and I came within inches of hitting it. [He puts both hands up in front of him like he's holding the steering wheel.] I was just about to take my hands off the wheel when I saw I'd made it. The next time by I could see the tire marks going up toward the wall."

Mark goes off to talk to someone, and I ask Mauricio, "Can you hear the rumbling sound the cars make?"

"I can't hear much in the car, only a whistling noise," he answers. "Even the engine note is way behind the car at those speeds."

"You've been doing some tire testing for Firestone. How long will it take before that begins to help you in races?"

"Probably at Vancouver," Mauricio says. "At Sebring we were testing the street-course tire. The front tire at this race is the one Zanardi liked at the test they had here a month ago. He probably had an advantage at Michigan because of a tire test he did there. If you're the one telling Firestone which tire you like, it definitely helps."

Wanting to Go Over the Wall

At 10:25 I'm in the pit lane walking toward Turn 1 to get a ride in a PPG pace car. In the 18-car pit box, Roy Wilkerson is by himself practicing changing tires. He's at the right rear of the car changing a tire again and again. He's sweaty and breathing hard, but he's determined to earn Gavin Hamilton's spot changing the outside rear tire on Mark's car.

Pace-Car Ride

I stand in line awhile and then get into a BMW driven by Pattie Neff. She got started in racing by driving street cars in autocrosses. Now she races in BMW club events. This is her first year on the pace-car team.

There are a lot of elevation changes at Mid-Ohio and I can feel the car get light over the brows. Pattie says, "You have to place the car precisely to do a good time."

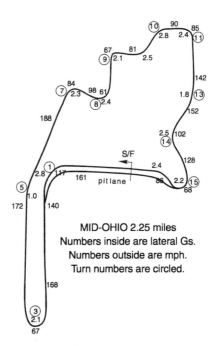

MID-OHIO 2.25 miles
Numbers inside are lateral Gs.
Numbers outside are mph.
Turn numbers are circled.

Friday Practice

I've been spending most of my time at the races in the pits and garage areas watching the crews work. Today I decide to walk over the bridge at Turn 1 and spend some time watching the cars on track. Of course, I'm still listening to the PacWest guys using my scanner. Standing on the outside of Turn 1 I can see the straight going up to the hairpin Turn 3 and the backstraight coming back down the hill to Turn 7.

Allen tells Mark to take a two-lap installation run and bed in a new set of brakes. Andy has similar instructions for Mauricio: "Morris, take as many laps as you need to bed in these rotors."

The green flag starts this session at 11:15. Whistles and cheers go up from the people in shorts and T-shirts standing or sitting on the grass all around me. These people like their racing!

Mark is the last driver out of the pit lane. He drives slowly through Turn 1 and accelerates hard up the hill toward Turn 3. Michel Jourdain Jr. causes an early red flag and the cars go back into the pit lane. I walk down the hill to the fence to watch the cars through the up-and-down part of the course, Turns 7, 8, and 9.

Mauricio says the car is pushing in the slow corners. Andy tells him, "I think we need to run some more to establish a baseline. When you get the push, is it before you get to the power or when you go to the power?"

Mauricio: "When I go into the power."

Andy: "I just raised the rear one flat because that's what the skids are telling us to do."

Mark comes in complaining about the boost fluctuating. "The gearbox is fine, but the brake pedal is too soft." Allen tells the crew to change the pop-off valve.

Mark: "There's too much push in the car mid to exit, especially in the mid-speed corners. A bit too much roll in Turn 1, in the rear, but I'm gonna try going up on the rear bar first and see if that cuts it down. That might help the push as well."

Mauricio comes back in saying the changes made the car worse. Andy says, "Understood. What I'd like to do then is take that change out, and I'll go two sweeps the other way. That should help the low-speed on the power. We'll change the rear wing next time."

Mauricio: "The track is terrible compared to when we tested here. The car is crashing more. It's like bang, bang, bang, because it's too stiff. Still it rolls more at the back. I don't feel the downforce I had at the back before. I don't like the way it feels at all. It's like I lost grip all around."

Andy: "Understood, Morris. I want to put more preload on the waste gate to improve the boost. I think the big change since the test is the front tires. We'll have to make some changes to accommodate that." Firestone has a new front tire for this race, the one Mauricio talked about that was developed from Zanardi's feedback during the tire test here.

Mark is still having boost problems. Allen asks him is he has any feeling for the car. "The car feels better with the bar. It's got a touch of looseness, just like under accel and from mid to about 65% into the turn, it looses a bit of rear grip. We could maybe come down a flat all around again, just to bring the ride heights into synch. I wouldn't want to go to two flats."

After the changes Mark says, "Watch out. I'm gonna lay some rubber out of the pit." He smokes the rear tires big time.

Mauricio is back in saying the car is still crashing down. "When I put the power down it rolls onto the outside rear." He and Andy discuss some changes.

Mark comes in again saying, "It's better, but it still doesn't feel correct. It's still got some problem with the engine, but it's cleaner. The tim doesn't seem to have any effect. There's a little bit too much pitch in the car. Under the braking there's too much pitch. It's unstable on entry. Through Turn 1 the balance is OK, but it's got too much movement fore and aft. It's lackin' a bit of low-speed grip on entry as well. The rear is hookin' up OK."

Mark continues to talk about the car. "It feels unstable on the entry to the corner, so when I go in I have to brake earlier than what I'd like to, and then, when that movement comes in, I don't take any good amount of front grip into the turns. Then I got a little bit of walk when I go in. If the front grip picks up then the rear of the car comes through and it feels a little bit unstable. After that it quiets itself down and I can carry it off the turn, but it doesn't feel as rosy as what we should be. Goin' up on the rear bar seems to be a little bit of help on entry, but actually I'm not sure it's not detrimental to us at the moment, because I think it might be makin' it a little bit too nervous at the rear, sheddin' a little bit of grip." This is vintage Mark Blundell feedback.

Andy tells Mauricio about a shock change: "I put some low-speed bump in the car which was helping at Sebring, so it should help here for that feeling of roll. It should also stop the rear coming down on the straights. I'm also going to take some rebound out at the rear because I think we're trying to hold the back of the car down too much. If you feel that hurts the car on entry you've still got the adjustment on the tim."

After a run on the track Andy asks Mauricio if he likes the changes. "I like the changes on the car." Then his voice fades into a bunch of white noise and whistles.

Mark Moore, Mo's chief mechanic, says, "This radio absolutely sucks. Dump the repeater."

The teams use a "repeater" in the transporters to receive, boost, and retransmit the radio signals. Maybe it's not working. I'm glad to know it's not just my scanner. At some tracks the radio sounds great. Here I agree with Mark; it sucks.

Right at the end of the session Mauricio runs out of gas and has to be towed back to pit lane. This was a tough practice session for the PacWest boys. Alex Zanardi, running as Mauricio said, on front tires that he helped to develop at this track, had the best lap with a 66.399-seconds lap. Gil de Ferran is second followed by Scott Pruett, Christian Fittipaldi, and Bryan Herta. Mo is in P9; Mark is P13.

Between Sessions

The garage area at Mid-Ohio is unique. The garage buildings look like rustic log cabins and they have stairs up to walkways above each garage, so the fans can look down on the teams as they work. Since each team thinks it has some secret techie tricks, this level of access is not smiled upon. The PacWest guys have their setup pads at the other end of the garages from the walkway, and they have to keep the cars covered more than usual.

During that session I heard reference to the "tim," so they must be using it here. I also see Trevor Jackson working with the equipment he uses to bleed the tim. The device takes a lot of time and effort, so it must work.

Allen McDonald, Al Bodey, and Mark Blundell

Friday Qualifying

The green flag flies at 3:02 p.m. for the 30-minute fast-guys' qualifying session. As Mauricio goes out Andy says, "Remember, Morris, tim has more adjustment in it this session."

Mo does well early in the session, holding down P3 with a 67.675-seconds lap. The PA announcer says he's visibly quick in the back part of the track. Mark is P7 with a lap at 67.901. Then, 7 minutes into the session, Bryan Herta is P1 followed by Scott Pruett and Greg Moore. Mauricio is P7 and Mark P10.

Mark comes in saying, "We got less grip going into Turn 1, and it's unnerving because it turns in and tucks in very quick and just makes the rear of the car, very quickly, try to overtake the front. You have to really catch it. Under brakin' it does a little bit better, but it's still the same goin' in. Over the bumps it feels good. Still, brakin' is the problem area for us, where we need to tidy up on. We still have too much push on entry and up to mid."

Allen: "Up 200 pounds on the front springs, please. Drop the front ride height a flat and a half. Do you want to take out a bit of front wing as well? Will that help you?"

Mark: "Maybe we should take some out. Also, in sixth gear we're on the limiter like halfway down the straight. We're way short on top."

Mauricio: "It's better than this morning. But it still needs some grip. Maybe we should do the changes at the back that we discussed. It's still touching."

Mark comes back after the stiffer front-spring change: "It's a little bit better in the high-speed stuff; in the lower speed it's about the same. Through 1 it's a bit of a tighter car through there; it turns in much quicker."

Allen: "Up two on the front springs. Down a flat and a half on the front ride height."

Mauricio is back in again saying, "The car is just sliding too much."

Andy: "What we're discussing here is whether to soften the shocks up a little all around to try to pick up a little grip. You're within two-tenths of fifth on the grid. We'll just put it back as it was with a fresh set of tires and give you the car you know."

Mauricio: "Ten-four; let's do that."

Andy: "Do you want the ride heights down again, Morris, or just leave those because of the problems we had?"

Mauricio: "Leave those."

Mark is still not happy with the car. "Still too much push in the car, Allen."

Allen: "What is the problem with the car?"

Mark: "Too much understeer, through 1 especially. The understeer level picked up as soon as I turned in. I couldn't come onto the gas early enough. On the slow-speed corners as well, still this lack of front grip, but with the bar stiffer, a lot more problems going into the corner. It's just carrying too much push on entry. I went up on tim two clicks, but the definition on clicks is not there. We need that better again. And the engine is still not running clean. There's still three or four points on the track where it falters."

Allen: "Did it feel better with the extra tim or not?"

Mark: "Gonna leave it in. I'm not gonna take it out. It went up with the bar as well at the same time."

Allen: "Do you want a turn of front wing just to help you with the push?"

Mark: "Give me a half a hole each side."

Allen: "All right, and you're going to go back on the bar, are ya? OK, go for it."

With a few minutes to go all the cars in this session are on the track trying for a time. Mauricio comes by on the pit straight and I hear him say, "Too much traffic, Andy."

Andy answers, "That's OK, there's still 3 minutes."

But neither Mauricio or Mark improve their times. The checkered flag ends qualifying at 3:33. Bryan Herta sets a new track record at 66.277 seconds. Zanardi is P1 followed by de Ferran, Moore, and Franchitti. Mo ends up ninth and Mark 13th. Mo gets out of the car and walks over to Andy, taking off his helmet. "We've got work to do," he says.

There was a breeze earlier, but the air is still and muggy now in the garage area. The 17-car goes on the setup pad. I ask Mark Moore what Mo meant by, "work to do."

"We're pretty close," Mark says, "but he's fighting the car. The tires are different since the test."

At 5:30 Mark Moore and the 17-crew are finishing up pit-stop practice in pit lane. The Formula Atlantic cars are on course qualifying. An hour later work is winding down in the PacWest garage so I head back to the motel. After a very mediocre dinner at Damon's, it's in the sack and to sleep.

SATURDAY

The drive to the track is easy today thanks to directions for a back-road route from truckie Mike Todd. I didn't sleep well at all, ending up just laying there worrying about getting the book project done by the end of the year. Sometimes I know I'm gathering some good stuff, and other times I wonder if people will think it's just a bunch of junk. Making my flight out of Columbus worries me too. It doesn't leave until 9 p.m., but the race doesn't start until 3 and the traffic could be horrible.

At 7 a.m. in the CART paddock the air is cool but humid. A hazy sunrise brightens the sky. We have a chance of thunderstorms later in the day. Tim Douthat is welding something in the Hollywood hauler. The cars are on the setup pads and the numbers are coming from the engineers.

Practice

The green flag waves at 9:25 to start this 1-hour practice session. Both PacWest cars are on track right away. I hear Control say, "The 18-car sounds rough."

Allen tells Mark, "Pit this lap."

Mark says, redundantly, "This engine is still not running right. It's got no grunt. It's flat. The boost is still variable. It's not brisk." The crew takes the sidepods off, and they begin to troubleshoot the engine. At 9:32 they fire it up but it still sounds rough. Ian Hawkins and Mark McArdle, Ilmor engineers, are looking worried. I hear Butch tell somebody to take all the preload out of the waste gates. Charlie Guilinger, Jeff Stafford, and Daryl Fox go to the garage to get the T-car ready.

Mauricio comes in off course and says to Andy, "Still got some push. It's a lot more push; it's even more undrivable than yesterday. Still quite a bit of roll at the back as well."

Andy: "The push in the car, is that after initial turn-in or when you get after the power again?"

Mauricio: "When I get into the gas, that's when I get the push."

Andy: "Is there pumping to the back of the car or is it more under control compared to yesterday in terms of ride?"

Mauricio: "The ride is softer, but the car is just lacking rear grip because of the roll, I feel, at the back."

Mark's car fires up again and sounds better. Butch radios back to the garage, "Charlie, you and Daryl hang on out there. We're just gonna go out for a lap and see if that fixed it." Mark goes back on track, but the engine sounds bad to me.

Andy is still talking to Mauricio: "We'll try and pick up some grip by coming down all around on the springs."

Mark Moore says, "Change all the springs, guys."

Andy tells Mark Moore, "Up one flat at the front and two flats at the rear."

Mark comes back in saying, "It sounds like it's on seven cylinders." The crew starts to change the spark plugs.

Mark Moore says, "Those guys are eatin' it. They should have been running their T-car by now."

Mauricio comes back on pit lane and stops, saying the car is still rolling too much. "It's definitely better now that it's softer at the back." Andy and Jim Hamilton go over the wall and look at the rear of the 17-car.

Andy: "Is it the roll angle that's the problem or is it the rate of roll?"

Mauricio: "It's the speed of the roll. Believe it or not there's less bounce with the softer springs."

Andy: "We have a theory about that [chuckles]. If you don't like your bar hooked up back there, let's do it with the shocks like we did it at Sebring. Did the basic balance change at all?"

Mauricio: "I feel I have less push at the exit."

Mark and Mauricio go back out at 9:49. The monitor shows Zanardi is P1 with Pruett and Herta right behind him.

I hear Control say black flag car-18. Mark exceeded the pit-lane speed and has to come in for a stop-and-go penalty that will cost him some track time. Al Bodey tells Mark, "Use your cruise-control button, please."

No one would explain the details of the cruise control to me, but I think it works like this: There are white stripes across the track at pit-in and pit-out. The driver pushes the button as he starts to pull out of the pit box, and the computer uses the wheel-speed sensor to control the speed of the car over the distance to pit-out. Coming into the pits the driver hits the button at pit-in and the computer controls the speed over the distance to the pit box.

The team has to input three numbers into the on-board computer system: the length in feet from pit-in to their pit box, the length from the pit box to pit-out, and the speed limit.

After the stop-and-go penalty, Mark lights up the rear tires leaving the pit box.

Next time Mo comes in he says, "I like the control I got at the back. The car is still too loose coming out, but now the roll is a little bit slower."

A red flag stops the session with 28 minutes to go. Andy: "I would like to take the bar off and come up with the shocks, and see if we can control it with the shocks, just for comparison right now."

Mauricio: "Let's do that."

Andy: "The looseness when you come out of the corner now, is it a flat slide, or still partly because the car is still too rolled over?"

Mauricio: "It's some roll and then it goes into a flat slide."

Mark also reports on changes made to his car. "We've got a hell of a lot more push in the car now. I mean, it's just doubled up. Basically the car is quieter turning into 1, but there's more push from the entry all the way to the exit of the corner. The grip seems to be a little bit more beneficial at turn-in, but now the grip falls away, and the understeer increases as we go through the turn. But it's not enough grip at turn-in, and there's too much understeer. The actual grip is improved.

"Going into the hairpin, it feels slightly better in terms of takin' the car in with some more front grip, but there's a lot of understeer in there now. Coming off the corner I'm pickin' up a few clicks of oversteer as well. The rear of the car is just falling over slightly as it comes off the turn. It doesn't feel like there's enough actual rake in the car. It needs some mechanical rake to get the car around the corner.

"Turn 7, again, it's a little bit easier goin' under braking, a little bit more front grip produced, but the understeer level is high. The back part of the course has massive levels of understeer. Over the crest of the hill, I'm actually havin' to back out of the throttle now because there's so much push I'm gonna go off the track. At 13 and 14 as well, because the understeer there is so big. The rear is just slightly rolling and falling over when we get so much lock on that the rear gives way as well, but it's the front end we need improving."

Mark Moore's guys are making changes to Mauricio's car, and he tells them, "Just take your time. It'll be 5 minutes at least. De Ferran's off at 6." I look on the monitor and Gil de Ferran's car is up on a tire barrier.

Allen tells Mark's crew, "Let's go down two on the front springs, please."

Andy: "After this run, Morris, I want to change tires. This set's now at 30 laps. Do you think we've reached the limit on softness with the car? We keep going down, and it keeps improving right now."

Mauricio: "I don't think we reached the limit yet." They make some changes. The course goes green again at 10:08 and Mauricio goes on course. Mark is out a minute later. Mo is P7 and Mark P17.

Another red flag stops the session, and both cars are back in after a few laps. Mark says the front of the car is too soft. Mauricio tells Andy the changes helped, but he still has a mid-corner push. Andy: "Let's come down 200 on the front springs only."

Allen suggests to Mark they try some rebound in the front shocks. The course goes green again at 10:17. Mauricio is P7; Mark P17. Mark improves to P14 and comes back in.

Allen: "How's the car?" (It sounds like "ow's tha cah?")

Mark: "It's still got a little bit too much understeer, Allen, but it's improved. The problem is it's jackin' down at the front. [This happens when they've adjusted the shocks toward too much rebound force. Every bump contracts the shock, and the spring is not strong enough to expand it before the next bump.] It's bottoming through Turn 1."

Allen: "In the rest of the corners, is that a good change or a bad change?"

Mark: "I'm still not sure that's the way to go. It still feels like the damping is way too soft. It's a benefit, but I don't think that's the right benefit for us at the moment. It's makin' it a little-bit pointy."

Allen: "What about going back halfway on that change and going up 100 pounds on the rear springs?"

Mark: "Yeah, OK, Allen."

Allen: "That's one softer on the high-speed and low-speed front rebound and up one on the rear springs, please."

Mauricio has improved to P4 with a lap of 67.732 seconds. The top three on the monitor are Herta, Zanardi, and Pruett. When Mauricio comes in he and Andy discuss changes. Andy says, "OK; well, let's just do the rear-end change to get a good read on it. We can come back on the front springs between sessions, or there might still be time before we do our sticker run." Mo goes out on the track with about 16 minutes to go in the session.

Mark comes back in saying he feels a lack of control. "The car feels a little bit soggy, you know? The front end is still touchin' down and the rear snaps out."

Allen: "Do you think it's worth a try going stiffer on the front bump then?"

Mark: "Maybe, just to get a feel for which way to go. At the moment there's just way too much movement."

For his sticker run Mauricio and Andy decide to add some front wing. "Give me two turns on the front wing, please Mark." Mo goes back out with about 7 minutes to go. He's P7 now.

Mark goes out also. Al Bodey tells him, "There's 6 minutes to go, Mark, and you can run 'til the end." He improves to P8 with a lap of 67.890 seconds.

Mauricio doesn't improve, but Mark does. The checkered waves at 10:52 a.m. The monitor shows Christian Fittipaldi is P1 followed by Herta, Boesel, Max Papis, and Zanardi. That can't be right. Jim Hamilton tells me there's some Timing and Scoring glitch. When the times are corrected, Zanardi is P1 followed by Herta, Mark, Franchitti, and Michael Andretti. Mauricio is 12th, a second off the pace.

The crew tows the cars back to the garages. The paddock is crowded with fans now, making it difficult to walk from one place to another. Lunch is served in a narrow aisle between the haulers. Mark is mobbed by autograph seekers, and he stops to sign posters and caps and whatever they push at him. As the season goes on his popularity increases, especially among the road-racing crowd. The oval fans don't know him, but the sporty-car fans remember him from Formula 1, and they come running for snapshots and autographs.

Jim Hamilton tells me the new Firestone tires for this race have them way behind. "We tried to back the car data in to see how the tire characteristics changed. That helped some, but not until today."

Mark Blundell's engine problem was a broken spark plug. I ask Butch why they didn't go to the T-car when they had that engine problem. "Well, ya gotta find what's wrong. The other car hasn't been on the track. It hasn't even been warm."

Final Qualifying

The slow-guys' session starts at 1 p.m., only a half-hour late. It's cooled off some, and there's a breeze moving the humid air around some. The fast guys get the green flag at 2:05. Mauricio goes right out while Mark waits for a clear track. Allen tells him, "Adjust the tim if you don't like it in braking."

Greg Moore spins in Turn 1 and crunches his left-rear suspension. He limps the whole way around the course getting back to his pit. A red flag stops the session and all the cars return to pit lane. When Mark comes in Allen asks, "How's the car?"

Mark: "Firstly, the engine still doesn't run properly. It's not what it should be. Balance wise, in 1, entry's a little bit better, but it's still got some push there from 25% to exit. It feels like I can go into the hairpin under braking slightly deeper, but I'm still lacking a bit of front grip. From mid to exit the rear's sliding out. I went down on the rear bar, but didn't get a chance to try it. I was also going to go two clicks on the tim."

Allen: "All right. Do you want to try a bit more rear-ride height?"

Mark nods agreement, and Allen asks Butch to raise the rear three flats.

Mauricio says there's too much roll in the car at the rear. Both cars go back out when a green flag restarts the session at 2:15. Mark comes back in with an engine problem. It sounds really bad.

When Mauricio comes off the track he tells Andy how the car feels and Andy says, "I want to take some low-speed rear rebound out."

Allen listens to Mark talk about the car and suggests going softer on the rear springs. Mark says, "Let's try that and see if it'll settle the rear down and hook us up a bit more. Let's give it a go." Al Bodey tells Mark to switch to another fuel slot that should fix some of the engine problems. Mark goes back out at 2:26.

Mauricio is back in saying the changes made no improvement. Andy says, "OK, Morris, your call. Do you want to leave it as it is, or go back to how the car was for the first run?"

Mauricio: "Go back the way it was. I also tried the front bar stiffer; that was worse."

Andy: "OK, shall we move the drop link to the soft position, so you've got the option to go softer?"

Mauricio: "Leave it like this. I'll just do a good lap the way I know the car."

He asks for a drink of water while they make the changes. Andy tells him, "You're the only person to improve so far. You're sixth with a 66.69. There's 7 minutes to go."

Both Mark and Mauricio go back on course on sticker tires. With 4 minutes to go Mauricio is P6 and Mark is P13. Bryan Herta set a new track record in qualifying yesterday, but most of the drivers, including Herta, haven't gone any quicker today.

Then Mauricio crashes at Turn 11. The replay on the TV monitor shows he lost it coming over a brow. "I'm OK, Andy," he says.

Mark comes in during the red flag, and they decide to make a spring change.

The 17-crew walks back up to the garage to get the spare parts ready to repair the car. They know the wrecker will bring the car on the hook right to the garage.

The 17-Car after Mauricio's Crash

The course goes green again. Allen tells Mark, "OK, there's just over 2 minutes to go. You're going to have to go for it to get in two timed laps." The monitor shows Mark 11th, and Mauricio third. These times turn out to be wrong again. Bryan Herta has the pole and Alex Zanardi will start on the outside front row. Mauricio will start sixth and Mark 13th.

Although Herta set his fast time on Goodyear tires, six of the top-10 cars are running Firestones. The bugaboo of the Goodyears is their "give up," meaning the deterioration in performance after a few laps. Bryan might be quick early on, but if his tires go off he'll drop back.

Switch to the T-Car

In the garage, Allen McDonald and Russ Cameron are hunkered down looking at Mauricio's car. The left-front corner is gone, and the rear wing knocked off.

Mo is here and I ask him what happened. "I just drove a bit too hard."

The crew is beginning to take components off of the primary car to install on the back-up. Chris Jaynes, Roscoe, and Dave Jacobs look over the gearbox case very carefully.

An hour later I ask Mauricio if it's a big deal to run the T-car in the race. "Not really. We were going to change the motor and brakes anyway. It broke the gearbox tail case, but that's OK. It didn't get to the exhaust headers. [There might not be many of the new trick headers around.]

"It pushed some inserts out of the nose, so we'll have a new tub [chassis] at the shop Monday morning. The underwing and sidepods will be repaired. The biggest thing is we don't have a spare front wing for the race. We only had two and I just crunched one."

Mark, Al Bodey, and Allen are at a table in intense conversation, with lots of pointing at pieces of paper and hand movements by Mark describing car behavior.

Turtle the Fireman

Racing is impossible without the work of hundreds of volunteers at each event. The corner workers are visible. We see them when we're at a race in person, and we see them on TV. The safety people, medical personnel, and firemen are less obvious.

"Turtle,"
Ross Tourtellotte

Today one of the firemen introduces himself to me and we talk. Ross Tourtelotte, known as Turtle, travels all over the world acting as a volunteer fireman at races, mainly Formula 1 and CART. He works as a paramedic and firefighter for the city of Shaumberg, Ill. This weekend he's assigned to Mauricio's pit.

Ross likes what he's doing and it certainly gets him right in the middle of things. That flashy helmet and visor is not just for show. "It's actually cooler with the visor down," he tells me.

Whenever the cars are on course, Ross pays attention and knows what's going on. He makes sure he has a bucket of water and a fire extinguisher handy. Whenever Roscoe puts fuel into Mauricio's car Ross is watching carefully, ready to go into action. He also helps me, making it easier for me to stand where I want to and see what I need to see without getting in the way. Ross is a subscriber to my newsletter and we had talked on the phone, but I had never met him until today.

SUNDAY

I'm up early again today and check out of the motel at 6:30 a.m. The sky is overcast and I get some sprinkles on the windshield on the way to the track. The Formula 1 race from Hungary is on the TV in the PacWest hospitality area. I see Damon Hill pass Michael Schumacher for the lead. How did that Arrows car go from being a dog to leading a race?

Warm-Up

The session starts at 11 a.m. It's still cloudy and breezy, but the sun breaks through now and then. Russ Cameron tells Mauricio to bed his brakes, and then come back in for an installation check. Mark and Mauricio come back in after a few laps. Mo says, "The tires are fine and the brakes feel good."

Mark gets a checkout and goes back on course. Allen tells him, "Don't forget your bars, and you've got the tim too." Al Bodey cues Mark to try a new fuel slot almost every lap. They're trying to find one he likes.

After halfway in the session Mauricio says it's oversteering. Andy asks, "With the car as it was then, before the change, what's the biggest problem?"

Mauricio: "It's understeer middle-corner, but less than when we qualified. I can live with it. It's the back coming out at the exit, a little bit of lack of traction."

Andy: "Let's not forget that these tires have about 28 or 30 laps. I could tighten up the diff a little bit if that would help the traction. In the mid-corner I'd like to try the front tire pressures that we talked about."

Mauricio: "Leave the diff."

Andy: "Remember we'd like to try slot two on the fuel. When you have a feel for that we'll go to slot zero. We've got about 10 minutes of green left."

Mark comes in saying, "I've gone up on the front bar to the mid and two more clicks on tim. That gives the car a little bit more support to the rear. It's still loose at the exit. We're not laying the power down that well. Mo lays the power down more efficiently than us. Under brakin' I can sneak up on him, but comin' off the turn he gets on the gas a bit earlier and stays with it. He comes off the corner nice and tight. We come off sideways. Also, with the bar a little bit stiffer, there's more push in 1."

Allen: "Would you like to try droppin' it a couple of flats, and see what that does?"

They make that change. Mark goes out with a few minutes to go and improves to P3 on his last timed lap. When he comes back onto pit lane Ando [John Anderson] talks him in for a simulated pit stop. Greg Moore is P1 for this session followed by Jimmy Vasser and Mark. Mauricio is P7. The times are a second and a half slower than qualifying.

Strategy

I'm trying to work out an exit strategy that will let me get out of here this afternoon and avoid the traffic on the two-lane roads that hook up to the interstate highway to Columbus. Coming in this morning I saw people parking cars right inside the gate. They will have a long walk to their cars, but then they'll get out the gate quickly.

Yesterday I was whining about the difficulty of getting on the road after the race to Gary Gerould, TV pit announcer. He has the same problem and came back

Roscoe Drives the Hollywood Tugger

this morning with a map he got from somewhere. It shows several back-road routes to the interstate. That should help. If I can get out of the media parking lot in a reasonable amount of time I'll make it to the airport OK.

I catch Ando eating some lunch and ask him about the race strategy. "The race is 83 laps, and we'll try to make it with two stops. The window will open at 25 to 27 laps. The history of yellow-flag laps here over the last five years averages to two full-course yellows for a total of eight laps. Last year de Ferran hit Mo in the rear. We'll be ready for an early stop on a yellow situation, if it will get us track position on the restart."

"What would an early stop do for you?" I ask.

The Tugger Tows the 17-Car to the Grid

"Well, we didn't qualify very well, and the lead pack tends to pull away here. If we get caught with them getting away we might stop early, so when they stop later, it might give us the lead."

Allen McDonald also says Mark's poor starting position dictates the race strategy. "We'd like to stretch the fuel window as much as possible. From where we are on the grid, we'll try something unusual if it makes sense."

Just before 2 o'clock Mauricio is here in the garage looking over his car. Both PacWest cars are finishing up on the setup pads. Outside the clouds look dark in three directions. I can feel some rain sprinkles.

Pre-Grid

Activity in the pit lane picks up now. It's 2:15, less than an hour before the race. Engines are warming and tuggers pull cars down from the garages and out onto the frontstraight. At 2:50 we're all on the racetrack in front of the pits, standing around among the gridded cars.

The 17-Car Crew on Pre-Grid

THE RACE

The front-row drivers, Bryan Herta and Alex Zanardi, have some history. Zanardi robbed Herta of a win at Laguna Seca last year with a banzai pass. Because the pit straight is so short this race starts on the long straight coming down from the hairpin, but the flagging during the race and the checkered flag happens on the pit straight.

After the pace laps the green flag waves at 3:05 and the race is on. Mauricio holds his sixth-place spot as Herta and Zanardi fight it out up front. Mark's race is over early. Despite many efforts, his engine is still not right. I hear Mark on the radio yelling, "It's cutting out."

Ando tells him to try another fuel slot. Al Unser Jr. is close behind Mark when the engine falters and his front wheels run up and over Mark's car, damaging the rear wing and sidepod.

Mark limps toward the pits. Ando asks, "Any damage?"

Mark replies, "It's a mess." When he gets to the pits the crew swarms over it and some start to bring spare parts. Then I see a wave-off at the rear of the car and somebody says, "The gearbox case is cracked." Mark gets out of the car.

After only 10 laps, Mauricio's engine sounds rough also. He says, "The engine is turning to shit."

Russ encourages him: "You're running as quick as the leaders. Keep it up."

On lap 19 Bryan Herta's hopes explode with his tire coming out of Turn 1. On the TV monitor we can see all of the left-rear suspension is gone. It was a big failure. This brings out the first all-course yellow and the cars all pit.

Russ tells Mauricio to stay out. I'm surprised. Is this another screw-up like Cleveland? Mauricio passes by the pit entrance but he's upset, saying he didn't hear Russ and got no instructions.

Russ tells him, "It looked like it was too early to come in. Let's stick to our plan. We'll do it in two stops. We have to stay with it." Russ is hoping the other cars will have to make three pit stops because this first one is too early.

Mauricio says he has a problem with the throttle. Russ tells him to go up two clicks on the boost. Mauricio says, "I'll go down first and then up when it stabilizes." The race restarts on lap 22 and Mauricio is the leader.

Russ says, "Stretch out the lead so we have a gap. We'll pit in six laps."

Mauricio pulls away from Zanardi and gets a lead of about 2.3 seconds in three laps. Then the interval is 2.6 seconds. He's light on fuel and gaining a few tenths of a second a lap.

Mo pits on lap 29. Ross Tourtelotte, the fireman, leans forward and grabs the handle of his water bucket when Mauricio comes into the pits.

After Mo's pit stop Alex Zanardi is the leader followed by Greg Moore and Dario Franchitti. Mauricio is 20th. It was a good pit stop, but they had to make sure the car got all the fuel it could take, and that's what takes the time.

The 18-crew is packing up the pit lane equipment. Mark talked to Allen for a few minutes, took care of some TV and print interviews, and left.

Mauricio works his way up the list and he's 15th on lap 47 when the next round of pit stops start under green. After all those stops he's in fourth spot and the 17-crew is hoping a good pit stop could put them in position to run until the end and finish well.

Mark Moore tells his guys, "OK; a full load of fuel, and by the numbers."

The pit stop looks good to me. After Mo storms back out on course, Chris Jaynes says, "We're close to emptying the tank. Good stop." They got all the fuel in so he can run to the finish now. The leaders are Zanardi, Moore, and Franchitti. Mauricio is 12th.

Russ tells Mauricio, "Jourdain Jr. is ahead of you and Parker [Johnstone] is behind. He's catching you."

Parker is the last driver on the lead lap and Zanardi passes him on lap 63. Russ tells Mo, "Push it. If Zanardi laps us we're finished."

Zanardi continues to catch up to Mauricio. Russ says, "We've worked too hard for him to get by now." Everyone in this part of the pits is rooting for Mauricio now. Even Turtle, the fireman, waves Mo on as he comes by.

Russ is still encouraging Mauricio on the radio, "Get by Jourdain. I know you're better than he is."

Jourdain Jr. yields to the pressure and spins off the course. An all-course yellow comes out and most cars pit for fuel. Mauricio improves from 12th to ninth. Zanardi had built enough of a lead over Greg Moore that after pitting for a splash of fuel he returns to the course in the lead even though Moore didn't pit. The order now is Zanardi, Moore, Rahal, Boesel, Vasser, de Ferran, Franchitti, Pruett, and Mauricio.

Russ continues to exhort Mauricio on during the caution period. "Are you packed up?"

Mauricio says, "I hear you but you're talking too fast."

The race restarts on lap 73. Mauricio passes Pruett and then Franchitti. With six laps to go Russ says, "Every car in front of you is running lean. You can get 'em."

Mauricio is pressing de Ferran for sixth spot. Maybe he can get by all these guys. The excitement is mounting. I'm wishing Mo on so hard I feel weak. The PA announcer talks about the drama with three laps to go.

But Mauricio doesn't have the time or the car to make up any more spots. Zanardi wins the race. Moore is second and Rahal third. Mauricio finishes seventh; Mark 26th. This gives Zanardi a clear lead in the championship points over Paul Tracy, Gil de Ferran, and Greg Moore.

At the checkered flag I grab my shoulder bag, say good-bye to a few people in the pits, and walk back toward the garage. I say, "See you in Elkhart" to a couple of guys working there and walk to the car.

The Formula Atlantic race has yet to run today, and that helps me get out of the parking lot. Within 10 minutes of getting in the car I'm driving out the gate. The line I'm in turns left, and I begin to look for the shortcut on the map Gary Gerould gave me. I turn right and go a ways before I realize I turned too soon. The map shows I need to go left at the next intersection, and when I get to it, there's another car looking lost. I wave "Follow me," at them and turn left. I can see where I am on the map, and it's clear sailing to the interstate and Columbus. Happiness is a quick exit.

Aftermath

Sitting in the gate area at the Columbus airport I think about the race and the 17-car's pit-stop strategy. That last yellow flag messed up the strategy, but it wouldn't have resulted in a win anyway. Other teams were saving fuel too, and some of them had qualified up front or were passing people for position during the race.

Even if that last yellow hadn't happened, Mauricio wouldn't have been able to catch Zanardi. He was just too far back. He probably would have gained some positions when cars ahead of him made a green-flag stop.

Still, you have to pass people to get to the front. Zanardi won even though he made one more stop in the pits than the second-place driver. Using the power of the Honda engine and his ability to pass, Zanardi built a lead that gave him the margin to stop for fuel. Greg Moore, Raul Boesel, and Mauricio couldn't pass people and conserve fuel at the same time.

CHAPTER 20
ROAD AMERICA

If it's Thursday, I must be flying to a race. Today, Aug. 14, I'm on a flight from SFO to Denver and then on to Milwaukee for the race at Road America. The team is staying at the Inn on Maritime Bay in Manitowoc, Wis. I get there about 7:30 p.m. after an hour and a half drive north from Milwaukee. The motel is right on the western shore of Lake Michigan.

A nice bar and restaurant at the motel proves to be good for evening socials. This first night I have a late dinner with some of the PacWest guys. Russ Cameron, the team crew chief and race strategist for Mauricio, tells me about the Mid-Ohio race. "I was certain those guys couldn't make it on two stops, but somehow they did. If there hadn't been a yellow and they were forced to pit at the end, we would have led and looked like heroes. But that didn't happen. I don't think we could have held off Zanardi anyway. He was strong.

"The mistake I made was not following standard procedure. I told Mo 'Don't pit.' Andy was certain we couldn't make it on fuel. When the leaders came in I yelled, 'Pit, pit, pit.' We were having radio problems, and he didn't hear me. Then we were committed."

"What did you learn?" I ask.

"Well, I guess if you're in the top six you have to do what the leaders do."

"The radios are really important, aren't they?"

"Yeah, they are," Russ says.

"I didn't realize that before this year," I say. "I haven't listened to the radio conversations that much before this season. I guess I'm surprised at the importance of the radio conversations and how many problems there are with the basic equipment."

"You're right," Russ says.

FRIDAY

I'm up at 5:45, out of the motel at 7, and at the track at 7:45. The drive is on good, two-lane farm roads. This is dairy country, and the towns are small and widely spaced. There's a light rain falling, and I have the windshield wipers going for the entire drive.

This is my first trip to this track. I stop on the way in and pick up my parking pass and the pass that gets me into the media center. The parking lot is right in front of the media center, and there's a tunnel under the track that takes me into the infield. When I come out of the tunnel I see the CART paddock starts to the left, and the Trans-Am and Formula Atlantic paddocks are to the right down the hill.

The hospitality motor coaches are on a hill above the CART paddock. I find the PacWest area and stow my gear. Then it's a walk back down the hill to the paddock and the PacWest garage area. Ando [John Anderson] is here and I ask him what was wrong with the engines at Mid-Ohio. "The ECM [Engine Control Module] was bad on Mark's car. We sent it back to VDS and they told us it had received a corrupted signal."

At 10:20 the sun is shinning through the clouds and the air is warming up some. As usual the garage area is between the two haulers, covered by tents anchored on the sides of the haulers. This is only Friday, but there are a lot of people here despite the rain.

The PacWest Garage Area

Practice

This session is scheduled for an 11 a.m. start, but at 11:15 there are some sprinkles of rain. This begins a weekend-long ritual of looking up to the sky, determining which direction the clouds are coming from, and predicting when the next rain will begin.

Allen McDonald tells me Mark will go out in the T-car in this first session. "That car was the race car at Mid-Ohio, and we want to make sure the engine problem we had there isn't a car problem. The ECM could have been affected by the power supply or something intermittent in the wiring harness."

At 11:22 the green flag starts the session. Sprinkles of rain come and go. Mauricio goes out saying the engine isn't running right. "There's a yellow light flashing on the dash. The engine is really rough. Something is really wrong. I'll be lucky to finish the lap."

When Mauricio comes in the crew takes the sidepods off and looks over the electronics. Andy says, "We're only allowed four sets of wets [rain tires] for the whole weekend, Morris. So if the track partly dries, I don't think we can afford to run around on these and chew them up."

Mauricio is incredulous. "What if it rains for the next two days? What are they going to do?"

Andy: "Good question."

A red flag stops the session. Mark gets out of the T-car and into his primary car. The course goes green again at 11:30 and Mauricio goes back out. His engine is still running poorly, however. "I'm not going to make it, Andy. This thing is getting worse."

He comes into the pits but no one is standing out in the pit lane to wave him in, so he misses the pit box and has to go back out on the track. "Nobody stands out there? That's great," Mauricio says disgustedly.

Andy suggests he take the short cut from Turn 5 to Turn 14, but he says, "I already went past that."

Mark Moore, Mo's chief mechanic, says, "We'll take off the engine cover and the left-hand sidepod. They're reprogramming a new ECU for it."

But then he says, "Never mind on that, guys. They said they can just plug in on the download and do it that way."

Andy explains to Mauricio: "OK, Morris. We've just plugged Charlie [Harris, Ilmor tech] in and we've rewritten a slot for the ECU which will bypass that switch." Something called the throttle safety switch is causing the problem.

Mark comes back off the track saying he's still having problems with the dash lights that alert him when the engine is getting near maximum revs. Allen asks him to get out of the car so they can look at all the sensors. Those lights are important because the drivers don't have time to look at the dash for rpm information to decide when they should shift gears.

Mauricio's engine fires up and he goes back out saying, "It feels better now."

Dave Jacobs, a mechanic on the 17-car, says, "OK everybody, regroup; the panic's over."

When Mauricio comes back in Andy asks him, "How's the track?"

Mauricio: "Getting drier. But it's not dry enough for slicks yet."

It's almost noon and the track is drying. Both Allen and Andy suggest changing to slicks. Mark asks if Stephen Kent can clean his windscreen and visor. Mark has been complaining about the cruise control and Al Bodey tells him, "There does seem to be some kind of failure going on with the cruise control. Ian's [Hawkins, Ilmor tech] not sure what it is, so you're going to have to watch it yourself for a while."

Greg Moore spins out after switching to slick tires, causing a red flag that stops the session. Max Papis spins in the same place and crashes into Greg's car. There's still 30 minutes to go in the session.

Andy cautions Mauricio about the drying track: "Looking on the monitor, it seems that at

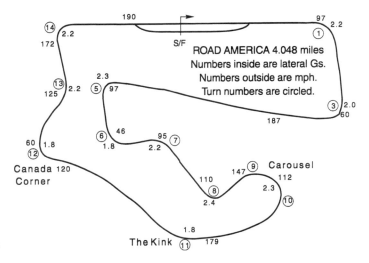

Canada Corner itself, right on the apex, there's some shadows being thrown on there by some trees, and it looks like there's a slight weeper there. It's still very wet. I think that's why both Moore and Papis lost it there. I think Michael almost lost it on his in-lap too. He got a bit loose there. Then Moore and Papis lost it at the same spot. This is the optional tire, by the way. Green flag."

Mauricio goes back out again at 12:03 p.m. Mark's putting his helmet back on, about to get back into his car. Michael Andretti is P1 with a lap of 2:03.525. That's 20 seconds off the pace, so the track is far from dry. As Mark pulls back on course, Butch Winkle, his chief mechanic, says, "OK; everybody back to their assigned jobs. Let's try to make this second half smooth."

Mauricio comes back in saying the engine is still hesitating and the brake pedal is very stiff. This last complaint must have something to do with the tim device, because Tim Neff, its inventor, goes to the rear of Mauricio's car and says on the radio, "Mo, can you take four clicks out of the rake control, please?"

Then Tim says, "Put your foot on the brake and hold it, please." They make some adjustments until Tim is satisfied with the tim.

Mark comes back in talking about boost and shift-light problems. "The boost has dropped off and it doesn't stay stable in terms of engine feel. You just can't feel it pulling crisply all the way through the range. It's just kinda intermittent. Also the car feels quite pointy now going into the quick stuff like Turn 1 and the Kink and the Carousel entry. You have to back out of the gas pedal, and then we go back into a push, but that's very early on with the tire temperatures and pressures low."

A red flag stops the session. Newcomer Charles Nearburg spins somewhere. I can feel drops of rain again. Mauricio says the engine is still cutting out. When he comes in his crew messes around with the sensors.

Mark also continues to have problems with his rpm lights. "I don't have enough time to keep looking down at the rpm and read it. If I don't have the lights, you have to give me something."

Allen: "All right. How's the car?"

Mark: "Basically we have to just keep trimming back on the tim. It's just too aggressive. That aggressiveness is coming in under braking, and it's snapping out on me. It's got too much push in the car, especially at the slower speeds."

Allen: "What about your rear roll bar? Can you go stiffer on that?"

Mark: "I can try that. I'd like to see what these tires are like. But the pedal is still sinking."

You'd never know it just listening to the conversations, but the PacWest drivers are turning the quickest laps right now. At 12:38 with about 9 minutes to go, Mauricio is P1 and Mark P2. They both go out on course for another run.

Mark comes back off course and Allen asks, "How's the car?"

Mark: "There's a lot of push in the car, especially on the initiation of braking into the corner. Then the rear of the car snaps out sideways. I'm braking real deep, but I can't actually control it. The rear snaps out, and there's not enough load on the front end. The front doesn't have enough grip to take the car down and in."

Allen: "We'll make some rear damper changes."

Mark goes back on track at 12:44 with about 3 minutes to go. The monitor shows him in P1 followed by Michael Andretti, Gil de Ferran, and Mauricio. Mo runs out of fuel on course. As he waits for a tow, Andy tells him, "That last lap didn't look too bad before you lost fuel pressure."

The drying track allowed quite a few drivers to set their best times in the last couple of minutes before the checkered flag. Raul Boesel has the best time of 104.208 seconds. Mark is P2 followed by de Ferran, Scott Pruett, and Alex Zanardi. Mauricio ends up 10th.

I say to Chris Jaynes, lead mechanic on Mo's car, "That was a crazy session, huh?"

"Tell me," he says. "We changed everything on the car — the throttle pot, sensors, plugs, coils, the ECU, the spark box, a bunch of stuff." A few minutes later the PacWest cars are back in the paddock on the setup pads. Mo's wife, Stella, is here with one of their twins, Bernardo.

Friday Qualifying

At 2:27 p.m. I'm in the pit lane waiting for the start of qualifying. Mark and Mauricio are both in this first group, the fast guys. Mauricio goes right out at the green flag at 3:32. Allen asks Mark, "Do you want to go out now or wait a bit?"

Mark: "I'll wait." As the other drivers begin to come down for the last turn, Mark goes out onto a clear track. As a result, his first timed lap is a 105.120 seconds, good for P1. Michael Andretti takes over P1 for a half-lap before Mark reclaims it with a time of 103.738. Mauricio is P4, then he takes over P1 and pits.

Andy tells him, "You're currently P1. Do we want to go to the changes we were talking about?"

Mauricio: "If we have to go back on that, can we do that?"

Andy: "Not quickly; it does take awhile to repressure the thing."

Mauricio: "If we have time to try, let's do it."

Andy: "Mark, will you take the engine cover off, please? We're going to dump the pressure from the mid-rear. I'd like to come up four flats on the rear pushrods please."

I think they're using an air spring on the third spring at the rear, what Andy calls "the mid-rear." An air spring has the advantage of low weight and a natural rising spring rate, but the seals necessary to hold high-pressure air can produce high frictional forces. Mo and Andy probably just decided to try some laps without the air spring so they can get a back-to-back comparison of the performance.

Mark comes in and reports on the car, "It's a little bit better so far; a bit more grip and it feels better under braking. It's just got a little bit of pointyness to the car at high speed, but I can carry it, it's OK. We could cut down a bit on the understeer level. There's too much understeer at Turn 7 and also coming through the 12, 13, 14 combination."

Mauricio: "Can you go through the changes, Andy?"

Andy: "We've taken the pressure out of the mid-rear, raised the rear four flats, reversed the rear wing Gurney flap, and dropped the front wing two and a half turns."

This information shows the benefit of the air spring. When he took the air out Andy had to raise the rear of the car four flats, about an eighth of an inch. The air spring lets him run the car lower, which gives more downforce from the underwing. Mauricio goes back on track. He's still P1 with a lap of 103.033. Mark is P2 followed by Scott Pruett, Gil de Ferran, and Raul Boesel.

Allen has changed front springs on Mark's car. He says to Mark, "If you like it, go for it, but now might not be the best time. If you go now and don't like the changes, come back in."

Mark: "I don't want to ruin the tires at the beginning of the run, so I don't know if I want to commit to the run right now. I think it's just too early to commit."

Allen: "All right. Well, we'll wait till 10 minutes to go then."

Mark: "What about the ride height with the new springs? Do we have to go higher?"

Allen: "From looking at the skids, no. I think we'll just get away with it."

Mauricio is back in at 3:52, still in P1. "It's touching a little bit more in middle corner going fast, and through the Carousel."

Andy: "How about the Kink? Is that too pointy or can we put some more wing into it?"

Mauricio: "Don't change the wing. The Kink is fine."

Andy: "If I just drop the rear ride height it's just going to make it push worse. So my recommendation would be to leave it."

Mauricio: "OK, I'll put in a little bit of tim."

Andy: "We can take some bump out of the front shocks if you think that might help."

Mauricio: "Leave it for now."

While the PacWest cars are waiting for the right time to go back for their last timed laps, Alex Zanardi has taken over P1 from Mauricio by 3-thousandths of a second. Mark goes out at 3:53 and Mauricio a minute later.

Partway through his out-lap Mo radios that his electronic dash has gone away. Dario Franchitti jumps to P1 and the times are coming down as the track continues to improve. With 3 minutes to go Mark is in P1 with a lap of 102.451 seconds. We're all standing in pit lane looking at the monitor on the PacWest scoring cart. I count 16 guys watching that monitor. Mark radios a question, "One more lap?"

Al Bodey answers, "Yes."

Andy tells Mauricio there's 1 minute and 40 seconds left in the session. I hear Mo say something about "traffic" as he goes by us on the pit straight. The checkered flag flies. This will be Mauricio's last timed lap. His chief mechanic, Mark Moore, leans against my shoulder, straining toward the monitor. Mauricio's car screams up the hill toward Start/Finish. The monitor flashes a change, and he did it! On his last lap he earned the provisional pole position. Whoops and hollers erupt behind me, and I turn to see a bunch of smiles and high fives and back slapping.

"I'm out of gas, Andy," Mo says on the radio. Now that's a perfect qualifying run — picking the right time with the right tires and the right amount of fuel on board.

A safety truck tows him in, and he gets out of the car in a crowd of PacWest guys. Mark is P2, and he goes over to congratulate Mauricio also. Mark Moore says to me, "He was flying blind; no shift lights or any of the dash functions."

Behind Mo and Mark on the provisional grid are Zanardi, Franchitti, and Andretti. Those are all Italian names but the nationalities are Italian, Scottish, and American.

Pole Press Conference

I walk back through the tunnel to the media center. At 5:20 the slow-guys' qualifying session is over and the press conference begins. Mo, Mark, and Alex Zanardi are sitting in director's chairs on a small podium just a foot higher than the floor. Zanardi is in his driving suit. Mauricio and Mark are in casual pants and polo shirts.

Mike Zizzo introduces Zanardi first. "We can make the car better for tomorrow, but these guys are going to do the same thing."

Mark is next. "The conditions were tough out there for everybody. One minute it was dry and the next it was raining. It's tough to get your rhythm. The team did a good job. We had some problems, but we did very well."

Zizzo says Mauricio broke the track record set last year by Jacques Villeneuve. This is his 16th consecutive top-10 start. "Did you use anything Mark learned this morning, since he was second-quick in that session?"

Mauricio: "Yeah, we did a little bit of that. We both had quite a difficult session in the morning. We compared data before the afternoon, but we did test here and we had two very good days of testing and our cars are running very similar to what we ran here in testing, unlike Mid-Ohio, where the tires were different from the test to the race. So, we were just starting from where we were at the test.

"We both feel there is more to come from our cars. I particularly didn't like the way the lap was and I had too much push in the car, but of course I'm happy for the team. It's the first time we've actually been one and two, and hopefully we can keep it that way tomorrow."

Zizzo opens the floor for questions and someone asks what problems they had in the morning session. Mauricio says, "I had just an electrical-related engine problem. It took a long time to find it. It turned out to be an external part. You have to change them one at a time to find out what it is. When you change too many things at once you can't tell what the problem is."

Mark: "My problem was electrical as well. Similar, but a little bit different. For instance, we lost a wheel-speed sensor, which was giving the black box some confused information. The weather conditions helped as Mauricio said because with all our troubles everyone else was in the pits also. It gave us a bit of breathin' space."

Another question is "Any thoughts as to why some of your colleagues were having difficulty staying on the track today?"

There is a span of silence with some nervous laughter. Mark says, "I'll let Alex answer that."

Zanardi rises to the occasion, laughing. "I guess the main factor was that the trees on the back section didn't let the track dry enough. You're all pumped up on a good lap and it's tough to slow down, but if you don't do that you may end up on the grass or in the fence."

There's a question about the track being too long to get a good lap out of the tires. Zanardi says, "I don't agree with that. We have more than one good lap with the Firestones. I hope it's not that way for the Goodyear guys."

All three of these drivers are on Firestones.

I ask Mauricio about his dash going out on his last run.

Mauricio: "I lost everything, but I don't really look at my dash a lot anyway. I didn't slow down. These days you have like Nintendo lights up at the top, and you can look at the lights most of the time. I wasn't going to stop and take the sidepods off and do all that. I'd rather drive with no dash. I just kept radioing in to see what lap times I did. That was important and I kept going quicker. They kept saying another 2-tenths and another tenth and then they told me that Mark was ahead and then Alex was ahead and I got ahead in the end."

"So the shift lights still worked?"

Mauricio: "Yes, they still worked."

Mark is asked about his neck. "No problem at all. The muscles are a little bit tight, but the problem is the actual nerves. I feel a lot more comfortable than I did at the last race."

The drivers are asked their impression of the track.

Mark: "I think this is a fantastic circuit. There are some mighty corners here, like the Kink and the Carousel, and Turn 1 is exhilarating. It's got a nice flow to it. When you get a circuit that flows it's a pleasure to drive. When you change the car you get some reward back in the course of a long lap. It's very rewarding for the driver. It gives me the impression of Spa [Formula 1 track in Belgium] for some reason, but it's not like Spa really."

Mauricio: "It's amazing to me that over 4 miles the cars are very close in times. When you're out there, at least I do it this way, you go through Turn 1 and you know you've done better than the previous lap and all behind you is a plus and you try all around, and then at Turn 13 under the bridge, it's incredibly fast there. The concentration to put everything into one lap and then you think you've done the maximum and you expect to be a half a second ahead of the other guys and it's just like half a tenth. It's unbelievable."

Zanardi: "It does remind me a lot of Spa. Maybe because the circuit is so long and the corners are pretty fast. When you go out the first laps you go much, much slower than what you end up doing later. The first time I went around Spa, actually at one point about three-quarters around, I thought am I lost? Have I took a wrong turn? [laughter] The lap was never-ending. I had the same feeling here."

Mauricio: "Here you rely a lot on mechanical grip rather than aerodynamic grip. That makes these cars slide a lot and you have to be more precise. Because it's long straights, you can't put too much wing in the car."

The press conference winds down, and I walk through the tunnel and back to the PacWest garage area. At 6 o'clock there are no engine changes going on. I talk to some of the guys and then head back to the car.

I meet some people for dinner at the restaurant in 52 Stafford, a small hotel in nearby Plymouth. Bill Krause and Bob Wilson work at Classic Motorbooks, my book distributor. Katie is Bill's wife and Tom is a friend. They've driven across Wisconsin from the Minneapolis area for the race, and want to know how the book is going. I get to tell some of the stories I've accumulated. It's a treat to step away from the track and spend some time with some nice people who are racing fans like myself.

SATURDAY

The sun is out this morning and the drive to the track is pleasant. At 7 a.m. I'm talking to Dr. Love, Tim Love, the gearbox guy for the 18-car, in the PacWest garage area.

"How are the gearboxes doing?"

Tim shows me crossed fingers on both hands and grins broadly. "So far, so good."

I laugh. "Sorry I asked."

"No, everything is all right," Tim says. "No problems. It's pretty amazing how good the gearboxes are. You can tell there's some flexing going on because of the way some of the gears wear, but you allow for it and replace parts before they break."

At 7:30 Dave Jacobs and Jim Reid crank the 17-car to get the oil and fuel pressure up before they start the engine. I ask Dave how late they were here last night. "We left here about 7:30 last night and left the motel this morning at 6:30. That's not bad."

Mike Todd Oils the Air Wrenches

Daryl Fox and I are talking and watching a Honda engine being dressed on the lift gate of the KOOL team next door. A red blanket hides the plenum from view. "Have they come up with anything new this year?"

"No," Daryl says. "I saw one the other day, and it looked the same. It's a heavy bugger though. Their cars are always about 20 pounds overweight. Reynard made the '97 car so light just for the Honda."

In the pit lane a while later Scott Simpson is polishing wheels. Mike Todd sits astride the pit wall oiling the air guns. He removes the air hose from each gun and drips a half-dozen drops of oil into the gun.

The 18-crew is practicing pit stops. Butch fumbles around and stops to laugh at himself. He takes off a glove and throws it on the ground. Mark Blundell gets into the teasing and points a water hose and threatens to hose them down. Then Mark and Allen McDonald talk together.

We have CART practice at 9 o'clock this morning and the atmosphere on pit lane begins to gain energy. Crews tow or push cars into pit boxes and motors are started and coaxed up to temperature. It's already warm, about 75 degrees and humid. The sky is mostly clear, but some clouds are blowing in from the southwest.

Saturday Practice

Jim Swintal's green flag starts this session at 9:01. The PacWest cars go out on track and then come back in for changes. Both driver/engineer teams deal with the usual problems: tire pressures, mechanical grip and balance in the slow corners, aero balance in the high-speed corners, and optimizing the ride height. About 10 minutes into the session I hear Andy say, "Red flag, Morris. Hiro's [Hiro Matsushita] gone into the kitty litter."

A while later Mauricio is P4 and Mark P9. Andy says to Mauricio, "The rear skid is getting a bit thin. Could you live with that being a bit higher? It would help the mid-corner balance."

Mauricio nods and Andy says, "Come up a flat at the rear, please, guys."

Mark comes in saying to Allen, "The changes I made during that run, one up on the rear bar and two clicks up on tim."

Allen: "Why did you go up on the rear bar, Mark?"

Mark: "To see whether I can stop the rear of the car from walking through the Carousel. Seems to be a little bit of help. Also, going up on the tim seems to bring a bit of push into the car, but it's still not where we were yesterday. We still don't have the level platform what we had then."

Allen: "Wonder if you could try the front bar next time?"

Allen sounds frustrated by Mark's seemingly whimsical use of the cockpit adjustments. Here he had been complaining of lack of grip at the rear coming off the corners. A stiffer rear sway bar is going to make that worse. On the next run Mark tries adjusting the front bar stiffer and says it makes the car push in the high-speed corners.

The session stops with a red flag at 9:37. Andy gives Mauricio some options. "I can come back up on the rear springs, which I think will help your push, and it will keep a flat car and you won't get so much of a rear ride-height reaction under braking. We are softer compared to last year. Or I can pull the rebound out of the rear. I'll pull that rebound out anyway since we're going to stiffer springs. As an alternative to that we can put some low-speed bump in the back."

It's almost 10 o'clock and Mauricio is P4 with Mark P8. The air is cooler now. The sky is overcast, and there's a gusty breeze. I feel a few light sprinkles.

With about 12 minutes to go Mauricio says he has some mid-corner understeer. Andy changes to some tires with only six laps on them, and Mo returns to the track. Then I hear on the scanner something about the 17-car stopping on course. I hear the word fire. Somebody nearby says, "Mo blew a motor."

The TV monitor shows the car pulling off track trailing lots of smoke. Andy says, "Do we have time to get the T-car, Mark? Just to scuff a set of race tires."

Gualter Salles goes off into a gravel trap, causing a red flag. Andy says, "Red flag, go for it. Hustle Mo back and we'll scuff a set." The 17-crew walks quickly back around the fence to the garage area and pushes the back-up car onto pit lane.

Dave Jacobs gets on a scooter and goes off to where Mauricio is still with the car. Mark Moore says, "Dave, have Mo come back on the scooter. You stay with the car and make sure they don't screw up the tires."

They put some of the current changes onto the 17x-car in the pit lane and Mo is in the car at 10:11, about 5 minutes since he stopped on course. The session restarts at 10:13 and Mark returns to the track. Mauricio starts the engine and sits waiting for the temperatures to come up. "Tell me when, Andy."

Andy: "When we get to 65." He means 65 degrees Celsius of course, the minimum oil temperature.

"OK, Morris," Andy says, and Mauricio goes back out at 10:15. His primary car comes in on the hook. The wrecker has to push slowly through the crowd in the paddock around the PacWest garage area. They set it down and Jimmy asks Mark Moore, "Should we start to disassemble it?" Mark shakes his head in the negative and they start to carefully look over the rear of the car.

Mauricio comes back in for another set of tires and goes out to scuff them. The checkered flag waves at 10:22. Scott Pruett has the fastest time of the session at 102.017 seconds. The remainder of the top five are Raul Boesel, Gil de Ferran, Alex Zanardi, and Michael Andretti. Mauricio is P8 and Mark P10.

Engine Thrash

At noon Mauricio is standing under the tent watching as a new engine goes into his primary car. Qualifying is scheduled to start at 12:30 with the slow guys first. Andy is nearby and he goes into his version of a rain dance, producing laughter all around. It works. The clouds are getting darker in the west and some sprinkles of rain begin. Mark Blundell does his own rain dance into the engineering room in the front of the Motorola transporter.

Mark Moore tells me Mauricio's engine blew a piston. "The Ilmor guys tried to boroscope that cylinder last night, but the

Russ Cameron Watches and Chris Jaynes Sits In the 17-Car as Mark McArdle and Blake Hamilton Work to Start the Engine

spark plug tightened up when they tried to take it out."

At 12:10 the new engine in the 17-car is cranking over but won't start. After a few tries I see a lot of worried looks. The Ilmor guys begin to show up one by one. At 12:20 the engine starts but doesn't sound right. Mark McArdle is leading the battle. He goes over to confer with Dyno Don.

Mauricio walks over to the gap between the tents and puts a hand out, palm up. He looks over at me, rolls his eyes toward the sky, looks down at the raindrops in his hand, and looks back at me smiling. Behind us the engine is still running bad. "It sounds like shit," Mauricio says to me, and then he notices some fans at the barriers calling to him wanting autographs. He walks over to them and begins to sign the stuff they hand him.

The engine finally fires up and sounds right. The Ilmor guys disperse now that the crisis is over. Jim Reid gets in the car and puts it in gear. The car is up on jack stands so he can run the engine through the gears. There aren't any rear wheels on the car, so the brake rotors just spin free in the open. They shut the engine off and start to put the underwing on the bottom of the car. The rain continues to sprinkle down.

Non-Qualifying

At 12:36 the slow-guys' group goes out to qualify. The rain is coming down a little harder, then it slacks up. The pavement in the pit lane looks about half wet. At 1 o'clock the rain stops and the sky in the west looks lighter. The 18-crew pushes their car onto pit lane. Andy tells me, "I'd like to get a set of race tires scuffed. You can see on the TV the backstraight is wet."

At 1:20 we get a short shower of larger drops and then the light rain

The 17-Car Crew (Dan Boyd Photo)
L. to R.: Mark Moore, Andy Natalie, Scott Simpson, Ron Endres, Trevor Jackson, Mauricio Gugelmin, Russ Cameron, Dave Jacobs, Andy Brown, Chris Jaynes, Jim Reid

continues. I put on my rain jacket. Marty Reid, pit announcer for ESPN, interviews Mauricio to start the TV coverage of this qualifying session. Mo's provisional-pole qualifying effort from yesterday will probably stand due to the wet track. That means a one-two start for the PacWest drivers.

The fast-guys' group starts at 1:30, and a few cars go out on track. At 1:37 as Mark drives out of the pit box Al Bodey says, "The wet slot is slot five, Mark." Mauricio also goes on track. Andy comes out of the engineering cart to stare at the sky in the west.

Both PacWest cars come back in after one lap. Mark says, "There's a big patch of dampness under the trees and the tires have spray coming off them. From the Carousel to the Kink is soaking wet still. You wouldn't be able to do anything."

Andy tells Mauricio, "Well, only 20 minutes to go then. Do you think it's worth it to check some wets for balance?"

Mauricio: "We could." Both he and Mark go out on sticker rain tires.

A bunch of us are watching the TV monitor. We can see the cars on course are spraying water off their tires. One by one the heads turn toward the west and look at the darkening skies. The guys look at each other and a few grins begin to appear.

Both cars come back in. Mark says, "If it's gonna dry you're going to have to be out with at least 6 or 7 minutes to go to have time for a hot lap. It's still bloody wet out there."

Mauricio calls Andy to the car to talk. There's 5 minutes to go.

With 3 minutes to go Mauricio goes out to scuff a set of rain tires. Gil de Ferran spins in Canada corner. At 2:02 the checkered flag ends the session. The PacWest guys gather round to shake hands and slap backs. Lots of grins showing. The race will start with a PacWest front row.

Five minutes later the rain is coming down hard.

The same three guys, Mauricio, Mark, and Zanardi, go to the media center for the pole press conference. All the questions were asked yesterday, and it's a less-interesting event. Someone asks Mauricio about the risks of starting the race in the rain. "It's dangerous for sure. I'd rather have Mark next to me than anyone else."

Mark sounds less attuned to teamwork. "We have to run our own race, but we have to be careful."

A famous watering hole near Road America is Siebken's Resort. On my way back to the motel I stop for a beer. It's early and the rain has just let up so not many people are there. Behind the bar decals and stickers with famous racing names from the past and present are stuck on the wall.

SUNDAY

At 7:30 a.m. I'm in the media center. The sky is overcast and the air cool and breezy, like before a summer storm. There were drops of rain on the windshield during the drive to the track. I had planned to stay in Manitowoc tonight and drive to Milwaukee Monday morning for my flight home, but instead I checked out this morning, and I'll drive to Milwaukee tonight and get a room at a motel near the airport.

At 8:15 I'm in the PacWest garage area talking to Roscoe, really Russ Grosshans, the 17-car gearbox guy. "This is what we work for," Roscoe says. "Race day. It can be great or it can be horrible, depending on what happens."

Both primary cars are on the setup pads. It's raining lightly, but it's a long time until the race starts at 3 o'clock. Andy tells me the engine drama yesterday was caused by a zero missing from a rev-limit table in the ECM. The engine thought it was on the rev limit even when it was idling. Above the rev limit, the ECM randomly drops signals to the ignition coils at the spark plugs, creating a controlled misfire that keeps the engine from producing power. That's why the engine sounded so bad.

The Formula Atlantics finish their warm-up session and the Dodge Neons go on course. I haven't had a pace-car ride around the track because the PPG pace cars are a mile away in the lower paddock, and I just haven't had the time to walk down there. I saw Wally Dallenbach, the chief steward, earlier and asked him if I could ride a lap with him this morning. He said fine so I go looking for him as the Neon session winds down.

Wally drives an inspection lap, not a fast one like the pace cars. The impression I get is one of natural terrain up and over hills and through valleys, and the gun-barrel path of the track through the trees. Wally worries aloud about the safety problems looming in the track's future. The racecourse is beautiful, for sure, and I hope CART races here for years to come, but the track management will have to spend some money on improvements.

At 10:15 the rain is coming down steadily. Mark Moore laughs at the Rahal crews already taking down their tents. "That's dumb. It's probably going to rain all day."

Warm-Up

The session starts at 10:32. All of us have on rain gear, and the drivers concentrate on getting comfortable with driving in the wet. Both Mark and Mo talk about helmet-visor details. Brakes are also a problem. On a wet track they can't really heat up the brakes, so the crews partially block the air ducts with duct tape. This creates the possibility of overheating the brakes so there is a lot of talk about brake temperatures, and Butch has his guys take the wheels off Mark's car at one point so they can check the temperature-sensitive paint on the rotors to see how hot they've been.

I hear Andy tell Mauricio that the Firestone rain tires have changed since Portland. I ask "Little Brett" Schilling, Firestone engineer, about the difference. "A small compound change," he says. Of course a small compound change could make a big difference in the tire.

A lot of cars spin in this session. Some just go off and on, while others hit the wall as Bryan Herta does at Turn 3, causing a red flag. About halfway in the session Mo and Mark almost come together on course. The TV monitor is on them at the time. Scott Simpson is watching and he turns to me and puts his thumb and forefinger together saying, "That close." An incident like that could cause a lot of unnecessary work for the crews.

Bruce McCaw is here in the scoring cart by himself. Both cars come in practicing a hot pit stop. With about 10 minutes to go Mark describes the conditions on the racetrack. "The track, there's no way we can run like this in the race. Through the Carousel and the Kink there's still puddles, and if you go through there 2 inches off line, you're going to be smack into the barrier, and you can't see. Do the visor and I'll go out and run some more."

There's another red flag at 11:14, and Mark Moore says, "Haven't we had enough of this?"

Mark comes in and Allen says, "Take us around for a lap, what you can see of it."

Mark: "Basically, all around the circuit is, under braking, just getting the car to have a little more front end. There's not enough download on the front of the car. The middle-corner grip is actually reasonable. The biggest issue then is trying to come off apex to exit with a flick oversteer."

Allen: "What about the high speed?"

Mark: "Around the Carousel it isn't too bad. The car starts to sit down and has some push there, but in the Kink you have to brake there, and it makes the car pointy as you go in."

Andy asks Mauricio, "Do you need more laps with the brakes?"

Mauricio: "No, they have to sand them down. If we're not going to do any changes, there's no point in going out there again. I feel the car is a bit stiff for these conditions, but I don't want to even touch it."

Andy: "It's a dry setup, so I'd like to leave it as it is, to be honest. Do you agree? Is there any point in making changes to the car?"

Mauricio: "It depends on what the weather's going to do. Right now it's raining like hell, but I'd rather have a car that might be a bit difficult for me in the wet, but if a lot of cars are running and it stops raining, my car should be better."

Andy: "I agree."

Mauricio: "This is one of the worst conditions I ever drove in my life, but we didn't put a wheel on the grass yet."

Andy: "Well, you're not going to get a timed lap with 5 minutes of green, so we might as well pull it back under the tent."

Mauricio: "Let's do that and then just monitor the weather." He gets out of the car.

Mark goes back out on track again with 5 minutes to go, but it's raining harder now. He comes right back in and Allen says, "All right, let's put it away." Alex Zanardi had the best lap of that session, a 135.917-seconds lap, 3 seconds quicker than Mauricio in P2. Mark is P7.

Trying to Stay Dry

Al Speyer, Firestone's director of motorsports, comes by the PacWest garage area to congratulate Mauricio on his pole position. Little Brett is here looking at the rain tires Mauricio ran in that session. "He just knocked the corners off. They're fine."

Ned Wicker, editor of *Indy Car Magazine*, interviews Mark and Mo on the PA system. "If you go into the first corner at the same time, who lifts?"

Mark says, "Technically Mo should get there first; he's in the pole position. After that we have to race our own race."

Mauricio's answer is, "There's room enough for both of us. It's a long race."

The Formula Atlantic race starts an hour late at 12:15 p.m. Their rain tires throw up huge rooster tails of spray. Mostly I hear the sound of their engines from under the PacWest tents. They have several short bursts of racing between droning periods of yellow flag.

I ask Russ Cameron about the race strategy. "It's all up in the air. It'll be two stops if it's wet, but it could take three in the dry. You could probably do it in two stops, if you run lean and get some yellows."

Daryl Fox in the Driver's Seat Under Cover

Jim Reid in the 17-Car Trying to Stay Dry

"What about the Goodyear rain tires?"

"It's tough to tell. It looks like the Firestones are better."

Allen McDonald says, "We've agonized over a full-wet setup, but we're not going to do it. We can't go with something Mark's not used to. The conditions are bloody miserable. I told him to let people pass him. Just motor around, and don't go off. That's a podium for sure.

"It's a dangerous track. Charlie Whiting [Formula 1 technical administrator] came over here a few years ago to look at the U.S. tracks and the possibility of having an F-1 race in the States. He said Mid-Ohio was a possibility, but Elkhart was no way. We're cranking some more front wing in on Mark's car to give it some grip in the wet."

The schedule shows gridding the CART cars starts at 1:45, but the rain is still coming down. The CART officials call the cars to the pre-grid anyway at 1:50. We all stand around in the rain for a while, and then I hear Wally's voice on my scanner saying, "Kirk [Russell], here's what I want to do. Announce that we're on a hold 'til the conditions improve."

Kirk comes on the radio saying, "All participants: One or more people can stay with the cars, but most people should go under cover."

An hour later it's still raining steadily and we're all hovering under the tents in the garage area. Ando tells me, "They won't start under these conditions. It's forecast to rain here 'til 4 or 5 p.m. We might have to race tomorrow."

Turtle the fireman is here again and I catch him napping during the rain.

At 3:20 they call the Neon Challenge drivers to their cars. The decision has been made to run that race, let them pump the water off the course, and hope the rain lets up for a late-afternoon start of the CART race.

They start the Neon race at 3:55. CART says be ready to start the race right after the Neons are through. Jim Hamilton, Mark Moore, and I are in the 17-car engineering cart watching an Indy Racing League race on the TV. The rain pelts down onto the vinyl covering.

Mark turns to Jim grinning and hooks a thumb at me. "I was talking to our writer here, and I told him I hope I can get a job after you come out with this book. Paul told me, 'Jim Hamilton said the same thing 3 months ago.'"

A Snoring Turtle

I burst out laughing. Jim just shakes his head and says, "I'm not talking to you anymore."

About 4:10 the rain stops, and the CART officials are going to checkered flag the Neon race and start the CART race at 4:30.

THE RACE

This will be a wet race, meaning all cars start on rain tires, and no tire changes are allowed until after the green flag. In addition the start will be single file for safety reasons.

We're all out on the frontstraight again at pre-grid. At 4:30 the national anthem is sung and the CART officials are waiting for the TV people to say they're ready. The jet-blower truck is on the mainstraight blowing the big puddles off the track. I can see clouds of water kicked up into spray by the exhaust of the jet engine. At 4:42 someone says, "Gentlemen, start your engines!"

I walk back to the PacWest pits and find a place right at a break in the pit wall. I can see a monitor, which is good because I can't see much of the cars as they flash by on the pit straight. This is a 50-lap race.

During the pace laps Mauricio says, "The only place that will be bad is where the trees are." Where the trees overhang the track they continue to drip water onto the surface.

Russ Cameron and Mauricio talk about the possibility of the track drying and Mo having to switch to slick tires. Russ says, "We'll be watching your lap times compared to the other competitors, but it's your call out there."

Jim Swintal starts the race at 4:52 and Mauricio leads into the first turn. An all-course yellow flag waves immediately, however, and the cars slow behind a pace car. Gualter Salles spun and collected Paul Tracy, who slid off course and flipped upside down.

Mark tells Ando, "These wets won't last long because there's no surface water out there. It's just greasy conditions."

Ando says, "OK, just hang on as long as you can then."

The race restarts on lap three. Mauricio builds up a slight lead over Mark. He's followed by Zanardi, Franchitti, and Michael Andretti. Zanardi gets off into the grass and Franchitti passes him for third.

Mauricio drives out to a lead of almost 2 seconds, but Mark begins to catch him up. Franchitti is pressing Mark. I can't tell if Mo is slowing or Mark is going faster.

On lap nine Mark comes out of the last turn quicker than Mauricio and passes him on the pit straight. Mark just draws away. I can see on the monitor that there is a dry line all around the track. The cars are running off line on the straights trying to find water to cool their tires. Nobody wants to stop earlier than lap 16, or they might have to make a late third stop for fuel.

If someone would take the risk to stop early and switch to slicks, that guy might get good track position after everyone else makes their pit stops. Michael Andretti takes that risk on lap 13, but he makes a mistake and spins off course before he gets enough heat in his tires. That causes a yellow flag at just the right time for everyone else to pit for fuel and slick tires.

Ando talks Mark into the pit box: "OK, you're lookin' for Butch. Nice and easy now. Easy. Easy. That's it. That's it. Stop!"

Coming out of the pits Dario Franchitti almost gets by Mark but he goes off at Turn 1 and hits the wall. This causes a yellow flag and after the restart Bryan Herta, who did not pit, is the leader followed by Mark, Zanardi, Mauricio, and de Ferran. Fernandez and Salles come together right after the start, causing another yellow flag. This time Herta pits, handing the lead back to Mark.

At the restart P.J. Jones and Hiro Matsushita crash together, and we have another yellow flag. This is boring.

Mark is saying he's got a big vibration when he brakes. Ando tells him to use the yellow-flag period to build up heat in the brakes and then let them cool. "Work away at 'em."

Mark says the car is bottoming, "It's knockin' the crap out of the front of the car."

Ando tells him to work with it and try to adjust the tim. "Use the button on the start if you have to. You're lookin' good."

Mark says, "Just to let you know, the clutch is going away, so at the next pit stop make sure to give me a good shove."

Ando: "Don't put it in gear with plenty of rpm on. See if you can get it cleanly. We'll have the boys on the rear wing give you a shove out. If you don't think it's going to go in, we'll give you a shove before you pull a gear. Don't crowd that pace car."

We have another restart on lap 24, but incredibly there's another crash. This time it's Jimmy Vasser and Parker Johnstone. Ando coaches Mark on the restarts: "You're looking pretty good on the last start. But you may want to let the pace car lead you a bit more."

Mark says Zanardi might have a little less aero drag in his car. "They catch us by the end of the straight."

Ando asks about the brakes, "How they lookin' now? Better?"

Mark: "Still vibratin', which is still a little bit of a problem. I want to go deeper into the corner and I can't. I need a little bit more work with the tires."

Ando: "Our experience is the more we use them, the quicker they get through that vibration. Keep us posted there. There's not much we can do but carry on."

Mark: "The pace car is too slow. The car is groundin' because there's no pressure in the tires. That's a big problem."

Ando: "OK; they're going to try to get the pace car to go faster."

Russ tells Mauricio, "For the restart go to slot four; after it settles down go to three."

Ando is still talking about the restart coming up. "We'll go green next time. Think about this one. You just need to time your run from behind the pace car. We want you to go to zero on the fuel as you come down that backstraight. OK, let's have a little wiggle there, mate. I know it's difficult for you, but we need more temp in those tires. This is going to be a perfect restart, this one. Don't get in a position where you got to slow down. Pace car is in. Green! Green!"

Mark and Mauricio both make good starts. Mo passes Zanardi into Turn 1 for second spot, but Zanardi repays the favor later that lap. The order is Mark, Zanardi, Mo, de Ferran, and Christian Fittipaldi.

Cars continue to go off the track and struggle back on, but on lap 35 Greg Moore tries to pass Bobby Rahal and crashes, bringing out an all-course yellow flag just when everyone needs to pit for fuel.

Russ asks Mauricio, "Do you want any changes?"

"No," says Mauricio.

As Mark comes down the pit lane with Zanardi right behind him, he yells, "Don't change tires." The stops look good but Zanardi gets out ahead of Mark. Mauricio goes back out still holding third.

Russ tells Mo, "Zanardi and Mark didn't change tires. You might have an advantage."

Mauricio: "I have to warm them up." Maybe that was a smart thing that Mark and Zanardi did. Their tires certainly aren't wearing in these conditions, and they didn't have to warm up new ones like Mauricio has to do.

Ando tells Mark, "Keep the pressure on him. Wait for the car to come to you."

Every time Mark comes by on the straight, Ando says something encouraging. "Get up on him. We need this fuel setting another lap. Get up there."

Zanardi builds a lead on Mark, then he goes off into the grass and Mark catches up and looks to have a chance at getting by. But three laps from the end Mark's engine lets go in a cloud of smoke and fire. His race is over.

Zanardi wins another race and celebrates with some tire-smoking doughnuts during his cool-off lap. Mauricio is second and de Ferran third.

The 18-crew shows little emotion when Mark pulls off course. They just begin to pack up the equipment. The 17-crew is happy with Mo's second place, but there is no whooping and hollering. It's not a win, and they're getting used to running up front.

I say good-bye to the guys and head for the victory-lane celebration outside the media center. Mauricio says he's glad to get the second place. He and Andy had the car set up for drier conditions, and he didn't have the car he needed to fight for the lead.

The race ended about 6:55 p.m. At 7:15 the podium ceremony is winding down, so I walk to the car and get into the line heading for a gate; I don't know which one. Fifteen minutes later I'm on a road south and then I turn onto another road headed east. Rain starts to hit the windshield shortly after I get on the interstate, and it persists all the way to Milwaukee.

After a night in a motel I catch my flight back home. I've got 10 days before the trip to Vancouver.

A Second-Place Trophy for Mauricio
(Dan Boyd Photo)

CHAPTER 21

VANCOUVER

The only real hassle I've had this year is the travel, so I'm glad the last three races of the season are in my time zone. The hop up to Vancouver, British Columbia, from the San Francisco airport is a treat because of the view of the mountains out of the right side of the plane. I usually don't need a car here, but I'm driving to Seattle Sunday after the race for the two-day party at Bruce McCaw's getaway, called Caledon. The guys have been anticipating this event in conversation for some time, so it must be a good time.

Our hotel in Vancouver, the Rosedale on Robson, is only a couple of blocks away from the track, so after I check in I walk over to the track. The PacWest garage area is busy as usual. All the guys are setting up equipment on pit lane or getting the cars ready for practice tomorrow. I usually don't get to see them put up the tents that mount off the sides of the transporters, but I'm here earlier today because of the short flight. Guys on top of the haulers attach the tent anchors, while others below thread the aluminum tubes that make up the frame into the tent material.

Mark's engine failure at Elkhart Lake was not an engine problem. A visor tear-off got into a cooler duct and blocked airflow. Ian Hawkins, Ilmor engineer assigned to the 18-car, could see the engine temperature go up as it overheated. "It's difficult just watching it die and not being able to do anything about it."

There seems to be some discussion of how Zanardi got out ahead of Mark after the second pit stop. Mark had a 2-second lead on the track, and his stop was a good one. Zanardi's win at Road America gives him a big lead in the championship points over Gil de Ferran. Paul Tracy is third, but the Penske chassis is outclassed by the Reynard.

Robson Street is the main drag in downtown Vancouver. I always enjoy walking here and watching the people. Unlike many American cities, I always feel safe here. There's good food in Vancouver also. After a pasta dinner I stop in an ice cream shop for some dessert. Later I talk to some PacWest people in the hotel bar.

Russ Cameron is the PacWest crew chief which means all the people who work on the cars or make or order parts for the cars work for him. It's a big job, and on top of that Russ is the race strategist for Mauricio. He's the guy who talks to Mo during races and calls the timing on the pit stops. He admits to me that sometimes the rah-rah he's saying to Mauricio during a race doesn't feel right. "I'm supposed to be saying things to motivate him and make him try harder, but he doesn't really need that."

"It seems to me that Mauricio is one of the most technical drivers in the series," I say. "He knows a lot about the car. But Blundell seems to be a better racer."

"Mauricio is still engineering the car in the race," Russ says. "He needs to just race it. I see Zanardi and Blundell really flogging the car, operating outside of the envelope. Mauricio is too comfortable in the car."

"Maybe he's too sympathetic with the equipment?"

"Could be."

FRIDAY

The sky is overcast this morning, as it is most of the time in the Pacific Northwest. The race weekends that I've been here have been mostly dry, and hopefully so will this one. The crews are just getting into the garage area at 7:30. The practice session doesn't start until 11.

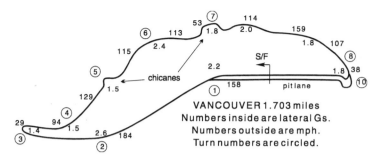

VANCOUVER 1.703 miles
Numbers inside are lateral Gs.
Numbers outside are mph.
Turn numbers are circled.

Later I ask Malcolm Oastler, the Reynard chief designer, how work is going on the design of the '98 car. "Pretty good, I think. I'll get a look at it this next week."

"It amazes me that you can continue to make significant improvements every year," I say.

"It is remarkable. We have good people and they work hard at it."

Pace-Car Ride

The sun is peeking in and out of the clouds, and the air is warming. At 9:15 I go to the pit lane and stand in line for a ride in a PPG pace car. My driver is Margy Eatwell again, but this time she's driving a Honda NSX. Several years ago I drove an NSX at Sears Point during a press demonstration event. It was impressive then, and it's impressive now.

The track is bumpy and the hard-braking areas at the end of the straights are curved, forcing the driver to brake while turning the car into the corner. That means the brake balance has to be just right or the drivers will flat-spot the right-front tires. The first chicane on the back side of the course has big curbs that can toss the car into the outer wall if the driver doesn't place the car precisely.

Friday Practice

A green flag starts the session at 11:02. Both PacWest cars go out and come back in for their installation checks. Paul Tracy spins in the hairpin, causing a red flag. I can see the bumps at Start/Finish bounce the cars badly. Some cars bounce more at the front than the rear, but mostly I see the rear of the cars moving.

The PacWest cars are in the last pit closest to pit-out and Turn 1. This is convenient for me, because I can see a monitor in the scoring cart or over someone's shoulder in the 18-car engineering cart, and I can see a big-screen TV across the frontstraight that shows me the on-track action. The cars come out of Turn 9 way off to my right and go into Turn 1 just in front of us. The Ganassi team, Alex Zanardi and Jimmy Vasser, are in the next two pit boxes to the right of us.

Mauricio comes in during a red flag saying his car is crashing down on the pit straight. "It feels too soft, but the pressures could be down. It's too early to do too much."

Andy: "The front pressure-sensors aren't working, but the rears are still a pound and a half or 2 pounds down. This won't be a long wait. They're pushing Tracy out of the way, so we'll be going green very soon."

Russ Cameron tells Mauricio, "Make sure you put some rubber down here, Mo." The course goes green at 11:14 and Mauricio smokes the rear tires on the way out.

When Mauricio comes back in he says the gear indicator on his dash is showing the wrong gears. "The car is just crashing down on the straights. I have to brake before the kink at the end of the straight. If I go at high speed through there, it wants to go straight into the wall."

Andy: "We'd like to jack the car up and run the car through the gears." The crew puts the car up on jack stands and manually rotates the rear wheels while Mo changes gears and calls out what gear his dash says he's in.

Andy: "Do you still have that pointy feeling? Rather than give the grip away by trying to come up on forces, we could just raise the front of the car."

Mauricio: "We should raise the front and the back, right now."

Andy: "OK, we'll do that. Let's make a run with that and then we'll change the gear pot." They raise the car two flats all around and Mauricio goes back on course.

Mark is in P2 at 11:20. He comes in and talks about the car. "The car has a lot of roll in it. It really gets upset. It's touchin' down and that's unsettlin' it. Squeezing on the power the rear of the car is rolling, and it's really unsettled now. It doesn't give up completely enough to really slide out, but it feels like it needs a little bit of support there. It's a little bit scary, 'cause it feels like the rear is going to jack around when it hits the bumps."

Colleen Howerton, Darla Elkins, and Michel Molin
Talk with Mark Blundell

Allen: "How's the gearbox?"

Mark: "Downshifts, really weak. What's happening is I try to shift, and it won't go down the box. Upshifts as well, it won't allow me to shift up. The last lap I hit the limiter in every gear. It's not popping out directly. The brake pedal is soft, Allen, as well."

Allen: "Where's the car touchin' down?"

Mark: "It feels like it's touching down a fair amount on the front end. It's touching down at the back as well. It gets to a certain speed and then it hits those bumps pretty hard."

Allen: "Try going full stiff on your front roll bar and see what you think." Allen says to go up on the ride height all around.

Mark: "The other thing is the wheelspin lights — they're on all the time. I don't know if that's the software installation or what."

That's the first I've heard about wheelspin lights, but it wouldn't be difficult. The on-board computer can compare the wheel speeds of a front and a rear wheel and turn on a series of lights as the speed difference increases. That would give the driver some help controlling the throttle out of the slow corners. Several years ago some teams used a traction control that worked similarly, dropping cylinder sparks like a rev limiter to control engine power and eliminate wheelspin off slow corners. That was outlawed, but there is no rule prohibiting a warning light.

Mark goes back out on course, but slides into the tires at the new chicane in the backstraight. After he can hear that Mark is all right, Allen asks about the car. Mark answers on the radio, still sitting in the car. "The wing and the suspension on the right-hand side is bent or broken."

The crew rolls up the 18x-car from behind the pits. The monitor shows Scott Pruett has the quick lap at 56.524 seconds, followed by Michael Andretti, Mark, Andre Ribeiro, and Jimmy Vasser. Mauricio is off the page.

The 18-crew continues to prepare the back-up car for Mark. The wrecker takes the primary car straight to the garage area. Butch tells Daryl to get the stuff off the car and bring it all to pit lane so they can install it in the 18x-car. The seat and steering wheel and cockpit padding have all been customized for Mark and need to go into the x-car. They immediately begin to repair the primary car in the garage area. Butch says, "Change that wishbone and get that car back out here."

Andy and Mauricio continue to try to dial in their car. Andy suggests they raise the car at the rear. He asks Mauricio if he feels any difference between left- and right-hand corners. Mauricio says, "The right-handers are understeering more."

Andy: "That's probably the tire pressures then." He adjusts the tire pressures and asks Mauricio to do a front sway bar scan on his next run. The course goes green again and Mauricio returns to the track. The engine in the 18x-car is warming. Alex Zanardi is P1 now.

At 11:43 Mauricio is back in, having improved to P12. Andy asks, "How was the crashing that time?"

Mauricio: "It's better, but there is a lot of amplitude in the car. I have the grip, but a lot of amplitude." Andy suggests a shock change.

Daryl radios Butch from the garage area saying they have the wishbone on and are installing a new steering arm. Butch says, "Just make sure everything adds up. OK?"

"Yeah, we're gonna put it on the pad and take camber and toe and all that," Daryl says. "We'll make sure everything's OK." Mark gets in the 18x-car and says the brake pedal is softer than the other car. He goes on course at 11:53. There's 23 minutes to go in the session. Mauricio drives back out also. He's now P8. Improving times have slipped Mark to P13.

When Mauricio comes back in, Andy asks about the shock change. "It's better. It helps the front and there's less amplitude."

Mark comes back in saying he's locking up the left-front brake all around the track. Allen prescribes some shock and ride-height changes. "Come out a turn and a half on the front shocktopussy, please. And go up another flat all 'round."

Mauricio returns to the circuit at 12:01. Mark is back out a minute later. There's 15 minutes to go. At 12:03 Russ Cameron radios Butch that the 18-car is repaired. "Do you want it on pit lane?"

"Just leave the car there," Butch says. "Bring the guys back out here."

Mauricio is back in, having moved up to P6. He says the front of the car is too stiff. Andy says, "What I'd like to do with the front, especially if you're still having problems under braking, is wind the shocktopussy out a little."

Mauricio: "That might help the braking; it might brake flatter."

Mark is back in at 12:07 saying, "I've lost a bit of front grip in terms of turn-in and precision. It's a catch 22. I still don't feel confident goin' into the corner harder and a bit deeper. The other thing is, when I get on the gas, the rear of the car can't recover. So when you go into a corner, the rear starts to come up and roll, and then when you have a direction change, it's still trying to recover from turning in so there you are trying to go the other way. It falls over itself and you come off the corner completely sideways, to the point that the tires are like... vibrating, trying to struggle for grip."

Allen: "OK. We'll make a rear damping change. Let's go stiffer on the rear low-speed bump, two sweeps, and the rear high-speed rebound, two sweeps stiffer. Do you want to do a sticker run?"

Mark: "I don't feel we're there with the car. The front of the car is still touchin' down way too much. I don't know if it's just too low, or we need some damping and it's just crashing through. I've got no confidence to go through some of these corners. The thing's just pickin' me up and chuckin' me across the road."

Allen: "OK, we'll make a front damping change as well. That will give us a feeling for the ride heights. Two sweeps of front low-speed and high-speed bump, please."

Mark and Mo are both back on track with about 8 minutes to go. Mauricio is P8 and Mark P16. Mark goes by on the frontstraight saying he's made an adjustment to the tim. A few minutes later Blake Hamilton, standing near me watching a monitor, flashes an index finger to Roy Wilkerson. Mauricio has jumped up to P1 with a lap of 55.340 seconds.

He goes by again asking Andy how much time is left. "Two minutes and 30 seconds, Morris. You're P1." Mauricio comes in saying he got behind Dario Franchitti and couldn't get a clear lap to improve the time. The checkered flag waves at 12:16. Mark ended up P17 in the primary car and P13 in the back-up.

Back in the garage area Charlie and Daryl are looking at the bent A-arm and steering arm from Mark's crash. They'll take the mounting blocks off the car and crack-check them.

Friday Qualifying

This session is scheduled for 2:30, but goes green at 2:59 p.m. The fast guys are first as usual on Friday. Mauricio goes right out on the track. Mark waits. As he pulls out, Allen says, "Don't forget your front bar." Five minutes into the session Mo is P1 with a lap time of 55.325 and Mark is P2. Vasser and de Ferran are close behind. Then Mark slows, and the car stops before reaching the pit box. There's some smoke at the rear. It looks like the engine blew.

The 18-crew, for the second session in a row, begins to switch components off the primary car to install on the back-up car. Mauricio comes back in saying the engine is cutting out. Andy says, "We're P4. Zanardi is fastest with a 54.8. Our fastest is a 55.3. There's no reason to change anything, because the pressures continue to build a little."

Mauricio: "I'm losing some grip. Nothing drastic, but I'm losing some grip." He goes back out at 3:11. Mark climbs up into the scoring cart with Bruce and Jolene. There's a red flag because of a spin and crash by Gil de Ferran. Mo comes back into his pit box.

Andy: "Do you need any changes to the rear ride height, Morris? Are we hitting about right back there now?"

Mauricio: "The rear ride-heights are about right. How are the tire pressures?"

Andy: "I saw 2 pounds up all 'round on the sensors at the end of the last lap."

Russ Cameron tells me that Mark won't run the T-car this session. "There are some things they don't want to change over to the T-car. He'll just wait 'til tomorrow."

Andy: "We can't really understand why you can't change the gears. As you back off you're so far off the throttle that it should allow the dog teeth to engage. We can't make any changes, really." The course goes green and Mauricio goes back out with 15 minutes to go. Zanardi is P1 followed by de Ferran, Jimmy Vasser, Scott Pruett, and Mauricio.

Mo comes back in and Andy makes some shock changes. Mo asks Andy if he should leave BOSS on. Andy says, "Yeah, leave it on, Morris. It's still learning." He can see from the transmitted data that the plenum pressure is still rising as the BOSS system optimizes the turbo boost.

The 17-crew puts on new primary tires and Mauricio goes on track with 9 minutes to go. After an out lap and a tire-warming lap, he starts a flyer and improves to 55.280 for P3. Mark is still in the scoring cart watching the monitor.

Mauricio tells Andy he'll drive a slow lap and then try another quick one. Bryan Herta jumps ahead of him and Mo slips to P6. Trying too hard, Mauricio locks up his brakes coming into the hairpin at the start of the pit straight. He has to use the pit entrance as a runoff. He motors through the pits and starts an out-lap. Andy tells him, "There's 2 minutes to go. You're P8."

Maybe he has enough time for one last timed lap. Then Greg Moore spins and hits a wall but drives the car away. "I've locked up something. I'm coming in," Mauricio says. He only improves a couple of tenths of a second, finishing the session in ninth spot. Mark slips to 12th. Zanardi has the provisional pole position with a lap of 54.184 seconds. Right behind him are Scott Pruett, Michael Andretti, and Jimmy Vasser.

Repairs

At 4 o'clock in the garage area the 18-crew is changing engines. The one out of the primary car has a jagged hole in the head right above an exhaust port. Some light sprinkles of rain are falling, but not enough to wet the ground. The slow-guys' qualifying group is still on track.

Mark was not happy with the way his gearbox worked today, so Dr. Love - Tim Love, the 18-car gearbox guy — is fooling around with the selector barrel. At 6 o'clock I ask Gavin Hamilton how long the engine changes will take. "We'll be done by 8."

Because of the engine changes the undertrays of both PacWest cars are laying out on stands. Malcolm Oastler is here again, so I ask him if the bottom of the '98 car will have any changes. He smiles at me and says, "All different." That amazes me. Air is air. How do they continue to learn how to get more downforce out of the bottom of the car?

SATURDAY

In the garage area at 7:15 the guys are at work prepping the cars for the 9 a.m. practice. The air is warm, about 70 degrees, and it's humid. The sky is cloudy to the west but the sun is coming up bright in the east. Walking in I noticed a patch on the frontstraight where they've tried to smooth down that bump at Start/Finish.

At 8:30 in the pit lane the Formula Atlantics are on course qualifying for their race later this afternoon. One of the Ganassi crews is practicing pit stops. The 18-car crew watches them intently. Maybe that's the team that beat them at Elkhart. Each of these guys knows every move it takes for him to do his job during a pit stop. Watching those other guys now, he can compare himself with the guy doing his job over there.

Morning Practice

The session starts at 9:02. The sky is overcast. Both PacWest cars go out and come back in for their installation checks. Within a few laps Bobby Rahal gets into the tires at one of the chicanes. A red flag stops the session, and Andy warns Mauricio to watch for Rahal as he's coming back into the pits. Rahal gets a push start and motors away. The course goes green again at 9:10.

Both Mark and Mauricio say the track feels like it has less grip than yesterday. Andy tells Mauricio, "The Atlantic guys are off their pace from yesterday as well." Five minutes later Dennis Vitolo goes into a run-off area somewhere, causing another red flag.

Mauricio says, "The tires came in eventually. I do have a bit more front grip than before, but I need to run a bit more and then see exactly where we are. There are a lot of cars out there and a lot of people going straight [down the run-offs at the turns] and making mistakes. It's hitting down at the kink before the hairpin, but I don't want to raise it yet."

Mark: "I'm on the gas all the way through that backstraight, but the rear of the car's got a helluva lot of movement. We gotta try and calm that down. It's still lacking some front grip on the low-speed turn-in."

Allen and Mark decide to make a change to the rear roll center. On the Reynard this can be done by turning the outboard mounting blocks around where the A-arm attaches to the hub, changing the height of the attachment. While that work goes on, Mark talks about how the car feels around the circuit. "At Turn 1 the balance is good. It's a bit quicker on turn-in and the entry into 2, the fast kink, it seems to have calmed down quite a bit. It needs a bit more damper control on the front end. There are a couple of bumps there where we could carry a bit more speed.

"Coming off there into the braking area, the rear of the car is gettin' a little bit unsettled. There's still a lack of front load as well, so the fronts are lockin' up. Lack of front grip, entry to mid. Secondary apex, I've got push and exit oversteer. I'm really limited as to how I can get on the gas there. The car still rolls a bit too much as we accelerate, and it carries a little bit of that into the chicane. It's still slightly better with the rear springs. As it is, the rear gives a little kick as it turns in. A little more front grip on turn-in, but we still need to improve that again.

"I need a little bit more response in direction change. Power out in that chicane, we've still got that sensation of roll building up in the rear. Secondary chicane, the front end is a little bit light under braking and at turn-in it kicks again on the rear. The direction change is weaker, and it enables me to come off that chicane cleaner. It still takes a little bit of a lift, but it's quicker now than it was yesterday.

"From there the rear just has too much movement, and the quicker we go the front gets some of its energy used up and by the time I'm into the braking area there's no suspension travel left. That's why it's hard for me to stop the car. We should be brakin' deeper, but there's nothing there to absorb the bumps. Turn-in is slow, the front end is still weak, and there's not enough grip on the second part of that corner." That's the best description of an entire lap I've heard all year.

Mark goes back on track after the roll-center change. He turns a lap at 56.244 seconds to earn P1. Then Mauricio takes over P1. Jimmy Vasser, Scott Pruett, and Alex Zanardi are all up at the top of the list. Mauricio comes in and Mark goes back on course.

Mauricio says, "The rear has a lot of amplitude. When I go out it takes two laps because the car is so high at the back it's just not gripping at all. It's just too high on the ride height. The back is scaring me." They make some changes, but I don't hear what they are.

Mark comes back in saying the roll-center change didn't make any difference at all. He's having problems shifting down through the gears into the corners. They decide to make a front geometry change. Gavin and Charlie work on the front suspension — the rear upper A-arm mount. Maybe they're making a caster change. Mark and Allen talk about the lap times today, which are 2 seconds slower than yesterday during qualifying. They don't know why.

Allen: "So, was that rear roll-center change a good move or a bad move?"

Mark: "I'm not so sure that I like it. It seems to make the car a little bit looser on entry, and also from the mid to the exit it feels like there's going to be more push in it. So in terms of overall balance the car feels slightly better, but I'm not sure the roll center's in its proper position."

Allen: "Given the amount of time we have, should we go back on that change?"

Mark: "Let's do that. Put the roll center back and make a front-end change."

They also change the gearshift pot on Mark's car to help his shift problem. With about 30 minutes to go Michel Jourdain Jr. is in P1. This is a surprise. I don't think he's ever been the fastest driver in a session before. Mauricio is in P7 and Mark P8. Mark goes out to try the shift change and comes right back in saying it's not better. They change the engine control unit.

Mauricio is having traction problems coming off the corners, so he and Andy decide to change rear springs. They must have gone stiffer because Andy tells Mark Moore to lower the car at the rear. At 9:48 with 17 minutes to go Alex Zanardi goes to P1. Mauricio is P5 and Mark P10.

Both Allen and Andy propose shock changes and Trevor Jackson has to hop back and forth between the cars tweaking the shock adjustments. Mauricio says he doesn't like the way his rear tires look.

Mark comes back in saying the shock adjustments didn't work, and Allen suggests they go back on the shock change. Mauricio comes off the track unhappy with the changes on his car also. Andy tells him he's going back on the spring and damper changes and will also go back to the original ride-height settings.

With about 7 minutes to go in the session both PacWest cars go back out. Andy tells Mauricio, "Evaluate this as quick as you can, and then we'll make a sticker run."

The top three now are Zanardi, Bryan Herta, and Bobby Rahal. Mo is P8 and Mark P12. Then Jimmy Vasser jumps to P1 and Mark goes to P2 with a lap of 55.184 seconds.

Mark comes by on the pit straight saying, "Front bar full stiff."

"Two laps left," Al Bodey tells him. The sun breaks through the clouds and warms my back as Mauricio storms by into Turn 1. That lap of 54.996 seconds bumps him up to P3. The checkered flag ends the session, but Mo gets to finish this timed lap. He comes by again and the monitor flashes him to P1 with a time of 54.769 seconds, still a half-second slower than qualifying yesterday. Mark is P4. The top five are Mo, Andre Ribeiro, Jimmy Vasser, Mark, and Alex Zanardi.

Charlie Guilinger, one of Mark's crew members, leans over toward Mauricio's crew and says, "Good job, guys."

I hear Andy on the radio tell Mauricio, "Good job, sir."

Final Qualifying

The slow-guys' group starts qualifying at 1:05 p.m. They finish at 1:38 and the safety trucks go on track for clean up and inspection. The green flag for the fast guys waves at 1:52. Allen says to Mark, "Slot seven on the fuel. You've got fuel for eight timed laps. Don't forget what we've done with tim. If you want to, you can readjust that if the situation demands it."

Bruce and Jolene are here in the scoring cart. After the first stint on track, Mark says the car has too much push. "Coming into the chicane, that little bit of lack of front grip makes me a little bit apprehensive on entry. I want to drive the car into the corner harder. That lack of front bite is not really giving me any confidence. It's not laying the power down that well either. I can't get on the gas early."

Allen asks the crew to change the front springs on Mark's car by 100 pounds, and Mark goes back out at 2:07. The monitor shows Zanardi is P1 now followed by Herta, Vasser, and Mauricio. Mark is P9.

Mauricio comes onto the pit lane talking as he's driving toward his pit box. "There's more roll in the back in the high-speed corners. But with new tires, I can live with it."

Andy: "OK, Morris. I can put a bit more bump in the rear shocks, if you think that would help."

Mauricio: "Ten-four. Just a little bit." One of the things I've learned this season is that "just a little bit" is a British unit of measure slightly smaller than "a little bit" which is smaller than "a bit."

Andy: "There's still 12 minutes of green left. It's a bit early, I feel, to go for the stickers right now. Do you want to just try this bump first?"

Mauricio: "We can wait for the tires."

Andy: "OK, I'm going to put two sweeps of low-speed bump in the rear shocks."

Mauricio goes back on track and Mark comes in, almost running over a Ganassi guy as he turns in for the pit box. He doesn't like the changes. Allen asks if he wants to go back on the spring change. Mark grimaces and says the changes might be making the car better over the bumps. They just change tires and Mark goes back out. "Don't forget your front bar and the tim," Allen says as he pulls out of the pit box.

"Nine minutes to go," says Al Bodey. Mauricio and Mark are still fourth and ninth. Mark improves to P7 with a lap of 54.600 seconds and radios that he's flat-spotted his rear tires. When he comes in Allen says, "OK, there's only 2 minutes left. We'll call it a day then."

Mauricio is still on track but can't do any better than fifth. Zanardi ends up on the pole position with a lap of 54.025 seconds. Bobby Rahal is P2 followed by Vasser, Michael Andretti, and Mauricio. Mark will start eighth on the grid tomorrow.

Race Prep

In the garage area both PacWest crews are changing engines. Mauricio is here and I ask him if he got all there was out of the car. "Yep. There must be a recipe for this place because [Al Unser] Junior and Michael [Andretti] are the only ones to ever win the race here. You have to accelerate well and brake well while you turn."

Ian Hawkins, the Ilmor engineer, answers my questions about the data acquisition built into their engine-management system. "We can record 30 channels if we want to but each one takes some extra memory, so we only use 16 to 18 channels at any one time. We need the memory because in case of a failure, we'd like to be able to see everything that happened during the last 2 minutes."

I watch the guys work on the cars for a while and then go back to the hotel. A dozen of us are talking in the hotel bar when the first television coverage of Princess Diana's death in a car wreck appears on the TVs. Some people stare at the screen intently, but most of us continue to talk racing as usual.

SUNDAY

I'm up at 5:30 a.m. and at the track at 7. I check out of the hotel but leave the car in the parking garage. I'll walk over there after the race and start my drive to Seattle. The sky is clear in the east this morning, but there are a few clouds in the west. The air is still and about 70 degrees. We're supposed to have a nice day.

Butch Winkle has an elastic wrap on his left wrist that starts across his palm and goes halfway up his forearm. "Yeah, I tore a tendon yesterday," he tells me. "We were having trouble with the rake control, and I yanked up on a wheel. It went 'pop' and the tendon just rolled up here." He points to a lump under the bandage. "I'll have an operation after the season, and they'll re-attach it."

"What about the pit stops?"

"Yeah, I'll still do that. It's not that bad. I'll get it wrapped tight. It'll hurt, but I won't feel it during the race."

I walk to the hospitality area and see Mauricio and Mark eating breakfast cereal. Back in the PacWest garage at 7:45, engines are firing up and warming. The primary cars are on the setup pads. The 18-crew is beginning to tear down their tent. Just after 8 o'clock I see Butch come back from CART medical with a tight wrap on his wrist.

At 8:20 I'm walking in the pit lane toward the PacWest pits at the far end. I see Tom Anderson, managing director of Ganassi Racing, standing in their pit box.

"Hey, Tom," I say. "At Elkhart, Zanardi was 2 seconds behind Blundell going into the pit lane for that last stop. He caught right up to Mark and then got out in front. How did that happen?"

"You can see it if you look at the tapes," Tom says. "Blundell slowed too much in the pit lane, and they took longer to get the fuel hose on. Neither car changed tires."

"Thanks for explaining that and congratulations," I say. "You guys are doing really well."

"Thanks," Tom says, smiling.

When I get to the PacWest pit box Al Bodey is there and I tell him what Tom said. "Randy got the hose in quick and the stop was OK. Either Mark slowed too much or Zanardi used him to shield himself from the radar gun and went over the pit lane speed limit."

Both PacWest crews are practicing pit stops. When I look back down pit lane, I see that almost all the teams are practicing stops.

Help for the Lights Team

Mark Moore tells me about how they all helped out the PacWest Indy Lights team after driver Robby Unser crashed yesterday. "We keep some parts in their transporter because we don't have enough room in ours. Somebody went over to the Lights paddock to get brake rotors late yesterday and came back saying they weren't going to be able to fix their car in time. We finished up here, and I went over there to help. Andy Natalie was already there working on the car with Jim Reid. A bunch of people pitched in: Tom Keene, Julian Karras, Randy, Ando, Roscoe, Jeff Horton, Charlie, Roy, Gavin, and I don't know who all. It looked like a plane wreck with everybody swarming all over it.

"Andy Natalie is new with us and I saw him working on the front of the car. I told Ziggy [Paul Harcus, the Lights team manager], 'I don't let him work on our car.' He just rolled his eyes. It didn't matter at that point. We really care about the Lights team. I'm always asking Ziggy, 'How's my car doing?' "

Warm-Up

The session starts at 9:09 and both PacWest cars go out. They do radio checks and come back in after a few laps. Ando coaches Mark as he comes in for a practice pit stop. Then Russ talks Mauricio into the pit box for his practice stop.

Mauricio says his brakes are making a noise. Andy asks if they are vibrating, and Mauricio says no, just noisy. "Red flag, Morris," says Andy. "Mark is actually off at the first chicane."

Mark says, "I just went in very slowly into the tires."

Andy: "Doesn't look like Mark has much damage. They pulled him out and push-started him. I expect we'll go green pretty soon."

Mark drives in to the pit box and talks about the car as the crew replaces the nose. "The brakes are locking pretty easily, into the hairpin and into the chicane as well." Allen makes some damper changes. They adjust the front shocktopussy. They also talk about Mark changing the cockpit adjustment on the tim, the rake control.

Mauricio is in at 9:32. "We could lower the front just a little bit."

Andy: "OK; I'll get the guys to do one flat. What about rear support on full tanks? Is that OK?"

Mauricio: "Fine."

Andy: "Did you do the front bar scan?"

Mauricio: "Yes, Andy."

Andy: "And what did you do with tim?"

Mauricio: "I went up with tim, probably three or four clicks. That was better. It would lock the fronts a little bit, but nothing drastic."

Andy: "OK. I'd like to try slot one this next run."

Mark goes back on track at 9:27. He's off the monitor page, having had little track time yet this session. He's back in a few laps later saying the brakes are still locking. Then he goes out on a new set of tires.

The checkered flag ends the session at 9:42. Zanardi is in P1 followed by Michael Andretti, Mauricio, Al Unser Jr., and Bobby Rahal. Mark is P12. Mauricio looks at his rear tires. Jim Hamilton and "Little Brett" Schilling are also looking at them.

Tim Neff walks out to Mauricio's car, sits down on his haunches, and sticks an arm under the rear cover to feel his namesake, the "tim" device. Someone is in the car changing the adjustment in the cockpit and Tim is feeling the results on the device itself.

Jim Hamilton tells me the optional Firestone tires are graining. "You can tell a lot about what's going on by looking at them. The angle of the graining indicates the input of forces to the tire. The tire is not just generating lateral forces, it's in a combination of spinning and slipping sideways. The races on the track yesterday increased the grip. It makes the bump effects worse."

Several knots of discussion form: Jim and Malcolm Oastler talk over the tires; Bruce and Mauricio huddle together. Then Mauricio and Andy discuss something. Andy greets Jolene. Then Andy, Tim, and Allen talk together.

Back in the Garage

At 10 o'clock I'm back in the garage area. The 18-crew has pulled their tent down off the Motorola transporter. The tent on the Hollywood hauler is still up. We get an early lunch at 11. I know Andy and Mauricio used the primary tires to qualify on Friday, but switched to optionals for yesterday's qualifying session. You have to start the race on the tires you use to qualify, so they took the risk of giving up Friday's time. "The optionals are better than the primes," Andy tells me. "The primes went off four-tenths in 30 laps with no advantage in initial stick. It's all power down and braking here."

Jim Hamilton and Malcolm Oastler
Talk about the Tires

I finally notice Roscoe has shaved his mustache. "I just didn't want to trim it," he says, "so I just shaved it all off." He looks younger, kind of baby-faced.

I see Jim Swintal, the starter, and ask him about the race start. "It's Zanardi on the pole and Rahal alongside him. I don't think Rahal will make the same mistake he made at Toronto."

Pre-Grid

The race is scheduled for a 1 p.m. start. At 12:30 I'm out on the frontstraight standing on pre-grid with the cars and crews. Carl Haas, owner of the Newman-Haas team, walks up and stares hard at Mauricio's car. The increase in performance of the PacWest team this year over last year cannot escape notice. Haas is staring at the machine, but he should be staring at the people.

Andy tells me the race is 100 laps, and the window for the first pit stop is at 28 to 34 laps. "We need about five yellow laps or we'll have to use the full-lean slot all the way. The pit stops are really important here."

THE RACE

On the second pace lap Ando tells Mark, "Zero on the fuel. Don't take any rubbish off these guys." Mauricio starts fifth and Mark eighth.

Mark Moore tells his crew, "Check all the guns and make sure the spare [gun] is on the wall."

The green flag waves at 1:08 p.m. Mauricio makes a great start, going into Turn 1 fast, pulling up on the outside of Michael Andretti in Turn 2, and driving by him before braking for the hairpin at Turn 3. Behind the leaders there's contact between cars. Paul Tracy is out of the race right away. A yellow flag slows the cars for three laps.

The race restarts with Alex Zanardi in the lead followed by Bobby Rahal, Jimmy Vasser, Mauricio, and Michael Andretti. Mark is P10. The order at the front stays the same until lap 15, when Zanardi locks up his brakes and goes straight at the hairpin Turn 3. He motors through the runoff and reenters in 23rd. Rahal is the leader now with Vasser pressing him and Mauricio catching Vasser.

Everyone is astounded that Zanardi would make a mistake like that while in the lead. I hear Control say, "He was just alone, wasn't he?"

Ando cheers Mark on: "Keep the pressure on there, pal. You're about 11 seconds from the leader."

Mark Moore makes the first tentative statement about a possible win. "I'd like to go to Caledon with a smile on my face."

On lap 24 Mark is in ninth place and says his rear tires are going off. Ando to Mark: "We're not too far away from our first stop. Hang in there. Keep the pressure on when you can." Scott Pruett is ahead of him and Andre Ribeiro right behind.

Rahal's Goodyear tires are going off and Vasser gets by him on lap 25. A few laps later Mauricio also passes Rahal, so Vasser is leading and Mauricio is second. Russ Cameron tells Mo, "Use the button if you need to pass."

On lap 34 the first pit stops begin. Mark comes in on lap 35 and so does Vasser. Mauricio stays out, gaining the lead. He pits on lap 37, and comes back on the track just behind Vasser. The pit stops looked great. The order now is Vasser, Mauricio, Andretti, de Ferran, and Greg Moore. Mark is eighth.

Vasser catches up to Al Unser Jr. in 15th and Junior doesn't want to go a lap down. Vasser is slowed enough so Mauricio is able to catch up. Vasser tries hard to pass Junior and we watch on the big-screen TV as Jimmy locks up a front tire going into one of the slow corners.

Mark Moore delivers another great one-liner: "Vasser getting held up just kills me."

Then Richie Hearn hits a barrier, bringing out an all-course yellow. During the caution period Mauricio closes up on Vasser. He and Russ talk about tire pressures and fuel slots. "Stay with these settings 'til after the last stop, and maybe we can turn it up after that."

Mark is having braking and gearbox problems, and Ando tells him to "soldier on."

The race restarts on lap 51. Zanardi has recovered to 10th. Then Scott Pruett and Adrian Fernandez get together going into the first chicane. Zanardi takes advantage of the yellow flag confusion to pass several drivers, including Mark, who yells about it into the radio. Ando's rational encouragement calms him down.

A full-course yellow flag bunches up the field again. Ando tells Mark, "Get right on Zanardi's tail. Let's see if we can put some pressure on him." The race goes green again on lap 56. The order is Vasser, Mauricio, Andretti, de Ferran, Moore, Zanardi, and Mark.

Tom Keene, the Hollywood transport driver, is handling Mauricio's pit board today, as usual. In addition to posting information on the pit board and holding it over the wall for Mo to read, Tom has been cheering Mauricio on all day. As Mo comes by Tom waves him on and I can see his mouth moving, so he's talking to Mauricio also.

Mark has a problem that turns out to be a puncture. He comes in for tires on lap 59, reentering the race in 13th. Vasser has a lead on Mauricio in second. Zanardi continues to pass cars, getting by Greg Moore on lap 60, de Ferran on lap 65, and Michael Andretti on lap 69. At lap 70 Jimmy Vasser is still leading with Mauricio in second challenged by Zanardi.

Zanardi makes a dive inside of Mauricio into the hairpin and Mauricio gives him room. Zanardi slides wide and Mauricio repasses him on the inside at the exit. That seems to take the steam out of Zanardi's run. The final pit stops begin and Vasser comes in on lap 74, giving Mauricio the lead. He and Zanardi pit together on lap 75.

The 17-crew pulls off a great pit stop, and Mauricio comes out on the track just in front of Vasser. Jimmy's tires are up to temperature, but Mauricio holds him off. Bryan Herta is the race leader, but he'll have to make another stop for fuel. The order now is Herta, Mauricio, Vasser, Zanardi, and Unser Jr.

Zanardi is still passing people, and it seems he has a chance to get to the front of the race with 20 laps to go. Amazingly, he goes down the escape road at Turn 3 again and stalls the car. He loses a lap, and ends up right behind the leaders. Zanardi closes on Mauricio. Russ tells him, "Zanardi is the car behind you. He's a lap down."

Once again, Mo is smart enough to let him by. But when Zanardi dives inside of Herta going into the first chicane, Herta doesn't give him room and they touch, putting Herta into the tires. He gets restarted and pits for fuel during the yellow flag.

When the race restarts Mauricio is in the lead and Vasser can't make any real challenge. Mark Moore says, "Just go win the f**kin' race, Morris."

Tom Keene, handling Mauricio's pit board, has gone from encouragement to advice. He's been waving his whole arm cheering Mo forward, but now that the 17-car is leading, Tom is leaning out over the wall touching his head with his forefinger to signal, "Use your head." This is, after all, a team sport.

The TV people start to gather around the PacWest pits. Derek Daly interviews Russ for the Canadian TV network.

Bryan Herta speeds by on the frontstraight, and Mark Moore has yet another great line: "He's just trolling for Zanardi."

With 10 laps to go I'm getting nervous. It's impossible to travel with all these people and not get emotionally involved. Mauricio is a great guy. He works hard for the team and deserves a win.

Zanardi is still passing people. He was ninth at the restart, but he's picking up a position almost every lap. I hear Control say, "White flag next time by for car 17."

Russ tells Mauricio, "White flag. Bring 'er home."

As he's crossing the finish line Mauricio yells and says, "It feels good."

I can hear Russ' voice crack with emotion as he yells, "Great job, Mo."

Both crews go over the wall to clap and yell and hug each other. Everyone runs off down the pit lane to where Mauricio will stop the car.

At the same time Mark is having his last problem of a tough day. On the last lap going into the last corner, Christian Fittipaldi spins and crashes in front of Mark. He manages to get by and actually picks up a position to seventh, but he doesn't sound happy on the radio.

Mauricio's crew surrounds him as he gets out of the car and shakes his hand or pounds his back. The TV people swarm over the group.

Victory Circle

On the way to the Victory Circle celebration I congratulate Andy and Russ, and everybody else I can find. The small, fenced-off compound in front of the podium is packed with smiling Hollywood, Motorola, and PacWest people as well as the usual horde of photographers. Mauricio comes in with a Brazilian flag someone has given him. I take a bunch of photos, and then get back out of the way of the champagne. After a while I head for the garage area to get my shoulder bag so I can make a getaway after the press conference.

Mauricio Enjoys his First Win

Press Conference

Jimmy Vasser finished second and Gil de Ferran third. They're at the table with Mauricio.

Mauricio says, "The team has been working very hard. In Portland I was in perfect position to win, and I made a small mistake that dropped me back and Mark got his first win. In this series, if everything is not 100% on that day, and that includes strategy, pit stops, and the car behaving consistently, maybe not the fastest car, but very consistent, you don't stand a chance of winning. The team today gave me the consistency. They gave me a fast car and I was able to keep my concentration and get my first win.

"I knew I could do it. Mark did it first and then you start worrying what's wrong, it doesn't happen. The team is the key. They give us the same equipment and support for both guys. You have to be careful that doesn't get you down too. You have to use it for motivation and keep pushing.

"I think qualifying really well all through this year has made my life easier in all the races. I think it was a matter of time. The hardest thing is the amount of people who keep asking you, 'When are you going to win your first one?' At least that's not going to happen now."

The press conference is winding down so I head out back to the hotel to start my drive south. On the way I remember Mauricio telling me about a Firestone tire test where he helped develop the street-course tire. The testing paid off today.

CALEDON: CELEBRATION

The drive to Caledon is uneventful except for the annoyingly long wait at the U.S. border. The directions to my motel, a Howard Johnson's in Everett, Wash., are clear, and I check in there first before I drive out to Caledon.

Caledon was a businessman's getaway that was going downhill when Bruce bought it. On 1,300 acres in the foothills of the Cascade Mountains north of Seattle, the spread has an 18-hole golf course, the largest quarter-scale railroad in the world, a go-kart track, and a lake where you can swim, boat, or fish. The lodge has its own disco, tavern, bar, soda fountain, seven bedrooms, and a full-time staff of three.

There are already a lot of cars parked around the drive when I get there. Spirits are high. A water-gun fight is going on in front of the house and the participants are enjoying themselves, soaking each other and anyone else they can find. I wuss out and go around the back of the house. Entering through the kitchen I find my way to the entrance hall where there are hundreds of commemorative T-shirts stacked on a table. The room assignments and schedule are posted on a corkboard. The furniture is heavy, polished, rustic chairs, tables and sofas that look solid and comfortable. Bowls of peanuts and M&Ms are handily placed.

Downstairs is the tavern, complete with juke box and pool table. A fully equipped soda fountain is in an adjacent room. Consumption of mass quantities has begun and I join in vowing to pace myself until a reasonable hour and drive safely back to the motel.

This is not a small party. The PacWest Group includes the Indy car team, the Indy Lights team, and the Super Touring team. That's about 80 people. Then there are the sponsors, friends, and hangers-on like myself. There are people here from Motorola, Mercedes-Benz, Chrysler Corp., and Ilmor. Reynard founders Adrian Reynard and Rick Gorne are here.

Mauricio's victory fuels a very high-energy party. Colleen Howerton, the PacWest business manager and daughter of CART Chief Steward Wally Dallenbach, had made a bet with Fuzzy, Jeff Horton. Colleen shaved Fuzzy's head into a mohawk after Mark's first win at Portland. She said she'd dye her hair red when Mauricio won.

Tonight's the night.

The hair ceremony happens on the deck off the big meeting room. At least 50 people hoot and holler while Fuzzy lathers up Colleen's hair with a colored mousse. Later, other team members join in and the drivers — Mauricio, Mark, David Donohue, and Robby Unser — are forced to be good sports and dye their hair also.

Most of the people my age are smart enough to lay back and let the team members celebrate. Not me. I've been hanging out with these people all year, so I join in. I get some great photos.

Mark Moore, Mo's crew chief, tells me he didn't allow himself to feel the Vancouver win until the car was through tech inspection. "The inspectors turned away, and I said, 'Is that it?' They said, 'Yeah,' and I yelled out, 'Awwright!' As far as I was concerned we didn't win 'til then."

My early exit doesn't happen and I end up crashing in a sleeping bag in a downstairs room. Early the next morning I feel good enough to drive and go back to the motel. Following the typed directions backwards is a sobriety test I would not have passed the evening before.

It's noon on Monday before I get to Caledon again. A few people are non-functional, but most are golfing or boating or karting. A buffet lunch on the patio looks good, but I can't overcome my nausea. The formal karting

Time to Get Silly!
Charlie, Allen, and Daryl

Kart Races

activities start about 3:30, and as we sign up we're given starting times. For the rest of the afternoon more than 50 people watch a series of heat races on the twisty, hilly kart course.

Racing people are risk-takers and they are also competitive, so the racing is sometimes serious. Several scrapes and bruises occur. After all the organized racing, Mauricio, Mark, David Donohue, Dominic Dobson, Robby Unser, Flavio de Andrade, and Jolene demonstrate the faster karts. Mauricio, especially, seems very comfortable on a shifter cart belonging to Dominic.

As these activities wind down, a dinner catered by a local restaurant begins. A band provides background music. The usually rainy Northwestern weather holds off today, and the dinner is outside on the lush back lawn by the first tee of the golf course.

Award presentations are next on the schedule, and we all take seats in the big meeting room. Bruce presents awards to the drivers and some crew members. Special gifts go to Adrian Reynard and Rick Gorne of Reynard Racing Cars, Paul Ray of Ilmor, Steve Potter of Mercedes-Benz of North America, Flavio de Andrade of Hollywood, Fred Tucker and Bob Schaul of Motorola, and Tim Culbertson of Chrysler.

The last item on the schedule is "Special Guest." This turns out to be the best ventriloquist in the world, Ron Lucas, with his very special friend Scorch, a teen-age, fire-breathing dragon.

Ron starts out with Scorch, changes to another puppet, and ends up using a sock over his hand. He performs while drinking water and blowing up a balloon. This guy is extremely talented and a great storyteller.

The cap on the evening is when Ron gets John [Ando] Anderson, vice president of race operations, on stage, and then puts a mask on him and uses him as a puppet. The mask just covers Ando's lower face and Ron operates the mouth. After some initial shyness, Ando gets into it and the act brings down the house.

The party winds down then, and I reluctantly drive back to the motel. I'm flying out early Tuesday morning. On my way to the motel I pass the Hollywood motor coach. The hospitality guys are on their way down south already.

Stephen Kent, Scorch, and Ron Lucas

CHAPTER 22

LAGUNA SECA

Part of a Monterey County, Calif., park on land that once belonged to Fort Ord, a U.S. Army training base, Laguna Seca Raceway has hosted road races for 30 years. It's a home track for me, the only CART track I've actually driven myself.

On Thursday morning, Sept. 4, I drive an hour and a half south of our house on the San Francisco Peninsula, getting to the track just before noon. As usual, I wander around talking to people and watching what's going on. This is the next-to-the-last race of the year, and Alex Zanardi will probably clinch the title here.

About 5:30 p.m. I check in at the Embassy Suites in Seaside, and after stowing my stuff in the room take advantage of the "Manager's Reception" to have a free glass of wine in the lobby atrium. PacWest people come through in bunches and some of them also have a drink and gather to sit and talk.

FRIDAY

CART practice isn't on the schedule until 11 a.m., but I'm awake at 6 and I'm at the track at 7:30. At 8 the Super Touring cars are on the track, and the PacWest crews are unzipping the tent sides in the garage area and getting to work.

At the hospitality area I see Mauricio, and he's pleased at the publicity he's gotten in Brazil since the win in Vancouver. "It made all the papers in Brazil — front page stuff — pictures and all." He's not a whoop-it-up guy, but his grin says he's truly happy with the attention.

The pit lane at Laguna slopes up from the hairpin Turn 11, ending almost at the top of the hill at Turn 1. About 9:30 a.m. I walk up under the bridge past the last pit and look down on Turn 3.

The track has made even more improvements since last year. The exit of Turn 3 is tight and the drivers tend to drop a wheel here and kick up dirt on the track. Some new rumble strips will make that less likely.

The hills here are brown and dead-looking, in contrast to the green places we've raced the last months. But those places, the American Midwest and the Pacific Northwest, get rain during the summer. In California there are two seasons — a short, wet winter and a long dry summer.

At 10:20 a.m. the 18-car crew is practicing pit stops in their pit box. The weather is sunny and very comfortable. It's about 75 degrees, and there's a light breeze from the southwest.

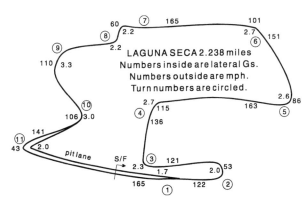

LAGUNA SECA 2.238 miles
Numbers inside are lateral Gs.
Numbers outside are mph.
Turn numbers are circled.

First Practice

Both the 17- and the 17x-cars are on pit lane. Mauricio will go out in the x-car first and do a few laps to bed in some new brake rotors. Then he'll get in the primary car for the remainder of the session.

Mauricio comes to pit lane at 10:45 and gets into each car so he can make sure the seat and pedals are how he wants them.

Just before 11 o'clock there's a delay while the safety crews clean the track surface. It's cooler now;

Jim Hamilton, Blake Hamilton, Dave Jacobs, Ron Endres, Scott Simpson, Mark Moore, and Trevor Jackson

the breeze has kicked up. The green flag starts the session at 11:02. Both PacWest cars are out right away and do radio checks around the course. Corner workers report fluid from the 17x-car, and when Mo brings it in the crew swarms around the back looking for the source.

Mark also comes in for his check-out, and he talks about the gearbox and a soft brake pedal and "a helluva lot of oil out there." Nothing is found leaking from the 17x-car and Mauricio goes back out at 11:08.

Allen asks Mark about the tire pressures. Mark answers, "Let me rush around a bit, and they'll come up." As Mark drives out of the pit box, Allen tells him to try the roll bars and "other things" to work on the balance of the car.

Mauricio brings the 17x-car in and gets into the primary car. He goes out for an installation lap and comes back in for a check. Andy asks if he still thinks the brakes on this car feel softer than the other. Mo says they'll be fine for the warm-up. "Softer won't be the word; there's just more travel initially."

At 11:19 a red flag interrupts the session. Hiro Matsushita has spun off course at Turn 6. Mauricio doesn't like the way the brakes feel. "They are acting very strange. Like if I lean on them, the fronts just lock like crazy.

"I want to undo the belts and do them again," he adds. "They're crushing my balls." Andy goes over the wall to look at the tires. Jim Reid helps Mo with his safety harness.

Zanardi is P1 followed by Mark, Michael Andretti, Christian Fittipaldi, and Paul Tracy. Allen asks Mark about the car. "Basically the car has got good turn-in, and it's a little bit detrimental to the rear because the rear of the car breaks loose on turn-in. As soon as you get the front turned in to the corner it's got a lot of push, especially in slow speeds; second gears, really bad push, just cannot control the front end. And even if you can, when you come off the gas it doesn't bring the front end back into line. The Corkscrew is hangin' a right rear up; it seems very high in the rear. So sometimes you're gettin' on the gas and it's just spinnin' up its wheels. Then when it hooks up, it gets out of shape.

"High speed, predominantly understeer, but again a little bit of pitch and there is a sensitivity on the turn-ins. I just want to use the front bar to see if we can stabilize the car and support the rear as well and flatten out the car on entry. We normally run a firmer brake pedal. It's a bit softer than we normally have."

Allen and Mark negotiate some changes. A green flag restarts the session at 11:30.

Another red flag gives the 17-crew a chance to check the tim device, which Mauricio thinks is operating incorrectly. When the session resumes Mauricio spins the tires out of the pit box. At the next red flag Mauricio complains of the braking attitude of the 17-car. "I went two clicks off again, but the back was jerking up and down under braking. The pedal is still too hard. And the kickback on the steering wheel is terrible coming down the hill."

Mark tells Allen: "I'm just trying to get a bit of feel as the tires are coming in. Predominately there's a push level increased in the higher-speed range. The slow speed into Turn 1 the car felt a little bit sweeter; obviously the tires are fresh. As I went through the second corner, Turn 3 and then 4 (he's referring to the map taped to his steering wheel), more push. I've got the bar on full stiff. It still lacks a bit of front end. Lockin' slightly under brakin' up at the top there, but maybe the pressures are still on the low side. Maybe we could drop the car slightly front and rear in ride height."

Allen: "What about the turn-in? Does the turn-in still feel sharp?"

Mark: "It still feels sharp comparison-wise to the other tires. It feels like there's goin' to be a little bit more grip on the front of the car proportionally."

Allen: "All right, 'til we get a better read maybe you can go back softer on the front bar or even go stiffer on the rear bar."

The course goes green again about 11:47. Mark is still P2, but Mauricio is struggling back in 25th. It's rare that Andy and Mauricio start out a weekend this far off on setup.

After only one lap Michael Andretti goes into the tire wall at the exit of Turn 2. We can see the replay on the monitors and on a huge big-screen TV on a pedestal right back of the pits. Michael's car bounces up in the air and ends up on top of the tire wall. He gets out shaking his head. Another red flag. This session is taking forever.

Mauricio explains to Andy as he comes into the pit lane, "Michael went into the wall. It's going to be another red. I don't have any damage. I managed to avoid him. I felt he wasn't going to make it passing me like that. I just went wide. It'll be a big red. He's up on the wall. That's a move for the last lap of the race. He tried to pass under braking on the inside on Turn 2. I left space for him, but he spun and started going backwards towards my line, but I went around on the outside. It's probably it's just that time on Friday." The session starts again at 12:01. Mauricio goes out, but the 18-car is still getting some adjustments.

One of the Newman-Haas crew jogs by with the seat parts out of Michael's car to put in the back-up car they're probably getting ready for him now.

I hear Mauricio complain about the car as he comes back in. This is the most frustrated I've ever heard him sound. "The car feels terrible, Andy. It's dragging all over the place. I can't stop. I took the tim all the way out. There's just no grip anywhere."

Andy: "Understood, Morris. Is it a similar feeling to the first day at Mid-Ohio?"

Mauricio: "It's worse than that, a lot worse. It feels very stiff, and there is no movement when I brake. It just locks up and goes EEE, EEE, EEE all the way to the apex." He makes squeaking noises to tell Andy how the car sounds. He's panting with exertion and frustration.

"I just pick up a little bit of understeer, but not much. There's no grip on the goddamn thing. I feel like it's just too stiff. Let's try the front bar as soon as we can."

Andy: "Understood Morris, but I think we need to soften the car up all 'round to start with. Let's do front and rear springs, guys."

Mauricio: "Andy, something is wrong with this car. It feels like the shocks are just solid."

Andy: "That could be the case at the rear, Mo, when you consider the settings we put on it."

The session restarts but another red flag flies at 12:11. Dennis Vitolo has spun and stalled.

Andy: "We put the alternate rear shocks on, which are the same shocks that we had at Mid-Ohio and Elkhart. I'm going to come down three (hundred pounds) on the front springs and come down two on the rear. This gives us the same split that worked here. This should pick us up some grip, but the main thing is that rear-shock change."

Mark: "The rear support level is slightly better in the middle of the corner, but that's primarily because I've got a bit of support in terms of a little less roll. It also does help me slightly turning in to the corner, but it's very slight. It might be working the rear tire a little bit too hard and make it go away from us.

"There's too much push in the car at this present point and the car, with these tires and the bar on full stiff, which may need to come down a snatch because of the level of understeer, especially at higher speeds. That's why I've gone off the road up there; it's just too much push and I couldn't hold it. I'm not sure if goin' up on the rear bar is the right way to do it at this moment in time. We need to find some front grip."

Allen: "What about more front wing, softer front springs?"

Mark: "Both at the same time? Just one or the other? We could probably handle a bit more front wing, to be honest. Just a bit more straightforward aero. I think we could cope with that, primarily in the infield here, 3, 4, 5. I think a bit of front wing will give us a bit more grip. I don't think it will hurt me much in turn-in; I think we should be able to carry it. I don't think we need a lot, but we need some."

Allen: "Good; shall we give you one turn?"

A nod from Mark.

The session restarts at 12:15 and Mark goes out, but the 17-car is still getting springs changed. The crew finishes up the 17-car, but Mauricio barely gets on course when Richie Hearn spins and there's another red flag. When Mo comes in he complains to Andy, "Still not to the grip level that I used to have around this place."

Andy: "We should consider that the track could have changed since we've last been here. I think at this stage, with 20 minutes left, I'd like to go on prime tires to give you a run with those to check balance."

Mauricio: "The car is still no grip at all, Andy. We have to improve a lot. The car is very different, just the feeling. Maybe we have to lower the front a little bit. I'm pushing in the middle of the corners. Under braking the car jumps up and down. The front, I don't feel the front coming down anywhere when I brake. I'll try the front bar before the session's over to see if leaning more on the front bar, that it'd help. It's bad to stop, the back is locking, so I have to stop early. Then I turn up, and in the middle of the corner, it's pushing and then it's flick oversteer. It's not together, and that's everywhere."

That's the longest feedback I've ever heard from Mauricio. They must have missed the starting setup by a ton. This could be interesting.

Andy: "The rear's jumping up, we need to get tim working again, if it's wound all the way out right now. Do you want to put the softer front spring in or do another run with this setup?"

Mauricio: "Let's do another run. I don't want to waste time in case they bring the car back quick. The tim's got to be worse, but I've been there, I've done that, and it was worse. Are the shocks too stiff? I know we've changed that. Could be it's gonna work, but as soon as I hit the brakes, the rear wheels just come off the ground."

Andy: "Let's come down a flat on the front rods, please, guys."

At 12:22 the track goes green again, and both PacWest cars go out. Allen made some shock changes to Mark's car and he's in P4. Mo is off the page in P23. CART decides it will throw the checkered at 12:30 and shorten the session because of all the red flags.

Mark comes in and Allen tells him there's 4 minutes left. "How's the car?"

Mark: "It's got a little bit more push. Coming down off the Corkscrew [Turn 8], the left-hander, it's increased the level of push through there and that's where the car gets loaded up and there's some little bumps in there, so it gets into a frequency and it drops off in grip. When I back off and go in there a bit slower and tighter it falls off the turn, but I'm losing a bit of entry speed. If I try to load the car up earlier, the front grip shallows off. It's still too much push in the car even in the high-speed corners."

Allen: "Maybe you should try the bar, going softer?"

Mark: "I can try that; that'll give us an indication. That change felt good; it's given me a bit of benefit, but we lost a level of grip still."

Allen: "How 'bout some more front wing?" A nod from Mark.

"Forget the shock change, please. Just give me a half-turn of front wing."

Mark: "I actually went up one step on the rear bar. Just to try to give myself a bit of load into the front. It just increased the level of push."

Both cars go out for the last run of the session at 12:37. Mauricio finally feels some grip and improves to P8 on the last timed lap. As he comes into the pit box after the checkered flag, he says, "It started to work, but Jesus Christ!" He gets out of the car at 12:35.

Al Bodey says to Allen, "This is the [pop-off] valve we want when we come back for qualifying."

Alex Zanardi is P1 at 68.757 seconds followed by Bryan Herta and Jimmy Vasser. Mark ends up sixth, a second slower than Zanardi.

In the garage area I ask Mark Morris what happened. "We started off softer than at the test in February, but it was way too stiff. It's a problem testing at a track so far ahead of the race." The cars go on the pads and some of the crew start lunch. I join them.

Friday Qualifying

At 3:27 p.m. the CART officials give the 5-minute sign in pit lane. I hear Butch on the radio: "We need a driver out here. If we don't get one, one of us is going to get in." Mark hurries up onto pit lane and gets into his car.

The fast guys are first on Fridays, and Mark and Mauricio are both in this session. They're both out on track at the green flag. I decide to watch this session from the top of pit lane, where I can see the cars come out of Turn 2 and go through Turn 3. The bridge blocks Turn 4 from view, but I can see them run down to Turn 5 and go up the hill to Turn 6.

Just for the hell of it I get out my stopwatch and take some section times, starting the watch as the cars come even with the end of the berm at the exit of Turn 2 and stopping it when they hit the shadow of the bridge near the turn-in point for Turn 4. This will give me a section time from the exit of Turn 2 to the exit of Turn 3, a 100-mph corner. I can't see a monitor up here, so I don't know who's turning the quickest times.

This section yields times around 7 seconds. The PacWest cars and Alex Zanardi are below 7, about 6.8. Most of the cars are right at 7 seconds or higher. Sure enough, at 3:30, 7 minutes into the session, I hear on my scanner that the order is Mauricio, Mark, and de Ferran.

Mark comes in saying the car is too loose. "I went up on the front bar because the car's too loose. It's still a little too sensitive on the front. The turn-in for the corners is particularly aggressive. The rear steps out. It's destabilizing me when it gets into the corner. It's too sharp on turn-in; too much movement."

During that last run I could see the front of Mark's car jerk toward the outside of the corner as he heads in for Turn 3. It looks like the front is washing out.

When Mauricio comes in the first time he complains of the car hitting the track "harder than this morning."

Andy: "What I'd like to do is take some low-speed bump out of the front of this car, Mo. That'll help it turn in and also help the mid-corner front grip."

Allen makes some damper changes to the 18-car and both drivers go out for another run. The order now is Zanardi, Pruett, Mauricio, and Greg Moore.

When Mauricio comes in, Andy says, "I'd like to do that bump change at the rear that we spoke about. What about the tire-pressure change, Morris?"

Mauricio: "That's helped the rear grip." Lots of squawks and squeals come over the scanner. Up here on this hill it must be worse than right down by the pit box.

Andy: "There's still 13 minutes to go, Morris. I want to make these bump changes and do another run before going to stickers."

Shortly after Mauricio goes on course, Greg Moore spins in Turn 2 and stalls, causing a red flag. Andy adds a turn of front wing to the 17-car. Allen makes some damper changes to Mark's car. A green flag restarts the session at 3:41.

When Mauricio comes in after that run, he sounds deflated and says, "I don't know about the rear bump. I can't tell if it's worse or better." Andy lowers the front of the car.

Mo says, "Take the bump out of the back."

Mark comes in and Allen back-tracks on the last changes and has the guys put sticker tires on the car. Mark talks about lack of support at the rear of the car. Allen gives him some choices. "We can either drop the rear a flat or take out a little bit of aero."

Mark: "We can drop the rear a flat just to give it a bit more grip." They do it.

Both cars are out with about 4 minutes to go. Mark improves right at the end of the session and the order is Zanardi, Pruett, Mark, Mauricio, and Greg Moore.

Reporters, both print and video, swarm around the drivers when they get out of the cars. I hear Mark say, "The car felt good. We made some good improvements. I'd like to do better tomorrow and get into the front row as opposed to the second."

Paddock Talk

Back in the garage area, I tell Mark I saw the front of the car jerk into Turn 3. He says that was him catching the rear of the car. "You want to brake late and the rear of the car wants to jump up and come around."

At 4:50 Butch gets his crew together, telling them "This is our race motor going in tonight." The 17-crew is also changing engines.

I talk to Tom Keene about his cheering on Mauricio during the race at Vancouver. "I was waving him toward the front all race. With two laps to go I was touching my head to tell him to use his head. I come here to win. I'm cheerin' my guy to a win. I don't come here to lose, Paul. I'm totally into racing."

I head back to the hotel to meet my wife, Pat, who drove down here this afternoon. We're invited to a dinner hosted by Firestone. Although we're familiar with the Monterey/Carmel area we've never eaten at this little restaurant, Triples, before, and we enjoy the food and talk. Trevor Hoskins, Firestone public relations manager, and his wife Judy sit at our table as do Tim Tuttle, *On Track* editor at large, and George Webster, a writer for *National Speed Sport News*.

SATURDAY

I'm up at 5:45 a.m. so I can get through in the bathroom before Pat needs it. I watch TV while she finishes getting ready. Reruns of Princess Di's funeral are on every channel. When we go outside to get in the car the sky is overcast, but the air isn't cold.

We're at the track at 7:30, and since this is her first race this year, I introduce Pat around in the PacWest hospitality area. Mauricio is gracious, as usual. We go to the garage area and I introduce her to some of the guys who aren't too busy.

The first practice is always early on Saturday. It's at 9 a.m. today, with the qualifying session at 12:30 p.m. At 8:45 we're in the pit lane and it's still overcast. We could get warm if the clouds burn off.

Mark Moore says they really got behind yesterday because they had the car way too stiff off the trailer. "We made some big changes last night."

At 9:04 Mark Blundell is in the pit lane joking with the crew. I ask Andy about missing the setup. "We started with the setup that was so fast here at the test in February, which is close to last year's race setup. The track could change as more rubber goes down and come back to us. We're prepared."

Practice

At 9:12 a green flag starts the Saturday practice session. Both PacWest cars are out immediately but Charles Nearburg spins and stalls, bringing out a red flag. Both cars come right back in, and Mark talks about how the tires are probably not up to temperature and pressure yet. Allen asks the crew to up the pressure "half a pound all 'round" to help them feel better for Mark during the next run.

The green flag flies again at 9:17 and Mauricio goes out with Mark following a minute later. For some reason Mark drives through the pit lane on the next lap, but doesn't stop in the pit box. Allen tells him, "Nice to see ya anyway, mate."

When Mo comes in after his next run he says, "The car is too high. It's pushing too much."
Andy: "Understood. How is the compliance in the braking areas now?"
Mauricio: "Better than yesterday, for sure. The rear grip is better than yesterday."

A red flag stops the session at 9:26. Andy: "After this run, Morris, I want to put the front bar on because that's what's helped to load the car on turn-in previously." They check the tim device and make sure it's working and adjusted correctly. There's a green flag at 9:30. Mark goes out but they're still working on changes to the 17-car.

Mauricio goes out at 9:32. There's 46 minutes to go and the monitor gives the order as Greg Moore, Bryan Herta, and Zanardi. I've turned off the channel to the 18-car. Andy and Mauricio are working uncharacteristically hard to dial in the setup, and I don't want to miss anything. Mark talks so much that if I listen to both channels I'll only hear him and miss most of what Andy and Mauricio say.

After that run Mauricio says, "All right, Andy, the car feels better. I feel like there's still more to go."

Andy: "OK; I'd like to come down another flat. How's the rear under braking today?"

Mauricio: "The rear is jumping up and down. I think I can deal with it with tim, but I have to get the car going better, and then I can adjust it."

Andy: "Give me 3 gallons, Roscoe." They're still working on the qualifying setup and keep a light load of fuel in the car.

Andy to Mauricio: "Once you've got the front where you want it, you might want to come out a couple of clicks on the tim."

At this point Mark is P14 and Mo P23. The clouds are breaking up and it's getting warmer. Tom Keene is on the 17-pit board across the way; Stephen Kent works the 18-board. Mark Moore is setting up some alternate shock/spring packages here on the pit wall.

I'm standing at a break in the pit wall right in the middle of the pits. To my right is the 18-car and to my left is the 17. I can look over my right shoulder and up at the big-screen TV, and to my left at the monitor sitting on the scoring cart. Not bad.

Turtle the fireman, actually Ross Tourtellotte, is here for this race, and he's working Mauricio's pit. Once again he helps me a lot by giving me room to work. I make sure I don't get in his way. As usual his shiny helmet and visor is a big hit with the photographers.

Mauricio comes in off the track at 9:42. "There is less traffic, but I don't think we gained. That's not what I really wanted."

Andy: "OK. We can go with softer front springs?"

Mauricio: "It's still better than yesterday. If I cut the car in, the rear gets out. The car is just not flowing the way I want it. If I miss the apex, or if I get off-line a little bit, it's just not working."

Andy: "Come up one and a half flats on the front rods, please. Morris, you want to turn BOSS off and come up four on the valve." A red flag stops the session. Mark is 13th fast in this session and Mo 17th.

Mauricio: "When I get off the brake into a turn the front comes up, and I start washing out. This is the biggest difference from when we tested here. There is very little movement on the front, then it comes up. It's just screwed up."

Andy: "Did you leave the front bar on its initial setting?"

Mauricio: "Full soft. If this doesn't work, we need to make a big step."

Andy: "We could look at the front shocks too, from what you're saying. The settings are low in line with what's been happening with the rest of the season, but here the front rebound has been a big help." There's a green flag at 9:48. Both cars go out.

Mark Moore comes from the garage area with another set of springs. Danny Sullivan, the TV announcer who drove for this team a couple of years ago, comes over to the scoring cart to talk to Ziggy Harcus and Steve Fusek. Ziggy was his chief mechanic when he drove for PacWest.

Mauricio is back in at 9:51. "It's worse; let's go the other way."

Andy: "Understood. Get those front springs on Mark, that we talked about, and let's come down three and a half flats on the front rods. I'll disconnect the front bar at the same time, Morris."

Mauricio: "Ten-four."

They must be going stiffer now, because they're lowering the ride height. The stiffer springs will hold the car up higher against the same aero loads. With stiffer springs they don't need the roll control of the front anti-roll bar.

There's a red flag at 9:54. Mauricio talks more about the car. He's frustrated.

At 9:58 the course goes green again, but after a couple of laps there's another red, stopping the session. The session is only half done an hour after it started. Cars are going off track and stalling or hitting walls almost constantly.

Mauricio: "Under braking I still don't feel the car has the same grip as when we tested. It's a little bit bouncy at the front. We have to look at the shocks. Maybe we need another shock change to keep the front down and see what that does."

Andy: "The front ride height?"

Mauricio: "It's all right. Down the hill it's hitting a little bit. To go lower would be difficult."

Andy: "Especially with this change on the shocks. Let's leave that as it is. We're still struggling with rear grip. The only other thing I can think of right now is more rake in the car and use the softer springs in the rear like we've done before. The softer springs to give us the grip so you can set the car on turn-in as well, and more rake for better mid-corner."

Mauricio: "That would help. I'd like to try that."

Andy: "This set of tires has 31 laps now, which is over a race stint. I think we should put another set on at this stage."

Mauricio: "More front rebound?"

Andy: "Yeah; put one sweep of high speed and six sweeps of low speed. The low speed is quite a way off."

Richie Hearn goes off on the outside of Turn 8, causing a red flag. Mark went out with the green flag, but the 17-crew is still making front spring and shock changes. The track is green again at 10:17. Mo goes out but Mark has come in on the red flag and his car is still getting changes. Mauricio is P14, but turns a lap of 1:10.78 for 14th and then 1:10.02 for P6.

Mauricio comes in saying, "I want to go another two at the rear. We need to improve a little bit the front grip. It feels just a little bit better. Maybe we could change the caster again for qualifying."

Andy: "We could probably do that now if you want to. While we do the rear spring change."

Mauricio: "Yes, I'd like to try that."

Andy: "Come up three flats on the rear rods, please. Do you want more shock control with these springs?"

Mauricio: "I'd like to try it like this."

Andy: "Think if we want to go back on any of those spring or shock changes we did, to help in mid-corner and in the braking areas. They might cut this session short, but we still have 16 minutes to go."

Mauricio: "We should go back on the front springs a little bit. There's a big difference on the steering. I'm sure I have more front grip."

Andy: "There would have been slight changes to camber and toe with the caster change. We need to make a run on this, I feel, before we make any more changes."

Mauricio: "Do it." He goes out with the green flag at 10:32. Then CART says the session will conclude at 10:42.

When Mo comes back in, Andy asks, "There's just over 6 minutes to go. We can just get a sticker run in, or do you want to make changes to the car?"

They talk about more changes and make some of them. Mauricio goes out for a final run. After the checkered flag he comes in and gets out of the car. It's been another disappointing session for the PacWest team. Bryan Herta is P1 followed by Zanardi, Greg Moore, and Raul Boesel. Mark is P12, a second slower than Herta, and Mauricio is a tenth of a second slower than Mark in P14.

Changes in the Lineup

Roy Wilkerson has replaced Gavin Hamilton as the outside-rear-tire changer on the 18-car. He came to the team in mid-season from a lead-mechanic position at Della Penna. Butch told me then that he knew Roy was quicker than Gavin, but he didn't think a change in mid-season would be productive.

"We had some practice pit stops at Elkhart," Roy tells me. "I did four and Gavin did four, and we did it again the next day. He had some stops that were faster than mine, but my overall average was better. I know Gavin really likes going over the wall. He's taken it pretty well, considering."

Big Setup Changes

The 17-car is undergoing some big changes. It looks to me like they're even changing the rocker arms in both the front and rear suspension. I know PacWest has some rockers designed and fabricated by Galmer in England. Rockers can be made to give different ratios of spring/shock movement vs. movement at the wheel.

It's 12:30 and qualifying is scheduled to start now, but support-series practice sessions have run long, and now CART says the final qualifying session won't start before 1 o'clock.

At 12:42 Mark Moore gets the qualifying setup sheet from the engineers. He calls his guys together and they talk about the work necessary to get the car ready for qualifying.

A few minutes later Andy comes out of the engineering office in the front of the Motorola hauler, and I go to talk to him. "Did you find a setup you like in that last session, or did you just run out of things to change?"

Andy smiles that silly grin he flashes just before he says something funny. "We changed everything but the Ackerman [the angle of the steering arms]."

"The track will change as it warms up and gets more rubber on it. How will you handle that?"

The grin again. "I just tell Morris we've got time for three runs, go to it. That's how you do that. It's called delegation."

"You do have some contingencies, don't you?"

"Yes." He's more serious now. "But there really isn't much time during a qualifying session."

Don Mullins and Greg Watson bring in the lunch from hospitality, and the crew eats when they have time. After everyone has eaten and the tables are clear I see Scott Simpson walk back and place the salt and pepper shakers together in the center of each table. Just a little attention to detail.

Final Qualifying

The slow guys are out first on Saturday and the green flag starts the session at 1:15 p.m. The monitor shows yesterday's times to start the session. The monitor order only changes when a driver turns a lap faster than his previous best. Mark is third and Mauricio fourth.

Michel Jourdain Jr. quickly jumps to P5 with a time almost a second better than he did yesterday afternoon. Maybe everyone will improve.

At 1:32 the 18-car rolls onto pit lane followed a few minutes later by the 17. Scott Simpson has two sets of sticker tires laid out for Mauricio, as does Randy Smay for Mark. Each team starts and warms the engine and places wet towels on the sidepods so the exhaust heat soak doesn't ruin the paint. At 1:48, with 3 minutes to go until the green flag starts the fast-guys' session, the engines are started for the final warm-up.

Near the end of the slow-guys' session the big-screen TV behind us shows a bizarre sequence of events. P.J. Jones is going slow out of Turn 6 when Max Papis, a fellow Toyota engine user, comes up behind him and makes some light contact before continuing. P.J. stops the car on course and starts to get out. Max finishes the lap and then, when he comes on P.J. again, slows and makes some gestures.

P.J., a big lad and a scrapper like his dad, throws his steering wheel at Max with enough accuracy to hit Max's helmet. Max drives off and they tow P.J. in to the pit lane. A good laugh to start an important qualifying session.

With a green flag at 2:08, both PacWest cars go on course. The sky is clear and sunny. There's a cool breeze from the west. I wonder if the guesses and compromises that Andy and Mauricio had to make will prove to be positive or negative.

Mark is back on pit lane first, followed by Mauricio. I hear Allen ask Mark, "OK, how's the car then?" and I disable that channel. I'd rather listen to Andy and Mo.

Mauricio: "I'm getting oversteer in some places, at the exits."

Andy: "How is the ride height?"

Mauricio: "It could go lower all 'round, a little bit."

Andy: "When you get the looseness is it right on exit? Are you on the power at that stage?"

Mauricio: "Right at exit, when I get on the gas."

Andy: "Seven gallons, please, Roscoe. Do you feel the car squatting when you want to put the power down?" Andy steps out of the end of the engineering cart, looks at Mauricio in the car, and uses his hand, dipping it palm down, to emphasize squat to Mo.

Mauricio: "It's a rolling, squatting feeling."

Andy: "What if I put some more low-speed bump in the rear to try to restore that? Do you think that will help?"

Mauricio: "Let's give it a try."

Andy: "That front wing we added, we went through how much that would move the center of pressure forward. Is that too far, do you think?"

Mauricio: "That's not too far."

Mark goes back out at 2:17. Changes continue on Mo's car.

Andy: "If this doesn't work we can also look at coming back to the rear springs that we liked this morning."

Mo goes out at 2:18, with 18 minutes to go in the session. The order is Zanardi, Herta, Pruett, Mark, and Mauricio. Then Herta jumps up to P1 with a 68.325-seconds lap. Neither PacWest driver has improved on his Friday time.

Mauricio comes back in saying, "The right-front tire is flat-spotted."

Andy: "Understood. Is Zanardi off? No, he's got going again. He'll be clear by the time you get there."

Andy makes some changes to the car saying, "There's a red flag for Greg Moore. He's blown an engine. There's still 11 minutes to go. I still think it's too early to go out on stickers. I'd like you to go out and feel these rear changes and come in, and we'll put the stickers right on."

The safety crews clean up at Turn 8 where Greg's engine let go. At the green flag Mark goes out again, but the shock changes aren't done on the 17-car.

Michael Andretti goes off course at 2:33, causing another red flag. Andy says, "One time by should be enough to evaluate this, Mo. The clock won't start 'til the first car's gone by."

Mauricio comes back in saying, "Just the tires."

Andy: "Understood. Three gallons, please, Roscoe. It'll be about 8 minutes when you come around, Morris. I've put fuel in to get you to the end of the session. I think we can go out as soon as it goes green. That should give you a good place on the track."

Mauricio: "Ten-four." His comments are more cryptic and sound less frustrated now that the car is more to his liking.

A green flag restarts the session at 2:40 with 8 minutes, 47 seconds to go. The PacWest cars go out and settle in, warming the tires with 73- and 74-seconds laps, then faster with 69-seconds times. The next couple of laps should be the best for the tires. Mo is 10th and Mark 13th. Bryan Herta is P1 with a 68.735. The monitor changes constantly as times rapidly improve.

Mark also turns a lap of 68.735 seconds, earning P4, and Mauricio a 68.769 for P5, just nipping Jimmy Vasser. One more lap to go. Surprisingly Herta lowers the lap record to 67.895 seconds. Neither of the PacWest cars improves on the last lap. Herta will start on the pole with his nemesis Zanardi outside him. Scott Pruett and Mark Blundell will be on the second row and Mauricio and Vasser the third.

Andy: "Fifth place, Mo. Good effort, mate. Good run there."

Mauricio: "I'm running out of fuel."

An Unplanned Engine Change

Back in the garage area I see engine changes starting, and when I ask, I learn that Greg Moore's engine failure has caused the PacWest team to change engines now when they had planned to use the engines they put in last night on Sunday for the warm-up and the race.

I ask Charlie Harris, an Ilmor engineer, what's going on.

"I just found out about it a minute ago. I'm glad we bring plenty of engines."

"How many is plenty?"

"We bring five engines per driver per weekend. We hope they only use two. There's a fresh one for the primary car to start the weekend and a change for the primary and the back-up; that's three. Then there's a practice spare and a race spare; that's five."

"That's a lot of rebuilds. How many people work at VDS [the Ilmor rebuild facility in Midland, Texas]?"

"Sixteen guys with tools in their hands and four support people."

Extra Oil

Between sessions I just stand around and watch what's going on, making notes and asking questions. This afternoon I notice Daryl Fox rigging an electric pump and tank in the sidepod of the 18-car. He has installed them with some power and control wiring and a hose leads from the tank to somewhere in the engine compartment. I don't get a chance to ask but I'll bet this is a make-up oil system. I heard talk earlier in the year that these engines use a lot of oil. They've installed an extra oil tank and during the race they tell the driver to turn it on so it can pump oil from that small tank to the larger one. Higher rpm also increases oil use, and I know they're revving them up to 15,000 rpm in qualifying.

Pat and I go back to the hotel, have a glass of wine down in the lobby, and then decide to order a room-service pizza. A NASCAR race is on the tube. We go to bed early. The Sunday morning warm-up is at 8 a.m.

SUNDAY

I'm up at 4:45 and get through in the bathroom so Pat can have at it. We pack up everything so we can check out as we leave. Outside at 6:50 we see it's foggy. That can be a problem. A few years ago the fog was so bad they had to delay the start of the race. It seems to me this will definitely affect the warm-up, at least.

The crews worked at the track last night 'til 7:30 and got here this morning at 6. In the garage area I see Butch Winkle, Mark's crew chief, has a clean wrap on the wrist he hurt at Vancouver. "Yeah; I just went over to CART medical, and they shot me up and rewrapped it for the race."

"When will you get it fixed?"

"In October. They said it would take a good three weeks to heal and it has to be in a cast, so I'll wait for the end of the season to do that."

It makes me think about the things I'm putting off 'til the three-week break after this race, and other things I'm delaying until after that last race. I guess that's part of the lifestyle. You do things when you have time. The cars and the races come first.

The 17-car is getting filled with fuel, and the 17x is on the setup pad. The 18- and 18x-cars are both in the garage area. There are a lot of Motorola and Hollywood people at this race, but it's a little early to expect to see them at the track.

Mark Moore tells me there are no big changes to Mo's car. "Just small spring changes. We got pretty close yesterday."

Warm-Up

At 7:30 the fog is still below the top of the big hill between the paddock and the Corkscrew. Wally Dallenbach, the chief steward, will let the drivers decide if they want to run in the fog. Green and yellow flags start the 30-minute session at 8 a.m., and the cars drive a lap behind Wally in his baby-puke-green Mercedes-Benz pace car. On the scanner I can hear PacWest radio checks and Control saying car 20 (Scott Pruett) spun and continued at Turn 2.

Control passes along comments from the drivers through their radio people to the CART officials in the pit lane. "Driver of car-6 [Michael Andretti] says it's OK. Junior [Al Unser Jr.] says he can race." Wally brings the pace car onto pit lane and they wave the green flag.

At 8:05 Mark comes in for his installation check. "Not much retardation. I need to get some heat in the brakes."

Mauricio also complains about his brakes — vibration and a soft pedal. Russ suggests to Andy that they tape the ducts half-shut, and they do that.

At 8:13 Mauricio comes in the pits and the 17-crew performs a practice pit stop.

Ando talks Mark in for a practice pit stop. "OK; look for Butch. You've got a clear pit. Straight down the middle. Swing 'er in. Straight down the center."

Mark says he's locking up the front wheels. Mauricio goes back on track. There's a red flag at 8:15 with half the session gone. After track cleanup the session restarts.

With 6 minutes to go in the session Mauricio has driven the 17-car to P1. He comes in as Mark goes back on track. Andy asks, "How's the balance?"

Mauricio: "Understeer. Probably the air is so bad. I like it pretty well." He goes out for a last run. The checkered flag flies at 8:34 a.m.

As Mauricio comes in to get out of the car he says, "We need to look at these brakes, Andy. They're vibrating like crazy still."

Ando talks Mark in for a last practice pit stop as Andy and Mauricio study the tires on the 17-car. The monitor shows the fast times in this session. Zanardi is P1 followed by Greg Moore and Mauricio. Mark ends up 16th, a second slower than Mo.

Up and down the pit lane engines go quiet one by one, and that noise is replaced by the whirring of wheel guns as some teams practice pit stops. The PacWest cars get towed back to the garage area. The sun is brightening the paddock, but I still can't see the top of the hill for the fog.

Silly Season

Parker Johnstone is having a tough time. This should have been a good year for him and Team Green. Tony Cicale came out of retirement to work as Parker's engineer. But things haven't clicked. Parker doesn't think the team is giving him what he needs, and the team seems to have given up on Parker. The owner, Barry Green, has gone public this weekend about the rift between the team and the driver. Parker spun twice during the warm-up, which was probably the result of a driver trying too hard in a car he's not comfortable driving.

Silly season is in full bloom. The PacWest drivers are signed for next year, and it looks to me like none of the top teams and drivers will make changes. One persistent, but unlikely, rumor is that Mario Andretti will start a team with his son, Michael, as driver.

Pre-Race Prep

At 9 the sun is beginning to burn away the fog, and the top of the hill is now visible. People are already up there staking out their spot for viewing the race.

I ask Russ Cameron, "What's the deal on the race strategy?"

"It's like Mid-Ohio," Russ says. "It's an 83-lap race and you've got one-lap pit windows if it goes all green. It'll be a two-stop race; pretty straightforward."

At 9:30 I see the 17-crew changing out the rotors on the primary car. The 18-car crew is doing the same thing.

I ask Allen McDonald about it. "There were some vibration problems during the warm-up. In low-grip situations the rotors don't bed in easily. We taped off the ducts, but that didn't do it."

"The first of the year you guys were using pre-bedded pads and rotors," I note. "But then you went back to bedding them on track, and you're still having problems."

"Yeah; maybe the pre-bedding didn't work either. We thought it did, but when we got to Detroit we had vibration problems."

"Is there any risk in changing them all out right before the race?"

"No; these are rotors we used in practice and qualifying."

That answer somehow doesn't sound right. It's still something that has to be done at the last minute that could cause a problem. I watch the guys changing out the rotors, and they're working carefully and are very focused on what they're doing.

Ten feet away from the intense work on the car are a couple of dozen Brazilians, chanting and clapping while they form groups to have pictures taken with a smiling Mauricio standing against the Hollywood transporter. True to form, Trevor Jackson is chatting with one of the pretty, Hollywood-costumed models.

Just before 10 Mauricio goes around his racecar and looks carefully at the rotor on each corner. We can hear the Indy Lights race starting. The cars are on their pace laps now and the noise level in the paddock goes up. Mark is talking to a couple of Motorola guys, Fred Tucker and Bob Schaul.

Talk with the Motorola Guys

After Mark moves on I walk over to talk to Tucker, who is executive vp/president and general manager of the automotive, electronics, and computer systems group at Motorola. "I didn't see you on those go-karts at Caledon."

He shakes his head and smiles. "I played golf; it was safer."

Bob Schaul, corporate vp and director of global markets, has walked over to join us. He's a big, balding guy, linebacker-size, with a mustache. "It didn't scare Bob off," I say. "He was right out there in the middle of it, spun off course, and bruised his leg even."

"Yeah; that was fun," Bob says, grinning.

"Sales guys seem to be able to do those things and come out OK," I say to Tucker, who's still shaking his head.

"It was a pretty risky deal, though, really," I continue. "I guess that's what racing is all about, is risk. The people in the middle of it seem to get used to it."

Tucker is still shaking his head. It's obviously way too risky for the way he looks at running an organization. At his level at Motorola, risk is something to be managed and reduced to an acceptable level with planning and contingencies. The sight of all those people, so important to the realization of PacWest's and Motorola's goals, running into trees and each other on those little buzzing, metal things probably made him cringe. I decide to change the subject.

"Fred, we've talked before about the way you guys allocate the cost of a program like the PacWest sponsorship. Does it make it any easier now that they're winning? Do the groups paying the bills feel like they're getting their money's worth?"

"Well, sure they do," he says. "Still, I pay the biggest amount because I'm the champion of the program. The consumer groups in Motorola, like cellular, pay a good amount. Some divisions don't get the benefit, and if they don't want to they don't pay anything. It was more difficult earlier on. Bob was the guy asking them to pay. If Bob couldn't get it, I'd make a call."

Nut and Bolt

At 10:15 Pat and I stand out of the way and watch Jim Reid "nut and bolt" the front of the 17-car. There's only a few different sizes of nuts and bolt heads and Jim knows them, so he gets the wrench sizes he needs all at one time from his toolbox. The tools are all Snap-On, brightly finished and handy. Jim is intensely focused as he carefully tightens each fastener a measured amount. He wants to make sure that each one is tight, and if one breaks during the check it's better for it to happen here and now than later on course.

Watching him, I think of what Mark Moore told me. "Jimmy's a little guy and sometimes they pick on him. They tease him for being slow too, but really, he's just being careful. He's the only one all year that hasn't made a mistake."

From talking to Jimmy myself, over caipirinhas in Rio, I know he drove racecars, and he was good at it as was Mark Moore. Like 99% of the good drivers, race wins and sponsor money didn't happen at the same time. Rubbing up against racing working with a team has to be almost as good as being in the seat.

The credentials Pat has this weekend get her into the pit lane, but not during the race. I need to go up there now, so I say good-bye and tell her to look for me here in the garage area after the race.

Pit Lane

In the pit lane I run into Jim Swintal, the CART starter. "So you've got the front row from hell here," I say, referring to Bryan Herta and Alex Zanardi. "How are you handling that?"

"I told them what I expect of them, and I think they're OK," Jim says. "I told them everybody thinks they'll mess it up."

"What if they do?"

"What if....say Alex jumps the start?" Jim offers. It sounds like a point on the tame end of the curve to me. "I think Wally would do something right away, maybe a stop-and-go penalty."

I say "Good luck" to Jim and walk back down the pit lane toward the PacWest pit boxes.

It's getting hotter now. There's a wind out of the northwest. The guys on the 18-crew push their car onto pit lane followed a few minutes later by the 17-crew. The stands are about one-third full, but the fans are shoulder-to-shoulder in the paddock behind me. They'll start moving to their seats soon. The noon start is only 45 minutes away.

Pre-Grid

At 11:30 a.m. all the cars are formed up on the straight, and the crews are standing around them. The drivers are being introduced.

I take a bunch of pictures as usual, and when they start the engines I go back over the barrier and take up my station at the break in the pit wall between the Hollywood and Motorola pit boxes. Turtle the fireman is here, and he helps me get into a good position. Actually this is one of the best situations I've had for a race. I can see both pits really well, and I can see the cars come out of Turn 11 and accelerate toward Start/Finish and up over the hill at Turn 1. I can lean forward a little and see a monitor on the scoring cart. Over my right shoulder about 20 feet in the air is the big TV screen showing the network line feed.

THE RACE

At 12:01 p.m. the cars are on their pace laps. The race is 83 laps around this up-and-down, twisty track. A spin will be disastrous today because the sandy run-off areas don't allow the cars to get back on track. The rear tires just spin and sink down into the sand.

"Check all your guns," Butch says to the 18-crew.

Ando says to Mark on the radio, "Get your temperatures up. Work the water and oil and brakes. We need a good start here. Zero on the fuel."

Russ tells Mauricio, "No passing 'til the stripe. Use the button at the start."

As the field comes around for the green flag, Control growls slowly, "They're starting to form up pret-ty nice."

The cars come around Turn 11, and Russ says to Mauricio, "Herta's pretty slow on the start."

Bryan Herta is on pole and just outside of him on the front row is his nemesis, Alex Zanardi. Scott Pruett and Mark are on the second row with Mauricio and Jimmy Vasser right behind them. Ando to Mark: "Watch your position before the flag flies, before you cross the line."

The crowd ramps up a yell as the cars accelerate, and Jim Swintal waves the green flag. "Green flag; green flag," says Russ.

Into the slow, double-apex, left-hand Turn 2, Mauricio creeps up inside Mark. Mark just turns in and Mo has to move left and give way, but not before he gets his left-front tire in the dirt. Vasser goes by Mark on the outside, leaving Mark and Mauricio in fifth and sixth spots. The order is Herta, Zanardi, Pruett, Vasser, Mark, and Mauricio.

These six cars stay together, pulling a 5-second gap from Mo to de Ferran in seventh place. About 10 laps into the race Mauricio complains of the car, "jumping up and down a lot. Lots of oversteer."

Russ comes back saying, "The pressures are up. Can you stand a little lower cold pressures?"

"Ten-four," comes the answer.

Shortly after, Russ tells Mauricio, "Herta's holding up Zanardi. You're closing the gap."

Then, "De Ferran has now caught you. Use the button."

Herta's tires are losing grip, and Zanardi is poking his nose inside or outside at every corner. Bryan is probably hoping to hold him off another eight or 10 laps so he can get a fresh set of tires.

On lap 16 Zanardi almost gets by, braking late into Turn 2 taking an outside line while Bryan hugs the inside to block a pass there. Bryan slides out a little and Zanardi gets a nose inside and squirts up even with Bryan going toward Turn 3. But Bryan is on the inside for this fast, flat, right-hander and Zanardi locks up his right-front tire trying to brake late. Herta dodges one bullet, but the other guys have closed up right behind Zanardi. Things are getting tight.

A lap later Zanardi goes by Herta on the inside at the entrance to Turn 5, a fast left turn exiting uphill. But he slides wide at the exit, and Herta repasses him retaining the lead. How many lives do Bryan's tires have?

On lap 20 what everyone was waiting for finally happens. Zanardi brakes late into Turn 2 again and goes around Bryan on the outside. It almost works, but Bryan has been saying all week he would give no quarter and he doesn't. He holds his line at the exit of Turn 2 and bumps Zanardi off into the dirt.

This is one of the really slow spots on the track and all six cars are bunched up. Herta bobbles too, and Pruett shoots by followed by Vasser and Zanardi. Mauricio gets by Mark at the same time, and they both pass Herta later that lap in Turn 6. The order now is Pruett, Vasser, Zanardi, Mo, Mark, and Michel Jourdain Jr.

Mark's car is pushing and Jourdain Jr. gets by him. Ando tells him to hang on 'til the pit stop. Both the PacWest cars pit at the same time and get out cleanly. The order after the stops is Vasser, Pruett, Zanardi, Mauricio, and Mark. Andre Ribeiro has worked his way up to sixth from 10th on the grid.

Ando tells Mark, "Hang in there. We need the fuel and we need those tires."

Russ to Mauricio, "Ribeiro is catching up. He's 5 or 6 seconds behind Mark, but he's very quick."

Ando cheers Mark on: "Keep pedaling. You're only 4 seconds behind Vasser in the lead. You're lookin' good. Just hang in there."

The 17-crew gets another set of tires up on the wall ready for the next stop. I notice the stands are completely full, and the hill behind me is colorfully dotted with groups of people sitting on blankets.

The order holds until lap 54 of 83 when Mauricio makes his second stop. Greg Moore, Zanardi, Pruett, and Ribeiro come in at the same time. Mo gets out ahead of Pruett — another good pit stop. Mark comes in a lap later at the same time as Vasser and de Ferran, and the 18-crew nails the stop. Vasser gets out first but both come out ahead of Zanardi and Mauricio. So it's Vasser, Blundell, Zanardi, Gugelmin, and Pruett.

One lap later Zanardi tries Mark inside at Turn 2, and Mark lets him slide out ahead of him, turning in as Zanardi goes off in the dirt once again. Mark and Mo are now in second and third behind race leader Vasser.

The TV crews start to come around. Bruce is sitting in the scoring cart just behind my left shoulder, and if I look over my other shoulder I can see him on the big screen as well. He appears calm, as usual.

Ando tells Mark to conserve fuel, but put the pressure on Vasser. Mark is pushing Jimmy with his nose right under the red car's rear wing going into the Corkscrew. Jimmy will have to make a mistake for Mark to be able to make a clean pass, and Mark's not going to take a chance knocking himself out of the race when he could finish second.

Mauricio is not in such good shape. Russ tells him to use the push-to-pass button only when he needs it. He's got brake problems also. The rear brakes just don't seem to be working like they should.

"What's with the fuel?" he asks.

Russ answers, "We need that 1 gallon we would have had if we had stayed out that extra lap." That's how tight the pit windows are here.

With less than 20 laps to go Ando tells Mark, "You got some traffic up ahead of Vasser. Use it when you can."

A few laps later Russ tells Mo, "One lap with the green switch up. One lap with the switch up."

Mauricio: "Let me know when I have to turn it off." I think the green switch powers the pump that transers the extra oil into the engine oil tank.

Mark is catching Mo and Russ tells him, "We're too tight on fuel. Do not use the button. Do not use the button."

With 10 laps to go Mauricio is still having brake problems. Russ tells him, "The temps are OK."

Tom Keene is once again working Mauricio's pit board, and he's waving Mo on every time he comes by. Finally the white flag is out, and it looks like a podium finish for both the PacWest drivers. That's a great big deal, seldom seen. Russ tells Mauricio, "Last lap. Zanardi is about 3 seconds behind you. Last lap."

Mo doesn't make it. His brakes give up as he tries to stop the car from 180 mph going into Turn 2. "I saw the Hollywood hospitality suite down there as I slid by," he told me later, "but I didn't have time to wave."

Both PacWest crews watch Mark come out of Turn 11 for the last time, and then they jump up and down, pumping hands and high-fiving in the pit lane. They'll settle for a second for Mark. Vasser wins and Zanardi gets third, clinching the '97 CART championship.

The big-screen TV shows Vasser and Zanardi waving at each other while they're still in their cars, coming down from the Corkscrew. Wheels touch and Jimmy spins into the bank before Turn 9 and stalls. Mark avoids the mess by driving around the outside, but in the excitement he misses the Victory Circle turnoff before Turn 10. Mark pulls into pit lane and they point him out onto the racecourse again. I head for Victory Circle myself.

Gary Gerould with the Blundell Family

When I get there the 18-crew is beating up on Mark as he gets out of the car. Mark's wife, Deborah, and both their boys are there. The Mercedes guys are handing out Manufacturer's Championship hats.

On my way to the post-race interview I stop back in the garage area. The 18-car is coming back from tech inspection. About 10 people hover around the back of the 17-car and one of them is Mauricio. He looks up at me, and I ask what happened. "Something with the brakes. I was losing some fluid in the rear. We're looking at it now."

Later I find out a brake caliper cross-over pipe leaked during the race, draining all the fluid. I wonder if that was a result of that last-minute rotor change?

Press Conference

Mike Zizzo, CART director of public relations, asks Mark to summarize the last nine laps.

Mark: "Actually, what was going through my mind was to win the race, and also a bit of frustration with a couple of backmarkers. Jimmy was the first one there and he got a bit of a better break. We got caught up with them and the gap to him kept expanding and getting smaller again. We certainly had the car. The guys did a great job, and we got the fastest lap of the race [70.960 seconds vs. 70.988 for Andre Ribeiro and 71.273 for Alex Zanardi].

"My thanks goes to the team. That second pit stop was the edge for us. They turned me in and out really quickly, and I'm very thankful for that. Jimmy had it today. We had a little bit there for him, but he was going to be a tough one to get by."

Zizzo asks Jimmy Vasser to tell us how that cool-off-lap accident happened.

"Well, Alex and I were jokin' around about it. He has a great thing with his doughnuts and all that. I figured, how am I going to top that? So I figured, if on the cool-off lap I just stuff it into the fence somewhere....[laughter stops the proceedings for a few minutes]. Maybe that'll make it on Sports Center.

"Actually, we were comin' down there side by side, and Alex took his hands off the wheel to clap or something, and we just touched a little bit. It spun me out. But Chip [Ganassi, team owner] didn't seem to mind too much."

After that I go back to the paddock and find Pat. We walk to our car and head home. No airplanes this weekend. The season finale at Fontana is next.

CHAPTER 23

FONTANA

This is the last race and I'm ready for it. It's been a long year. The travel is a huge hassle. My 10 a.m. flight from San Francisco International to Ontario is canceled, but there's another one at 1:30 p.m. Flights back from Ontario were full when I booked my travel three weeks ago, so I have to come back from John Wayne Airport in Costa Mesa, Calif. That's only an hour drive south from the California Speedway in Fontana. The last flight is at 8 p.m. and that should give me plenty of time, especially since the race starts at noon Pacific time.

My flight takes off on time and an hour later we're in Southern California. Surprise! It's raining, an uncommon occurrence in L.A. in September. Due to a global weather condition called El Niño, the Pacific Ocean water off California is 10 degrees warmer than usual, almost 70 degrees Fahrenheit. Because of this, a hurricane named Nora has drifted farther north than usual, bringing rain and floods to the Southwest.

The California Speedway

A short drive on the freeway east brings me to Cherry Avenue, where I exit north into a very unattractive industrial area full of trucks and razor-wired fences. The California Speedway looms large on the left, and I turn into the main gate. After a visit to the credential office for my parking pass and a press-room sticker for my hardcard, I drive through a tunnel under Turn 4 to the infield.

The drainage system is handling the rain run-off pretty well. Since it doesn't rain much in this area many malls and parking lots omit drainage, and you have to wade through puddles when water occasionally falls from the sky.

After a short walk I find the PacWest garage area. The 18- and 17-crews flew in yesterday and are finishing up a day of car prep. Jim Hamilton tells me his dynamic analysis software predicted a change that worked well when they were here at the test a couple of weeks ago. "I walked the track and drove it in a van to get a feel for the bumps. I ran it through my software and something came up that was decidedly unconventional. We tried it and Mo liked it. It's one thing for a simulation to predict what we all think we know, but quite another to predict an unconventional change that actually works."

I walk around and talk to people for another hour and then drive to our hotel in San Bernadino, 10 miles east on Interstate 10. In the hotel bar I learn that Robby Gordon is here to replace Dario Franchitti in Carl Hogan's car, and Parker Johnstone is probably out in Barry Green's KOOL car next year. That's too bad. I like Parker.

Russ Cameron is in the bar with his laptop computer combining drinking a cool beer with planning next year's pit equipment. The team is having meetings on '98 improvements this weekend. I ask him whether the techie stuff — shocks and engine developments — have helped or hurt this year.

"The tech stuff is a mixed bag," Russ says. "I think the engine has been an advantage. Some engine software, like BOSS, we had to learn how to use and it's a small advantage, but you don't want to be without it. The shocks and the other hydraulic systems have helped, but we don't have a way to develop them without putting them on a car during a race weekend, and that's really not the way to do it.

"I really feel if you had two good drivers, and we do, and a good bunch of people, and we do, you could run a pretty standard Reynard. The Ilmor motor and Firestone tires helped a lot this year." A couple more beers, more conversation, and it's bedtime.

FRIDAY

Leaving for the track about 6:30 a.m. I decide to avoid the notoriously fickle L.A. freeways and take the back way to the track on Foothill Boulevard, which used to be the main highway through these parts, U.S. Route 66. Two blocks from the hotel I turn left, drive a couple of miles, and there it is, a four-lane street lined with old motels and eating spots, most of which are now closed and boarded up.

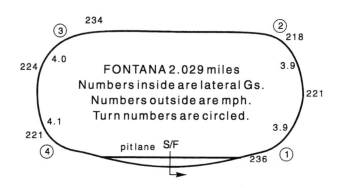

The sun is coming up as I drive in the track gate. I find a convenient parking spot and walk into the paddock. The track is dry, but occasional drizzle has caused CART to cancel rookie practice and delay Indy Lights practice.

At 10:15 the Indy Lights cars are on the track, and Mark Blundell is here on pit lane watching the 18-crew practice pit stops. CART practice is scheduled to start at 11 a.m. Ron Endres, Trevor Jackson, and Andy Natalie push the 17-car into the pit box. Pit location is about three-quarters the length of pit road from pit-in, almost to Turn 1. The press room is, conveniently for me, right behind us. My feet will appreciate this. The Indy Lights practice session is checkered at 10:21, and the PPG pace cars go on course.

At 10:50 the 17-car gets towed back to the garage to fix a fuel leak. The 2-foot-square wet spot caused by the spilled methanol slowly evaporates during the next few minutes. The car comes back as the session goes onto a 5-minute sign.

Friday Practice

I put on my headphones and fire up the scanner. Everything is dry but the sky is still darkly overcast and a light mist comes and goes. At 11:02 Wally Dallenbach is in the pace car and he's telling Control, "Go when you're ready. We're not taking any chances this morning."

The session starts with the cars circulating behind Wally in his orangish-green Mercedes. At the first race at Homestead he told me he wondered if he would ever get used to the color. I haven't. The drivers all say conditions are fine and they go green, but a car slows on course causing a yellow flag. Mauricio and Mark are still on pit lane. When Mark got in the car he felt the brake pedal was too soft, so they're bleeding the brakes. After they've finished the left side Stephen Kent comes along spraying brake cleaner on the fittings and carefully wiping them off with a white paper shop towel.

Mauricio is out at 11:17. I can hear Mark saying "pressure, pull" on the radio as the bleeding goes on. He's out on track at 11:19.

Mauricio is back in a couple of minutes later. "The car is a little bit loose, so I moved the weight jacker a little bit. Could be just a [tire] pressure thing."

Andy: "I'm watching these [tire pressures] and thinking we should help them a fraction." Andy asks the crew to increase the tire pressures and Mo goes back out.

There's another yellow flag, and when Mo comes back in he says it's still "a little bit on the loose side."

Andy: "We have changed the aero settings just a tad. I think we should take some front wing out too. Do you want a half degree or more?"

Mauricio: "OK, take a full degree to start."

Mark comes in saying the pedals are jammed and the boost isn't coming up. He and Allen decide the tires aren't up to temperature and pressure yet and make no changes.

I decide to walk down to Turn 1 and look for the bumps there. Track employees and gates are everywhere, but my hardcard and media sticker get me right through to the area just behind the inside track wall. The bright green grass is wet from the rain yesterday and there are some puddles with an oily stain floating on top.

The course goes green as I get to Turn 1. The concrete wall is about 4-and-a-half-feet tall and a foot thick. The cars are still 100 feet away but they look fast from here, and I can hear a deep rumbling like at Michigan, louder from some cars than others. The Penske cars are louder it seems. I don't see any bumps. To my eye the cars just glide along smoothly.

I can still hear the radio conversations with the scanner. When Mauricio comes back in he tells Andy, "The car is turning in fine, gets to the middle corner fine, and then on the exit it gets light. I don't think the rear is secure. It needs some more downforce."

Andy: "OK. What I'd like to try is that low-speed shock change we were talking about. I think that will really help you."

Mauricio: "Ten-four, but I don't want to try to do too much, Andy, because of the circuit, with this rain and all the pollution and stuff. They need to blow the circuit off."

They make the shock change and he goes back out at 11:34 a.m. Then they throw a yellow for a track inspection, and when Mo comes back in he says, "I really couldn't feel the shock change that you did. When I go across a patch that has a line the car just goes loose there. We need to put more wing on, Andy."

A safety truck stops on the track right in front of me and a guy gets out to pick up something off the track. The big, electric signboard on the track fence above the safety truck flashes driver names, car numbers, and driver statistics. Then it tells me how to find Lost and Found. The Safety-1 truck comes back home to a break in the wall to my left, and the course goes green again at 11:40. I see Mauricio roll by, picking up speed slowly. Mark goes by a minute later. I can smell hamburgers grilling somewhere up-wind, probably cooked by someone at one of the campers parked along the fence behind me.

Mark come back into the pit box at 11:42. "The car basically feels pretty good. The front end's got less push than we had at the test. The rear feels a bit more stable but it's got a little bit more roll in it now. When you turn in to the corner it feels like the rear just falls over slightly. I can feel a little bit of softness in the car at that point. It's no problem, but it's just touching down toward the rear of the car, especially going into 1. Turns 3 and 4, the balance feels pretty good. There's just something there; it's the rear of the car that's not giving me enough to get stuck on the gas pedal all around the turn. I'm just havin' to breathe it slightly."

Allen: "What's the exact reason for that?"

Mark: "Just a little bit of insecurity, and I think it's because there's just too much roll on the rear of the car. I think it's OK, but it just gives me the feelin' that it's going to go and go a little bit more, and I'm just monitoring it with the gas pedal if you know what I mean. It just feels a little bit uncomfortable, but it's slight."

Allen: "OK; let's go up one on the rear springs, please."

Mark: "Could you just check the skids? And also the front-left tire. Is it OK or has it got a patch on it? I locked it up coming down onto pit lane."

Allen: "It looks OK. What about the track conditions?"

Mark: "It's very dusty out there; I mean you can see the amount of shit we're throwing up with the traffic circulatin.' It's very bad. The grip level sure feels there, but for us it's reducing push."

Allen: "OK, just to confirm, we're at the same rear ride height."

Mark goes out on course. From that conversation it seems to me he's pretty comfortable with the way the car's handling. A 100-pound spring change is a small correction, and he's not being spooked by the "nervous rear" I've heard so much of this year. Of course he still finds a lot of things to say about the car but that's his style, and if he's this comfortable this early in the weekend he could do very well in the race.

Mauricio has been out on track and comes back in at 11:52. He's not as happy as Mark, saying "It's pushing. It's not as good as it was at the test."

Andy: "We've found the limit of this valve, so I'd like to change to the other one. How's the bottoming?"

Mauricio: "About the same."

Mark comes back in and Allen asks, "Is that any better?"

Mark: "It promoted more push in the car but the push is more consistent all the way around. It just jumped up a level, especially in 1 and 2, but also coming out of the 3/4 exit, there's more push in the car as well. The car feels a little bit more stable, which I guess is surprising in some ways, but maybe it gives me a bit more confidence entering into the corner. With more gas on it's just a little more push. The funny thing is, going into 1 and 2 it feels like the car's touching down harder. I'm carrying a bit more commitment in, it's touchin' down, and then it's gettin' the front of the car to skip. It's a small amount, but it's there and you lose a little front grip with that skip. There's a small vibration as well on the tires."

Allen: "All right, so what's your worst problem?" This is one of the ways Allen tries to sort out what he should be working on next from all of Mark's talk.

Mark: "The front end basically. Going into 1 and 2 with a bit of commitment, there the car's just touchin down a bit too aggressively, just givin' it that skip on the front end and you lose front-end grip. Then with the understeer level being increased now, you just have to be prepared to get on the right line, and if I've got the right line I can carry it all the way out, but there's too much push at that point."

Allen: "Well, the first thing we'll do is raise the car a flat all 'round. All right? Could we go up a flat all 'round, please?"

Mark: "It's a bit shy of revs as well, Al, and also boost. It's only up to 40 and it's a bit temperamental at that."

Allen: "I think with the revs we're OK. What with the way the wind is, we're just being very careful, mate. The push, you remember we were talking about the front bump? How about we go down on that a little bit and see if that gives you some front grip?"

Mark: "Yeah, we can try that. Just another problem we need to make an observation of, on the speed on the dash, because I got my right hand down on the wheel, I can't see the speed when I come into the pit. I'm way off where I should be in terms of gettin' speed down on the marker. I'm goin' to fly in way too quick."

They talk about the electronic dash and ways to fix it later. Just after noon Richie Hearn crashes in Turn 4, causing a yellow flag. He's driving a new Swift for the first time. The billboard across the track from me flashes one huge word, "ACCIDENT."

Mark says his visor is dirty. "Can't hardly see out of it already."

I decide to walk back to the pit box and get there about 12:13. The monitor shows Zanardi is P1 with a lap of 235.858 followed by Scott Pruett, Mauricio, Greg Moore, and Mark. I can see some blue sky through the overcast now, and it's getting warmer. The session goes green again about 12:14. There's been a lot of yellows, so there's still 53 minutes to go.

Mark has been out on course and comes back in. "It's less push, but now the turn-in is not quite as cute; it's not as sweet going in. From that point on there's just a lack of front grip. It just doesn't generate enough grip for me, and I've got too much push too early in the turn."

Allen: "Let's give it a half-turn of front wing then. Maybe just changing the aero balance or something. [Mark nods in the car.] Let's give it a half-turn both sides, please, front wing. If this doesn't work we'll go back on the bump change, but it was a favorable change at the test. So let's give this a run."

Mauricio goes out and improves to P2 with a lap of 31.006 seconds, 235.580 mph. The next lap is even faster at 236.884. Zanardi is still P1.

When Mo comes in he tells Andy, "That gave the rear a little bit more stability; that's the right way to go." Maybe he's talking about the low-speed shock change they made earlier. My scanner only picks up one channel at a time, and with many conversations going at the same time I miss things I'd like to know. I turn off the CART channel to concentrate on the PacWest conversations.

Mark is back in for another set of tires. He's in P5 now. "It feels like it doesn't have enough support when you lean on it into the turn. It feels like that right-hand side is just a little too weak.

It gives it that nasty skip. I've got the commitment going in. I've got too much lock on coming off the mid to the exit."

Allen: "I want to try a back-to-back with this set [of tires], so I don't want to change anything. All right? We're hopin' to run on these, so we need to run them now."

Mauricio goes back out at 12:29 and Mark follows a minute later. Then there's a yellow for a track inspection. When he comes in Mark complains about the mirror vibration. "Maybe we could glue the lens in the shell if that's what's movin'."

I turn the CART channel on again and I hear one of the pit officials say the 21-team, Richie Hearn's crew, "respectfully requests that the parts are returned to the pit or paddock when clean-up is complete."

Safety 3 comes back saying they had to unload all the stuff they picked up. "There was so much of that debris that they had to unload it back at their safety station so they could perform their duties. The team can take a cart out there and pick it up. If they choose to wait, we'll bring it in at the end of the session."

The monitor says Zanardi is still P1 followed by Mauricio, Scott Pruett, Parker Johnstone, and Bobby Rahal.

Mauricio says his visor is sandblasted. "I can hardly see."

Andy: "There's still 38 minutes of green. Is that going to be a problem? For the rest of the session?"

Mauricio: "No; maybe it's better not to see where you're going."

Andy: "This isn't another of my setups, where you just shut your eyes and hope, is it?"

Mauricio's eyes smile at Andy through the visor opening.

Andy: "Green flag."

It's 12:38 p.m. Mark Moore, the 17-car chief mechanic, waves Mauricio out and then stands there in the middle of the pit box with his fists on his belt and his elbows out. Mark is a strong, blocky guy who takes up a lot of space anyway, but right now he looks like that whole pit box is his and nobody better mess with it.

At 12:42 Juan Fangio II slows to a stop on course, causing a yellow flag. When Mark comes in he says, "It still seems to be consistent with losing a little bit of grip all the way through the radius of the turn. Where I notice it a lot is going into 3, turn-in and the thing just does a little skip on the entry there, which is, we haven't really felt that before."

Allen: "Well, when we picked that up is when we softened up the front-right damping, so let's go back on that. Can we go back on that, please, Trevor? One stiffer, high-speed and low-speed."

Mauricio tells Andy: "It's pushing a little bit too much; probably something good for a race situation. I moved some of the weight. You can see it. I reckon we could trim [smaller angle of attack on the wings and/or smaller Gurney flaps for less downforce, less drag] a little bit."

Mauricio is still P2 behind Zanardi. Mark is P7. Jim Hamilton walks over to the 18-car and looks hard at the front tires. Mauricio asks Andy about the pressures. Andy says, "The pressures built a lot better." The session returns to green, and both cars go out at 12:46.

After a few laps Mark improves to P3. Then, as Mauricio comes out of Turn 4, I hear him say, "It's a good one, Andy." It sounds like he's excited, for him anyway. And so he should be. The lap is 30.555 seconds, 239.057 mph. That puts him all alone in P1. A 30-second lap on a 2-mile track!

Mauricio comes in saying, "It's got a little push; the difference was I got a nice line. Actually on the backstraight I thought the engine was gonna blow up. The whole car was just shaking like crazy."

Then we see Zanardi come sliding down the frontstraight, having crashed in Turn 3 or 4. He gets out and walks down the banking. The crowd cheers as only a race crowd can when it feels the excitement of a crash and the relief at seeing a driver walk away unhurt.

The TV replays show that Patrick Carpentier lost it low in Turn 3 and hit the wall. Michael Andretti saw Carpentier crash in front of him and backed out of the throttle. Zanardi, right behind Michael, probably thought he was going into the pits and went high to pass. He almost T-boned Carpentier. A loose wheel from the crash hit Zanardi's right-front wheel, knocking it off the car and causing Zanardi to crash into the wall. The TV replay shows his car going nose up along the wall like it wants to take off. A nasty but natural result of 235 mph on a 2-mile oval.

Mauricio is out of the car. It's going to be a long clean-up. He calls for the Bell Helmet rep and asks for another visor to replace his grit-blasted one. I look at his car and see the windscreen is almost opaque. The leading edge of the front wing is covered with a tough tape, but where the tape ends near the nose the paint has been blasted off. The leading edges of the rear-view mirrors are devoid of paint. All this is evidence of a lot of gritty crap out there on the track. Why can't they clean that off?

There's still 26 minutes to go in this session that seems to go on forever. The track goes green again at 1:19. Mauricio and Mark are getting back into their cars and they're on course again at 1:21. The monitor shows the 17-car in P1 followed by Zanardi, Mark, Parker, Vasser, and Greg Moore. Mauricio quickly turns a lap at 30.618 seconds, almost as quick as his best. He's making this look easy.

Incredibly the next lap is faster — 30.555 seconds. Then we hear him on the radio as he comes to the Start/Finish line again. "Another good one, Andy!" he yells. He's right; 30.416 seconds, 240.150 mph. I think that's the fastest lap ever in an Indy car.

There's a yellow flag for a track inspection and both cars come in. Mauricio says, "There's more mechanical grip, Andy. We got some roll, but we're probably about there. It's nice. I don't even feel the thing is touching."

Mark is also close to his optimum setup. He can hardly find anything at all wanting with the car. "It's touchin' down a little bit, just in 1 and 2. It's also just a little less responsive on turn-in going into 3, but very slight, very marginal. Maybe we can check the skids to see whether they show us any signs, but overall grip and balance feel pretty good."

Amazing. I don't remember Mark ever sounding so satisfied. Look out! This could be a one-two finish for PacWest.

Allen says to Mark, "So you think it's a pretty good race setup like this?" I think he's surprised too.

Mark: "It's pretty reasonable, to be honest. The car is just a little bit more effective in those bumps. I'd like to get a longer run and get mixed into some traffic and see whether the car's still in balance."

Andy needs to run some BBS wheels to see how they perform vs. the OZ wheels. "Let's give this the five laps they're asking for. It's basically a qualifying run they're asking for, a scuffing. We'll just scuff this set."

There's a green flag at 1:34 and both cars go out. Mauricio comes back in after the BBS run and Andy tells him, "All right, Morris, I think we can go back to the pad."

Allen to Mark, "Let's call it a day there. Eh? Shall we take it to Valvoline, please, Butch, and then we'll put it on the pad. Well, mate, well done."

Mark doesn't get out before talking about the last possible nit that can be improved. "When I was running there with Bobby [Rahal], he was holding me up, and there's just a little bit too much push. It's just hard to get underneath him and commit to the line. Maybe a little trim on the front aero might get it OK." And he finally gets out of the car.

Mark and Mark Jr. with Some Movie Stars

Back in the garage area Mauricio is joking about saying "It's a good one" on the radio. "Maybe I'll start calling out the lap speed like calling your shots in pool."

"You must be pretty comfortable in the car, running that many laps that fast," I say.

"It's definitely not comfortable going that fast," he says. "It's scary."

Someone else says, "Pretty good for a stock motor and only 14,000 rpm. The qualifying motor goes in tonight."

"I walked down to Turns 1 and 2, and I didn't see any bumps," I say to Mark. "The cars look really smooth through there."

"They're there," Mark say, raising his eyebrows. "I can feel them, I'll tell you."

Andy says Mauricio had a tow on those good laps. "Pruett saw him coming and backed off, but it was too late."

Russ Cameron tells me the vibration Mauricio talked about was probably turbulence, maybe from the car he was drafting. "But he can go pretty good on his own. He did a 237.9 scuffing tires without a draft."

The afternoon session is scheduled for 3 p.m. but CART now says it won't start before 3:45 because of delays.

Carbon Fiber Brake Rotor Used
At Superspeedways

Friday Afternoon Practice

At 3:15 the 17- and 18-cars are in their pit boxes. It's still overcast and there's a light wind from the northwest. We could still have some sprinkles. The session goes green at 3:46. Mo is getting in his car but Mark is just walking up. A few minutes later Mark is in the car and Allen tells him, "We're scuffing tires, Mark. It's the baseline setup."

Both cars are out at 3:50. Mark is back in right away because the left-hand mirror is pointing down at the sidepod. That gets fixed quickly, but there's a yellow right away caused by another Toyota engine coming apart. Max Papis has slowed on course.

Al Bodey makes a reference to Mark about Papis being "your cooking partner." They have been doing some cooking episodes for TV. Mark says somebody else did the cooking.

Andy asks Mauricio, "Did you feel any difference in traffic?"

Mauricio: "Not really." That's good news.

The course finally goes green again at 3:58. Mauricio is trying a set of turning vanes in front of the sidepods. He reports a lot of vibration though, and they come off. Vanes like that generate a vortex that can decrease aerodynamic drag and create an aero seal along the outside, lower corner of the sidepods. Evidently these are no help because they take them off right away.

Tire scuffing continues. They could run new tires, called "stickers" because of the paper labels on them which quickly wear off. My guess is that on this track at the high temperatures expected during the race they need the hardening of the compound caused by that one initial heat cycle during scuffing.

Some wind has come up and there's a lot of dark, gritty dust blowing around on pit lane. Maybe this is condensed smog, the precipitation indigenous to the region.

Mark comes in at 4:08 and Allen asks, "How's the car now, Mark?"

Mark: "It's pretty good. I think it's just the wind making the car turn in a little bit quicker than what we were having this morning. Just getting up to speed I have to be careful on the out-lap and the next lap it's a little bit sweeter."

Mark complains to Scott Ellison, a CART pit steward, about Scott Pruett working with his teammate, Raul Boesel, to get a tow and not getting out of Mark's way when he was trying to overtake them.

It's sunny now. There's a dark cloud bank to the west and the sun is shining over the top of it. Mauricio is P11 and Mark P14. Jimmy Vasser is P1 with a lap average speed of 238.

Mark comes in from a run at 4:17 and Allen asks, "All right, how's the car?" It sounds like, "Awright, ows tha cah?"

Mark: "With the wind as it is, it's really not giving me any trouble turnin' the car in. The car really doesn't seem to be too much of an issue, especially in 1 and 2. So I guess it feels OK as far as the balance goes."

Allen: "I guess we don't dick with it then, eh?"

Mark comes back with some complaints about the brakes that can't be fixed in pit lane. He goes back out at 4:19. Butch, the 18-car chief mechanic, asks Randy, the tire guy, how many more sets to scrub. Randy shows him three fingers. Mauricio is P3 now with Mark P10. With 36 minutes to go in the session the monitor shows Vasser is still P1 followed by his teammate, Zanardi.

Mark is back on pit lane at 4:23. He's improved slightly to P9. Mauricio comes in also, saying the car is still vibrating but less than before. A yellow flag stops the session.

Andy: "We've got a yellow out; let's do these two sets of primes for a rim comparison. Let's go to set 10." They're still trying to see if the BBS wheels are better than the OZ rims. Mauricio says he's bottoming a little bit more than this morning. Mainly this session, both cars are scuffing tires for the race.

Mark has been trying fuel maps that run the engine lean to save on fuel consumption. He doesn't like the way it feels and explains why. "The thing I don't like is when I have to breathe it, when I have to lift out and get back on it again, then it doesn't come on clean, it like falters. So can I whine now?"

At 4:47 Mauricio has improved to P3 with a lap of 237 mph. As the crew puts on yet another set of tires to scuff, Jim Reid goes under the car to inspect the skids. I can smell the spray paint as he comes out and marks on the paper form that shows the wear pattern.

Mark is in P12, not really going for speed during the scuffing. Allen says, "We got one more set. You want to try this right-front bump change just to see what it does?"

Mark agrees and Allen tells Trevor to come up one sweep on the high- and low-speed bump on the right-front shock. Andy sends Mauricio out on a 20-lap run. "I'll give a countdown every five laps."

A yellow flag interrupts the session. When Mauricio comes back in he asks about the vibration he's had intermittently. Andy says, "We feel it's the tires, Mo, because both sets we ran first thing this afternoon we ran this morning with no problem."

Mauricio: "When they warm up a bit they get better. Could be there's something in the back end of the car. Something is wrong at the left rear." Within a minute there are 10 people at the rear of the 17-car looking at everything and jerking on the suspension members trying to find the source of the vibration. They don't find anything, so they button it back up. There's a green flag again at 4:59, and Mo goes out to continue his long run.

Mark is back in at 5:06. Allen asks, "How was that?"

Mark: "Still OK. It's just another crappy run. I just couldn't get any room out there. The car feels well balanced. It felt like there's a little more front end in there. At the moment I think I'd take the package we had the previous run. It seemed a bit more consistent."

Allen: "All right. That's it. We'll call it a day then."

At 5:08 there's a yellow flag because Juan Fangio II is slow on course, and Mauricio comes back in. Andy asks, "Was that OK?"

Mauricio: "That's OK. The tires feel good to me." They put on another set of tires to scuff.

The course goes green at 5:15 and Mo rolls off. Then Alex Zanardi crashes for the second time today, causing another yellow flag. If he destroyed another car he's out of a ride. Maybe that's good. There's some reason for two crashes in one day.

Mauricio comes in saying, "The vibration is just terrible, Andy. Each set is different and I hate to have any vibration in the car."

Andy: "I agree, especially around here." Mauricio gets out of the car.

Vasser's 239.968-mph lap is the fast one in this session. His teammate Alex Zanardi is P2 followed by Scott Pruett. Mark ends up in P5 with Mauricio in P6. Back in the garage area Russ tells me the vibration is a balance problem that Firestone is working on.

Press Conference

At 5:40 there is a press conference with the three drivers who have the top lap times for the first day. Mauricio's 240.150-mph lap this morning is still quickest overall. Vasser and Zanardi are second and third on combined speeds from both sessions.

Mauricio and Jimmy are here in the conference room in the paddock. Zanardi is still getting checked out by the medical staff. Here are a few comments from the drivers in response to media questions.

"Do you need to draft to get those speeds?"

Mauricio: "I can do 237 laps by myself, but you have to have a tow to do better."

"How difficult is passing?"

Jimmy: "Passing will be difficult in the race. You have to get it done before the turns."

"Are you comfortable in the car?"

Mauricio: "Nobody is comfortable at these speeds. I'm not. We're pushing the laws of physics."

"What about the damage from the grit on course?"

Mauricio: "I'll have to add some tearoffs maybe. We'll make it through the race but it will be tough. It's much worse here than at Michigan."

Jimmy: "It just doesn't rain enough here to wash it off."

"Tires?"

Mauricio: "It's the same Firestone tires as at the test. The wear is fine. We could go half the distance on the same set."

"How long does it take to warm up the tires?"

Mauricio: "There's not a problem. I can go flat right out of the pits. When I get to Turn 3 I can stay flat out through there."

Jimmy: "I can't." He looks at Mauricio as if to say, "Are you sure you can do that?"

At 5:47 Alex Zanardi arrives with the Ganassi Racing PR guy, Michael Knight.

"It was an exciting day," Alex says, humorous as ever. "I don't know what happened in the second crash. In the middle of the corner the rear of the car went away. We'll have to check the data. I've run out of cars."

Jimmy: "I've got one for ya."

Alex: "I'll wait 'til tomorrow to see if I can drive. It's not pleasant being a passenger at 230. It's thanks to Malcolm Oastler, who designed this car, that I'm still here."

Prep for Qualifying

Back in the garage at 5:55, both PacWest cars get new engines. These are the qualifying engines that will also be used for practice tomorrow morning.

I put my hand on the windscreen of the 17-car. I thought it would just be polished, but it's rough like sandpaper and you can barely see through it. It's really torn up. Russ Cameron says they may have to cut the windscreen down some so the drivers can see the side mirrors without looking through the screen.

I talk to David Bruns, the Swift designer. He's not happy with their first season with the new car. "I guess that first race was an aberration. We just haven't done well enough to make people think they need a Swift to win. Changing from a Reynard looks like too much of a risk."

I really like David. No whining.

Randy Smay tells me the 18-car scuffed nine sets of tires today. Andy Brown says they scuffed four sets with the 17-car and they've got three more to do tomorrow.

SATURDAY

I leave the hotel at 6:40 a.m. and get to the track just after 7. The beauty of the San Gabriel Mountains that mark the north wall of the Los Angeles basin is usually hidden by the nasty brown smog generated by the interaction of sunlight, ozone, and unburned hydrocarbons from car exhaust. This morning we get a rare treat. The rain has scrubbed the air clean and the sun illuminates the pink peaks while it's still dark down here in the valley.

In the Hollywood hospitality area I see Mauricio and Stella, his wife. I tell him I couldn't see any bumps in Turn 1. "Well, I can feel them. The bump into Turn 1 is bad, but I can avoid it by going higher. The Turn 2 bump you can't avoid."

"That was fun watching Jimmy's reaction in the press conference when you said you're flat on your out lap."

"He's running less wing than me, but I'll run less in qualifying."

In the garage area I see the back-up cars on the pads. Butch says the other cars are on pit lane "ready to go."

"How's the wrist?" I ask.

"It gets fixed next Tuesday."

"I see Gavin practicing on the right front. Will he be there during the race?"

"No, he's just doing the practice sessions. I don't want to use the wrist 'til I have to. They'll wrap it for me real tight Sunday morning, and I won't feel it because of the adrenaline."

Allen McDonald is having a bowl of cereal, and I tell him it seemed like Mark liked the car so much he didn't have anything to gripe about but the mirrors.

Allen laughs. "He was pretty pleased with it, wasn't he?"

Stephen Kent tells me he has to replace some of the decals on the cars because of the grit blasting.

Saturday Practice

The 1-hour CART practice session goes green at 9 a.m. Both PacWest cars go out and come back in for installation checks. The sky is clear and sunny. Allen tells Mark, "Go out and do a reasonably long run." Both cars go back out at 9:06.

When Mo comes back in Andy says, "I really would like to give our qualifying setup a run to check balance now. Let's change to set 12B."

I walk down to Turn 1 again to try to spot the bumps Mauricio and Mark were talking about yesterday. OK, I see a shiny spot in Turn 1 way up the track. It's shiny because the cars are bottoming and polishing the surface. That must be it.

Mauricio comes back in, reporting to Andy: "The balance is fine."

Andy: "Understood. Just give this set like a dummy qualifying run and see if that sliding was, in fact, the age of those other tires, and then we'll start trimming."

I take off the headphones so I can hear what the cars really sound like. There's a big whoosh and the scream of the engine. With the headphones on I can hear the low-frequency rumbling.

Mo comes in off course and Andy asks, "Are we OK to start trimming?"

Mauricio: "Ten-four."

Andy: "OK, we'll have to change a control box as well so it'll be a slightly longer stop. We're going to go to another set of tires and go to that wing adjustment we talked about."

There are two women in CART shirts here constantly looking at the track surface through binoculars. They're scanning the track for debris. The sun is hot and the sky is hazy, but there's a nice breeze from the south.

Allen sends Mark out. "We'll be scrubbing in these tires, so do a maximum of 10 laps."

Andy: "Is the bottoming OK, Morris?"

Mauricio: "Yeah, the bottoming is fine."

Andy: "Did you do the front wing, Mark?"

Mauricio: "First step, Andy?"

Andy: "That's correct."

Mauricio goes out at 9:26. There's about 35 minutes to go in the session. Yesterday they worked on a fast baseline setup for the car. Now, with a light load of fuel, they'll start to trim out the car aerodynamically, trying to get higher speeds. They'll set the wings to lower angles of attack and that will give less drag, but also less downforce. Mauricio will go toward the setup that will give him maximum speed while retaining control. At the same time Mo doesn't want to put much time on this engine. It's a qualifying-spec motor geared to turn 15,000 rpm. He doesn't want to use it up in this practice session.

Mark: "We're in the ballpark. It's a little bit like Michigan. The engine gets up there and it struggles to find its revs. If you can get a tow it brings it up into it and it's easy. We'll have to look at it in fifth gear."

Mauricio comes in and Andy asks, "Are we ready to go to the next level, or do you want to try this with the revs first?"

Mauricio: "On my own I'll probably be all right, but we're very close on the limit here."

Andy: "OK. Well that's what we need, is running on our own right now. Set 14, please. No, set eight, please."

Mauricio: "What else do you want to do? Because soon I want to park this car."

Andy: "Understood. We'll try the revs now and see what you think of that. After that we ought to try the other valve. This one hasn't quite found its limit yet. I'd like you to punch this one up two clicks. And we've just got one more set to scuff after that. You need to go to slot seven [full fuel, max rpm] for this run and probably use fourth gear [the lowest gear to run the engine at max rpm]."

Mauricio goes out at 9:32. I clock him with my stopwatch at a 30.50 or 239 mph.

When he comes back in he says, "I don't want to try any different downforce levels. I think we're about on the limit."

Andy: "Understood. We've got the best of that valve, so I want to try the other valve now. We'll just do two more runs on the last two sets of tires, and we're done."

Mauricio goes out for a couple of laps and comes in. The CART officials checking pit-lane speeds with a radar gun report that Mo went too fast.

Mauricio: "63? I wasn't there yet. I reckon they gettin' the number wrong, but I'll do a drive-through if they want."

Andy: "We're gonna go back to slot zero, Morris, back to fifth gear to scuff these two sets."

Russ Cameron says to go out and come in and go out again to satisfy the speeding penalty. Mauricio says, "They are wrong. I'll do it. But they are wrong."

Russ: "That's what I told them, but they said it was 69 mph."

Mauricio: "I was going less than 69 before the pit limit starts. I can see it on the dash. They should know where they're pointing that thing."

As he comes back in Mauricio says to Andy, "Do we really have to do two more sets?"

Andy: "You can just do four laps. Two each is all we need."

Mauricio: "That last set? I want them re-balanced. They're not bad, but they're not perfect."

It's 9:44 with 16 minutes to go in the session. Andy doesn't put fuel in because he wants to see the total amount of fuel this car can pick up and use from the fuel cell.

Mauricio comes back in after only one lap because of a yellow flag. He has one last set of tires to scuff. "I'm not running any more after this one. No more new ideas."

Andy, his voice smiling: "Well, there is just one thing we haven't looked at."

Mauricio: "We should put you in the car, Andy."

Andy: "Cut the radio chatter, please. This is a serious business."

Mauricio says he smells something burning. "Please don't let this thing burn at the back."

CART has shortened the session, so there's 4 minutes left.

Andy: "You just used a half a gallon on that one lap, so we still should be OK on fuel. Just go out, do three laps and in."

Mauricio: "I want to talk to the CART guys, 'cause they waste my time this session."

Russ: "I went down there. Billy [Kamphausen] knows. He's down there trying to sort them out. They tried to say our data must be wrong. I told them I'm sure our data is right."

Mauricio goes out for those last three laps. When he comes in I hear him say. "Sit [That's it.]." He's in P1 with an amazing lap of 242.333 mph. Vasser is P2 at a 240.347 followed by Mark, who drove a lap at 239.795 mph.

Back in the Garage

I ask Andy Brown about temperature changes. "It's likely to be much warmer for qualifying a couple of hours from now. Do you make any changes to the car?"

"I don't try to make guesses on the weather," Andy says. "If you ignore weather changes you're only off the amount it changes. If you guess, you could be off twice that much."

At 11:30 lunch is here and each guy eats as he gets a break in his work. Mark Moore is eating but still thinking. He asks Scott Simpson where the tire set is that they've decided to use for the qualifying run. Scott says the tires are in the pit box. "Would you go get 'em and bring 'em here?" Mark asks. "We'll use 'em on the pad."

There are slight differences tire-set to tire-set and Mark wants to make sure the qualifying setup that goes on the car is exactly right. He'll put those tires on the car when it goes on the setup pad.

At 11:45 the 17- and 18-cars are on the setup pads. We're hearing rumors that Arie Luyendyk will be brought in to replace Alex Zanardi in the Ganassi car. Alex destroyed both his cars and he's not feeling up to driving in the race. The Ganassi team has prepared Jimmy Vasser's backup car for Arie. This is a controversial move because of the CART/IRL squabble. Luyendyk has always been a good oval driver and has driven for Ganassi before.

Qualifying

A few minutes before noon the qualifying session is almost underway. Instead of drawing for the qualifying order, the cars are arranged along the pit wall in order of increasing speed. Mauricio will be the last to make his run. I'm told the way they did it is to average the best speeds from the three sessions for each driver. The place where Alex Zanardi's car should be is empty. If Arie drives in the race tomorrow, he'll start from the back of the field.

Both the PacWest cars are using OZ wheels because they have an aerodynamic advantage. One set is brightly polished and one is matte black. The polished set is on the 17-car. Mark Moore says, "I told them the shiny ones would look good in the pole photo."

Jimmy Vasser is in the second-fastest place, and Mark is fourth-fast after the Zanardi blank spot. Jimmy and Mark are on sticker, optional Firestone tires. Mauricio is running scuffed optionals. As more cars make their qualifying runs the CART officials delivering the pop-off valves come down the line. Ron and Chris install one on the 17-car very carefully, using Loctite on the bolts.

At 1 p.m. Mark is in his car and Mauricio gets in his. Mo is very methodical about his preparation and gets everything just how he wants it. His lips purse and twitch sideways in a way I've not noticed before. Mauricio is extremely focused and intent on this qualifying run. He told me earlier that a 500-mile race is very special.

Scott Simpson checks the tire pressures. He kids Mark Moore, "I didn't get that valve cap on tight and you didn't catch it. I did that just to see if you'd find it." Scott laughs more than Mark.

As more drivers make their runs the knot of photographers and media people move down the line toward us. There's a low wall on the track-side of pit lane and another higher, stronger wall between the pit wall and the grass lining the track. The space in between is wide enough to walk in; that's where the guys manning the pit boards stand. I see the Lola guys, as usual, standing there now. Chris Saunders, the aero guy, and Ben Bowlby, the chief designer, make a habit of moving down the line during qualifying to look at each car and see how it's set up.

At 1:06 Mark is on course. His fastest lap is a 30.942 for 236.067 mph, 3 mph slower than this morning. That earns him sixth place for the moment.

Jimmy Vasser is next and he takes over first place with a 239.222-mph lap. That's the average speed Mauricio has to beat for the pole.

Mauricio is the last qualifier. With his first timed lap he takes over the number-one position with a lap average of 239.41 mph. His next lap is even quicker, 240.94 mph. Before he gets to the Start/Finish line he knows it's a quick one. I hear him yell, "Yeeehaaah!" He has the pole for the first-ever California 500 at Fontana.

As I walk down the pit lane toward the inspection area where the CART officials will check to see that the car is legal, Bruce is walking ahead of me. Teddy Mayer, managing director of Penske Cars, Ltd., steps out of one of the Penske pit boxes and congratulates Bruce. Chuck Sprague, Team Penske general manager, joins in with a smiling handshake of his own. These people are fierce competitors, but they recognize and acknowledge achievement.

The car is up off the ground getting scrutinized and a bunch of people are congratulating Mauricio. Gary Gerould, ABC pit announcer, smiles as he says to me, "A little bit of history; the closed-course speed record."

The awards and festivities go on for another hour. The drivers who won pole positions during the year are given a car key for each pole, and now they get to see which one fits a new car. Bryan Herta's key opens the door and he gets the car.

At 2:30 the pole press conference is held in the paddock conference room. Mauricio and Jimmy Vasser are there to talk to the media. Mike Zizzo, CART director of public relations, introduces Mauricio by saying, "The quickest today for the qualifying for the Marlboro 500 presented by Toyota with a speed of 240.942 in the Hollywood PacWest Mercedes on Firestones, the fastest official qualifying lap in auto racing history. That tops the 237.4 set by Luyendyk at the '96 Indy 500. He also sets the all-time fastest unofficial lap this morning at 242.333. All three drivers in here today topped the record. We also had 14 drivers today top the CART record of 234.665 set by Vasser at last year's Marlboro 500 at Michigan. This is Mo's third career pole, 20th consecutive top-10 start, including 13 top-fives, the 12th pole for Firestone, sixth for Mercedes. He gets 10 grand from Marlboro for the pole, but you'll like this number, $105,000 available if he wins from the pole tomorrow. Mo, can you tell us about the fastest lap in history? Tell us about your emotions about this."

Jimmy is in civvies with his sunglasses up on his forehead, long hair hanging down over his face and ears. Bryan Herta has on a cap and driver suit, but the suit is unzipped and rolled down to his waist, showing an off-white Nomex underwear top. In contrast Mauricio has his driving suit zipped up and he looks fresh and crisp with a neat haircut and a red Hollywood cap.

"240 is a magic number," he says. "It's a great achievement for the PacWest team today and I hope we'll have a great race tomorrow."

The drivers all agree they'd be more comfortable with averages in the 220s.

Prep for Race Day

Back in the garages at 3:15 the PacWest crews are changing engines in both the primary cars. The qualifying engines come out and the race motors go in.

In the press room I watch some of the Indy Lights race. They're running 60 mph slower than the CART cars — in the 180s — but the race is extremely exciting. They can run close together, actually getting four abreast at times. To me this proves you don't need these ridiculous speeds for good racing. I don't understand why the people running CART and IRL and F1 don't realize this. What we fans want is good-sounding cars dicing with each other and getting sideways.

Fastest Lap Ever!
(Dan Boyd Photo)

At 3:30 I'm in the PacWest garage watching the cars being prepared for tomorrow's race. I manage to get in Roscoe's way as he changes gears in the 17-car transmission. He just smiles at me as I stumble out from between him and his toolbox.

At 4:30 Arie Luyendyk is in a Ganassi car for the first time during a special practice session. He turns a 226 without much trouble. It's possible Mauricio could bump Jimmy Vasser out of third place in the season championship. Maybe Ganassi wants to run two cars to keep that from happening. Or maybe there is some contractual agreement with sponsors to run both cars no matter what.

Down the pit lane in the PacWest pit boxes, Jeff Stafford and Mike Todd lay down the duct-tape stripes to aid the drivers in stopping right on the marks during the race tomorrow.

A dinner of cold cuts is served in between the transporters at 5:45. I fix myself a sandwich now so when I get back to the hotel I won't have to go eat somewhere. I'm going to go to bed early tonight.

RACE DAY

As usual I wake up early on race day. I'm excited and there's no use lying here trying to go back to sleep. I get up and get after it. I have to pack and check out, but I leave the hotel at 6 a.m. and get to the track a half-hour later. There's a thin crescent moon above the rising sun. This is the last time today this place will look pretty. It's going to be smoggy and hot as hell!

Jim Swintal tells me he hasn't had a chance to talk to the front-row drivers, Jimmy and Mauricio, because he was flagging the Indy Lights race yesterday afternoon during the CART drivers' meeting. "I'm sure they'll be fine. I'm not worried about Mo and Jimmy."

At 7:30 on the mainstraight just under the flagger's stand there's a photo shoot for the front row, the 17-car of Mauricio and Jimmy Vasser's 1-car. The sun is shining low and bright directly from Turn 1. It takes the whole crew to push the 17-car up the bank. I take a bunch of photos.

Warm-Up

The warm-up session is scheduled for an 8 a.m. start, and it goes off on time. The first time in for Mark he says the steering wheel feels funny. "More right-hand down than yesterday."

Mauricio says, "It's hard to see where I'm going with this sun."

Allen tells Mark they've got two sets of tires to scrub. Andy wants Mauricio to try both fifth and sixth gears while they scrub some tires also.

After a run Mauricio says, "I guess the pressures must be a bit low. 'Cause I'm bottoming a little bit and it's pushing a little bit. Probably just because of that."

Andy: "This next set of tires is a second scuff. [Two heat cycles in the tire make it harder so it will take higher temperatures.] I'm going to help the pressures a bit if you think it would be useful for information. It would just take the bottoming out. Shall we put a pound down the right side, please, Scott? And we need to do a waste-gate change before we can find the limit of this valve. This will be the last run for this car."

Ando talks Mark into the pit box as he comes in from a run. "Down the middle. Down the center. Stop on Butch's hands. Stop."

Mark: "There is a little bit more push in the car, especially between 1 and 2. It's more prominent there, but I don't know whether it's conditions, with the track a little bit colder. Maybe we could try something to see if we could trim it out maybe. Maybe a bit of front wing if we need that for the race."

Allen: "One more run and then we'll park it. If you've still got push then try the front roll bar, softening up that and also the weight jacker, take a bit of weight off the right front."

Andy: "OK, Mo, are we happy with this car? Can we get into the T-car now?"

Mauricio: "I'm happy with this. I'm not happy with this switch though [the oil-transfer switch]. I'm going to switch it off now." Mauricio gets out of the racecar and into the T-car to scuff some tires.

Ando talks Mark in after a run and Allen asks him, "That feel better?"

Mark: "Feels like it's a little bit cleaner comin' off the corner, but it's makin' it a little bit nervous turnin' in. It's a quicker turn-in, which gives me a bit of unease when I turn the car in and load it up initially. I'd like to try it again this next run, just to see if it's OK."

Allen: "We can't really do any more. That's it, mate. We're out of laps."

Mark: "Maybe we should take half of that change back out? Takin' into mind the conditions where we'll be this afternoon."

Allen: "All right, then, boys. That's it for this morning."

There's a yellow flag at 8:18. Somebody stalled on course. The monitor shows the order for this session is Vasser, Ribeiro, Moore, Mauricio, and Scott Pruett. Mark is P9. The track goes green again at 8:22. Mark is out of his car and gone from pit lane.

Andy: "One run to get this set of scuffs up to speed and see if they're OK and that'll be it."

Mauricio goes out in the T-car at 8:23. A lot of cars are getting pushed off pit lane back to the garage area.

But that's not the last run. They change the pop-off valve and make one more run in the T-car. They have to hurry to make the valve change and get in the laps. Mo goes out at 8:32.

Andy: "Up 10 on the boost, Morris." After looking at the data coming from the car he says, "Up four on the boost, Morris."

The checkered flag flies at 8:34. Mark Moore says, "He was faster in the T-car. We did an awesome job on that. Maybe we should run this one now — start at the back." I can hear the smirk in his voice.

Mauricio had only gone 232 mph in the racecar, but turned a lap at 235 in the back-up for P3 behind Vasser and Ribeiro. Arie Luyendyk is fifth in the session at 234 mph. Mark is P13 at 231.

Race Prep

Back in the garage I ask Mauricio about the differences in the two cars. "The T-car pushed less; the racecar motor is better."

Trevor takes the tiny Gurneys off the front wing so he can clean the grit trapped under the leading edges. Mauricio says the track is just as dirty today as it was the last two days. Maybe this grit really is precipitated smog. Maybe it falls like dew during the night.

The wind is from the east now and it's hot and very dry. It's what Southern California folks call a Santa Ana wind. It'll be over 100 degrees today. I need to make sure I drink enough water. If I'm not peeing every hour or so, I'm not drinking enough.

Pre-Race Meeting

The pre-race meeting is moved back from 10 to 10:30. I don't usually want to be in those meetings, but today I've asked Ando if I can be there. A PacWest car could easily win this race, and I don't want to miss anything!

At 10:30 we all crowd into the engineering office in the front of the Motorola transporter. Both drivers are here in their suits. Ando and Russ are the race strategists for Mark and Mauricio. There are two engineers and a data-acquisition guy for each car. Jim Hamilton is the software guru. Charlie Harris is here representing Ilmor. Ziggy Harcus and Roberto Trevisan from the Lights team are here because they'll be spotters today in addition to Steve Fusek. Two Motorola people are here including Bob Schaul. Almost 20 of us are crammed into this little cubical.

Russ says the cars need to be gridded in pit lane at 11:15, and "Start your engines!" is at 12:01. CART moved the pit-signal board and they talk about that. Ando tells Ziggy and Roberto to say as much as they want on the spotter channel. "Tell where the drivers should be going if there's a crash — high or low."

Russ presents the race history of the Michigan 500 because this is the first race here. That race averages seven yellow flags for a total of 50 laps. Because of the slow 60-mph pit speed a pit stop costs a lot of time, so they want to use the yellows and avoid green-flag pit stops. If the fuel tank is less than half full when a yellow flag waves they'll come in for fuel and tires. Al Bodey says, "If there's a yellow at lap 206, we could make it home."

Ando says, "We need to stay with the leaders and pit when they do, if it's right for us. We'll have the T-cars parked behind the pits in case we have to use them."

Pre-Grid

At 11 a.m. I'm on pit lane and it's getting hot. The stands are about one-third full. At 11:19 I ride the 17-tugger as Trevor drives, pulling the car down pit lane toward Turn 1. This is the pole car, I remind myself. The Valvoline truck is there and all the cars get a top-off. A few bubbles dance up into the jug indicating a small amount of fuel went into the car.

Bob Varsha, ABC and ESPN anouncer, is talking intently into a camera on the pit side, taping a segment of the race program that will be shown tape-delay later this evening. In between shots Bob wipes his face free of sweat. One of the electric billboards says "LOOK UP," and I see some sky divers drifting down onto the grass between the pit wall and the frontstraight.

Steve Fusek tells me that Mo's T-car was faster this morning because it was 0.040-inch lower than the primary car when they put it back on the setup pad after the session.

At 11:40 the drivers are in black Toyota convertibles going out on the track for an introduction lap. Mauricio and Stella are in the last one.

Jim Reid tells me, "These cars really haven't run much, and we send 'em off for 500 miles."

Charlie Harris, an Ilmor engineer, introduces me to one of the VDS engine builders. "Paul, this is Scott Mount. He built the motor that won the pole."

I shake Scott's hand and say, "Way to go. How long have you been at VDS?"

"Seven years," Scott says with a grin.

"Did you build this race motor too?"

"No. I build the Bettenhausen race motors, and they're out because Carpentier crashed."

I thank Charlie for introducing Scott to me. It's fun to meet the people behind the scenes. There's a lot of hard work and dedication here that doesn't get enough recognition.

At 11:52 Mauricio comes to the car. The stands are about 70% full. I walk back down the grid to the 18-car to take some pictures there. Mark is getting in. They start the engines on time and I go back to the 18-car pits, where I'm going to stay during the race.

Actually I've got a pretty good spot for this race. The PacWest pit boxes are on either side of a 20-foot break in the pit wall. The scoring cart where Bruce and Jolene are sitting is in the 18-pit just toward Turn 1 from the break in the wall. I'm standing right behind the pit wall wedged in between the cart and the barrier at the break. If I lean back and look to the left I can see a TV monitor in the scoring cart. Off to my right is the huge pylon showing all the car numbers in race order. I can walk back and forth between the PacWest pits easily.

THE RACE

The cars go out for their pace laps and Ando is already telling Mark, "Make fuel."

Russ tells Mo, "Slot zero on the fuel."

Brett Schilling, "Little Brett," one of the Firestone engineers, is standing on the other side of the barrier from me. He says the track temperature is 130 degrees.

The cars come around for the start but one of the Toyotas has blown up, and they start the race on a yellow flag. I can see on the monitor it's Juan Fangio II up in flames. I feel sorry for Juan. He's a nice guy and a great driver.

Ando tells Mark, "There's a lot of oil dry on the backstraight."

Mauricio says, "The blower is out and they're going to have to blow that shit. It's going to be awhile; three-four laps at least."

Mark is gridded in eighth with Michael Andretti alongside in seventh. Ando tells Mark, "You and Michael will be good buddies before this is over."

"I reckon," Mark says.

A couple of cars at the back of the field pit for a fuel top-up. "Good gamble," Russ says. If they stay out after others pit and get a lucky yellow flag they could get good track position.

As Arie Luyendyk pulls out of a Ganassi pit box, fire breaks out in his pit about 75 feet to my left. One crewman gets doused with a bunch of water, but seems OK.

Ando tells Mark, "It's a double-file restart; get some temp into the old girl." The green flag restarts the race at the start of lap 11. It's 11:29 p.m.

Two laps later Paul Tracy crashes in Turn 4, bringing out another yellow flag. I hear Ziggy telling Mark to go high. Mark says, "There's crap everywhere." Mo says it's a big mess.

The next green flag comes on lap 22. I'm hoping the race gets going this time. Mauricio is leading, and he builds a gap between himself and Jimmy Vasser in second. Mark is eighth, yelling into his radio, "Push, gotta push."

Ando tells him to soften the front bar. "Play with the car."

Michael Andretti moves up through the field and on lap 39 the order is Mauricio, Michael, Jimmy, Michel Jourdain Jr., Andre Ribeiro, and Mark.

Another crash causes a yellow flag. I can see on the monitor that Arie Luyendyk has crashed. Arnd Meier spun and collected him. I hear "code three" on the radio, so someone is hurt. There's a call for an ambulance.

Russ tells Mauricio to stay out. "The pits are closed."

Mark reports, "A level-four push in traffic. Pretty bad. The car's still got level-three push with no traffic. Pretty bad. I went up one notch on the front bar, one notch stiffer. That stabilized it more on turn-in, but it actually increased the push." Of course stiffer on the front bar would increase the push. He went the wrong way. He should have softened it like Ando told him.

Allen: "Would you like a bit of front wing?"

CART conversation covers up the answer. Ziggy reports they haven't got Arie out of the car yet. It could be bad. Then I hear Control say, "We won't need the helicopter." Arie Luyendyk is probably not hurt seriously.

On lap 41 the pits open up and everyone comes in. Ando talks Mark in. "Get that clutch workin.' Look for Butch. Right down the centerline ["Roight down the centerloin" is what I hear.]. Set 'er up. Set 'er up. Easy now. Easy. Stop!"

Mauricio is coming in also and he says the engine won't rev; it's stuck at 9,000 rpm. Michael passed him coming into the pits and gets out ahead of him. When the race order gets sorted out Michael is in P1 followed by Mauricio, Vasser, Jourdain, Mark, and Ribeiro.

Mauricio is upset Michael passed him. "He was too fast in the pit lane. He was 80 miles per hour for 50 yards. That's bullshit. Go shout at those people."

Ziggy says they've got Arie out and into the ambulance.

Russ says, "Mo, it's fairly simple. There was a flash fire in the plenum. If this happens again, just lift out of the throttle and get right back in."

Andy adds some more advice: "Do not de-clutch. Just get out of the throttle."

Mauricio: "Ten-four."

Ando tells Mark the telemetry isn't working and they can't see the fuel numbers that show how much methanol the engine is using. He'll have to read them off the dash and tell them over the radio.

They go green again on lap 51. Ten laps later Mark is P6 and has relayed the fuel information. Ando tells him to go to sixth gear. "We need that fuel."

Greg Moore has moved up and is challenging Mark, who's still complaining of a push. Ando tells him to use his front bar and weight jacker, but Mark goes the wrong way with the bar again. Moore gets past but Vasser falls back and Mark passes him to maintain sixth spot. Mauricio catches Michael and tries to pass but can't.

On lap 78 Ando tells Mark, "Five laps to the next pit stop."

Mark says the car is vibrating and the right-rear tire looks bad.

Both PacWest cars pit under green and get out all right. I see a small burst of flame on Mark's sidepod. The water spray was a little late, but it put out the fire.

The order on lap 89 is Ribeiro, Andretti, Mauricio, Moore, and Mark. Ando tells Mark there are some blisters on the right-rear tire that came off his car at the last stop.

Allen tells him, "The tire pressures are coming up higher than Firestone expected. We're making adjustments."

Russ is telling Mauricio about the blisters on his tires also.

This order holds until lap 100 when Michael Andretti pits unexpectedly, falling back in the field. Mauricio is in P2 behind Ribeiro, and Tom Keene, working the pit board, is waving at Mo and pointing toward the front. A few laps later Michael pits again and retires with overheating.

The PacWest cars pit under green again on lap 115, falling back to seventh and 10th. Unfortunately there's a yellow flag for debris on course a few laps later. I hear Butch say, "Shit."

Tasman teammates Ribeiro and Adrian Fernandez are running one-two now, a surprising result given the problems they've had this year. Andre is in a Reynard. Adrian is still flogging a Lola, but he's got a new bottom on the car that must be a big improvement.

With the restart on lap 125 Mo is fifth and Mark eighth. The wind out of the east is really hot now, and a lot of gritty dust is blowing around on pit lane.

Mauricio falls back the next few laps and Mark passes him. The order on lap 130 is Ribeiro, Fernandez, Gil de Ferran, Vasser, Moore, Mark, and Mauricio.

Mo's right-rear tire is blistering and he wants to come in and change it. He does that on lap 136. It's a good stop and he only drops two spots to ninth.

I walk over to the 17-pit and see a line of quarter-sized blisters around the middle of the tire. Some Goodyear guys are back of the pits looking hard at the wounded Firestones. At this point in the race de Ferran and Christian Fittipaldi are the only guys on Goodyears in the top 10.

The tires are definitely the story today. I walk over to Paul Ray, Ilmor vice president, and say, "The tire god giveth and then taketh away."

He smiles and nods. They spend millions of dollars and many man-years developing engine improvements that are good for a couple of tenths, while the tire guys mix up some more black stuff and get a half-second a lap.

Over the next 30 laps Mauricio moves up as others pit. Mark comes in on lap 154. His right-rear has some tiny blisters. Allen McDonald goes to talk to Brett. On lap 168 Ando is encouraging Mark to get around Bobby Rahal, who's a lap down but ahead of Mark on the track.

"Let's put the old fella down a lap." He does.

Mo's in third behind Ribeiro and de Ferran when he pits on lap 173. The right-rear tire that comes off his car is blistered. On lap 176 the order is Ribeiro, de Ferran, Vasser, Mark, and Moore. Mo and Rahal are a lap down in sixth and seventh. It's 2:30 p.m. and very hot. I'm drinking from a plastic bottle hung from my belt. There's a bunch more water bottles on ice by the 17-pit, thank goodness.

Ando talks Mark in for his fifth pit stop on lap 190. "Turn the switch on, come in straight. Steady; steady; OK. Turn the switch off." They're transferring oil from that extra tank to the main oil tank.

When Mark's back on course, Ando tells him, "Get the pace up there. We want that time. We got to go here. Walk up smartly. We've got 57 laps to go. We're going down to the wire."

Ribeiro still leads and de Ferran is second. Mauricio is third followed by Rahal. Mark is fifth followed by Vasser.

Fifteen laps later Ribeiro and de Ferran have pitted, putting Mauricio and Mark one-two on course. The PacWest cars circulate in the top spots and it's all smiles around me in the pits. Even Bruce almost looks excited. Jolene, ever the cheerleader, is yelling and pumping her fists in the air. Ando tells Mark, "One more pit stop; we need that track position."

Then Ribeiro spins in Turn 2 and hits the inside wall on the backstraight. He's OK. The track goes yellow and pit stops start.

Russ yells to Mo, "We're ready for ya. Full load of fuel, guys."

Ando talks to Mark: "We're one-two. We need this one here. This will be our last segment."

Russ to Mauricio: "Go for that green switch and transfer your oil."

Mauricio: "I'm starting it right now. Switching it on right now."

Russ: "Ten-four; we'll have it on for a minute and a half."

Mark asks, "Will this be enough fuel to go to the end?"

Ando: "It should be. You just have to be careful with it. We're lookin' real fat."

Mauricio gets out second behind de Ferran and Russ tells him, "I think we can make it on fuel. Just save those tires and hold your position." The order is de Ferran, Mo, Mark, Vasser, and Greg Moore.

They restart on lap 214. Mauricio passes de Ferran into Turn 1 for the lead. But Mark falls back as first Vasser and then Moore get by him. He stays in fifth spot as Greg Moore passes Vasser and then de Ferran to challenge Mauricio for the lead. This is an exciting race. Any one of a bunch of different guys could win it.

Mark is complaining of a push and Ando is sounding more angry at Mark than I've ever heard. "Get with the program. Use the weight jacker."

Mark passes de Ferran on lap 227 and moves up on Vasser.

Mauricio has a problem. In his mirrors he can see a dark line growing on his right-rear tire. He tells Russ, who says, "Just try and hang in there. Twenty-two to go. Try to hang on to it."

Mauricio: "It's getting worse."

Russ: "Is there any way to hang on another 20 laps? Even if you lose a few positions. We're gonna lose so much if you pit."

Mauricio: "You must be f**cking joking."

Russ, giving up, "Come on in then. Come on in. Pit. Change the tires. No fuel, no fuel." The stop is quick but the engine stalls on the way out. Mauricio comes out in eighth spot, a lap down.

Ando to Mark, "Get up there. We're P3 with Vasser in front for position."

Greg Moore is leading the race. Maybe this will be his third win of the year.

Stephen Kent, working Mark's pit board, is waving him on now.

I'm watching the monitor more now because anything could happen, and I can only see the cars as they go by on the last part of the frontstraight. Mark is in third closing on Vasser. Then, with 11 laps to go, Moore's car puffs a big cloud of smoke and he slows. Vasser gets out of the throttle expecting a yellow flag. Mark goes around Jimmy on the outside. Moore goes off course quickly and there's no yellow. Vasser recovers, but Mark's in the lead now and pulling away. He turns a lap of 233 mph vs. Jimmy's 226. Mo is up to fourth, but he's a long way behind Vasser.

At the white flag Ando tells Mark, "Two miles."

As Mark comes across the Start/Finish line I hear him scream into the radio, "YYEEEOOOWWW! WAAHHOOO! We won a superspeedway!"

All the PacWest people are jumping up and down and beating each other on the backs. Even Bruce is pumping his fists in the air and yelling.

Russ tells Mo, "P4. Good job. That gives you fourth in the championship as well. Awesome."

The 18-crew is running down pit lane toward the victory circle. As they get there Mark is coming to a stop, and I hear him on the radio yelling, "I love all of ya."

I get there in time to hear Mark and the crew yelling, "Show me the money."

Scott Simpson, Mauricio's tire guy, tells me Andy was going down in pressure a half pound at a time. "I tried to tell him to go in bigger steps, but he wouldn't."

I walk over to tech inspection where the 18-crew is pushing the winning car in for a check. The right-rear tire has quarter-sized blisters, so Mark's last run was not without problems. I take a photo and step into the media conference room. Butch, Mark's chief mechanic, is sitting there in a chair trying to draw some relief from the air conditioning.

"The pit stops looked good," I say after congratulating him.

"They were good, especially at the end when we needed them."

"Mark really went for it at the end, didn't he?"

"He really did," Butch says, looking tired but smiling. "He got slack in the middle of the race, but then at the end when he saw the front, he was really fast. That tire is blistered bad. Mo came in and replaced a set with smaller blisters than that."

The Winning Car with a
Blistered Tire

Post-Race Press Conference

At 3:50 they start the press conference with Mark and Adrian Fernandez, the third-place finisher, here. Jimmy Vasser, who placed second, has some heat-exhaustion problems and we're told he will be here soon.

Adrian speaks first and talks about a good result ending a difficult season for the Tasman team. "We got a new part from the Lola guys, and the car felt more stable. I had some blisters today. It was good running behind my teammate, Andre. This was a great result for our team."

Mark is asked to comment on the last 10 laps of his third victory this season.

"We had a very good car underneath us, and like the other race at Michigan, we were waiting for the end of the race to make our move. Jimmy had a good car there, but I think I would have found a way around him. Then Greg's engine let go, and I saw it spit some things out of the back of it into Turn 1. He very quickly went up high and Jimmy backed out, and at that point I backed out as well because it looked like Greg's engine might spill some oil and put us into the wall. Coming out of 2 I assessed the situation very quickly, and I could see there were no yellow flags around. I also got a good message from John Anderson, who was calling my race. He said there were no flags, just go for it. Jimmy faltered and we made the move, and the rest is history as they say. It's very unfortunate for Greg, but I guess that turns the tables from Detroit. But, uh, that's the way it happened."

The questions from the press gets more detailed but seem to concentrate on trying to get the drivers to say the track was dangerous, too fast. Of course it is, but why ask the drivers? The people who build new racetracks like this design them around the NASCAR races that makes them money. Indy cars race on these tracks because the track is here and it takes drivers to drive them. None of this will change until some drivers are killed, and even then only the rules will be changed. The tracks cost too much money to be changed.

Tires

Mark Blundell with the Trophy
(Dan Boyd Photo)

Mark won with bigger blisters on his tires than on the tires Mauricio had given up the lead to replace. How can that be?

Allen McDonald explained it to me this way: "Mo sets his car up more free than Mark does. Mo's on the verge of oversteer, and he likes that feeling. When his tires blistered it oversteered more and made the car undrivable for him. He had to replace them.

"Mark doesn't like the car with that much oversteer. We always have a little push dialed into it. That actually helped him today because when the right-rear tire blistered, the increase in oversteer just decreased the push some, it didn't go all the way to oversteer. He was still able to race the car even with the blisters."

And race it he did.

Tires were a huge factor in this race. On race day it was just a little too hot for the Firestone tires and they suffered. They were, however, on the first four cars at the end of the race. Firestone had a faster tire than Goodyear today, as it has had most of this year. In fact, one ex-Goodyear guy told me he is "stunned" the company hasn't responded better to Firestone's successes. Two Goodyear-shod CART teams, Team Rahal and Della Penna Motorsports, announced a switch to Firestones for next season during this race weekend.

I'm Outa Here

OK, that's it. I walk back through the garage area and tell some of the PacWest guys I'll see them in a couple of weeks, in Indy, when we all get to drive the racecars. Then I go to the hospitality motor coaches, pick up my stuff, and walk to the car.

I'm in the car at 4:20 and head for an airport for the last time this season. Amazingly traffic moves fairly consistently leaving the track. I've got a map and I try to tell where I'm being routed, but I lose track. Finally I see signs for Interstate 15 South and follow them.

An hour later, after driving through the smog and traffic conditions ranging from stopped to 80 mph, I pull into the Hertz lot at John Wayne Airport in Costa Mesa.

At the United counter I find I can get an earlier flight with a first-class upgrade. In the nearest restroom I wash the grit off my face and take a leak. I managed my moisture well today. A call to Pat alerts her I'll be early.

Later, drinking a glass of wine waiting for the plane to take off, I decide this was a hell of a season. Now if the book would only write itself!

CHAPTER 24

DRIVING THE CAR

One of the ways PacWest is different from other teams is the way it shows appreciation for the people in the family, and the most extravagant event of this type is referred to as "The Driving Experience." Not long after I came on the scene someone asked me if I would get to "drive the car." At the time I just said I hope so.

Toward the end of the season the event began to be a popular topic of conversation among the crew, and I was thinking a lot about it myself. Just before the last race at Fontana I received a fax from Steve Fusek inviting me to the PacWest Racing Group 1997 "Driving Experience."

I fly to Indianapolis on Tuesday, October 14, and go in to the shop the next morning. My invitation says I'm scheduled to drive in the 11 a.m. to 1 p.m. time slot. After visiting people in the shop, I drive a short way east of the city to the Mt. Comfort airport. Good directions to the airport came with the invitation, but a PacWest sign at the highway exit makes it difficult to get lost. It's a cool day, but the sun is shining in between clouds.

The Hollywood motor coach and hospitality enclosure is all set up, and Dave Loik, the PacWest chef, is cooking lunch. Greg Watson, Don Mullin, Chris Wood, and Justin Poynter man the hospitality area as usual. Victoria Vanderwell signs me in, and says I can probably get in a car right away. I walk past a chain-link fence onto the rough concrete typical of airports. To my left is the Super Touring transporter and on the right the Hollywood CART transporter. They've laid out a couple of short courses using orange traffic cones. The Super Touring course looks tight and twisty like an autocross, and the Indy car course is a D-shaped oval, but they are running it clockwise. Jeff Oster, the hospitality manager, tells me he had to buy five million dollars worth of personal liability insurance for this event. That's more coverage than they needed, but the airport required that amount.

This is the second day of the three-day event, and things are running along smoothly. The engineering office in the front of the Motorola transporter serves as our change room. About 20 driving suits hang from the ceiling, and helmets, shoe boxes, and gloves line the tables and shelves. I find a suit that looks big enough and put it on along with size 10 shoes. A 7 3/8 helmet fits all right, so I grab some gloves and step down the into the staging area under the awning right next to the transporter.

Casey Eason, one of the PacWest data acquisition guys, and two of the Ilmor engineers, Charlie Harris and Ian Hawkins, are working the data acquisition equipment. Charlie and Ian are baby-sitting the Ilmor/Mercedes-Benz engines. They have them rev-limited to 10,500 rpm and there are probably other adjustments to the fuel and ignition maps to make the engines more forgiving for us wankers.

Casey tells me, "Mark [Blundell] set up the course and did a 15.0 second lap that stood till a guy over here from McLaren turned a 14.9. Mark went back out and drove it in 14.7. That's stood up so far." I'm certainly not worried about a time. I just hope I don't look too stupid.

Driving the Reynard

PacWest does things right. When my turn comes, there are stickers saying HANEY in black block letters that go on the cockpit sides of the Hollywood car over Mauricio's more permanent name. Charlie Guilinger, Russ Grosshans, Gavin Hamilton, and Daryl Fox are crewing. I know Russ by his nickname, Roscoe. They put one of the name tags on the car upside down, laughing about how that would tell them who's in the car when it's upside down.

Somebody's on-course in the Motorola car, and I'm up next. Charlie takes me to a whiteboard to look at a sketch of the cockpit that shows me the ignition switch location and the gear shift actuation. They tell me to get in, so I stand in the seat with both feet—the molded seat for Mauricio has been removed so us bigger people can fit—and sit down sliding my feet forward to the pedals. Charlie, Roscoe, and Gavin are helping me. Charlie belts me in and they're all hunkered down around the front of the car telling me things I immediately forget. I'm very excited.

Is This Guy Intense or Scared?

The cockpit is snug but comfortable. The gear shift lever is a sturdy black stalk with a bulge at the top. My right hand fits easily around it. Gavin says, "It takes a good sharp pull. Don't baby it."

Charlie says I should drive it like a go kart, left foot braking and using my right foot for the throttle. He says to rest my left foot on the dead pedal when it isn't on the brake. I move my feet around to feel the pedals as instructed. The brake pedal is very hard, solid. I'm surprised how comfortable I feel. There's just enough room in here, no more.

The guys snap the steering wheel on the shaft, and tell me about the dash readouts and the lights that will tell me when to shift if I want to do that. "You can just run it in second gear if you want," somebody tells me.

The other car is coming off the course, so Charlie turns on the ignition switch, telling me to give the engine some revs, "Nobody wants to rev the engine enough." The starter goes in the gearbox and turns the engine over. Gavin is standing out in front of the car, and he pumps his hand up and down telling me to give it some gas. The engine fires up with a now-familiar sound, and I goose it a few times. They push the car forward and I press the gearshift forward to put it in gear. Gavin signals and yells, "Pull it back, not forward."

I pull it back into first and let out the clutch. It stalls, of course. Not enough throttle. It's all too strange. I just don't have time to absorb the instructions. I stall it again. The guys are very patient. Finally I get the right combination of throttle and clutch and pull out onto the course.

The steering feels soft and easy, very direct, but not really as precise as I expected. I like seeing the front tires right out there on either side of my ankles. I go slow the first lap and then gave it a little throttle. The engine feels very powerful. On the slow end of the oval the engine has trouble at low revs and lurches the car back and forth which pushes my foot on and off the throttle making it worse. I can't go any faster there or the car understeers badly.

The far turn is faster and I build some speed on the short back stretch. After a few laps I try some more throttle, and the rear just slides right out to the left. The car spins 180 degrees and the engine stalls. Everything happened too quick for me. I didn't even feel the rear end coming around, it just jumped out there. The same thing happens at least twice more. On one of the spins I think I got on the throttle and the brake at the same time. I should have started off left-foot braking like Charlie suggested, but I didn't.

Every time I screw up the guys bring a starter over on a tugger and they fire up the engine. I stall it a couple more times before I relax and slip the clutch enough. After a few more laps, I get going a little faster and I start getting more comfortable. Nigel Bloom waves the checkered flag, and I finish the lap slowly and pull in beside the tent.

"Way to go," somebody says as I get out. My legs are trembling, but my face is grinning. Casey hands me a printout of my fastest lap, 17.96 seconds, Not bad, really.

I never saw the readouts on the dash, I was just too busy watching the front tires and the orange cones. The rear end never gave me any warning when it came around in a spin. I'm sure I was just too jerky on the throttle. These cars reward smoothness, and I didn't show any of that. I shifted a couple of times but didn't really use the extra speed after the shift.

On Course Between Spins
Dan Boyd Photo

They take off the HANEY stickers and give them to me. Mary Fusek hands me a video tape her husband, Ron, has taken, and Dan Boyd, the PacWest photographer, tosses me a roll of film. Ron hands me my own camera he used to take some extra photos.

As usual it was a letdown afterward. I tell myself I could/should have done better, at least not stalled so much. But it was definitely fun and a unique opportunity. Changing back into my jeans I notice I'm sweaty. Other people are there looking for suits and changing. More than 200 people drove the cars those three days.

Driving the Dodge Super Touring Car

Later I suit up again for a ride in the PacWest Super Touring Dodge Stratus. Getting in is actually more difficult than getting in the Indy car because of the roll cage, and I'm not nearly as comfortable in the car. My knees are bent up and my feet twisted into a strange position. The seating is probably just right for the regular drivers, Dominic Dobson and David Donohue.

The crew guys buckle me in and show me the controls. This gearbox is also sequential, but 1st is forward and the other gears are back. I don't remember about neutral. They fire it up and I ease out. This clutch is much less difficult to slip—less power, more clearance and travel.

The course is a very tight layout, narrow and twisty, and I can't see the front tires as in the other car. The engine is super responsive and very loud. They told me you have to be going straight before you get on the throttle, with front wheel drive. It understeers badly if I ask the tires to turn and accelerate at the same time. One portion of the course allows enough speed to try shifting, and it works great, no clutch, up and down. A couple of times I plow down some cones, but a spin isn't going to happen with the front wheels driving. What is most fun is staying on the throttle and shifting into third gear. The car just keeps accelerating. The Super Touring series is gone now, so I'm glad I got to drive one of the cars.

Last Laps

I hang around the rest of the afternoon watching people take their turns and talking to all the guys. The fast times of the day are Chris Griffis, Daryl Fox, and Casey. At 5 p.m. it's getting cooler as the sun goes down. Bruce suits up for his ride, using his classic, black, open-faced helmet. He gets going pretty fast, enough so, when he spins on the front part he goes through the cones and into the grass ten feet or so. Like all of us he's got a big smile on his face when he climbs out to the car.

Then it's John Anderson's turn. They've save Ando for last because he's rough on the car. Steve Fusek tells me, "He's OK at the start, but then he gets frustrated." I'm not sure what he's talking about, but that's what happens. The first few laps are slow and careful, then he carries too much speed into the slow corner at the end of the straight nearest us, and goes spinning backwards off into the grass, way off into the grass. A few more sane laps and he drives a 16.17

lap, very good. Then he just starts spinning doughnuts raising clouds of white smoke. People either laugh or shake their heads, or both.

When Ando gets out of the car his rear tires are showing cord almost the whole way across the tread. I notice the fabric doesn't look high-tech at all, more like khaki cotton twill. Mark Blundell is right there asking Ando, "Did you use the bars? What about the weight jacker? Eh, mate?" Everybody laughs at that.

The next morning I spend some time at the shop and then go back out to the airport. Colleen Howerton, the office manager, is nervous before her turn. When she gets in the car she says, "The third Dahlenbach in an Indy car." Mary hands her a video tape as she gets out after her run and Colleen says, "This is going right to Daddy." Colleen's dad is CART Chief Steward, Wally Dahlenbach and her brother, Wally Jr. drives in NASCAR Winston Cup now.

It had to happen and it finally does, the engine in the Motorola car succumbs to the abuse with a bang and a cloud of gray smoke. Ironically Blake Hamilton, the guy who dresses all the engines, is driving when it lets go. He feels terrible.

The event is now down to one car and the pace slows. Guys who haven't had their turn yet begin to worry they might miss out. Dave Jacobs is new to PacWest this year and he's been suited up for a while. Dave's patience is giving way to nervousness. His wife, Kathy, seems as relieved as Dave when the time comes. After his laps Dave is all smiles, beaming to everyone and jabbering about how much fun it is just like we all did.

David Donohue, the Super Touring driver who won that championship for PacWest takes a turn and looks very smooth and fast. He turns a bunch of laps in the 15 second range with a best of 15.2. He carries a lot of speed into the fast far turn. If I had another lap I'd shift up on that side of the course as David does and try to go faster into that corner. That's where the speed is.

I begin to realize this is my last event with the PacWest people, and the realization makes me look around with more awareness. I try to focus on each person and get an image in my mind that will help me describe them in the months of writing coming up. My eyes fill up with emotion and I put on my sunglasses so no one can see.

The safety crew is lounging on a tugger in the middle of the cones, so I go out to visit with them. It's Boomer, Dr. Love, Mark Moore, and Roscoe sitting on the tugger in between chasing cones. Nigel Bloom is still flagging. I feel very comfortable here with them trading jokes and watching people go out in the cars and do the same silly things I did. I say as much and Nigel laughs, "Hey, Paul, we didn't mind all the stalls and spins, at least you were trying."

"Hey, guys," I say, "I'll be at few of the races next year. Can I get a ride on the tugger sometime?"

"Sure, Paul," Tim Love answers and others say it too, "You can ride on the tugger."

Roscoe says, "Hey, next year we can go back to doing things like we used to, Paul won't be here." We all laugh and I wonder how much truth and how much teasing is in that statement, and whether any of us really know the answer. Jim Hamilton, in his scientific language, put it this way early in the year, "You're the observer in the Heisenberg Principle of Uncertainty. Just being there changes the environment."

It's getting time for me to leave for the airport and I tell Mark Moore. "Hey, I've got to go pretty soon. Am I going to get to see you drive?"

"OK," Mark says, "I might as well."

We walk over to the transporter and Mark just tells them, "Paul's got to go and he wants to see me drive." As if my wish were their command, Mark is next in the car. A former top-level driver in Formula Atlantic, he shows remarkable smoothness and quickly gets going well in the fast parts of the course. He's especially smooth on the throttle which I now know is a must to keep from spinning a car with this much power. Mark's best lap is 16.1 seconds. He's beaming a squint-eyed grin as he gets out of the car, and I shake his hand.

I've got to go now and I feel the emotion again, knowing I'm going to miss being with this bunch of people. The travel was stressful, and it was a lot of work. The hardest work is yet to come putting the book together in the next three months. I had a great time this season, and I learned a lot about racing and racing people.

The one thing I'm most proud of is the way I was allowed to fit into the group, the way people accepted me, the PacWest guys and the CART people. I guess we're all racers. We like each other because we're all crazy in the same direction.

CHAPTER 25

EPILOGUE

PacWest took a huge step forward in 1997, from a mid-pack, occasional performer to a team that was at the top of the chart in almost every track session. Mauricio Gugelmin finished fourth in championship points with one win and three poles. Mark Blundell earned sixth spot in the season points with three wins. Here are some other statistics:

Team Points
1. Ganassi	339
2. PacWest	247
3. Patrick	193
4. Penske	188
5. Newman-Haas	169

Team Race Wins
1. Ganassi	6
2. PacWest	4
3. Penske	3
4. Forsythe	2
5. Newman-Hass	1

Team Laps Led
1. Ganassi	492
2. PacWest	349
3. Penske	336
4. Newman-Haas	200
5. Rahal	191

Total Laps (2259 possible)
1. Gugelmin	2,172
2. De Ferran	2,110
3. Vasser	2,061
4. Pruett	1,981
5. Zanardi	1,930
6. Boesel	1,926
7. Blundell	1,919
8. Rahal	1,883

Team Total Laps
1. PacWest	4,091
2. Ganassi	4,030
3. Patrick	3,907
4. Rahal	3,700
5. Newman-Haas	3,415

Combined Qualifying Times of All 17 Tracks
1. Gugelmin	14 min 40.050 seconds
2. Pruett	14:42.263
3. De Ferran	14:42.672
4. Andretti	14:43.908
5. Moore	14:44.170
6. Herta	14:44.664
7. Vasser	14:45.447
8. Blundell	14:45.743

Total Race Miles (3948.187 possible)
1. Gugelmin	3,785.292
2. De Ferran	3,708.764
3. Vasser	3,553.319
4. Pruett	3,469.189
5. Blundell	3,443.265

Team Total Race Miles
1. PacWest	7,228.557
2. Ganassi	6,910.758
3. Patrick	6,699.876
4. Rahal	6,459.517
5. Newman-Haas	5,817.924

Average Qualifying Postition
1. Gugelmin	4.2
2. Pruett	7.1
3. De Ferran	7.2
4. Moore	8.1
5. Andretti	8.4
6. Herta	8.9
Vasser	8.9
8. Rahal	9.2
9. Blundell	9.6

Post-Season Events

Mark Blundell was named *Autosport* magazine's British Competition Driver of the Year. Mark was selected by the readers of *Autosport*, England's weekly motorsports magazine, from a group that included all British drivers who compete at the in international level in Formula 1, CART and rallying. He nosed out David Coulthard, driver for the McLaren Formula 1 team. This shows the affection the English have for Mark as well as the growing popularity of CART racing in Europe and around the world.

"The competition in America is very tough," Blundell told the packed, turn-away audience that jammed into the Great Room at London's Grosvenor House for the 16th annual *Autosport* Awards. "To win this from the F1 boys means a lot. Winning races is what its all about. Winning the championship is the next step. We are going to be strong, but it's going to be tough."

At this same *Autosport* event Mauricio Gugelmin received a special award for his 240-mph qualifying lap at Fontana.

The Engine Manufacturers Championship

Winning the CART engine manufacturers championship meant a lot to Mercedes-Benz. Steve Potter, manager of sports marketing for Mercedes-Benz of North America, confirms the importance. "The CART engine championship is a big deal to Mercedes-Benz. The '94 Indy 500-winning car [Penske chassis with the push-rod M-B/Ilmor V-8 engine] is prominently displayed in their museum at Stuttgart. The CART series is not as big as Formula 1 for Mercedes-Benz, but it's the next biggest thing for them worldwide. The United States is the biggest market for Mercedes-Benz cars outside of Germany and the CART series is U.S.-based but it has global exposure. They are enormously pleased and proud of this achievement."

Drivers Are Different

I'm sure the reader noticed the difference in the way the two PacWest drivers go about their business. Mauricio is very analytical and works with Andy Brown, his engineer, to get the most performance from the car. His ability to discern the relative performance of the many combinations of tire, engine, aerodynamic, and suspension tweaks enables him to start the races at the front of the grid. As several people pointed out in these pages these same analytical capabilities might actually limit his ability to win races. Mark Blundell is less sensitive to technical changes, but when he has a car that's drivable and he can get among the leaders, he wins the race.

What's not so obvious is both drivers benefit from the other. Mark's ability to win provides the end result the sponsors pay for and motivates everyone on the team. Mauricio's technical sensitivity and hard work during testing allows the development of a car that's capable of winning. Mark couldn't win if he didn't have the technical components and detail setups that Mauricio develops. Mauricio wouldn't really know that his cars are capable of winning if Mark wasn't proving it.

At times I'd laugh when I heard what Mark was saying about the car. While Andy and Mauricio were executing their plan with tens of words, Mark would talk for minutes, talk so long it sounded like he was contradicting himself, understeer and oversteer all at once at the same place in the corner. But Allen McDonald, knowing the directions Andy and Mauricio were going, almost always found a change that made Mark feel better in the car and able to drive it faster.

"I'm not an engineering driver,..." Mark told me. "...I get the best out of the car what's underneath me...I relay whatever the car is doing underneath me...I'm not there to fix it. I'm there to drive it 100% and to give 100% feedback."

There is a state of mind I call racer prejudice, and I found myself drifting in that direction this season. Mauricio is the perfect racer. He's handsome, quick with a smile and a joke, and a hard worker. Whenever he's in the car he's driving it as fast as he can and he can feel the effect of changes to the car. He's warm and appreciative of his crew and all the people on the team.

Mark suffers by comparison. He doesn't feel every shock tweak and spring change. He talks long and hard in great detail about everything he can think of that might make some sense to somebody. Probably because he can't feel small differences, he doesn't work as hard at tests as Mauricio does. But after all, winning races is what counts, and he won three of them this year. And he'll win more in the future.

It's Easy to Screw Up

In racing there's more opportunity to make mistakes than to look smart. Racecars are extremely complicated. Even small changes in air or track temperature or tire condition can drastically affect the level of grip the car generates and the balance of the car and the way the car feels to the driver. The crews can screw up preparing the car or fumble during pit stops, the engineers can make setup mistakes, and the drivers have an opportunity to screw up every foot of every lap. Even if everyone does a perfect job another driver can make a mistake and involve other drivers in a crash. In that sense it is a cruel sport.

This year when Mark Blundell had a chance to win a race he didn't screw up. He had many opportunities to make a mistake during those laps in the rain at Portland. Other drivers made it extremely difficult to get by them. But Mark leaned on them and clawed at the course until he got around. The finish was the closest in Indy car history, with Mark just edging out Gil de Ferran and Raul Boesel.

Mark's win at Toronto, his second of the season, was another example of him having a lot of opportunities to screw up. Bobby Rahal's overzealous run inside Dario Franchitti at the first corner knocked them both out of the race and gave Mark the lead. In spite of serious challenges from Alex Zanardi, the '97 CART champion, Mark maintained a lead of several seconds, conserving fuel at the same time and driving lap after lap without a mistake. This happened on a street course with different types of pavement and lined with unforgiving concrete barriers.

That Sunday at Fontana there was once again a lot of chances to screw up, but Mark won instead. He acted like he had given up in the middle of the race but Ando and the 18-car crew kept him in the hunt and his animal competitiveness took over in the end.

I have to admit that at midseason I thought Mark was a hopeless wanker. If the second half of his season had gone like the first half, I would probably still think poorly of him and so would a lot of other people. Instead, his performance makes us look dumb.

Big Stories in 1997

1. Alex Zanardi's pure talent and willingness to drive the car hard. The Ganassi team gave him a car he could flog and they executed great pit stops.

2. Firestone domination of Goodyear. I'm sure there's a technical story here, but the tire guys are very tight-lipped. Maybe neither company knows why Firestone tires were better. I did hear a rumor that the Japanese-manufactured Firestones can use a chemical that is now illegal in this country. I learned a lot about tires this year but it still doesn't add up to much total knowledge. Tire design and development is extremely complicated and performance is subjective.

3. The domination of the series by the Reynard chassis made Penske and Lola look inept, and makes it difficult for Swift to earn customers. There is something about the way a Reynard handles the air under the car that gives it a downforce advantage. The '98 Penske chassis will be the only car designed to take advantage of the all-new, tiny Ilmor engine. Reynard has to design its car for the largest engine, still the Honda. I think the charismatic leadership of Adrian Reynard and the superb people he's assembled will continue to dominate, unless their Formula 1 sortie derails the Indy car effort.

4. PacWest's movement from mid-pack to front runner. It's all about good people and managing resources.

5. Mark Blundell's emergence as a race winner. Not much more to say there.

6. Tim Neff's shocks and other hydraulic goodies were a distinct advantage for PacWest. Jim Hamilton's "vertical-mode" analysis software helped them and he's just scratching the surface of this area. Jim left PacWest to engineer Scott Pruett at Patrick Racing in 1998. If the Cosworth engines can hold together Scott could win the championship in '98.

It's ironic that Tim Neff's success has created waves of interest in shocks and spurred increased development at all the top teams. If PacWest doesn't follow up with increased resources in this very complicated area they could actually have created for themselves an area in which to fall behind.

7. The Ilmor/Mercedes-Benz engine has to be a big story also. The Honda might still be the most powerful engine, but it's also the biggest and heaviest. Ilmor founders, Mario Illien and Paul Morgan, have created by far the most sophisticated, elegant, and powerful engine in this racing series.

The '98 Season?

The new Reynard chassis, Ilmor/M-B engine, and Firestone tires will benefit PacWest in '98. The Firestone engineers like working with Mauricio and that will result in race tires that feel good to him. The team will benefit from the track time during testing and the prior knowledge of the tires on race weekends. Tim Neff will continue to develop shocks and other hydraulic systems. PacWest has a great bunch of people who now know what it takes to win.

But when I was at the PacWest shop in October it looked to me like PacWest had already lost its momentum. I think championships are won in the off-season. Nigel Mansell won in 1993 because he came over here after driving almost daily in Formula 1. Newman-Haas stepped up its testing program at a time when most Indy car drivers took the winter months off. Penske won the 1994 championship because the team spent the winter in intense testing with their push-rod Indy 500 engine.

In October PacWest had lost Jim Hamilton and had hired no other technical people. The team didn't get its first '98 Reynard chassis until just before Christmas. Scott Pruett and Jim Hamilton had been testing their new cars for a month.

A team's success creates recruiting pressures on everyone. When I was at the PacWest shop for the Driving Experience most of the crew and engineers were talking about getting phone calls, but most were saying they were happy where they were. The plus side of that is that good people from other teams will be knocking on PacWest's door trying to get onto a winning team.

All considered, I think PacWest will win championships, but not in 1998.

Other Comments

The CART people are great. I was always treated professionally by the CART race officials and I had a lot of fun with them. Unfortunately the CART owners are hurting the sport and the series. Letting the Indy Racing League split off was really dumb. The owners have too many conflicts of interest with ownership of engine manufacturers and racetracks and chassis manufacturers on top of their race team and CART franchise ownership. It looks to me like these people are addicted to winning. I see adolescent macho posturing with the goal of personal advantage instead of long-range business planning for the good of the sport and the series. Building racetracks that are potential killers is the worst symptom of the owners' poor judgment.

Bruce McCaw is a notable exception among the owners, as are the few ex-little guys who have pulled themselves up with hard work and real entrepreneurial spirit. I'm talking about Derrick Walker, Tony Bettenhausen, Barry Green, John Della Penna, Bobby Rahal, and Steve Horne. I still remember seeing Steve and Christine Horne walking hand-in-hand from the track to the the motel in Australia. They've got everything they own tied up in that team. At the same time Penske Racing can spend another $5 million of someone else's money on a whim.

The CART owners have to start thinking past next week. The cars have to be slowed and rules stability maintained. The CART race administrators and officials are mainly volunteers. With 19 races in 1998 the critical positions need to be full-time with competitive wages and benefits. This is the best racing in the world and it deserves permanent, full-time officials.

Here in January 1998 I'm looking forward to CART Spring Training at Homestead in a few weeks. I can't wait to see the new hardware. And I'll get to see all my friends.

INDEX

People who appear in the text many times have the word "various" indicating that the pages are too numerous to report fully. All PacWest CART people are listed on the organization charts on pages 11 and 12.